W9-BNK-564

6. Can a local account be used in a trust relationship? Explain.

7. In a complete trust domain model that uses 4 different domains, what is the total number of trust relationships required to use a complete trust domain model?

Exam Questions

The following questions are similar to those you will face on the Microsoft exam. Answers to these questions can be found in section Answers and Explanations, later in the chapter. At the end of each of those answers, you will be informed of where (that is, in what section of the chapter) to find more information..

1. ABC Corporation has locations in Toronto, New York, and San Francisco. It wants to install Windows NT Server 4 to encompass all its locations in a single WAN environment. The head office is located in New York. What is the best domain model for ABC's directory services implementation?

   A. Single-domain model

   B. Single-master domain model

   C. Multiple-master domain model

   D. Complete-trust domain model

2. JPS Printing has a single location with 1,000 users spread across the LAN. It has special printers and applications installed on the servers in its environment. It needs to be able to centrally manage the user accounts and the resources. Which domain model would best fit its needs?

A. Single-domain model

B. Single-master domain model

C. Multiple-master domain model

D. Complete-trust domain model

5. What must be created to allow a user account from one domain to access resources in a different domain?

A. Complete Trust Domain Model

B. One Way Trust Relationship

C. Two Way Trust Relationship

D. Master-Domain Model

Answers to Review Questions

1. Single domain, master domain, multiple-master domain, complete-trust domain. See section, Windows NT Server 4 Domain Models, in this chapter for more information. (This question deals with objective Planning 1.)

2. One user, one account, centralized administration, universal resource access, synchronization. See section, Windows NT Server 4 Directory Services, in this chapter for more information. (This question deals with objective Planning 1.)

6. Local accounts cannot be given permissions across trusts. See section, Accounts in Trust Relationships, in this chapter for more information. (This question deals with Planning 1.)

Answers and Explanations: For each of the Review and Exam questions, you will find thorough explanations located at the end of the section. They are easily identifiable because they are in blue type.

Exam Questions: These questions reflect the kinds of multiple-choice questions that appear on the Microsoft exams. Use them to become familiar with the exam question formats and to help you determine what you know and what you need to review or study more.

Suggested Readings and Resources

The following are some recommended readings on the subject of installing and configuring NT Workstation:

1. Microsoft Official Curriculum course 770: *Installing and Configuring Microsoft Windows NT Workstation 4.0*

   • Module 1: Overview of Windows NT Workstation 4.0

   • Module 2: Installing Windows NT Workstation 4.0

2. Microsoft Official Curriculum course 922: *Supporting Microsoft Windows NT 4.0 Core Technologies*

   • Module 2: Installing Windows NT

   • Module 3: Configuring the Windows NT Environment

3. *Microsoft Windows NT Workstation Resource Kit Version 4.0* (Microsoft Press)

   • Chapter 2: Customizing Setup

   • Chapter 4: Planning for a Mixed Environment

4. Microsoft TechNet CD-ROM

   • *MS Windows NT Workstation Technical Notes*

      • MS Windows NT Workstation Deployment Guide – Automating Windows NT Setup

      • An Unattended Windows NT Workstation Deployment

5. Web Sites

   • www.microsoft.com/train_cert

Suggested Readings and Resources: The very last element in each chapter is a list of additional resources you can use if you wish to go above and beyond certification-level material or if you need to spend more time on a particular subject that you are having trouble understanding.

MCSE

Second Edition

Networking Essentials

Exam: 70-058

New Riders

GLENN BERG

MCSE Training Guide:
Networking Essentials, Second Edition

International Standard Book Number: 1-56205-919-X

Library of Congress Catalog Card Number: 98-86317

First Printing: September, 1998

Printed in the United States of America

00   99   98   4   3   2   1

Trademarks

Warning and Disclaimer

EXECUTIVE EDITOR
Mary Foote

ACQUISITIONS EDITOR
Sean Angus

DEVELOPMENT EDITOR
Chris Zahn

MANAGING EDITOR
Sarah Kearns

PROJECT EDITOR
Mike La Bonne

COPY EDITORS
Margo Catts
Cliff Shubs

INDEXER
Chris Barrick

TECHNICAL EDITORS
Joe Reeves
Edward Tetz

SOFTWARE DEVELOPMENT SPECIALIST
Jack Belbot

PRODUCTION
Betsy Deeter
Becky Stutzman

Contents at a Glance

PART V Final Review

PART VI Appendixes

Table of Contents

PART II: Planning

5 Network Adapter Cards   195

6 Connectivity Devices and Transfer Mechanisms   221

7 Transport Protocols   251

PART III: Implementation

10 Managing and Securing a Microsoft Network   343

PART V: Final Review

Fast Facts: Networking Essentials Exam   449

PART VI: Appendixes

About the Author

Glenn Berg's first experience with a computer came in 1982 with the purchase of a Commodore VIC 20. From this machine Glenn went on to an Apple Mac +. With this massive computing power, Glenn spent many an hour hooking up to a mainframe at the University to run statistical models. In the early 1990s, Glenn started working on Sun stations while earning his masters degree and then moved over to Novell networks. From there he continued on into the world of Microsoft NT and other networking systems.

Glenn is Microsoft (MCSE, MCT), Novell (CNE, CNI), Lotus (CLP), and A+ certified. He is currently a trainer with PBSC in Canada, and has traveled extensively around North America and the world delivering courses on Networking. His main area of interest lies in the integration of different network systems.

Glenn is known for making the computer and networking learning experience fun and entertaining, with emphasis on always bringing the real world into the classroom and making people enjoy thinking.

About the Technical Editors

Edward Tetz graduated in 1990 from Saint Lawrence College in Cornwall, Ontario, with a diploma in business administration. He spent a short time in computer sales, which turned into a computer support position. He has spent the last seven years performing system and LAN support for small and large organizations. In 1994, he added training to his repertoire. He is both a Microsoft Certified Trainer and a Microsoft Certified Systems Engineer. He has experience with Apple Macintosh, IBM OS/2, and all Microsoft operating systems. He is currently an information technology coordinator and an instructor for PBSC Computer Training Centres, delivering certified training in most Microsoft products.

Joe Reeves works for Today's Computers Business Center in Marietta, Ohio, as a network design and support engineer certified as an MCSE, and as a Compaq ASE. He has taught classes on Microsoft products ranging from Windows NT to Office. He has also been featured on television as a stand-up comic. He'd like to thank his supporters, **Mark Eakle** (for direction), his wife, **Debbie**, for her patience and understanding, and special thanks to his daughter, **Lydia Marie**, for being a kid. Joe's email address is **jreeves@citynet.net**.

Dedication

*I dedicate this book to my wife, **Colleen**, the biggest inspiration in my life, and my parents, **Linda** and **Terje*** for their lifelong support. I also wish to mention my brothers, ***Kyle*** and ***Erik***, who make me more competitive.*

Acknowledgments

I thank **Sean Angus** and **New Riders** for giving me the opportunity to write this book. I really thank **Chris Zahn** for his development editing. Chris taught me a lot and gave a ton of support. I thank **Ed Tetz** and **Joe Reeves** for their technical editing. They kept me straight and gave lots of great feedback. I also thank my wife, **Colleen**, for her never-ending support. And both of us are thankful for the constant rain that made it easier to stay inside to write this book.

Tell Us What You Think!

As the reader of this book, *you* are our most important critic and commentator. We value your opinion and want to know what we're doing right, what we could do better, what areas you'd like to see us publish in, and any other words of wisdom you're willing to pass our way.

As the Executive Editor for the Certification team at Macmillan Computer Publishing, I welcome your comments. You can fax, email, or write me directly to let me know what you did or didn't like about this book—as well as what we can do to make our books stronger.

Please note that I cannot help you with technical problems related to the topic of this book, and that due to the high volume of mail I receive, I might not be able to reply to every message.

When you write, please be sure to include this book's title and author, as well as your name and phone or fax number. I will carefully review your comments and share them with the author and editors who worked on the book.

Fax: 317-581-4663

Email: certification@mcp.com

Mail: Executive Editor
        Certification
        Macmillan Computer Publishing
        201 West 103rd Street
        Indianapolis, IN 46290 USA

How to Use This Book

New Riders Publishing has made an effort in the second editions of its Training Guide series to make the information as accessible as possible for the purposes of learning the certification material. Here, you have an opportunity to view the many instructional features that have been incorporated into the books to achieve that goal.

CHAPTER OPENER

Each chapter begins with a set of features designed to allow you to maximize study time for that material.

List of Objectives: Each chapter begins with a list of the objectives as stated by Microsoft.

Objective Explanations: Immediately following each objective is an explanation of it, providing context that defines it more meaningfully in relation to the exam. Because Microsoft can sometimes be vague in its objectives list, the objective explanations are designed to clarify any vagueness by relying on the authors' test-taking experience.

OBJECTIVES

Microsoft provides the following objectives for "Connectivity":

Add and configure the network components of Windows NT Workstation.

▶ This objective is necessary because someone certified in the use of Windows NT Workstation technology must understand how it fits into a networked environment and how to configure the components that enable it to do so.

Use various methods to access network resources.

▶ This objective is necessary because someone certified in the use of Windows NT Workstation technology must understand how resources available on a network can be accessed from NT Workstation.

Implement Windows NT Workstation as a client in a NetWare environment.

▶ This objective is necessary because someone certified in the use of Windows NT Workstation technology must understand how NT Workstation can be used as a client in a NetWare environment and how to configure the services and protocols that make this possible.

Use various configurations to install Windows NT Workstation as a TCP/IP client.

▶ This objective is necessary because someone certified in the use of Windows NT Workstation technology must understand how TCP/IP is important in a network environment and how Workstation can be configured to use it.

CHAPTER 4

Connectivity

OUTLINE

Chapter Outline: Learning always gets a boost when you can see both the forest and the trees. To give you a visual image of how the topics in a chapter fit together, you will find a chapter outline at the beginning of each chapter. You will also be able to use this for easy reference when looking for a particular topic.

STUDY STRATEGIES

▶ Disk configurations are a part of both the planning and the configuration of NT Server computers. To study for Planning Objective 1, you will need to look at both the following section and the material in Chapter 2, "Installation Part 1." As with many concepts, you should have a good handle on the terminology and know the best applications for different disk configurations. For the objectives of the NT Server exam, you will need to know only general disk configuration concepts—at a high level, not the nitty gritty. Make sure you memorize the concepts relating to partitioning and know the difference between the system and the boot partitions in an NT system (and the fact that the definitions of these are counter-intuitive). You should know that NT supports both FAT and NTFS partitions, as well as some of the advantages and disadvantages of each. You will also need to know about the fault-tolerance methods available in NT—stripe sets with parity and disk mirroring—including their definitions, hardware requirements, and advantages and disadvantages.

Of course, nothing substitutes for working with the concepts explained in this objective. If possible, get an NT system with some free disk space and play around with the Disk Administrator just to see how partitions are created and what they look like.

You might also want to look at some of the supplementary readings and scan TechNet for white papers on disk configuration.

▶ The best way to study for Planning Objective 2 is to read, memorize, and understand the use of each protocol. You should know what the protocols are, what they are used for, and what systems they are compatible with.

As with disk configuration, installing protocols on your NT Server is something that you plan for, not something you do just because it feels good to you at the time. Although it is much easier to add or remove a protocol than it is to reconfigure your hard drives, choosing a protocol is still an essential part of the planning process because specific protocols, like spoken languages, are designed to be used in certain circumstances. There is no point in learning to speak Mandarin Chinese if you are never around anyone who can understand you. Similarly, the NWLink protocol is used to interact with NetWare systems; therefore, if you do not have Novell servers on your network, you might want to rethink your plan to install it on your servers. We will discuss the uses of the major protocols in Chapter 7, "Connectivity." However, it is important that you have a good understanding of their uses here in the planning stage.

Study Strategies: Each topic presents its own learning challenge. To support you through this, New Riders has included strategies for how to best approach studying in order to retain the material in the chapter, particularly as it is addressed on the exam.

INSTRUCTIONAL FEATURES WITHIN THE CHAPTER

These books include a large amount and different kinds of information. The many different elements are designed to help you identify information by its purpose and importance to the exam and also to provide you with varied ways to learn the material. You will be able to determine how much attention to devote to certain elements, depending on what your goals are. By becoming familiar with the different presentations of information, you will know what information will be important to you as a test-taker and which information will be important to you as a practitioner.

EXAM TIP

Only One NTVDM Supports Multiple 16-bit Applications Expect at least one question about running Win16 applications in separate memory spaces. The key concept is that you can load multiple Win16 applications into the same memory space only if it is the initial Win16 NTVDM. It is not possible, for example, to run Word for Windows 6.0 and Excel for Windows 5.0 in one shared memory space and also run PowerPoint 4.0 and Access 2.0 in another shared memory space.

Exam Tip: Exam Tips appear in the margins to provide specific exam-related advice. Such tips may address what material is covered (or not covered) on the exam, how it is covered, mnemonic devices, or particular quirks of that exam.

Note: Notes appear in the margins and contain various kinds of useful information, such as tips on the technology or administrative practices, historical background on terms and technologies, or side commentary on industry issues.

---

8   Chapter 1   PLANNING

INTRODUCTION

Microsoft grew up around the personal computer industry and established itself as the preeminent maker of software products for personal computers. Microsoft has a vast portfolio of software products, but it is best known for its operating systems.

Microsoft's current operating system products, listed here, are undoubtedly well-known to anyone studying for the MCSE exams:

❖ Windows 95

❖ Windows NT Workstation

❖ Windows NT Server

NOTE

Strange But True   Although it sounds backward, it is true: Windows NT boots from the system partition and then loads the system from the boot partition.

Some older operating system products—namely MS-DOS, Windows 3.1, and Windows for Workgroups—are still important to the operability of Windows NT Server, so don't be surprised if you hear them mentioned from time to time in this book.

Windows NT is the most powerful, the most secure, and perhaps the most elegant operating system Microsoft has yet produced. It languished for a while after it first appeared (in part because no one was sure why they needed it or what to do with it), but Microsoft has persisted with improving interoperability and performance. With the release of Windows NT 4 which offers a new Windows 95-like user interface, Windows NT has assumed a prominent place in today's world of network-based computing.

WINDOWS NT SERVER AMONG MICROSOFT OPERATING SYSTEMS

WARNING

Don't Overextend Your Partitions and Wraps   It is not necessary to create an extended partition on a disk; primary partitions might be all that you need. However, if you do create one, remember that you can never have more than one extended partition on a physical disk.

As we already mentioned, Microsoft has three operating system products now competing in the marketplace: Windows 95, Windows NT Workstation, and Windows NT Server. Each of these operating systems has its advantages and disadvantages.

Looking at the presentation of the desktop, the three look very much alike—so much so that you might have to click the Start button and read the banner on the left side of the menu to determine which operating system you are looking at. Each offers the familiar Windows 95 user interface featuring the Start button, the Recycling

---

Objective Coverage Text: In the text before an exam objective is specifically addressed, you will notice the objective is listed and printed in color to help call your attention to that particular material.

Warning: In using sophisticated information technology, there is always potential for mistakes or even catastrophes that can occur through improper application of the technology. Warnings appear in the margins to alert you to such potential problems.

STEP BY STEP

5.1 Configuring an Extension to Trigger an Application to Always Run in a Separate Memory Space

1. Start the Windows NT Explorer.

2. From the View menu, choose Options.

3. Click the File Types tab.

4. In the Registered File Types list box, select the desired file type.

5. Click the Edit button to display the Edit File Type dialog box. Then select Open from the Actions list and click the Edit button below it.

6. In the Editing Action for Type dialog box, adjust the application name by typing **cmd.exe /c start /separate** in front of the existing contents of the field (see Figure 5.15).

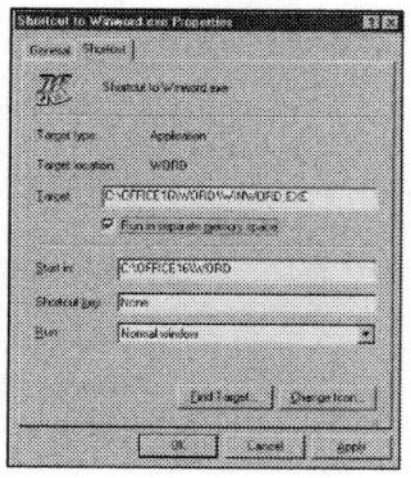

FIGURE 5.15
Configuring a shortcut to run a Win16 application in a separate memory space.

Step by Step: Step by Steps are hands-on tutorial instructions that walk you through a particular task or function relevant to the exam objectives.

Figure: To improve readability, the figures have been placed in the margins so they do not interrupt the main flow of text.

14   Chapter 1   PLANNING

You must use NTFS if you want to preserve existing permissions when you migrate files and directories from a NetWare server to a Windows NT Server system.

Windows 95 is Microsoft's everyday workhorse operating system. It provides a 32-bit platform and is designed to operate with a variety of peripherals. See Table 1.1 for the minimum hardware requirements for the installation and operation of Windows 95. Also, if you want to allow Macintosh computers to access files on the partition through Windows NT's Services for Macintosh, you must format the partition for NTFS.

MAKING REGISTRY CHANGES

To make Registry changes, run the REGEDT32.EXE program. The Registry in Windows NT is a complex database of configuration settings for your computer. If you want to configure the Workstation service, open the HKEY_LOCAL_MACHINE hive, as shown in Figure 3.22.

The exact location for configuring your Workstation service is

HKEY_LOCAL_MACHINE\System\CurrentControlSet\Services\
LanmanWorkstation\Parameters

To find additional information regarding this Registry item and others, refer to the Windows NT Server resource kit.

This summary table offers an overview of the differences between the FAT and NTFS file systems.

REVIEW   BREAK

Choosing a File System

But if the system is designed to store data, mirroring might produce disk bottlenecks. You might only know whether these changes are significant by setting up two identical computers, implementing mirroring on one but not on the other, and then running Performance Monitor on both under a simulated load to see the performance differences.

This summary table offers an overview of the differences between the FAT and NTFS file systems.

In-Depth Sidebar: These more extensive discussions cover material that perhaps is not as directly relevant to the exam, but which is useful as reference material or in everyday practice. In-Depths may also provide useful background or contextual information necessary for understanding the larger topic under consideration.

Review Break: Crucial information is summarized at various points in the book in lists or tables. At the end of a particularly long section, you might come across a Review Break that is there just to wrap up one long objective and reinforce the key points before you shift your focus to the next section.

CASE STUDIES

Case Studies are presented throughout the book to provide you with another, more conceptual opportunity to apply the knowledge you are developing. They also reflect the "real-world" experiences of the authors in ways that prepare you not only for the exam but for actual network administration as well. In each Case Study, you will find similar elements: a description of a Scenario, the Essence of the Case, and an extended Analysis section.

CASE STUDY: REALLY GOOD GUITARS

ESSENCE OF THE CASE

Here are the essential elements in this case:

- need for centralized administration
- the need for WAN connectivity nation-wide
- a requirement for Internet access and e-mail
- the need for Security on network shares and local files
- an implementation of Fault-tolerant systems

SCENARIO

Really Good Guitars is a national company specializing in the design and manufacturer of custom acoustic guitars. Having grown up out of an informal network of artisans across Canada, the company has many locations but very few employees (300 at this time) and a Head Office in Churchill, Manitoba. Although they follow the best traditions of hand-making guitars, they are not without technological savvy and all the 25 locations have computers on-site which are used to do accounting, run MS Office applications, and run their custom made guitar design software. The leadership team has recently begun to realize that a networked solution is essential to maintain consistency and to provide security on what are becoming some very innovative designs and to provide their employees with e-mail and Internet access.

RGG desires a centralized administration of its

continues

Essence of the Case: A bulleted list of the key problems or issues that need to be addressed in the Scenario.

Scenario: A few paragraphs describing a situation that professional practitioners in the field might face. A Scenario will deal with an issue relating to the objectives covered in the chapter, and it includes the kinds of details that make a difference.

Analysis: This is a lengthy description of the best way to handle the problems listed in the Essence of the Case. In this section, you might find a table summarizing the solutions, a worded example, or both.

CASE STUDY: PRINT IT DRAFTING INC.

continued

too, which is unacceptable. You are to find a solution to this problem if one exists.

ANALYSIS

The fixes for both of these problems are relatively straightforward. In the first case, it is likely that all the programs on the draftspeople's workstations are being started at normal priority. This means that they have a priority of 8. But the default says that anything running in the foreground is getting a 2-point boost from the base priority, bringing it to 10. As a result, when sent to the background, AutoCAD is not getting as much attention from the processor as it did when it was the foreground application. Because multiple applications need to be run at once without significant degradation of the performance of AutoCAD, you implement the following solution:

1. On the Performance tab of the System Properties dialog box for each workstation, set the Application Performance slider to None to prevent a boost for foreground applications.

2. Recommend that users keep the additional programs running alongside AutoCAD at a minimum (because all programs will now get equal processor time).

The fix to the second problem is to run each 16-bit application in its own NTVDM. This ensures that the crashing of one application will not adversely affect the others, but it still enables interoperability between the applications because they use OLE (and not shared memory) to transfer data. To make the fix as transparent as possible to the users, you suggested that two things be done:

1. Make sure that for each shortcut a user has created to the office applications, the Run in Separate Memory Space option is selected on the Shortcut tab.

2. Change the properties for the extensions associated with the applications (for example, .XLS and .DOC) so that they start using the /separate switch. Then any file that is double-clicked invokes the associated program to run in its own NTVDM.

CHAPTER SUMMARY

KEY TERMS

Before you take the exam, make sure you are comfortable with the definitions and concepts for each of the following key terms:

- FAT
- NTFS
- workgroup
- domain

This chapter discussed the main planning topics you will encounter on the Windows NT Server exam. Distilled down, these topics revolve around two main goals: understanding the planning of disk configuration and understanding the planning of network protocols.

◆ Windows NT Server supports an unlimited number of inbound sessions; Windows NT Workstation supports no more than 10 active sessions at the same time.

◆ Windows NT Server accommodates an unlimited number of remote access connections (although Microsoft only supports up to 256); Windows NT Workstation supports only a single remote access connection.

Key Terms: A list of key terms appears at the end of each chapter. These are terms that you should be sure you know and are comfortable defining and understanding when you go in to take the exam.

Chapter Summary: Before the Apply Your Learning section, you will find a chapter summary that wraps up the chapter and reviews what you should have learned.

EXTENSIVE REVIEW AND SELF-TEST OPTIONS

At the end of each chapter, along with some summary elements, you will find a section called "Apply Your Learning" that gives you several different methods with which to test your understanding of the material and review what you have learned.

Chapter 1 PLANNING 23

APPLY YOUR LEARNING

This section allows you to assess how well you understood the material in the chapter. Review and Exam questions test your knowledge of the tasks and concepts specified in the objectives. The Exercises provide you with opportunities to engage in the sorts of tasks that comprise the skill sets the objectives reflect.

Exercises

1.1 Synchronizing the Domain Controllers

The following steps show you how to manually synchronize a backup domain controller within your domain. (This objective deals with Objective Planning 1.)

Time Estimate: Less than 10 minutes.

1. Click Start, Programs, Administrative Tools, and select the Server Manager icon.

2. Highlight the BDC (Backup Domain Controller) in your computer list.

3. Select the Computer menu, then select Synchronize with Primary Domain Controller.

12.2 Establishing a Trust Relationship between Domains

The following steps show you how to establish a trust relationship between multiple domains. To complete this exercise, you must have two Windows NT Server computers, each installed in their own domain. (This objective deals with objective Planning 1.)

Time Estimate: 10 minutes.

1. From the trusted domain select Start, Programs, Administrative Tools, and click User Manager for Domains. The User Manager.

FIGURE 1.2
The login process on a local machine.

2. Select the Policies menu and click Trust Relationships. The Trust Relationships dialog box appears.

4. When the trusting domain information has been entered, click OK and close the Trust Relationships dialog box.

Review Questions

1. List the four domain models that can be used for directory services in Windows NT Server 4.

2. List the goals of a directory services architecture.

3. What is the maximum size of the SAM database in Windows NT Server 4.0?

4. What are the two different types of domains in a trust relationship?

5. In a trust relationship which domain would contain the user accounts?

Exercises: These activities provide an opportunity for you to master specific hands-on tasks. Our goal is to increase your proficiency with the product or technology. You must be able to conduct these tasks in order to pass the exam.

Review Questions: These open-ended, short-answer questions allow you to quickly assess your comprehension of what you just read in the chapter. Instead of asking you to choose from a list of options, these questions require you to state the correct answers in your own words. Although you will not experience these kinds of questions on the exam, these questions will indeed test your level of comprehension of key concepts.

6. Can a local account be used in a trust relationship? Explain.

7. In a complete trust domain model that uses 4 different domains, what is the total number of trust relationships required to use a complete trust domain model?

Exam Questions

The following questions are similar to those you will face on the Microsoft exam. Answers to these questions can be found in section Answers and Explanations, later in the chapter. At the end of each of those answers, you will be informed of where (that is, in what section of the chapter) to find more information..

1. ABC Corporation has locations in Toronto, New York, and San Francisco. It wants to install Windows NT Server 4 to encompass all its locations in a single WAN environment. The head office is located in New York. What is the best domain model for ABC's directory services implementation?

A. Single-domain model

B. Single-master domain model

C. Multiple-master domain model

D. Complete-trust domain model

2. JPS Printing has a single location with 1,000 users spread across the LAN. It has special printers and applications installed on the servers in its environment. It needs to be able to centrally manage the user accounts and the resources. Which domain model would best fit its needs?

A. Single-domain model

B. Single-master domain model

C. Multiple-master domain model

D. Complete-trust domain model

5. What must be created to allow a user account from one domain to access resources in a different domain?

A. Complete Trust Domain Model

B. One Way Trust Relationship

C. Two Way Trust Relationship

D. Master-Domain Model

Answers to Review Questions

1. Single domain, master domain, multiple-master domain, complete-trust domain. See section, Windows NT Server 4 Domain Models, in this chapter for more information. (This question deals with objective Planning 1.)

2. One user, one account, centralized administration, universal resource access, synchronization. See section, Windows NT Server 4 Directory Services, in this chapter for more information. (This question deals with objective Planning 1.)

6. Local accounts cannot be given permissions across trusts. See section, Accounts in Trust Relationships, in this chapter for more information. (This question deals with Planning 1.)

Exam Questions: These questions reflect the kinds of multiple-choice questions that appear on the Microsoft exams. Use them to become familiar with the exam question formats and to help you determine what you know and what you need to review or study more.

Answers and Explanations: For each of the Review and Exam questions, you will find thorough explanations located at the end of the section. They are easily identifiable because they are in blue type.

Suggested Readings and Resources

The following are some recommended readings on the subject of installing and configuring NT Workstation:

1. Microsoft Official Curriculum course 770: *Installing and Configuring Microsoft Windows NT Workstation 4.0*

   • Module 1: Overview of Windows NT Workstation 4.0

   • Module 2: Installing Windows NT Workstation 4.0

2. Microsoft Official Curriculum course 922: *Supporting Microsoft Windows NT 4.0 Core Technologies*

   • Module 2: Installing Windows NT

   • Module 3: Configuring the Windows NT Environment

3. *Microsoft Windows NT Workstation Resource Kit Version 4.0* (Microsoft Press)

   • Chapter 2: Customizing Setup

   • Chapter 4: Planning for a Mixed Environment

4. Microsoft TechNet CD-ROM

   • *MS Windows NT Workstation Technical Notes*

     • MS Windows NT Workstation Deployment Guide – Automating Windows NT Setup

     • An Unattended Windows NT Workstation Deployment

5. Web Sites

   • www.microsoft.com/train_cert

   • www.prometric.com/testingcandidates/ assessment/chosetest.html (take online

Suggested Readings and Resources: The very last element in every chapter is a list of additional resources you can use if you want to go above and beyond certification-level material or if you need to spend more time on a particular subject that you are having trouble understanding.

Introduction

MCSE Training Guide: Networking Essentials, Second Edition is designed for advanced end-users, service technicians, and network administrators with the goal of certification as a Microsoft Certified Systems Engineer (MCSE). The "Networking Essentials" exam (70-058) measures your ability to implement, administer, and troubleshoot information systems that incorporate Windows 95 as well as any of the BackOffice family of products. According to Microsoft, the exam covers only the networking knowledge and skills common to both Windows 95 and BackOffice products.

WHO SHOULD READ THIS BOOK

This book is designed to help you meet the goal of certification by preparing you for the "Networking Essentials" exam.

This book is your one-stop shop. Everything you need to know to pass the exam is in here, and Microsoft has approved it as study material. You do not *need* to take a class in addition to buying this book to pass the exam. However, depending on your personal study habits or learning style, you may benefit from taking a class in addition to the book or buying this book in addition to attending a class.

This book also can help advanced users and administrators who are not studying for the exam but are looking for a single-volume reference on networking.

HOW THIS BOOK HELPS YOU

This book conducts you on a self-guided tour of all the areas covered by the "Networking Essentials" exam and teaches you the specific skills you need to achieve your MCSE certification. You'll also find helpful hints, tips, real-world examples, exercises, and references to additional study materials. Specifically, this book is set up to help you in the following ways:

◆ **Organization.** This book is organized by major exam topics and individual exam objectives. Every objective you need to know for the "Networking Essentials" exam is covered in this book. We attempted to make the information accessible in several different ways:

  • The full list of exam topics and objectives is included in this introduction.

  • Each chapter begins with a list of the objectives being covered in that particular chapter.

  • Each chapter also begins with an outline that provides you an overview of the material and the page numbers where particular topics can be found.

  • We've also repeated the objective at the beginnig of the section where the material most directly relevant to it is covered.

  • This information on where the objectives are covered is also conveniently condensed in the tear card at the front of this book.

◆ **Instructional Features**. This book has been designed to provide you with multiple ways to access and reinforce the exam material. The features include the following:

- *Objective Explanations.* As mentioned above, each chapter begins with a list of the objectives covered in the chapter. In addition, immediately following each objective is an explanation of it in context that defines it more meaningfully.

- *Study Strategies.* The beginning of the chapter also includes strategies for how to approach studying and retaining the material in the chapter, particularly as it is addressed on the exam.

- *Exam Tips.* Exam tips appear in the margin to provide specific exam-related advice. Such tips may address what material is covered (or not covered) on the exam, how it is covered, mnemonic devices, or particular quirks of that exam.

- *Reviews Breaks and Summaries.* Crucial information is summarized at various points in the book in lists or tables. Each chapter ends with a summary as well.

- *Key Terms.* A list of key terms appears at the end of each chapter.

- *Notes.* These appear in the margin and contain various kinds of useful information like tips on the technology or administrative practices, historical background on terms and technologies, or side commentary on industry issues.

- *Warnings.* In using sophisticated information technology, there is always the potential for mistakes or even catastrophes that can occur through improper application of the technology. Warnings appear in the margin to alert you to such potential problems.

- *In-Depth Sidebars.* These more extensive discussions cover material that is perhaps not as directly relevant to the exam, but which is useful as reference material and/or in everyday practice. In-depths may also provide useful background or contextual information necessary for understanding the larger topic under consideration.

- *Step by Steps.* These are hands-on tutorial instructions that step you through a particular task or function relevant to the exam objectives.

- *Exercises.* Found at the end of the chapters in the "Apply Your Learning" section, Exercises may include additional tutorial material as well as other types of problems and questions.

- *Case Studies.* Case studies are presented throughout the book. They provide you with another, more conceptual opportunity to apply the knowledge you are developing. Each case study includes a description of a scenario, the essence of the case, and an extended analysis section. The case studies reflect the "real-world" experiences of the authors in ways that prepare you not only for the exam but for actual network administration as well.

◆ **Extensive practice test options.** The book provides numerous opportunities for you to assess your knowledge and practice for the exam.

- *Review Questions.* These open-ended questions appear in the "Apply Your Learning" section that appears at the end of each chapter. They allow you to quickly assess your comprehension of what you just read in the chapter. Answers to the questions are provided later in the section.

- *Exam Questions.* These questions also appear

in the "Apply Your Learning" section. They reflect the kinds of multiple-choice questions that appear on the Microsoft exams. Use them to practice for the exam and to help you determine what you know and what you need to review or study further. Answers and explanations for them are provided.

- *Practice Exam.* A practice exam is included in the "Final Review" section. The final review and the practice exam are discussed below.

- *Top Score.* The Top Score software included on the CD-ROM provides further practice questions.

◆ **Final Review.** This part of the book provides you

> **NOTE**
>
> **Top Score**   For a complete description of New Riders' Top Score test engine, please see Appendix D, "Using the Top Score Software."

with three valuable tools for preparing for the exam:

- *Fast Facts.* This condensed version of the information contained in the book will prove extremely useful for last-minute review.

- *Study and Exam Tips.* Read this section early on to help you develop study strategies. It also provides you with valuable exam-day tips and information on new exam/question formats like adaptive tests and simulation-based questions.

- *Practice Exam.* A full practice exam is included. Questions are written in the styles used on the actual exam. Use it to assess your readiness for the real thing.

The book includes other features like a section titled

"Suggested Reading and Resources" at the end of each chapter that directs you toward further information that could aid you in your exam preparation or your actual work. There are several valuable appendixes as well, including a glossary (Appendix A), an overview of the Microsoft certification program (Appendix B), and a description of what is on the CD-ROM (Appendix C). These and all the other book features mentioned above will provide you with thorough preparation for the exam.

For more information about the exam or the certification process, contact Microsoft:

Microsoft Education: (800) 636-7544

Internet: `ftp://ftp.microsoft.com/Services/MSEdCert`

World Wide Web: `http://www.microsoft.com/train_cert`

CompuServe Forum: GO MSEDCERT

WHAT THE NETWORKING ESSENTIALS EXAM (#70-058) COVERS

The "Networking Essentials" exam (70-058) covers the four main topic areas represented by the conceptual groupings of the test objectives. Each chapter represents one or more of these main topic areas. The exam objectives are listed by topic area in the following sections.

Standards and Terminology

◆ Define common networking terms for LANs and WANs.

◆ Compare a file and print server with an application server.

◆ Compare user-level security with access permission assigned to a shared directory on a server.

◆ Compare a client/server network with a peer-to-peer network.

◆ Compare the implications of using connection-oriented communications with connectionless communications.

◆ Distinguish whether SLIP or PPP is used as the communications protocol for various situations.

◆ Define the communication devices that communicate at each level of the OSI model.

◆ Describe the characteristics and purpose of the media used in IEEE 802.3 and IEEE 802.5 standards.

◆ Explain the purpose of NDIS and Novell ODI network standards.

Planning

◆ Select the appropriate media for various situations.

Media choices include:

- Twisted-pair cable
- Coaxial cable
- Fiber-optic cable
- Wireless

Situational elements include:

- Cost
- Distance limitations
- Number of nodes

◆ Select the appropriate topology for various token-ring and Ethernet networks.

◆ Select the appropriate network and transport protocol or protocols for various token-ring and Ethernet networks.

Protocol choices include:

- DLC
- AppleTalk
- IPX
- TCP/IP
- NFS
- SMB

◆ Select the appropriate connectivity devices for various token-ring and Ethernet networks.

Connectivity devices include:

- Repeaters
- Bridges
- Routers
- Brouters
- Gateways

◆ List the characteristics, requirements, and appropriate situations for WAN connection services.

WAN connection services include:

- X.25
- ISDN
- Frame relay
- ATM

Implementation

◆ Choose an administrative plan to meet specified needs, including performance management, account management, and security.

◆ Choose a disaster recovery plan for various situations.

◆ Given the manufacturer's documentation for the network adapter, install, configure, and resolve hardware conflicts for multiple network adapters in a token-ring or Ethernet network.

◆ Implement a NetBIOS naming scheme for all computers on a given network.

◆ Select the appropriate hardware and software tools to monitor trends in the network.

Troubleshooting

◆ Identify common errors associated with components required for communications.

◆ Diagnose and resolve common connectivity problems with cards, cables, and related hardware.

◆ Resolve broadcast storms.

◆ Identify and resolve network performance problems.

HARDWARE AND SOFTWARE NEEDED

As a self-paced study guide, this book was designed with the expectation that you will use Windows 95 and Windows NT 4.0 as you follow along through the

exercises while you learn. The theory covered in *MCSE Training Guide: Networking Essentials, Second Edition* is applicable to a wide range of network systems in a wide range of actual situations, and the exercises in this book encompass that range.

Your computer should meet the following criteria:

◆ On the Microsoft Hardware Compatibility List

◆ 486DX2 66-Mhz (or better) processor for Windows NT Server

◆ 340-MB (or larger) hard disk for Windows NT Server, 100 MB free and formatted as NTFS

◆ 3.5-inch 1.44-MB floppy drive

◆ VGA (or Super VGA) video adapter

◆ VGA (or Super VGA) monitor

◆ Mouse or equivalent pointing device

◆ Double-speed (or faster) CD-ROM drive (optional)

◆ Network Interface Card (NIC)

◆ Presence on an existing network, or use of a 2-port (or more) mini-port hub to create a test network

◆ Microsoft Windows 95

◆ Microsoft Windows NT Server version 4.0 (CD-ROM version)

It is somewhat easier to obtain access to the necessary computer hardware and software in a corporate business environment. It can be difficult, however, to allocate enough time within the busy workday to complete a self-study program. Most of your study time will occur after normal working hours, away from the everyday interruptions and pressures of your regular job.

ADVICE ON TAKING THE EXAM

More extensive tips are found in the Final Review section titled "Study and Exam Prep Tips," but keep this advice in mind as you study:

◆ **Read all the material.** Microsoft has been known to include material not expressly specified in the objectives. This book has included additional information not reflected in the objectives in an effort to give you the best possible preparation for the examination and for the real-world network experiences to come.

◆ **Do the Step by Steps and complete the Exercises in each chapter.** They will help you gain experience using the Microsoft product. All Microsoft exams are task- and experience-based and require you to have used the Microsoft product in a real networking environment.

◆ **Use the questions to assess your knowledge.** Don't just read the chapter content; use the questions to find out what you know and what you don't. Study some more, review, and then assess your knowledge again.

◆ **Review the exam objectives.** Develop your own questions and examples for each topic listed. If you can make and answer several questions for each topic, you should not find it difficult to pass the exam.

Remember, the primary objective is not to pass the exam—it is to understand the material. After you understand the material, passing the exam should be simple. Knowledge is a pyramid; to build upward, you need a solid foundation. This book and the Microsoft Certified Professional programs are designed to ensure that you have that solid foundation.

Good luck!

NOTE

Preparation Includes Practice
Although this book is designed to prepare you to take and pass the Networking Essentials certification exam, there are no guarantees. Read this book, work through the questions and exercises, and when you feel confident, take the Practice Exam and additional exams using the Top Score test engine. This should tell you whether or not you are ready for the real thing.

When taking the actual certification exam, make sure you answer all the questions before your time limit expires. Do not spend too much time on any one question. If you are unsure about an answer, answer the question as best you can and mark it for later review, when you have fin-

NEW RIDERS PUBLISHING

The staff of New Riders Publishing is committed to bringing you the very best in computer reference material. Each New Riders book is the result of months of work by authors and staff who research and refine the information contained within its covers.

As part of this commitment to you, the NRP reader, New Riders invites your input. Please let us know if you enjoy this book, if you have trouble with the information or examples presented, or if you have a suggestion for the next edition.

Please note, however, that New Riders staff cannot serve as a technical resource during your preparation for the Microsoft certification exams or for questions about software- or hardware-related problems. Please refer instead to the documentation that accompanies the Microsoft products or to the applications' Help systems.

If you have a question or comment about any New Riders book, there are several ways to contact New Riders Publishing. We will respond to as many readers as we can. Your name, address, or phone number will never become part of a mailing list or be used for any purpose other than to help us continue to bring you the best books possible. You can write to us at the following address:

New Riders Publishing
Attn: Publisher
201 W. 103rd Street
Indianapolis, IN 46290

If you prefer, you can fax New Riders Publishing at (317) 581-4663.

You also can send e-mail to New Riders at the following Internet address:

certification@mcp.com

Thank you for selecting *MCSE Training Guide: Networking Essentials, Second Edition*!

STANDARDS AND TERMINOLOGY

Chapter 1 targets the following objectives in the Standards and Terminology section of the Networking Essentials exam:

Compare a client/server network with a peer-to-peer network.

▶ This objective makes sure you are familiar with the two main network classification models.

Define common networking terms for LANs and WANs.

▶ The purpose of this objective is to make sure people working in the networking field understand the difference between a local area network (LAN) and a wide area network (WAN). These terms are the main topics of discussion throughout this chapter.

Compare a file and print server with an application server.

▶ This objective makes sure you are aware of the different types of servers in the field of networking.

CHAPTER 1

Networking Terms and Concepts

OUTLINE

▶ You need to be very familiar with the terminology used throughout this chapter. This terminology serves as a basis for the rest of the book and for the exam.

▶ Many different services are explained in this book. Be prepared to understand the key differences between a file and print server and an application server, as well as the differences between client/server and peer-to-peer networks. Remember that a file and print server or an application server can be part of either a client/server or peer-to-peer network.

▶ Keep in mind that this chapter presents the big picture—a 50,000-foot overview of networking—while at the same time introducing basic terminology and definitions that need to be memorized.

INTRODUCTION

As one of the required exams in the Microsoft MCSE certification program, the exam for Networking Essentials challenges your knowledge of computer networking components, theory, and implementation. This chapter is generic in the sense that it is not specific to any one software or hardware vendor; instead, it introduces you to some of the basic and rudimentary terms and concepts used when discussing networking. Real-world examples are provided whenever possible. Study this chapter carefully; you will use these terms and concepts throughout the rest of this book and in the real world, no matter which networking model or system is being discussed. Although most of this chapter's examples are given in terms of Microsoft solutions, all other successful networking models must accomplish these same tasks.

This chapter begins with a definition of networking. It then moves on to cover three different computing models used by various systems throughout the world. The discussion next turns to the two main types of network models and then covers how networks are classified based on various factors. The chapter goes on to describe the various services that a network can offer.

In general, this chapter helps the reader understand some of the broad classifications into which networks can fall. An appropriate analogy might be motor vehicle classification—you should think in terms of car, truck, or bus instead of a detailed description such as a 1969 Ford Mustang or a 1998 Honda Accord.

The integration of network services within personal desktop operating systems and the public emergence of the worldwide network, also known as the Internet, have generated incredible momentum in the movement to get connected. Networks have become the primary means of disseminating information in most modern offices and even in some homes.

NETWORKING CONCEPTS AND COMPONENTS

Networking is the concept of sharing resources and services. A network of computers is a group of interconnected systems sharing resources and interacting using a shared communications link (see Figure 1.1). A *network*, therefore, is a set of interconnected systems with something to share. The shared resource can be data, a printer, a fax modem, or a service such as a database or an email system. The individual systems must be connected through a pathway (called the *transmission medium*) that is used to transmit the resource or service between the computers. All systems on the pathway must follow a set of common communication rules for data to arrive at its intended destination and for the sending and receiving systems to understand each other. The rules governing computer communication are called *protocols*.

In summary, all networks must have the following:

◆ A resource to share (resource)

◆ A pathway to transfer data (transmission medium)

◆ A set of rules governing how to communicate (protocols)

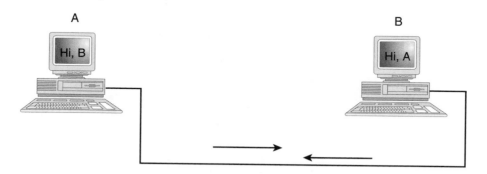

FIGURE 1.1
In its simplest form, a computer network is two or more computers sharing information across a common transmission medium.

Having a transmission pathway does not always guarantee communication. When two entities communicate, they do not merely exchange information; rather, they must understand the information they receive from each other. The goal of computer networking, therefore, is not simply to exchange data but to understand and use data received from other entities on the network.

An analogy is people speaking (see Figure 1.2). Just because two people can speak, it does not mean they automatically can understand each other. These two people might speak different languages or interpret words differently. One person might use sign language, while the other uses spoken language. As in human communication, even though you have two entities who "speak," there is no guarantee they will be able to understand each other. Just because two computers are sharing resources, it does not necessarily mean they can communicate.

Because computers can be used in different ways and can be located at different distances from each other, enabling computers to communicate often can be a daunting task that draws on a wide variety of technologies.

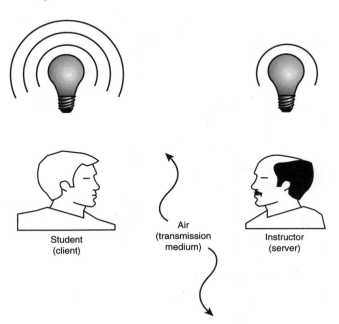

Student
(client)

Air
(transmission
medium)

Instructor
(server)

FIGURE 1.2
Human communication is like a network.

The two main reasons for using computer networking are to provide services and to reduce equipment costs. Networks enable computers to share their resources by offering services to other computers and users on a network. The following are specific reasons for networking PCs:

◆ Sharing files

◆ Sharing printers and other devices

◆ Enabling centralized administration and security of the resources within the system

◆ Supporting network applications such as electronic mail and database services

You will learn more about these important network functions later in this chapter.

MODELS OF NETWORK COMPUTING

After you have the necessary prerequisites for network communication, a structure must be put in place that organizes how communication and sharing occurs. Three methods of organization, or models, generally are recognized. The following are the three models for network computing:

◆ Centralized computing

◆ Distributed computing

◆ Collaborative or cooperative computing

These three models are the basis for the various types of computer networks you learn about in this book. The following sections discuss the three models for network computing.

Centralized Computing

The first computers were large, expensive, and difficult to manage. Originally, these large mainframe computers were not networked as you are familiar with today. Jobs were entered into the system by reading commands from card decks. The computer executed one job at a time and generated a printout when the job was complete. Terminals, which came later, provided the user with a new mechanism to interact with the centralized computer. These terminals, however, were merely input/output devices that had no independent processing power. All processing still took place on the central mainframe, (see Figure 1.3) hence the name *centralized computing*. Networks, therefore, served little purpose other than to deliver commands to and get results from the powerful centralized processing device. To this day, large mainframe systems are still being operated around the world, most often by governments and large corporations. An example of centralized computing to which everyone can relate is using an ATM machine. ATMs function as terminals. All processing is done on the mainframe computer to which the ATMs are connected. In summary, the centralized computing model involves the following:

◆ All processing takes place in the central mainframe computer.

◆ Terminals are connected to the central computer and function only as input/output devices.

This early computing model worked well in large organizations that could justify the need for these expensive computing devices. One of

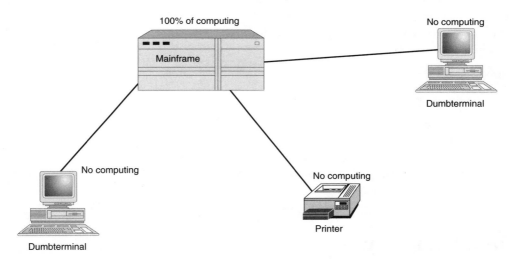

FIGURE 1.3
In centralized computing all the processing is done by a central computer.

the drawbacks, however, was that the mainframes were not flexible in their placement (some were the size of a large room) and did not scale down to meet the needs of smaller organizations. New ways of sharing information were necessary to allow computing power to be shared efficiently on smaller networks.

Distributed Computing

As personal computers (PCs) were introduced to organizations, a new model of *distributed computing* emerged. Instead of concentrating computing at a central device, PCs made it possible to give each worker an independent, individual computer. Each PC could receive input and could process information locally, without the aid of another computer (see Figure 1.4).

This meant that groups who previously had found the cost of a mainframe environment to be prohibitive were now able to gain the benefits of computing at a far lower cost than that of a mainframe. These PCs, however, did not have the computing power of a mainframe. Thus, in most instances, a company's mainframe could not be replaced by a PC.

An analogy might help clarify the difference between the two computing models. A mainframe, which uses a centralized computing model, is like a bus. A bus is a large, powerful vehicle used to transport many people at once. Everyone goes to one location—the bus—to be transported. In the same way, everyone must work

> **NOTE**
>
> **Personal Computer Terminology.**
> The term *PC* initially referred to a specific device—the IBM PC computer. Over time, *PC* has become a generic term referring to any desktop computer. Some purists, however, still use the term *PC* to refer to an IBM-compatible workstation computer and use the term *Mac* to refer to a computer from Apple.

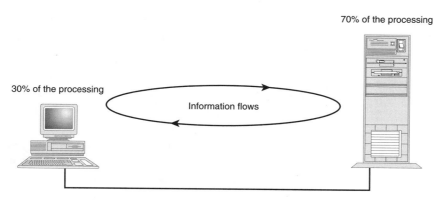

70% of the processing

30% of the processing

Information flows

FIGURE 1.4
Distributed computing.

through or at a mainframe computer. A personal PC, which uses distributed computing, is like a motorcycle. It transports one person at a time. (Yes, I know a motorcycle can transport two people, but think of it as only having one seat.) Each person can use his own motorcycle to go somewhere without worrying about the other users. PCs enable individuals to work at their own computers rather than through a single large computer.

In summary, distributed computing involves the following:

◆ Multiple computers capable of processing independently

◆ Task completion by the local computer or other computers on the network

Distributed computing was a major step forward in how businesses leveraged their hardware resources. It provided smaller businesses with their own computational capabilities, enabling them to perform less-complex computing tasks on the smaller, relatively inexpensive machines.

Collaborative Computing

Also called cooperative computing, *collaborative computing* enables computers in a distributed computing environment to share processing power in addition to data, resources, and services. In a collaborative computing environment, one computer might borrow processing power by running a program on another computer on the network. Or, processes might be designed so they can run on two or more computers. Collaborative computing cannot take place without a network to enable the various computers to communicate.

A person browsing the Internet is an example of collaborative computing. On the Internet, Web servers actively use resources to give your computer information about how a Web page should look, includings its colors, its font sizes, and what graphics should display. Your computer uses its processing power to interpret this information and to display it in the format intended by the designer. Another example of collaborative computing is Microsoft server-based products such as Exchange Server or SQL Server. For both of these products, requests originate from intelligent client software (which uses the processor power of the workstation it is running on) but then are serviced from server software running on a Windows NT server. The server then processes the request using its own resources and passes the results back to the client. Processor and memory resources on both the client and the server are utilized in the completion of the task.

In the future, you can expect collaborative computing to provide even greater amounts of computing power. This might happen through a new capability of computers to detect which PCs are idle on the network and to harness the CPU power or RAM of the idle PCs for use in processing.

In summary, collaborative computing involves the following:

◆ Multiple computers cooperating to perform a task

◆ Software designed to take advantage of the collaborative environment

Network Models: Comparing Client/Server and Peer-to-Peer Networking Configurations

Compare a client/server network with a peer-to-peer network.

Networks generally fall into one of two broad network categories:

◆ Client/server networks

◆ Peer-to-peer networks

It is important to remember that one type of networking configuration is not necessarily better than another. Each type of networking model has its own strengths and weaknesses.

Client/Server-Based Networking

A client/server network consists of a group of user-oriented PCs (called *clients*) that issue requests to a server. The client PC is responsible for issuing requests for services to be rendered. The server's function on the network is to service these requests. Servers generally are higher-performance systems that are optimized to provide network services to other PCs. The server machine often has a faster CPU, more memory, and more disk space than a typical client machine.

Some examples of client/server-based networks are Novell NetWare, Windows NT Server, and Banyan Vines. Some common server types include file servers, mail servers, print servers, fax servers, and application servers. In a client/server network, the server machines often are not even set up to do the tasks that a client machine can do. (On a Novell or Banyan server, for example, a person cannot run a spreadsheet from the server console. Other systems, such as Windows NT and UNIX machines, enable a person to do this even though it is not the intended use of the system).

Eating at a restaurant is analogous to a client/server model. You, the customer, are a client. You issue requests for meals, drinks, and dessert. The waiter is the server. It is the waiter's job to service those requests.

Although this discussion should have made it clear how they differ, people often confuse mainframe computing with a client/server-based network. The two approaches to computing are not the same, however. In mainframe computing, the dumb terminal does not process any requests. It simply acts as an interface to receive input and to display output. Only the mainframe computer can process information. In a client/server model, the client PC can process information, but certain services are offloaded to the server machine. The server machine's role is simply to process the requests made for these services by the client. In short, a client/server-based network is one in which certain tasks run on and utilize the resources of one machine while others utilize another machine, each according to its functional role.

An example of a client/server system is Microsoft Exchange Server. Your PC is responsible for constructing and displaying email messages, to name a couple of the possible tasks. The Exchange server is responsible for delivering outgoing email and for receiving email intended for you.

In summary, the client/server model is a network in which the role of the client is to issue requests and the role of the server is to service requests.

Peer-to-Peer Networking

A peer-to-peer network consists of a group of PCs that operate as equals. Each PC is called a *peer*. The peers share resources (such as files and printers) just like in a server-based network, although no specialized or dedicated server machines exist. In short, each PC can act as a client or a server. No one machine is set up with a higher-powered set of devices, nor is any one PC set up simply to provide one service (such as storing files). Small networks—usually with fewer than 10 machines—can work well in this configuration. In larger networks, companies usually move to a server-based network because many clients requesting to use a shared resource can put too much strain on one client's PC. Examples of peer-to-peer networks include Windows for Workgroups, Windows 95, and Windows NT Workstation.

Many actual network environments consist of a combination of server-based and peer-to-peer networking models. In the real world, companies often grow from a peer-to-peer network into a client/server-based network. The following analogy might help you better understand the use of each type of network.

A small company of 10 employees might choose to implement a car-pool strategy. Let's say four employees get together, and each takes a turn driving the other three employees to work. This is analogous to a peer-to-peer network. Just like a peer-to-peer network, in which no one PC is responsible for dedicating itself to providing a service, no one car is dedicated to providing transportation.

As the company grows to 400 employees, it might be decided that the number of employees justifies the purchase of a dedicated ride-pool van with a dedicated driver. This is analogous to a client/server network, in which a dedicated machine is used to provide a service. In this example, the company has dedicated a van to providing a ride-share service.

As you can see in this analogy, no single network model fits all situations. A car pool in a small company is an efficient and cost-effective way to get people to work. A bus probably is not economically feasible for a small company. In a big company, however, the use of a bus becomes feasible. Peer-to-peer networks can work well for small workgroups. Client/server networks provide the necessary resources for larger groups of users.

LOCAL AND WIDE AREA NETWORKS

Define common networking terms for LANs and WANs.

Networks come in all shapes and sizes. Network administrators often classify networks according to geographical size. Networks of similar size have many similar characteristics, as you will learn in later chapters. The following are the most common size classifications:

◆ Local area networks (LANs)

◆ Wide area networks (WANs)

These size classifications are described in the following sections.

Local Area Networks (LANs)

A *local area network (LAN)* is a group of computers and network communication devices interconnected within a geographically limited area, such as a building or a campus. LANs are characterized by the following:

◆ They transfer data at high speeds (higher bandwidth).

◆ They exist in a limited geographical area.

◆ Connectivity and resources, especially the transmission media, usually are managed by the company running the LAN.

Wide Area Networks (WANs)

A *wide area network (WAN)* interconnects LANs. A WAN can be located entirely within a state or a country, or it can be interconnected around the world.

WANs are characterized by the following:

◆ They exist in an unlimited geographical area.

◆ They usually interconnect multiple LANs.

◆ They often transfer data at lower speeds (lower bandwidth).

◆ Connectivity and resources, especially the transmission media, usually are managed by a third-party carrier such as a telephone or cable company.

NOTE

WANs Are Interconnected LANs.
This interconnection often is represented by a line going into a cloud. This is because the company running the network typically has only a general idea of the path that the data will take on its journey to the other LAN segment. All the company knows is that the data enters the cloud on one side and exits the other side.

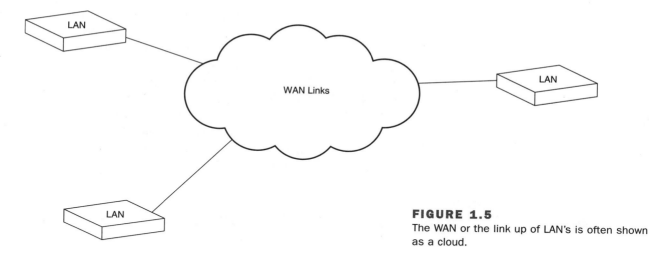

FIGURE 1.5
The WAN or the link up of LAN's is often shown as a cloud.

WANs can be further classified into two categories: enterprise WANs and global WANs. An *enterprise WAN* connects the widely separated computer resources of a single organization. An organization with computer operations at several distant sites can employ an enterprise WAN to interconnect the sites. An enterprise WAN can combine private and commercial network services, but it is dedicated to the needs of a particular organization. A *global WAN* interconnects networks of several corporations or organizations. Other terms that describe networks include *municipal area network (MAN)*—a connected network that spans the geographic boundaries of a municipality—and *campus area network (CAN)*—a network that spans a campus or a set of buildings. These terms often lead to confusion because people are not sure whether they refer to the company's own network of computers or its connection to the outside world.

INTRANETS AND INTERNETS

In recent years, two new terms have been introduced: internet and intranet. A company that has a LAN has a network of computers. As a LAN grows, it develops into an internetwork of computers, referred to as an internet.

In the 1990s, graphical utilities (or browsers) were developed to view information on a server. Today, the two most popular forms of this utility are Microsoft's Internet Explorer and Netscape's Navigator. These browsers are used to navigate the Internet (note the capital I). This terminology initially led to much confusion in the industry because an *internet* is a connection of LANs, and the *Internet* is the connection of servers on various LANs that is available to various browser utilities. To avoid this confusion, the term *intranet* was coined. This term describes an internetwork of computers on a LAN for a single organization; the term *Internet* describes the network of computers you can connect to using a browser—essentially, an internetwork of LANs available to the public.

NETWORK SERVICES

Network services are the basic reason we connect computers. Services are what a company wants to have performed or provided. Based on the services a company wants to utilize, the company purchases a specific program and operating system. This section describes some of the most common services available on computer networks.

Basic Connectivity Services

The PCs in a network must have special system software that enables them to function in a networking environment. The first network operating systems really were add-on packages that supplied the networking software for existing operating systems such as MS-DOS or OS/2. More recent operating systems, such as Windows 95 and Windows NT, come with the networking components built in.

An analogy might help you differentiate fully integrated systems from add-ons. A box can hold goods, but it is not specifically designed to go anywhere. You can place a set of logs on the ground to act as rollers for the box, thus providing a mechanism for transporting or moving the box. This is similar to how old network systems used to work. Newer operating systems are like trucks. A truck is designed from the ground up with a chassis that supports a box to move goods. The box and the mechanism for transportation (the chassis) are integrated from the beginning; they are designed to operate with each other.

Client and server machines require specific software components. A computer that is strictly a server often cannot provide any client functionality. On a Novell server or a Banyan server, for example, a user cannot use the server for word processing. This is not always the case, however; Microsoft's NT Server and UNIX servers can run client programs.

A computer in a peer-to-peer network functions as both a client and a server; thus, it requires both client and server software. Operating systems such as Windows NT Workstation and Windows 95, both of which are peer-to-peer network operating systems, include dozens of services and utilities that facilitate networking. Some of these components are discussed in other chapters, and some are beyond the scope of the Networking Essentials exam. (You'll learn about them when you study for the Windows NT Server or Windows NT Workstation exam.) This section introduces you to a pair of key network services—the redirector service and the server service—that are at the core of all networking functions.

Redirector Service

A network client must have a software component called a *redirector*. In a typical standalone PC, I/O requests pass along the local bus to the local CPU. The redirector intercepts I/O requests within the client machine and checks whether the request is directed toward a service on another computer. If it is, the redirector directs the request toward the appropriate network entity. The redirector enables the client machine to send information out of the computer, provided that a transmission pathway exists.

In some operating environments, the redirector is called the *requester*. The workstation service acts as a redirector on Windows NT systems. In the field, people often refer to a redirector as a *client*. To connect a Windows 95 machine to a Windows NT machine, for example, it often is said, "Install the Microsoft Client for Microsoft Networks." If you want this Windows 95 machine to connect to a Novell server, you might say, "Install a Novell Client on the Windows 95 machine" (see Figure 1.6).

Server Service

A network server machine must have a component that accepts I/O requests from clients on the network and that fulfills those requests

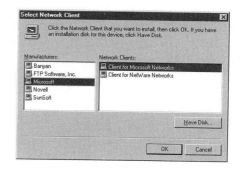

FIGURE 1.6

The dialog box on a Windows 95 machine that shows a redirector being installed.

by routing the requested data back across the network to the client machine. In Windows NT, the server service performs the role of fulfilling client requests.

File Services

Compare a file and print server with an application server.

File services enable networked computers to share files with each other. This capability was one of the primary reasons networking of personal computers initially came about. File services include all network functions dealing with the storage, retrieval, or movement of data files. File services enable users to read, write, and manage files and data. This includes moving files between computers and archiving files and data.

This section begins by defining file services and then moves on to other related topics such as file transfers, file storage, data migration, file archiving, and file update synchronization.

File services are an important part of client/server and peer-to-peer networks. Computers providing files services are referred to as file servers (see Figure 1.7). Two types of servers exist: dedicated and non-dedicated. *Dedicated servers* do nothing but fulfill requests to network clients. These servers commonly are found in client/server environments. *Non-dedicated servers* do double duty. They enable a user to go onto the machine acting as a file server and request the use of files from other machines; at the same time, they give files to users who request them from other computers on the network (see Figure 1.7). Non-dedicated file servers often are found in peer-to-peer networks. An example of a non-dedicated server is a Windows 95 machine that accesses files from other computers on the network and that provides access to its hard drive for other computers.

Dedicated file servers have the following benefits:

◆ Files are stored in a specific place where they can be reliably archived.

◆ Central file servers can be managed more efficiently because there is a single point of storage.

◆ Central file servers can contain expensive high-performance hardware that expedites file services and makes file servers more reliable.

◆ The cost of specialized file server technology is shared by a large number of users.

◆ Centralized networks are more scalable.

The following drawbacks, however, should be considered with regard to centralized file services:

◆ When all data is stored on a single server, a single point of failure exists. If the server fails, all data becomes unavailable.

◆ Because all clients contend for file services from a single source, average file-access times might be slower with a centralized file server than when files are stored on individual local hard drives.

Centralized file services generally are best for organizations that want to achieve the highest levels of centralized control for their data.

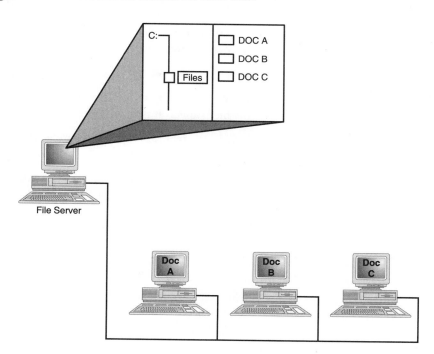

FIGURE 1.7

A file server stores files for users on other network machines.

Do not confuse centralized file services with centralized computer models. The terms *centralized* and *distributed* in this context describe the utilization method of processor resources, file resources, or administrative tasks. A single administrator, for example, can watch over a network with a single file server and many PC clients. This network utilizes centralized administration and provides centralized file access. Because the clients do their own processing, the network itself fits under the distributed computing model.

In a peer-to-peer network environment, most computers can share their files and applications with other computers, provided that a service is installed on the machine allowing them to do this. The sharing of services must be established for each individual computer, and each user must have the skills required to manage the networking services on her PC. Because services are being provided by many different computers, users must be aware of which computers are providing which services. Clearly, the skills and responsibility required in this situation are greater than for centralized file services. This is in contrast to a client/server model, in which the network often has one or more dedicated people to manage the servers.

The following are advantages of distributed file storage:

◆ No single point of failure exists. When a computer fails, only the files stored on that computer become unavailable.

◆ Individuals typically experience faster access to files located on their local machines than to files on centralized file servers.

◆ No specialized server hardware is required. File services can be provided with standard PCs.

The following are disadvantages related to distributed file storage:

◆ It is more difficult to manage the file service because there is not a single file location.

◆ File services provided by peers typically are not as fast or as flexible as file services provided by a central file server specifically designed for that purpose.

◆ Instead of upgrading one central file server when higher performance is needed, you must upgrade each computer.

Organizations tend to choose peer-to-peer networking for two reasons. The first reason is a desire to network with their current stock of PCs without the expense of a centralized server. Another reason is that a peer-to-peer network is an informal networking approach that fits the working style of many organizations. Microsoft implements peer-to-peer networking components in Windows for Workgroups, Windows 95, and Windows NT Workstation. All of these operating systems are capable of sharing and accessing network resources without the aid of a centralized server. These systems are not optimized for file and printer sharing, however; this sort of network structure is recommended only for smaller networks with limited security concerns.

File Transfer Services

Without a network, the options are limited for transferring data between computers. You can, of course, exchange files on floppy disks. This process is called *sneaker-net* because it consists of networking by physically running around and hand-delivering floppy disks from desk to desk. Otherwise, you can use communication software to dial up another computer and transfer files using a modem or a direct serial connection. With a network, users have constant access to high-speed data transfer without leaving their desks or dialing another computer. Making a file accessible on a network is as easy as moving it into a shared directory.

Another important file-management task of the network operating system (NOS) is providing and regulating access to programs and data stored on the file server's hard drive. This is known as *file sharing*. File sharing is another main reason companies invest in a network. Companies can save money by purchasing a single network version of an application rather than many single-user versions. Placing data files created by employees on a file server also serves several purposes including security, document control, and backup.

Centralized document control can be critical for a company in which a document might need to be revised several times. In an architectural firm, for example, the design of a building might be created by using a drafting program such as AutoCAD. The architects might produce several versions of the building plan as the client comes to a decision. If the plan is stored on the individual computers of each architect, the firm might not know which is the most recent version of the plan. An older version might have the most recent date (because of a backup, for example). If the plan is saved on a file server, however, each architect can access and work on the same file.

Most networks have some form of centralized file storage. For many years, companies have used the *online storage* approach to file storage. In the online storage scenario, data is stored on hard disks that are accessible on demand. The files that can be accessed on a server are limited to the amount of available hard drive space. Hard drives are fast, but even with drive prices decreasing in recent years, the cost to store megabytes of data this way can still be fairly high. Hard drives also have another disadvantage. Generally, they cannot be removed for off-site storage or exchange or to build a library of files that are seldom required but must be fairly readily available.

Another common approach to file storage is *offline storage*, which consists of removable media that are managed manually. After data is written to a tape or an optical disk, the storage medium can be removed from the server and can be shelved. Users who require offline data might need to know which tape or optical disk to request. Some systems provide indexes or other aids that make requesting the proper offline storage element automatic. A system operator still has to retrieve the tape or disk, however, and mount it on the server.

When the slow response of offline storage is unacceptable, a *near-line storage* approach can be used. Near-line storage employs a machine, often called a *jukebox*, to manage large numbers of tapes or optical disks automatically. The proper tape or disk is retrieved and mounted by the jukebox without human intervention. With near-line storage, huge amounts of data can be made available with only slight delays and at a much lower cost than storing the data on hard drives.

Data Migration

Data migration is a technology that automatically moves infrequently used data from online storage to near-line or offline storage. The criteria for moving files can include when the files were last used, the owner of the files, the files' sizes, and a variety of other factors. An efficient data-migration facility makes it easier to locate migrated files. Figure 1.8 illustrates one approach to data migration. Data migration is used when dealing with near-line storage systems.

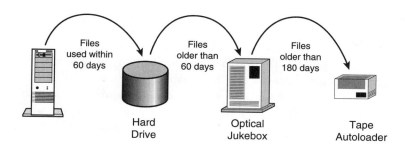

FIGURE 1.8
Data migration.

File Archiving

File archiving (also known as *backup*) is offline storage primarily geared toward creating duplicate copies of online files. These backup copies serve as insurance against minor or major system failures. A redundant copy is made of important system, application, and data files.

Generally, network administrators enable file archiving from a centralized location. A single site, for example, can back up all the servers on a network. Many current backup systems also offer the capability to back up various client workstations, making it feasible to archive all files on the network to a central facility. This makes archiving possible whether the files are located on network servers or on the clients. This archive is then stored in a safe location. A duplicate often is made and placed off the premises in case of disaster.

File-Update Synchronization

In its simplest form, *file-update synchronization* ensures that all users have the most recent copy of a file. File-update synchronization services can monitor the date and time stamps on files to determine which files were saved most recently. By tracking the users who access the file—along with the date and time stamps—the service can update all copies of the file with the most recent version.

In some cases, however, file-update synchronization can be considerably more involved. In a modern computing environment, it is not always feasible for all users to access all files in real time. A salesman, for example, might carry a notebook computer for entering orders. Dialing the central LAN every time an order needs to be entered is impractical; the salesman can enter orders offline (while disconnected from the network) and can store them in the laptop. That evening, he can call the central LAN, log in, and transmit all the day's orders at once.

During this process, files on the LAN must be updated to reflect new data in the salesman's portable computer. The salesman's PC also might need to be updated with order confirmations or new pricing information. The process of bringing the local and remote files into agreement also is called file-update synchronization.

File-update synchronization becomes considerably more challenging when additional users are sharing data files simultaneously. Complex mechanisms must be in place to make sure users do not accidentally overwrite each other's data. In some cases, the system simply flags files that have multiple conflicting updates, and a human must reconcile the differences. In Windows 95 and Windows NT 4.0, the My Briefcase program provides this service.

Printing Services

After file services, printing is probably the second biggest incentive for installing a LAN. The following are some of the many advantages of network print services:

- ◆ Many users can share the same printers. This capability is especially useful with expensive devices such as color printers and plotters.

- ◆ Printers can be located anywhere, not just next to a user's PC.

- ◆ Queue-based network printing is more efficient than direct printing because the workstation can begin to work again as soon as a job is queued to the network.

- ◆ Modern printing services enable users to send facsimile (fax) transmissions through the network to a fax server.

In this book, print services are defined as a network service that controls and manages access to printers and plotters (see Figure 1.9).

Application Services

Application services enable applications to leverage the computing power and specialized capabilities of other computers on a network.

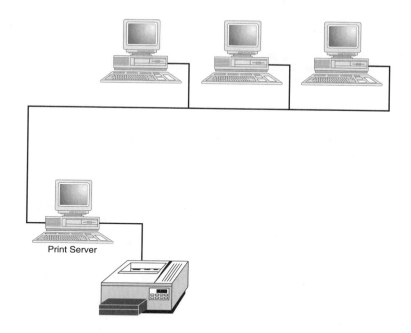

Business applications, for example, often must perform complex statistical calculations beyond the scope of most desktop PCs. Statistical software with the required capabilities might need to run on a mainframe computer or on a minicomputer. The statistical package, however, can make its capabilities available to applications on users' PCs by providing an application service.

The client PC sends the calculation request to the statistics server. When the results become available, they are returned to the client. This way, only one computer in an organization needs to have the expensive software license and processing power required to calculate the statistics, but all client PCs can benefit.

Application services enable organizations to install servers that are specialized for specific functions (see Figure 1.10). Some of the more common application servers are database servers, messaging/communication servers, groupware servers, and directory servers.

Application servers are an effective strategy for making a network more scalable. Additional application servers can be added as new application needs emerge. If more power is necessary for an application, only the application server needs to be upgraded. A database server, for example, can grow from a PC to a multiprocessor RISC

FIGURE 1.10

An application server runs all or part of an application on behalf of a client and then transmits the result to the client for further processing.

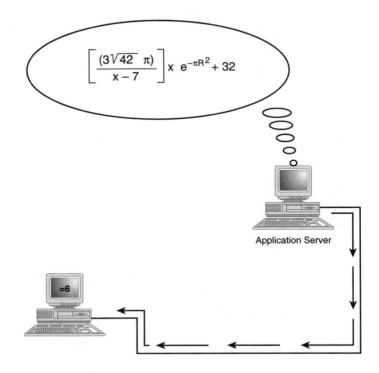

system running UNIX or Windows NT without requiring many (or even any) changes to the client PCs.

If demand for a server-based application begins to affect a server's performance, it's easy to move the application to a different server or even to dedicate a server specifically to that application. This isolates the application, enabling it and applications on the other server to run more efficiently. This type of scalability is one of the advantages of a LAN architecture.

Database Services

Database servers are the most common type of application servers. Because database services enable applications to be designed in separate client and server components, such applications frequently are called client/server databases.

With a client/server database, the client and server applications are designed to take advantage of the specialized capabilities of client and database systems, as described here:

◆ The client application manages data input from the user, generation of screen displays, some of the reporting, and data-retrieval requests sent to the database server.

◆ The database server manages the database files; adds, deletes, and modifies records in the database; queries the database and generates the results required by the client; and transmits results back to the client. The database server can service requests for multiple clients at the same time.

Database services relieve clients of most of the responsibilities for managing data. A modern database server is a sophisticated piece of software that can perform the following functions:

◆ Provide database security

◆ Optimize the performance of database operations

◆ Determine optimum locations for storing data without requiring clients to know where the data is located

◆ Service large numbers of clients by reducing the amount of time any one client spends accessing the database

◆ Distribute data across multiple database servers

Microsoft SQL Server and Oracle are two examples of applications that run at the server but are able to perform tasks requested by clients. Because of the way these applications were designed, both require a *back-end*, or server, component and a *front-end*, or client, component.

Distributed databases are becoming increasingly popular. They enable portions of databases to be stored on separate server computers, which may be in different geographic locations. This technique, known as *distributed data*, looks like a single logical database to users, but it places the data users need in the most accessible location. East coast sales data, for example, might be located on a database server in Boston; West coast sales data might be on a server in San Diego. Special database mechanisms must be in place to keep data synchronized in the copies of the database.

More simply, databases can be replicated. Complete copies of a database can be stored in various locations. This provides a redundancy factor because disaster is unlikely to strike all copies at once. In addition, database replication improves application response time over low-bandwidth connections because users can access the database on the LAN rather than over a comparatively slow WAN link.

As shown in Figure 1.11, the most popular strategies for replicating databases are the following:

◆ *Master-driven updates.* A single master server receives all updates and, in turn, updates all replicas.

◆ *Locally driven updates.* Any local server can receive an update and is responsible for distributing the change to other replicas.

Messaging/Communication Services

Messaging/communication services generally transfer information from one place to another. This communication of information can be broken down into three subareas:

◆ Email

◆ Voice mail

◆ Fax services

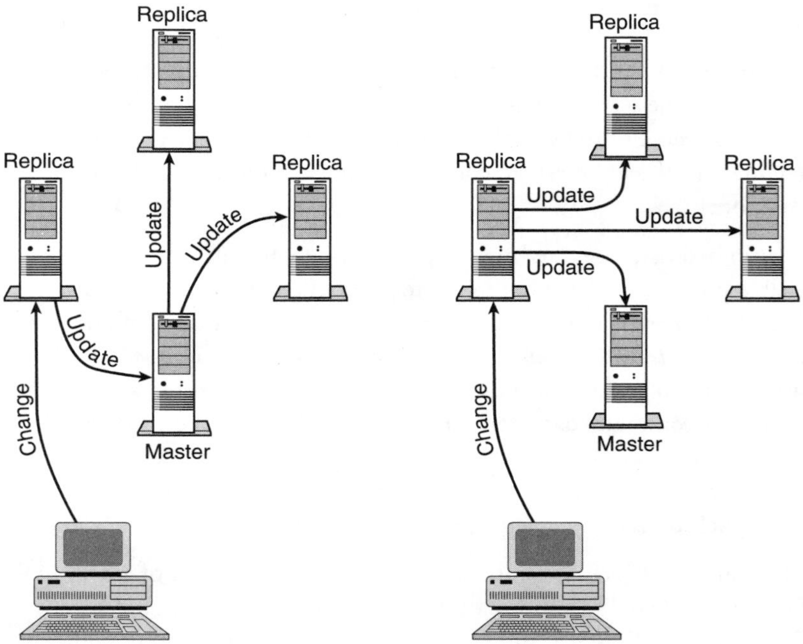

FIGURE 1.11
Master-driven and locally driven database replications.

Email

Email systems can service any size group from a local workgroup to a corporation to the world. By installing email routing devices, you can transfer mail smoothly and efficiently among several LANs. Email also can be routed to and received from the Internet. This enables users in dozens of countries throughout the world to exchange electronic messages.

Early text-based email has given way to elaborate systems that support embedded sound, graphics, and even video data.

Some of the major email packages include Microsoft's Exchange Server, Novell's GroupWise, and Lotus Notes.

Voice Mail

Voice mail enables you to connect your computer to a telephone system and to incorporate telephone voicemail messages with your PC. The technical term for this is *telephony*. This often involves moving your voicemail messages from the phone system to the LAN and enabling the computer network to distribute this information to different clients.

Fax Services

Fax services enable you to send or receive faxes from your computer. This is similar to printing in that your can "print" the document to a fax device. Fax services, however, can take on more complicated features including the capability to send faxes to a central fax server and to receive faxes from the phone system to a central fax device. That device then delivers the fax message to your PC. This all occurs automatically.

Groupware

Groupware is a relatively recent technology that enables several network users to communicate and to cooperate when solving a problem through shared document management. Interactive conferencing, screen sharing, and bulletin boards are examples of groupware applications. Groupware essentially is the capability for many users to work on one or more copies of a document together. Examples of applications with groupware features are Microsoft Exchange, Novell's GroupWise, and Lotus Notes.

Directory Services

Directory services, also known as the x.500 standard, provide location information for different entities on the network. Their main function is to act as an information booth, directing resource requests on the network to the location of the resource. When a client is requesting to use a printer or to find a server or even a specific application, the directory service tells the client where the resource is on the network and whether the resource is available (see Figure 1.12).

This is a service that more and more networking systems are moving towards. As networking systems have developed, they have begun to include this feature. This is similar to a large company having an information desk, whereas a small company probably would not.

Examples of computer systems that use directory services include Novell NetWare 4.11, Banyan VINES, Microsoft Exchange Server, and the soon-to-be-released Windows NT 5.0.

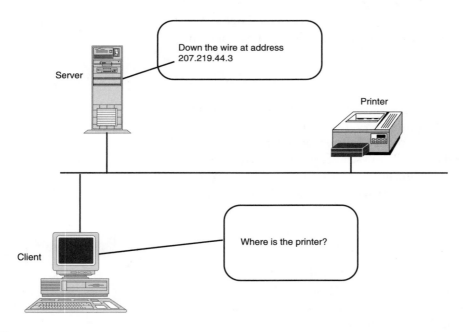

FIGURE 1.12

Directory services tells clients the location of resources on the network.

Security Services

Another service provided by networks is security. Security is one of the most important elements involved in a network. When users share resources and data on a network, they should be able to control who can access the data or resource and what the user can do with it. An example of this is a file showing the financial records of a company. If this file is on a file server, it is important to be able to control who has access to the file. One step further, who is able to read and change the file also is a crucial consideration. This same example also applies to a shared printer. You might want to specify who can use the expensive color laser printer or, more specifically, when a person can use this printer. As you can see, security is an important service on a network. Network administrators spend a great deal of time learning and setting up security.

Security services often deal with a user account database or something like the aforementioned directory services. This database of users often contains a list of names and passwords. When a person wants to access the network, he must log on to the network. Logging on is similar to trying to enter an office building with a security guard at the front door. Before you can enter the building, you must verify who you are against a list of people who are allowed access.

Security services often are intermingled with other services. Some services added to a network can utilize the security services of the system onto which they have been installed. An example of this is Microsoft Exchange Server. This messaging product can utilize the security services of an existing Windows NT Server. An example of a product that does not need to utilize an existing security system is Lotus Notes. Lotus Notes has its own independent security system.

This topic is discussed in more detail in Chapter 10, "Managing and Securing a Microsoft Network."

NETWORK TERMS IN THE AGE OF THE INTERNET

Computers process information. Networked computers process information with each other. This information can be processed centrally (mainframe), in distributed fashion, or collaboratively (network). When referring to a network of computers, the term LAN is

continues

continued

used; when describing how computers are connected over large areas, the term WAN is used. These terms often are expressed as "Our intranet is connected to the Internet." This translates to "Our corporate network is connected to the global network known as the Internet."

One of the main reasons to have a network of computers is so shared services are available to many users at once. These tasks can range from storing and retrieving files to printing documents to running databases or email. These services can be located on dedicated machines (client/server) or can be distributed on all the client machines (peer-to-peer). In reality, a company does not say "I want this type of network." It simply finds a solution for its business needs. Based on this solution, the client gets a LAN or a WAN that runs services following either a client/server or a peer-to-peer model of networking. This enables them to process information in some fashion.

CASE STUDY: MATCHING NETWORK TYPE TO COMPANY NEEDS

ESSENCE OF THE CASE

The following two issues are at hand:

- What details do you need from the company for you to make an informed decision?

- Based on this detailed information, will you recommend a peer-to-peer network or a client/server network?

SCENARIO

You have an initial meeting scheduled with two companies that have no computers.

All you know about these companies going into the meeting is that each wants to install a network to increase its productivity. They want to know whether to install a peer-to-peer network or a client/server network. They also want to know what details you need before a decision can be made. You need to decide which type of network to install in each case.

ANALYSIS

When analyzing a computer network, it is most important to address the types of functions the company performs and the size of the company.

CASE STUDY: MATCHING NETWORK TYPE TO COMPANY NEEDS

Is it a small office with one or two employees? Is it a large corporation with many people performing information gathering? Is it a company that simply will use the network as an access point to go out onto the Internet? What percentage of the work force uses computers?

Based on the function and size of a company, you can determine which services it needs. This is because a company does not buy a network, so to speak; it purchases a business solution. A network model is chosen based on the business solution instead of choosing a network model first.

The following two companies provide examples of this principle.

The Veterinarian Clinic

A small veterinarian clinic has just set up shop in town. This company has three employees. There is a front desk person who books appointments and does billing, and there are two veterinarians. These three people need to share simple files that make up the case file of the pet in question. These three people also share a small printer for printing out client bills.

A firm such as this can easily get by with a simple peer-to-peer network. Installing Windows 95 on all three machines and connecting them together to form a small LAN provides the three employees with the shared resources they need to perform their job functions.

The Large Sales Organization

A large sales organization has a huge inventory database that is continuously updated by all 140 sales representatives. This database is central to the existence of the firm. This company wants to have a fax device to which all salespeople can fax and three printers to handle all the sales orders.

This company more than likely should go with a client/server model. It has a large number of people working in the office. All these people need access to a central database, several printers, and one fax device. Ideally, this company should purchase dedicated servers to handle each of the three services the company wants to incorporate into a network environment. Because the company is very dependent on the existence of this database, it definitely needs some form of security service running on the servers. Strong security services typically are found in client/server models.

Based on the services to be provided and the size of the organization, you can begin the process of conceptualizing a network. As these examples illustrate, you should start with the services needed and work your way out to the network model instead of jumping right into the network topology, the operating system, and so on.

CHAPTER SUMMARY

This chapter has introduced you to a number of terms commonly used in computer networking. It also has addressed many of the basic networking structures you need to understand as an administrator. In doing so, this chapter has provided a general framework you can use when analyzing a network in terms of its general design and the function it is trying to serve or perform.

In this chapter, the exam objective "Define common networking terms for LANs and WANs" was addressed throughout. The "Compare a client/server network with a peer-to-peer network" objective was covered in the section "Network Models: Comparing Client/Server and Peer-to-Peer Networking Configurations." Finally, the exam objective "Compare a file and print server with an application server" was covered in the sections "File Services" and "Application Services."

KEY TERMS

- network
- transmission medium
- protocol
- centralized computing
- distributed computing
- collaborative or cooperative computing
- client/server
- peer-to-peer
- local area network (LAN)
- wide area network (WAN)
- campus area network (CAN)
- municipal area network (MAN)
- Internet
- intranet
- redirector service
- server service
- file service
- file transfer
- data migration
- file archiving
- file-update synchronization
- printing services
- application server
- database services
- message/communication services
- email
- voice mail
- fax services
- groupware
- directory services
- security services

APPLY YOUR LEARNING	

The following sections enable you to assess how well you understood the material in this chapter. The exercises provide you with opportunities to engage in the sorts of tasks that comprise the skill sets the objectives reflect. The review questions both review and test you on the major concepts discussed in the chapter. The exam questions test your knowledge of the tasks and concepts specified in the objectives in a fashion similar to the Microsoft exams. Answers to the review and exam questions follow in the answers sections.

For additional review- and exam-type questions, see the Top Score test engine on the CD-ROM that came with this book.

Exercises

1.1   Logging On as a Peer

Objective: To explore the distinction between logging on locally and logging on to a domain from Windows NT Workstation. This exercise demonstrates the use of a security service.

Estimated time: 15 minutes

1. Boot a domain-based Windows NT Workstation computer. Press Ctrl+Alt+Del to reach the Logon Information dialog box.

2. The box labeled Domain should display the name of the Windows NT domain to which the Windows NT Workstation belongs. This option logs you in using the domain account database located on a domain controller. Click the down arrow to the right of the Domain box. At least one other option—the name of the workstation itself—should appear in the domain list. This

option logs you in using the workstation's local account database. The local account database is completely separate from the domain database, and it only gives you access to the local computer.

If the workstation is a member of a peer-to-peer workgroup instead of a domain, the local logon option is the only option. In fact, if a Windows NT workstation is a member of a workgroup, the Domain box doesn't even appear in the Logon Information dialog box—you automatically log on to the local account database.

3. Select the computer name in the Domain box. Enter a username and a password for the local account.

If you rarely or never use the local logon option, you may not remember a username or a password for a local account. If you can't remember a local username and password, log on to the domain from the workstation and find a local account using the workstation's User Manager application (in the Administrative Tools group). Double-click an account name to check the properties. Reset the password if necessary. You need to log in as Administrator to do this.

4. After you successfully log on to the local workstation account, you operate as a peer in a peer-to-peer network would operate. Your credentials will carry you no farther than the local system. Try to access another network computer using Network Neighborhood. Windows NT displays a dialog box asking for a username and a password. The computer you are accessing validates your credentials separately.

APPLY YOUR LEARNING

1.2   Seeing Where a Redirector Is Installed

Objective: To see where a redirector is installed on a Windows 95 machine.

Estimated time: 10 minutes

1. Power up your Windows 95 PC.

2. Right-click the Network Neighborhood icon and choose the Properties option.

3. Select the Configuration tab.

4. In the Configuration page, click the Add button.

5. Select the Client component in the Select Network Component Type box. After you have done this, click the Add button.

6. The next dialog box is the Select Network Client dialog box. This is the dialog box you interact with when installing a redirector on Windows 95. On the left-hand side of the dialog box is a list of various manufacturers that have supplied Windows 95 with redirectors to connect to their systems. The right-hand side of the dialog box shows a list of the redirectors, or clients, that each vendor has supplied.

7. Select Microsoft on the left-hand side of the dialog box where it says Manufacturers.

8. On the right-hand side of the dialog box under the heading Network Clients, you see two clients that Microsoft supplies. (Some machines might see three or more.) One of these clients is Client for Microsoft Networks, a redirector to connect Microsoft Windows 95 machines with other Windows 95 machines and Windows NT computers. The other client, Client for NetWare Networks, enables a Windows 95 machine to connect to a Novell server.

9. Select the Cancel button three times to close all the dialog boxes.

1.3   Exploring the NT Workstation Service

Objective: To examine the effect of stopping Windows NT's redirector—the Workstation service.

Estimated time: 15 minutes

1. Log on to a Windows NT Workstation system as an administrator.

2. Browse a shared directory on another computer using Network Neighborhood or the Network Neighborhood icon in Explorer. You should see a list of the files on the shared directory.

3. From the Start menu, click Settings and choose Control Panel. Double-click the Services icon to start the Control Panel Services application.

4. From the Control Panel Services application, scroll down to the Workstation service and click the Stop button. This stops the Workstation service on your computer. Windows NT asks whether you also want to stop some other dependent services. Click Yes.

5. Now try to access the shared directory using Network Neighborhood. Without the redirector (the Workstation service), you are unable to access the other computers on the network.

Review Questions

1. What are three types of computing done in networks?

2. What are two main classifications of networks?

3. List five services that networks provide.

APPLY YOUR LEARNING

Exam Questions

The following questions test your knowledge of the information in this chapter. For additional exam help, see the Top Score software on the CD-ROM that came with this book. You also can visit Microsoft's Certification site at www.microsoft.com/train_cert.

1. Your client computer isn't able to access services on other network PCs. The problem is with your client computer is:

   A. The reflector

   B. The redirector

   C. The server service

   D. None of the above

2. You need to add a server to your domain to compensate for the shortage of disk space on many of the older machines. What type of computer will you be adding?

   A. A peer

   B. An application server

   C. A file and print server

   D. Both A and C

3. You have a small office of computers. Each machine is responsible for its own security. What type of network are you running?

   A. Peer-to-peer

   B. Cooperative

   C. WAN

   D. None of the above

4. You need to add a server to your network that will provide services designed to alleviate the problems caused by slow processor speeds on many of the older machines. What type of server will you be adding?

   A. A peer

   B. An application server

   C. A file and print server

   D. Both A and C

5. You are designing a small network for a single office. The network will have nine users, each operating from one of nine networked PCs. The users are all accustomed to working with computers. What type of networking model is the best solution?

   A. Server-based

   B. Peer-to-peer

   C. A combination of A and B

   D. Any of the above

6. You are designing a small network for a single office. The network will have approximately 19 users who will roam freely among the 14 participating PCs. What type of networking model is the best solution?

   A. Client/server

   B. Peer-to-peer

   C. A combination of A and B

   D. Any of the above

APPLY YOUR LEARNING

7. Which type of network is most likely confined to a building or a campus?

   A. Local area

   B. Metropolitan area

   C. Wide area

   D. Departmental

8. Which of the following can concurrently provide and request services?

   A. Server

   B. Client

   C. Peer

   D. None of the above

9. Which file service is responsible for creating duplicate copies of files to protect against file damage?

   A. File transfer

   B. File-update synchronization

   C. File archiving

   D. Remote file access

10. Which two of the following are file services?

    A. Archiving

    B. File segmenting

    C. Update synchronization

    D. Data integrity

11. Which three statements are true regarding application services?

    A. Clients request services.

    B. Application services are responsible for running Microsoft Office.

    C. Application servers can be optimized to specialize in a service.

    D. Multiple services can be offered by the same server PC.

12. Which three statements are true regarding database services?

    A. A database server improves data security.

    B. All data must be located on the main database server.

    C. Database performance can be optimized.

    D. Database services enable multiple clients to share a database.

13. Which are the two most popular strategies for replication databases?

    A. Offline migration

    B. File-update synchronization

    C. Locally driven update

    D. Master server update

14. Which three are advantages of a centralized approach to providing file services?

    A. Centralized files can be readily archived.

    B. It provides the best possible performance.

    C. Management is efficient.

    D. The cost of high-performance, high-reliability servers can be spread across many users.

APPLY YOUR LEARNING

15. Which two are advantages of a distributed approach to providing file services?

    A. There is no central point of failure.

    B. It's less difficult to manage than a complex, centralized server.

    C. It's easily scaled to improve performance for all users.

    D. Specialized equipment is not required.

16. You want to install some services that will utilize your network computers more efficiently.

    Required Result: The bulk of the computer processing needs to be performed by the main network server.

    Optional Result 1: You want all changes to the software to be administered centrally.

    Optional Result 2: Printing needs to be done from a central location.

    Suggested Solution: You install Microsoft Office off your central file server. You also share the printer on the central file server and provide all your users with access.

    A. This solution obtains the required result and both optional results.

    B. This solution obtains the required result and one of the optional results.

    C. This solution obtains the required result.

    D. This solution does not satisfy the required result.

17. You have advanced network users that will work on a new network you are to install.

    Required Result: Users need to be able to share their hard drives.

    Optional Result 1: Users need to be able to access each other's printers.

    Optional Result 2: The network model should require very little training of any new users.

    Suggested Solution: Implement a peer-to-peer network using Windows 95.

    A. This solution obtains the required result and both optional results.

    B. This solution obtains the required result and one of the optional results.

    C. This solution obtains the required result.

    D. This solution does not satisfy the required result.

Answers to Review Questions

1. Three types of computing are centralized, distributed, and collaborative (cooperative) computing. See the section "Models of Network Computing."

2. The two main classifications of networking are client/server and peer-to-peer networking. See the section "Network Models: Comparing Client/Server and Peer-to-Peer Networking Configurations."

3. The following are some of the possible services provided by a network:

- File services

- Print services

- Database services

- Messaging services

- Communication services

- Security services

- Directory services

For more information on this topic, see the section "Network Services."

Answers to Exam Questions

1. **B.** A server service runs a server machine. A redirector is run on a client machine. See the section "Basic Connectivity Services."

2. **C.** A file server is a server that provides file services to a user. An application server runs programs for users. A file server often is called a file and print server because it usually provides both file and printing services. See the sections "File Services" and "Printing Services."

3. **A.** Because there is no central server, this classification is known as a peer-to-peer network. See the section "Peer-to-Peer Networking."

4. **B.** An application server is responsible for running processor-dependent applications. See the section "Network Services."

5. **B.** A peer-to-peer network commonly is the solution for small networks. See the section "Peer-to-Peer Networking."

6. **A.** Roaming users are usually best supported by a client/server model. See the section "Client/Server-Based Networking."

7. **A.** A local area network (LAN) usually is defined by a network confined to a building or a campus. See the section "Local Area Networks (LANs)."

8. **C.** A peer is a machine that both provides and requests services. See the section "Peer-to-Peer Networking."

9. **C.** File archiving, also known as tape backup, is responsible for this. See the section "File Services."

10. **A, C.** B is a term that could be used to describe a function of the hard drive not the file service. D is a function of fault tolerance (discussed later in this book). See the section "File Services."

11. **A, C, D.** When Microsoft Office is stored on a file server, the server is performing file services. See the section "Application Services."

12. **A, C, D.** Not all data must be stored on the main database server. See the section "Database Services."

13. **C, D.** A and B are file services. See the section "Database Services."

14. **A, C, D.** A person will get faster file access if the files are stored locally. See the section "File Services."

15. **A, D.** B is incorrect because it is often more difficult to manage. C is incorrect because it is often harder to scale. See the section "File Services."

16. **D.** By installing Microsoft Office on a central file server, you are enabling all changes to the

APPLY YOUR LEARNING

software to be administrated centrally, satisfying optional result 1. By sharing out a printer—using your printing services—you satisfy optional result 2. The required result is not met by installing Microsoft Office on a file server; the file server is not processing the Microsoft Office program. The file server is simply passing files down to the workstations. It is the workstations that are doing all the processing.

17. **B.**   A peer-to-peer network enables users to share their hard drives and printers. This satisfies the required result and optional result 1. Peer-to-peer networks, however, do require more training for users than client/server networks. This is because users need to be trained to manage their shared resources.

Suggested Readings and Resources

The following is recommended reading in the area of networking terms and concepts:

1. Tanenbaum, Andrew. *Computer Networks.* Prentice Hall, 1996.

2. *Advances in Local and Metropolitan Area Networks*, William Stallings (editor). IEEE Computer Society, 1994.

3. Derfler, Frank and Les Freed. *How Networks Work.* Ziff Davis, 1996.

4. Hayes, Frank. *Lan Times Guide to Interoperability (Lan Times).* Osborne-McGraw Hill, 1994.

5. Wheeler, Tom, Alan Simon, and Thomas Wheeler. *Open Systems Handbook.* AP Proffessional, 1994.

Chapter 2 targets the following objectives in the Standards and Terminology section of the Networking Essentials exam:

Define the communication devices that communicate at each level of the OSI model.

▶ The purpose of this exam objective is to make sure that you are able to identify what devices on a network work within what levels of the OSI model.

Compare the implications of using connection-oriented communications with connectionless communications.

▶ This exam objective addresses whether a person understands how a connection-oriented type of communication differs from a connectionless form of communication.

Distinguish whether SLIP or PPP is used as the communications protocol for various situations.

▶ The purpose of this objective is to make sure you understand where, when, and for what reasons one would use SLIP or PPP as a communications protocol.

Describe the characteristics and purpose of the media used in IEEE 802.3 and IEEE 802.5.

▶ This question is asked to assess whether a person is aware of two of the more popular implementations of the IEEE 802.x set of standards.

Explain the purpose of the NDIS and Novell ODI network standards.

▶ This objective is included to make sure that a person is aware of the differences between the NDIS standard used by Microsoft networks and the ODI standard used by Novell Networks.

CHAPTER 2

Networking Standards

OUTLINE

This chapter presents an overview of the OSI model used in networking. Follow these approaches to studying the material in this chapter:

▶ You should understand the general functionality of each layer of the OSI model that is presented.

▶ You should be able to identify what networking component, whether it is a device or a standard, operates at each level of the OSI model.

If you understand the ODI model in these ways, you should be ready to take this section of the exam.

INTRODUCTION

Before servers can provide services to clients, communications between the two computers must be established. Beyond the cables connecting the computers together, numerous processes operate behind the scenes to keep things running smoothly. For these processes to operate smoothly in a diverse networking environment, the computing community has settled on several standards and specifications that define the interaction and interrelation of the various components of network architecture. This chapter explores some of those standards. It begins by exploring the Open Systems Interconnection (OSI) reference model. This has become an industry blueprint for defining the different components that are involved in networking. This is an important model to learn, because all networking components and functionality are referenced within this model. In fact, the remaining chapters of this book are organized around the OSI model.

The chapter then moves from the OSI reference model to other industry standards that often encompass several areas of the OSI model at once. These standards include the Serial Line Internet Protocol (SLIP), Point-to-Point Protocol (PPP), the IEEE 802 standards, Network Driver Interface Specification (NDIS), and Open Data-Link Interface (ODI). The chapter concludes with a case study applying exam-specific objectives in a real-world setting.

As noted in the study strategies for this chapter, the best approach to the material covered in this chapter is to keep a "big picture" perspective in mind as you read through the OSI model. Focus on the fact that the OSI model is a framework to explain concepts. This chapter serves as a general framework, discussing general concepts used throughout the rest of this book. Other chapters refer back to this chapter to explain why different services and components function the way that they do. This chapter also provides a great framework for identifying and addressing real-world networking problems and issues that may arise.

STANDARDS

The network industry uses two types of standards: *de facto standards* and *de jure standards*. To understand the concept of open systems architecture, you must be familiar with the concepts of de facto and de jure standards.

De facto standards arise through widespread commercial and educational use. These standards often are proprietary and usually remain unpublished and unavailable to outside vendors. Unpublished and unavailable standards are known as *closed system standards*. Published and accessible standards, on the other hand, are known as *open system standards*. Through the growing acceptance of the concept of interoperability, many closed, proprietary systems (such as IBM's Systems Network Architecture) have started to migrate toward open system standards. Certainly, de facto standards are not always closed system standards. Some examples of proprietary open system standards include Novell's NetWare network operating system and Microsoft's Windows.

The second type of standards, de jure standards, are nonproprietary, which means that no single company creates them or owns the rights to them. De jure standards are developed with the intent of enhancing connectivity and interoperability by making specifications public so that independent manufacturers can build to such specifications. TCP/IP, which is discussed in more detail in Chapter 7, "Transport Protocols," is an example of a nonproprietary de jure standard.

> **NOTE**
>
> **Open System Standard**   By saying that Microsoft has an open system standard, this does not mean that Microsoft has published its source code for its products. What this means is that Microsoft supplies other developers with the commands they need to enable their products to interact with Microsoft products. These sets of commands are also known as Software Development Kits or SDKs. Microsoft supplies SDKs for virtually all its products.

Several permanent committees comprised of industry representatives develop de jure standards. Some examples of these committees are the IEEE (Institute of Electrical and Electronic Engineers) and the IRTF (Internet Engineering Task Force). Although these committees are supported by manufacturer subscriptions, and in some cases government representatives, they are intended to represent the interests of the entire community and thus remain independent of any one manufacturer's interests. Subscribing to de jure standards reduces the risk and cost of developing hardware and software for manufacturers. After a standard has been finalized, a component manufacturer subscribing to it can develop products with some confidence that the products will operate with components from other companies that also subscribe to the same standards.

An example of a de jure standard is the set of rules that guide how web pages are transferred between computers or how files are transferred between systems. These de jure standards are created by the IRTF to facilitate communication between different systems. One problem of de jure standards, though, is the possibility of a vendor choosing to follow only part of a given standard. The frequent result is a product that claims to conform to the standard, but that in reality fails to operate with other products in the way one might believe or expect.

Standards Organizations and the ISO

The development and implementation of de jure standards is regulated by standards organizations. For example, the CCITT (this is a French acronym that translates to the International Consultative Committee for Telegraphy and Telephony) and the Institute of Electrical and Electronic Engineers (IEEE), among other organizations, are responsible for several prominent network standards that support the International Standards Organization's objective of network interoperability.

The International Standards Organization (ISO)—whose name is derived from the Greek prefix *iso*, meaning "same"—is located in Geneva, Switzerland. ISO develops and publishes standards and coordinates the activities of all national standardization bodies. In 1977, the ISO initiated efforts to design a communication standard based on the open systems architecture theory from which computer networks would be designed. This model came to be known as the Open Systems Interconnection (OSI) model. This model has become an accepted framework for analyzing and developing networking components and functionality.

Rules and the Communication Process

Networks rely on many rules to manage information interchange. Some of the procedures governed by network standards are as follows:

- ◆ Procedures used to communicate the establishment and ending of communication

◆ Signals used to represent data on the transmission media

◆ Types of signals to be used

◆ Access methods for relaying a signal across the media

◆ Methods used to direct a message to the intended destination

◆ Procedures used to control the rate of data flow

◆ Methods used to enable different computer types to communicate

◆ Ways to ensure that messages are received correctly

Network communication is very similar to human communication. People follow sets of rules when they talk to one another. As a society, people have mechanisms in place to get the attention of others, to let them know that someone is talking to them, and to establish when they finish talking. They also have methods for verifying that the information passed along to a person was received and understood by that person.

Like human communicaton, computer communication is an extremely complex process, one that is often too complex to solve all at once using just one set of rules. As a result, the industry has chosen to solve different parts of the problem with compatible standards so that the solutions can be put together like pieces of a puzzle—a puzzle that comes together differently each time to build a complete communication approach for any given situation.

THE OSI REFERENCE MODEL

Having a model in mind helps you understand how the pieces of the networking puzzle fit together. The most commonly used model is the Open Systems Interconnection (OSI) reference model. The OSI model, first released in 1984 by the International Standards Organization (ISO), provides a useful structure for defining and describing the various processes underlying networking communications.

The OSI model is a blueprint for vendors to follow when developing protocol implementations. The OSI model organizes communication protocols into seven levels. Each level addresses a narrow portion of the communication process. Figure 2.1 illustrates the levels of the OSI model.

FIGURE 2.1
The OSI model has seven layers.

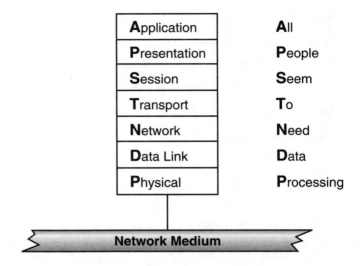

Although you will examine each level in detail later in this chapter, a quick overview is in order. Layer 1, the Physical layer, or Hardware layer, as some call it, consists of protocols that control communication on the network media. Essentially, this layer deals with how data is transferred across the transmission media. At the opposite end, Layer 7, the Application layer, interfaces the network services with the applications in use on the computer. These services, such as file and print services, are discussed in Chapter 1. The five layers in between—Data Link, Network, Transport, Session, and Presentation—perform intermediate communication tasks. In essence the OSI model is a framework that describes how a function from one computer is transmitted to another computer on the network.

It is important to remember that the OSI model is not a blueprint for how to design something; that is, it does not tell you how your network card is suppose to operate. Instead, the OSI model is a framework in which various networking components can be placed into context. Many networking professionals rely on the OSI model when troubleshooting in unfamiliar situations. These professionals may be dealing with systems not familiar to them, but by referring to the OSI model they are able to at least narrow down the issues at hand.

How Peer OSI Layers Communicate

Communication between OSI layers is both vertical within the OSI layers, and also horizontal between peer layers in another computer (see Figure 2.2). This is important to understand, because it affects how data is passed within a computer, as well as between two computers.

When information is passed within the OSI model on a computer, each protocol layer adds its own information to the message being sent. This information takes the form of a *header* added to the beginning of the original message. The sending of a message always goes down the OSI stack, and hence headers are added from the top to the bottom (see Figure 2.3).

When the message is received by the destination computer, each layer removes the header from its peer layer. Thus at each layer headers are removed (*stripped*) by the receiving computer after the information in the header has been utilized. Stripped headers are removed in the reverse order in which they were added. That is, the last header added by the sending computer, is the first one stripped off and read by the receiving computer.

In summary, the information between the layers is passed along vertically. The information between computers is essentially horizontal, though, because each layer in one computer talks to its respective layer in the other computer.

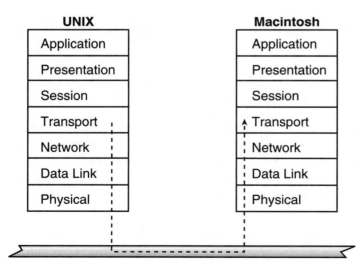

FIGURE 2.2
Each layer in the OSI model communicates with its peer layer on the other computer's protocol stack.

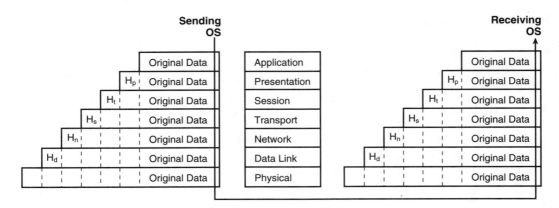

H_p = Presentation Header
H_t = Transport Header
H_s = Session Header
H_n = Network Header
H_d = Data Link Header

FIGURE 2.3

Each layer, except the Physical layer, adds a header to the frame as it travels down the OSI layers, and removes it as it travels up the OSI layers.

It should probably be noted that the Physical layer does not append a header on to the information, because this layer deals with providing a transmission route between computers. An analogy to this is when one sends a courier package. To send a package, you place documents into an envelope (header no. 1). This envelope is addressed (header no. 2). The courier company places its documentation on the package (header no. 3). This package is then moved down the road in a vehicle (the transmission pathway). At the receiving end, the recipient strips off the courier documentation (removing header no. 3), then strips off the package and addressing, (the removal of headers no. 2 and no. 1), and now has the documents at hand.

Protocol Stacks

The OSI model (and other non-OSI protocol standards) break the complex process of network communication into *layers*. Each layer represents a category of related tasks. A protocol stack is an implementation of this layered protocol architecture. The protocols and services associated with the protocol stack interact to prepare, transmit, and receive network data.

It is important to understand just what is meant by the terms "protocol" and "protocol stack." Often when people talk about protocols, they mention terms such as TCP/IP or IPX. This terminology can be misleading, for although these terms refer to protocols, they are a specific type of protocol: transport protocols. These transport protocols often do not encompass the entire mechanism for transferring communications. Transport protocols are discussed in Chapter 7.

Two computers must run compatible protocol stacks before they can communicate, because each layer in one computer's protocol stack must interact with a corresponding layer in the other computer's protocol stack. For example, refer to Figure 2.2. It shows the path of a message that starts in the Transport layer. The message travels down the protocol stack, through the network medium, and up the protocol stack of the receiving computer. If any layer in the receiving computer cannot understand or is not compatible with the corresponding layer of the sending computer, the message cannot be delivered.

To place this concept into perspective, imagine two people wishing to communicate. If one is blind and the other is deaf, there will be a communication problem. Both people need to convey the thought through some form of media. However, the blind person uses voice to transmit, which requires the receiving person to use hearing, while the deaf person uses sign language to transmit, which requires the receiving person to use sight.

Now if you put the idea of communicating into a layered model, one layer constitutes the idea or need to communicate, one layer is responsible for transmitting, and one layer is responsible for receiving the information. Both these people are using a mechanism to transmit and receive, but the mechanisms are incompatible. In essence, these two individuals are running different protocol stacks; they use different systems at the layers that need to mesh.

CONCEPTUALIZING THE LAYERS OF THE OSI MODEL

The following sections provide a more detailed exposition of each of the seven layers of the OSI model.

OSI Physical Layer Concepts

Although the OSI Physical layer does not define the media used, this layer is concerned with all aspects of transmitting and receiving data on the network media. By not defining the media, this layer is not responsible for saying whether a cable should be made of silver, copper, or gold. Specifically, the Physical layer is concerned with transmitting and receiving bits. This layer defines several key characteristics of the Physical network, including the following:

◆ Physical structure of the network (physical topology)

◆ Mechanical and electrical specifications for using the medium (not the medium itself)

◆ Bit transmission, encoding, and timing

Although the Physical layer does not define the physical medium, it defines clear requirements that the medium must meet. These specifications differ depending on the physical medium. Ethernet for UTP, for example, has different specifications from coaxial ethernet. You learn more about network transmission media in Chapter 3, "Transmission Media." In Chapter 4, "Network Topologies and Architectures," you learn more about physical topologies. This chapter is intended to give you an overview of the OSI model and which components work at each layer. The following sections examine in detail the components that operate at each layer, presenting this detailed information from the bottom of the OSI model upwards.

Components That Operate at This Level—Repeaters

Define the communication devices that communicate at each level of the OSI model.

A *repeater* is a network device that repeats a signal from one port onto the other ports to which it is connected (see Figure 2.4). Repeaters operate at the OSI Physical layer. A repeater does not filter or interpret anything; instead, it merely repeats (regenerates) a signal, passing all network traffic in all directions. Signals become weaker the farther they travel down a transmission medium, so repeaters are used to extend the distance between network stations. The term used to describe the loss of a signal's strength is *attenuation*.

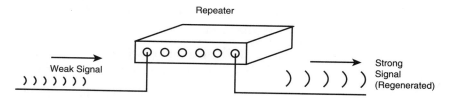

Repeater

Weak Signal

Strong
Signal
(Regenerated)

FIGURE 2.4
A repeater regenerates a weak signal.

A repeater operates at the OSI Physical layer because a repeater doesn't require any information from the upper layers of the OSI model to regenerate a signal. Therefore, the repeater doesn't have to pass the frame to upper layers where addresses and other parameters are interpreted. A repeater merely passes along bits of data, even if a data frame is corrupt. The primary purpose of a repeater is to enable the network to expand beyond the distance limitations of the transmission medium. (See Chapter 3 for more details on the lengths associated with transmission mediums.)

The advantages of repeaters are that they are fairly inexpensive and simple. In addition, although they cannot connect networks with dissimilar data frames (such as a Token Ring network to an Ethernet network), some repeaters can connect segments with similar data frame types but dissimilar cabling (such as twisted pair and coaxial cable).

OSI Data Link Layer Concepts

As you learned in the preceding section, the OSI Physical layer is concerned with moving messages between two machines. Network communication, however, is considerably more involved than moving bits from one device to another. In fact, dozens of steps must be performed to transport a message from one device to another.

Real messages consist not of single bits but of meaningful groups of bits. The Data Link layer receives messages, called *frames*, from upper layers. A primary function of the Data Link layer is to disassemble these frames into bits for transmission and then to reconstruct the frames from the bits received.

The Data Link layer has other functions as well, such as addressing, error control, and flow control for a single link between network devices. (The adjacent Network layer, described later in this chapter, handles the more complex tasks associated with addressing and delivering packets through routers and across an internetwork.)

The IEEE 802 standard (discussed in more detail in Chapter 4, divides the Data Link layer into two sublayers:

◆ *Media Access Control (MAC)*. The MAC sublayer controls the means by which multiple devices share the same media channel for the transmission of information. This includes contention methods (see Chapter 4), or how data is transferred from a device, such as the network card, to the transmission medium. The MAC layer can also provide addressing information for communication between network devices. (This is covered in more detail in the discussion of the Network layer).

◆ *Logical Link Control (LLC)*. The LLC sublayer establishes and maintains links between communicating devices.

Hardware Access at the Data Link Layer

As the preceding section mentions, the Data Link layer's MAC sublayer provides an interface to the network adapter card. The details necessary to facilitate access to the network through the adapter card are thus assigned to the Data Link layer. Some of these details include the access control method (for example, contention or token passing, described in Chapter 4) and the network topology.

The Data Link layer also controls the transmission method (for example, synchronous or asynchronous) used to access the transmission medium. See Chapter 6, "Connectivity Devices and Transfer Mechanisms," for more on synchronous and asynchronous communications.

Addressing at the Data Link Layer

The Data Link layer maintains device addresses that enable messages to be sent to a particular device. The addresses are called *physical device addresses*. Physical device addresses are unique addresses associated with the networking hardware in the computer. In most cases (for example, Ethernet and Token Ring), the physical device address is burned into the NIC (network interface card) at the time the card is manufactured. Other devices, such as ARCNet, require the changing of DIP switches on the card to set a hardware address.

The standards that apply to a particular network determine the format of the address. Because the address format is associated with the media access control method used, physical device addresses are frequently referred to as *MAC addresses*.

Packets on LANs are typically transmitted so that they are available to all devices on the network segment. Each device reads each frame far enough to determine the device address to which the frame is addressed. If the frame's destination address matches the device's own physical address, the rest of the frame is received. If the addresses do not match, the remainder of the packet is ignored. This is the case for all transmissions except for those sent as broadcasts. All devices on the network receive these broadcasts.

Bridges can be used to divide large networks into several smaller ones. Bridges use physical device addresses to determine which frames to leave on the current network segment and which to forward to devices on other network segments. Bridges are discussed further later in this chapter and in even more detail in Chapter 6.

Because they use physical device addresses to manage frame routing, bridges function at the level of the Data Link layer and are Data Link layer connectivity devices.

Error and Flow Control at the Data Link Layer

Several of the protocol layers in the OSI model play a role in the overall system of flow control and error control for the network. Flow control and error control are defined as follows:

◆ *Flow control.* Flow control determines the amount of data that can be transmitted in a given time period. Flow control prevents the transmitting device from overwhelming the receiver.

◆ *Error control.* Error control detects errors in received frames and requests retransmission of frames.

Error control of network communications often occurs at several different layers in the OSI model. At the Data Link layer, however, error control consists simply of confirmation that the receiving computer got all the packets the sending computer transmitted. Compare this to the transmission of physically shipped goods. When a company receives a shipment of goods one of the first things it does is see whether the correct number of boxes arrived and whether these boxes are damaged. This is essentially the type of error control that happens at the Data Link layer of the OSI model. But this error control in itself does not guarantee that the information being received by one computer is all there. Consider the model of the shipped boxes again: Just because all boxes arrived does not mean that the contents of all the boxes were correctly packed or that the merchandise in the boxes will work.

The Data Link layer's LLC sublayer provides error control and flow control for single links between communicating devices. The Network layer (described in the section titled "OSI Network Layer Concepts") expands the system of error control and flow control to encompass complex connections that include routers, gateways, and internetworks.

Components That Operate at This Level— Bridges

Define the communication devices that communicate at each level of the OSI model.

A *bridge* is a connectivity device that operates at the OSI Data Link layer. The messaging parameters available at the Data Link layer enable a bridge to pass a frame in the direction of its destination without simultaneously forwarding it to segments for which it was not intended. In other words, a bridge can filter network traffic. This filtering process reduces overall traffic because the bridge segments the network, passing frames only when they can't be delivered on the local segment and passing frames to only the segment for which they are intended.

Figure 2.5 depicts a simple bridge implementation. In this process, a bridge filters traffic by tracking and checking the Data Link layer's MAC sublayer addresses of incoming frames. The bridge monitors the source addresses of incoming frames and builds an address table that shows which nodes are on each of the segments. When a data frame arrives, the bridge checks the frame's destination address and forwards the frame to the segment that contains the destination device or *node*. If the destination node exists on the same segment as the source node, the bridge stops the frame so it doesn't pass unnecessarily to the rest of the network. If the bridge can't find the destination address in its address table, it forwards the frame to all segments except the source segment.

To understand the role a bridge plays, think of a bridge as similar to a bridge with a toll booth on a street. The toll booth operator knows which houses are on either side of the bridge. Based on this scenario, when a person walks down the street and approaches the toll booth, the toll booth operator either lets this person pass or stops him. If this person is going to a house on the other side of the bridge, the toll booth operator allows the person to pass. If the intended house number is not on the other side of the bridge, the person is not allowed to pass. Remember, the walker's position is on the same street the whole time. This will be important for you to remember when the Network layer in the OSI model is discussed.

In some cases, a bridge can also perform the same functions that a repeater performs, if this feature is built into the bridge, including expanding cabling distance and linking dissimilar cable types. In addition, a bridge can improve performance and reduce network traffic by splitting the network and confining traffic to smaller segments.

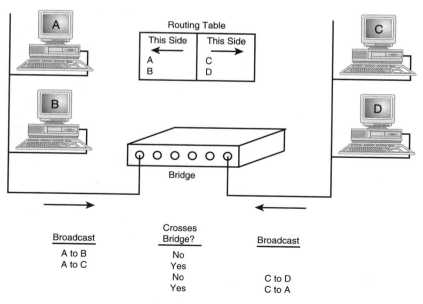

FIGURE 2.5

Bridges isolate traffic on a single network segment.

So far the Physical and Data Link layers have been discussed. These layers are concerned with connecting devices together and getting information onto the transmission media. The next layer up in the OSI model is concerned with how data is routed to different parts of the network. This is a function of the Network layer.

OSI Network Layer Concepts

As you learned in the preceding section, the Data Link layer deals with communication between devices on the same network. Physical device addresses are used to address data frames, and each device is responsible for monitoring the network and receiving frames addressed to that device.

The Network layer handles communication with devices on logically separate networks that are connected to form *internetworks*. Because internetworks can be large and can be constructed of different types of networks, the Network layer utilizes routing algorithms that guide packets from their source to their destination networks. For more about routing and routing algorithms, see Chapter 6.

Within the Network layer, each network in the internetwork is assigned a *network address* that is used to route packets. The Network layer manages the process of addressing and delivering packets on internetworks.

Network Layer Addressing

You have already encountered the Data Link layer's physical device addresses that uniquely identify each device on a network. On larger networks, it is impractical to deliver network data solely by means of physical addresses. (Imagine if your network adapter had to check every packet sent from anywhere on the Internet to look for a matching physical address.) Larger networks require a means of routing and filtering packets to reduce network traffic and minimize transmission time. The Network layer uses *logical network addresses* to route packets to specific networks on an internetwork.

Logical network addresses are assigned during configuration of the networks. A network installer must make sure that each network address is unique on a given internetwork. The rules for governing how these addresses are assigned are discussed in greater detail in Chapter 6.

The Network layer also supports *service addresses*. A service address specifies a channel to a specific process on the destination PC. The operating systems on most computers can run several processes at once. When a packet arrives, you must determine which process on the computer should receive the data in the packet. You do so by assigning service addresses, which identify upper-layer processes and protocols. These service addresses are included with the physical and logical network addresses in the data frame. (Some protocols refer to service addresses as *sockets* or *ports*.)

To understand the many types of addresses used in networking, take a step back and analyze our information so far. The analogy to be used here is that of a house on a street in a residential neighborhood. Imagine the address of the house is 1263 Main Street, Seattle, Washington. As far as the postal system is concerned, all this information is the "address." In networking, the different components that really make up the address have names. The MAC address is similar to the house number—1263. The network address is similar to the street name—Main Street. Further information regarding the address—Seattle, Washington, in this case—is analogous to the logical network address.

A service address is similar to a room in a building. If you are delivering a packet to a company, often this package needs to go one step beyond just the front door. You can think of a service address representing a room or a department within a building, such as Apartment 404, 1263 Main St., Seattle, Washington.

Some service addresses, called *well-known addresses*, are universally defined for a given type of network. These well-known addresses are often used for services that are shared between many different vendors. An example of this would be a web service address. Many different vendors develop web servers and web browsers. For these components to operate with one another, a *well-known address* is needed.

Other service addresses are defined by the vendors of the network service in question. This is often the case when a vendor has some proprietary service. In that case, only the vendor supplies the means for communicating between the various components. An example of this could be the service address between the cash register at a department store and the database the cash register is updating.

Delivering Packets

Many internetworks often include redundant data paths that you can use to route messages. Typically, a packet passes from the local LAN segment of the source PC through a series of other LAN segments, until it reaches the LAN segment of the destination PC. The OSI Network layer oversees the process of determining paths and delivering packets across the internetwork.

This is similar to when you drive from your house to work. You can probably take a variety of routes, depending upon the events on the roadways, such as road work or traffic jams. Based on these conditions, you choose the route to take. This type of decision-making is what is done at the network level.

Chapter 6 describes some of the routing algorithms used to determine a path. The following sections introduce some of the basic switching techniques. Switching techniques are mechanisms for moving data from one network segment to another. These techniques are as follows:

◆ Circuit switching

◆ Message switching

◆ Packet switching

Circuit Switching

Circuit switching establishes a path that remains fixed for the duration of a connection (see Figure 2.6). Much as telephone switching equipment establishes a route between two telephones, circuit-switching networks establish a path through the internetwork when the devices initiate a conversation. These paths tend to be reliable and fast in performance.

Circuit switching provides devices with a dedicated path and a well-defined bandwidth, but circuit switching is not free of disadvantages. First, establishing a connection between devices can be time-consuming. Second, because other traffic cannot share the dedicated media path, bandwidth might be inefficiently utilized. This can be compared to having a telephone conversation, yet not speaking. You are using the line, thus not allowing others to use it, but you are not transmitting any data. Finally, circuit-switching networks must have a surplus of bandwidth, so these types of switches tend to be expensive to construct.

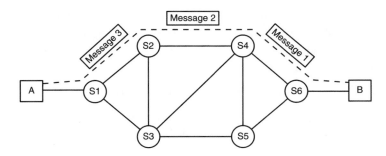

FIGURE 2.6
Circuit switching establishes a constant path between devices, much like a telephone connection.

Message Switching

Message switching treats each message as an independent entity. Each message carries address information that describes the message's destination, and this information is used at each switch to transfer the message to the next switch in the route. Message switches are programmed with information concerning other switches in the network that can be used to forward messages to their destinations. Message switches also may be programmed with information about the most efficient routes. Depending on network conditions, different messages may be sent through the network by different routes, as shown in Figure 2.7.

Message switching transfers the complete message from one switch to the next, where the message is stored before being forwarded again. Because each message is stored before being sent on to the next switch, this type of network frequently is called a *store-and-forward network*. The message switches often are general-purpose computers and must be equipped with sufficient storage (usually hard drives, or RAM) to enable them to store messages until forwarding is possible.

Message switching is commonly used in email because some delay is permissible in the delivery of email. Message switching uses relatively

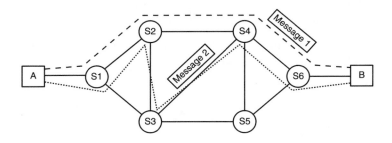

FIGURE 2.7
Message switching forwards the complete message, one switch at a time.

low-cost devices to forward messages and can function well with relatively slow communication channels. Other applications for message switching include group applications such as workflow, calendaring, and groupware.

Message switching offers the following advantages:

◆ Data channels are shared among communicating devices, improving the efficiency of available bandwidth.

◆ Message switches can store messages until a channel becomes available, reducing sensitivity to network congestion.

◆ Message priorities can be used to manage network traffic.

◆ Broadcast addressing uses network bandwidth more efficiently by delivering messages to multiple destinations.

The chief disadvantage of message switching is that message switching is not suited for real-time applications, including data communication, video, and audio.

Packet Switching

In packet switching, messages are divided into smaller pieces called *packets*. Each packet includes source and destination address information so that individual packets can be routed through the internetwork independently. As you can see in Figure 2.8, the packets that make up a message can take very different routes through the internetwork.

So far, packet switching looks considerably like message switching, but the distinguishing characteristic is that packets are restricted to a size that enables the switching devices to manage the packet data entirely in memory. This eliminates the need for switching devices to store the data temporarily on disk. Packet switching, therefore, routes packets through the network much more rapidly and efficiently than is possible with message switching.

Several methods of packet switching exist. Two common methods of packet switching are as follows:

◆ Datagram

◆ Virtual circuit

These two methods are discussed in the following sections.

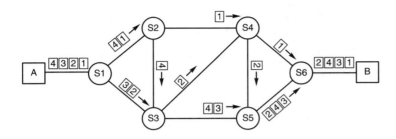

FIGURE 2.8
Packet switching breaks a packet up into many
different pieces that are routed independently.

Datagram Packet Switching

Datagram services treat each packet as an independent message.
Each packet is routed through the internetwork independently, and
each switch node determines which network segment should be
used for the next step in the packet's route. This capability enables
switches to bypass busy segments and take other steps to speed
packets through the internetwork (refer to Figure 2.8).

Datagrams are frequently used on LANs. Network layer protocols
are responsible for delivering the frame to the appropriate network.
Then, because each datagram includes destination address information (in most cases this is the MAC address), devices on the local
network can recognize and receive appropriate datagrams.

Packet switching meets the need to transmit large messages with the
fairly small frame size that can be accommodated by the Physical
layer. The Network layer is responsible for fragmenting messages
from upper layers into smaller datagrams that are appropriate for the
Physical layer. The Network layer is also responsible for reconstruct-
ing messages from datagrams as they are received.

Virtual Circuit Packet Switching

Virtual circuits operate by establishing a formal connection between
two devices in communication. When devices begin a session, they
negotiate communication parameters, such as maximum message
size, communication windows, and network paths. This negotiation
establishes a *virtual circuit*, which is a well-defined path through the
internetwork by which the devices communicate. This virtual circuit
generally remains in effect until the devices stop communicating.

Virtual circuits are distinguished by the establishment of a logical
connection. *Virtual* means that the network behaves as though a
dedicated physical circuit has been established between the communicating devices. Even though no such physical circuit actually

exists, the network presents the appearance of a physical connection to the devices at the ends of the circuit.

Virtual circuits are frequently employed in conjunction with connection-oriented services, which are discussed later in this chapter.

Packet switching offers the following advantages:

◆ Packet switching optimizes the use of bandwidth by enabling many devices to route packets through the same network channels. At any given time, a switch can route packets to several different destination devices, adjusting the routes as required to achieve the best efficiency.

◆ Because entire messages are not stored at the switches prior to forwarding, transmission delays are significantly shorter than those encountered with message switching.

Although the switching devices do not need to be equipped with large amounts of hard drive capacity, they might need a significant amount of real-time memory. In addition, the switching devices must have sufficient processing power to run the more complex routing protocols required for packet switching. A system must be in place by which devices can recognize when packets have been lost so that retransmission can be requested.

Connection-Oriented and Connectionless Modes

Compare the implications of using connection-oriented communications with connectionless communications.

The OSI Network layer determines the route a packet will take as it passes through a series of different LANs from the source PC to the destination PC. The complexity and versatility of Network layer addressing gives rise to two different communication modes for passing messages across the network, both of which are recognized under OSI:

◆ *Connection-oriented mode.* Error correction and flow control are provided at internal nodes along the message path.

◆ *Connectionless mode.* Internal nodes along the message path do not participate in error correction and flow control.

To understand the distinction between connection-oriented and connectionless communications, you must consider an important distinction between the OSI model's Data Link and Network layers. In theory, the Data Link layer facilitates the transmission of data across a single link between two nodes. The Network layer describes the process of routing a packet through a series of nodes to a destination on another link on the network. An example of this latter scenario is a message passing from a PC on one LAN segment through a series of routers to a PC on a distant part of the network. The internal nodes forwarding the packet also forward other packets between other end nodes.

In connection-oriented mode, the chain of links between the source and destination nodes forms a kind of logical pathway connection. The nodes forwarding the data packet can track which packet is part of which connection. This enables the internal nodes to provide flow control as the data moves along the path. For example, if an internal node determines that a link is malfunctioning, the node can send a notification message backward, through the path to the source computer. Furthermore, because the internal node distinguishes among individual, concurrent connections in which it participates, this node can transmit (or forward) a "stop sending" message for one of its connections without stopping all communications through the node. Another feature of connection-oriented communication is that internal nodes provide error correction at each link in the chain. Therefore, if a node detects an error, it asks the preceding node to retransmit.

Connectionless mode does not provide these elaborate internal control mechanisms; instead, connectionless mode relegates all error-correcting and retransmitting processes to the source and destination nodes. The end nodes acknowledge the receipt of packets and retransmit if necessary, but internal nodes do not participate in flow control and error correction (other than simply forwarding messages between the end nodes).

The advantage of connectionless mode is that connectionless communications can be processed more quickly and more simply because the internal nodes only forward data and thus don't have to track connections or provide retransmission or flow control.

The differences between connection-oriented and connectionless modes of communication may be easier to understand by analogy.

Imagine talking to someone and then having her reaffirm that she understood what you have told her after each sentence. Connectionless mode is like having a conversation with someone, but the speaker just carries on and assumes that the listener understands. Connection-oriented is slower, yet more reliable. Connectionless is faster, but has less capability to correct errors (misunderstandings in the conversation example) as they occur.

Connectionless mode does have its share of disadvantages, however, including the following:

- Messages sometimes get lost due to an overflowing buffer or a failed link along the pathway.

- If a message gets lost, the sender doesn't receive notification.

- Retransmission for error correction takes longer because a faulty transmission can't be corrected across an internal link.

It is important to remember that the OSI model is not a set of rules for communication; the OSI model is a framework in which models of communication are explained. As such, individual implementations of connectionless protocols can attenuate some of the preceding disadvantages. It is also important to remember that connection-oriented mode, although it places much more emphasis on monitoring errors and controlling traffic, doesn't always work either. Ultimately, the choice of connection-oriented or connectionless communications mode depends on interoperability with other systems, the premium for speed, and the cost of components.

Gateway Services

Routers can handle interconnection of networks whose protocols function in similar ways. When the rules differ sufficiently on the two networks, however, a more powerful device is required.

A *gateway* is a device that can translate the different protocols used by different networks. Gateways can be implemented starting at the Network layer or at higher layers in the OSI model, depending on where the protocol translation is required.

Components That Operate at This Level— Routers

Define the communication devices that communicate at each level of the OSI model.

A *router* is a connectivity device that operates at the OSI Network layer (see Figure 2.9). The information available at the Network layer gives a router far more sophisticated packet-delivery capabilities than a bridge provides. As with a bridge, a router constructs a routing table, but the Network layer addressing information (discussed earlier in this chapter) enables routers to pass packets through a chain of other routers, or even choose the best route for a packet if several routes exist. (See Chapter 6 for more information on routers and how they operate.)

To understand the function of routers, it might be useful to compare them directly to a concept you should already understand at this point, that of a bridge. A bridge separates a LAN segment without changing the LAN address. Think of a bridge on a street used to cross a river. Even though you cross the bridge, you are still on the same street. A router is more like an intersection. Think of three

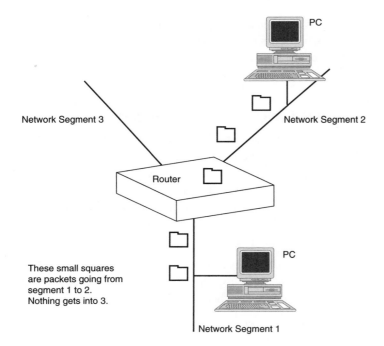

FIGURE 2.9
Routers move packets onto different segments.

streets converging to a single intersection. No matter which path you take from your current street, you end up on a new street. The router's functionality is to direct the traffic down the correct street at the intersection.

A hybrid device called a *brouter* combines some characteristics of a router and a bridge. A brouter routes routable protocols using information available at the Network layer and acts as a bridge for non-routable protocols. A *routable protocol* is a protocol that can pass through a router. TCP/IP and IPX/SPX are examples of routable protocols. (See Chapter 7 for more information.)

OSI Transport Layer Concepts

The Transport layer, the next layer of the OSI model, can implement procedures to ensure the reliable delivery of messages to their destination devices. The term "reliable" does not mean that errors cannot occur; instead, it means that if errors occur, they are detected. If errors such as lost data are detected, the Transport layer either requests retransmission or notifies upper-layer protocols so that they can take corrective action.

The Transport layer enables upper-layer protocols to interface with the network but hides the complexities of network operation from them. One of the functions of the Transport layer is to break large messages into segments suitable for network delivery.

Transport Layer Connection Services

Some services can be performed at more than one layer of the OSI model. In addition to the Data Link and Network layers, the Transport layer can take on some responsibility for connection services. The Transport layer interacts with the Network layer's connection-oriented and connectionless services and provides some of the essential quality control features. Some of the Transport layer's activities include the following:

◆ *Repackaging*. When large messages are divided into segments for transport, the Transport layer must repackage the segments when they are received before reassembling the original message.

◆ *Error control*. When segments are lost during transmission or when segments have duplicate segment IDs, the Transport layer must initiate error recovery. The Transport layer also detects corrupted segments by managing end-to-end error control using techniques such as checksums.

◆ *End-to-end flow control.* The Transport layer uses acknowledgments to manage end-to-end flow control between two connected devices. Besides negative acknowledgments, some Transport layer protocols can request the retransmission of the most recent segments.

OSI Session Layer Concepts

The next OSI layer, the Session layer, manages dialogs between two computers by establishing, managing, and terminating communications. As illustrated in Figure 2.10, dialogs can take three forms:

◆ *Simplex dialogs.* These dialogs are responsible for one-way data transfers only. An example is a fire alarm, which sends an alarm message to the fire station but cannot (and does not need to) receive messages from the fire station.

◆ *Half-duplex dialogs.* These dialogs handle two-way data transfers in which the data flows in only one direction at a time. When one device completes a transmission, this device must "turn over" the medium to the other device so that this second device has a turn to transmit. In a similar fashion, CB radio operators converse on the same communication channel. When one operator finishes transmitting, he must release his transmit key so that the other operator can send a response.

◆ *Full-duplex dialogs.* This third type of dialog permits two-way simultaneous data transfers by providing each device with a separate communication channel. Voice telephones are full-duplex devices, and either party to a conversation can talk at any time. Most computer modems can operate in full-duplex mode.

Costs rise for half- and full-duplex operation because the more complex dialog technologies are naturally more expensive. Designers of communications systems, therefore, generally use the simplest dialog mode that satisfies the communication requirements.

FIGURE 2.10
Simplex, half-duplex, and full-duplex communication modes.

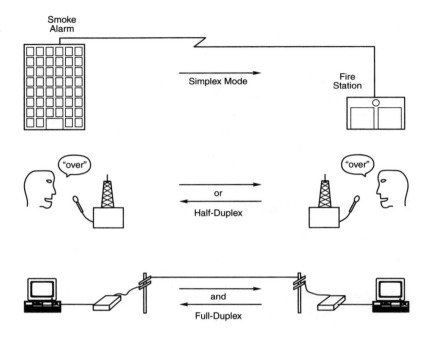

Half-duplex communication can result in wasted bandwidth during the intervals when communication is turned around. On the other hand, using full-duplex communication generally requires a greater bandwidth than half-duplex communication.

The Session layer also marks the data stream with checkpoints and monitors the receipt of those checkpoints. In the event of a failure, the sending PC can retransmit, starting with the data sent after the last checkpoint, rather than resend the whole message.

Session Layer Session Administration

A *session* is a formal dialog between a service requester and a service provider. Sessions have at least four phases:

◆ *Connection establishment.* In this phase, a service requester requests initiation of a service. During the setup process, communication is established and rules are agreed upon.

◆ *Data transfer.* With all the rules agreed upon during setup, each party to the dialog knows what to expect. Communication is therefore efficient, and errors are easy to detect.

◆ *Connection release.* When the session is completed, the dialog is terminated in an orderly fashion.

◆ *Error Correction.* Error Correction is also done at the Session layer. It checks for errors in the reassembled packets received from the Transport layer.

The connection establishment phase establishes the parameters for the communication session. Actually, the connection establishment phase is comprised of several tasks, including the following:

◆ Specification of required services that are to be used

◆ User login authentication and other security procedures

◆ Negotiation of protocols and protocol parameters

◆ Notification of connection IDs

◆ Establishment of dialog control, as well as acknowledgment of numbering and retransmission procedures

After the connection is established, the devices involved can initiate a dialog (data transfer phase). As well as exchange data, these devices exchange acknowledgments and other control data that manage the dialog.

The Session layer can also incorporate protocols to resume dialogs that have been interrupted. After a formal dialog has been established, devices recognize a lost connection whenever the connection has not been formally released. Therefore, a device realizes that a connection has been lost when the device fails to receive an expected acknowledgment or data transmission.

Within a certain time period, two devices can reenter the Session that was interrupted but not released. The connection release phase is an orderly process that shuts down communication and releases resources on the service provider.

OSI Presentation Layer Concepts

The Presentation layer deals with the syntax, or grammatical rules, needed for communication between two computers. The Presentation layer converts system-specific data from the Application

What "Presentation" Means in the Presentation Layer The name "Presentation layer" has caused considerable confusion in the industry because some people mistakenly believe that this layer presents data to the user. However, the name has nothing to do with displaying data. Instead, this function is performed by applications running above the Application layer.

The Presentation layer is so named because it presents a uniform data format to the Application layer. As a matter of fact, this layer is not commonly implemented because applications typically perform most Presentation layer functions.

layer into a common, machine-independent format that supports a more standardized design for lower protocol layers.

The Presentation layer also attends to other details of data formatting, such as data encryption and data compression.

On the receiving end, the Presentation layer converts the machine-independent data from the network into the format required for the local system. This conversion could include the following:

◆ *Data formatting.* This is the organization of the data. This topic is actually broken down into four subtopics:

- *Bit-order translation.* When binary numbers are transmitted through a network, they are sent one bit at a time. The transmitting computer can start at either end of the number. Some computers start at the *most significant digit (MSD)*; others start at the *least significant digit (LSD).* Essentially this has to do with whether information is read from right to left or from left to right.

- *Byte-order translation.* Complex values generally must be represented with more than one byte, but different computers use different conventions to determine which byte should be transmitted first. Intel microprocessors, for example, start with the least significant byte and are called *little endian.* Motorola microprocessors, on the other hand, start with the most significant byte and are called *big endian.* Byte-order translation might be needed to reconcile these differences when transferring data between a computer with an Intel processor and a Motorola processor.

- *Character code translation.* Different computers use different binary schemes for representing character sets. For instance: *ASCII,* the American Standard Code for Information Interchange, is used to represent English characters on all microcomputers and most minicomputers (see Figure 2.11); *EBCDIC,* the Extended Binary Coded Decimal Interchange Code, is used to represent English characters on IBM mainframes (see Figure 2.12); and *Shift-JIS* is used to represent Japanese characters.

- *File syntax translation.* File formats differ between computers. For instance, Macintosh files actually consist of two

7-Bit ASCII Character Set

8				0	0	0	0	0	0	0	0
7				0	0	0	0	1	1	1	1
6				0	0	1	1	0	0	1	1
5				0	1	0	1	0	1	0	1
4	3	2	1								
0	0	0	0	NUL	DLE	SP	0	@	P	`	p
0	0	0	1	SOH	DC1	!	1	A	Q	a	q
0	0	1	0	STX	DC2	"	2	B	R	b	r
0	0	1	1	ETX	DC3	#	3	C	S	c	s
0	1	0	0	EOT	DC4	$	4	D	T	d	t
0	1	0	1	ENQ	NAK	%	5	E	U	e	u
0	1	1	0	ACK	SYN	&	6	F	V	f	v
0	1	1	1	BEL	ETB	'	7	G	W	g	w
1	0	0	0	BS	CAN	(	8	H	X	h	x
1	0	0	1	HT	EM	)	9	I	Y	i	y
1	0	1	0	LF	SUB	*	:	J	Z	j	z
1	0	1	1	VT	ESC	+	;	K	[	k	{
1	1	0	0	FF	FS	,	<	L	\	l	|
1	1	0	1	CR	GS	_	=	M	]	m	}
1	1	1	0	SO	RS	.	>	N	^	n	~
1	1	1	1	SI	US	/	?	O	_	o	DEL

8-Bit IBM Extended ASCII

8				1	1	1	1	1	1	1	1
7				0	0	0	0	1	1	1	1
6				0	0	1	1	0	0	1	1
5				0	1	0	1	0	1	0	1
4	3	2	1								
0	0	0	0	Ç	É	á		¿	─	‡	
0	0	0	1	ü	æ	í	±	¡		ß	±
0	0	1	0	é	Æ	ó		¬	"	,	≥
0	0	1	1	â	ô	ú	|	├	"	„	≤
0	1	0	0	ä	ö	ñ	¥	─	'	Σ	Ù
0	1	0	1	à	ò	Ñ	µ	+	'	Â	I
0	1	1	0	å	û	ª	┤	╞	÷	Ê	
0	1	1	1	ç	ù	º	╗	«	╫	Á	≈
1	0	0	0	ê	ÿ	¿		»	╜	Ë	°
1	0	0	1	ë	Ö	©	╣		Ÿ	È	·
1	0	1	0	è	Ü		║	╨	/		-
1	0	1	1	ï	¢	´	ª	╥	░	Î	√
1	1	0	0	î	£	¨	a	╠	‹	∞	ⁿ
1	1	0	1	ì	¥	¡		═	›	ø	²
1	1	1	0	Ä	₧	«			fi		■
1	1	1	1	Å	ƒ	»	ø		fl		

FIGURE 2.11
ASCII character code, used by PCs.

EDIBIC Character Code

8				0	0	0	0	0	0	0	0	1	1	1	1	1	1	1	1
7				0	0	0	0	1	1	1	1	0	0	0	0	1	1	1	1
6				0	0	1	1	0	0	1	1	0	0	1	1	0	0	1	1
5				0	1	0	1	0	1	0	1	0	1	0	1	0	1	0	1
4	3	2	1																
0	0	0	0	NUL	DLE	DS		SP	&	—									0
0	0	0	1	SOH	DC1	SOS			/			a	j			A	J		1
0	0	1	0	STX	DC2	FS	SYN					b	k	s		B	K	S	2
0	0	1	1	ETX	DC3							c	l	t		C	L	T	3
0	1	0	0	PF	RES	BYP	PN					d	m	u		D	M	U	4
0	1	0	1	HT	NL	LF	RS					e	n	v		E	N	V	5
0	1	1	0	LC	BS	EOB	UC					f	o	w		F	O	W	6
0	1	1	1	DEL	IL	PRE	EOT					g	p	x		G	P	X	7
1	0	0	0		CAN							h	q	y		H	Q	Y	8
1	0	0	1		EM							i	r	z		I	R	Z	9
1	0	1	0	SMM	CC	SM			!	:									
1	0	1	1	VT				.	$	,	#								
1	1	0	0	FF	IFS		DC4	<	*	%	@								
1	1	0	1	CR	IGS	ENQ	NAK	(	)	-	,								
1	1	1	0	SO	IRS	ACK		+	;	>	=								
1	1	1	1	SI	IUS	BEL	SUB	|	¬	?	"								

FIGURE 2.12
EDIBIC character code, used by IBM mainframes.

N O T E

Many vendors incorporate *Unicode* in their products. Unicode, a 16-bit code that can represent 65,536 characters in English and other languages, is organized into code pages devoted to the characters required for a given language. Unicode improves the portability of products between different language environments.

related files called a data fork and a resource fork. PC files, on the other hand, consist of a single file.

◆ *Encryption.* Encryption puts data into a form unreadable by unauthorized users. Encryption takes on two main forms:

   • *Public key.* This uses a rule of encryption (the key) and a known value. The manipulation of the key with a known value produces a mechanism for decrypting data.

   • *Private key.* This encryption uses one key. All components that have the key can decrypt the data.

The redirector service operates at the OSI Presentation layer.

OSI Application Layer Concepts

The Application layer of the OSI reference model is concerned with providing services on the network, including file services, print services, application services such as database services, messaging services, and directory services among others.

A common misunderstanding is that the Application layer is responsible for running user applications such as word processors. This is not the case. The Application layer, however, does provide an interface whereby applications can communicate with the network. It is this interface that is often referred to as the Application Programming Interface (API). Some examples of APIs include MAPI (Messaging Programming Interface) and TAPI (Telephony Application Programming Interface).

The Application layer also advertises the available services that your computer has to the network. An example of this is when you double-click on the Network Neighborhood Icon in Windows 95 or Windows NT. The resulting picture shows a list of computers that have services available to network users. (The security service of these computers determines whether or not a user has access.)

The nature of these services is beyond the scope of this chapter. In general, you would take a course or read a book to understand how to manage different services on a network. Examples of these services include Windows NT security, file and printing management, SMTP mail, fax servers, and ODBC connectivity. This book covers some of the basics of Windows NT Security in Chapter 10, "Managing and Securing a Microsoft Network."

PUTTING THE OSI MODEL IN PERSPECTIVE

To put the whole OSI model into context, begin by assuming that you are sitting at your PC, using Microsoft Word, and you have just elected to print the document to a printer attached to your neighbor's computer.

The word processor sends the print job down to the redirector (Presentation layer). From here it goes to get information about its destination. This information is contained in the Session layer, where a session was established by your neighbor's computer. At this point the data is broken up into smaller chunks of information (Transport layer). From here it is addressed, so it can get to the other computer (Network Layer). At this point it is sent to the network card (Data Link layer) so that the print job can be converted into signals that run down the network cable (Physical layer).

From this point it may pass between several repeaters if the network cable is going a long distance. The packets of data may also go through various bridges if they are on a network segment that is heavily populated with machines. These packets containing the print job may also go through various routers, if the destination printer is on another network segment in the office.

At this point, the packets containing the print job arrive at the network card of the destination computer with the printer. From here the signals from the network cable are converted back into a format that the computer can understand (Data Link layer). Then the information on the intended address is verified as indicating the receiving computer (Network layer). At this point packets are reassembled to form a proper job (Transport layer). During the receiving of the packets, the destination computer must know when it has received the complete the print job (Session layer). Finally, the information is presented to the Print Service (the Application layer).

In the real world, you usually can pick individual OSI layer components at the Physical (transmission media types, repeaters), Data Link (network card, network card drivers and bridges), Network (routers and brouters) and Application (services you wish to have on your network) levels. Typically, the Transport, Session, and Presentation layers are built into the networking components of operating systems or programs that are used and do not present a set of alternatives from which to choose.

STANDARDS THAT UTILIZE MULTIPLE LEVELS OF THE OSI MODEL

The discussion in most of this chapter has focused on the explanation of the OSI model and its seven levels. This chapter has discussed what occurs at each level, and in some cases, has given examples of components that operate at these different levels.

The remainder of this chapter looks at some other standards or protocols that are common features of networks. These standards often encompass several layers of the OSI model at once. The three broad standards that will be examined are the following:

- ◆ SLIP and PPP
- ◆ The IEEE 802 suite of standards
- ◆ NDIS and ODI

When working with Microsoft networks, you will come across these standards on more than one occasion when dealing with connectivity issues.

Serial Line Internet Protocol (SLIP) and Point-to-Point Protocol (PPP)

Distinguish whether SLIP or PPP is used as the communication protocol for various situations.

Two other standards vital to network communication are *Serial Line Internet Protocol (SLIP)* and *Point-to-Point Protocol (PPP)*. SLIP and PPP were designed to support dial-up access to networks based on the Internet transport protocols. SLIP is a simple protocol that functions at the Physical layer, whereas PPP is a considerably enhanced protocol that provides Physical layer and Data Link layer functionality. The relationship of both to the OSI model is shown in Figure 2.13.

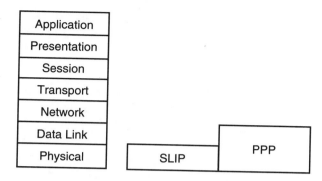

FIGURE 2.13
The relationship between SLIP, PPP, and the OSI model.

Developed to provide dial-up TCP/IP connections, SLIP is an extremely rudimentary protocol that suffers from a lack of rigid standardization in the industry, which sometimes hinders different vendor implementations of SLIP from operating with each other.

Windows NT supports both SLIP and PPP from the client end using the Dial-Up Networking application. On the server end, Windows NT RAS (Remote Access Service) supports PPP but doesn't support SLIP. In other words, Windows NT can act as a PPP server but not as a SLIP server.

SLIP is most commonly used on older systems or for dial-up connections to the Internet via SLIP-server Internet hosts.

PPP was defined by the Internet Engineering Task Force (IETF) to improve on SLIP by providing the following features:

◆ Security using password logon

◆ Simultaneous support for multiple protocols on the same link

◆ Dynamic IP addressing

◆ Improved error control

Different PPP implementations might offer different levels of service and negotiate service levels when connections are made. Due to its versatility, interoperability, and additional features, PPP is presently surpassing SLIP as the most popular serial-line protocol.

Certain dial-up configurations cannot use SLIP for the following reasons:

◆ SLIP supports the TCP/IP transport protocol only. PPP, however, supports TCP/IP, as well as a number of other transport

NOTE

RAS and Dial-Up Networking
Windows NT RAS is a dial-up service that ships with Windows NT. This service is known as Dial-Up Networking in Windows 95, and essentially enables one to connect computer systems using telephone lines. Anytime you dial up an ISP (Internet Service Provider), you are experiencing functionality similar to RAS.

protocols, such as NetBEUI, IPX, AppleTalk, and DECnet. In addition, PPP can support multiple protocols over the same link.

◆ SLIP requires static IP addresses. Because SLIP requires static—or preconfigured—IP addresses, SLIP servers do not support Dynamic Host Configuration Protocol (DHCP), which assigns IP addresses dynamically, or when requested. (DHCP enables clients to share IP addresses so that a relatively small number of IP addresses can serve a larger user base.) If the dial-up server uses DHCP to assign an IP address to the client, the dial-up connection won't use SLIP.

◆ SLIP does not support dynamic addressing through DHCP. SLIP connections, therefore, cannot dynamically assign a WINS or DNS server.

Windows NT RAS (using PPP) offers a number of other interesting features, including the following:

◆ *PPP Multilink Protocol.* Multilink enables a single connection to use several physical pathways of the same type (such as modems, ISDN lines, and X.25 cards). Utilizing multiple pathways for a single connection increases bandwidth and, therefore, performance.

◆ *NetBIOS Gateway.* A RAS server can connect a client running the NetBEUI protocol with a TCP/IP or IPX network by serving as a NetBIOS gateway.

◆ *IPX or IP Router.* A RAS server can act as a router for IPX/SPX and TCP/IP networks. (See Chapter 6 for more information on routers.)

THE IEEE 802 FAMILY

The Institute of Electrical and Electronic Engineers (IEEE) is one of the largest professional organizations in the world, and is extremely influential with regard to setting standards. In February of 1980, the IEEE implemented a task force to develop a set of standards for connectivity between Network Interface Cards (NICs) and transmission media. This task force was known as the 802 committee. This 802 committee was broken down into several different subcommittees

Origin of the 802 Number The IEEE decided to name the 802 family set of standards "802" because it was in February of 1980 that they started this project of standardization.

that were each responsible for some different implementation of data transfer that occurs at the Data Link level of the OSI model. These IEEE standards have also been adopted by ISO, and they are referred to as ISO 8802. The IEEE 802 series of standards, as well as all the other IEEE standards and research, can be found at http://standards.ieee.org/802/index.html.

Thirteen workgroups oversee the 802 standards. Each workgroup is assigned a specific mandate in the area of LAN/MAN connectivity they are to analyze. Figure 2.14 illustrates the position each standard occupies in the OSI reference model.

IEEE 802.1

This standard is actually one that goes beyond the Data Link layer of the OSI model. This is a general standard for network management, and provides network management standards to the other 802 standards in the OSI model. This standard actually covers all layers from the Physical to the Transport layer.

IEEE 802.2

The IEEE 802.2 standard defines an LLC sublayer that is used by other lower-layer protocols. Because these lower-layer protocols can use a single LLC protocol layer, Network layer protocols can be designed independently of both the network's Physical layer and MAC sublayer implementations.

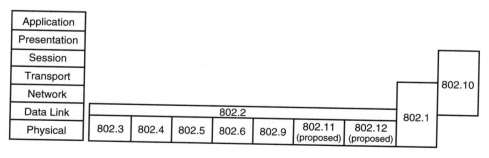

FIGURE 2.14
The relationship between the IEEE 802 standards and the OSI model.

The LLC appends to packets a header that identifies the upper-layer protocols associated with the frame. This header also declares the processes that are the source and destination of each packet.

The workgroup for this set of standards is currently inactive.

IEEE 802.3

The IEEE 802.3 standard defines a network derived from the ethernet network originally developed by Digital, Intel, and Xerox. This standard defines characteristics related to the MAC sublayer of the Data Link layer and the OSI Physical layer. With one minor distinction—frame type—IEEE 802.3 Ethernet functions identically to DIX Ethernet v.2. These two standards can even coexist on the same cabling system, although devices using one standard cannot communicate directly with devices using the other.

The MAC sublayer uses a type of contention access called *Carrier Sense Multiple Access with Collision Detection* (CSMA/CD). This technique reduces the incidence of collision by having each device listen to the network to determine whether it's quiet ("carrier sensing"); a device attempts to transmit only when the network is quiescent. This reduces but does not eliminate collisions because signals take some time to propagate through the network. As devices transmit, they continue to listen so they can detect a collision should it occur. When a collision occurs, all devices cease transmitting and send a "jamming" signal that notifies all stations of the collision. Then, each device waits a random amount of time before attempting to transmit again. This combination of safeguards significantly reduces collisions on all but the busiest networks.

IEEE 802.4

The 802.4 standard describes a network with a bus physical topology that controls media access with a token mechanism. This standard was designed to meet the needs of industrial automation systems but has gained little popularity. Both baseband and broadband (using 75-ohm coaxial cable) configurations are available.

The workgroup for this set of standards is currently inactive.

IEEE 802.5

The IEEE 802.5 standard was derived from IBM's Token Ring network, which employs a ring logical topology and token-based media access control. Data rates of 1, 4, and 16Mbps have been defined for this standard. More discussion on Token Ring will be seen in Chapter 4.

IEEE 802.6

The IEEE 802.6 standard describes a MAN standard called *Distributed Queue Dual Bus (DQDB)*. Much more than a data network technology, DQDB is suited to data, voice, and video transmissions. The network is based on fiber-optic cable in a dual-bus topology, and traffic on each bus is unidirectional. When operated in pairs, the two buses provide a fault-tolerant configuration. Bandwidth is allocated by using time slots, and both synchronous and asynchronous modes are supported.

The workgroup for this set of standards is currently inactive.

IEEE 802.7

This standard deals with integrating broadband solutions into a network environment. This standard is currently under development.

The workgroup for this set of standards is currently inactive.

IEEE 802.8

This standard deals with methods of implementing fiber optic technology into networking environments. This standard is currently under development.

IEEE 802.9

The IEEE 802.9 standard supports a 10Mbps asynchronous channel, along with 96 64Kbps (6Mbps total bandwidth) channels that can be dedicated to specific data streams. The total bandwidth is

16Mbps. This standard is called *Isochronous Ethernet (IsoEnet)* and is designed for settings with a mix of bursty and time-critical traffic.

IEEE 802.10

This standard deals with security and encryption standards. This standard is currently under development.

IEEE 802.11

IEEE 802.11 is a standard for wireless LANs and is currently under development. A CSMA/CD method has been approved, but the final standard is pending.

IEEE 802.12

The IEEE 802.12 standard is based on a 100Mbps proposal promoted by AT&T, IBM, and Hewlett-Packard. Called *100VG-AnyLAN*, the network is based on a star-wiring topology and a contention-based access method whereby devices signal the wiring hub when they need to transmit data. Devices can transmit only when granted permission by the hub. This standard is intended to provide a high-speed network that can operate in mixed ethernet and token-ring environments by supporting both frame types.

IEEE 802.14

The 802.13 designation is not used, hence the last standard is known as 802.14. This standard is for transmitting data over cable TV lines. The committee is currently looking at a hybrid fiber/coax media. This is one of the up and coming areas for fast Internet access from a person's home.

IEEE 802.3 and IEEE 802.5 Media

Describe the characteristics and purpose of the media used in the IEEE 802.3 and IEEE 802.5.

IEEE 802.2 (topology independent), IEEE 802.3 (based on Ethernet), and IEEE 802.5 (based on token ring) are the most commonly used IEEE 802 standards. Carefully read the following overview of the media each uses; Microsoft expects you to describe the characteristics and purpose of the media used in IEEE 802.3 and IEEE 802.5 for the Networking Essentials exam. (Chapters 3 and 4 discuss Ethernet and token-ring media in greater detail.)

The IEEE 802.3 Physical layer definition describes signaling methods (both baseband and broadband), data rates, media, and topologies. Several Physical layer variants also have been defined. Each variant is named following a convention that states the signaling rate (1 or 10) in Mbps, baseband (BASE) or broadband (BROAD) mode, and a designation of the media characteristics.

The following list details the IEEE 802.3 variants of transmission media:

◆ *1BASE5*. This 1Mbps network utilizes UTP cable with a signal range up to 500 meters (250 meters per segment). A star physical topology is used.

◆ *10BASE5*. Typically called Thick Ethernet, or Thicknet, this variant uses a large diameter (10mm) "thick" coaxial cable with a 50-ohm impedance. A data rate of 10Mbps is supported with a signaling range of 500 meters per cable segment on a physical bus topology.

◆ *10BASE2*. Similar to Thicknet, this variant uses a thinner coaxial cable that can support cable runs of 185 meters. (In this case, the "2" indicates only an approximate cable range.) The transmission rate remains at 10Mbps, and the physical topology is a bus. This variant typically is called Thin Ethernet, or Thinnet.

◆ *10BASE-F*. This variant uses fiber-optic cables to support 10Mbps signaling with a range of 4 kilometers. Three sub-categories include *10BASE-FL* (fiber link), *10BASE-FB* (fiber backbone), and *10BASE-FP* (fiber passive).

◆ *10BROAD36*. This broadband standard supports channel signal rates of 10Mbps. A 75-ohm coaxial cable supports cable runs of 1,800 meters (up to 3,600 meters in a dual-cable configuration) using a physical bus topology.

NOTE

Some disagreement exists in the industry regarding the proper use of the name "Ethernet." Xerox has placed the name "Ethernet" in the public domain, which means that no one can claim authority over it. Purists, however, often claim that "Ethernet" refers to only the original Digital-Intel-Xerox standard. More frequently, however, the term designates any network based on CSMA/CD access-control methods.

Usually, it is necessary to be specific about the standard that applies to a given network configuration. The original standard is called Ethernet version 2 (the older version 1 is still in occasional use) or Ethernet-II. The IEEE standard is distinguished by its committee title as 802.3.

This distinction is important because Ethernet version 2 and 802.3 Ethernet use incompatible frame types. Devices using one frame type cannot communicate with devices using the other frame type.

◆ *10BASE-T.* This variant uses UTP cable in a star physical topology. The signaling rate remains at 10Mbps, and devices can be up to 100 meters from a wiring hub.

◆ *100BASE-X.* This proposed standard is similar to 10BASE-T but supports 100Mbps data rates.

The IEEE 802.5 standard does not describe a cabling system. Most implementations are based on the IBM cabling system, which uses twisted-pair cable wired in a physical star. See Chapters 3 and 4 for more information on Token Ring cabling and topologies.

NDIS AND ODI

Explain the purpose of NDIS and Novell ODI network standards.

The *Network Driver Interface Specification (NDIS)*, a standard developed by Microsoft and 3Com Corp., describes the interface between the network transport protocol and the Data Link layer network adapter driver. The following list details the goals of NDIS:

◆ To provide a vendor-neutral boundary between the transport protocol and the network adapter card driver so that a NDIS-compliant protocol stack can operate with a NDIS-compliant adapter driver.

◆ To define a method for binding multiple protocols to a single driver so that the adapter can simultaneously support communications under multiple protocols. In addition, the method enables you to bind one protocol to more than one adapter.

The *Open Data-Link Interface (ODI),* developed by Apple and Novell, serves the same function as NDIS. Originally, ODI was written for NetWare and Macintosh environments. Like NDIS, ODI provides rules that establish a vendor-neutral interface between the protocol stack and the adapter driver. This interface also enables one or more network drivers to support one or more protocol stacks.

Essentially NDIS and ODI are standards to which a person wishing to develop a driver for a network card or a protocol will adhere. Standards are similar to how cars are manufactured. Cars destined for England are designed with the steering wheel on the right-hand side of the car. Cars for North America are designed with the steering wheel on the left-hand side of the car. This standard does not change the function of the car or the steering wheel; conforming to it simply ensures that the car will function properly for each country's driving environment. NDIS and ODI are similar. Neither standard changes the function of the network card or the network card's driver, they simply are standards enabling the network card to function in each operating system's environment.

CASE STUDY: WHAT DEVICE SHOULD BE USED: A REPEATER, BRIDGE, OR ROUTER?

ESSENCE OF THE CASE

The facts of the case are as follows:

- Too much traffic on the network is the problem, slowing access and bringing the productivity of the workers down.

- You must be able to define the purpose or function of a repeater, bridge, and router if you are to see which device is a solution for the problem.

- To be able explain why you are proposing which device to implement, you need to understand at which layer in the OSI model different components or services run.

- You want to make sure that the solution you are going to provide to the company is not going to become obsolete with the advent of new technology.

SCENARIO

This case study addresses the decisions involved in determining when a LAN should implement a repeater, bridge, or router. The company in question is a medium-size firm with roughly 100 employees. They are currently running a LAN utilizing a single cable segment. The users of this LAN are finding that it is taking a relatively long time to download files from one of their two centralized file servers. This company has two distinct groups: the sales group and the support group. Each group accesses its own server. Due to the long waits, the company has called you in to explore various options for speeding up the throughput on the LAN. The owners of the company have heard of the terms "repeater," "bridge," and "router," and say that their LAN supplier has mentioned that their company should purchase all three devices.

ANALYSIS

This case study is real-world applicable, but also puts into perspective the following two exam objectives:

continues

CASE STUDY: WHAT DEVICE SHOULD BE USED: A REPEATER, BRIDGE, OR ROUTER?

continued

- Define the communication devices that communicate at each level of the OSI model.
- Describe the characteristics and purpose of the media used in IEEE 802.3 and IEEE 802.5.

The first thing to analyze is which of the three devices can be used to isolate the network traffic.

The repeater, which operates at the physical level of the OSI model, is definitely ruled out. You do so because a repeater is used to regenerate a signal that has degenerated over distance. The repeater has nothing to do with isolating or lessening network traffic.

Both a bridge, which operates at the Data Link level, and a router, which operates at the Network level of the OSI model, could be used. As was discussed in the Data Link section, a bridge can isolate network traffic on a single network segment. By putting a bridge on the LAN, and placing the sales group on one side and the support group on the other, with their respective servers on each side, the problems with response time brought on by network traffic should be alleviated. That is, network traffic from one group will not interfere with another group.

A router could also isolate network traffic, but this would require dividing the network into two separately addressed network segments (one for sales and one for the support group). Recall that routers operate at the Network layer of the OSI model. They utilize network addresses to determine the location of a network segment on the network. Because routers must evaluate packets based upon network addresses, data transferred from one network segment to another incurs a small amount of overhead. Also, because routers need to be programmed to be aware of the different segment (either by using a routing protocol or manually), the network's administrator requires a higher level of expertise than that required to administer a bridge. Not all transport protocols are routable (see Chapter 7), and routers normally do not forward broadcasts, thus these conditions may play a role in determining whether a router is a feasible option.

Also, routers usually cost more than bridges, and thus are best suited for networks with more than two segments. On this basis alone, the best option here is that of the bridge. It provides the solution that your client is looking for—that of faster access—at a lower cost than a router. It also requires less administration and is slightly more efficient in this situation.

One issue in the "Essence of the Case" section asked you to make sure that the technology you are purchasing does not become obsolete. To check for potential obsolescence, go to the IEEE web site and look up the developments of the various standards being investigated by the IEEE in one of its workgroups. The type of network this company uses (that is, Ethernet, Token Ring or ARCNet) is not mentioned in this case study. But this information is important to know, because it affects which 802 standard you need to research.

CHAPTER SUMMARY

This chapter discussed some of the important standards that define the networking environment. An understanding of these standards is essential for understanding the networking topics discussed in later chapters. This chapter covered the following:

◆ The OSI model

◆ SLIP and PPP

◆ The IEEE 802 Standards

◆ NDIS and ODI

Later chapters in this book look more closely at related topics, including transmission media, topologies, and connectivity devices.

KEY TERMS

• International Standards Organization (ISO)

• Open Systems Interconnection (OSI)

• Physical layer

• Data Link layer

• Network layer

• Transport layer

• Session layer

• Presentation layer

• Application layer

• Serial Line Internet Protocol (SLIP)

• Point-to-Point Protocol (PPP)

• IEEE

• IEEE 802 family

• circuit switching

• message switching

• packet switching

• datagram packet switching

• virtual circuit packet switching

• connection-oriented mode

• connectionless mode

• gateway

• Network Data Link Interface Standard (NDIS)

• Open Data Link Interface (ODI)

APPLY YOUR LEARNING	

Exercises

2.1 SLIP and PPP in Dial-Up Networking

Objective: Explore the Dial-Up Networking application and learn how to configure Dial-Up Networking for SLIP or PPP.

Estimated time: 10 minutes

1. From the Windows NT Start menu, choose Programs/Administrative Tools and select Dial-Up Networking. The Dial-Up Networking application enables you to connect to another computer as a dial-up client using SLIP or PPP.

   To get the full effect of this exercise, RAS, TCP/IP, NWLink, and NetBEUI must be installed on your system and must be enabled for dial-out connections. If they already are, proceed to Step 7. Exercise 7.1 in Chapter 7 describes how to install protocols. To enable the protocols for dial-out connections, follow these steps:

2. Start the Control Panel Network application and select the Services tab. If Remote Access Service isn't installed, click the Add button to install it.

3. Double-click on Remote Access Service in the Services tab (or select Remote Access Service and click Properties).

4. In the Remote Access Setup dialog box, click the Configure button and make sure either the Dial Out Only or Dial Out And Receive Calls button is selected under Port Usage. Click OK.

5. In the Remote Access Setup dialog box, click the Network button. Select dial out protocols NetBEUI, TCP/IP, and IPX. Click OK.

6. Click Continue in the Remote Access Setup dialog box.

7. In the Dial-Up Networking main screen, click the New button to set up a new connection. The New Phonebook Entry dialog box appears. The tabs of the New Phonebook Entry dialog box enable you to enter a phone number, modem information, security information, and a login script. In addition, you can enter information about the dial-up server to which you are connecting. Click the Server tab when you are finished.

8. In the Dial-Up Networking Server tab, click the arrow to the right of the box labeled Dial-up server type. Note that the default option is PPP: Windows NT, Windows 95 Plus, Internet. PPP enables you to connect to a Windows NT RAS server, a Windows 95 machine with the Windows 95 Plus Dial-up Server feature, or a server with an Internet-style TCP/IP configuration.

9. In the Dial-up server type box, select the SLIP: Internet option. (TCP/IP must be installed on your machine.) Examine the rest of the Server tab options. The other protocols (IPX/SPX and NetBEUI) should be grayed out, as should software compression. Your only protocol option is TCP/IP. Check the TCP/IP check box and click the TCP/IP Settings button. Note the boxes for a static IP address and static DNS and WINS server addresses. Click Cancel.

10. In the New Phonebook Entry Server tab, click the down arrow to the right of the Dial-up server type box and choose PPP: Windows NT, Windows 95 Plus, Internet. Note that the IPX/SPX Compatible and NetBEUI protocol options are now available (if they are installed on your system and enabled for dial-out connections—see preceding note), as are software compression and PPP LCP extensions. Select the

APPLY YOUR LEARNING

TCP/IP protocol and click the TCP/IP Settings button. Note that under a PPP connection, the TCP/IP Settings dialog box contains option buttons for a server-assigned IP address and server-assigned name server addresses.

11. Click Cancel to exit TCP/IP Settings, Cancel to exit New Phonebook Entry, and Close to exit Dial-Up Networking.

2.2 Finding IEEE Standards on the Internet

Objective: Find information on the Internet about the emergence of new standards dealing with the 802 series of standards.

Estimated time: 30 minutes

1. On a computer that is connected to the Internet, open up your web browser.

2. In the Location pane, type in the following URL: www.ieee.org

3. On the welcome screen, click on the area of the graphic that says Standards. (Because web pages are continually being redeveloped, there may not be a "standards" area to click on the web page. If this is the case, do a search on the web page for 802).

4. On the new window, scroll down until you see a standards list referencing 802, LAN, and MAN (the exact wording may change at any given time, so looking for these key words should be directive enough) and click on that topic.

5. On the list of 802 series of standards, explore what is new for the 802.3 and 802.5 set of standards.

Review Questions

1. Explain the difference between a router, a repeater, and a bridge.

2. What are the seven layers of the OSI model?

3. What are the three main purposes of NDIS and ODI?

4. What are three main differences between PPP and SLIP?

5. In one sentence, explain the difference between standards 802.3 and 802.5.

Exam Questions

1. The OSI model organizes communication protocols into how many layers?

   A. 3

   B. 7

   C. 17

   D. 56

2. The layers of the OSI model (in order) are included in which of the following choices?

   A. Physical, Data Link, Network, Transport, System, Presentation, Application

   B. Physical, Data Link, Network, Transport, Session, Presentation, Application

   C. Physical, Data Link, Network, Transform, Session, Presentation, Application

   D. Presentation, Data Link, Network, Transport, Session, Physical, Application

APPLY YOUR LEARNING

3. In the OSI model, what is the relationship of a layer (N) to the layer above it (layer N+1)?

   A. Layer N provides services for layer N+1.

   B. Layer N+1 adds a header to information received from layer N.

   C. Layer N utilizes services provided by layer N+1.

   D. Layer N has no effect on layer N+1.

4. Which option best describes the condition of two different computer types that can communicate?

   A. They conform to the OSI model.

   B. They are both using TCP/IP.

   C. They are using compatible protocol stacks.

   D. They are a Macintosh and a UNIX workstation.

5. Which three of the following statements regarding protocol stacks are true?

   A. A given protocol stack can run on only one computer type.

   B. Layers add headers to packets received from higher layers in the protocol stack.

   C. A protocol stack is a hierarchical set of protocols.

   D. Each layer provides services for the next highest layer.

6. Which protocol layer enables multiple devices to share the transmission medium?

   A. Physical

   B. Data Link

   C. Session

   D. Network

7. Which switching method employs virtual circuits?

   A. Message

   B. Circuit

   C. Packet

   D. All the above

8. Which OSI layer is concerned with data encryption?

   A. Network

   B. Transport

   C. Session

   D. Presentation

9. Which switching method makes the most efficient use of network bandwidth?

   A. Message

   B. Circuit

   C. Packet

   D. All methods are about equal

10. What is another name for a message-switching network?

   A. Connectionless

   B. Datagram

   C. Store-and-forward

   D. Virtual circuit

APPLY YOUR LEARNING

11. Which two statements about virtual circuits are true?

    A. They are usually associated with connection-oriented services.

    B. A virtual circuit represents a specific path through the network.

    C. A virtual circuit appears to the connected devices as a dedicated network path.

    D. Virtual circuits dedicate a communication channel to a single conversation.

12. Which switching method fragments messages into small units that are routed through independent paths?

    A. Message

    B. Packet

    C. Circuit

    D. Neural

13. Which two of the following methods of dialog control provide two-way communication?

    A. Simple duplex

    B. Simplex

    C. Half-duplex

    D. Full-duplex

14. Dialog control is a function of which layer of the OSI reference model?

    A. Network

    B. Transport

    C. Session

    D. Presentation

15. Which three of the following are functions of session administration?

    A. Connection establishment

    B. Checksum error detection

    C. Data transfer

    D. Connection release

16. Which two of the following are functions of connection establishment?

    A. Resumption of interrupted communication

    B. Verification of logon name and password

    C. Determination of required services

    D. Acknowledgment of data receipt

17. Which two of the following are possible functions of the Presentation layer?

    A. Data encryption

    B. Presentation of data on display devices

    C. Data translation

    D. Display format conversion

18. Which three of the following are possible functions of the Application layer?

    A. Network printing service

    B. End-user applications

    C. Client access to network services

    D. Service advertisement

APPLY YOUR LEARNING

19. PPP operates at which two of the following OSI layers?

    A. Physical

    B. Data Link

    C. Network

    D. Transport

20. SLIP supports which of the following transport protocols?

    A. IPX/SPX

    B. NetBEUI

    C. TCP/IP

    D. All the above

21. IEEE 802.3 is associated with which of the following network architectures?

    A. Token Ring

    B. Ethernet

    C. Internet

    D. None of the above

22. IEEE 802.5 is associated with which of the following network architectures?

    A. Token ring

    B. Ethernet

    C. Internet

    D. None of the above

23. NDIS describes the interface between which two components?

    A. User

    B. Network transport protocol

    C. Physical layer

    D. Network adapter driver

24. Routers operate at which layer of the OSI model?

    A. Transport

    B. Network

    C. Data Link

    D. Physical

25. Which type of communication provides flow control at internal nodes?

    A. Transport

    B. Internal

    C. Connection-oriented

    D. Internet

26. Which answer best describes support over serial line communication under the TCP/IP transport protocol?

    A. SLIP

    B. PPP

    C. Both A and B

    D. None of the above

27. 10BASE-T networks are defined in which standard?

    A. IEEE 802.1

    B. IEEE 802.5

    C. Both A and B

    D. None of the above

APPLY YOUR LEARNING

28. You notice that on your network the response time is very slow. You wish to solve this problem.

    Primary Objective: You are using protocols that are not routable, hence there cannot be any changes in network addresses.

    Secondary Objective: The device needs to require no user intervention.

    Secondary Objective: The device needs to operate at the Data Link layer.

    Suggested Solution: You install a router in the middle of the network cable.

    A. This solution meets the primary objective and both secondary objectives.

    B. This solution meets the primary objective and one secondary objective.

    C. This solution meets the primary objective.

    D. This solution does not meet the primary objective.

Answers to Review Questions

1. A repeater is used to regenerate a signal. It is used primarily to extend a cable length beyond its recommended capacity. A repeater does not route information onto other network segments, or isolate traffic on a cable segment. A repeater operates at the Physical layer of the OSI model. See the section titled "Components That Operate at This Level—Repeaters."

   A bridge is responsible for isolating traffic within a given cable segment. Some bridges can also do the task of a repeater and regenerate a signal on a cable. A bridge does not route data onto different network segments. A bridge operates at the Data

   Link layer of the OSI model. See the section titled "Components That Operate at This Level—Bridges."

   A router is used to route data onto different network segments. It can perform the role of a bridge as well, but if this is the case, then it is called a brouter. A router operates at the Network level of the OSI model. See the section titled "Components That Operate at This Level—Routers."

2. The seven layers of the OSI model are as follows:

   • Physical

   • Data Link

   • Network

   • Transport

   • Session

   • Presentation

   • Application

   See the section titled "The OSI Reference Model."

3. NDIS is a standard developed by Microsoft and 3Com Corp. ODI has the same function, but it was developed by Novell and Apple. The three main features are as follows:

   • It was designed to provide a vendor-neutral boundary between the transport protocol and the network adapter card driver.

   • It enables one network card to support multiple protocol stacks.

   • It enables one protocol stack to be shared by multiple network cards.

   See the section titled "NDIS and ODI."

4. SLIP and PPP are designed to support dial-up networking. PPP is more advanced than SLIP, because the SLIP protocol has no rigid standardization. Windows NT cannot act as a SLIP server.

   PPP has all the capabilities of SLIP, but also provides the following:

   • Security using password logon

   • Simultaneous support for multiple protocols on the same link

   • Dynamic IP addressing

   • Improved error control

   See the section titled "Serial Line Internet Protocol (SLIP) and Point-to-Point Protocol (PPP)."

5. 802.3 is an Ethernet standard, whereas 802.5 is a Token-Ring standard.

   See the section titled "The IEEE 802 Family."

Answers to Exam Questions

1. **B**. The OSI model has only seven layers. See the section titled "The OSI Reference Model."

2. **B**. Answers A and C each mention a non-existent layer (System and Transform). D references the OSI model in the incorrect order. See the section titled "The OSI Reference Model."

3. **A**. A lower layer in the OSI model provides services to the layer above it. See the section titled "How Peer OSI Layers Communicate."

4. **C**. All layers in the OSI model must be compatible with one another for two computers to communicate. Answers A, B, and D do not describe situations where total conformity exists. See the section titled "The OSI Reference Model."

5. **B, C, D**. A is incorrect because a given protocol stack can run on many different computer types. See the section titled "Protocol Stacks."

6. **B**. Transmission media sharing is done at the Data Link layer of the OSI model. See the section titled "OSI Data Link Layer Concepts."

7. **C**. Only packet switching employs virtual circuits. See the section titled "Delivering Packets."

8. **D**. Data encryption is a function of the Presentation level. See the section titled "OSI Presentation Layer Concepts."

9. **C**. Packet switching can make the best use of network bandwidth. See the section titled "Packet Switching."

10. **C**. The other three answers do not relate to message switching. Store-and-forward is a common term that is used to describe message-switching. See the section titled "Message Switching."

11. **A, C**. Answers B and D are the opposite of virtual circuits. See the section titled "Virtual Circuit Packet Switching."

12. **B**. A does not use small packets. C uses only one path. D has to do with physiology. See the section titled "Delivering Packets."

13. **C, D**. A and B provide only one-way communication. See the section titled "OSI Session Layer Concepts."

14. **C**. This is one of the functions of the Session layer. See the section titled "OSI Session Layer Concepts."

APPLY YOUR LEARNING

15. **A, C, D**. Checksum error detection is done at the Data Link layer of the OSI model. See the section titled "OSI Session Layer Concepts."

16. **B, C**. Session establishment is at the start of a session. A is in the middle of a session. D is during a session. See the section titled "OSI Session Layer Concepts."

17. **A, C**. B and D are functions of operating systems, and are not part of the OSI model. See the section titled "OSI Presentation Layer Concepts."

18. **A, C, D**. Application layer has to do with services, not desktop applications. See the section titled "OSI Application Layer Concepts."

19. **A, B**. PPP is a lower-layer protocol that encompasses both the Physical and Data Link layers of the OSI model. See the section titled "Serial Line Internet Protocol (SLIP) and Point-to-Point Protocol (PPP)."

20. **C**. Only PPP supports all; SLIP supports only TCP/IP. See the section titled "Serial Line Internet Protocol (SLIP) and Point-to-Point Protocol (PPP)."

21. **B**. 802.3 is an IEEE Ethernet standard. See the section titled "IEEE 802.3."

22. **A**. 802.5 is an IEEE Token-Ring standard. See the section titled "IEEE 802.5."

23. **B, D**. NDIS is a standard to which network card drivers should be written. The NDIS standard addresses the Data Link layer of the OSI model. See the section titled "NDIS and ODI."

24. **B**. This is the layer at which routers operate, because routers are concerned with forwarding packets to devices on different networks based on each packet's network address. See the section titled "Components That Operate at This Level—Routers."

25. **C**. One purpose of connection-oriented communications is flow control. All the other answers are not types of communications describing flow control. See the section titled "OSI Session Layer Concepts."

26. **C**. Both SLIP and PPP provide TCP/IP support. PPP also provides support for NetBEUI and NWLink as well, whereas SLIP does not. See the section titled "Serial Line Internet Protocol (SLIP) and Point-to-Point Protocol (PPP)."

27. **D**. It is defined in the 802.3 standard. See the section titled "IEEE 802.3."

28. **D**. Adding a router accomplishes none of the objectives. A router needs to supply more than one network address. A router requires user input to program network addresses into it. A router operates at the Network Layer of the OSI model.

Suggested Readings and Resources

1. Tanenbaum, Andrew. *Computer Networks.* Prentice Hall, 1996.

2. Henshall, John. *Open Up OSI: An Illustrated Guide.* Ellis Horwood Ltd., 1993.

3. Simon, Alan, Tom Wheeler, and Thomas Wheeler. *Open Systems Handbook.* AP Professional, 1994.

PLANNING

Chapter 3 targets the first objective in the Planning section of the Networking Essentials exam:

Select the appropriate media for various situations. Media choices include twisted-pair cable, coaxial cable, fiber-optic cable, and wireless.

Situational elements include cost, distance limitations, and number of nodes.

▶ This chapter focuses on one exam objective and the many issues that stem from it. This is due to amount and complexity of the material associated with the topic of Transmission Media. It is just as important to know the advantages and disadvantages of different transmission media and in what situations to use them as it is to simply understand the characteristics of each transmission medium.

CHAPTER 3

Transmission Media

STUDY STRATEGIES

▶ Be able to compare and contrast one transmission media with another. Always think in terms of which form of transmission media best suits the needs of the network. These needs take into account the following:

- The distances the network needs to cover
- The type of electromagnetic interference that needs to be overcome

- The impenetrable barriers that may force you to use a wireless media
- The relative costs of the transmission media and whether or not they are justifiable

▶ Read the chapter with these criteria in mind and pay particular attention to the tables presented. This provides you with a solid understanding of the topic of Transmission Media as it is addressed on the exam.

INTRODUCTION

On any network, the various entities must communicate through some form of media. Human communication requires some sort of media, whether it is technologically based (as are telephone wires) or whether it simply involves the use of our senses to detect sound waves propagating through the air. Likewise, computers can communicate through cables, light, and radio waves. Transmission media enable computers to send and receive messages but, as in human communication, do not guarantee that the messages will be understood.

This chapter discusses some of the most common network transmission media. One broad classification of this transmission media is known as *bounded media*, or cable media. This includes cable types such as coaxial cable, shielded twisted-pair cable, unshielded twisted-pair cable, and fiber-optic cable. Another type of media is known as *boundless media*; these media include all forms of wireless communications. To lay the groundwork for these issues, the chapter begins with an introduction to the frequencies in the electromagnetic spectrum and a look at some important characteristics of the transmission media that utilize these different frequencies to transmit the data.

TRANSMISSION FREQUENCIES

Transmission media make possible the transmission of the electronic signals from one computer to another. These electronic signals express data values in the form of binary (on/off) impulses, which are the basis for all computer information (represented as 1s and 0s). These signals are transmitted between the devices on the network, using some form of transmission media (such as cables or radio) until they reach the desired destination computer.

All signals transmitted between computers consist of some form of electromagnetic (EM) waveform, ranging from radio frequencies through microwaves and infrared light. Different media are used to transmit the signals, depending on the frequency of the EM waveform. Figure 3.1 illustrates the range of electromagnetic waveforms (known as the electromagnetic spectrum) and their associated frequencies.

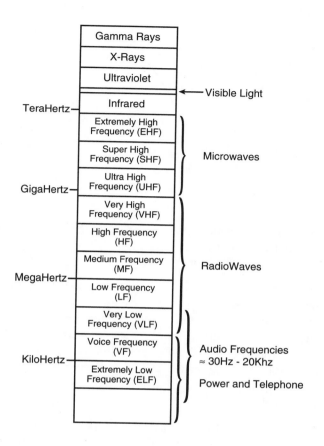

FIGURE 3.1
The electromagnetic spectrum.

The electromagnetic spectrum consists of several categories of waveforms, including radio frequency waves, microwave transmissions, and infrared light.

The frequency of a wave is dependent upon the number of waves or oscillations that occur during a period of time. An example that all people can relate to is the difference between a high-pitched sound, such as a whistle, and a low-pitch sound such as a fog horn. A high-pitched sound has a very high frequency; in other words, numerous cycles of oscillation (or waves) occur each second. Whereas, a low frequency sound, such as the fog horn, is based on relatively few cycles or waves per second (see Figure 3.2). Although sound is not an example of electromagnetic energy (it's mechanical energy), the principles are similar.

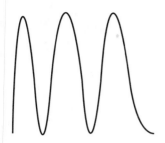

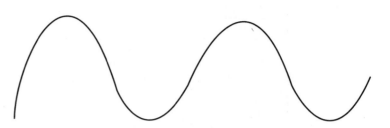

High frequency

Low frequency

FIGURE 3.2
High frequency and low frequency waves.

Radio frequency waves are often used for LAN signaling. Radio frequencies can be transmitted across electrical cables (twisted-pair or coaxial) or by radio broadcast.

Microwave transmissions can be used for tightly focused transmissions between two points. Microwaves are used to communicate between earth stations and satellites, for example, and they are also used for line-of-sight transmissions on the earth's surface. In addition, microwaves can be used in low-power forms to broadcast signals from a transmitter to many receivers. Cellular phone networks are examples of systems that use low-power microwave signals to broadcast signals.

Infrared light is ideal for many types of network communications. Infrared light can be transmitted across relatively short distances and can be either beamed between two points or broadcast from one point to many receivers. Infrared and higher frequencies of light also can be transmitted through fiber-optic cables. A typical television remote control uses infrared transmission.

The next sections examine the major factors you should consider when evaluating what type of transmission media should be implemented.

TRANSMISSION MEDIA CHARACTERISTICS

Each type of transmission media has special characteristics that make it suitable for a specific type of service. You should be familiar with these characteristics for each type of media:

- ◆ Cost

- ◆ Installation requirements

- ◆ Bandwidth

- ◆ Band usage (baseband or broadband)

- ◆ Attenuation

- ◆ Immunity from electromagnetic interference

These characteristics are all important. When you design a network for a company, all these factors play a role in the decision concerning what type of transmission media should be used.

Cost

One main factor in the purchase decision of any networking component is the cost. Often the fastest and most robust transmission media is desired, but a network designer must often settle for something that is slower and less robust, because it more than suffices for the business solution at hand. The major deciding factor is almost always price. It is a rare occasion in the field that the sky is the limit for installing a network. As with nearly everything else in the computer field, the fastest technology is the newest, and the newest is the most expensive. Over time, economies of scale bring the price down, but by then, a newer technology comes along.

Installation Requirements

Installation requirements typically involve two factors. One is that some transmission media require skilled labor to install. Bringing in a skilled outside technician to make changes to or replace resources on the network can bring about undue delays and costs. The second has to do with the actual physical layout of the network. Some types of transmission media install more easily over areas where people are spread out, whereas other transmission media are easier to bring to clusters of people or a roaming user.

N O T E **Using the Term "Bandwidth"** The term "bandwidth" also has another meaning. In the communications industry, bandwidth refers to the range of available frequencies between the lower frequency limit and the upper frequency limit. Frequencies are measured in Hertz (Hz), or cycles per second. The bandwidth of a voice telephone line is 400–4,000Hz, which means that the line can transmit signals with frequencies ranging from 400 to 4,000 cycles per second.

N O T E As you know, everything in computers is represented with 1s and 0s. We use 1s and 0s to represent the bits in the computer. However, be sure to remember that transmission media is measured in megabits per second (Mbps), not megaBYTES per second (MBps). The difference is eight-fold, as there are 8 bits in a byte.

Bandwidth

In computer networking, the term *bandwidth* refers to the measure of the capacity of a medium to transmit data. A medium that has a high capacity, for example, has a high bandwidth, whereas a medium that has limited capacity has a low bandwidth.

Bandwidth can be best explained by using water hoses as an analogy. If a half-inch garden hose can carry water flow from a trickle up to two gallons per minute, then that hose can be said to have a bandwidth of two gallons per minute. A four-inch fire hose, however, might have a bandwidth that exceeds 100 gallons per minute.

Data transmission rates are frequently stated in terms of the bits that can be transmitted per second. An Ethernet LAN theoretically can transmit 10 million bits per second and has a bandwidth of 10 megabits per second (Mbps).

The bandwidth that a cable can accommodate is determined in part by the cable's length. A short cable generally can accommodate greater bandwidth than a long cable, which is one reason all cable designs specify maximum lengths for cable runs. Beyond those limits, the highest-frequency signals can deteriorate, and errors begin to occur in data signals. You can see this by taking a garden hose and snapping it up and down. You can see the waves traveling down the hose get smaller as they get farther from your hand. This loss of the wave's amplitude represents attenuation, or signal degradation.

Band Usage (Baseband or Broadband)

The two ways to allocate the capacity of transmission media are with *baseband* and *broadband* transmissions. Baseband devotes the entire capacity of the medium to one communication channel. Broadband enables two or more communication channels to share the bandwidth of the communications medium.

Baseband is the most common mode of operation. Most LANs function in baseband mode, for example. Baseband signaling can be accomplished with both analog and digital signals.

Although you might not realize it, you have a great deal of experience with broadband transmissions. Consider, for example, that the TV cable coming into your house from an antenna or a cable provider is a broadband medium. Many television signals can share the bandwidth of the cable because each signal is modulated using a separately assigned frequency. You can use the television tuner to select the frequency of the channel you want to watch.

This technique of dividing bandwidth into frequency bands is called frequency-division multiplexing (FDM) and works only with analog signals. Another technique, called time-division multiplexing (TDM), supports digital signals. Both of these types of multiplexing are discussed in the next section.

Figure 3.3 contrasts the difference between baseband and broadband modes of operation.

Multiplexing

Multiplexing is a technique that enables broadband media to support multiple data channels. Multiplexing makes sense under a number of circumstances:

◆ *When media bandwidth is costly.* A high-speed leased line, such as a T1 or T3, is expensive to lease. If the leased line has sufficient bandwidth, multiplexing can enable the same line to carry mainframe, LAN, voice, video conferencing, and various other data types.

◆ *When bandwidth is idle.* Many organizations have installed fiber-optic cable that is used to only partial capacity. With the proper equipment, a single fiber can support hundreds of megabits—or even a gigabit or more—of data per second.

◆ *When large amounts of data must be transmitted through low-capacity channels.* Multiplexing techniques can divide the original data stream into several lower-bandwidth channels, each of which can be transmitted through a lower-capacity medium. The signals then can be recombined at the receiving end.

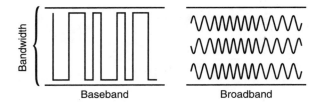

FIGURE 3.3
Baseband and broadband transmission modes.

Multiplexing refers to combining multiple data channels for transmission on a common medium. *Demultiplexing* refers to recovering the original separate channels from a multiplexed signal.

Multiplexing and demultiplexing are performed by a multiplexer (also called a mux), which usually has both capabilities.

Frequency-Division Multiplexing

Figure 3.4 illustrates frequency-division multiplexing (FDM). This technique works by converting all data channels to analog form. Each analog signal can be modulated by a separate frequency (called a "carrier frequency") that makes it possible to recover that signal during the demultiplexing process. At the receiving end, the demultiplexer can select the desired carrier signal and use it to extract the data signal for that channel.

FDM can be used in broadband LANs. (A standard for Ethernet also exists.) One advantage of FDM is that it supports bidirectional signaling on the same cable. That is, a frequency can originate from both ends of the transmission media at once.

Time-Division Multiplexing

Time-division multiplexing (TDM) divides a channel into time slots that are allocated to the data streams to be transmitted, as illustrated in Figure 3.5. If the sender and receiver agree on the time-slot assignments, the receiver can easily recover and reconstruct the original data streams.

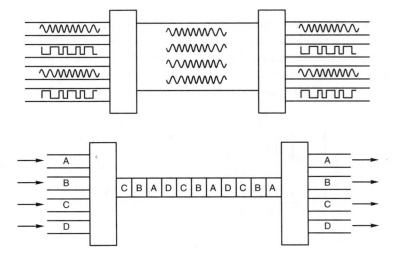

FIGURE 3.4
Frequency-division multiplexing.

FIGURE 3.5
Time division multiplexing steams data depending on the data's allocated time slots.

TDM transmits the multiplexed signal in baseband mode. Interestingly, this process makes it possible to multiplex a TDM signal as one of the data channels on an FDM system.

Conventional TDM equipment utilizes fixed time divisions and allocates time to a channel, regardless of that channel's level of activity. If a channel isn't busy, its time slot isn't being fully utilized. Because the time divisions are programmed into the configurations of the multiplexers, this technique is often referred to as synchronous TDM.

If using the capacity of the data medium more efficiently is important, a more sophisticated technique, statistical time-division multiplexing (StatTDM), can be used. A stat-mux uses the time-slot technique but allocates time slots based on the traffic demand on the individual channels, as illustrated in Figure 3.6.

Notice that Channel B is allocated more time slots than Channel A, and that Channel C is allocated the fewest time slots. Channel D is idle, so no slots are allocated to it. To make this procedure work, the data transmitted for each time slot includes a control field that identifies the channel to which the data in the time slot should be assigned.

Attenuation

Attenuation is a measure of how much a signal weakens as it travels through a medium, as discussed in Chapter 2. This book doesn't discuss attenuation in formal terms, but it does address the impact of attenuation on performance.

Attenuation is a contributing factor to why cable designs must specify limits in the lengths of cable runs. When signal strength falls below certain limits, the electronic equipment that receives the signal can experience difficulty isolating the original signal from the noise present in all electronic transmissions. The effect is exactly like trying to tune in distant radio signals. Even if you can lock on to the

FIGURE 3.6

Statistical time-division multiplexing allocates timeslots based on a channel's traffic demand.

signal on your radio, the sound generally still contains more noise than the sound for a local radio station. As mentioned in the previous chapters, repeaters are used to regenerate signals; hence one solution to deal with attenuation is to add a repeater.

Electromagnetic Interference

Electromagnetic interference (EMI) consists of outside electromagnetic noise that distorts the signal in a medium. When you listen to an AM radio, for example, you often hear EMI in the form of noise caused by nearby motors or lightning. Some network media are more susceptible to EMI than others.

Crosstalk is a special kind of interference caused by adjacent wires. Crosstalk occurs when the signal from one wire is picked up by another wire. You may have experienced this when talking on a telephone and hearing another conversation going on in the background. Crosstalk is a particularly significant problem with computer networks because large numbers of cables often are located close together, with minimal attention to exact placement.

CABLE MEDIA

For the Networking Essentials exam, you need to know how to make decisions about network transmission media based on some of the factors described in previous sections of this chapter. The following sections discuss three types of network cabling media, as follows:

- ◆ Coaxial cable
- ◆ Twisted-pair cable
- ◆ Fiber-optic cable

Later in this chapter, you will learn about some of the wireless communication forms.

Coaxial Cable

Coaxial cables were the first cable types used in LANs. As shown in Figure 3.7, coaxial cable gets its name because two conductors share

NOTE

Mixing Media Some large networks use combinations of media. When you mix and match different types of media, difficulties can arise, largely because mixed media require a greater level of expertise and training on the part of the network support staff. As the number of media types increases, your own responsibilities increase—when a problem arises on the LAN, the number of areas you must investigate increases dramatically when mixed transmission media are involved.

a common axis; the cable is most frequently referred to as a "coax." A type of coaxial cable that you may be familiar with is your television cable.

The components of a coaxial cable are as follows:

◆ A *center conductor*, although usually solid copper wire, is sometimes made of stranded wire.

◆ An *outer conductor* forms a tube surrounding the center conductor. This conductor can consist of braided wires, metallic foil, or both. The outer conductor, frequently called the shield, serves as a ground and also protects the inner conductor from EMI.

◆ An *insulation layer* keeps the outer conductor spaced evenly from the inner conductor.

◆ A plastic encasement (jacket) protects the cable from damage.

Types of Coaxial Cable

The two basic classifications for coaxial cable are as follows:

◆ Thinnet

◆ Thicknet

The following sections discuss Thinnet and Thicknet coaxial cabling.

Thinnet

Thinnet is a light and flexible cabling medium that is inexpensive and easy to install. Table 3.1 illustrates some Thinnet classifications.

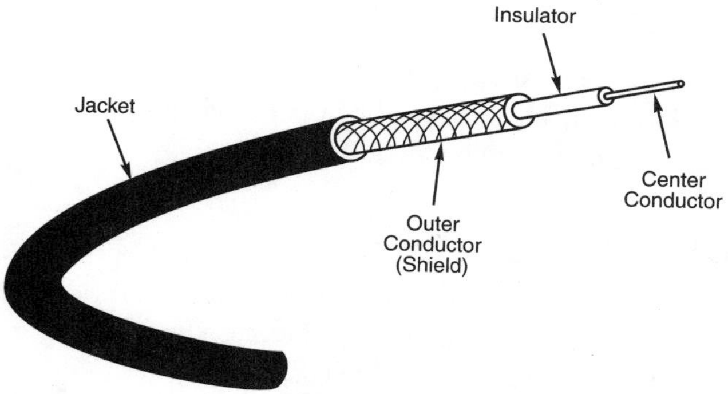

NOTE **Impedance** All coaxial cables have a characteristic measurement called *impedance*, which is measured in ohms. Impedance is a measure of the apparent resistance to an alternating current. You must use a cable that has the proper impedance in any given situation.

FIGURE 3.7

The structure of coaxial cable consists of four major components.

Note that Thinnet falls under the RG-58 family, which has a 50-ohm impedance. Thinnet is approximately .25 inches (6 mm) in thickness.

TABLE 3.1

THINNET CABLE CLASSIFICATIONS

Cable	Description	Impedance
RG-58/U	Solid copper center	50-ohm
RG-58 A/U	Wire strand center	50-ohm
RG-58 C/U	Military version of RG-58 A/U	50-ohm
RG-59	Cable TV wire	75-ohm
RG-62	ARCnet specification	93-ohm

Thinnet cable can reliably transmit a signal for 185 meters (about 610 feet).

Thicknet

Thicknet (big surprise) is thicker than Thinnet. Thicknet coaxial cable is approximately 0.5 inches (13 mm) in diameter. Because it is thicker and does not bend as readily as Thinnet, Thicknet cable is harder to work with. A thicker center core, however, means that Thicknet can carry more signals a longer distance than Thinnet. Thicknet can transmit a signal approximately 500 meters (1,650 feet).

Thicknet cable is sometimes called Standard Ethernet (although other cabling types described in this chapter are used for Ethernet also). Thicknet can be used to connect two or more small Thinnet LANs into a larger network.

Because of its greater size, Thicknet is also more expensive than Thinnet. However, Thicknet can be installed relatively safely outside, running from building to building.

Coaxial Characteristics

You should be familiar with the installation, cost, bandwidth, and EMI resistance characteristics of coaxial cable. The following sections discuss some of the characteristics of coaxial cable.

Installation

Coaxial cable is typically installed in two configurations: daisy-chain (from device to device—Ethernet) and star (ARCnet). The daisy chain is shown in Figure 3.8.

The Ethernet cabling shown in the figure is an example of Thinnet, which uses RG-58 type cable. Devices connect to the cable by means of T-connectors. Cables are used to provide connections

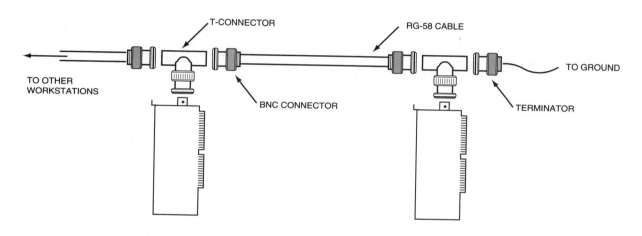

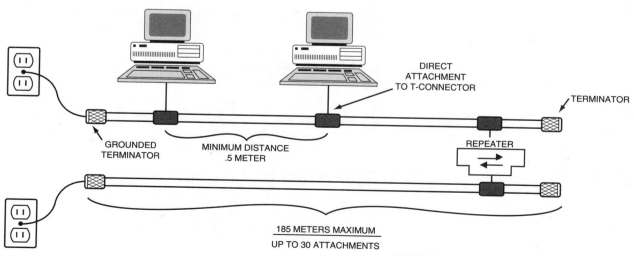

FIGURE 3.8
Coaxial cable wiring configuration.

between T-connectors. One characteristic of this type of cabling is that the ends of the cable run must be terminated by a special connector, called a terminator. The terminator contains a resistor that is matched to the characteristics of the cable. The resistor prevents signals that reach the end of the cable from bouncing back and causing interference.

Coaxial cable is reasonably easy to install because the cable is robust and difficult to damage. In addition, connectors can be installed with inexpensive tools and a bit of practice. The device-to-device cabling approach can be difficult to reconfigure, however, when new devices cannot be installed near an existing cabling path.

Cost

The coaxial cable used for Thinnet falls at the low end of the cost spectrum, whereas Thicknet is among the more costly options. Detailed cost comparisons are made later in this chapter in "Summary of Cable Characteristics."

Capacity

LANs that employ coaxial cable typically have a bandwidth between 2.5Mbps (ARCNet) and 10Mbps (Ethernet). Thicker coaxial cables offer higher bandwidth, and the potential bandwidth of coaxial is much higher than 10Mbps. Current LAN technologies, however, don't take advantage of this potential. (ARCNet and Ethernet are discussed in greater detail in Chapter 4, "Network Topologies and Architectures.")

EMI Characteristics

All copper media are sensitive to EMI, although the shield in coax makes the cable fairly resistant. Coaxial cables, however, do radiate a portion of their signal, and electronic eavesdropping equipment can detect this radiated signal.

Connectors for Coaxial Cable

Two types of connectors are commonly used with coaxial cable. The most common is the British Naval Connector (BNC). Figure 3.9 depicts the characteristics of BNC connectors and Thinnet cabling.

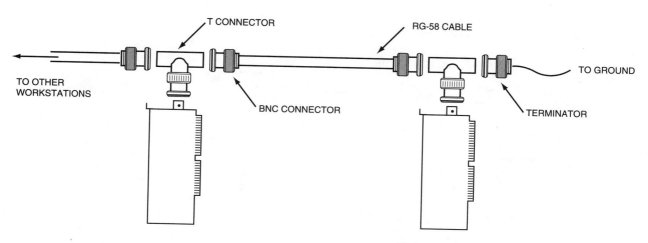

FIGURE 3.9
Thinnet is connected using BNC T-connectors.

Key issues involving Thinnet cabling are

◆ A BNC T-connector connects the network board in the PC to the network. The T-connector attaches directly to the network board.

◆ BNC cable connectors attach cable segments to the T-connectors.

◆ A BNC barrel connector connects to Thinnet cables.

◆ Both ends of the cable must be terminated. A BNC terminator is a special connector that includes a resistor that is carefully matched to the characteristics of the cable system.

◆ One of the terminators must be grounded. A wire from the connector is attached to a grounded point, such as the center screw of a grounded electrical outlet.

In contrast, Thicknet uses N-connectors, which screw on rather than use a twist lock (see Figure 3.10). As with Thinnet, both ends of the cable must be terminated, and one end must be grounded.

Workstations don't connect directly to the cable with Thicknet. Instead, a connecting device called a transceiver is attached to the Thicknet cable. This transceiver has a port for an AUI connector (which looks deceivingly like a joystick connector), and an AUI cable (also called a transceiver cable or a drop cable) connects the workstation to the Thicknet medium. Transceivers can connect to Thicknet cables in the following two ways:

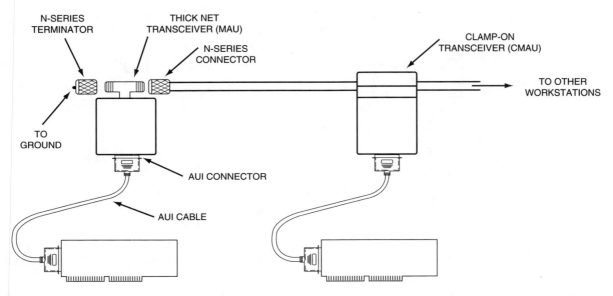

FIGURE 3.10
Connectors and cabling for Thicknet.

◆ Transceivers can be connected by cutting the cable and splicing N-connectors and a T-connector on the transceiver. Because it is so labor-intensive, this original method of connecting is used rather infrequently.

◆ The more common approach is to use a clamp-on transceiver, which has pins that penetrate the cable without the need for cutting it. Because clamp-on transceivers force sharp teeth into the cable, they frequently are referred to as vampire taps.

You can use a transceiver to connect a Thinnet LAN to a Thicknet backbone.

Coax and Fire Code Classifications

The space above a drop ceiling (between the ceiling and the floor of a building's next level) is extremely significant to both network administrators and fire marshals. This space (called the plenum—see Figure 3.11) is a convenient place to run network cables around a building. The plenum, however, is typically an open space in which air circulates freely, and, consequently, fire marshals pay special attention to it.

The most common outer covering for coaxial cabling is polyvinyl chloride (PVC). PVC cabling gives off poisonous fumes when it burns. For that reason, fire codes prohibit PVC cabling in the

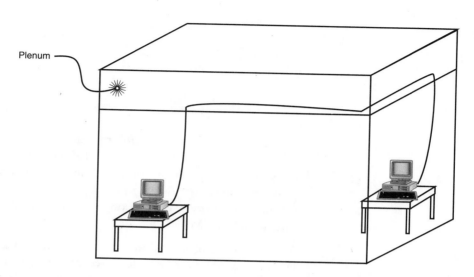

FIGURE 3.11
The plenum—the space between the drop-down ceiling of a room and its actual ceiling—is often a convenient spot for placing network cabling.

plenum because poisonous fumes in the plenum can circulate freely throughout the building.

Plenum-grade coaxial cabling is specially designed to be used without conduit in plenums, walls, and other areas where fire codes prohibit PVC cabling. Plenum-grade cabling is less flexible and more expensive than PVC cabling, so it is used primarily where PVC cabling can't be used.

Twisted-Pair Cable

Twisted-pair cable has become the dominant cable type for all new network designs that employ copper cable. Among the several reasons for the popularity of twisted-pair cable, the most significant is its low cost. Twisted-pair cable is inexpensive to install and offers the lowest cost per foot of any cable type. Your telephone cable is an example of a twisted-pair type cable.

A basic twisted-pair cable consists of two strands of copper wire twisted together (see Figure 3.12). The twisting reduces the sensitivity of the cable to EMI and also reduces the tendency of the cable to radiate radio frequency noise that interferes with nearby cables and electronic components, because the radiated signals from the twisted wires tend to cancel each other out. (Antennas, which are purposely designed to radiate radio frequency signals, consist of parallel, not twisted, wires).

FIGURE 3.12
Twisted-pair cabling.

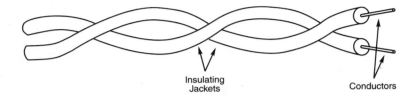

Twisting of the wires also controls the tendency of the wires in the pair to cause EMI in each other. As noted previously, whenever two wires are in close proximity, the signals in each wire tend to produce crosstalk in the other. Twisting the wires in the pair reduces crosstalk in much the same way that twisting reduces the tendency of the wires to radiate EMI.

A twisted-pair cable is used in most cases to connect a PC to either a HUB or a MAU. Both of these devices are discussed in Chapter 6, "Connectivity Devices and Transfer Mechanisms." Two types of twisted-pair cable are used in LANs: shielded and unshielded, as explained in the following section.

Shielded Twisted-Pair (STP) Cable

Shielded twisted-pair cabling consists of one or more twisted pairs of cables enclosed in a foil wrap and woven copper shielding. Figure 3.13 shows IBM Type 1 cabling, the first cable type used with IBM Token Ring. Early LAN designers used shielded twisted-pair cable because the shield performed double duty, reducing the tendency of the cable to radiate EMI and reducing the cable's sensitivity to outside interference.

Coaxial and STP cables use shields for the same purpose. The shield is connected to the ground portion of the electronic device to which the cable is connected. A ground is a portion of the device that serves as an electrical reference point, and usually, it is literally connected to a metal stake driven into the ground. A properly grounded shield prevents signals from getting into or out of the cable.

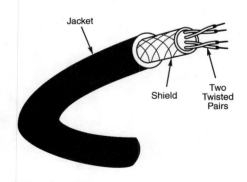

The picture in Figure 3.13 is an example of IBM Type 1 cable, an STP cable, and includes two twisted pairs of wire within a single shield. Various types of STP cable exist, some that shield each pair individually and others that shield several pairs. The engineers who design a network's cabling system choose the exact configuration. IBM designates several twisted-pair cable types to use with their Token Ring network design, and each cable type is appropriate for a

FIGURE 3.13
A shielded twisted-pair cable.

given kind of installation. A completely different type of STP is the standard cable for Apple's AppleTalk network.

Because so many different types of STP cable exist, describing precise characteristics is difficult. The following sections, however, offer some general guidelines.

Cost

STP cable costs more than thin coaxial or unshielded twisted-pair cable. STP is less costly, however, than thick coax or fiber-optic cable.

Installation

Naturally, different network types have different installation requirements. One major difference is the connector used. Apple LocalTalk connectors generally must be soldered during installation, a process that requires some practice and skill on the part of the installer. IBM Token Ring uses a so called unisex or hermaphrodite data connector (the connectors are both male and female), which can be installed with such common tools as a knife, a wire stripper, and a large pair of pliers (see Figure 3.14).

In many cases, installation can be greatly simplified with prewired cables—cables precut to length and installed with the appropriate connectors. You must learn to install the required connectors, however, when your installation requires the use of bulk cable. The installation of cables has been regulated or made part of building codes in some areas, to be performed only by a certified cable

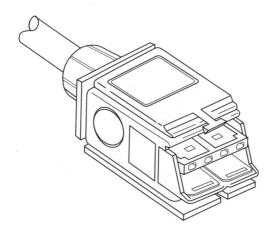

FIGURE 3.14
An IBM Data connector, also known as a hermaphrodite connector.

installer. You should check the regulations regarding this in your area before beginning the installation of any cable.

CONNECTOR TYPES

Most connectors require two connector types to complete a connection. The traditional designation for connector types is male and female. The male connector is the connector with pins, and the female connector has receptacles into which the pins insert. In a standard AC wall outlet, for example, the outlet itself is female and the plug on the line cord is male.

These designations originated when electrical installation was a male province so the terms "male" and "female" are being replaced gradually. A commonly used alternative is "pins and sockets."

The IBM data connector is called a unisex or hermaphrodite connector because the connector has both pins and sockets. Any IBM data connector can connect to any other IBM data connector.

STP cable tends to be rather bulky. IBM Type 1 cable is approximately ½ inch (13 mm) in diameter. Therefore, cable paths cannot hold nearly as many STP cables as they can when a thinner medium is used.

Capacity

STP cable has a theoretical capacity of 500Mbps, although few implementations exceed 155Mbps with 100-meter cable runs. The most common data rate for STP cable is 16Mbps, which is the top data rate for Token Ring networks.

Attenuation

All varieties of twisted-pair cable have attenuation characteristics that limit the length of cable runs to a few hundred meters, although a 100-meter limit is most common.

EMI Characteristics

The shield in STP cable results in good EMI characteristics for copper cable, comparable to the EMI characteristics of coaxial cable. This is one reason STP might be preferred to unshielded twisted-pair cable in some situations. As with all copper cables, STP is still sensitive to interference and vulnerable to electronic eavesdropping.

Connectors for STP

AppleTalk and Token Ring networks can be cabled using UTP cable and RJ-45 connectors (described later in this chapter), but both networks originated as STP cabling systems. For STP cable, AppleTalk also employs a DIN-type connector. Figure 3.15 shows an IBM connector connected to a network card having a DIN (DB-9) connector using a STP cable.

The IBM Data Connector is unusual because it doesn't come in two gender configurations. Instead, any IBM Data Connector can be snapped to any other IBM Data Connector. The IBM cabling system is discussed later in this chapter.

Unshielded Twisted-Pair (UTP) Cable

Unshielded twisted-pair cable doesn't incorporate a braided shield into its structure. However, the characteristics of UTP are similar in many ways to STP, differing primarily in attenuation and EMI. As shown in Figure 3.16, several twisted pairs can be bundled together in a single cable. These pairs are typically color-coded to distinguish them.

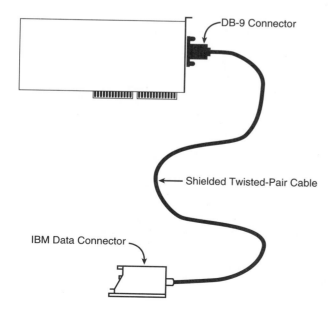

FIGURE 3.15
A drop cable using a DB-9 connector to connect to the Network Interface Card (NIC), and having IBM Data Connector ready to be attached to a MAU.

FIGURE 3.16
A multipair UTP cable.

Telephone systems commonly use UTP cabling. Network engineers can sometimes use existing UTP telephone cabling (if it is new enough and of a high enough quality to support network communications) for network cabling.

UTP cable is a latecomer to high-performance LANs because engineers only recently solved the problems of managing radiated noise and susceptibility to EMI. Now, however, a clear trend toward UTP is in operation, and all new copper-based cabling schemes are based on UTP.

UTP cable is available in the following five grades, or categories:

◆ *Categories 1 and 2.* These voice-grade cables are suitable only for voice and for low data rates (below 4Mbps). Category 1 was once the standard voice-grade cable for telephone systems. The growing need for data-ready cabling systems, however, has caused Categories 1 and 2 cable to be supplanted by Category 3 for new installations.

◆ *Category 3.* As the lowest data-grade cable, this type of cable generally is suited for data rates up to 10Mbps. Some innovative schemes utilizing new standards and technologies, however, enable the cable to support data rates up to 100Mbps. Category 3, which uses four twisted pairs with three twists per foot, is now the standard cable used for most telephone installations.

◆ *Category 4.* This data-grade cable, which consists of four twisted-pairs, is suitable for data rates up to 16Mbps.

◆ *Category 5.* This data-grade cable, which also consists of four twisted-pairs, is suitable for data rates up to 100Mbps. Most new cabling systems for 100Mbps data rates are designed around Category 5 cable.

The price of the grades of cable increase as you move from Category 1 to Category 5.

In a UTP cabling system, the cable is only one component of the system. All connecting devices are also graded, and the overall cabling system supports only the data rates permitted by the lowest-grade component in the system. In other words, if you require a Category 5 cabling system, all connectors and connecting devices must be designed for Category 5 operation.

The installation procedures for Category 5 cable also have more stringent requirements than the lower cable categories. Installers of Category 5 cable require special training and skills to understand these more rigorous requirements.

UTP cable offers an excellent balance of cost and performance characteristics, as discussed in the following sections.

Cost

UTP cable is the least costly of any cable type, although properly installed Category 5 tends to be fairly expensive. In some cases, existing cable in buildings can be used for LANs, although you should verify the category of the cable and know the length of the cable in the walls. Distance limits for voice cabling are much less stringent than for data-grade cabling.

Installation

UTP cable is easy to install. Some specialized equipment might be required, but the equipment is low in cost and its use can be mastered with a bit of practice. Properly designed UTP cabling systems easily can be reconfigured to meet changing requirements.

As noted earlier, however, Category 5 cable has stricter installation requirements than lower categories of UTP. Special training is recommended for dealing with Category 5 UTP.

Capacity

The data rates possible with UTP have pushed up from 1Mbps, past 4 and 16Mbps, to the point where 100Mbps data rates are now common.

Attenuation

UTP cable shares similar attenuation characteristics with other copper cables. UTP cable runs are limited to a few hundred meters, with 100 meters (a little more than 300 feet) as the most frequent limit.

EMI Characteristics

Because UTP cable lacks a shield, it is more sensitive to EMI than coaxial or STP cables. The latest technologies make it possible to use UTP in the vast majority of situations, provided that reasonable care is taken to avoid electrically noisy devices such as motors and fluorescent lights. Nevertheless, UTP might not be suitable for noisy environments such as factories. Crosstalk between nearby unshielded pairs limits the maximum length of cable runs.

Connectors for UTP

The most common connector used with UTP cables is the RJ-45 connector shown in Figure 3.17. These connectors are easy to install on cables and are also extremely easy to connect and disconnect. An RJ-45 connector has eight pins and looks like a common RJ-11 telephone connector. They are slightly different sizes, however, and won't fit together: an RJ-11 has only four pins.

Distribution racks, trays, shelves, and patch panels are available for large UTP installations. These accessories enable you to organize network cabling and also provide a central spot for expansion and reconfiguration. One necessary accessory, a jack coupler, is a small device that attaches to a wall plate or a patch panel and receives an RJ-45 connection. Jack couplers can support transmission speeds of up to 100Mbps.

Fiber-Optic Cable

In almost every way, fiber-optic cable is the ideal cable for data transmission. Not only does this type of cable accommodate extremely high bandwidths, but it also presents no problems with EMI and supports durable cables and cable runs as long as several kilometers. The two disadvantages of fiber-optic cable, however, are cost and installation difficulty. Despite these disadvantages, fiber-optic cable is now often installed into buildings by telephone companies as the cable of choice.

The center conductor of a fiber-optic cable is a fiber that consists of highly refined glass or plastic designed to transmit light signals with little loss. A glass core supports a longer cabling distance, but a plastic core is typically easier to work with. The fiber is coated with a cladding or a gel that reflects signals back into the fiber to reduce signal loss. A plastic sheath protects the fiber (see Figure 3.18).

A fiber-optic network cable consists of two strands separately enclosed in plastic sheaths. One strand sends and the other receives. Two types of cable configurations are available: loose and tight

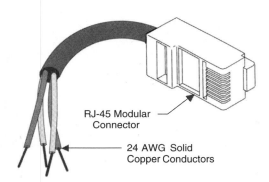

FIGURE 3.17
An RJ-45 connector.

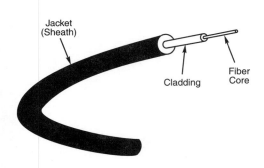

FIGURE 3.18
A fiber-optic cable.

configurations. Loose configurations incorporate a space between the fiber sheath and the outer plastic encasement; this space is filled with a gel or other material. Tight configurations contain strength wires between the conductor and the outer plastic encasement. In both cases, the plastic encasement must supply the strength of the cable, while the gel layer or strength wires protect the delicate fiber from mechanical damage.

Optical fiber cables don't transmit electrical signals. Instead, the data signals must be converted into light signals. Light sources include lasers and light-emitting diodes (LEDs). LEDs are inexpensive but produce a fairly poor quality of light suitable for only less-stringent applications.

The end of the cable that receives the light signal must convert the signal back to an electrical form. Several types of solid-state components can perform this service.

One of the significant difficulties of installing fiber-optic cable arises when two cables must be joined. The small cores of the two cables (some are as small as 8.3 microns) must be lined up with extreme precision to prevent excessive signal loss.

NOTE **Lasers** A laser is a light source that produces an especially pure light that is monochromatic (one color) and coherent (all waves are parallel). The most commonly used source of laser light in LAN devices is called an injection laser diode (ILD). The purity of laser light makes lasers ideally suited to data transmissions because they can work with long distances and high bandwidths. Lasers, however, are expensive light sources used only when their special characteristics are required.

Fiber-Optic Characteristics

As with all cable types, fiber-optic cables have their share of advantages and disadvantages.

Cost

The cost of the cable and connectors has fallen significantly in recent years. However, the electronic devices required are significantly more expensive than comparable devices for copper cable. Fiber-optic cable is also the most expensive cable type to install.

Installation

Greater skill is required to install fiber-optic cable than to install most copper cables. Improved tools and techniques, however, have reduced the training required. Still, fiber-optic cable requires greater care because the cables must be treated fairly gently during installation. Every cable has a minimum bend radius, for example, and fibers are damaged if the cables are bent too sharply. It also is important to not stretch the cable during installation.

Capacity

Fiber-optic cable can support high data rates (as high as 200,000Mbps) even with long cable runs. Although UTP cable runs are limited to less than 100 meters with 100Mbps data rates, fiber-optic cables can transmit 100Mbps signals for several kilometers.

Attenuation

Attenuation in fiber-optic cables is much lower than in copper cables. Fiber-optic cables are capable of carrying signals for several kilometers.

EMI Characteristics

Because fiber-optic cables don't use electrical signals to transmit data, they are totally immune to electromagnetic interference. The cables are also immune to a variety of electrical effects that must be taken into account when designing copper cabling systems.

When electrical cables are connected between two buildings, the ground potentials (voltages) between the two buildings can differ. When a difference exists (as it frequently does), the current flows through the grounding conductor of the cable, even though the ground is supposed to be electrically neutral and no current should flow. When current flows through the ground conductor of a cable, the condition is called a *ground loop*. Ground loops can result in electrical instability and various other types of anomalies. Because fiber-optic cable is immune to electrical effects, the best way to connect networks in different buildings is by putting in a fiber-optic link segment. Fiber-optic cable also makes a great backbone for larger networks.

Because the signals in fiber-optic cable are not electrical in nature, they cannot be detected by the electronic eavesdropping equipment that detects electromagnetic radiation. Therefore, fiber-optic cable is the perfect choice for high-security networks.

Summary of Cable Characteristics

The table below summarizes the characteristics of the four cable types discussed in this section.

COMPARISON OF CABLE MEDIA

Cable Type	Cost	Installation	Capacity	Range	EMI
Coaxial Thinnet	Less than STP	Inexpensive/easy	10Mbps typical	185 m	Less sensitive than UTP
Coaxial Thicknet	Greater than STP, less than fiber	Easy	10Mbps typical	500 m	Less sensitive than UTP
Shielded twisted-pair (STP)	Greater than UTP, less than Thicknet	Fairly easy	16Mbps typical up to 500Mbps	100 m typical	Less sensitive than UTP
Unshielded twisted-pair (UTP)	Lowest	Inexpensive/easy	10Mbps typical up to 100Mbps	100 m typical	Most sensitive
Fiber-optic	Highest	Expensive/difficult	100Mbps typical	10s of kilometers	Insensitive

When comparing cabling types, remember that the characteristics you observe are highly dependent on the implementations, such as the network cards, hubs, and other devices used. Engineers once thought that UTP cable would never reliably support data rates above 4Mbps, but 100Mbps data rates are now common.

Some comparisons between cable types are fairly involved. For example, although fiber-optic cable is costly on a per-foot basis, it may be the most cost-effective alternative when you need to run a cable for many kilometers. To build a copper cable many kilometers in length, you need to install repeaters at several points along the cable to amplify the signal. These repeaters could easily exceed the cost of a fiber-optic cable run.

IBM Cabling

IBM assigns separate names, standards, and specifications for network cabling and cabling components. These IBM cabling types roughly parallel standard forms used elsewhere in the industry, as Table 3.2 illustrates. The AWG designation in this table stands for the American Wire Gauge standard, a specification for wire gauges. Higher gauge wire is thinner; lower gauge wire is thicker.

IBM provides a unique connector (mentioned earlier in this chapter) that is of both genders—any two of the same type can be connected together. IBM also uses other types of connectors, such as the standard RJ-45 used in many office environments.

TABLE 3.2

IBM CABLING TYPES

Cable Type	Description	Comment
Type 1	Shielded twisted-pair (STP)	Two twisted pairs of 22AWG wire in braided shield
Type 2	Voice and data	Two twisted pairs of 22AWG wire for data and braided shield, and two twisted pairs of 26AWG for voice
Type 3	Voice	Four solid UTP pairs; 22 or 24AWG wire
Type 4	Not defined	
Type 5	Fiber-optic	Two 62.5/125-micron multi-mode fibers
Type 6	Data patch cable	Two twisted pairs of 26AWG wire, dual foil, and braided shield
Type 7	Not defined	
Type 8	Carpet grade	Two twisted pairs of 26 AWG wire with shield for use under carpets
Type 9	Plenum grade	Two twisted pairs, shielded (see previous discussion of plenum-grade cabling)

This list of IBM cable types is important, as many shops and documentation often reference cable types using the IBM classification.

WIRELESS MEDIA

The extraordinary convenience of wireless communications has placed an increased emphasis on wireless networks in recent years. Technology is expanding rapidly and will continue to expand into the near future, offering more and better options for wireless networks.

Presently, you can subdivide wireless networking technology into three basic types corresponding to three basic networking scenarios:

◆ *Local area networks (LANs).* Occasionally you will see a fully wireless LAN, but more typically one or more wireless machines function as members of a cable-based LAN.

◆ *Extended local networks.* A wireless connection serves as a backbone between two LANs. For instance, a company with office networks in two nearby but separate buildings could connect those networks using a wireless bridge.

◆ *Mobile computing.* A mobile machine connects to the home network using cellular or satellite technology.

The following sections describe these technologies and some of the networking options available with each.

> **NOTE**
>
> **Point-to-point Connectivity** Wireless point-to-point communications are another facet of wireless LAN technology. Point-to-point wireless technology specifically facilitates communications between a pair of devices (rather than attempting to achieve an integrated networking capability). For instance, a point-to-point connection might transfer data between a laptop and a home-based computer or between a computer and a printer. Point-to-point signals, if powerful enough, can pass through walls, ceilings, and other obstructions. Point-to-point provides data transfer rates of 1.2 to 38.4Kbps for a range of up to 200 feet indoors (or one third of a mile for line-of-sight broadcasts).

Reasons for Wireless Networks

Wireless networks are especially useful for the following situations:

◆ Spaces where cabling would be impossible or inconvenient. These include open lobbies, inaccessible parts of buildings, older buildings, historical buildings where renovation is prohibited, and outdoor installations.

◆ People who move around a lot within their work environment. Network administrators, for instance, must troubleshoot a large office network. Nurses and doctors need to make rounds at a hospital.

◆ Temporary installations. These situations include any temporary department set up for a specific purpose that soon will be torn down or relocated.

◆ People who travel outside of the work environment and need instantaneous access to network resources.

◆ Satellite offices or branches, ships in the ocean, or teams in remote field locations that need to be connected to a main office or location.

Wireless Communications with LANs

For some of the reasons described earlier in this chapter, it is often advantageous for a network to include some wireless nodes. Typically, though, the wireless nodes are part of what is otherwise a traditional, cable-based network.

An access point is a stationary transceiver connected to the cable-based LAN that enables the cordless PC to communicate with the network. The access point acts as a conduit for the wireless PC. The process is initiated when the wireless PC sends a signal to the access point; from there, the signal reaches the network. The truly wireless communication, therefore, is the communication from the wireless PC to the access point. Use of an access point transceiver is one of several ways to achieve wireless networking. Some of the others are described in later sections.

This is similar to when you use your remote control for your TV. Think of the remote control unit in your hand as the computer, and the area on the TV set that receives the signal as your access point, or stationary receiver.

You can classify wireless LAN communications according to transmission method. The four most common LAN wireless transmission methods are as follows:

◆ Infrared

◆ Laser

◆ Narrow-band radio

◆ Spread-spectrum radio

◆ Microwave

The following sections look briefly at these important wireless transmission methods. Because of vast differences in evaluation criteria such as costs, ease of installation, distance, and EMI characteristics, these items are evaluated at the end of this section in a summary table. (Bandwidth usage is not evaluated because wireless media is not a bound communication media.)

Infrared Transmission

You use an infrared communication system every time you control your television with a remote control. The remote control transmits pulses of infrared light that carry coded instructions to a receiver on the TV. This technology also is used for network communication.

Four varieties of infrared communications are as follows:

◆ *Broadband optical telepoint.* This method uses broadband technology. Data transfer rates in this high-end option are competitive with those for a cable-based network.

◆ *Line-of-sight infrared.* Transmissions must occur over a clear line-of-sight path between transmitter and receiver.

◆ *Reflective infrared.* Wireless PCs transmit toward a common, central unit, which then directs communication to each of the nodes.

◆ *Scatter infrared.* Transmissions reflect off floors, walls, and ceilings until (theoretically) they finally reach the receiver. Because of the imprecise trajectory, data transfer rates are slow. The maximum reliable distance is around 100 feet.

Infrared transmissions are typically limited to within 100 feet. Within this range, however, infrared is relatively fast. Infrared's high bandwidth supports transmission speeds of up to 10Mbps.

Infrared devices are insensitive to radio-frequency interference, but reception can be degraded by bright light. Because transmissions are tightly focused, they are fairly immune to electronic eavesdropping. Infrared transmissions are commonly used for LAN transmissions, yet can also be employed for WAN transmissions as well.

Laser Transmission

High-powered laser transmitters can transmit data for several thousand yards when line-of-sight communication is possible. Lasers can be used in many of the same situations as microwave links (described later in this chapter), but do not require an FCC license. On a LAN scale, laser light technology is similar to infrared technology. Laser light technology is employed in both LAN and WAN transmissions, though it is more commonly used in WAN transmissions.

> NOTE
>
> **FCC License** An FCC license is required to use certain radio frequencies. Some of these reserved frequencies are the ones airline pilots and police communications utilize.

Narrow-Band Radio Transmission

In narrow-band radio communications (also called single-frequency radio), transmissions occur at a single radio frequency. The range of narrow-band radio is greater than that of infrared, effectively enabling mobile computing over a limited area. Neither the receiver nor the transmitter must be placed along a direct line of sight; the signal can bounce off walls, buildings, and even the atmosphere, but heavy walls, such as steel or concrete enclosures, can block the signal.

Spread-Spectrum Radio Transmission

Spread-spectrum radio transmission is a technique originally developed by the military to solve several communication problems. Spread-spectrum improves reliability, reduces sensitivity to interference and jamming, and is less vulnerable to eavesdropping than single-frequency radio. Spread-spectrum radio transmissions are commonly used for WAN transmissions that connect multiple LANs or network segments together.

As its name suggests, spread-spectrum transmission uses multiple frequencies to transmit messages. Two techniques employed are frequency hopping and direct sequence modulation.

Frequency hopping switches (hops) among several available frequencies (see Figure 3.19), staying on each frequency for a specified interval of time. The transmitter and receiver must remain synchronized during a process called a "hopping sequence" for this technique to work. Range for this type of transmission is up to two miles outdoors and 400 feet indoors. Frequency hopping typically transmits at up to 250Kbps, although some versions can reach as high as 2Mbps.

Direct sequence modulation breaks original messages into parts called chips (see Figure 3.20), which are transmitted on separate frequencies. To confuse eavesdroppers, decoy data also can be transmitted on other frequencies. The intended receiver knows which frequencies are valid and can isolate the chips and reassemble the message. Eavesdropping is difficult because the correct frequencies are not known, and the eavesdropper cannot isolate the frequencies carrying true data. Because different sets of frequencies can be selected, this technique can operate in environments that support other transmission activity. Direct sequence modulation systems operating at 900MHz support bandwidths of 2–6Mbps.

Spread-spectrum radio transmissions are often used to connect multiple LAN segments together, thus it is often a WAN connection.

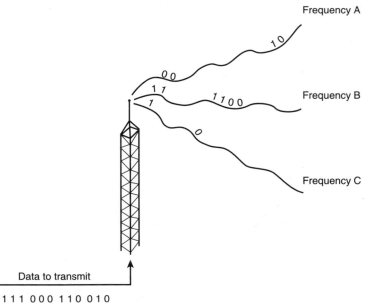

FIGURE 3.19

Frequency hopping transmits data over various frequencies for specific periods of time.

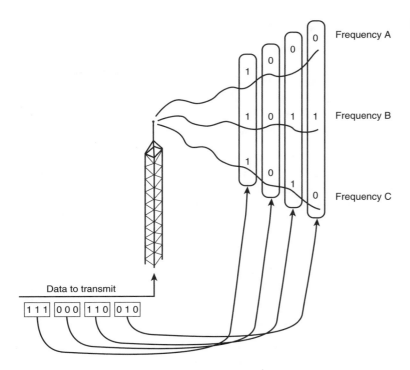

FIGURE 3.20
Direct sequence modulation.

WIRELESS BRIDGES

Wireless technology can connect LANs in two different buildings into an extended LAN. This capability is, of course, also available through other technologies (such as a T1 line—discussed in Chapter 6—or a leased line from a telephone provider), but depending on the conditions, a wireless solution is sometimes more cost-effective. A wireless connection between two buildings also provides a solution to the ground potential problem described in a note earlier in this chapter.

A wireless bridge acts as a network bridge, merging two local LANs over a wireless connection. (See Chapter 2, "Networking Standards," and Chapter 6 for more information on bridges.) Wireless bridges typically use spread-spectrum radio technology to transmit data for up to three miles. (Antennae at each end of the bridge should be placed in an appropriate location, such as a rooftop.) A device called a long-range wireless bridge has a range of up to 25 miles.

Microwave

Microwave technology has applications in all three of the wireless networking scenarios: LAN, extended LAN, and mobile networking. As shown in Figure 3.21, microwave communication can take two forms: terrestrial (ground) links and satellite links. The frequencies and technologies employed by these two forms are similar, but distinct differences exist between them.

Mobile computing is a growing technology that provides almost unlimited range for traveling computers by using satellite and cellular phone networks to relay the signal to a home network. Mobile computing typically is used with portable PCs or personal digital assistant (PDA) devices.

Three forms of mobile computing are as follows:

◆ *Packet-radio networking.* The mobile device sends and receives network-style packets via satellite. Packets contain a source and destination address, and only the destination device can receive and read the packet.

◆ *Cellular networking.* The mobile device sends and receives cellular digital packet data (CDPD) using cellular phone technology and the cellular phone network. Cellular networking provides very fast communications.

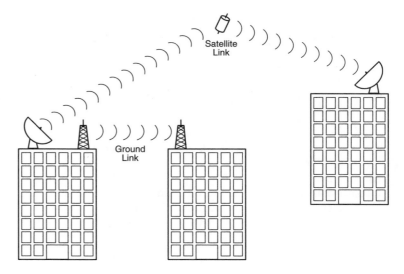

FIGURE 3.21
Terrestrial and satellite microwave links.

◆ *Satellite station networking.* Satellite mobile networking stations use satellite microwave technology, which is described later in this chapter.

Terrestrial Microwave

Terrestrial microwave communication employs earth-based transmitters and receivers. The frequencies used are in the low gigahertz range, which limits all communications to line-of-sight. You probably have seen terrestrial microwave equipment in the form of telephone relay towers, which are placed every few miles to relay telephone signals across a country.

Microwave transmissions typically use a parabolic antenna that produces a narrow, highly directional signal. A similar antenna at the receiving site is sensitive to signals only within a narrow focus. Because the transmitter and receiver are highly focused, they must be adjusted carefully so that the transmitted signal is aligned with the receiver.

A microwave link is used frequently to transmit signals in instances in which it would be impractical to run cables. If you need to connect two networks separated by a public road, for example, you might find that regulations restrict you from running cables above or below the road. In such a case, a microwave link is an ideal solution.

Some LANs operate at microwave frequencies at low power and use nondirectional transmitters and receivers. Network hubs can be placed strategically throughout an organization, and workstations can be mobile or fixed. This approach is one way to enable mobile workstations in an office setting.

In many cases, terrestrial microwave uses licensed frequencies. A license must be obtained from the FCC, and equipment must be installed and maintained by licensed technicians.

Terrestrial microwave systems operate in the low gigahertz range, typically at 4–6GHz and 21–23GHz, and costs are highly variable depending on requirements. Long-distance microwave systems can be quite expensive but might be less costly than alternatives. (A leased telephone circuit, for example, represents a costly monthly expense.) When line-of-sight transmission is possible, a microwave link is a one-time expense that can offer greater bandwidth than a leased circuit.

Costs are on the way down for low-power microwave systems for the office. Although these systems don't compete directly in cost with cabled networks, microwave can be a cost-effective technology when equipment must be moved frequently. Capacity can be extremely high, but most data communication systems operate at data rates between 1 and 10Mbps. Attenuation characteristics are determined by transmitter power, frequency, and antenna size. Properly designed systems are not affected by attenuation under normal operational conditions; rain and fog, however, can cause attenuation of higher frequencies.

Microwave systems are highly susceptible to atmospheric interference and also can be vulnerable to electronic eavesdropping. For this reason, signals transmitted through microwave are frequently encrypted.

Satellite Microwave

Satellite microwave systems relay transmissions through communication satellites that operate in geosynchronous orbits 22,300 miles above the earth. Satellites orbiting at this distance remain located above a fixed point on earth.

Earth stations use parabolic antennas (satellite dishes) to communicate with satellites. These satellites then can retransmit signals in broad or narrow beams, depending on the locations set to receive the signals. When the destination is on the opposite side of the earth, for example, the first satellite cannot transmit directly to the receiver and thus must relay the signal through another satellite.

Because no cables are required, satellite microwave communication is possible with most remote sites and with mobile devices, which enables communication with ships at sea and motor vehicles.

The distances involved in satellite communication result in an interesting phenomenon: Because all signals must travel 22,300 miles to the satellite and 22,300 miles when returning to a receiver, the time required to transmit a signal is independent of distance on the ground. It takes as long to transmit a signal to a receiver in the same state as it does to a receiver a third of the way around the world. The time required for a signal to arrive at its destination is called propagation delay. The delays encountered with satellite transmissions range from 0.5 to 5 seconds.

Unfortunately, satellite communication is extremely expensive. Building and launching a satellite can cost easily in excess of a billion dollars. In most cases, organizations share these costs or purchase services from a commercial provider. AT&T, Hughes Network Services, and Scientific-Atlanta are among the firms that sell satellite-based communication services.

Satellite links operate in the low gigahertz range, typically at 11–14GHz. Costs are extremely high and usually are distributed across many users when communication services are sold. Bandwidth is related to cost, and firms can purchase almost any required band-width. Typical data rates are 1–10Mbps. Attenuation characteristics depend on frequency, power, and atmospheric conditions. Properly designed systems also take attenuation into account. (Rain and atmospheric conditions might attenuate higher frequencies.) Microwave signals also are sensitive to EMI and electronic eaves-dropping, so signals transmitted through satellite microwave fre-quently are encrypted as well.

Earth stations can be installed by numerous commercial providers. Transmitters operate on licensed frequencies and require an FCC license.

Comparisons of Different Wireless Media

The summary table below compares the different types of Wireless communication media in terms of cost, ease of installation, distance and "other issues."

TABLE 3.3
COMPARISON OF WIRELESS MEDIA

Cable Type	Cost	Installation	Distance	Other Issues
Infrared	Cheapest of all the wireless	Fairly easy, may require line-of-sight	Under a kilometer	Can attenuate due to fog and rain
Laser	Similar to infrared	Requires line-of-sight	Can span several kilometers	Can attenuate due to fog and rain
Narrow-band radio	More expensive than infrared and laser; may need FCC license	Requires trained technicians and can involve tall radio towers	Can span hundreds of kilometers	Low-power devices can attenuate; can be eavesdropped upon; can also attenuate due to fog, rain, and solar flares
Spread-spectrum radio	More advanced technology than narrow band radio, thus more expensive	Requires trained technicians and can involve tall radio towers	Can span hundreds of kilometers	Low-power devices can attenuate; Can also attenuate due to fog, rain, and solar flares
Microwave	Very expensive, as requires link up to satellites often	Requires trained technicians and can involve satellite dishes	Can span thousands of kilometers	Can be eavesdropped upon; can also attenuate due to fog, rain, and solar flares

CASE STUDY: ANALYZING TRANSMISSION MEDIA NEEDS

ESSENCE OF THE CASE

The essential facts and features of this case are as follows:

- Cost is an issue in Part 1.

- Cost and distance are an issue in Part 2.

- Security of data and speed is an issue in Part 3.

- Traveling remote locations are the issue in Part 4.

SCENARIO

The purpose of this case study is to put this entire chapter into perspective. You saw from the previous two chapters that a network is a connected set of devices. These can be computers, printers, and servers, to name just a few of the possible devices. These devices are networked so that users can utilize different services on the network. These services might be file and print services, databases, or communication services. To connect all these services together, some form of transmission media must exist between the devices on the network. As seen in Chapter 2, "Networking Standards," the transmission media operate at the Physical layer of the OSI model. This chapter presented many forms of transmission media.

To apply your knowledge of transmission media, analyze the following evolving company. Notice how the company's business evolution leads to different transmission media selections, regardless of the services used by the company. Remember, whether a company is trying to give file and print access to its users or access to a

database, some form of transmission media is needed to connect the users of the services to the services themselves. The case study is divided into four parts, each part representing a growth stage of the company. The company in question is called Mining Enterprises, and does geological surveying.

Part 1

To begin with, Mining Enterprises is a small company with fifteen employees. They have just opened shop in a small office complex. They need to install a LAN, because they have an informational database that all the employees use, for purposes of payroll, accounting, and for the geological informational database. Because money is fairly tight, the company decides to spend as little as possible to set up its network.

Part 2

Now, two years after installing its first LAN, Enterprise Mining needs to expand. Business has been very good, and employees are extremely productive working on an efficient LAN. The problem is, though, that there is no office space left for Enterprise Mining on its present floor, so it needs to expand onto the 22nd floor. (It is currently on the 2nd floor.) Enterprise Mining needs to connect its LAN on the second floor with the LAN on the 22nd floor. Although business is good, Enterprise Mining is still a little tight for cash.

Part 3

It is now five years later. Enterprise Mining has expanded even further. It now operates on eight different floors. Each floor is almost like its own

CASE STUDY: ANALYZING TRANSMISSION MEDIA NEEDS

business unit, but a fair bit of data is still transferred between the different floors. Also, some industrial espionage rumors have begun to circulate, so security is of importance. The budget can be sacrificed to a degree for security, but the sky is not the limit.

Part 4

The company has expanded into washing carpets as well (nothing like a diversified company). They now have a fleet of trucks that roam around town, downloading information between the head office and the trucks. The carpet cleaning business is very competitive, and Enterprise Mining does not want the competition to be able to intercept any information.

ANALYSIS

Part 1

No requirements are mentioned that necessitate the use of wireless media. Because costs are the main concern, the possible bounded transmission media choices available are UTP, STP, Fiber, or coaxial cable. The fiber cable is the most expensive option, whereas UTP is the cheapest. STP and coaxial fall somewhere between. The media of choice for Part 1 is UTP, unless they were encountering some form of EMI that would require a transmission media that has better shielding.

Part 2

Cost is still an issue, but so is distance. Two solutions are possible. One is to go with the cheapest cable type, but place a repeater on this cable. This solution needs a cost estimate for the price of cable and a repeater.

Another alternative is to move to a Thinnet or Thicknet coax cable. The Thicknet cable costs more than the Thinnet, and is probably not needed to span the 20 floors difference. This solution involves only cable costs and no repeater costs.

The cost of laying the cable should be the same in both cases. You would probably find that the price of the Thinnet coax cable would be the cheapest alternative in this case.

Part 3

Because data transfer between the eight business units is heavy, we probably would like to use something with high bandwidth capability. The decision would undoubtedly reflect a choice to use a bound transmission media again. The higher bandwidths are found in coaxial cable and fiber-optic cable. Between these two options, fiber-optic cable has a better resistance to eavesdropping. Because security is a concern, a choice to use fiber optical cable is likely.

Part 4

This situation definitely leads to the use of some form of wireless media. These vans probably are moving around all the time and do not have a line of sight with the head office. Due to the movement, infrared and laser technologies should be ruled out. Because the vans are probably going to be out of urban areas at times, this rules out cellular media as well. This leaves either a microwave solution or some type of radio transmission.

continues

CASE STUDY: ANALYZING TRANSMISSION MEDIA NEEDS

continued

In analyzing microwave options, terrestrial microwave could be an option, but this technology is used primarily to connect stationary sites. Satellite microwave would probably be too costly as an option.

Of the two remaining options (narrow-band radio and spread-spectrum radio) spread-spectrum radio offers a higher level of security. This is the option most likely to be selected.

CHAPTER SUMMARY

KEY TERMS

Before taking the exam, make sure you are familiar with the definitions of and concepts behind each of the following key terms. You can use the glossary (Appendix A) for quick reference purposes.

- transmission media
- bounded media
- boundless media
- electromagnetic spectrum
- Electromagnetic Interference (EMI)
- bandwidth
- attenuation
- baseband
- broadband
- multiplexing
- frequency-division multiplexing
- time-division multiplexing

This chapter examined the characteristics of some common network transmission media. As explained in Chapter 2, transmission media falls under the Physical layer of the OSI model. Regardless of what services a network is providing, there must be some mechanism to connect to these services.

This chapter provided some of the features of popular transmission media. This chapter analyzed these features along the following terms:

- ◆ Cost
- ◆ Ease of installation
- ◆ Distance limitation
- ◆ Bandwidth usage
- ◆ EMI characteristics

The major classifications of transmission media were broken down into the following categories:

- ◆ Cable Media
  - UTP
  - STP
  - Coaxial Cable
  - Fiber Optic

CHAPTER SUMMARY

◆ Wireless Media

- Infrared

- Laser

- Narrow-band radio

- Spread-spectrum radio

- Microwave

Each form of transmission media was analyzed and compared in terms of each evaluation criteria. The purpose of this chapter was not to show which transmission media is best, but how each form of transmission media had a unique set of characteristics that made it adaptable to different situations and different sets of evaluation criteria.

Cable media are often cheaper than wireless media, yet cable media are also limited in the distances they can cover. Wireless media are often more susceptible to EMI than fiber-optic cable is, but wireless media are not subject to the accessibility and other installation problems faced by cable. In conclusion, each transmission media should be evaluated in terms of the obstacles one will face in trying to relay a signal from one device on the network to another.

- coaxial cable

- Thinnet

- Thicknet

- T-connector

- vampire clamp

- twisted-pair cable

- unshielded twisted-pair cable (UTP)

- shielded twisted-pair cable (STP)

- fiber-optic cable

- IBM cabling

- wireless media

- infrared transmissions

- laser transmissions

- narrow-band radio

- spread-spectrum radio

- terrestrial microwave

- satellite microwave

APPLY YOUR LEARNING

Exercises

3.1 Choosing Transmission Media

Objective: To explore the possibilities of different transmission media being used for different network setups.

Estimated time: 25 minutes

This chapter presented a wide range of transmission media possibilities. The purpose of this exercise is to explore situations where different transmission media could be used.

1. Company A wants to set up a LAN. There is EMI present in the building. What choices are available to this company? What may be the cheapest solution for this company?

   Possible Solutions:

   Almost all LANs use some form of bound media. The five main choices in terms of cheapest to most expensive are UTP, Thinnet, STP, Thicknet, and fiber-optic. To actually solve this question, one would need to test the degree of EMI interference. After the magnitude of this EMI is established, you can reduce the number of the cable types that are possibilities. For example, if the EMI was such that only Thicknet and fiber-optic cable were feasible options, you would probably select Thicknet to be your cable of choice, because it is the cheapest solution of the two.

2. Company B wants to connect two sites together. These sights are miles apart, with no line of sight between the two buildings. The company has no access rights on the land between the buildings. What transmission media would be available to them?

Possible Solutions:

Sites that are far apart, that do not have the right to lay cable between their buildings, need to select some form of wireless media. Possible solutions that do not require a line of sight are

- Narrow-band radio transmission
- Spread-spectrum radio transmission
- Satellite microwave

3.2 Shopping for Network Cabling

Objective: Explore the prices and availability of network cabling media in your area. Obtain a real-world view of cabling options.

Estimated time: 15 minutes

This chapter discussed the advantages and disadvantages of common network transmission media. In this exercise, you'll explore how network installation professionals perceive the differences between the cabling types. Remember that the cabling types discussed in this chapter are all tied to particular network topologies and architectures. You may want to read through Chapter 4, "Network Topologies and Architectures," before attempting this exercise.

1. Call a local computer store (preferably a store that provides network installations) and ask for some basic information on network cabling. Ask about coaxial Thinnet and Thicknet, UTP, and STP. Learn with which type the store prefers to work and in what situations they would recommend each of the types. Ask for pricing on Thinnet PVC and plenum-grade cable. Try to get a feeling for how the real world perceives the cabling types described in this chapter.

APPLY YOUR LEARNING

2. Computer vendors generally are busy people, so try to be precise. Don't imply that you're getting ready to buy a whole network (unless you are). Just tell them you're trying to learn more about network cabling—vendors are often happy to share their knowledge. If they're helpful, remember them the next time you need a bid.

Review Questions

1. What are the two types of twisted pair media?

2. What are the names of two common types of coaxial cable?

3. What is a major benefit of fiber-optic cable? What is a major drawback of fiber-optic cable?

4. What are some reasons a wireless media would be chosen over a bound media?

Exam Questions

1. Which two of the following are true about coaxial Thinnet?

   A. Thinnet cable is approximately 0.5 inches thick.

   B. Thinnet has 50-ohm impedance.

   C. Thinnet is sometimes called Standard Ethernet.

   D. Thinnet cable includes an insulation layer.

2. Transceivers for Thicknet cables are often connected using what device?

   A. Ghost taps

   B. Vampire taps

C. Witch widgets

D. Skeleton clamps

3. Which two of the following are true about UTP?

   A. You can use an RJ-11 connector with an RJ-45 socket.

   B. UTP has the highest cost of any cabling system except Thinnet.

   C. Telephone systems use UTP.

   D. UTP is more sensitive to EMI than Thinnet.

4. Which of the following is not a permissible location for coaxial PVC cabling?

   A. A bathroom

   B. Above a drop ceiling

   C. Outside

   D. Along an exterior wall

5. UTP Category 3 uses how many twisted pair(s) of cables?

   A. 1

   B. 2

   C. 4

   D. 8

6. Transmission rates of what speed are typical for fiber-optic cables?

   A. 10Mbps

   B. 25Mbps

   C. 100Mbps

   D. 500Mbps

APPLY YOUR LEARNING

7. What is a transceiver that connects a wireless node with the LAN?

   A. An access provider

   B. An access point

   C. A Central Access Device (CAD)

   D. A Wireless Access Device (WAD)

8. What type of transmissions are designed to reflect the light beam off walls, floors, and ceilings until it finally reaches the receiver?

   A. Reflective infrared

   B. Scatter infrared

   C. Spread-spectrum infrared

   D. None of the above

9. Which three of the following are forms of mobile network technology?

   A. Cellular

   B. Packet-radio

   C. UTP

   D. Satellite station

10. Which of the following cable types supports the greatest cable lengths?

   A. Unshielded twisted-pair

   B. Shielded twisted-pair

   C. Thicknet coaxial cable

   D. Thinnet coaxial cable

11. What are two advantages of UTP cable?

   A. Low cost

   B. Easy installation

   C. High resistance to EMI due to twists in cable

   D. Cabling of up to 500 meters

12. What are two benefits of shielding in a cable?

   A. Reduction in signal attenuation

   B. Reduction in EMI radiation

   C. Reduction in sensitivity to outside interference

   D. None of the above

13. What are two disadvantages of fiber-optic cable?

   A. Sensitive to EMI

   B. Expensive hardware

   C. Expensive to install

   D. Limited in bandwidth

14. Which cable type is ideal for connecting between two buildings?

   A. UTP

   B. STP

   C. Coaxial

   D. Fiber-optic

15. What do radio transmissions require more of as frequency increases?

   Increasingly _____.

   A. Attenuated

   B. Rapid

   C. Line-of-sight

   D. Sensitive to electromagnetic interference

APPLY YOUR LEARNING

16. Which two statements are true of microwave systems?

    A. Microwave transmissions do not attenuate under any conditions.

    B. All microwave systems operate in the low-gigahertz range.

    C. Microwave signals are sensitive to EMI and electronic eavesdropping.

    D. Unlike most other types of radio transmitters, microwave transmitters don't need to be licensed.

17. For what are DIN Connectors primarily used?

    A. Connecting UTP cables

    B. Cabling Macintosh computers to AppleTalk networks

    C. Connecting devices with Thick-wire Ethernet

    D. None of the above

18. Which two connectors are frequently used with STP cable?

    A. T-connectors

    B. RJ-45 connectors

    C. IBM unisex connectors

    D. AppleTalk DIN connectors

19. Which two connectors are commonly used with coaxial cable?

    A. DB-25 connectors

    B. T-connectors

    C. ST-connectors

    D. BNC connectors

20. Which two statements are true of Thinnet cabling?

    A. A T-connector must be used to connect the PC's network board to the network.

    B. Either end of the cable can be terminated, but not both ends.

    C. BNC connectors cannot be used.

    D. One terminator must be grounded.

21. Which form of spread-spectrum media breaks data into chips, which are transmitted on separate frequencies?

    A. Frequency hopping

    B. Data spread

    C. Frequency circulation

    D. Direct sequence modulation

22. What wireless system typically operates in the low gigahertz range?

    A. Laser

    B. Terrestrial microwave

    C. Infrared

    D. Audible sound

23. What is the term used to describe the time required for a signal to arrive at its destination in a satellite microwave system?

    A. Propagation delay

    B. Modulation delay

    C. Transmit delay

    D. Session delay

24. You are to choose a transmission media type for a network. The capacity for intruders to "sniff" information from the network is a major concern. Also EMI is a major consideration.

    Primary Objective: The transmission media must be capable of transferring the data over ten miles.

    Secondary Objective: Electrical lightning storms are common in the area, so the transmission media needs to be independent of the weather.

    Secondary Objective: The transmission media needs to be relatively inexpensive.

    Suggested Solution: Implement the network using fiber-optic cabling.

    A. This solution meets the primary objective and both secondary objectives.

    B. This solution meets the primary objective and one secondary objective.

    C. This solution meets the primary objectives.

    D. This solution does not satisfy the primary objective.

Answers to Review Questions

1. The two major types of twisted pair cabling are shielded twisted-pair (STP) and unshielded twisted-pair (UTP). STP has better EMI protection.

2. The two most common types of coax cable are Thinnet and Thicknet.

3. The major benefits of fiber-optic cable are immunity to EMI, high bandwidth, and the long distances that a cable can run.

The major drawback with fiber-optic cable is its cost.

4. Some typical situations that call for wireless media are

   • Spaces where cabling would be impossible or inconvenient. These include open lobbies, inaccessible parts of buildings, older buildings, historical buildings where renovation is prohibited, and outdoor installations.

   • People who move around a lot within their work environments. Network administrators, for instance, must troubleshoot a large office network. Nurses and doctors need to make rounds at a hospital.

   • Temporary installations. These situations include any temporary department set up for a specific purpose that soon will be torn down or relocated.

   • People who travel outside the work environment and need instantaneous access to network resources.

   • Satellite offices or branches that need to be connected to a main office or location.

Answers to Exam Questions

1. **B, D**. Thinnet cable includes an insulation layer and needs a 50-ohm terminator. See "Thinnet" under "Cable Media" section in this chapter.

2. **B**. A vampire clamp is used to clamp a transceiver onto a Thicknet cable. See "Thicknet" under "Cable Media" section in this chapter.

APPLY YOUR LEARNING

3. **C, D**. Telephone cable is UTP, and UTP has the highest sensitivity to EMI. See "Unshielded Twisted-Pair (UTP) Cable" under "Cable Media."

4. **B**. PVC emits toxic fumes when it burns and is not permitted in plenum spaces. See "Coax and Fire Code Classifications" under "Cable Media."

5. **C**. Category 3 UTP uses 4 pairs of twisted-pair cables. See "Unshielded Twisted-Pair (UTP) Cable" under "Cable Media."

6. **C**. Standard transmission rates for fiber-optic cable are 100Mbps. See "Fiber-Optic Cable" under "Cable Media."

7. **B**. The function of an access point is to relay information between a transceiver and the LAN. See "Wireless Communications with LANs" under "Wireless Media."

8. **B**. Scatter infrared does not require line of sight. See "Infrared Transmission" under "Wireless Media."

9. **A, B, D**. UTP is not a wireless technology. Compare the sections titled "Cable Media" and "Wireless Media."

10. **C**. Thicknet supports the greatest lengths of all the cable types listed. See "Thicknet" under "Cable Media."

11. **A, B**. C has to do with crosstalk; D is not true. See "Unshielded Twisted-Pair (UTP) Cable" under "Cable Media."

12. **B, C**. B and C are why shielding is used. See the section "Cable Media."

13. **B, C**. A and D are not a factor with fiber-optic cable. See "Fiber-Optic Cable" under "Cable Media."

14. **D**. Fiber is the preferred medium between buildings when using a bound transmission media. See "Fiber-Optic Cable" under "Cable Media."

15. **C**. The higher the frequency, the more of a line of sight is required. See "Wireless Communications with LANs" under "Wireless Media."

16. **B, C**. A is simply false, and D is incorrect because microwave transmissions do need to be licensed. See "Wireless Media."

17. **B**. A DIN is used by Macintosh computers. See "Connectors for STP" under "Cable Media."

18. **C, D**. A is for coaxial cables, whereas B is used primarily with UTP. See the section "Cable Media."

19. **B, D**. T connectors attach to the BNC connector. See "Coaxial Cable" under "Cable Media."

20. **A, D**. Both ends need to be terminated, hence B is incorrect. BNC connectors are used, hence C is incorrect. See "Coaxial Cable" under "Cable Media."

21. **D**. Spread-spectrum media uses frequency hopping in general. The data is spread across different frequencies when being transmitted. This spread of the data is circulated between the different frequencies being used. The actual term to describe this is direct-sequence modulation. See "Spread-Spectrum Radio Transmission" under "Wireless Media."

22. **B**. All other answers operate at a lower frequency range. See "Microwave" under "Wireless Media."

23. **A**. "Propagation delay" is the term used to explain the delay that occurs when data is transmitted within a satellite microwave system. This delay causes a delay of a session being established and

APPLY YOUR LEARNING

of data being transmitted. See "Satellite Microwave" under "Wireless Media."

24. **B.** Fiber-optic cable enables the network to span many miles as well as be immune to weather conditions. The last secondary objective will not be met, because fiber optic cable solutions are among the most expensive solutions to implement on the market.

Suggested Readings and Resources

1. Kayata Wesel, Ellen. *Wireless Multimedia Communications: Networking Video, Voice, and Data.* Addison-Wesley, 1997.

2. Horak, Ray, Uyless Black, and Mark Miller. *Communication Systems and Networks: Voice,* *Data, and Broadband Technologies.* IDG Books, 1996.

3. Black, Uyless. *Computer Networks: Protocols, Standards, and Interfaces—The Professional's Guide.* Prentice-Hall, 1993.

Chapter 4 targets one multi-part objective in the Planning section of the Networking Essentials exam:

Select the appropriate topology for various token-ring and ethernet networks.

▶ This objective is necessary because token-ring or ethernet networks can utilize different physical and logical topologies. This exam objective points out the need for you to be able to identify which topology should be used by a token-ring or ethernet network given different circumstances or environmental conditions.

CHAPTER 4

Network Topologies and Architectures

STUDY STRATEGIES

▶ This chapter addresses physical and logical topology types. You can deploy a range of different physical and logical topologies on your network. Token-ring and ethernet networks can utilize some, but not necessarily all, of these different physical and logical topologies. Be aware of the advantages and disadvantages of the different topologies and which ones can be used by and with token-ring or ethernet networks.

INTRODUCTION

Networks come in a few standard forms or architectures, and each form is a complete system of compatible hardware, protocols, transmission media, and topologies. A *topology* is a map of the network. It is a plan for how the cabling will interconnect the nodes, or devices, and how the nodes will function in relation to one another. Several factors shape the various network topologies, and one of the most important is the choice of an access method. An *access method* is a set of rules for sharing the transmission medium. This chapter describes two of the most important categories of access methods: *contention* and *token passing*. You learn about *CSMA/CD* and *CSMA/CA*, two contention-based access methods, and about some of the fundamental topology archetypes. This chapter then looks at ethernet, token-ring, ARCNet, and FDDI networks. These types of networks all utilize either a contention-based or token-passing access method.

The exam objective being addressed focuses on a selection of the appropriate topology for either ethernet or token-ring architectures. As you read this chapter be very aware of the differences between a physical and logical topology, because these terms mean different things. Pay particular attention to the cabling specifications used by the different topologies. ARCNet and FDDI are discussed in this chapter so that the subject of network topologies and architectures can be addressed completely.

ACCESS METHODS

An *access method* is a set of rules governing how the network nodes share the transmission medium. The rules for sharing among computers are similar to the rules for sharing among humans in that they both boil down to a pair of fundamental philosophies: 1) *first come, first served* and 2) *take turns*. These philosophies are the principles defining the three most important types of media access methods:

◆ *Contention*. In its purest form, *contention* means that the computers are contending for use of the transmission medium. Any computer in the network can transmit at any time (first come, first served).

◆ *Polling.* One device is responsible for polling the other devices to see whether they are ready for the transmission or reception of data.

◆ *Token passing.* The computers take turns using the transmission medium.

As you can imagine, contention-based access methods can give rise to situations in which two or more of the network nodes try to broadcast at the same time and the signals collide. Specifications for contention-based access methods include procedures for how to avoid collisions and what to do if a collision occurs. This section introduces the CSMA/CD and CSMA/CA access methods.

On most contention-based networks, the nodes are basically equal. No node has a higher priority than other nodes. A new access method called *demand priority*, however, resolves contention and collisions and in so doing accounts for data type priorities. This section also describes demand priority access.

Contention

In pure contention-based access control, any computer can transmit at any time. This system breaks down when two computers attempt to transmit at the same time, in which case a collision occurs (see Figure 4.1). Eventually, when a network gets busy enough, most attempts to transmit result in collisions and little effective communication can take place.

Mechanisms are usually put into place to minimize the number of collisions. One mechanism is *carrier sensing*, whereby each computer listens to the network before attempting to transmit. If the network is busy, the computer refrains from transmitting until the network quiets down. This simple "listen before talking" strategy can significantly reduce collisions.

Another mechanism is *carrier detection*. With this strategy, computers continue to listen to the network as they transmit. If a computer detects another signal that interferes with the signal it's sending, it stops transmitting. Both computers then wait a random amount of time and attempt to retransmit. Unless the network is extremely busy, carrier detection along with carrier sensing can manage a large volume of transmissions.

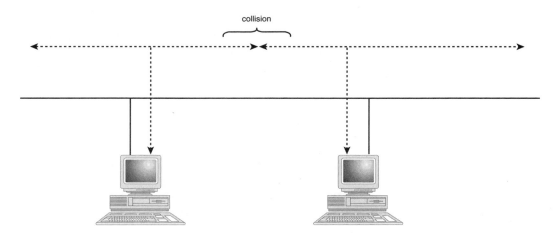

FIGURE 4.1
A collision on a contention-based network.

Carrier detection and carrier sensing used together form the protocol used in all types of ethernet: *Carrier Sense Multiple Access with Collision Detection (CSMA/CD)*. CSMA/CD limits the size of the network to 2,500 meters. At longer distances, the broadcast-sensing mechanisms don't work—a node at one end can't sense when a node at the other end starts to broadcast.

Apple's LocalTalk (See Chapter 7, "Transport Protocols," for more details) network uses the protocol *Carrier Sense Multiple Access with Collision Avoidance (CSMA/CA)*. Collision avoidance uses additional techniques to further reduce the likelihood of collisions. In CSMA/CA, each computer signals a warning that says it is *about* to transmit data, and then the other computers wait for the broadcast. CSMA/CA adds an extra layer of order, thereby reducing collisions, but the warning broadcasts increase network traffic, and the task of constantly listening for warnings increases system load.

CSMA/CD can be compared to trying to walk across the street and almost being hit by a car. If you are almost hit by a car, then you wait a few moments before trying to cross again. CSMA/CA is similar, but in this case you send your friend across the street first. If your friend is almost hit by a car, then you wait. If a car does not hit him, then you proceed.

Although it sounds as if contention methods are unworkable due to the risk of collisions, contention (in particular CSMA/CD in the form of ethernet) is the most popular media access control method on LANs. In fact, no currently employed LAN standards utilize pure contention access control without adding some mechanism to reduce the incidence of collisions.

Contention is a simple protocol that can operate with simple network software and hardware. Unless traffic levels exceed about 30% of bandwidth, contention works quite well. Contention-based networks offer good performance at low cost.

Because collisions occur at unpredictable intervals, no computer is guaranteed the capability to transmit at any given time. Contention-based networks are called *probabilistic* because a computer's chance of being permitted to transmit cannot be precisely predicted. Collisions increase in frequency as more computers use the network. When too many computers use the network, collisions can dominate network traffic, and few frames are transmitted without error.

All computers on a contention-based network are equal. Consequently, it's impossible to assign certain computers higher priorities and, therefore, greater access to the network.

Contention access control is well-suited for networks that experience bursts in traffic (such as large intermittent file transfers, for instance) and have relatively few computers.

Polling

Polling-based systems require a device (called a *controller*, or *master device*) to poll other devices on the network to see whether they are ready to either transmit or receive data as seen in Figure 4.2. This access method is not widely used on networks because the polling itself can cause a fair amount of network traffic. A common example of polling is when your computer polls its printer to receive a print job.

Token Passing

Token passing utilizes a frame called a *token*, which circulates around the network. A computer that needs to transmit must wait until it receives the token, at which time the computer is permitted to transmit. When the computer is done transmitting, it passes the token frame to the next station on the network. Figure 4.3 shows how token passing is implemented on a token-ring network. Token-ring networks are discussed in greater detail later in this chapter in the section titled "Token Ring."

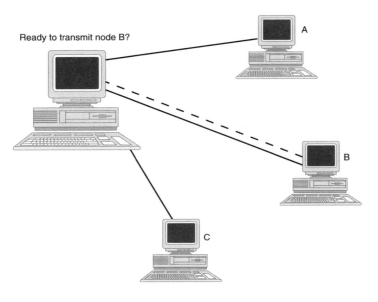

Ready to transmit node B?

FIGURE 4.2
An example of polling-based access.

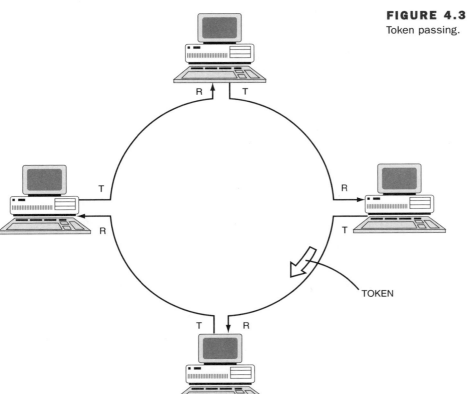

FIGURE 4.3
Token passing.

TOKEN

Several network standards employ token passing access control:

◆ *Token ring.* The most common token-passing standard, embodied in IEEE standard 802.5.

◆ *IEEE standard 802.4.* Implemented infrequently; defines a bus network that also employs token passing. ARCNet can deploy this standard, as is shown later in the chapter in the section titled "ARCNet."

◆ *FDDI.* A 100Mbps fiber-optic network standard that uses token passing and rings in much the same manner as 802.5 token ring.

Token-passing methods can use station priorities and other methods to prevent any one station from monopolizing the network. Because each computer has a chance to transmit each time the token travels around the network, each station is guaranteed a chance to transmit at some minimum time interval.

Token passing is more appropriate than contention under the following conditions:

◆ *When the network is carrying time-critical data.* Because token passing results in more predictable delivery, token passing is called *deterministic*.

◆ *When the network experiences heavy utilization.* Performance typically falls off more gracefully with a token-passing network than with a contention-based network. Token-passing networks cannot become gridlocked due to excessive numbers of collisions.

◆ *When some stations should have higher priority than others.* Some token-passing schemes support priority assignments.

Comparing Contention and Token Passing

As an access control mechanism, token passing appears to be clearly superior to contention. You'll find, however, that ethernet, by far the dominant LAN standard, has achieved its prominence while firmly wedded to contention access control.

Token passing requires a variety of complex control mechanisms to work well. The necessary hardware is considerably more expensive than the hardware required to implement the much simpler contention mechanisms. The higher cost of token-passing networks is difficult to justify unless the special features are required.

Because token-passing networks are designed for high reliability, building network diagnostic and troubleshooting capabilities into the network hardware is common. These capabilities increase the cost of token-passing networks. Organizations must decide whether this additional reliability is worth the extra cost.

Conversely, although token-passing networks perform better than contention-based networks when traffic levels are high, contention networks exhibit superior performance under lighter load conditions. Passing the token around (and other maintenance operations) eats into the available bandwidth. As a result, 10Mbps ethernet and 16Mbps token-ring networks perform comparably well under light load conditions, but the ethernet costs considerably less.

Figure 4.4 illustrates the performance characteristics you can expect from each access control method.

NOTE

Token-Passing Throughput Figure 4.4 implies that token-passing throughput eventually reaches a zero level, but that cannot happen, regardless of the loading conditions. Although a station's access to the network might be limited, the workstation is guaranteed the right to add itself to the reservation list on each circuit. It may take several more circuits of the token before the station's data is actually sent, but it will be sent.

NOTE

Hubs A hub is a device on the network that connects many short cables together. It is discussed in detail in Chapter 6, "Connectivity Devices and Transfer Mechanisms."

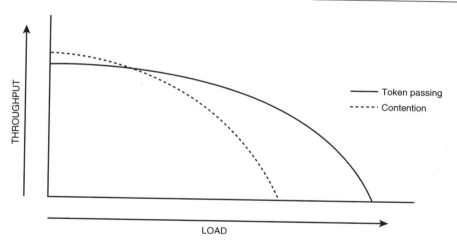

FIGURE 4.4
Comparison of contention and token passing.

Demand Priority

Demand priority is an access method used with the new 100Mbps 100VG-AnyLAN standard. Although demand priority is officially considered a contention-based access method, demand priority is considerably different from the basic CSMA/CD ethernet. In demand priority, network nodes are connected to hubs, and those hubs are connected to other hubs. Contention, therefore, occurs at the hub. (100VG-AnyLAN cables can actually send and receive data at the same time.) Demand priority provides a mechanism for prioritizing data types. If contention occurs, data with a higher priority takes precedence.

NETWORK TOPOLOGIES

A topology defines the arrangement of nodes, cables, and connectivity devices that make up the network. Two categories form the basis for all discussions of topologies:

◆ *Physical topology*. Describes the actual layout of the network transmission media.

◆ *Logical topology*. Describes the logical pathway a signal follows as it passes among the network nodes.

Another way to think about this distinction is that a physical topology defines the way the network *looks*, and a logical topology defines the way the *data passes* among the nodes. At a glance this distinction may seem nit-picky, but as you will learn in this chapter, the physical and logical topologies for a network can be very different. A network with a star physical topology, for example, may actually have a bus or a ring logical topology.

In common usage, the word "topology" applies to a complete network definition, which includes the physical and logical topologies and also the specifications for elements such as the transmission medium. The term *topology* as used in Microsoft's test objectives for the Networking Essentials exam is not limited to the physical and logical topology archetypes (that is, the design or layout) described in this section. It applies to the complete network specifications (such as 10BASE-T or 10BASE5) described in the "Ethernet" and "Token Ring" sections of this chapter.

Physical and logical topologies can take several forms. The most common and the most important for understanding the ethernet and token-ring topologies (described later in this chapter) are the following:

- ◆ Bus topologies
- ◆ Ring topologies
- ◆ Star topologies
- ◆ Mesh topology

The following sections discuss each of these important topology types.

Bus Topologies

A *bus physical topology* is one in which all devices connect to a common, shared cable (sometimes called the *backbone*). A bus physical topology is shown in Figure 4.5.

If you think the bus topology seems ideally suited for the networks that use contention-based access methods such as CSMA/CD, you are correct. Ethernet, the most common contention-based network architecture, typically uses bus as a physical topology. Even 10BASE-T ethernet networks (described later in this chapter) use the bus as a logical topology but are configured in a star physical topology.

FIGURE 4.5
A bus physical topology.

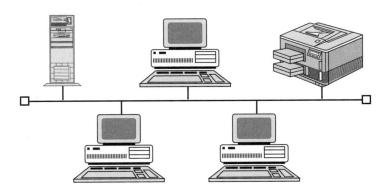

Most bus networks broadcast signals in both directions on the backbone cable, enabling all devices to directly receive the signal. Some buses, however, are unidirectional: Signals travel in only one direction and can reach only downstream devices. Recall from Chapter 3, "Transmission Media," that a special connector called a *terminator* must be placed at the end of the backbone cable to prevent signals from reflecting back on the cable and causing interference. In the case of a *unidirectional bus*, the cable must be terminated in such a way that signals can go down the cable but do not reflect back up the cable and reach other devices, causing disruption.

Ring Topologies

Ring topologies are wired in a circle. Each node is connected to its neighbors on either side, and data passes around the ring in one direction only (see Figure 4.6). Each device incorporates a receiver and a transmitter and serves as a repeater that passes the signal on to the next device in the ring. Because the signal is regenerated at each device, signal degeneration is low.

Ring topologies are ideally suited for token-passing access methods. The token passes around the ring, and only the node that holds the token can transmit data.

Ring physical topologies are quite rare. The ring topology is almost always implemented as a logical topology. Token ring, for example, the most widespread token-passing network, always arranges the nodes in a physical star (with all nodes connecting to a central hub), but passes data in a logical ring (see Figure 4.7).

You get a closer look at token ring later in this chapter in the section titled "Token Ring."

Star Topologies

Star topologies require that all devices connect to a central hub (see Figure 4.8). The hub receives signals from other network devices and routes the signals to the proper destinations. Star hubs can be interconnected to form *tree*, or *hierarchical*, network topologies.

As mentioned earlier, a star physical topology is often used to implement a bus or ring logical topology (refer to Figure 4.5).

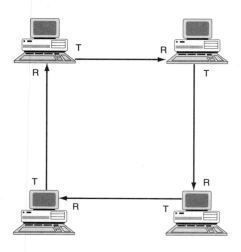

T = TRANSMIT
R = RECEIVE

FIGURE 4.6
A ring topology.

> **NOTE**
>
> **The Star Physical Topology**   A *star physical topology* means that the nodes are all connected to a central hub. The path the data takes among the nodes and through that hub (the logical topology) depends on the design of the hub, the design of the cabling, and the hardware and software configuration of the nodes.

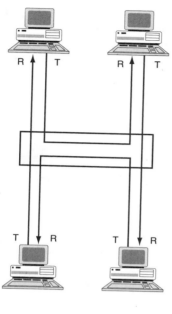

FIGURE 4.7
A logical ring configuration in a physical star.

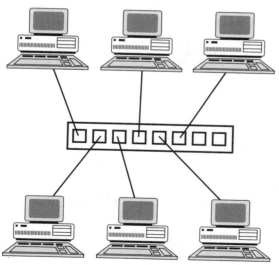

FIGURE 4.8
A star topology.

Mesh Topology

A popular test subject is the mesh topology. A *mesh* topology (see Figure 4.9) is really a hybrid model representing an all-channel sort of physical topology. It is a hybrid because a mesh topology can incorporate all the topologies covered to this point. It is an all-channel topology in that every device is directly connected to every other device on the network. When a new device is added, a connection to all existing devices must be made. This provides for a great deal of fault tolerance, but it involves extra work on the part of the network administrator. That is, if any transmission media breaks, the data transfer can take alternative routes. However, cabling becomes much more extensive and complicated.

FIGURE 4.9
A mesh topology.

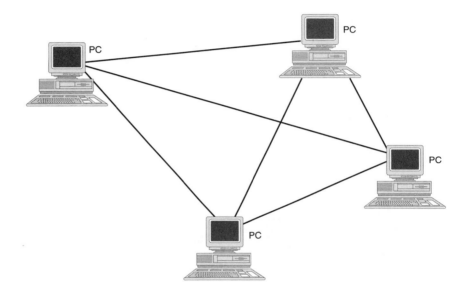

These different connections can be the same (all ethernet) or different (a mix of ethernet and token ring).

NETWORK ARCHITECTURES

A network architecture is the design specification of the physical layout of connected devices. This includes the cable being used (or wireless media being deployed), the types of network cards being deployed, and the mechanism through which data is sent on to the network and passed to each device. Network architecture, in short, encompasses the total design and layout of the network.

Ethernet

Ethernet is a very popular local area network architecture based on the CSMA/CD access method. The original ethernet specification was the basis for the IEEE 802.3 specifications (see Chapter 2, "Networking Standards"). In present usage, the term "ethernet" refers to original ethernet (or Ethernet II, the latest version) as well as the IEEE 802.3 standards. The different varieties of ethernet networks are commonly referred to as *ethernet topologies*. Typically, ethernet networks can use a bus physical topology, although, as mentioned earlier, many varieties of ethernet such as 10BASE-T use a star physical topology and a bus logical topology. (Microsoft uses the term "star bus topology" to describe 10BASE-T.)

Ethernet networks, depending on the specification, operate at 10- or 100Mbps using baseband transmission. Each IEEE 802.3 specification (see Chapter 2) prescribes its own cable types.

Later sections in this chapter examine the following ethernet topologies:

- ◆ 10BASE2
- ◆ 10BASE5
- ◆ 10BASE-T
- ◆ 10BASE-FL
- ◆ 100VG-AnyLAN
- ◆ 100BASE-X

Note that the name of each ethernet topology begins with a number (10 or 100). That number specifies the transmission speed for the network. For instance, 10BASE5 is designed to operate at 10Mbps, and 100BASE-X operates at 100Mbps. "BASE" specifies that baseband transmissions are being used. The "T" is for unshielded twisted-pair wiring, "FL" is for fiber optic cable, "VG-AnyLAN" implies Voice Grade, and "X" implies multiple media types.

Ethernet networks transmit data in small units called *frames*. The size of an ethernet frame can be anywhere between 64 and 1,518 bytes. Eighteen bytes of the total frame size are taken up by frame overhead, such as the source and destination addresses, protocol

> NOTE
>
> **Ethernet Origins** The origins of ethernet are commemorated in the initials DIX, a 15-pin connector used to interface ethernet components. The acronym "DIX" derives from the combination of leading letters of the founding ethernet vendors: Digital, Intel, and Xerox.

information, and error-checking information. There are many different types of ethernet frames, such as the Ethernet II, 802.2, and 802.3 frames to name a few. It is important to remember that 802.2 and 802.3 are IEEE specifications on how information is transferred onto the transmission media (Data Link layer) as well as the specification on how the data should be packaged. More information on frame types is discussed in Chapter 5, "Network Adapter Cards."

A typical Ethernet II frame has the following sections:

- *Preamble.* A field that signifies the beginning of the frame.
- *Addresses.* A field that identifies the source and destination addresses for the frame.
- *Type.* A field that designates the Network layer protocol.
- *Data.* The data being transmitted.
- *CRC.* Cyclical Redundancy Check for error checking.

These parts of the frame are illustrated in Figure 4.10.

The term "ethernet" commonly refers to original ethernet (which has been updated to Ethernet II) as well as the IEEE 802.3 standards. Ethernet and the 802.3 standards differ in ways significant enough to make standards incompatible in terms of packet formats, however. At the Physical layer, ethernet and 802.3 are generally compatible in terms of cables, connectors, and electronic devices.

Ethernet generally is used on light-to-medium traffic networks and performs best when a network's data traffic transmits in short bursts. Ethernet is the most commonly used network standard.

One advantage of the linear bus topology used by most ethernet networks (this doesn't apply to star bus networks such as 10BASE-T) is that the required cabling is minimized because a separate cable run to the hub for each node is not required. One disadvantage is that a break in the cable or a streaming network adapter card can bring

Preamble	Address	Type	Data	CRC

FIGURE 4.10
A sample of part of an Ethernet II frame.

down the entire network. Streaming is more frequently referred to as a *broadcast storm*. A broadcast storm occurs when a network card fails and the transmitter floods the cable with traffic, like a faucet stuck open. At this point, the network becomes unusable. See Chapter 12, "Troubleshooting," for more on broadcast storms.

Ethernet Cabling

You can use a variety of cables to implement ethernet networks. Many of these cable types, such as Thinnet, Thicknet, UTP, and STP, are described in Chapter 3. Ethernet networks traditionally have used coaxial cables of several different types. Fiber-optic cables now are frequently employed to extend the geographic range of ethernet networks.

The contemporary interest in using twisted-pair wiring has resulted in a scheme for cabling that uses unshielded twisted-pair (UTP). The 10BASE-T cabling standard uses UTP in a star physical topology. (10BASE-T is discussed later in this chapter.)

Ethernet remains closely associated with coaxial cable. Two types of coaxial cable still used in small and large environments are Thinnet (10BASE2) and Thicknet (10BASE5). Thinnet and Thicknet ethernet networks have different limitations that are based on the Thinnet and Thicknet cable specifications. The best way to remember the requirements for ethernet cable types is to use the 5-4-3 rule of thumb for each cable type.

The 5-4-3 rule (see Figure 4.11) states that the following can appear between any two nodes in the ethernet network:

◆ Up to 5 segments in a series

◆ Up to 4 concentrators or repeaters

◆ 3 segments of cable (coaxial only) that contain nodes

The following subsections describe some of the characteristics of cable types used in ethernet topologies.

10BASE2

The 10BASE2 cabling topology (Thinnet) generally uses the on-board transceiver of the network interface card to translate the signals to and from the rest of the network. Thinnet cabling, described

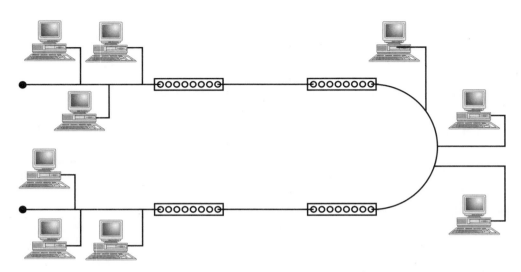

FIGURE 4.11
The 5-4-3 rule: 5 segments on a LAN, 4 connection devices (hubs or repeaters), and only 3
populated segments.

in Chapter 3, uses BNC T-connectors that attach directly to the network adapter. Each end of the cable should have a terminator, and
you must use a grounded terminator on one end (see Figure 4.12).

The main advantage of using 10BASE2 in your network is cost.
When any given cable segment on the network doesn't have to be
run farther than 185 meters (607 feet), 10BASE2 is often the cheapest network cabling option.

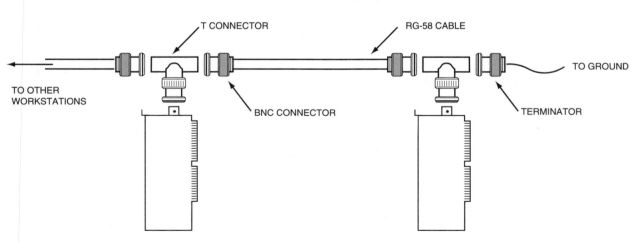

FIGURE 4.12
T connector and a BNC connector.

10BASE2 is also relatively simple to connect. Each network node connects directly to the network cable with a T-connector attached to the network adapter. For a successful installation, you must adhere to several rules in 10BASE2 ethernet environments, including the following:

◆ The minimum cable distance between clients must be 0.5 meters (1.5 feet).

◆ *Pig tails*, also known as *drop cables*, from T-connectors shouldn't be used to connect to the BNC connector on the network adapter. The T-connector must be connected directly to the network adapter.

◆ You may not exceed the maximum network segment limitation of 185 meters (607 feet).

◆ The entire network cabling scheme cannot exceed 925 meters (3,035 feet).

◆ The maximum number of nodes per network segment is 30 (this includes clients and repeaters).

◆ A 50-ohm terminator must be used on each end of the bus with only one of the terminators having either a grounding strap or a grounding wire that attaches it to the screw holding an electrical outlet cover in place.

◆ You may not have more than five segments on a network. These segments may be connected with a maximum of four repeaters, and only three of the five segments may have network nodes.

> **EXAM TIP**
>
> **Metric Conversion** You should be able to translate cable segment lengths from feet to meters or from meters to feet. A meter is equivalent to 39.37 inches or 3.28 feet.

Figure 4.13 shows two network segments using 10BASE2 cabling. For more on 10BASE2's Thinnet cabling, see Chapter 3.

10BASE5

The 10BASE5 cabling topology (Thicknet) uses an external transceiver to attach to the network adapter card (see Figure 4.14). The external transceiver clamps to the Thicknet cable (as described in Chapter 3). An Attachment Universal Interface (AUI) cable runs from the transceiver to a DIX connector on the back of the network adapter card. As with Thinnet, each network segment must be terminated at both ends, with one end using a grounded terminator. The components of a Thicknet network are shown in Figure 4.15.

FIGURE 4.13
Two segments using 10BASE2 cabling.

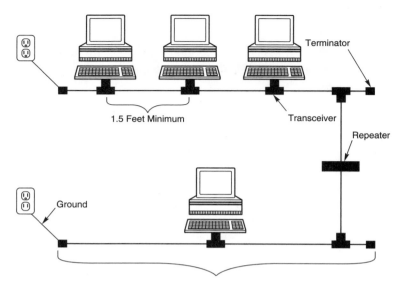

FIGURE 4.14
Two segments using 10BASE5 cabling.

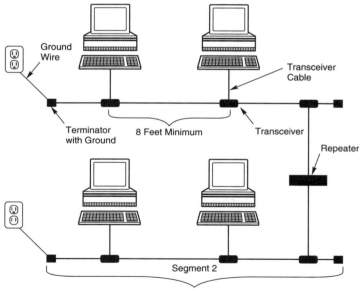

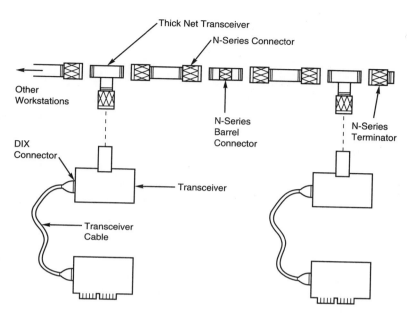

FIGURE 4.15
Components of a Thicknet network.

The primary advantage of 10BASE5 is its capability to exceed the cable restrictions that apply to 10BASE2. 10BASE5 does pose restrictions of its own, however, which you should consider when installing or troubleshooting a 10BASE5 network. As with 10BASE2 networks, the first consideration when you troubleshoot a 10BASE5 network should be the established cabling rules and guidelines. You must follow several additional guidelines, along with the 5-4-3 rule, when configuring Thicknet networks, such as the following:

◆ The minimum cable distance between transceivers is 2.5 meters (8 feet).

◆ You may not go beyond the maximum network segment length of 500 meters (1,640 feet).

◆ The entire network cabling scheme cannot exceed 2,500 meters (8,200 feet).

◆ One end of the terminated network segment must be grounded.

◆ Drop cables (transceiver cables) can be as short as required but cannot be longer than 50 meters from transceiver to computer.

◆ The maximum number of nodes per network segment is 100. (This includes all repeaters.)

The length of the drop cables (from the transceiver to the computer) is not included in measurements of the network segment length and total network length.

As Chapter 3 mentions, Thicknet and Thinnet networks are often combined, with a Thicknet backbone merging smaller Thinnet segments. (See Chapter 3 for more on 10BASE5's Thicknet cabling.)

10BASE-T

The trend in wiring ethernet networks is to use unshielded twisted-pair (UTP) cable. 10BASE-T, which uses UTP cable, is also one of the more popular implementations for ethernet. It is based on the IEEE 802.3 standard. 10BASE-T supports a data rate of 10Mbps using baseband.

10BASE-T cabling is wired in a star topology. The nodes are wired to a central hub, which serves as a multiport repeater (see Figure 4.16). A 10BASE-T network functions logically as a linear bus. The hub repeats the signal to all nodes, and the nodes contend for access to the transmission medium as if they were connected along a linear bus. The cable uses RJ-45 connectors, and the network adapter card can have RJ-45 jacks built into the back of the card (An RJ-45 connector looks very similar to a telephone plug.)

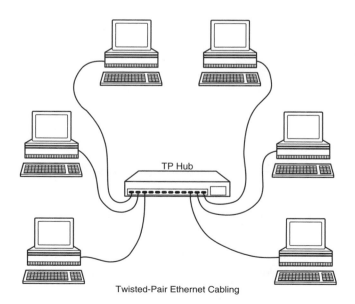

Twisted-Pair Ethernet Cabling

FIGURE 4.16
A 10BASE-T network wired in a star topology.

10BASE-T segments can be connected using coaxial or fiber-optic backbone segments. Some hubs provide connectors for Thinnet and Thicknet cables (in addition to 10BASE-T UTP-type connectors).

By attaching a 10BASE-T transceiver to the AUI port of the network adapter, you can use a computer set up for Thicknet on a 10BASE-T network.

The star wiring of 10BASE-T provides several advantages, particularly in larger networks. First, the network is more reliable and easier to manage because 10BASE-T networks use a concentrator (a centralized wiring hub). These hubs are "intelligent" in that they can detect defective cable segments and route network traffic around them. This capability makes locating and repairing bad cable segments easier.

Networks with star wiring topologies can be significantly easier to troubleshoot and repair than bus-wired networks. With a star network, you can isolate a problem node from the rest of the network by disconnecting the cable and directly connecting it to the cable hub. If the hub is considered intelligent, management software developed for that hub type, as well as the hub itself, can disconnect the suspect port. Another benefit to this is that one bad cable segment does not affect the entire network, only the machine connected to that bad cable.

10BASE-T enables you to design and build your LAN one segment at a time, growing as your network needs to grow. This capability makes 10BASE-T more flexible than other LAN cabling options.

10BASE-T is also relatively inexpensive to use compared to other cabling options. In some cases in which a data-grade phone system has already been used in an existing building, the data-grade phone cable can be used for the LAN.

The rules for a 10BASE-T network are as follows:

◆ The maximum number of computers on a LAN is 1,024.

◆ The cabling should be UTP Category 3, 4, or 5. (Shielded twisted-pair cabling, STP, can be used in place of UTP.)

◆ The maximum unshielded cable segment length (hub to transceiver) is 100 meters (328 feet).

◆ The cable minimum distance between computers is 2.5 meters (8 feet).

◆ The minimum distance between a hub and a computer, or between two hubs, is 0.5 meters (1.5 feet).

10BASE-FL

10BASE-FL is a specification for ethernet over fiber-optic cables. The 10BASE-FL specification calls for a 10Mbps data rate using baseband.

The advantages of fiber-optic cable (and hence, the advantages of 10BASE-FL) are discussed in Chapter 3. The most important advantages are long cabling runs (10BASE-FL supports a maximum cabling distance of about 2,000 meters) and the elimination of any potential electrical complications. Another advantage is that the number of nodes a segment can handle with 10BASE-FL is far greater than the maximum supported by 10BASE-T, 10BASE2, and 10BASE5.

100VG-AnyLAN

100VG-AnyLAN is defined in the IEEE 802.12 standard. *IEEE 802.12* is a standard for transmitting ethernet and token-ring packets (IEEE 802.3 and 802.5) at 100Mbps. 100VG-AnyLAN is sometimes called 100BASE-VG. The "VG" in the name stands for "voice grade." 100VG-AnyLAN cabling uses four twisted-pairs in a scheme called *quartet signaling.*

The section titled "Demand Priority," earlier in this chapter, discussed 100VG-AnyLAN's demand priority access method, which provides for two priority levels when resolving media access conflicts.

100VG-AnyLAN uses a *cascaded star* topology, which calls for a hierarchy of hubs. Computers are attached to *child hubs*, and the child hubs are connected to higher-level hubs called *parent hubs* (see Figure 4.17).

The maximum length for the two longest cables attached to a 100VG-AnyLAN hub is 250 meters (820 ft). The specified cabling is Category 3, 4, or 5 twisted-pair or fiber-optic. 100VG-AnyLAN is compatible with 10BASE-T cabling.

NOTE

The Upgrade Path Both 100VG-AnyLAN and 100BASE-X (see the following section) can be installed as a Plug and Play upgrade to a 10BASE-T system.

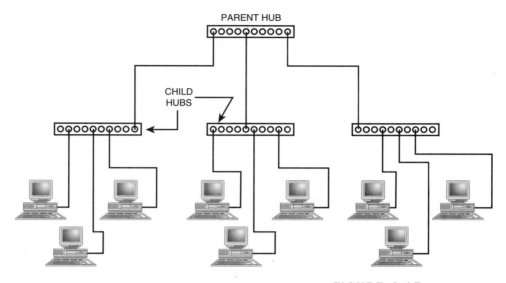

FIGURE 4.17
Cascaded star topology.

100BASE-X

100BASE-X uses a star bus topology similar to 10BASE-T's.
100BASE-X provides a data transmission speed of 100Mbps using
baseband.

The 100BASE-X standard provides the following cabling specifications:

- ◆ *100BASE-TX.* Two twisted pairs of Category 5 UTP or STP.

- ◆ *100BASE-FX.* Fiber-optic cabling using 2-strand cable.

- ◆ *100BASE-T4.* Four twisted-pairs of Category 3, 4, or 5 UTP.

100BASE-X is sometimes referred to as *Fast Ethernet.* Like 100VG-
AnyLAN, 100BASE-X provides compatibility with existing
10BASE-T systems and thus enables plug-and-play upgrades from
10BASE-T.

In summary, ethernet networks use the following cable types:

- ◆ 10BASE2

- ◆ 10BASE5

- ◆ 10BASE-T

R E V I E W   B R E A K

◆ 10BASE-FL

◆ 100VG-AnyLAN

◆ 100BASE-X

  • 100BASE-TX

  • 100BASE-FX

  • 100BASE-T4

Token Ring

Token ring uses a token-passing architecture that adheres to the IEEE 802.5 standard, as described earlier. The topology is physically a star, but token ring uses a logical ring to pass the token from station to station. Each node must be attached to a concentrator called a *multistation access unit (MSAU or MAU).*

In the earlier discussion of token passing, it may have occurred to you that if one computer crashes, the others will be left waiting forever for the token. MSAUs add fault tolerance to the network, so that a single failure doesn't stop the whole network. The MSAU can determine when the network adapter of a PC fails to transmit and can bypass it.

Token-ring network interface cards can run at 4Mbps or 16Mbps. Although 4Mbps cards can run at that data rate only, 16Mbps cards can be configured to run at 4 or 16Mbps. All cards on a given network ring must run at the same rate. If all cards are not configured this way, either the machine connected to the card cannot have network access, or the entire network can be ground to a halt.

As shown in Figure 4.18, each node acts as a repeater that receives tokens and data frames from its nearest active upstream neighbor (NAUN). After the node processes a frame, the frame transmits downstream to the next attached node. Each token makes at least one trip around the entire ring and then returns to the originating node. Workstations that indicate problems send a *beacon* to identify an address of the potential failure.

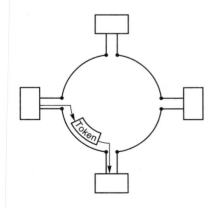

FIGURE 4.18
Operation of a token ring.

Token Ring Cabling

Traditional token-ring networks use twisted-pair cable. The following are standard IBM cable types for token ring:

◆ *Type 1.* A braided shield surrounds two twisted pairs of solid copper wire. Type 1 is used to connect terminals and distribution panels or to connect between different wiring closets that are located in the same building. Type 1 uses two STPs of solid-core 22 AWG wire for long, high-data-grade transmissions within the building's walls. The maximum cabling distance is 101 meters (331 feet).

◆ *Type 2.* Type 2 uses a total of six twisted pairs: two are STPs (for networking) and four are UTPs (for telephone systems). This cable is used for the same purposes as Type 1, but enables both voice and data cables to be included in a single cable run. The maximum cabling distance is 100 meters (328 feet).

◆ *Type 3.* Used as an alternative to Type 1 and Type 2 cable due to its reduced cost, Type 3 has unshielded twisted-pair copper with a minimum of two twists per inch. Type 3 has four UTPs of 22 or 24 AWG solid-core wire for networks or telephone systems. Type 3 cannot be used for 16Mbps token-ring networks. It is used primarily for long, low-data-grade transmissions within walls. Signals don't travel as fast as with Type 1 cable because Type 3 doesn't have the shielding that Type 1 uses. The maximum cabling distance (according to IBM) is 45 meters (about 148 feet). Some vendors specify cabling distances of up to 150 meters (500 feet).

Type 3 cabling (UTP) is the most popular transmission medium for token ring. A token-ring network using Type 3 (UTP) cabling can support up to 72 computers. A token-ring network using STP cabling can support up to 260 computers.

The minimum distance between computers or between MSAUs is 2.5 meters (8 feet).

A patch cable is a cable that connects MSAUs. Patch cables are typically IBM Type 6 cables that come in standard lengths of 8, 30, 75, or 150 feet. (A Type 6 cable consists of two shielded 26-AWG twisted-pairs.) You can also get patch cables in custom lengths. You can use patch cables to extend the length of Type 3 cables or to

> **NOTE**
>
> **MAU vs. Hub** People often confuse a MAU with a hub. A MAU is strictly used in a token-ring network. It is involved with the token generation and with facilitating the passing of a token between machines. A hub is used in ethernet. It is used to connect drop cables from various workstations. These two items are not interchangeable.

connect computers to MSAUs. Patch cables have an IBM connector at each end.

Token-ring adapter cables can have an IBM data connector at one end and a nine-pin connector at the other end, or they can use UTP cables with RJ-45 connectors on each end. Adapter cables connect client and server network adapters to other network components that use IBM data connectors. The type of connectors you need for a token-ring network depends on the type of cabling you're using. Type 3 cabling uses RJ-11 or RJ-45 connectors. (Media filters, if necessary, can convert the network adapter to RJ-11 or RJ-45 format.) Meanwhile, Type 1 and 2 cabling use IBM Type A connectors.

Token-ring networks come in a few sizes and designs. A *small movable* token-ring system supports up to 12 MSAUs and uses Type 6 cable to attach clients and servers to IBM Model 8228 MSAUs. Type 6 is flexible but has limited distance capabilities. The characteristics of Type 6 cable make it suitable for small networks and for patch cords.

A *large nonmovable* system supports up to 260 clients and file servers with up to 33 MSAUs. This network configuration uses IBM Type 1 or Type 2 cable. The large nonmovable system also involves other wiring needs, such as punch panels or distribution panels, equipment racks for MSAUs, and wiring closets to contain the previously listed components.

The MSAU is the central cabling component for IBM Token-Ring networks. The 8228 MSAU was the original wiring hub developed by IBM for its IBM Token-Ring networks. (IBM names all its hardware with numbers.) Figure 4.19 shows 8228 MSAUs. Each 8228 has ten connectors, eight of which accept cables to clients or servers. The other connectors are labeled RI (ring in) and RO (ring out). The RI and RO connectors are used to connect multiple 8228s to form larger networks. The last RO must be connected to the first MAU's RI.

8228s are mechanical devices that consist of relays and connectors. Their purpose is to switch clients in and out of the network. Each port is controlled by a relay powered by a voltage sent to the MSAU from the client. When an 8228 is first set up, each of these relays must be initialized with the setup tool that is shipped with the unit. Insert the setup tool into each port and hold it there until a light indicates that the port is properly initialized.

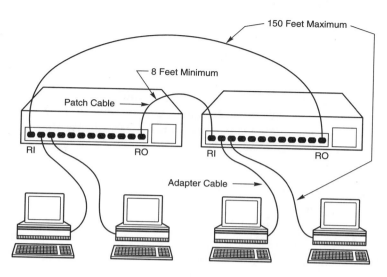

Token Ring Cabling

When you connect a token-ring network, make sure you do the following:

1. Initialize each port in the 8228 MSAU by using the setup tool shipped with the MSAU.

2. If you're using more than one MSAU, connect the RO port of each MSAU with the RI port of the next MSAU in the loop.

3. Connect the last RO with the first RI to complete the loop so that the MSAUs form a circle or ring.

Passing Data on Token Rings

As this chapter has already described, a frame called a token perpetually circulates around a token ring (see Figure 4.20). The computer that holds the token has control of the transmission medium. The actual process is as follows:

1. A computer in the ring captures the token.

2. If the computer has data to transmit, it holds the token and transmits a data frame. A token-ring data frame contains the fields listed in Table 4.1.

3. Each computer in the ring checks to see whether it is the intended recipient of the frame.

4. When the frame reaches the destination address, the destination PC copies the frame to a receive buffer, updates the frame status field of the data frame (see step 2), and puts the frame back on the ring.

In 16Mbps token-ring networks, the sending device can utilize an optional enhancement, known as *early token release*. This is where the sending device issues a token immediately after sending a frame, not waiting for its own header to return. This speeds up the data transfers on the network.

5. When the computer that originally sent the frame receives it from the ring, it acknowledges a successful transmission, takes the frame off the ring, and places the token back on the ring.

TABLE 4.1

TOKEN-RING DATA FRAME FIELDS

Field	Description
Start delimiter	Marks the start of the frame
Access control	Specifies priority of the frame; also specifies whether the frame is a token or a data frame
Frame control	Media Access Control information
Destination address	Address of receiving computer
Source address	Address of sending computer
Data	Data being transmitted
Frame check sequence	Error-checking information (CRC)
End delimiter	Marks the end of the frame
Frame status	Tells whether the destination address was located and whether the frame was recognized

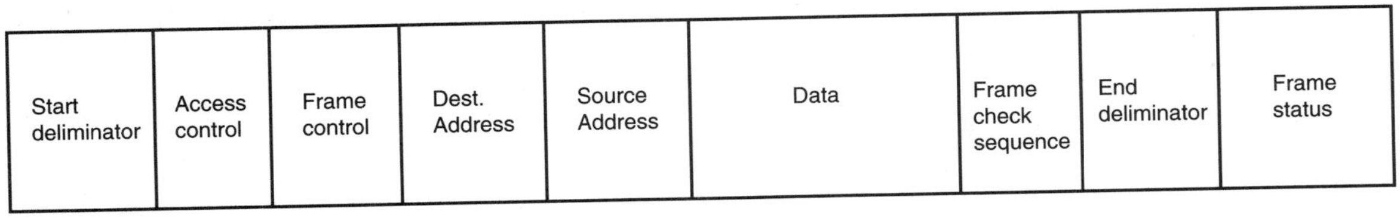

Start deliminator	Access control	Frame control	Dest. Address	Source Address	Data	Frame check sequence	End deliminator	Frame status

FIGURE 4.20
A token ring frame.

The Beaconing Process

Generally, the first station that is powered up on a token-ring network automatically becomes what is called the *active monitor* station. The responsibility of the active monitor station is to announce itself to the next active downstream station as the active monitor station and request that station to announce itself to its next active downstream station. The active monitor station sends this beacon announcement every seven seconds.

After each station announces itself to its next active downstream neighbor, the announcing station becomes the nearest active upstream neighbor (NAUN) to the downstream station. Each station on a token-ring network has an upstream neighbor as well as a downstream neighbor.

After each station becomes aware of its NAUN, the beaconing process continues every seven seconds. If, for some reason, a station doesn't receive one of its expected seven-second beaconed announcements from its upstream neighbor, it attempts to notify the network of the lack of contact from the upstream neighbor. It sends a message out onto the network ring, which includes the following:

- ◆ The sending station's network address
- ◆ The receiving NAUN's network address
- ◆ The beacon type

From this information, the ring can determine which station might be having a problem and then attempt to fix the problem without disrupting the entire network. This process is known as *autoreconfiguration*. If autoreconfiguration proves unsuccessful, there may be a Ring Purge issued by the active monitor, forcing all computers to stop what they are doing and resynchronize with the ring. *If both these mechanisms fail,* manual correction becomes necessary. Figure 4.21 shows a token-ring network utilizing the beaconing process.

ARCNet

ARCNet is an older architecture that is not found too often in the business world, but does have a presence in many older networks and school systems who often receive hand-me-downs from the business sector.

FIGURE 4.21
Token-ring beaconing.

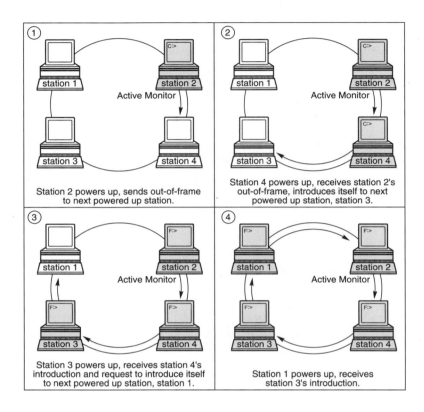

ARCNet utilizes a token-passing protocol that can have a star or bus physical topology. These segments can be connected with either active or passive hubs. ARCNet, when connected in a star topology, can use either twisted pair or coaxial cable (RG-62). If coaxial cable is used to create a star topology, the ends of the cable can be attached directly to a BNC connector, without a terminator. When in a bus topology, ARCNet uses a 93-ohm terminator, which is attached to each end of the bus in a similar fashion to an ethernet bus.

Each ARCNet card has a set of DIP switches built onto it. You can change the setting of these DIP switches to give each card a separate hardware address. (This is covered in more detail in Chapter 5.) Based upon these addresses, tokens are passed to the card with the next highest address on the network. Due to this "access to the net-work passing," ARCNet shares some characteristics with a token passing network.

Some important facts about ARCNet are as follows:

- ◆ ARCNet uses a 93-ohm terminator. (Ethernet uses a 50-ohm terminator.)

- ◆ ARCNet uses a token-like passing architecture, but does not require a MAU.

- ◆ The maximum length between a node and an active hub is 610 meters. (Hubs are discussed in more detail in Chapter 5, "Connecting Devices.")

- ◆ The maximum length between a node and a passive hub is 30.5 meters.

- ◆ The maximum network segment cable distance ARCNet supports is 6100 meters.

- ◆ ARCNet can have a total of only 255 stations per network segment.

FDDI

FDDI is very similar to token ring in that it relies on a node to have the token before it can use the network. It differs from token ring in that it utilizes fiber-optic cable as its transmission media, allowing for transmissions of up to 100Km. This standard permits up to 100 devices on the network with a maximum distance between stations of up to 2 kilometers (see Figure 4.22).

FDDI has two different configurations: Class A and B. Class A uses two counteracting rings. Devices are attached to both rings. If one of these rings develops a fault, the other ring can still be used to transmit data. Class B uses a single ring to transmit data.

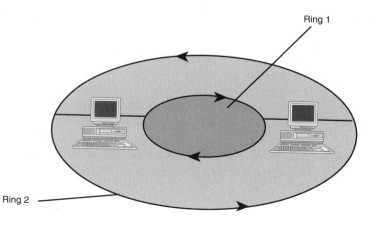

FIGURE 4.22
An FDDI Network.

CASE STUDY: SMALL-COMPANY TOPOLOGY

ESSENCE OF THE CASE

These are the essential facts:

- Fast access to the database server is needed by all parties.

- Data is transferred in very small amounts, but access on the network is constant by almost all 100 employees.

- The company wants to minimize the effects of transmission media failure on the network.

- Walls between groups cannot be drilled through, so all cable must go around the wall.

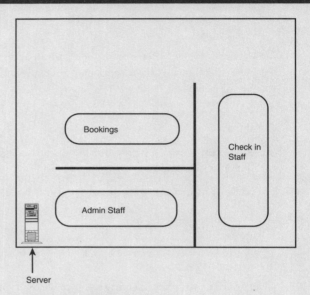

FIGURE 4.23
Physical layout

SCENARIO

You are responsible for deciding upon a topology for a small airline company's network. This company has 80 employees. The physical layout of the building that this airline company is located in is seen in Figure 4.23.

The information that flows through this company consists mostly of airline reservations. The company is using a Microsoft NT server with a SQL server database running on it. The database is accessed by each of three groups in this Airline. These are: Group 1—Reservation and Booking, Group 2—Check-in, and Group 3—Administrative. Each group is separated from each of the others by an impenetrable wall, with no access over or through the wall. The only way to physically move anything from one group to another is to go around the wall. The greatest distance between the server and a PC is 80 meters.

All three groups have important functions, and no one group can really afford to have delays in receiving information from the server. The Reservation and Bookings staff cannot afford to have the clients wait to book a flight, which may cause lost sales. They also must be able to process persons waiting at the terminal or else flights leave late. Thus they need quick access to the database server. The check-in staff has to be able to quickly access the database on the server to check in customers, so that flights will not be delayed. The Administrative staff has to be able to access the database server quickly to deal with complaints and lost luggage. Because the airline does not run flights constantly, a lot of people tend to be on the network at one time, or very few. Also, the amount of data transferred on the network by each user is relatively small (how

CASE STUDY: SMALL-COMPANY TOPOLOGY

much information is really on an airline ticket?), but all the users are continually accessing the network when the flights are running. Only a handful would be continually accessing the network during those times that the flights are not running.

Because this is a competitive market, this airline company cannot afford to have the network go down.

ANALYSIS

This case study is a good example of how to deal with a real-world issue as well as how to address the exam topic of "Select the appropriate topology for various token-ring and ethernet networks."

One of the first questions needing to be asked is whether this network should use contention access or token passing. Fast access to the server is needed by all parties in question. Both contention-based systems and token-ring systems can give fast access to the network, but as the network load increases, one would find that a token-ring system would start to perform better. If the load on the system is very high, the token-ring solution is the best, because it guarantees all parties equal access to the network at once. The drawback to token ring is that it has a higher price tag than that of ethernet.

If the decision is made to use token ring, the topology of choice is going to be a physical star. A physical star is nice, in that if a patch cable is broken, this does not affect other nodes on the network. If the decision is made to go with ethernet, there are two options for the physical topology: a bus or a star. The benefits of a physical star are the same for ethernet as for token-ring.

A bus physical topology has the disadvantage that if any segment is broken, the entire network segment fails, affecting all parties. Furthermore, this point of failure is difficult to trace. Thus, due to the requirements of the company, in that they want to minimize the effects on the network due to failure of the transmission media, a bus topology should be ruled out.

To this point, your options have come down to the physical star ethernet or the token ring. The final issue to resolve is the type of cable to use in each situation.

For the ethernet solution, the 10BASE2 and 10BASE5 are ruled out, because they are used in a bus topology. 10BASE-T meets the requirements, because it supports cable runs of up to 100 meters, and you are not be going farther than 80 meters. Both 100BASE-X and 100BASE-AnyLAN can also be used, but these alternatives cost more than the 10BASE-T, and the data amounts transmitted are very small, hence there is probably not a strong reason to justify the extra cost.

For the token-ring network, Type 1 and 2 cables would work. The IBM standards for Type 3 do not allow the cable run to go past 45 meters; it is therefore too short. In addition, Type 3 does not support 16Mbps. For this reason, even if an approved vendor version that supported lengths up to 150 meters were used, Type 3 would probably be too slow.

To narrow down the cable type even further, in the Token-Ring network, Type 2 cable is more expensive than Type 1, hence, the preferred option is Type 1.

continues

CASE STUDY: SMALL-COMPANY TOPOLOGY

continued

In summary, the following two solutions have been proposed:

- Ethernet running 10BASE-T
- Token ring running Type 1 cable

Between these options there is no correct answer. Token ring costs more than the ethernet solution, but at the same time gives faster access to the users during peak usage. The company would need to evaluate whether the higher cost is worth the better performance of the network during peak time usage. A smart next step would be to see what other airlines of the same size are experiencing when they use either one of the topologies.

CHAPTER SUMMARY

KEY TERMS

- Contention
- Polling
- Token passing
- Physical topology
- Logical topology
- Bus topology
- Ring topology
- Star topology
- Mesh topology
- Ethernet
- Token ring
- ARCNet
- FDDI
- 10BASE2
- 10BASE5
- 10BASE-T
- 10BASE-FL
- 100VG-AnyLAN
- 100BASE-X

This chapter examined some common network topologies. You learned about the basic access methods, such as *contention, polling,* and *token passing.* This chapter then described some fundamental topology archetypes (bus, ring, and star) and discussed the differences between physical and logical topologies. Lastly, the chapter described the common varieties of ethernet and token-ring networks, as well as information on ARCNet and FDDI networks.

Just as you did in Chapter 2, you should review this chapter in its entirety. Questions concerning different network topologies are often stated in terms of comparing the features between the two topologies.

In short, ethernet topologies

- ◆ Are contention based
- ◆ Often employ a 10BASE or 100BASE cable types
- ◆ Can be employed in a physical star or bus topology

Token-ring networks

- ◆ Use a token passing access method
- ◆ Use an IBM type of cabling standard
- ◆ Mostly use a physical star topology

APPLY YOUR LEARNING

Exercises

4.1 Matching Topologies to Applications

Objective: Practice associating network topologies with appropriate uses.

Time estimated: 10 minutes.

Match the topology to the application. For this exercise, you should be familiar with the material in this chapter and also in Chapter 3.

1. 10BASE2
2. 10BASE5
3. 10BASE-T
4. 10BASE-FL
5. 100BASE-X
6. Token Ring

A. You are looking for an inexpensive network with the maximum flexibility for future expansion. You want to utilize existing data-grade phone lines for some segments.

B. Your network encompasses three buildings. The longest segment length is 450 meters. You want to minimize cost. The difference in electrical ground potential between the buildings is not a problem.

C. Your company encompasses three buildings. The longest segment length is 1,800 meters. In previous networking attempts, you have experienced problems with the ground potential differences between the buildings.

D. You are designing a network for an airline ticket office. Employees query the database constantly, so the network utilization rate is extremely high.

The network must be very reliable and capable of self-corrective action to isolate a malfunctioning PC.

E. You work in a small office with 12 PCs. You are looking for an inexpensive networking solution. The computers are spaced evenly throughout the office (approximately 3–5 meters between workstations). You want to minimize the total amount of cabling.

F. Your company colorizes Hollywood movies. Huge, digitized movie files, such as Bringing Up Baby or The Jazz Singer, must pass quickly through the network so they arrive with extreme dispatch at colorizing workstations. Very high transmission speeds are required. Your company is reaping huge profits, so the cost of cabling is no concern.

The correct responses are as follows:

1. E
2. B
3. A
4. C
5. F
6. D

Review Questions

1. Explain the difference between a logical and a physical topology.

2. Explain the difference between a physical bus topology and a physical star topology.

3. Explain the difference between contention-based, polling, and token-passing access methods.

APPLY YOUR LEARNING

Exam Questions

1. CSMA/CD uses which two of the following techniques to control collisions?

   A. Nodes broadcast a warning before they transmit.

   B. Nodes listen for a clear line before they transmit.

   C. Nodes request and are given control of the medium before transmitting.

   D. Nodes listen while they transmit and stop transmitting if another signal interferes with the transmission.

2. What is the maximum size of a 10BASE5 network?

   A. 100 meters

   B. 300 meters

   C. 1,500 meters

   D. 2,500 meters

3. By what type of network is CSMA/CA commonly used?

   A. Microsoft networks

   B. LocalTalk networks

   C. Fast Ethernet networks

   D. 10BASE5 networks

4. Which three of the following network architectures use the token-passing access method?

   A. IEEE 802.4

   B. FDDI

   C. Token-ring

   D. IEEE 802.3

5. If you see a group of networked computers connected to a central hub, you know that the network has what type of physical topology?

   A. Ring

   B. Star

   C. Bus

   D. Can't tell

6. If you see a group of networked computers connected to a central concentrator, you know that the network has what type of logical topology?

   A. Ring

   B. Star

   C. Bus

   D. Can't tell

7. Which topology uses fiber-optic cable?

   A. 10BASE2

   B. 10BASE5

   C. 10BASE-T

   D. None of the above

8. Which topology uses Thicknet cable?

   A. 10BASE2

   B. 10BASE5

   C. 10BASE-T

   D. None of the above

APPLY YOUR LEARNING

9. Which topology uses UTP cable?

   A. 10BASE2

   B. 10BASE5

   C. 10BASE-T

   D. None of the above

10. Which topology uses Thinnet cable?

    A. 10BASE2

    B. 10BASE5

    C. 10BASE-T

    D. None of the above

11. 10BASE5 networks consisting of a single cable segment cannot exceed what maximum length?

    A. 185 meters

    B. 300 meters

    C. 500 meters

    D. 1,000 meters

12. Which two of the following are characteristics of a 10BASE-T network but not a 10BASE2 network?

    A. T-connector

    B. Central hub

    C. UTP

    D. BNC

13 What is sometimes called "Fast ethernet"?

    A. 10BASE-T

    B. 10BASE5

    C. 100VG-AnyLAN

    D. 100BASE-X

14. A token-ring network using STP cabling can support how many computers?

    A. 60

    B. 260

    C. 500

    D. 1,024

15. What field of a token-ring frame is updated by the destination PC?

    A. Destination address

    B. Frame check sequence

    C. End delimiter

    D. Frame status

16. Which two of the following statements are true?

    A. Coax ethernet is a physical bus and a logical bus.

    B. 10BASE-T ethernet is a physical bus and a logical bus.

    C. Coax ethernet is a physical star and a logical bus.

    D. 10BASE-T ethernet is a physical star and a logical bus.

17. What is the single biggest advantage of using 10BASE-T when network segments don't have to exceed 185 meters?

    A. It is relatively simple to connect.

    B. Drop cables can be used, making it easier to troubleshoot.

APPLY YOUR LEARNING

C. Each node connects directly to the coaxial cable.

D. It is the least expensive of the cabling options.

18. Which three of the ethernet topologies require that each end of the bus be terminated?

A. 10BASE2

B. 10BASE5

C. 10BASE-T

D. 10BASE-FL

19. Which of the following is not an advantage of using 10BASE-T for cabling a network?

A. It is easier and more reliable to manage.

B. Centralized hubs make it easier to detect bad cable segments.

C. Beaconing helps to isolate cable breaks.

D. It is relatively inexpensive to use.

20. You are required to select a topology for the corporate network's backbone. Your decision, which is to look at only inter-server (not workstation) connectivity, needs to reflect speed and fault tolerance.

Primary Objective: The topology needs to have total fault tolerance, in case of a cable break.

Secondary Objective: Large data throughput is required.

Secondary Objective: The topology does not need to span a distance of more than 25 meters.

Suggested Solution: Implement the network using fiber-optic cabling.

A. This solution meets the primary objective and both secondary objectives.

B. This solution meets the primary objective and one secondary objective.

C. This solution meets the primary objective.

D. This solution does not meet the primary objective.

21. You wish to install a network that can handle large traffic volumes.

Primary Objective: The topology needs to be deterministic. That is, you need to be able to calculate the effect that the addition of new computers will have on the network.

Secondary Objective: Each station is not generating large amounts of data, but will be continuously generating small amounts of data. The topology needs to be capable of evenly distributing access time to the network.

Secondary Objective: The topology does not need to accommodate more than 244 computers.

Suggested Solution: Implement the network using a token-ring network.

A. This solution will obtain the required result and both optional results.

B. This solution will obtain the required result and one of the optional results.

C. This solution will obtain the required result.

D. This solution does not satisfy the required result.

| APPLY YOUR LEARNING |

Answers to Review Questions

1. A logical topology is the logical path that a signal follows on the transmission media. A physical topology is the physical layout of the transmission media. See "Network Topologies."

2. A physical bus is a cable segment that is a straight line, although in actual practice this cable segment is often snaked around its surroundings. A physical star has a center hub, with cable segments running out from the hub to the devices connected to the hub. See "Bus Topologies" and "Star Topologies."

3. Contention-based access methods employ either a CSMA\CD or a CSMA\CA method. CSMA\CD accesses the network without regard to other devices on the network. CSMA\CA polls the network first to see whether the media is currently busy.

   The polling access method polls different devices to see whether they are waiting to transmit or receive information. A computer accessing a printer often does this.

   Token-passing requires a device to be in possession of a token before transmitting data onto the network. See "Access Methods."

Answers to Exam Questions

1. **B, D.** A is CSMA/CA, and C is indicative of token ring. The purpose of CSMA/CD is to listen before transmitting and then stop if a collision occurs. See the section titled "Contention" under the topic of "Access Methods."

2. **D.** A 10BASE5 network is capable of spanning up to 500 meters on a single segment. Because you can add repeaters, and based on the 5-4-3 rule (5 cable segments connected by 4 repeaters and only three of these segments can be populated), a 10BASE5 network can span up to 2500 meters. See the section titled "10BASE5."

3. **B.** Apple's LocalTalk networks utilize this contention mechanism. See the section titled "Contention" under the topic of "Access Methods."

4. **A, B, C.** D is an ethernet standard defined by the IEEE. See the section titled "Token Passing" under the topic of "Access Methods."

5. **B.** A is a logical topology and B does not use a hub for connecting. See the section titled "Star Topologies" under the topic of "Physical and Logical Topologies."

6. **D.** The logical topology could either be a ring or bus. See the topic titled "Physical and Logical Topologies."

7. **D.** 10BASE-FL is fiber-optic. See the topic titled "Ethernet."

8. **B.** A is coaxial Thinnet cable and C is twisted-pair cable. See the topic titled "Ethernet."

9. **C.** C is twisted pair, which is what UTP is. See the topic titled "Ethernet."

10. **A.** 10BASE2 is often referred to as Thinnet cable. See the topic titled "Ethernet."

11. **C.** Thicknet cables can go only 500 meters before needing a repeater. See the topic titled "Ethernet."

APPLY YOUR LEARNING

12. **B, C**. A and D are used on coaxial cable. Twisted-pair cable goes into a hub, and another term for twisted-pair cable is Unshielded Twisted Pair (UTP). See the topic titled "Ethernet."

13. **D**. This is the other term for 100BASE-X. See the topic titled "Ethernet."

14. **B**. The maximum number of devices for a token ring using STP is 260. See the topic titled "Token Ring."

15. **D**. A, B, and C are either generated by the source PC or read by the destination PC. See the topic titled "Token Ring."

16. **A, D**. B is incorrect because it says "physical bus," C is incorrect because it says "physical star." See the topic titled "Ethernet" and the topic titled "Token Ring."

17. **D**. A could be correct, but this would be dependent upon the network layout; therefore this is not always an advantage. B is incorrect, because drop cables are not used. C is incorrect, because 10BASE-T does not use coaxial cable. See the topic titled "Ethernet."

18. **A, B, D**. Terminators are not used in 10BASE-T. See the topic titled "Ethernet."

19. **C**. Beaconing is done on a token-ring network. See the topic titled "Token Ring."

20. **D**. The only topology that supports total fault tolerance is a mesh topology, where every computer is connected to every other computer, using an independent connection. A fiber-optic network could be the transmission media of choice and does both secondary objectives, but does not satisfy the primary objective. See the section titled "Network Topologies."

21. **A**. The primary objective and both secondary objectives are indicative of a token ring network. See the section titled "Token Ring."

Suggested Readings and Resources

1. Tannenbaum, Andrew. *Computer Networks.* Prentice-Hall, 1996.

2. Derfler, Frank, Jr. and Les Freed. *How Networks Work.* Ziff-Davis Press, 1996.

Chapter 5 targets the following objectives in the Implementation section of the Networking Essentials exam (it has been included here in the Planning part to be consistent with the organization of the chapters reflecting the layers of the OSI model):

Given the manufacturer's documentation for the network adapter, install, configure, and resolve hardware conflicts for multiple adapters in a token-ring or ethernet network.

▶ As a network professional, it is vital that you have the ability to not only install and configure network adapter cards, but also to resolve hardware conflicts between network adapter cards and other adapters and peripherals. If these conflicts exist and are not resolved, your network adapter card will not function, thereby preventing your device from connecting to the network.

CHAPTER 5

Network Adapter Cards

STUDY STRATEGIES

▶ The topic of network adapters requires you to know how to accomplish the following tasks:

    • Installing a network adapter card
    • Configuring a network adapter card
    • Resolving hardware conflicts

▶ While there is factual knowledge to be learned concerning this objective, make sure you work your way through the Step-by-steps and Exercises in this chapter. That kind of hands on experience is important to answering exam questions on this topic.

INTRODUCTION

When devices are attached to a network, some mechanism must exist for transferring the information from one device to a transmission medium so that the other device or devices on the network can receive the information. Likewise, the receiving device must also have some mechanism to receive this information from the transmission medium, so that it can process the information. This chapter and Chapter 6, "Connectivity Devices and Transfer Mechanisms," describe to you the function and workings of some of the common devices used to attach components to the network's transmission medium. This chapter examines the role of the *network adapter card*, also known as a *network interface card* (NIC). Because a network adapter card is the most common mechanism for attaching PCs to a network, it is deserving of an entire chapter. The following chapter, Chapter 6, explains some of the other more common devices used to transmit data in a network.

A network adapter card is a hardware device that installs in a PC and provides an interface from a PC to the transmission medium. Most PC networks, including ethernet, token-ring, and ARCNet, use network adapter cards. The network adapter card is thus an essential part of networking, and an understanding of network adapter cards is crucial for any networking professional.

This chapter begins by explaining the mechanisms used to transfer data from the PC to the transmission medium. From there, configurable options on a network card are examined. That section explains the different properties that are configurable on a network adapter card. The next section of the chapter goes on to explain the installation of a network adapter card, and the chapter concludes with ways to resolve hardware conflicts.

DEFINING THE WORKINGS OF A NETWORK ADAPTER CARD

A network adapter card links a PC with the network cabling system (see Figure 5.1). The network adapter card fits into one of the PC's expansion slots. The card has one or more user-accessible ports to which the network cabling medium is connected.

FIGURE 5.1
An example of a network adapter card.

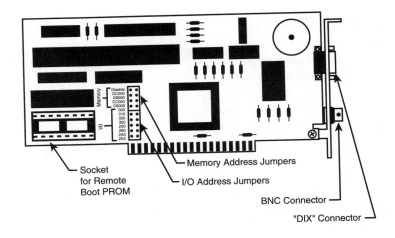

Network adapter cards play an important role on the network. They are responsible for translating data from a device on the network—mostly computers—and converting this data into some form of signal that can be transmitted across the transmission medium. To enable you to understand the full functionality of the network adapter card, the specific functions of what the network card does must each be addressed.

Preparing and Sending Data

All network cards perform the function of preparing and sending data from a computer to the transmission medium. This data, when inside the computer, travels along the bus of a computer in parallel form. This data can move at 8, 16, or 32 bits at a time. The network card must convert these signals coming to it in parallel form, into a serial signal that can travel across the transmission medium. Likewise, when data is received, this serial form of data that is in the signal must be converted into a parallel form matching the bus type (8, 16, or 32 bit) being used by the receiving device.

DATA BUSES

The *data bus* is a pathway inside your computer that carries data between the hardware components. Four data bus architectures are used in Intel-based PCs: the 8-bit bus or Industry Standard Architecture (ISA), the 16-bit bus Extended Industry Standard

Architecture (EISA), the 32-bit bus known as the Micro Channel (MCA), and the 32-bit bus also known as the Peripheral Component Interconnect (PCI). In recent models, PCI and EISA are the most common data bus architectures. ISA is a (more limited) predecessor of EISA. Micro Channel is a data bus developed by IBM for the PS/2 series that never caught on because it needed to be licensed from IBM by other equipment manufacturers.

The mechanism of this data conversion is handled in two ways. First, when data is coming from the computer, to be prepared to be sent out on the network, the network adapter card's driver, or software interface, is responsible for converting this data into a format that can be understood by the network adapter card. As explained in Chapter 2, "Networking Standards," this standard was either NDIS or ODI, depending on whether you were going to interface with a Microsoft operating system (NDIS) or a Novell operating system (ODI).

The second part of the data conversion is performed by the physical network card itself. It is here that the actual data that has been passed along from the computer is converted into a serial format using either a digital, analog, or light signal. The network card not only converts the data into this signal, but it also is responsible for accessing the transmission medium and forming a channel to conduct the signals onto the network. In essence, a network card is like the doorway to the network for the PC or other device.

How a Network Card Works

To enable you to fully appreciate how a network card functions, two important concepts must be explained. These are *signals* and *clocking*.

Signals

Two basic types of signals are used with transmission media: analog and digital.

Analog Signals

Analog signals (seen in Figure 5.2) constantly vary in one or more values, and these changes in values can be used to represent data. Analog waveforms frequently take the form of sine waves.

FIGURE 5.2
An example of an analog signal.

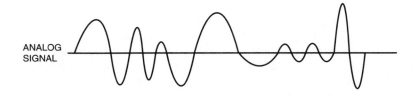

The two characteristics that define an analog waveform are as follows:

◆ *Frequency.* Indicates the rate at which the waveform changes. Frequency is associated with the wavelength of the waveform, which is a measure of the distance between two similar peaks on adjacent waves. Frequency generally is measured in Hertz (Hz), which indicates the frequency in cycles per second. Frequency is illustrated in Figure 5.3.

◆ *Amplitude.* Measures the strength of the waveform. Amplitude is illustrated in Figure 5.4.

Each of these characteristics—frequency and amplitude—can be used to encode data.

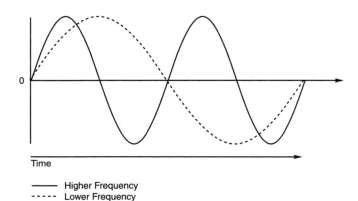

FIGURE 5.3
These two analog waveforms differ in frequency.

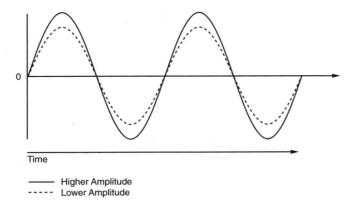

FIGURE 5.4
These two waveforms differ in amplitude.

Digital Signals

Digital signals are different than analog signals in that digital signals have two discrete states. These states are either "off" or "on." An example of how a digital signal is represented is seen in Figure 5.5.

Clocking

Clocking is the mechanism used to count and pace the number of signals being sent and received. Signals are expected to be sent in a continuous flow, representing the start and ending of the data. Clocking is the mechanism used by the network adapter card to determine how much data has been sent. For example, if a network card is designed to transmit data at 20,000 Megahertz a second, other cards receiving this data will also read the data at 20,000MHz a second. Clocking is a mechanism used by all network adapter cards to measure how much data has been sent or received.

A good example of clocking is when a person taps his feet to keep the time to music. The person doing the tapping expects a set number of music beats per measure; computer network cards also expect so many signals per second.

A clocking mechanism used by some network cards is *oversampling*. With oversampling, the receiving network adapter card samples, or

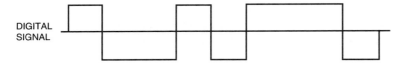

FIGURE 5.5
An example of a digital signal.

reads the signals, at a higher frequency than that at which the data is sent. This capability is programmed into the card by the manufacturers because the clock used on the sending adapter card can drift apart from that of the receiving adapter card. Oversampling enables the clocking mechanism to determine when this drifting apart is happening so that it can correct the clocking rates.

Measurement of the Signal

To this point you are aware that a network card transmits data and that this data is transmitted between devices across some transmission medium. The network adapter card's role is to convert data from one PC to signals, or convert signals back to understandable data for the PC. These signals are either analog or digital. You also know that clocking is used to count the signals. The last step to understand is the mechanism used by the network adapter card to read the signals. It should be no big surprise at this point that the mechanisms can be grouped into two common methods: digital and analog.

Measurement of Digital Signals

Digital signals use one of two common measurement mechanisms: current state or state transition. The manufacturer builds these measurement capabilities into the network adapter card.

Current State

Current state is a mechanism that uses the clock count to analyze the current state of the signal during that count. Thus the signal is either "on" or "off" during the clock count. Figure 5.6 shows the idea of current state measurement.

As seen in Figure 5.6, during each count, the state of the digital signal is either "on" or "off." Changes in the voltages happen during changes in the count. Common digital signal schemes for this sampling mechanism are also known as Polar, Unipolar, and Biphase.

State Transition

State transition is a more common form of data measurement of digital signals. This form of measurement is used on ethernet networks utilizing copper cables. This form of measurement tends to be less

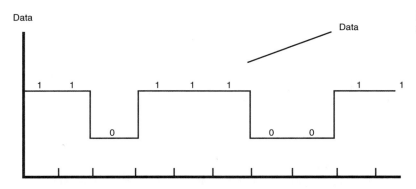

Data

Data

| 1 | 1 | | 1 | 1 | 1 | | 1 | 1 |

0

0   0

Time in thousandths of a second

FIGURE 5.6
Current state measurement.

prone to signal disruptions and also does not rely as much on the strength of a signal.

State transition relies on the change of the state of a network signal to represent a new transmission of data. Recall that in current state the length of time a signal is on or off indicates whether the signal represents a 1 or a 0. State transition represents a 1, for example, every time the state of the signal changes on a count, but a 0 is represented every time the state of the signal does not change during a count.

Common state transmission measurement standards are Manchester, Differential Manchester, and Biphase Space.

Measurement of Analog Signals

Analog, much like digital, signals also follow a similar mechanism of measurement of signals. The main difference between digital and analog signals is that digital signals have two discrete states—"on" and "off"—and analog signals can change frequencies.

Current State

Two mechanisms using current state measurement technologies are the Frequency Shift Keying (FSK) and Amplitude Shift Keying (ASK). FSK uses a change in frequency to indicate a change in data, whereas ASK uses a change in amplitude to indicate a change in data. An example of Frequency Shift Keying is shown in Figure 5.7.

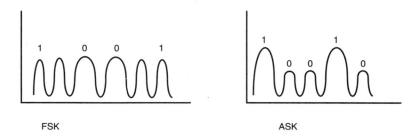

State Transition

State transition of a frequency is the measurement of a frequency's phase during a clock count. A *phase* is a difference in transition of a frequency. The *transition* of a frequency is the change between two frequencies. Figure 5.8 illustrates this.

An example of phase measurement is that a 1 may be represented by a 90 degree phase shift, and a 0 by no phase shift.

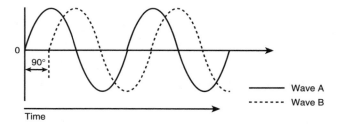

INSTALLING NETWORK ADAPTER CARDS

Given the manufacturer's documentation for the network adapter, install, configure, and resolve hardware conflicts for multiple network adapters in a token-ring or ethernet network.

The details of how to install a network adapter card might depend on the card, the operating system, or the hardware platform, but the steps are basically the same. To install a network adapter card, you must follow these steps:

1. Physically plug the card into the expansion slot, configuring jumpers and DIP switches as required (see the next section).

2. Install the network adapter card driver.

3. Configure the operating system so that the network adapter card doesn't conflict with other devices (see the next section).

4. Bind the network adapter to the required protocols (see Chapter 7, "Transport Protocols," for more information).

5. Attach the network cable to the card.

Depending on whether the network adapter card's hardware is plug-and-play and if the operating system being used is also plug-and-play, some of these steps might happen automatically when you plug a card into the slot and start your system. Windows NT is not really plug-and-play-capable, so when you install a network adapter card after the operating system is in place, you might have to spend some time with steps 2–4. Be warned, though: Even the presence of plug-and-play devices on plug-and-play systems does not guarantee the automation of installing hardware.

To install a network adapter card driver in Windows NT, follow these steps:

STEP BY STEP

5.1 Installing a Network Adapter Card Driver in Windows NT

1. Click the Start button and choose Settings/Control Panel. Double-click the Control Panel Network application. In the Control Panel Network application, choose the Adapters tab (see Figure 5.9).

2. In the Adapters tab (refer to Figure 5.9), click the Add button to invoke the Select Network Adapter dialog box (see Figure 5.10). Choose the adapter model from the list or click the Have Disk button to install a driver that isn't listed. Windows NT asks for the location of the Windows NT installation CD-ROM.

3. Windows NT attempts to detect the adapter and then might prompt you for additional information (see the section titled "Configuring Network Adapter Cards" later in this chapter).

continues

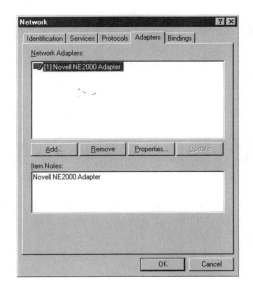

FIGURE 5.9
The Control Panel Network Adapters tab.

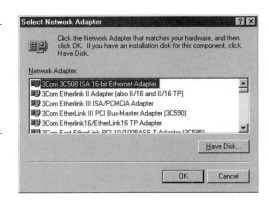

FIGURE 5.10
The Select Network Adapter dialog box.

continued

4. When the installation is complete, shut down Windows NT and restart.

5. Use the Network application's Bindings tab to check and set protocol bindings for the new adapter (see Chapter 7).

NOTE

Make sure the adapter is compatible with your version of Windows NT. To do so, check the Windows NT Hardware Compatibility list or consult the manufacturer.

NOTE

The Relationship Between Data Bus and Processor Type   The data bus architecture is generally independent of the processor type. Two Pentium machines from different vendors might have different data bus architectures, although PCI has essentially become the standard.

NOTE

Jumpers and DIP Switches   Jumpers are small connectors that bridge across predetermined terminal points (pins) on the card itself to hardwire the card for certain user-defined settings, such as the IRQ setting. DIP (dual inline package) switches are small switches (usually in groups) that, like jumpers, can configure the card for user-defined settings.

Before you buy a network adapter card, you must make sure it has the correct data bus architecture for your PC and the correct connector type for your transmission medium. It must support the operating system you are running on the computer into which it is being installed.

Almost all PCs use one of four basic data bus architectures: ISA, EISA, PCI, and Micro Channel. (Refer to the In-depth on data bus architectures earlier in this chapter.) These architectures are not necessarily compatible. For example, a Micro Channel card doesn't work on an EISA system and, in fact, doesn't even fit in the slot, so when you buy a card for an expansion slot, be ready to tell the vendor what type of data bus architecture you have available on your system.

Chapter 3, "Transmission Media," discussed some basic LAN network cabling types. The network adapter is responsible for transmitting in accordance with the specifications of the transmission medium. The adapter card also must supply a connector that is compatible with the cabling system. (See Chapter 3 for more information on Ethernet and token-ring cabling and connectors.) Some boards offer connectors for more than one cabling type, in which case you must configure jumpers or DIP switches or use software to set the active type.

CONFIGURING NETWORK ADAPTER CARDS

You must configure your operating system so that it can communicate with the network adapter card. Most plug-and-play adapter cards configure themselves and, in conjunction with the operating system running, assign resources to themselves. In many cases, though, you must manually configure the adapter card. These settings are configured through jumper or DIP switch settings, or by using some form of software, so that the network card can communicate with the operating system.

To communicate, the operating system and the network adapter must agree on certain important parameters, called resource settings. Some common resource settings for a network adapter are as follows:

- IRQ
- Base I/O port address
- Base memory address
- DMA channel
- Boot PROM
- MAC address
- Ring speed (token-ring cards)
- Connector type

IRQ

The *IRQ (Interrupt Request Line)* setting reserves an interrupt request line for the adapter to use when contacting the CPU. Devices make requests to the CPU using a signal called an *interrupt*. Each device must send interrupts on a different interrupt request line. Interrupt request lines are part of the system hardware. The IRQ setting (such as IRQ3, IRQ5, or IRQ15) defines which interrupt request line the device is to use. By convention, certain IRQ settings are reserved for specific devices. Different adapter cards provide numerous available IRQs from which you can choose. Be careful, though: Some network cards are very limited in the different IRQs that they have available, and may offer only IRQs that are currently being used by other devices on your system.

Base I/O Port Address

The *base I/O port address* defines a memory address through which data flows to and from the adapter. The base I/O port address functions more like a port, defining a channel between the adapter and the processor.

Base Memory Address

The *base memory address* is a place in the computer's memory that marks the beginning of a buffer area reserved for the network adapter. Not all network adapter cards use the computer's RAM, and therefore not all adapters require a base memory address setting.

DMA Channel

The DMA or Direct Memory Access channel is an address used for quicker access to the CPU by the adapter card. Many devices, including network cards, often enable you to choose between DMA channels 1 through 7, or have the channel disabled. Not all network cards have the capability to set DMA channels.

Boot PROM

Some network adapter cards are equipped with a Boot PROM (Programmable Read Only Memory). This Boot PROM enables the network card to boot up and connect over the network, because the Boot PROM has the necessary connection software to use. This feature is often used by diskless workstations, because they have either no hard drives or floppy drives onto which to store connection software.

MAC Address

As discussed in Chapter 2, using the MAC address burnt into each network card is one of the several ways to establish addresses for nodes on the network. These addresses are hexadecimal in nature and are unique for each card. The IEEE is responsible for assigning these addresses to each network card manufacturer. In some cases, you can reassign a new MAC address for the network adapter card. In the case of ARCNet cards, DIP switches are used to set the network card's address.

Ring Speed

In the case of token-ring networks, the ring speed must be set on the token-ring card. The possible values for this are either 4Mbps or 16Mbps. It is very important that the correct ring speed is set, because an incorrect ring speed prevents your computer from connecting onto the network, or it also can cause the entire network to fail.

Connector Type

Some network cards have different connectors from which you can choose. A common example is an ethernet card with both a BNC connector and an RJ45 connector. Some network cards require that the connector to be used must be specified. Other network cards self-adjust to the connector being used.

Any effort to configure a network adapter card should begin with the card's vendor documentation. The documentation tells you which resource settings are available for you to set, and it might recommend values for some or all of the settings. Some network cards have a default setting, in which all settable values are set to defaults recommended by the factory.

The actual process of configuring the operating system to interact with a network adapter card depends on the operating system. A plug-and-play operating system such as Windows 95, when used with a plug-and-play-compatible network adapter card, may perform much of the configuring automatically. In Windows NT, you can often configure adapter card resource settings through the Control Panel Network application's Adapters tab. (Not all adapter cards are configurable through this interface.) The Windows NT Diagnostics application in the Administrative Tools group (see Exercise 5.2 at the end of the chapter) indicates the resource settings that are currently available.

RESOLVING HARDWARE CONFLICTS

Hardware conflicts are caused when the devices on the system compete for the same system resources, such as interrupt request lines,

Plug-and-Play It is important to note that plug-and-play (sometimes facetiously called plug-and-pray by its critics) is still relatively new technology for Microsoft-based systems. Ideally, Windows 95 should configure a plug-and-play-compatible card without much user intervention, but in some cases, you might still face configuration problems. This occurs because many plug-and-play devices are simply not coded correctly to work with plug-and-play operating systems.

base I/O port addresses, and base memory addresses. An improperly configured device can cause a hardware conflict with other devices, so you must make sure that each device has exclusive access to the required system resources. An example of common resources and the devices assigned to them is seen in Table 5.1.

Other devices installed into a computer that often take up resources are sound cards, modems (discussed in Chapter 6), scanners, and CD-ROM controllers.

In Windows NT, a hardware conflict might evoke a warning message from the system or an entry in the Event Log (see Chapter 12, "Troubleshooting"). If you experience a hardware conflict, use Windows NT Diagnostics (see Exercise 5.2) to check resource settings for system devices. Then change the resource settings of any conflicting devices.

In Windows 95, use Device Manager (see the following Step by Step) to spot hardware conflicts and track resource settings.

TABLE 5.1

COMMON RESOURCE ALLOCATION ON A PC

Resources	IRQ	I/O Address	Memory	DMA
System Timer	0			
Key Board	1	060-06F		
VGA display	2/9	3C0-3CF	A0000-AFFFF	0
COM2	3	2F8-2FF		
COM1	4	3F8-3FF		
LPT2	5	278-27F		
Floppy Controller		3F0-3F7		
LPT1	7	378-37F		
Math coprocessor	13	0F0-0F8		
Primary hard drive controller	14	1f0-1f8		
Secondary hard drive controller	15	170-177		

STEP BY STEP

5.2 Using Device Manager

Windows 95 includes a utility called Device Manager that displays system devices by type, looks for resource conflicts, and provides an interface for checking and changing resource settings.

To access Device Manager, follow these steps:

1. Click the Start button and choose Settings, Control Panel.

2. In the Windows 95 Control Panel, double-click the System application.

3. Choose the Device Manager tab in the System Properties dialog box.

4. Device Manager displays system devices in a tree format. Click on the plus sign next to a device type to view the installed devices. Double-click on an installed device (or choose the device and click the Properties button) for a Properties dialog box, such as the one shown in Figure 5.11.

   Also, by selecting the computer icon and clicking the properties button, you see a list of all resource usage for Memory addresses, IRQs, DMA channels, and Input/Output settings.

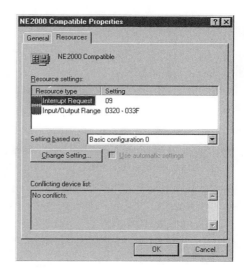

FIGURE 5.11
An adapter card's Properties dialog box in Device Manager.

If you can't pinpoint a resource conflict by using Windows NT Diagnostics, Windows 95's Device Manager, or some other diagnostic program, try removing all the cards except the network adapter and then replacing the cards one by one. Check the network with each addition to determine which device is causing the conflict.

CASE STUDY: WORKING WITH ADAPTER CARDS IN AN ESTABLISHED NETWORK

ESSENCE OF THE CASE

The facts for this case study are as follows:

- You have no documentation for the following:

  - What hardware is installed on these computers

  - What software is installed on the systems

  - How the network is configured

- You have no software for these cards; this includes configuration software or the drivers themselves.

- Based upon the description of the network adapter cards, you know that this network is a token-ring network.

- The network card manufacturer is Intel.

SCENARIO

You have been contacted by a firm to come in and attach all 10 of their new PCs to their existing token-ring network. However, the network adapter cards they want to use have been stripped out of old computers and are being reused in the new PCs. You try to obtain the detailed records of the network, but find that no one has been keeping records, thus you are going to have to obtain all information to install and configure these network adapter cards on your own. The network adapter cards are software-configurable, but a thorough search has failed to turn up the software needed to configure these network cards. You can see from the writing on the network adapter card that it is an Intel Token Express 16/4. What are the steps you would take to attach these computers to the network?

ANALYSIS

This case study is an example of a problem that almost all network professionals have encountered in their lives. This problem is made extra unique, for one issue is that you must not only resolve any hardware, or possible hardware conflicts, but you must also somehow obtain the software to configure these token-ring cards.

The approach to take in this situation is as follows: First, you need to acquire the software to configure these cards. Often network adapter card manufactures place the configuration software and drivers up on the web. But this is not always the case. Numerous network card manufacturers make "compatible" network cards, yet the software does not always work with the cards with which they are reported to be compatible. Another issue with network adapter cards is that in some cases no identifiable markings are on the network adapter card to enable you to even identify the manufacturer or model of the card. In this case study you are at least able to determine that this card is an Intel Token Express 16/4.

In this case, if you go to Intel's Web site and do a search for the keywords of "Intel Token Express 16/4," you get a list back that includes a downloadable compressed file containing the drivers and configuration software for this card.

CASE STUDY: WORKING WITH ADAPTER CARDS IN AN ESTABLISHED NETWORK

After obtaining this compressed file, you should uncompress it. The first thing you should look for is whether any information files are available that may note installation issues concerning the network adapter card. These issues can range from what hardware is incompatible with this network adapter card to what software may not work with these cards. This information is often found in the README.TXT or READ.ME file or may be part of the configuration software. To resolve these conflicts if they exist, you should check whether any of the PCs in which you are installing these network adapter cards contain this problematic software or hardware. If these components exist, you should either replace them or find a possible software fix.

The next step in this installation process, assuming the machines are running Windows 95 or Windows NT, is to go to either the Device manager (Windows 95) or the Windows NT Diagnostics (Windows NT) to determine what resources (that is, IRQ, DMA, I/O, and so forth) are not being used. Based upon this information, the proper values for the network card can be chosen. Because this network is a token-ring network, you should check to make sure that you select the correct ring speed at which the card should operate.

CHAPTER SUMMARY

This chapter examined the network adapter card—an essential component in ethernet and token-ring networks. The network adapter card performs several functions, including preparing, sending, and controlling the flow of data to the network transmission medium. To address these issues, this chapter focused on the following main issues:

◆ Defining the workings of a network adapter card

◆ How to install a network card

◆ How to configure a network adapter card

◆ How to resolve hardware conflicts

When you prepare for the exam, pay particular attention to the last three points, because it is on these issues that the exam objective focuses. The first point was included to give you needed background and a better understanding of the functionality of a network adapter card.

KEY TERMS

- Data bus
- Analog signal
- Digital signal
- Clocking
- Current state
- State transmission
- IRQ
- Base I/O port address
- Base memory address
- DMA channel
- Boot PROM
- MAC address
- Ring speed
- Connector type

APPLY YOUR LEARNING

Exercises

5.1 Network Adapter Resource Settings

Objective: Become familiar with the process of configuring network adapter resource settings in Windows NT.

Estimated time: 10 minutes

Earlier in this chapter, you learned how to install a network adapter card driver by using the Windows NT Network application. You can also use the Network application to check or change the resource settings for an adapter that is already installed.

1. Click the Start button and choose Settings/Control Panel. Double-click the Windows NT Control Panel Network application.

2. In the Network application, click the Adapters tab.

3. Select the network adapter that is currently installed on your system and click the Properties button.

4. The Network Card Setup dialog box then appears on your screen (see Figure 5.12).

5. In the Network Card Setup dialog box, you can change the resource settings as required. You might want to use the Windows NT Diagnostics application to look for available settings (see Exercise 5.2). Don't change the settings unless you're experiencing problems, though, because you could introduce a hardware conflict with another device.

6. Click Cancel to leave the Network Card Setup dialog box and click Cancel again to leave the Network application.

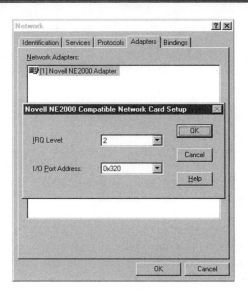

FIGURE 5.12
A Network Card Setup dialog box.

5.2 Windows NT Diagnostics

Objective: Learn to check resource settings through Windows NT Diagnostics.

Estimated time: 10 minutes

Windows NT Diagnostics tabulates a number of important system parameters. You can use Windows NT Diagnostics to help resolve resource conflicts for network adapters.

1. Click the Start button and choose Programs/Administrative Tools. Choose Windows NT Diagnostics from the Administrative Tools menu.

2. Windows NT Diagnostics provides several tabs with information on different aspects of the system. Choose the Resources tab (see Figure 5.13).

APPLY YOUR LEARNING

FIGURE 5.13
The Windows NT Diagnostics Resource tab.

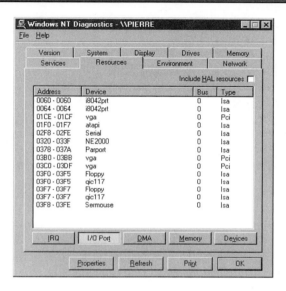

FIGURE 5.14
The Windows NT Diagnostics Resource tab—
I/O port setting

3. Figure 5.13 displays the IRQ settings for system devices. (Note that the network adapter card for which the resource settings were displayed is listed here beside IRQ2.) The buttons at the bottom of the screen invoke views of other resource settings. Click on a button to see the associated list. Figure 5.14 shows the I/O Port list.

You can't change any values in Windows NT Diagnostics. You can only view services, devices, statistics, and settings. Changes to devices can be done from their respective control panel applets. Network cards are often configurable from the Network applet and SCSI devices are changed under the SCSI applet, to name two examples. However, not all devices can be configured from their respective applets. Some require you to use manufacturer-supplied software or even adjust jumper settings to make any configuration changes.

Review Questions

1. What type of signal has a discrete state?

2. What are the configurable options on a network card?

3. What can be set on a token-ring card but not on an ethernet card?

4. What is caused by an incorrect setting on a network card?

Exam Questions

1. In Windows NT, what is a utility you can use to install network adapter card drivers?

   A. Windows NT Diagnostics

B. The System application

C. Device Manager

D. None of the above

2. What must a user sometimes configure to hard-wire resource settings on a network adapter card?

   A. Jumpers

   B. Resource switches

   C. Needle connectors

   D. None of the above

3. Which two of the following are common data bus architectures?

   A. EISA

   B. Pentium

   C. Plug-and-play

   D. PCI

4. Which resource setting gives the device a channel for contacting the CPU?

   A. IRQ

   B. Base I/O port address

   C. Base memory address

   D. None of the above

5. Which resource setting defines a means for passing data to the adapter?

   A. IRQ

   B. Base I/O port address

   C. Base memory address

   D. None of the above

6. Which resource setting specifies a serial communications port for the network adapter?

   A. IRQ

   B. Base I/O port address

   C. Base memory address

   D. None of the above

7. Which resource setting locates a buffer for the adapter in the computer's RAM?

   A. IRQ

   B. Base I/O port address

   C. Base memory address

   D. None of the above

8. Which two of the following enable you to check the resource settings for a network adapter card in Windows NT?

   A. Device Manager

   B. The Network application

   C. Windows NT Diagnostics

   D. The System application

9. Which of the following enables you to change the resource settings for a network adapter card in Windows NT?

   A. Device Manager

   B. The Network applet

   C. Windows NT Diagnostics

   D. The System applet

APPLY YOUR LEARNING

10. What are three duties of the network adapter card?

    A. Preparing data

    B. Sending data

    C. Identifying problems with the cabling medium

    D. Controlling the flow of data

11. On ethernet networks, data flows from the network adapter card to the transmission medium in what form?

    A. Parallel

    B. Serial

    C. Either A or B

    D. None of the above

12. Of the following IRQs, which would be a recommended IRQ setting for a network adapter card?

    A. IRQ14

    B. IRQ2

    C. IRQ1

    D. IRQ5

13. A user complains that after having a network card installed in his system, he is knocked off the network whenever he prints. What is the most likely solution to this problem?

    A. The printer's cable is plugged into the network card.

    B. The newly installed network card's IRQ is in conflict with the printer port's IRQ.

    C. The newly installed network card is not seated correctly.

    D. The newly installed network card's IRQ is in conflict with the sound card's IRQ.

14. A computer's network adapter card is not functioning. You suspect a resource conflict with another device. The operating system being used by the computer is Windows 95.

    Primary Objective: Make the network adapter card work.

    Secondary Objective: Learn what resources are being used by the network adapter card.

    Secondary Objective: Change the resource settings on the network adapter card.

    Suggested Solution: You go into Windows NT Diagnostics and view the resource configuration information. Based upon this information, you reset the network adapter card's resources in the Network section of Windows NT diagnostics.

    A. This solution meets the primary objective and both secondary objectives.

    B. This solution meets the primary objective and one secondary objective.

    C. This solution meets the primary objective.

    D. This solution does not meet the primary objective.

Answers to Review Questions

1. Digital signals have discrete states. These two discrete states are "on" and "off." Analog signals follow a wave pattern that has both amplitude and frequency. See the section titled "Signals."

2. Most common configurable options on a network card are:

   • IRQ

   • I/O port

   • Memory address

   • DMA

   • MAC address

   • Connector type

   • Ring speed (token ring)

   See the section titled "Configuring Network Adapter Cards."

3. A token-ring card can set the ring speed, which is not an option on an ethernet card. Some ethernet cards can set their data transfer rates between 10Mbps and 100Mbps, but this is not the same as ring speed. The options for ring speed are 4Mbps and 16Mbps. Incorrect setting of this can cause the card to be inoperable or can shut down the entire network. See the section titled "Ring Speed."

4. An incorrect setting on a network card causes one of several things to occur:

   First: An incorrect setting can cause the network adapter card to not function.

   Second: An incorrect setting can cause another device on the computer to not function, because this other device may also be using the resource set on the network adapter card. As this happens, the network adapter may or may not also function.

   Third: An incorrect setting can cause another device on the network to not function, as well as

all possibilities stated in the second scenario. See the section titled "Resolving Hardware Conflicts."

Answers to Exam Questions

1. **D**. The correct answer would be the Network icon in Control panel. B is not used to configure network adapters. C can be used in Windows 95. See the section titled "Installing Network Adapter Cards."

2. **A**. Jumpers are used to configure resource settings on network adapter cards. Other valid options could also have been DIP switches and software configuration utilities. See the section titled "Configuring Network Adapter Cards."

3. **A, D**. B is a processor type; C is an architecture standard to which devices can conform. See the section titled "Defining the Workings of a Network Adapter Card."

4. **B**. A is used to signal the processor that a device is ready to use the processor. C is a storage area for storing data that is passing to and from the device. See the section titled "Configuring Network Adapter Cards."

5. **B**. A is used to signal the processor that a device is ready to use the processor. Data is passed along the Base I/O port address. C is a storage area for storing data that is passing to and from the device. See the section titled "Configuring Network Adapter Cards."

6. **D**. A serial communication port is specified as a COMx port, where x typically ranges from 1-4. See the section titled "Configuring Network Adapter Cards."

APPLY YOUR LEARNING

7. **C.** A is used to signal the processor that a device is ready to use the processor. C is used for buffering data on a computer's RAM. See the section titled "Configuring Network Adapter Cards."

8. **B, C.** Using the Device Manager and the system application (where Device Manager is actually found) are methods of checking for resource settings in Windows 95. See the section titled "Resolving Hardware Conflicts."

9. **B.** Only through the network application can resource changes be made. All other answers are read-only utilities found in Windows 95 and NT. It should be noted that some devices do not allow changes to be made through the Network Application. See the section titled "Resolving Hardware Conflicts."

10. **A, B, D.** Problems with the cable medium are addressed with specific diagnostic utilities that are discussed in Chapter 11, "Monitoring the Network." See the section titled "Defining a Network Adapter."

11. **B.** The bits are sent out one after the other, just as they are in a com port. In parallel form bits are sent out eight at a time. See the section titled "Preparing Data."

12. **D.** IRQ 1 is used by the Keyboard; IRQ2 is used by the display adapter; IRQ14 is used by the Primary Hard drive Controller. See the section titled "Configuring Network Adapter Cards."

13. **B.** If a network card's IRQ is set to the same one used by the printer, the printer can cause the adapter card to not function anymore, thus causing a user's computer to be knocked off the network. A would not even enable the network card or printer to work in the first place. C would cause the network card to not function at all. Answer D would cause conflicts between the sound card and Network adapter card. See the section titled "Configuring Network Adapter Cards."

14. **D.** NT Diagnostics is a utility that enables one to view only configuration information. Nothing can be set through this utility. Also, there could be many reasons why the network adapter card is not functioning. It could be broken, unplugged from the network, incompatible with the operating system, or have a resource conflict with another device. The proposed solution satisfies only the first secondary objective. See the section titled "Resolving Hardware Conflicts."

Suggested Readings and Resources

1. Anderson, Douglas T. *The network interface card technical guide.* Micro House, 1993.

2. Derfler, Frank J., Jr., *Using Networks.* Que, 1998.

   • Chapter 5: LAN Adapters: The Hardware Heart of the LAN.

Chapter 6 targets the following objective in the Planning section of the Networking Essentials exam:

Select the appropriate connectivity devices for various token–ring and Ethernet networks. Connectivity devices include repeaters, bridges, routers, brouters, and gateways

▶ This exam topic was briefly highlighted in Chapter 2, "Networking Standards." In this chapter, a more in-depth analysis is done on the different devices that are used on various token-ring and Ethernet networks. In this chapter, besides simply addressing the role of each connectivity device, emphasis is placed on comparing and contrasting the devices in terms of when one would be used versus another.

CHAPTER 6

Connectivity Devices and Transfer Mechanisms

STUDY STRATEGIES

▶ When reading this chapter be very aware of the differences that each connectivity device plays. Some connectivity devices can perform multiple roles. If you can address when and why a certain connectivity device needs to be used, you will have no problems addressing the exam topic being presented by this chapter.

INTRODUCTION

People sometimes think of a network as a single, local cabling system that enables any device on the network to communicate directly with any other device on the same network. A network by this definition, however, has no connections to other remote networks.

An internetwork consists of multiple independent networks that are connected and can share remote resources. These logically separate but physically connected networks can be dissimilar in physical type and topology. The device that connects the independent networks together may need a degree of "intelligence" because it may need to determine when packets will stay on the local network or when they will be forwarded to a remote network.

This chapter examines some important connectivity devices. In order to facilitate your understanding of what these devices actually do, the chapter begins by explaining the concept of addressing. This is an important concept to understand in order to differentiate between different connectivity devices that exist on the network. In the following sections, you learn about modems, repeaters, bridges, routers, brouters, and gateways. Some of this material also appears in Chapter 2, "Networking Standards," in the discussion of communication devices and OSI. In Chapter 2, the main emphasis was where the different connectivity devices were situated within the OSI model. Here the emphasis is more on the function of the different connectivity devices, and when one would use them. The chapter concludes with a section discussing different routing algorithms.

ADDRESSING

Before a discussion of devices is warranted, addressing of a network must be explored further. Addressing a network is important, because it is by this mechanism that devices on the network are located and identified.

A network is similar to a city. A city has buildings and it has streets. Now imagine a city in which no two streets had the same name. Each street name must be unique. Now imagine a city that not only had unique names for each street, but also a unique address for each building on its street (this should not be too difficult).

A network is like a street. All buildings on a single street share the same street name that they reside on. Or in other words, all devices on a network segment share the same network address. Thus there are two distinct forms of addresses here: the logical network address and the node address that is physically part of the device.

All packets that go on to a network have within them the source address information and destination address information. Some packets are not routable; therefore they will not contain a source or destination network address in them. The details of routing will be covered in Chapter 7, "Transport Protocols."

These concepts have been touched on in previous chapters, but it is important that you understand these two concepts here, as the function of different devices on the network is dependent upon device (or hardware) addresses and logical network addresses. As seen in the previous chapter, device addresses in terms of a network card were either burnt onto, or programmed into, the network card by the manufacturer. These addresses could also be set with software by some network card manufacturers, or could be set through DIP switches, as in the case of ARCNet cards. This chapter will address different routing protocols used to discover the existence of different logical addresses on the network, whereas the next chapter will address rules that different transport protocols conform to when addressing networks.

MODEMS

Standard telephone lines can transmit only analog signals. Computers, however, store and transmit data digitally. Modems can transmit digital computer signals over telephone lines by converting them to analog form.

Converting one signal form to another (digital to analog in this case) is called modulation. Recovering the original signal is called demodulation. The word "modem" derives from the terms modulation/demodulation.

Modems can be used to connect computer devices or entire networks that are at distant locations. (Before digital telephone lines existed, modems were about the only way to link distant devices.)

Some modems operate constantly over dedicated phone lines. Others use standard public switched-telephone network (PSTN) dial-up lines and make a connection only when one is required.

Modems enable networks to exchange email and to perform limited data transfers, but the connectivity made possible is extremely limited due to the limited bandwidth most modems offer. Modems don't enable networks to connect to remote networks, like a router, to directly exchange data. Instead modems act like network cards in that they provide an access point onto the transmission medium, in this case the telephone lines, in order to send analog signals to another device, most likely another modem, on the network.

Until recently, modem manufacturers used a parameter called baud rate to gauge modem performance. The baud rate is the oscillation speed of the sound wave transmitted or received by the modem. Although baud rate is still an important parameter, recent advances in compression technology have made it less meaningful. Some modems now provide a data transfer rate (in bits per second—a more meaningful measure of network performance) that exceeds the baud rate. In other words, you can no longer assume the baud rate and the data transfer rate are equal.

Modems are classified according to the transmission method they use for sending and receiving data. The two basic types of modems are as follows:

◆ Asynchronous modems

◆ Synchronous modems

The following sections describe asynchronous and synchronous transmission.

NOTE

Other Modem Uses Modems don't necessarily need to connect through the PSTN. Short-haul modems frequently are used to connect devices in the same building. A standard serial connection is limited to 50 feet, but short-haul modems can be used to extend the range of a serial connection to any required distance.

Many devices are designed to operate with modems. When you want to connect such devices without using modems, you can use a null-modem cable, which connects the transmitter of one device to the receiver of the other device.

Asynchronous Transmission

Asynchronous transmission does not use a clocking mechanism to keep the sending and receiving devices synchronized. Instead, this type of transmission uses bit synchronization to synchronize the devices for each frame that is transmitted.

In bit synchronization, each frame begins with a start bit that enables the receiving device to adjust to the timing of the transmitted signal. Messages are kept short so that the sending and receiving devices do not drift out of synchronization for the duration of the message. Asynchronous transmission is most frequently used to transmit character data and is ideally suited to environments in which characters are transmitted at irregular intervals, such as when users enter character data.

Figure 6.1 illustrates the structure of a typical frame used to transmit character data. This frame has four components:

- ◆ *A Start bit.* This component signals that a frame is starting and enables the receiving device to synchronize itself with the message.

- ◆ *Data bits.* This component consists of a group of seven or eight bits when character data is being transmitted.

- ◆ *A parity bit.* This component is optionally used as a crude method of detecting transmission errors.

- ◆ *A stop bit or bits.* This component signals the end of the data frame.

Asynchronous transmission is a simple, inexpensive technology ideally suited for transmitting small frames at irregular intervals. Because start, stop, and parity bits must be added to each character being transmitted, however, overhead for asynchronous transmission is high—often in the neighborhood of nearly 20 to 30 percent. This high overhead wastes bandwidth and makes asynchronous transmission undesirable for transmitting large amounts of data.

Asynchronous transmission is frequently used for PC-to-PC and terminal-to-host communication. Modems use asynchronous transmission. Data in these environments is often of the bursty, character-oriented nature that is ideal for asynchronous communication. Asynchronous transmission generally requires less expensive hardware than synchronous transmission.

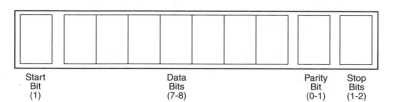

FIGURE 6.1

The structure of an asynchronous frame consists of four key bit components.

Synchronous Transmission

Synchronous transmission eliminates the need for start and stop bits by synchronizing the clocks on the transmitting and receiving devices. This synchronization is accomplished in two ways:

◆ By transmitting synchronization signals with data. Some data encoding techniques, by guaranteeing a signal transition with each bit transmitted, are inherently self-clocking.

◆ By using a separate communication channel to carry clock signals. This technique can function with any signal-encoding technique.

Figure 6.2 illustrates the two possible structures of messages associated with synchronous transmission.

Both synchronous transmission methods begin with a series of synch signals, which notify the receiver of the beginning of a frame. Synch signals generally utilize a bit pattern that cannot appear elsewhere in messages, ensuring that the signals always are distinct and easily recognizable by the receiver.

A wide variety of data types can be transmitted. Figure 6.2 illustrates both character-oriented and bit-oriented data. Notice that under synchronous transmission, multiple characters or long series of bits can be transmitted in a single data frame. Because the transmitter and receiver remain in synchronization for the duration of the transmission, frames may be very long.

When frames are long, parity is no longer a suitable method for detecting errors. If errors occur, multiple bits are more likely to be affected, and parity techniques are less likely to report an error. A more appropriate error-control technique for synchronous transmission is the cyclic redundancy check (CRC). In this technique, the

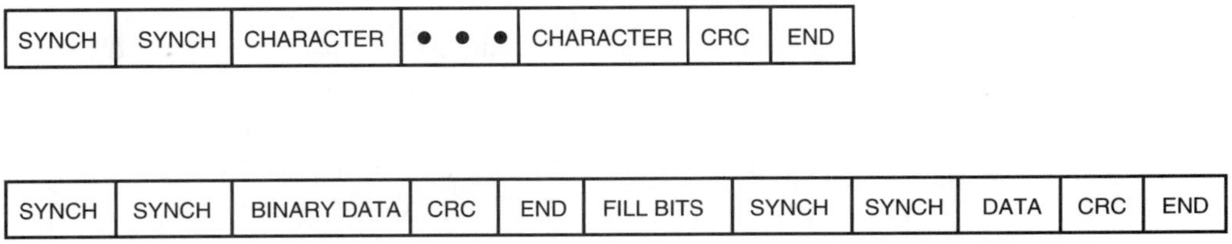

SYNCH	SYNCH	CHARACTER	● ● ●	CHARACTER	CRC	END

SYNCH	SYNCH	BINARY DATA	CRC	END	FILL BITS	SYNCH	SYNCH	DATA	CRC	END

FIGURE 6.2
Structures of synchronous transmission.

transmitter uses an algorithm to calculate a CRC value that summarizes the entire value of the data bits. This value is then appended to the data frame. The receiver uses the same algorithm, recalculates the CRC, and compares the CRC in the frame to the CRC value it has calculated. If the values match, the frame almost definitely was transmitted without error.

When synchronous transmission links are idle, communicating devices generally send fill bits to the devices synchronized.

Synchronous transmission offers many advantages over asynchronous transmission. The overhead bits (synch, CRC, and end) comprise a smaller portion of the overall data frame, which provides for more efficient use of available bandwidth. Synchronization improves error detection and enables the devices to operate at higher speeds.

The disadvantage of synchronous transmission is that the more complex circuitry necessary for synchronous communication is more expensive. Network adapter cards commonly employ synchronous transmission methods.

REPEATERS

As you learned in Chapter 3, "Transmission Media," all media attenuate the signals they carry. Each media type, therefore, has a maximum range that it can reliably carry data. The purpose of a repeater is to extend the maximum range for the network cabling.

A repeater is a network device that repeats a signal from one port onto the other ports to which it is connected (see Figure 6.3). Repeaters operate at the OSI Physical layer. (Refer to "The OSI Reference Model" section in Chapter 2.) A repeater does not filter or interpret—it merely repeats (regenerates) a signal, passing all network traffic in all directions.

A repeater doesn't require any addressing information from the data frame because a repeater merely repeats bits of data. This means that if data is corrupt, a repeater will regenerate the signal anyway. A repeater will even repeat a broadcast storm caused by a malfunctioning adapter (see Chapter 12, "Troubleshooting").

The advantages of repeaters are that they are inexpensive and simple. Also, although they cannot connect networks with dissimilar data

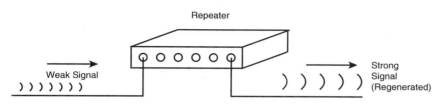

FIGURE 6.3
A repeater regenerates a weak signal.

frames (such as a token-ring network and an Ethernet network), some repeaters can connect segments with similar frame types but dissimilar cabling.

Figure 6.4 shows the use of a repeater to connect two Ethernet cable segments. The result of adding the repeater is that the potential length of the overall network is doubled.

Some repeaters simply amplify signals. Although this increases the strength of the data signal, it also amplifies any noise on the network. In addition, if the original signal has been distorted in any way, an amplifying repeater cannot clean up the distortion.

Certainly, it would be nice if repeaters could be used to extend networks indefinitely, but all network designs limit the size of the network. The most important reason for this limitation is signal propagation. Networks must work with reasonable expectations

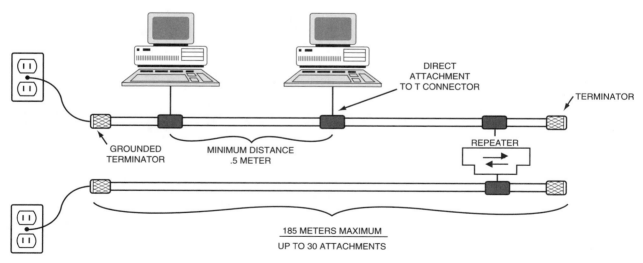

FIGURE 6.4
Using a repeater to extend an Ethernet LAN.

about the maximum time a signal might be in transit. This is known as *propagation delay*—the time it takes for a signal to reach the farthest point on the network. If this maximum propagation delay interval expires and no signals are encountered, a network error condition is assumed. Given the maximum propagation delay allowed, it is possible to calculate the maximum permissible cable length for the network. Even though repeaters enable signals to travel farther, the maximum propagation delay still sets a limit to the maximum size of the network. Repeaters also follow the 5-4-3 rule. That is five segments connected by four repeaters, with no more than 3 of the segments being populated.

HUBS

Hubs, also called wiring concentrators, provide a central attachment point for network cabling (see Figure 6.5). Hubs come in three types:

◆ Passive

◆ Active

◆ Switching

The following sections describe each of these types in more detail.

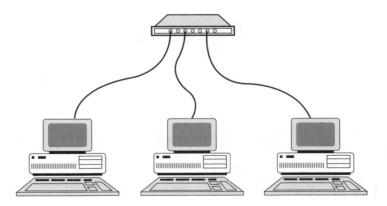

FIGURE 6.5
A network wired to a central hub.

Passive Hubs

Passive hubs do not contain any electronic components and do not process the data signal in any way. The only purpose of a passive hub is to combine the signals from several network cable segments. All devices attached to a passive hub receive all the packets that pass through the hub.

Because the hub doesn't clean up or amplify the signals (in fact, the hub absorbs a small part of the signal), the distance between a computer and the hub can be no more than half the maximum permissible distance between two computers on the network. For example, if the network design limits the distance between two computers to 200 meters, the maximum distance between a computer and the hub is 100 meters.

As you might guess, the limited functionality of passive hubs makes them inexpensive and easy to configure. That limited functionality, however, is also the biggest disadvantage of passive hubs. Often small networks use passive hubs, due to the fact that there are few machines on the LAN and small distances between them. Hubs follow the 5-4-3 rule, where no more than 5 network segments can be connected to 4 hubs with only 3 of them being populated. This is seen in Figure 6.6.

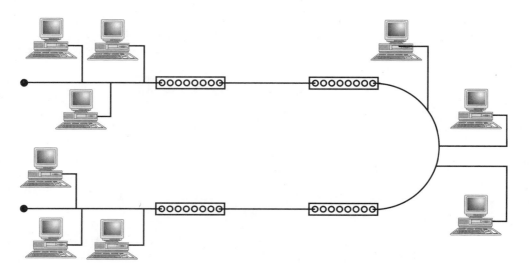

FIGURE 6.6

5-4-3 rule: 5 segments connected with 4 hubs, and only 3 segments are populated.

Active Hubs

Active hubs incorporate electronic components that can amplify and clean up the electronic signals that flow between devices on the network. This process of cleaning up the signals is called signal regeneration. Signal regeneration has the following benefits:

◆ The network is more robust (less sensitive to errors).

◆ Distances between devices can be increased.

These advantages generally outweigh the fact that active hubs cost considerably more than passive hubs.

Earlier in this chapter, you learned about repeaters, devices that amplify and regenerate network signals. Because active hubs function in part as repeaters, they occasionally are called multiport repeaters.

Intelligent Hubs

Intelligent hubs are enhanced active hubs. Several functions can add intelligence to a hub:

◆ *Hub management*. Hubs now support network management protocols that enable the hub to send packets to a central network console. These protocols also enable the console to control the hub; for example, a network administrator can order the hub to shut down a connection that is generating network errors.

◆ *Switching*. The latest development in hubs is the switching hub, which includes circuitry that very quickly routes signals between ports on the hub. Instead of repeating a packet to all ports on the hub, a switching hub repeats a packet only to the port that connects to the destination computer for the packet. Many switching hubs have the capability of switching packets to the fastest of several alternative paths. Switching hubs are replacing bridges and routers on many networks.

In essence, a switching hub acts like a very fast bridge, which is what is described in the next section. Switching hubs are the most expensive of hubs on the market. Often they are simply referred to as *Switches*. As for the exam, think of all types of hubs as simply a hub.

BRIDGES

Bridges, on the other hand, can extend the maximum size of a network. Although the bridged network in Figure 6.7 looks much like the earlier example of a network with a repeater, the bridge is a much more flexible device. Bridges operate at the MAC sublayer of the OSI Data Link layer (see Chapter 2).

A repeater passes on all signals that it receives. A bridge, on the other hand, is more selective and passes only those signals targeted for a computer on the other side. A bridge can make this determination because each device on the network is identified by a unique physical address.

Each packet that is transmitted bears the address of the device to which it should be delivered. The process works as follows (refer to Figure 6.7):

1. The bridge receives every packet from either side of it on LAN A.

> **N O T E**
>
> **Physical Addresses of Network Adapter Cards** Remember that the physical address of network adapter cards are often burnt onto the card, where as in the case of ARCNet, it is set by DIP switches. See Chapter 5 for more details on this issue.

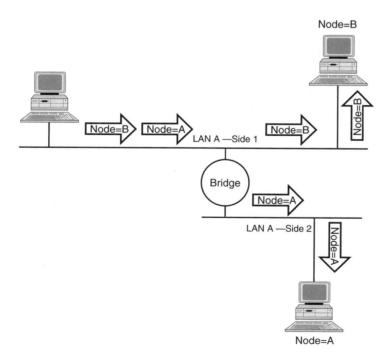

FIGURE 6.7
Separating signals on a LAN segment with a bridge.

2. The bridge references an internal table of addresses. This table is either learned by the bridge, from previous packet deliveries on the network, or manually programmed into the bridge.

3. Packets on LAN A – Side 1 that are addressed to devices on LAN A – Side 1 and packets on LAN A – Side 2 that are addressed to devices on LAN A – Side 2, are not passed along to the other side by the bridge. These packets can be delivered without the help of the bridge.

4. Packets on LAN A – Side 1 addressed to devices on LAN A – Side 2 are retransmitted, by the bridge to LAN A – Side 2 for delivery. Similarly, the appropriate packets on LAN A – Side 2 are retransmitted to LAN A – Side 1.

Bridges come in two main forms. One type of bridge is what is known as a *transparent or learning bridge.* This type of bridge is transparent to the device sending the packet. At the same time this bridge will learn over time what devices exist on each side of it. This is done by the bridge's ability to read the Data-Link information on each packet going across the network. By analyzing these packets, and seeing the source MAC address of each device, the bridge is able to build a table of which devices exist on what side of it. There usually is a mechanism for a person to go in and also program the bridge with address information as well. Learning bridges function as described in step 2, automatically updating their address tables as devices are added to or removed from the network. Ethernet networks almost always use a transparent bridge.

Another type of bridge is a *source routing bridge.* This type of bridge is employed on a token-ring network. A source routing bridge is a bridge that reads information appended to the packet by the sending device. This additional information in the packet will state the route to the destination segment on the network. A source routing bridge will analyze this information to determine whether or not this stream of data should or should not be passed along.

Bridges accomplish several things. First, they divide busy networks into smaller segments. If the network is designed so that most packets can be delivered without crossing a bridge, traffic on the individual network segments can be reduced. If the Accounting and Sales departments are overloading the LAN, for example, you might divide the network so that Accounting is on one segment and Sales on another. Only when Accounting and Sales must exchange packets does a packet need to cross the bridge between the segments.

Bridges also can extend the physical size of a network. Although the individual segments still are restricted by the maximum size imposed by the network design limits, bridges enable network designers to stretch the distances between segments and extend the overall size of the network. A general rule of thumb for deciding which side of a bridge a device should be placed on is that 80% of the device's traffic should be destined to devices on the same side of the bridge that the device in question resides on.

Bridges, however, cannot join LANs that are utilizing different network addresses. This is because bridges operate at the Data Link layer of the OSI model and depends on the physical addresses of devices and not at the Network layer which relies on logical network addresses.

Bridges sometimes are also used to link a LAN segment through a synchronous modem connection to another LAN segment at a remote location. A so-called remote bridge minimizes modem traffic by filtering signals that won't need to cross the modem line (see Figure 6.8).

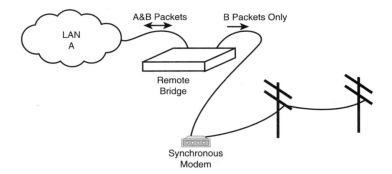

FIGURE 6.8
A remote bridge acts as a synchronous modem.

ROUTING

An internetwork consists of two or more physically connected independent networks that are able to communicate. The networks that make up an internetwork can be of very different types. For example, an internetwork can include Ethernet and token-ring networks.

Because each network in an internetwork is assigned an address, each network can be considered logically separate; that is, each network functions independently of other networks on the internetwork. Internetwork connectivity devices, such as routers, can use network address information to assist in the efficient delivery of messages. Delivering packets according to logical network address information is called routing. The common feature that unites internetwork connectivity devices (routers and brouters) is that these devices can perform routing. The following list details some common internetwork connectivity devices:

- ◆ Routers
- ◆ Brouters

Each of these devices is discussed in the following sections.

Routers

Bridges are suitable for relatively simple networks, but bridges have certain limitations that become more significant in complex network situations. One limitation of bridges is that packets intended for all people on a subnet, also known as a broadcast, are received by every single device on the network. By being able to section off a LAN segment into different network segments, routers allow you to control and group devices that work together to be on the same network segment.

Consider the network in Figure 6.9. Both bridges are aware of the existence of Node B, and both can pick up the packet from Net A and forward it. At the very least, the same packet can arrive twice at Node B.

A worse case, however, is that these relatively unintelligent bridges can start passing packets around in loops, which results in an ever-increasing number of packets that circulate on the network and never reach their destinations. Ultimately, such activity can (and will) saturate the network.

An algorithm, called the spanning tree algorithm, enables complex Ethernet networks to use bridges while redundant routes exist. The algorithm enables the bridges to communicate and construct a logical network without redundant paths. The logical network is reconfigured if one of the paths fails.

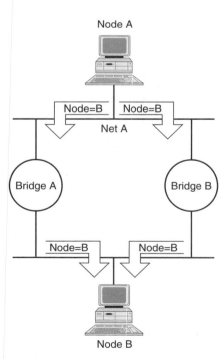

FIGURE 6.9
A complex network with bridges.

Another problem is that the bridges cannot analyze the network to determine the fastest route over which to forward a packet. When multiple routes exist, this is a desirable capability, particularly in wide area networks (WANs), where some routes are often considerably slower than others.

Routers organize the large network in terms of logical network segments. Each network segment is assigned an address so that every packet has both a destination network address and a destination device address.

Routers are more "intelligent" than bridges. Not only do routers build tables of network locations, but they also use algorithms to determine the most efficient path for sending a packet to any given network. Even if a particular network segment isn't directly attached to the router, the router knows the best way to send a packet to a device on that network. In Figure 6.10, for example, Router A knows that the most efficient step is to send the packet to Router C, not Router B.

Notice that Router B presents a redundant path to the path Router A provides. Routers can cope with this situation because they exchange routing information to ensure that packet loops don't occur. In Figure 6.10, if Router A fails, Router B provides a backup message path, thus making this network more robust.

One consequence of all the processing a router performs on a packet is that routers generally are slower than bridges.

You can use routers to divide large, busy LANs into smaller segments, much as you can use bridges. But that's not the only reason to select a router. Routers also can connect different network types. An example of this would be a router that connected a token-ring segment with the Ethernet segments. On such networks, a router is the device of choice, as a bridge cannot perform this function.

The protocols used to send data through a router must be specifically designed to support routing functions. IP, IPX, and DDP (the AppleTalk Network-layer protocol) are routable transport protocols. NetBEUI is a non-routable transport protocol. Transport protocols will be discussed in greater detail in Chapter 7.

Because routers can determine route efficiencies, they usually are employed to connect a LAN to a wide area network (WAN). WANs frequently are designed with multiple paths, and routers can ensure that the various paths are used most efficiently.

NOTE

Internetworks Recall that an internetwork consists of two or more logically separate but physically connected networks. By this definition, any network segmented with routers is an internetwork.

FIGURE 6.10

An internetwork: A series of networks separated by routers.

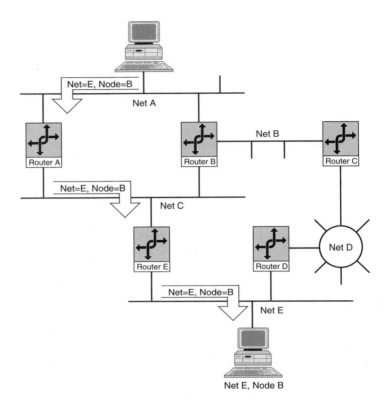

The Network layer functions independently of the physical cabling system and the cabling system protocols—independently, that is, of the Physical and Data Link layers. This is the reason that routers easily can translate packets between different cabling systems. Bridges, on the other hand, cannot translate packets in this way because they function at the Data Link layer, which is closely tied to physical specifications.

Routers come in two general types:

◆ *Static Routers.* These routers do not determine paths. Instead, you must configure the routing table, specifying potential routes for packets.

◆ *Dynamic Routers.* These routers have the capability to determine routes (and to find the optimum path among redundant routes) based on packet information and information obtained from other routers.

To determine the best path for a packet, routers employ some form of routing algorithm. Some common routing algorithms are discussed in the following sections.

Brouters

A brouter is a router that also can act as a bridge. A brouter attempts to deliver packets based on network protocol information, but if a particular Network layer protocol isn't supported, the brouter bridges the packet using device addresses.

GATEWAYS

The term "gateway" originally was used in the Internet protocol suite to refer to a router. Today, the term "gateway" more commonly refers to a system functioning at the top levels of the OSI model that enables communication between dissimilar protocol systems. A gateway generally is dedicated to a specific conversion, and the exact functioning of the gateway depends on the protocol translations it must perform. Gateways commonly function at the OSI Application layer, but actually can operate at any level of the OSI model.

Gateways connect dissimilar environments by removing the layered protocol information of incoming packets and replacing it with the packet information necessary for the dissimilar environment (see Figure 6.11).

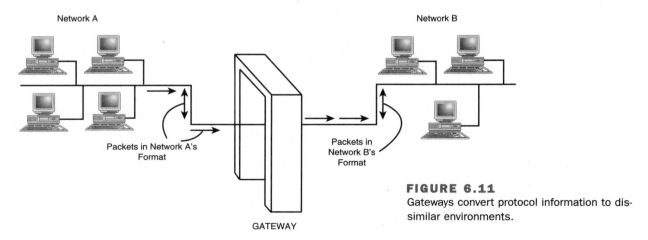

FIGURE 6.11
Gateways convert protocol information to dissimilar environments.

Gateways can be implemented as software, hardware, or a combination of both. An example of a gateway is often seen in email systems. When you send email, say from Microsoft Exchange to someone on the Internet, a gateway is responsible for converting the Microsoft Exchange message contents and addressing, to one that is compatible with the SMTP (Internet) message format and addressing.

DYNAMIC ROUTING APPLIED— ROUTING ALGORITHMS

Routing refers to the process of forwarding messages through internetworks of LANs. In some cases, routing information is programmed into the routing devices. However, preprogrammed, or static, routers cannot adjust to changing network conditions. Most routing devices, therefore, are dynamic, which means that they have the capability of discovering routes through the internetwork and then storing the route information in route tables.

Route tables do not store only path information. They also store estimates of the time, cost or calculated distance taken to send a message through a given route. This time estimate is known as the cost of a particular path. Some of the methods of estimating routing costs are as follows:

- *Hop count.* This method describes the number of routers that a message might cross before it reaches its destination. If all hops are assumed to take the same amount of time, the optimum path is the path with the smallest hop count.

- *Tic count.* This method provides an actual time estimate, where a tic is a time unit as defined by the routing implementation.

- *Relative expense.* This method calculates any defined measure of the cost (including the monetary cost) to use a given link.

After costs are established, routers can select routes, either statically or dynamically, as follows:

- *Static route selection.* This selection method uses routes that have been programmed by the network administrator.

◆ *Dynamic route selection.* Under this selection method, routing cost information is used to select the most cost effective route for a given packet. As network conditions change and are reflected in routing tables, the router can select different paths to maintain low costs.

Two common methods of discovering routes are distance vector routing and link-state routing. Both are discussed in the following sections. It should be mentioned that some networks are too large to implement dynamic routing, as the routing tables would get too large. In cases like this, reliance on static routing tables (those that are manually inputted) is needed. The Internet is a great example of systems that rely on static routing tables.

Distance Vector Routing

Distance vector routers advertise their presence to other routers on the network. Periodically, each router on the network broadcasts the information in its routing table. Other routers can use this information to update their own router tables.

Figure 6.12 illustrates how the process works. In the figure, Server S3 learns that Server S2 can reach Server S1 in one hop. Because S3 knows that S2 is one hop away, S3 knows that its cost to reach S1 through S2 is two hops.

Distance vector routing is an effective algorithm, but it can be fairly inefficient. Because changes must ripple through the network from

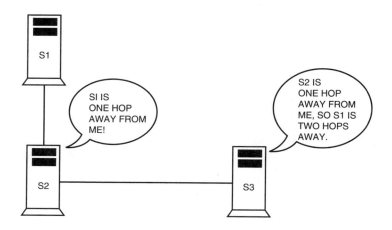

FIGURE 6.12
Distance vector routing.

router to router, it might take a while for a change to become known to all routers on the network. In addition, the frequent broadcasts of routing information produce high levels of network traffic that can hurt performance on larger networks.

Link-State Routing

Link-state routing reduces the network traffic required to update routing tables. Routers that are newly attached to the network can request routing information from a nearby router.

After routers have exchanged routing information about the network, routers broadcast messages only when something changes. These messages contain information about the state of each link the router maintains with other routers on the network. Because routers keep each other updated, complete network routing updates are not needed often.

CASE STUDY: BRIDGES OR ROUTERS?

ESSENCE OF THE CASE

The essence of the case is as follows:

- Should this company use bridges or routers?
- Explain the benefits and costs of each device.
- Do not focus on the details such as topology or cable types but raise these issues where applicable.

SCENARIO

You are involved in the planning stages of a network that is about to be placed within a company. There is concern over whether to utilize bridges or routers within the network. Actual cabling types, topologies, and protocols are not the primary concern at this planning event, but

you are to address these issues where applicable when making your presentation to the planning team. Your job is to present a brief summary of the benefits and costs of using bridges or routers.

ANALYSIS

If you were in this situation you would need to explain the function of a bridge and a router to the company. You should also make sure that this company is aware that bridges and routers compliment each other; they are not necessarily replacements for each other.

Bridges have the following features. They are transport protocol independent (see Chapter 7 for more information on transport protocols). Bridges also are not management intensive, as they usually in most cases do not require any configuration information. They will learn the

CASE STUDY: BRIDGES OR ROUTERS?

network segment, once they are attached. Bridges are often cheaper to purchase than a router. The main purpose of using bridges in an Ethernet network is to reduce collisions, whereas in a token-ring network, they are used to bridge rings together. A possible replacement for a bridge could be a switch, also known as a switched hub. However, switched hubs tend to cost more than a bridge.

The problem with a bridge is that a bridged network is reliant on the transmission medium properties as to the number of nodes that can be on the network. Also, bridges are ideally supposed to follow the 80/20 industry rule of thumb. That is 80% of a node's traffic should be on its side of the bridge. Only 20% of a node's traffic should go to the other side of the bridge. A bridge has no method of locating devices either. That is, because it relies only on MAC addresses, and not on any logical grouping address (network address), bridges are not ideal for large networks.

Routers require more manual intervention than bridges. They often cost more, and they are dependent upon transport protocols in order to function. The ideal thing about routers is that they can connect different LANs together to form an internetwork. Thus one can have a network of several different transmission media and topologies. One can also connect more devices together, utilizing different LANs, than possible when only having one network segment.

In large networks, routers are most often used in order to logically group devices, or because different transmission media are being used to connect different segments of a network. Bridges are often placed on the individual network

segments of a network in order to reduce collisions on that particular network segment.

One issue that would involve the use of routers would be if the router was to be static or dynamic. A dynamic router would need to use some form of dynamic routing protocol. Once a selected protocol was to be established, a particular router from a vendor could be selected.

In short, characteristics of bridges are:

- Bridges are cheaper than routers.
- Bridges usually do not require any manual intervention.
- Bridges do not extend the number of devices that can go on a transmission medium.
- Bridges have no method of locating devices on the cable segment.
- Learning bridges are used on Ethernet networks, whereas Source Routing bridges are used on token-ring networks.

Issues concerning routers are:

- Routers cost more than bridges.
- Routers often will require manual intervention to configure them.
- Routers will connect different LAN segments together, allowing a network to grow beyond the limitations of one transmission medium.
- Routers can use logical addresses to locate devices on the network.
- Routers can be used to connect Ethernet to token-ring networks.

CHAPTER SUMMARY

KEY TERMS

- Internetwork
- Modem
- PSTN
- Asynchronous Modems
- Synchronous Modems
- Concentrator
- Active Hub
- Intelligent Hub
- Transparent Bridge
- Learning Bridge
- Spanning Tree Algorithm
- Static Router
- Dynamic Router
- Hop count
- Tic count
- Relative expense
- Distance Vector Routing
- Link State Routing
- Repeaters
- Bridges
- Routers
- Brouter
- Gateways

This chapter examined some of the connectivity devices that network engineers use to expand, optimize, and interconnect networks. These devices have some similarities, but each is designed for a specific task, as described in the following list:

- ◆ *Repeaters*. Repeaters regenerate a signal and are used to expand LANs beyond cabling limits.

- ◆ *Bridges*. Bridges know the side of the bridge on which a node is located. A bridge passes only packets addressed to computers across the bridge, so a bridge can thus filter traffic, reducing the load on the transmission medium.

- ◆ *Routers*. Routers forward packets based on a logical (as opposed to a physical) address. Some routers can determine the best path for a packet based on routing algorithms.

- ◆ *Gateways*. Gateways function under a process similar to routers except that gateways can connect dissimilar network environments. A gateway replaces the necessary protocol layers of a packet so that the packet can circulate in the destination environment.

You should be familiar with the features of these connectivity devices and with their relative advantages and disadvantages for the Networking Essentials exam.

This chapter also analyzed several forms of transmission used by devices such as network cards and modems, both asynchronous and synchronous, and concluded with different types of routing algorithms used by routers, those being Distance Vector and Link State routing.

There are two major points to keep in mind about the material in this chapter. The first is that the devices discussed, particularly repeaters, bridges and routers, are not competing technologies but complementary technologies. The second is that, although the exam objective does not specifically identify transmission types and routing algorithms, it is important to be aware of them as a network professional. These topics were included in this chapter because it is the devices in this chapter that use these routing algorithms and transmission methods.

APPLY YOUR LEARNING

Exercises

6.1 Equipment Costs

Objective: Learn the costs of different hardware used on a network.

Estimated Time: 10 minutes

The purpose of this exercise is to call up a vendor and find out the prices of different components used on the network. Possible companies that you may ask for, that produce these devices are Cisco, Bay Networks, Intel and 3Com, to name but a few.

The main purpose is to find out the difference between the prices of a Repeater, Hub, and Router. If the company you call does not have the exact device as listed, substitute with one that is close.

When asking about the Routers, ask if these are passive or active routers. If the quotes you receive are for active routers, ask which routing algorithms the router supports.

Use the following table:

Item	Description	Price
Repeater	- 10BASE-T Cable	$_____
	- 10BASE-2 Cable	$_____
HUB	- 20 port passive (Ethernet)	$_____
	- 20 port active (Ethernet)	$_____
	- 20 port switched hub (Ethernet)	$_____
MAU	- 20 port MAU for token-ring	$_____
Router	- 3 connections, all for Ethernet	$_____
	- 1 ISDN connection and one token-ring connection	$_____

6.2 Configuring an Asynchronous Device

Objective: Learn how to configure parameters on an asynchronous modem within Windows 95.

Estimated Time: 10 minutes

1. Select the Start button, move to the Settings option and then select the Control Panel option.

2. Double click on the modem icon.

3. If you have a modem already installed, proceed to step 8. If you do not have a modem installed, a modem installer wizard opens up.

4. From the Install New Modem dialog box, check Don't detect my modem; I will select it from a list option and then click on the Next button.

5. From the Install New Modem dialog box, select the "(Standard Modem Types)" option under the Manufacturers list, and also select the Standard 28800bps Modem option under Types list. Then click on the Next button. (As we will not actually use the modem, it does not matter if you actually have a physical modem attached to your PC.)

APPLY YOUR LEARNING

6. In the Install New Modem dialog box, select Communications Port (Com3) under the Select the port to use with this modem list. Then click on the Next button.

7. Click on the Finish button.

8. In the Modem Properties dialog box select the Standard 28800bps Modem or your previously installed modem. Then click on the Properties button.

9. Select the Connection tab.

Examine the Connection preferences options. It is here that you can adjust for how many stop bits are to be used as well as the number of data bits and the parity type. All of these are options that control the amount of overhead used in an asynchronous communication method.

Review Questions

1. When discussing Repeaters, Bridges, and Routers, which device relies on logical network addresses, physical hardware addresses, or does not use addresses at all?

2. Describe the difference between synchronous and asynchronous transmissions.

3. Describe the difference between static and dynamic routing.

4. What is the difference between distance vector routing and link-state routing?

Exam Questions

1. Your LAN includes computers in two rooms at different ends of the company office. The cables connecting the rooms exceed the maximum cabling distance for the transmission medium, and the network is experiencing problems due to signal loss in the long cables. What would be the cheapest and simplest solution?

   A. Router

   B. Repeater

   C. Bridge

   D. Brouter

2. Your Ethernet LAN is experiencing performance problems due to heavy traffic. What would be a simple solution?

   A. Gateway

   B. Repeater

   C. Bridge

   D. Router

3. What routing algorithm enables bridges to operate on a network with redundant routes?

   A. Distance vector

   B. Link-state

   C. Spanning tree

   D. Learning tree

APPLY YOUR LEARNING

4. You need to connect a token-ring LAN with an Ethernet LAN. To do so, you will need what type of device?

    A. Bridge

    B. Gateway

    C. Repeater

    D. Hub

5. You need to connect a token-ring and an Ethernet LAN segment. To do so, you will need what type of device?

    A. Repeater

    B. Bridge

    C. Remote bridge

    D. Router

6. What device uses an address table to determine where to send a packet?

    A. Bridge

    B. Router

    C. Both A and B

    D. None of the above

7. Which three of the following are advantages of active hubs over passive hubs?

    A. They can regenerate network signals.

    B. LAN ranges can be extended.

    C. They are less expensive.

    D. They function as repeaters.

8. Which networks can use MAUs?

    A. Ethernet

    B. ARCnet

    C. Token-ring

    D. All the above

9. Which two of the following features can add intelligence to a hub?

    A. Signal regeneration

    B. Network-management protocols

    C. Multiport repeaters

    D. Switching circuitry

10. Which two statements are true of repeaters?

    A. Repeaters filter network traffic.

    B. Repeaters extend network distances.

    C. Repeaters regenerate signals.

    D. Repeaters operate at the OSI Data Link layer.

11. Which three statements are true of bridges?

    A. Bridges amplify and regenerate signals.

    B. Bridges can connect logically separate networks.

    C. Bridges use device address tables to route messages.

    D. Bridges divide networks into smaller segments.

APPLY YOUR LEARNING

12. Which of the following connectivity devices is the least expensive?

    A. Repeater

    B. Bridge

    C. Router

    D. Gateway

13. Which of the following connectivity devices uses logical addresses?

    A. Repeater

    B. Bridge

    C. Router

    D. None of the above

14. Which of the following connectivity devices connects dissimilar networking protocol environments?

    A. Repeater

    B. Bridge

    C. Router

    D. Gateway

15. What type of router requires a human-configured routing table?

    A. Explicit router

    B. Satic router

    C. Simple router

    D. Bridge

16. On what level of the OSI does a hub reside?

    A. Physical

    B. Network

    C. Application

    D. Transport

17. On what level of the OSI does a bridge reside?

    A. Data Link

    B. Physical

    C. Network

    D. Presentation

18. At what level does a Router live?

    A. Network

    B. Physical

    C. Application

    D. Data Link

19. At what level of the OSI does a Gateway live?

    A. Physical and Data Link

    B. Physical

    C. It can operate at multiple levels throughout the OSI model.

    D. Network and Data Link

Answers to Review Questions

1. Repeaters operate at the Physical layer of the OSI model. Repeaters do not rely on any type of address at all, as their function is to simply regenerate a signal, regardless of where the signal is destined to go.

   Bridges operate at the Data Link layer of the OSI model. Bridges analyze the hardware addresses, or MAC addresses, of the source and destination devices on each packet. Based upon these MAC addresses, a packet will be allowed through a bridge if that device is on the other side, or not through a bridge if the device is not on the other side of the bridge.

   Routers utilize logical network addresses to define separate network segments. These logical network addresses are usually assigned by the network administrator, and will follow specific naming conventions, depending upon the protocol being used.

   See the sections titled "Repeaters," "Bridges," and "Routing."

2. Asynchronous transmission utilizes a start and a stop bit when sending data, as there is no clocking being done. Up to 30% of the signals being transmitted can be the overhead of the start bit, stop bit, and the error correcting mechanism. Modems use asynchronous transmissions.

   Synchronous transmissions, allow for the removal of the overhead associated with asynchronous transmissions. It can accomplish this by encoding clocking signals in the data, or by using a separate communication channel to send the clocking signal. Network cards utilize synchronous transmissions.

   See the sections titled "Asynchronous Transmission" and "Synchronous Transmission."

3. Static routing requires manually entering routing tables into a router, so that the router knows which paths house different networks.

   Dynamic routers share routing information with each other automatically. Routers do this by using either a link-state or distance vector routing protocol.

   See the section titled "Routing."

4. Distance vector routing uses broadcasts at periodic intervals to announce the presence of the routes to other routers. Distance vector routing is effective, but can produce significant amounts of traffic on a large network.

   In link state routing, newly attached routers can request information, as soon as something on the network changes. It is an ideal routing protocol to use on a large network, but usually requires more manual configuration than distance vector routing.

   See the section titled "Dynamic Routing Applied—Routing Algorithms."

Answers to Exam Questions

1. **B.** Routers, brouters, and bridges are designed to isolate traffic, not regenerate signals to exceed cable distance recommendations. See the section titled "Repeaters."

2. **C.** Bridges and routers are solutions to isolate traffic. A bridge is a more simple solution than a router as bridges often do not need to be configured. See the section titled "Bridges."

APPLY YOUR LEARNING

3. **C.** A and B are router algorithms. D just sounds good. See the sections titled "Bridges" and "Routers."

4. **B.** Gateways are what are used to connect dissimilar systems. See the section titled "Gateways."

5. **D.** See the answer above.

6. **C.** Both bridges and routers consult an address table when determining where a packet is to be sent. For more information see the sections titled "Bridges" and "Routers."

7. **A, B, D.** Active hubs are more expensive than passive hubs. See the section titled "Hubs."

8. **C.** MAUs are used in token-ring networks. See the section titled "Hubs."

9. **B, D.** A and C are functions of a repeater, not an Intelligent hub. See the section titled "Hubs."

10. **B, C.** D is incorrect as a repeater operates at the Physical level of the OSI model. A is incorrect as repeaters do not filter traffic. See the section titled "Repeaters."

11. **A, C, D.** B is incorrect as this is the function of a router. See the section titled "Bridges" and the one titled "Routers."

12. **A.** Repeaters tend to be the cheapest of all four options. See the section titled "Repeaters."

13. **C.** Only routers use logical addresses. See the sections titled "Routing" and "Addressing."

14. **D.** Gateways are responsible for connecting dissimilar networking environments. See the section titled "Gateways."

15. **B.** There are two types of routers, static and dynamic. Static routers require human intervention. See the section titled "Routers."

16. **A.** Hubs operate at the Physical layer of the OSI model. See the section titled "Hubs."

17. **A.** Bridges operate at the Data Link layer of the OSI model. See the section titled "Bridges."

18. **A.** Routers operate a the the Network layer of the OSI model. See the section titled "Routing."

19. **C.** Gateways operate at many different layers of the OSI model. See the section titled "Gateways."

Suggested Readings and Resources

1. Derfler, Frank J., Jr. *Using Networks.* Que, 1998.
   - Chapter 10: Lan Portals

2. Ford, M. *Internetworking Technologies Handbook.* Macmillan Technical Publishing, 1997.

Chapter 7 targets the following objectives in the
Planning and Implementation sections of the
Networking Essentials exam:

Select the appropriate network and transport protocols for various token-ring and Ethernet networks. Protocols include DLC, AppleTalk, IPX, TCP/IP, NFS, and SMB.

▶ When devices communicate over the network, they
   must utilize some form of transport protocol or set
   of rules to move data from one device to another.
   This exam objective reflects the need for you to
   know the transport protocols that are used most
   often with Windows 95 and Windows NT.

Implement a NetBIOS naming scheme for all computers on a given network.

▶ Microsoft networking components rely on the
   capability to reference other machines on the network using NetBIOS names. This exam objective
   makes it clear that you must have the ability to deal
   with NetBIOS naming rules for computers.

CHAPTER 7

Transport Protocols

▶ This chapter presents two important exam topics. The first topic is concerned with different protocols, or sets of rules, used in networking. The second objective focuses on NetBIOS names and naming conventions used by Microsoft's networked operating systems.

▶ To give a full account of the first exam topic, many different protocols are presented. In preparing for the exam, pay particular attention to the features and functions of each of the six protocols listed. But also be aware of what the other protocols accomplish to ensure you do not confuse one protocol with another.

▶ With the second exam topic on NetBIOS names, be aware of what characters are not allowed, and what general naming conventions are followed.

INTRODUCTION

In Chapter 2, "Networking Standards," you learned that the design of network protocols is usually done in pieces, with each piece solving a small part of the overall problem. By convention, these protocols are regarded as layers of an overall set of protocols, called a *protocol suite* or a *protocol stack*. A protocol stack often covers the entire OSI reference model.

As Chapter 2 describes, the *OSI reference model* is a standard describing the activities at each level of a protocol stack. The OSI reference model is useful as a conceptual tool for understanding protocol layering. Chapters 3 through 6 have built upon the OSI reference model from the bottom up. This chapter discusses in detail the components that operate at the Network layer through the Application layer.

This chapter examines a variety of actual transport protocols and protocol suites, such as TCP/IP and IPX/SPX. Although some protocol stacks have been designed in strict conformance with the OSI reference model, full OSI compliance is not usually the norm. Many of these protocol stacks have their origins in the days before the OSI model, and thus can be matched only loosely to the seven-layer OSI model. The main use of the OSI reference model is as a conceptual framework for understanding network communication and comparing various types of protocols.

This chapter begins by reviewing and placing into context the information learned from the previous chapters. The analysis begins with an examination of packets and protocols, as well as protocols and their reference back to the OSI model. From that point, the transport protocols of TCP/IP, IPX/SPX, NetBEUI, AppleTalk, and DLC are examined. When analyzing these transport protocols, issues such as addressing, routing mechanisms, and services are addressed. The chapter continues by examining NetBIOS naming schemes that are used in Microsoft networks. From there, networking as a whole is applied to the Windows NT model.

PACKETS AND PROTOCOLS

Before investigating protocols and protocol stacks, take a moment to quickly review some of the protocol-related issues discussed in previous chapters.

The purpose of a network is to exchange information among computers, and protocols are the rules by which computers communicate. Computers, like humans, can adopt any number of systems for passing messages, as long as the sending and receiving computers are using the same (or compatible) rules. Computers, therefore, must agree on common protocols before they can communicate. Failing to do so would create a bewildering situation similar to what you'd face if you read a book in Russian to a listener who speaks only Cherokee.

You can classify the many tasks that network protocols must oversee into a few basic categories. Think of these categories chronologically, as a series of steps (each step including a collection of related tasks) that must take place before the data can reach the transmission medium. These steps are the layers of a protocol stack, as described in Chapter 2. In one sense, the term *layer* is more than metaphorical. Each layer of the stack (the Application layer, the Presentation layer, and so on) adds a layer of information to the packet; the corresponding layer of the receiving computer needs to process the incoming packet.

The purpose of the layering structure is to enable vendors to adapt to specific hardware and software components without having to recreate the entire protocol stack.

Protocols describe the way in which network data is encapsulated in packets on the source end, sent via the network to a destination, and then reconstructed at the destination into the appropriate file, instruction, or request. Breaking network data into packet-sized chunks provides smoother throughput because the small packets don't tie up the transmission medium as a larger unit of data might. Also, packets simplify the task of error detection and correction. Each file is checked separately for errors, and if an error is discovered, only that packet (rather than a whole file) must be retransmitted.

The exact composition of a network packet depends on the protocols you're using. In general, network packets contain the following:

NOTE

Standards and Protocols The NDIS and ODI standards greatly simplify the task of finding common protocols. NDIS and ODI (described in Chapter 2) enable several transport protocols to operate simultaneously through the same network adapter card.

◆ *Header.* The header signifies the start of the packet and contains a bundle of important parameters, such as the source and destination address and time/synchronization information.

◆ *Data.* This portion of the packet contains the original data being transmitted.

◆ *Trailer.* The trailer marks the end of the packet and typically contains error-checking (Cyclical Redundancy Check, or CRC) information.

As the data passes down through the protocol layers, each layer performs its prescribed function, such as interfacing with an application, converting the data format, or adding addressing and error-checking parameters. (Chapter 2 examines the functions of the OSI protocol layers.) As you learn in this chapter, actual working protocol stacks don't always comply exactly with the OSI model—some, in fact, predate the OSI model—but the concepts and terminology of the OSI model are nevertheless useful for describing protocol functions.

When the packet reaches the transmission medium, the network adapter cards of other computers on the network segment examine the packet, checking the packet's destination address. If the destination address matches the PC's address, the network adapter interrupts the processor, and the protocol layers of the destination PC process the incoming packet (see Figure 7.1).

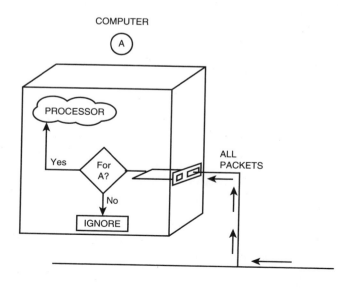

FIGURE 7.1

The network adapter card checks whether the destination address matches the PC's address.

PROTOCOLS AND PROTOCOL LAYERS

Many of the addressing, error-checking, retransmission, and acknowledgment services most commonly associated with networking take place at the Network and Transport OSI layers. (Refer to Chapter 2.) Protocol suites are often referred to by the suite's main Transport and Network protocols. In TCP/IP, for instance, TCP is a Transport layer protocol and IP is a Network layer protocol. (Note, however, that TCP/IP predates OSI and diverges from OSI in a number of ways.) IPX/SPX is another protocol suite known by its Transport and Network layer protocols, but the order of the protocols is backward from the way the protocols are listed in TCP/IP. IPX is the Network and Transport layer protocol; SPX is the Transport layer protocol.

The lower Data Link and Physical layers of the OSI model provide a hardware-specific foundation, addressing items such as the network adapter driver, the media access method, and the transmission medium. Transport and Network layer protocols such as TCP/IP and IPX/SPX rest on that Physical and Data Link layer foundation, and, with the help of the NDIS and ODI standards, multiple protocol stacks can operate simultaneously through a single network adapter. (Refer to the discussion of NDIS and ODI in Chapter 2.)

Upper-level protocols, those from the Network layer and higher, allow for the connection of services and the services themselves. This can imply routing programs, addressing schemes, and File and Print services.

This chapter describes the common protocol suites and many of the important protocols associated with them. In addition to TCP/IP and IPX/SPX, some of the common Transport and Network layer protocols are the following:

◆ *NWLink.* Microsoft's version of the IPX/SPX protocol essentially spans the Transport and Network layers.

◆ *NetBEUI.* Designed for Microsoft networks, NetBEUI includes functions at the Network and Transport layers. NetBEUI isn't routable and therefore doesn't make full use of Network layer capabilities.

◆ *AppleTalk Transaction Protocol (ATP)* and *Name Binding Protocol (NBP).* ATP and NBP are AppleTalk Transport layer protocols.

◆ *Data Link Control (DLC).* This is used to connect to IBM Mainframes and Hewlett-Packard JetDirect printers.

TCP/IP—Internet Protocols

Select the appropriate network and transport protocols for various token-ring and ethernet networks. Protocols include the following: DLC, AppleTalk, IPX, TCP/IP, NFS, and SMB.

The TCP/IP protocol suite (also commonly called the Internet protocol suite) was originally developed by the United States Department of Defense (DoD) to provide robust service on large internetworks that incorporate a variety of computer types. Part of the main purpose of this protocol was for it to be hardware-independent. In some literature, the TCP/IP protocol suite is referred to as the DoD model. In recent years, the Internet protocols constitute the most popular network protocols currently in use.

One reason for the popularity of TCP/IP is that no one vendor owns it, unlike the IPX/SPX, DNA, SNA, or AppleTalk protocol suites, all of which are controlled by specific companies. TCP/IP evolved in response to input from a wide variety of industry sources. Consequently, TCP/IP is the most open of the protocol suites and is supported by the widest variety of vendors. Virtually every brand of computing equipment now supports TCP/IP. This has lead to some problems, though. Because TCP/IP is an open standard, sometimes one vendor's implementation of TCP/IP does not work with another's implementation.

Much of the popularity of the TCP/IP protocols comes from their early availability on UNIX. The protocols were built into the Berkeley Standard Distribution (BSD) UNIX implementation. Since then, TCP/IP has achieved universal acceptance in the UNIX community and is a standard feature on all versions of UNIX.

Figure 7.2 illustrates the relationship of the protocols in the Internet suite to the layers of the OSI reference model. Notice that the suite doesn't include protocols for the Data Link or Physical layers. TCP/IP was designed to be hardware-independent and thus is able to work over established standards such as ethernet, token-ring, and ARCnet, to name but a few lower OSI layer standards. Over time, TCP/IP has been interfaced to the majority of Data Link and Physical layer technologies.

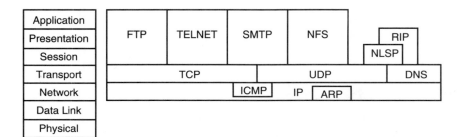

FIGURE 7.2
TCP/IP or the "Internet Protocol Suite."

The Internet protocols do not map cleanly to the OSI reference model. The DoD model was, after all, developed long before the OSI model was defined. The model for the Internet protocol suite has four layers (refer to Figure 7.2). From this model, you can see the approximate relationships of the layers. The DoD model's layers function as follows (see Figure 7.3).

◆ The *Network Access* layer corresponds to the bottom two layers of the OSI model. This correspondence enables the DoD protocols to coexist with existing Data Link and Physical layer standards.

◆ The *Internet* layer corresponds roughly to the OSI Network layer. Protocols at this layer move data between devices on networks.

◆ The *Host-to-Host* layer can be compared to the OSI Transport layer. Host-to-Host protocols enable peer communication between hosts on the internetwork. (At the time these protocols were designed, personal computers and workstations didn't exist, and all network computers were host computers. As a result, devices on TCP/IP networks are typically referred to as hosts. The concept of a client/server relationship didn't exist, and all communicating hosts were assumed to be peers.)

◆ The *Process/Application* layer embraces functions of the OSI Session, Presentation, and Application layers. Protocols at this layer provide network services.

One huge advantage of using TCP/IP is that TCP/IP is required for communication over the Internet; thus the Internet can be used as a communication backbone. One disadvantage is that the size of the protocol stack makes TCP/IP difficult to implement on some older machines. (Present-day PC models should have no problem running TCP/IP.) TCP/IP has traditionally been considered slower than other

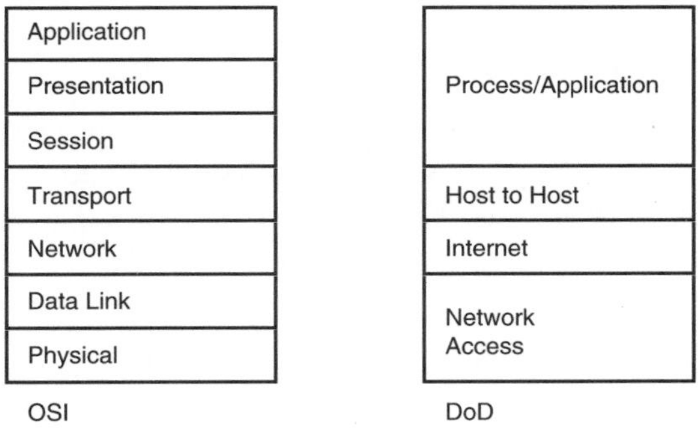

Application
Presentation
Session
Transport
Network
Data Link
Physical

OSI

Process/Application
Host to Host
Internet
Network Access

DoD

FIGURE 7.3
A comparison of the TCP/IP layers to the OSI model.

protocol stacks, because data must be analyzed up to the Network layer of the OSI model to be evaluated. But again, the power of the newer machines overcomes much of this difficulty.

A large number of protocols are associated with TCP/IP. These different protocols are grouped into the following unofficial categories:

◆ General TCP/IP Transport Protocols

◆ TCP/IP Services

◆ TCP/IP Routing

Several of these are discussed briefly in the following sections. TCP/IP is a complex topic, the scope of which runs beyond this book and the Networking Essentials exam. Microsoft has a full certification exam on their version of TCP/IP. The "Suggested Readings and Resources" section at the end of this chapter suggests several good sources on this topic and TCP/IP in general.

General TCP/IP Transport Protocols

This subsection covers general protocols dealing with the addressing and transportation of packets across the LAN using TCP/IP. All services and routing issues that fall into the TCP/IP protocol stack use one or more of these Network or Transport layer protocols.

Addressing in TCP/IP

One of the first aspects of transport protocols that needs to be discussed is how the protocols address entities on the network. As discussed several times previously in this book, there are two main forms of addresses: a node address and a logical network address. A node address is the address of the entity or device on the network, whereas the logical network address is the segment on the network to which the node is attached.

TCP/IP uses a unique numbering scheme that encapsulates the network and node address into a set of numbers. This number is what is known as an IP address. All devices on a network that runs the TCP/IP protocol suite need a unique IP address.

An IP address is a set of four numbers, or octets, that can range in value between 0 and 255. Each octet is separated by a period. Some examples are shown here:

◆ 34.120.66.79

◆ 200.200.20.2

◆ 2.5.67.123

◆ 107.219.2.34

These addresses are actually broken down into three distinct classes. These are known as class A, class B, and class C addresses.

Class A IP addresses contain a number between 1 and 127 before the first dot. Some examples are 3.3.6.8, 102.100.77.8, and 23.23.45.67. In a class A address, this first octet represents the network address, and the last three octets represent the node or host number. Hence an IP address of 69.23.104.200 would represent host number 23.104.200 on network 69.

Class B and C addresses follow a similar principal to that exemplified in the class A addresses. In the case of a class B address, the first octet can range in value from 128 to 191, but it is the first two octets that make up the network address, and the last two octets that make up the host ID. In the case of a class C address, the first octet can range in value from 192 to 223, and the first three octets make up the host ID.

There are class D and E addresses as well. For these addresses, the first octet is a number greater than 223. These addresses are not currently available to be used and are reserved for other purposes.

In summary, the differences in the classes of the IP addresses reside in which numbers are to be used in the first octet, which octets represent the Network ID, and which numbers represent the host ID.

Table 7.1 shows three examples, one from each class of address.

TABLE 7.1

CLASSES AND ADDRESSES

Class	IP Address	Network ID	Host ID
Class A	102.44.7.100	102.0.0.0	X.44.7.10
Class B	131.107.4.6	131.107.0.0	X.X.4.6
Class C	200.9.88.250	200.9.88.0	X.X.X.250

The topic of TCP/IP addressing goes well beyond the scope of the information covered in this book. As noted above, it is covered in more detail in books and courses that focus on TCP/IP.

One last thing to be aware of when discussing IP addresses is the fact that every device on the network—that is, every computer, printer, router, or any other device that can be specifically attached—needs a unique IP address. In other words, everything needs an IP address and no two IP addresses can be the same in a given network. If they were, you would end up with two devices on the network that have the same network and host ID.

Internet Protocol (IP)

The Internet Protocol (IP) is a connectionless protocol that provides datagram service, and IP packets are most commonly referred to as IP datagrams. IP is a packet-switching protocol that performs the addressing and route selection. An IP header is appended to packets, which are transmitted as frames by lower-level protocols. IP routes packets through internetworks by utilizing routing tables that are referenced at each hop. Routing determinations are made by consulting logical and physical network device information, as provided by the Address Resolution Protocol (ARP).

IP performs packet disassembly and reassembly as required by packet size limitations defined for the Data Link and Physical layers being implemented. IP also performs error checking on the header data using a checksum, although data from upper layers is not error-checked.

Transmission Control Protocol (TCP)

The Transmission Control Protocol (TCP) is an internetwork connection-oriented protocol that corresponds to the OSI Transport layer. TCP provides full-duplex, end-to-end connections. When the overhead of end-to-end communication acknowledgment isn't required, the User Datagram Protocol (UDP) can be substituted for TCP at the Transport (host-to-host) level. TCP and UDP operate at the same layer.

TCP corresponds to SPX in the NetWare environment (see the "NetWare IPX/SPX" section). TCP maintains a logical connection between the sending and receiving computer systems. In this way, the integrity of the transmission is maintained. TCP detects any problems in the transmission quickly and takes action to correct them. The trade-off is that TCP isn't as fast as UDP, due to the number of acknowledgments received by the sending host.

TCP also provides and assumes message fragmentation and reassembly and can accept messages of any length from upper-layer protocols. TCP fragments message streams into segments that can be handled by IP. This process enables the application being used to not break up the data into smaller blocks. IP still can perform fragmentation for UDP packets and further fragmentation for TCP packets. When used with IP, TCP adds connection-oriented service and performs segment synchronization, adding sequence numbers at the byte level.

In addition to message fragmentation, TCP can multiplex conversations with upper-layer protocols and can improve use of network bandwidth by combining multiple messages into the same segment. Each virtual-circuit connection is assigned a connection identifier called a port, which identifies the datagrams associated with that connection.

User Datagram Protocol (UDP)

The User Datagram Protocol (UDP) is a connectionless Transport (host-to-host) layer protocol. UDP does not provide message acknowledgments; rather, it simply transports datagrams.

Like TCP, UDP utilizes port addresses to deliver datagrams. These port addresses, however, aren't associated with virtual circuits and merely identify local host processes. UDP is preferred over TCP when high performance or low network overhead is more critical than reliable delivery. Because UDP doesn't need to establish, maintain, and close connections, or control data flow, it generally outperforms TCP. The downfall in UDP is that it does not perform as reliably as TCP when transmitting data; thus, UDP is often used when transmitting smaller amounts of data.

UDP is the Transport layer protocol used with the Simple Network Management Protocol (SNMP), the standard network management protocol used with TCP/IP networks. UDP enables SNMP to provide network management with a minimum of network overhead.

Address Resolution Protocol (ARP)

Three types of address information are used on TCP/IP internetworks:

◆ *Physical addresses.* Used by the Data Link and Physical layers.

◆ *IP addresses.* Provide logical network and host IDs. IP addresses consist of four numbers typically expressed in dotted-decimal form.

◆ *Logical node names.* Identify specific hosts with alphanumeric identifiers, which are easier for users to recall than the numeric IP addresses. An example of a logical node name is MYHOST.COM.

Given an IP address, the Address Resolution Protocol (ARP) can determine the physical address used by the device containing the IP address. ARP maintains tables of address resolution data and can broadcast packets to discover addresses on the network segment or use previously cached entries. The physical addresses discovered by ARP can be provided to Data Link layer protocols. All addresses in the ARP table are only local addresses. Any non-local address contains the hardware address of the local port on the router that is used to access that non-local segment.

Internet Control Message Protocol (ICMP)

The Internet Control Message Protocol (ICMP) enhances the error control provided by IP. Connectionless protocols, such as IP, cannot detect internetwork errors, such as congestion or path failures. ICMP can detect such errors and notify IP and upper-layer protocols. A network card that is generating an error often delivers a message to other network cards, via an ICMP packet.

TCP/IP Services

This section focuses on some of the TCP/IP services that exist within the TCP/IP protocol suite. These services are just some of the more common ones that you would deal with on a Microsoft network.

Dynamic Host Configuration Protocol (DHCP)

When dealing with IP addressing, it can be very management-intensive to manually assign IP addresses and subnet masks to every computer on the network. The Dynamic Host Configuration Protocol (DHCP) enables automatic assignment of IP addresses. This is usually performed by one or more computers (DHCP Servers) that assigns IP addresses and subnet masks, along with other configuration information, to a computer as it initializes on the network.

Most routers are configured not to forward broadcasts. DHCP, however, exchanges information by issuing broadcasts. A DHCP server, therefore, needs to be on each segment. An alternative to placing a DHCP server on each segment is to have a DHCP relay agent that forwards on the client's broadcast request for an IP address to a DHCP server on another segment.

Domain Name System (DNS)

The Domain Name System (DNS) protocol provides host name and IP address resolution as a service to client applications. DNS servers enable humans to use logical node names, utilizing a fully qualified domain name structure, to access network resources. Host names can be up to 260 characters long.

Windows Internet Naming Services (WINS)

Windows Internet Naming Service (WINS) provides a function similar to that of DNS, with the exception that it provides NetBIOS names to IP address resolution. This is important, because all of Microsoft's networking requires the ability to reference NetBIOS names. Normally NetBIOS names are obtained with the issuance of broadcasts, but because routers normally do not forward broadcasts, a WINS server is one alternative that can be used to issue IP addresses to NetBIOS name requests.

File Transfer Protocol (FTP)

The File Transfer Protocol (FTP) is a protocol for sharing files between networked hosts. FTP enables users to log on to remote hosts. Logged-on users can inspect directories, manipulate files, execute commands, and perform other commands on the host. FTP also has the capability of transferring files between dissimilar hosts by supporting a file request structure that is independent of specific operating systems.

Simple Mail Transfer Protocol (SMTP)

The Simple Mail Transfer Protocol (SMTP) is a protocol for routing mail through internetworks. SMTP uses the TCP and IP protocols.

SNMP doesn't provide a mail interface for the user. Creation, management, and delivery of messages to end users must be performed by an email application.

Remote Terminal Emulation (TELNET)

TELNET is a terminal emulation protocol. TELNET enables PCs and workstations to function as dumb terminals in sessions with hosts on internetworks. TELNET implementations are available for most end-user platforms, including UNIX (of course), DOS, Windows, and Macintosh OS.

Network File System (NFS)

Network File System (NFS), developed by Sun Microsystems, is a family of file-access protocols that are a considerable advancement over FTP and TELNET. Because Sun made the NFS specifications available for public use, NFS has achieved a high level of popularity.

NFS consists of two protocols:

◆ *eXternal Data Representation (XDR)*. Supports encoding of data in a machine-independent format. C programmers use XDR library routines to describe data structures that are portable between machine environments.

◆ *Remote Procedure Call (RPC)*. Functions as a service request redirector that determines whether function calls can be satisfied locally or must be redirected to a remote host. Calls to remote hosts are packaged for network delivery and transmitted to RPC servers, which generally have the capability of servicing many remote service requests. RPC servers process the service requests and generate response packets that are returned to the service requester.

TCP/IP Routing Protocols

The following sections describe two of the most common routing protocols used by TCP/IP.

Routing Information Protocol (RIP)

The Routing Information Protocol (RIP) in the TCP/IP suite is not the same protocol as RIP in the NetWare suite, although the two serve similar functions. Internet RIP performs route discovery by using a distance-vector method, calculating the number of hops that must be crossed to route a packet by a particular path.

Although it works well in localized networks, RIP presents many weaknesses that limit its utility on wide-area internetworks. RIP's distance-vector route discovery method, for example, requires more broadcasts and thus causes more network traffic than some other methods. The entire route table is also sent out on the broadcast, causing large amounts of traffic as route tables become large. The Open Shortest Path First (OSPF) protocol, which uses the link-state route discovery method, is gradually replacing RIP. (See Chapter 6, "Connectivity Devices and Transfer Mechanisms," for more on routing.)

Open Shortest Path First (OSPF)

The Open Shortest Path First (OSPF) protocol is a link-state route-discovery protocol that is designed to overcome the limitations of RIP. On large internetworks, OSPF can identify the internetwork topology and improve performance by implementing load balancing and class-of-service routing.

NetWare IPX/SPX

The protocols utilized with NetWare are summarized in Figure 7.4. The NetWare protocols have been designed with a high degree of modularity. This modularity makes the NetWare protocols adaptable to different hardware and simplifies the task of incorporating other protocols into the suite. Windows NT doesn't use the IPX/SPX suite to communicate with NetWare resources. Microsoft instead developed a clone of IPX/SPX called NWLink—IPX/SPX Compatible Transport. IPX/SPX is generally smaller and faster than TCP/IP and, like TCP/IP, it is routable. However, it operates down to the Data Link layer of the OSI model so it is more dependent upon hardware devices than the TCP/IP protocol.

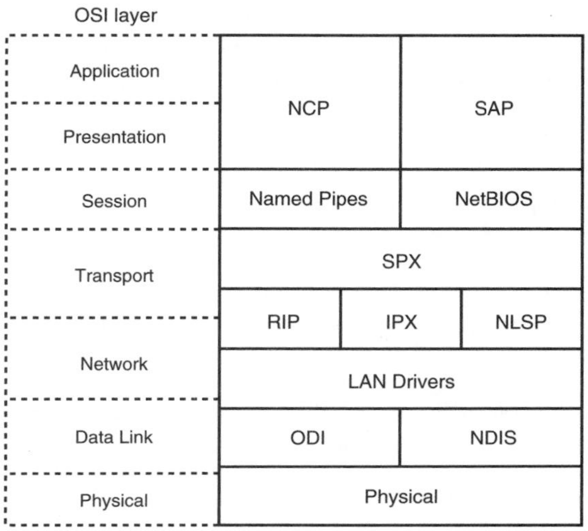

OSI layer

Application / Presentation	NCP	SAP
Session	Named Pipes	NetBIOS
Transport	SPX	SPX
Network	RIP / IPX / NLSP	LAN Drivers
Data Link	ODI	NDIS
Physical	Physical	Physical

FIGURE 7.4
The NetWare protocol architecture.

General IPX/SPX Transport Protocols

The following subsections deal with protocols in the IPX/SPX protocol suite that relate back to the Network and Transport layers of the OSI model.

Addressing in IPX

Addressing in IPX/SPX (NWLink) is much simpler than that in TCP/IP. IPX/SPX also has two distinct addresses: a host address and a network address. Unlike TCP/IP, the host address, or ID, is often something that is not configured by the administrator.

The host address in IPX/SPX is based on the hardware address of the network adapter card used by the device attaching to the network. These addresses are hexadecimal in nature, and address ranges used by network adapter cards are assigned by the IEEE. Usually the first two to three sets of numbers indicate the manufacturer of the network adapter card.

Two examples of these addresses are:

44-45-53-54-00-00

07-00-4d-55-64-3e

As for the network address, this logical address is assigned by the administrator of the cable segment. Usually when a server or router is installed, the logical network address is assigned by the administrator (see Exercise 7.2 for an example). The logical network address is an eight-character hexadecimal address. Some possible examples include:

903E0467

BEEF0000

E8012000

Again, any set of hexadecimal values is acceptable, but each network address must be unique on the internetwork.

In general, addresses in an IPX/SPX network are often represented as Host address : Network Address, as seen below:

55-66-00-e4-7a : E8022000

This address represents Host 55-66-00-e4-7a on Network E8022000.

IPX

The *Internetwork Packet Exchange Protocol (IPX)* is a Network layer protocol that provides connectionless (datagram) service. (IPX was developed from the XNS protocol originated by Xerox.) As a Network layer protocol, IPX is responsible for internetwork routing and for maintaining network logical addresses. Routing uses the RIP protocol (described later in this section) to make route selections. IPX provides similar functionality as UDP does in the TCP/IP protocol suite.

IPX relies on hardware physical addresses found at lower layers to provide network device addressing. IPX also uses *sockets*, or upper-layer service addresses, to deliver packets to their ultimate destinations. On the client, IPX support is provided as a component of the older DOS shell and the current DOS NetWare requester. Windows 3.1 utilizes the DOS shell client, whereas Windows 95 and Windows NT supports IPX if you install a Novell-supplied client. Microsoft-supplied clients use the NWLink transport protocol supplied by Microsoft.

SPX

Sequenced Packet Exchange (SPX) is a Transport layer protocol that extends IPX to provide connection-oriented service with reliable delivery. Reliable delivery is ensured by the retransmittal of packets in the event of an error. SPX is derived from a similar SPX protocol in the XNS network protocol suite.

SPX establishes virtual circuits called *connections*. The connection ID for each connection appears in the SPX header. A given upper-layer process can be associated with multiple-connection IDs.

SPX is used in situations where reliable transmission of data is needed. SPX sequences the packets of data. Missing packets or packets that don't arrive in the order in which they were sent are detected immediately. In addition, SPX offers connection multiplexing, which is used in the printing environment. Many accounting programs, for example, call upon the services of SPX to ensure that data is sent accurately. On the client, SPX support is provided as a component of the older DOS shell and of the current NetWare requester. SPX provides functionality similar to that of TCP in the TCP/IP protocol suite.

As a network administrator, you do not often get to pick whether you wish to use IPX or SPX. It is often the applications one uses that are preprogrammed to use one or the other. For example, in most Novell networks, all file transfers are done using IPX. In the case of printing, SPX is the protocol used.

Frame Type

When dealing with the IPX/SPX protocol suite, frame type is an important issue. Frame type deals with the issue of how the data is read by the adapter card. As you have seen in earlier chapters, data is transmitted in digital format within a computer, and the network card converts this digital information into a signal. This signal not only contains the data being transferred, but also headers of information being used by all the protocols in the OSI seven layers. When this data arrives at its destination, it gets converted from a signal back into a recognizable format understood by the computer.

Frame type has to do with interpreting the bits of data as they come in. As you will see in the following five sections, each of the five frame types orders the information in the data differently than the other frame types. Two computers not running the same frame type cannot communicate.

When installing the IPX/SPX (or Microsoft's NWLink) protocol on a system, the frame type will either be automatically detected or must be manually assigned. Most modern computers can run multiple frame types at once.

The frame types to be discussed below include:

◆ 802.2

◆ 802.3

◆ Ethernet II

◆ Ethernet_SNAP

◆ Token-Ring

◆ Token-Ring_SNAP

802.2

The 802.2 frame type is the default frame type used on ethernet networks by all NetWare versions from 3.12 and onwards. What this means is that this is the frame type these networking products use by default. Figure 7.5 shows an initial breakdown of an 802.2 packet.

802.3

This was the default frame type used in all Novell NetWare products from 3.11 and earlier. Figure 7.6 shows a breakdown of an 802.3 packet. The 802.3 packet is the same as an 802.2 packet, except that the 802.3 packet does not contain the Destination Service Access Point, Source Service Access Point, or Control bits.

Ethernet II

Ethernet II frame types are similar to 802.3 frame types, except they contain a type field rather than a length field (see Figure 7.7). This frame type can also be used with TCP/IP and AppleTalk.

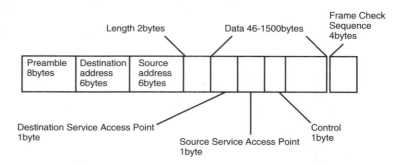

FIGURE 7.5
An 802.2 frame type packet.

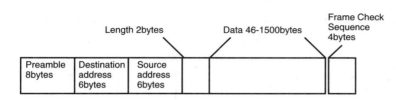

FIGURE 7.6
An 802.3 frame type packet.

FIGURE 7.7
An Ethernet II frame type packet.

Ethernet_SNAP

Ethernet_SNAP can be used for TCP/IP and AppleTalk Phase II
transport protocols, as well as IPX/SPX (see Figure 7.8).

Token-Ring

Token-ring frames are of two types. One is used to carry management information; the other is used to transfer data. Token-ring
frames are used on token-ring networks, and not ethernet networks.

Token-Ring_SNAP

A variation of the token-ring frame type is called token-ring_SNAP.
The token-ring_SNAP provides a function similar to that of the eth-
ernet_SNAP frame type, but for token-ring networks.

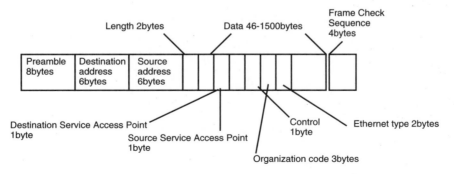

FIGURE 7.8
An Ethernet_SNAP frame type packet.

IPX/SPX Services

IPX/SPX services are similar to those used by TCP/IP in that they provide a service to the user rather than being solely concerned with transport issues. These services presented usually require the use of either IPX or SPX as their transport mechanism, although recently the capability to port these services over to TCP/IP has been included. Two services are briefly discussed in the following subsections. These are SAP and NCP.

Service Advertising Protocol (SAP)

With *Service Advertising Protocol (SAP),* a device provides location information by indicating what services it is offering. Devices can see each other on the network by listing the SAPs each server issues. In the case of NetWare, by default a SAP is issued every minute, telling other computers what service the server is offering, as well as on which node on what network this server is located.

NetWare Core Protocol (NCP)

The *NetWare Core Protocol (NCP)* provides numerous function calls that support network services, such as file service, printing, name management, file locking, and synchronization. NetWare client software interfaces with NCP to access NetWare services. NCP is to NetWare networks as SMB is to Microsoft networks (see the section titled "Server Messaging Blocks" later in this chapter).

NCP is a high-level protocol built into the NetWare operating system kernel. NCP covers aspects of the Session, Presentation, and Application layers of the OSI reference model and has its own miniature language that programmers use when writing applications for the NetWare environment. The commands that NCP understands are associated primarily with access to files and directories on a file server.

IPX/SPX Routing

This section looks at some of the more common routing protocols that can be used in a network running IPX/SPX.

Router Information Protocol (RIP)

The *Router Information Protocol (RIP)* uses the distance vector route discover method to determine hop counts to other devices. Like

IPX, RIP was developed from a similar protocol in the XNS protocol suite. RIP is implemented as an upper-layer service and is assigned a socket (service address). RIP is based directly on IPX and performs Network layer functions.

NetWare Link Services Protocol (NLSP)

NetWare Link Services Protocol (NLSP) is a link-state routing protocol used by routers (NetWare servers with two or more adapter cards can act as routers) to advertise networks when their address tables change.

NetBEUI

NetBEUI is a transport protocol that serves as an extension to Microsoft's Network Basic Input/Output System (NetBIOS). Because NetBEUI was developed for an earlier generation of DOS-based PCs, it is small, easy to implement, and fast. It is actually the fastest transport protocol available with Windows NT. Because it was built for small, isolated LANs, however, NetBEUI is non-routable, making it somewhat anachronistic in today's diverse and interconnected networking environment. NetBEUI is also a broadcast-based protocol and as such can cause congestion in larger networks.

Fortunately, the NDIS standard enables NetBEUI to coexist with other routable protocols. For instance, you could use NetBEUI for fast, efficient communications on the LAN segment and use TCP/IP for transmissions that require routing (see Exercise 7.2).

AppleTalk

AppleTalk is the computing architecture developed by Apple Computer for the Macintosh family of personal computers. Although AppleTalk originally supported only Apple's proprietary LocalTalk cabling system, the suite has been expanded to incorporate both ethernet and token-ring Physical layers. Within Microsoft operating systems, AppleTalk is only supported by Windows NT Server. Windows NT Workstation and Windows 95 do not support AppleTalk. AppleTalk cannot be used for Microsoft-to-Microsoft operating system communication. It can be used only through Windows NT servers supporting Apple clients.

AppleTalk originally supported networks of limited scope. The *AppleTalk Phase II* specification issued in 1989, however, extended the scope of AppleTalk to enterprise networks. The Phase II specification also enabled AppleTalk to coexist on networks with other protocol suites. Figure 7.9 presents a layered perspective of the AppleTalk protocols.

The LocalTalk, EtherTalk, and TokenTalk Link Access Protocols (LLAP, ELAP, and TLAP) integrate AppleTalk upper-layer protocols with the LocalTalk, ethernet, and token-ring environments.

Apple's *Datagram Deliver Protocol (DDP)* is a Network layer protocol that provides connectionless service between two sockets. A *socket* is the AppleTalk term for a service address. A combination of a device address, network address, and socket uniquely identifies each process.

DDP performs network routing and consults routing tables maintained by Routing Table Maintenance Protocol (RTMP) to determine routing. Packet delivery is performed by the data link protocol operating on a given destination network.

The *AppleTalk Transaction Protocol (ATP)* is a connectionless Transport layer protocol. Reliable service is provided through a system of acknowledgments and retransmissions. Retransmissions are initiated automatically if an acknowledgment is not received within a specified time interval. ATP reliability is based on transactions. A transaction consists of a request followed by a reply. ATP is responsible for segment development and performs fragmentation and reassembly of packets that exceed the specifications for lower-layer protocols. Packets include sequence numbers that enable message reassembly and retransmission of lost packets. Only damaged or lost packets are retransmitted.

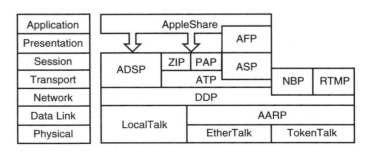

FIGURE 7.9
The AppleTalk protocol suite.

The *AppleTalk File Protocol (AFP)* provides file services and is responsible for translating local file service requests into formats required for network file services. AFP directly translates command syntax and enables applications to perform file format translations. AFP is responsible for file system security, and verifies and encrypts logon names and passwords during connection setup.

AppleShare is a client/server system for Macintosh. AppleShare provides three primary application services:

◆ The *AppleShare File Server* uses AFP to enable users to store and access files on the network. It logs in users and associates them with network volumes and directories.

◆ The *AppleShare Print Server* uses NBP and PAP to support network printing. NBP provides name and address information that enables PAP to connect to printers. The AppleShare Print Server performs print spooling and manages printing on networked printers.

◆ The *AppleShare PC* enables PCs running MS-DOS to access AppleShare services by running an AppleShare PC program.

Data Link Control (DLC)

The Data Link Control (DLC) protocol does not provide a fully-functioning protocol stack. In Windows NT systems, DLC is used primarily to access Hewlett-Packard JetDirect network-interface printers. DLC also provides some connectivity with IBM mainframes and for the Windows NT remoteboot service used by Diskless Windows 95 workstations. DLC is not a protocol that can be used to connect Windows NT or 95 computers together.

RELATING PROTOCOL STACKS TOGETHER

Discussing protocol stacks can be a very daunting exercise because many different protocols exist at every layer in the OSI model and make up the entire stack.

As was described during the discussion of TCP/IP, IPX/SPX, and NetBEUI, these protocol stacks are separated into three areas (except for NetBEUI). These areas are:

◆ Transport protocols

◆ Services offered

◆ Routing protocols

The transport protocols are the rules or standards used by the protocol stack to facilitate the movement of data between different devices. The services offered are some of the unique network services offered by each protocol stack. The routing protocols are designed to enable dynamic routing. The actual address format is based upon either TCP/IP (four octets of numbers) or IPX/SPX (network address was eight-character hexadecimal).

The interesting aspect of protocol stacks is the services they offer. Take TCP/IP for example. TCP/IP was developed to connect dissimilar machines together, and to provide services that could be used by these interconnected machines.

Another example would be that of FTP. This service was developed to transfer files from one machine to another. Thus an FTP client and an FTP server service were developed. The specification between these two programs was made public. If you programmed your FTP client to the open standards, it would interoperate with the FTP service that was also programmed to the open standards. Both the client and the service were designed to only "hook into" or operate with the TCP and IP Transport and Network layers of the protocol stack. That is, the FTP client or service is not programmed to operate with the NetBEUI transport protocol, for example.

The same analogy can be applied to NCP. NCP packets are designed to communicate with a NetWare server. Novell developed the NCP standard, and this standard is designed to operate only with IPX; thus communication to a Novell NetWare server cannot be done over NetBEUI or TCP/IP, because the NCP protocol is not designed to interoperate with these transport protocols.

NOTE

NetWare and TCP/IP   Add-ons to NetWare enable it to utilize TCP/IP, and the new NetWare version 5 is also being designed to use TCP/IP.

Server Messaging Blocks (SMB)

One protocol that is slightly independent is Microsoft's Server Messaging Blocks (SMB). SMB's are Microsoft's equivalent to NCP packets. Like NCP packets, SMB's operate at the Application layer of the OSI model.

SMBs enable machines on a Microsoft network to communicate with one another. Through the use of SMBs, File and Print services can be shared. SMBs can use TCP/IP, NWLink (IPX/SPX), or NetBEUI, because SMBs utilize a NetBIOS interface when communicating. For more information on NetBIOS names, see the following section.

NETBIOS NAMES

Implement a NetBIOS naming scheme for all computers on a given network.

NetBIOS is an interface that provides NetBIOS-based applications with access to network resources. Every computer on a Windows NT network must have a unique name for it to be accessible through the NetBIOS interface. This unique name is called a computer name or a NetBIOS name.

NetBIOS Background

NetBIOS (Network Basic Input/Output System) is an application interface that provides PC-based applications with uniform access to lower protocol layers. NetBIOS was once most closely associated with the NetBEUI protocol—*NetBEUI*, in fact, is an abbreviation for NetBIOS Extended User Interface. In recent years, however, other vendors have recognized the importance of providing compatibility with PC-based applications through NetBIOS, and NetBIOS is now available with many protocol configurations. For instance, such terms as "NetBIOS over IPX" or "NetBIOS over TCP/IP" refer to the protocols used with NetBIOS.

All of Microsoft's networking architecture references NetBIOS names, thus it can be said that Microsoft Networking uses a NetBIOS interface to access components on the network.

Assigning NetBIOS Names

On a NetBIOS network, every computer must have a unique name. The computer name must be 15 characters long or fewer. A

NetBIOS name can include alphanumeric characters and any of the following special characters:

!@#$%^&()-_'{}.~

Note that you cannot use an asterisk or all periods in a NetBIOS name. It is also not recommended to use spaces in NetBIOS names as well, as some applications are not able to work with a space in a NetBIOS name. Also, NetBIOS names are not case-sensitive.

Within these character limitations, you can choose any name for a PC. The rule of thumb is to choose a name that helps you to identify the computer. Names such as PC1, PC2, and PC3 are difficult to visualize and easy to confuse. Likewise, names such as MYPC or WORTHLESSPC could confuse you in the long run, especially if you have many computers on your network. For these reasons, names that include a hook relating the name of the owner or the location of the computer generally are more effective. Consider the following names, for example:

◆ BILLS_PC

◆ MARKETINGPC

◆ LUNCHROOM_PC

◆ BILLS_LAPTOP

You must specify a computer name for a Windows NT or Windows 95 computer at installation. The computer name then becomes part of the network configuration. In either Windows NT or Windows 95, you can change the name of the computer through the Control Panel Network application. (See the following Review Break and Step-by-Steps 7.1 and 7.2.)

R E V I E W   B R E A K

A NetBIOS computer name must:

◆ Be unique

◆ Consist of 15 or fewer characters

◆ Consist of either alphanumeric characters or the characters !@#$%^&()-_'{}.~

STEP BY STEP

7.1 Changing a Computer's Name in Windows NT

You designate a computer name for your PC when you install the operating system. You can change the computer name later through the Control Panel Network application, but you must have Administrative privileges on a Windows NT computer to change the computer name. Anyone can change the NetBIOS name on a Windows 95 computer. To change a NetBIOS computer name, follow these steps:

1. Click the Start button and choose Settings, Control Panel.

2. In Windows NT Control Panel, double-click the Network application.

3. In the Network application's Identification tab, click on the Change button. The subsequent Identification Changes dialog box is shown in Figure 7.10.

4. Change the computer name in the text box labeled Computer Name and click OK.

As with Windows NT, Windows 95 enables you to change the computer name after installation by using the Control Panel Network application. To change the name, follow these steps:

STEP BY STEP

7.2 Changing the Computer Name in Windows 95

1. Click the Start button and choose Settings, Control Panel.

2. In the Windows 95 Control Panel, double-click the Network application.

3. In the Network application, choose the Identification tab.

4. To change the computer name, edit the text in the Computer name text box (see Figure 7.11).

WARNING

Changing Names of Windows NT Computers in a Domain Changing the names of Windows NT computers that are in a domain can have serious consequences. Problems such as authentication not working and applications not functioning can occur. Consult an administrator before doing this.

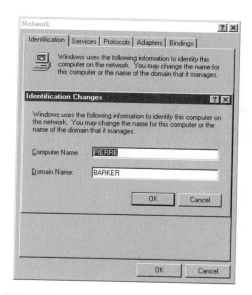

FIGURE 7.10

Windows NT's Identification Changes dialog box enables you to change the computer name.

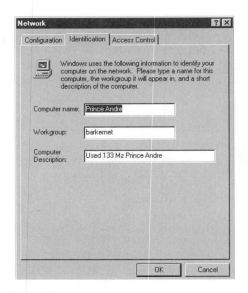

FIGURE 7.11
The Identification tab of the Windows 95 Network dialog box enables you to change the computer name.

A computer on a NetBIOS network must have a NetBIOS computer name. The NetBIOS name is configured at installation and, in Windows NT or Windows 95, can be changed later through the Control Panel Network application. Computers use the NetBIOS name (sometimes combined with a share name or a path name) to locate resources on the network.

Finding Resources on Microsoft Networks

The Universal Naming Convention is a standard for identifying resources on Microsoft networks. A UNC path consists of the following components:

◆ A NetBIOS computer name preceded with a double backslash (left-leaning slash)

◆ The share name of a shared resource located on the given PC (optional—see Chapter 10 for more details concerning shares)

◆ The MS-DOS–style path of a file or a directory located on the given share (optional)

Elements of the UNC path are separated with single backslashes. The following list details some legal UNC names:

```
\\BILL's_PC
\\WEIGHTRM\ACCOUNTS
\\PET_DEPT\CATS\SIAMESE.TXT
```

Various Windows NT commands use UNC paths to designate network resources. For instance,

```
net view \\PET_DEPT
```

enables you to view the shared resources on the computer with the NetBIOS name PET_DEPT. The command

```
net use G: \\PET_DEPT\CATS
```

maps the shared directory CATS on the computer PET_DEPT to drive G:.

CASE STUDY: SELECTING PROTOCOL STACKS

ESSENCE OF THE CASE

The essence of the case is as follows:

- Summarize the protocol stacks

- Address the benefits of the protocol stack

- Address the issues with the protocol stack

- Address the possibility of connecting to the Internet in the future

- Address the possibility of Novell servers in the future

SCENARIO

You have been invited into a network planning session. A new corporate-wide internetwork is being rolled out. The network will consist of Microsoft Windows NT Servers and Windows 95 workstations. The only service you are aware will be running on the internetwork is File and Print services. All computers need to be able to connect with all other computers on the internetwork, thus a routable protocol needs to be used. Possible future changes to the network include connection to the Internet or the addition of some Novell servers. You are to make a summary of which protocol stacks should be used on the network. Basically you are to recommend a type of protocol, describe why it should be implemented, and explain the benefits and any concerns about using this protocol.

ANALYSIS

Basically, five protocol stacks are supported by Windows NT Server and four by Windows 95. TCP/IP, NWLink (IPX/SPX), NetBEUI, and DLC are supported by both operating systems, and AppleTalk is supported by Windows NT Server.

If Novell servers are to be added to the internetwork in the future, NWLink should be used. If they will connect to the Internet, TCP/IP may need to be used.

The five protocols are analyzed in the following sections.

DLC

This protocol is not an option to connect the computers together. This protocol would only be added if there was to be some IBM mainframe connectivity or if there were some Hewlett-Packard JetDirect printers to be managed. Because neither of these options were specified, there is no reason to install this protocol on the machines.

AppleTalk

AppleTalk is only supported by Windows NT Server, and only for communications between Windows NT Server and Apple clients. Because this protocol cannot be used for communication between Microsoft machines, and no Apple computers are on the network, there is no reason to install this protocol stack.

continues

CASE STUDY: SELECTING PROTOCOL STACKS

continued

NetBEUI

NetBEUI is a protocol that is supported by all the Microsoft operating systems. It is a fast protocol that really requires no management to maintain. The only downfall is that NetBEUI is a non-routable protocol. An additional protocol would be needed for all LAN segments to intercommunicate. (As a side note, the networked game of Hearts cannot function unless the NetBEUI protocol is installed.)

TCP/IP

The TCP/IP protocol stack meets several criteria. It is a routable protocol and is the protocol needed to go out on the Internet. It does not, however, allow access to the Novell NetWare servers if they are added in the future.

TCP/IP is a management-intensive protocol. To ease the management issues, planning must be done. If the network is supposed to connect to the Internet, unique IP addresses must be obtained from an Internet Service Provider (ISP). Also, careful programming of the routers is necessary for internetwork connectivity to work.

Another issue that may need to be addressed is whether the network will use DHCP to allocate IP addresses on the network. If this is the case, a DHCP server must be placed on each subnet, unless a relay agent is placed on the subnet to forward requests to a DHCP server on a remote subnet.

Another issue would be the use of a WINS server. Microsoft networking uses NetBIOS names to communicate all networking functions. NetBIOS names need to be resolved to IP addresses so that the transport stack of TCP/IP can move the networking communication. NetBIOS names can be resolved on a local subnet through the use of broadcasts, but remote NetBIOS names cannot be resolved. By using a WINS server, this issue can be centrally managed.

NWLink (IPX/SPX)

Using NWLink enables the Windows NT and 95 machines to communicate with each other and across the routers. It also enables the computers to talk to any Novell servers that may be installed on the network. It does not, however, enable communication with the Internet.

An issue to consider with NWLink is what frame type is to be used on the network. Some equipment cannot handle certain frame types, thus it would be important to get a list of all hardware being used on the network to see whether it is compliant with the frame type to be chosen. It would be a good recommendation to choose the 802.2 frame type, because this is the current IEEE recommended standard.

Conclusion

There is no compellingly correct answer. It looks as if NWLink and TCP/IP are both contenders. Until the company makes a decision to either go onto the Internet and/or use Novell servers, a single protocol cannot be favored over another.

CASE STUDY: IMPLEMENTING A NETBIOS NAMING CONVENTION

ESSENCE OF THE CASE

The essence of the case is as follows:

- You are to assign NetBIOS names to all computers on the network.

- You do not need to follow any predetermined conventions.

SCENARIO

You are to implement a NetBIOS naming convention for the network. You are free to use what names you feel are suitable.

ANALYSIS

Being able to freely assign NetBIOS names can be a pleasure and a pain. The pleasure is that you are able to leave your own personal mark on the network. The naming convention that you choose is the one that others follow. The pain is that other network administrators may criticize your decisions.

When naming computers with NetBIOS names, recall that only three rules need to be followed:

- All names must be unique.

- Names cannot be more than 15 characters long.

- Alpha-numeric characters and the characters !@#$%^&()-_{}.~ are allowed.

There are no right or wrong names (unless you break the rules for characters). There are, however, efficient and inefficient names. Efficient names enable an administrator or support person to identify the location of the computer easily on the network. An inefficient name does not enable one to locate the computer on the network. Try to be descriptive and use something that follows corporate naming traditions.

FS1, FS1, APPS_SERV, and PRINT_SERV are all valid names that could be used for servers. All your servers should be locked up in a server room, so the name does not necessarily need to describe the location, but instead be descriptive of the function of the server.

F1PC3, ACCTDEPT#5 and ALVINSPC all are descriptive in location. F1PC3 could describe that this is the third PC on the first floor. ACCT-ROOM#5 could mean the fifth PC in the Accounting department. ALVINSPC of course means Alvin's PC. Again, all PC names ought to be descriptive so that the unique identifier also provides useful information such as location and/or function.

CHAPTER SUMMARY

KEY TERMS

- Packet
- Protocol
- TCP/IP
- Internet Protocol (IP)
- Transmission Control Protocol (TCP)
- User Datagram Protocol (UDP)
- Address Resolution Protocol (ARP)
- Internet Control Message Protocol (ICMP)
- Dynamic Host Configuration Protocol (DHCP)
- Windows Internet Naming Service (WINS)
- File Transfer Protocol (FTP)
- Simple Mail Transport Protocol (SMTP)
- Remote Terminal Emulation (Telnet)
- Network File System (NFS)
- Routing Information Protocol (RIP)
- Open Shortest Path First (OSPF)
- IPX/SPX
- NWLink
- Internetwork Packet Exchange (IPX)
- Sequenced Packet Exchange (SPX)
- 802.2 frame
- 802.3 frame
- Ethernet II frame type
- Ethernet_SNAP frame
- Token-ring frame
- Token-ring_SNAP frame
- Service Advertising Protocol (SAP)
- NetWare Core Protocol (NCP)
- NetWare Link Services Protocol (NLSP)
- NetBEUI
- AppleTalk
- Data Link Control (DLC)
- Server Messaging Blocks (SMB)

This chapter examined network protocols and protocol suites. The chapter began with an introduction to protocol stacks. You then learned about some of the most common protocol suites, as follows:

- *TCP/IP.* The Internet protocol suite

- *IPX/SPX.* A protocol suite used for Novell NetWare networks

- *NetBEUI.* A non-routable protocol used on Microsoft networks

- *AppleTalk.* The Apple Macintosh protocol system

- *DLC.* A protocol that Windows NT networks use to connect with HP JetDirect printers and IBM mainframes

During the discussion on the protocol suites, analysis was focused on the addressing schemes used by each suite, as well as the smaller components and their functions within each protocol suite.

The NDIS interface standard (discussed in Chapter 2) enables a single computer to bind one network adapter to more than one protocol system. This provides great versatility and interoperability in today's diverse networking environment.

The chapter also discussed NetBIOS names and naming conventions. You saw that all Microsoft machines on a network use NetBIOS names and that these names have some rules regarding their construction.

APPLY YOUR LEARNING

Exercises

7.1 Installing Network Protocols in Windows NT

Objective: Become familiar with the procedure for installing and removing protocols in Windows NT.

Estimated Time: 15 minutes

1. You can install, configure, remove, and manage network protocols by using the Network application in Windows NT's Control Panel. Click the Start menu and choose the Settings/Control panel. Then double-click the Network application icon.

   Another way to reach the Network application is to right-click the Network Neighborhood icon and choose Properties.

2. In the Network application, choose the Protocols tab (see Figure 7.12). The Network Protocols box displays the protocols currently installed on the system.

3. If TCP/IP is installed on your system, select TCP/IP Protocol and choose Properties to invoke the Microsoft TCP/IP Properties dialog box (see Figure 7.13). Note the several tabs that provide various configuration options. Close the Microsoft TCP/IP Properties dialog box and select the NetBEUI protocol (if it is installed) in the Network application's Protocols dialog box. Note that the Properties button is grayed. Try double-clicking the NetBEUI icon in the box's list of protocols. A message says `Cannot configure the software component`. Unlike TCP/IP, NetBEUI is not user-configurable.

   If TCP/IP and NetBEUI aren't installed on your system, you can install them by using the procedure described in steps 4 and 5 of this exercise and then delete them later.

4. To add a protocol, click on the Add button in the Network application's Protocols tab. Select a protocol from the protocol list in the Select Network

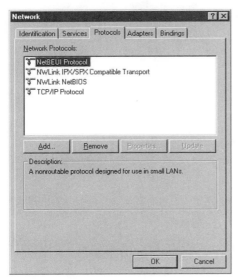

FIGURE 7.12
Network application's Protocols tab.

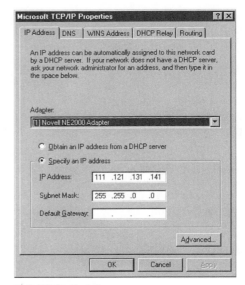

FIGURE 7.13
The Microsoft TCP/IP Properties dialog box.

APPLY YOUR LEARNING

Protocol dialog box (see Figure 7.14). Click on OK to install the protocol. Windows NT may prompt you for the location of the Windows NT installation disk. Type in the location or drive letter of the installation files and click OK. If you are installing a protocol that requires some configuration (such as TCP/IP or NWLink), Windows NT asks you for the necessary information.

5. Windows NT asks you to restart your system. Shut down your system and restart. Return to the Network application's Protocols tab and see whether the protocol is properly installed.

6. To remove a protocol, select the protocol from the Network Protocols list and click on the Remove button.

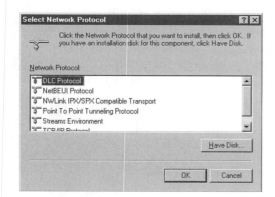

FIGURE 7.14
The Select Network Protocol dialog box.

7.2   Network Bindings

Objective: Become familiar with the process for enabling and disabling network bindings and changing network access order.

Estimated Time: 10 minutes

In Chapter 2, you learned about NDIS and the concept of network bindings. A binding is an association

between protocol layers that enables those layers to behave like a protocol stack. By binding a transport protocol such as TCP/IP (which operates at the Transport and Network levels) to a network adapter (which operates at the Data Link and Physical layers) you provide a conduit for the protocol's packets to reach the network and thus enable the protocol to participate in network communications. NDIS lets you bind multiple protocols to a single adapter or multiple adapters to a single protocol.

1. Click the Start button and choose Settings, Control Panel. In Windows NT's Control Panel, double-click the Network application icon and choose the Bindings tab (see Figure 7.15).

2. Click the Show Bindings down arrow to access the drop-down list. Note that you can display bindings for services, protocols, or adapters. A service bound to a protocol bound to an adapter provides a complete pathway from the local system to the network.

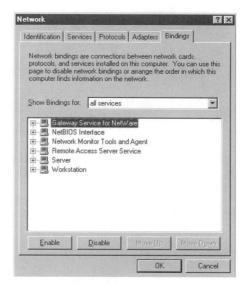

FIGURE 7.15
Network application's Bindings tab.

APPLY YOUR LEARNING

3. Click on the plus sign next to the Workstation service. The Workstation service is the Windows NT redirector (refer to Chapter 1, "Networking Terms and Concepts"), which redirects requests from the local system to the network. The protocols currently bound to the Workstation service appear in a list below the Workstation icon. Click on the plus sign next to one of the protocols. The network adapters bound to the protocol now appear in the tree (see Figure 7.16).

4. The protocols and their associated adapters represent potential pathways for the Workstation service to access the network. Windows NT prioritizes those pathways according to the order in which they appear in the Bindings tab. For the configuration shown in Figure 7.16, for example, Windows NT attempts to use the NetBEUI protocol with the Workstation service before attempting to use NWLink. The Move Up and Move Down buttons let you change the access

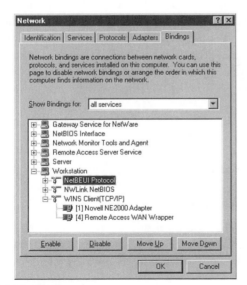

FIGURE 7.16
Inspect binding information by using the Bindings tab.

order. Select a protocol under the Workstation service. Try the Move Up and Move Down buttons to change the position of the protocol in the access order. (Don't forget to restore the protocol to its original position before leaving the Bindings tab.)

5. The Enable and Disable buttons let you enable or disable a protocol for a given service, because you may not wish people using a particular protocol to use a certain service. Disable a protocol (for instance, NetBEUI) for the Workstation service. Now click the plus sign next to the Server service. Note that although the protocol is disabled for the Workstation service, it is still enabled for the Server service. Re-enable the protocol under the Workstation service and close the Network application.

7.3 Mapping a Network Drive

Objective: Use the NetBIOS-based UNC path to map a drive letter to a network share.

Estimated Time: 10 minutes

1. Double-click Windows NT's Network Neighborhood application. Locate another computer for which network shares have been defined.

   Another useful tool for finding network shares is the Server Manager application in Windows NT Server's Administrative Tools group. To use this tool, click the Start menu and choose Programs, Administrative Tools, Server Manager.

2. Click the Start menu and go to the Windows NT command prompt. (Choose Programs, Command Prompt.)

3. Enter the following command:

   net view

APPLY YOUR LEARNING

4. The net view command lists the NetBIOS names of computers in your domain. Look for the computer you located using Network Neighborhood in Step 1.

5. Type the following command:

    net view \\computername

    where computername is the NetBIOS name of the computer you located in Step 1. This command lists the network shares available on the computer.

6. Locate a directory share in the share list. Then type the following command:

    net use * \\computername\sharename

    where computername is the NetBIOS name of the computer you located in Step 1, and sharename is the name of the share you located in the preceding step. The asterisk maps the next available drive letter to the share. You could also specify a particular drive letter (followed by a colon) rather than the asterisk. A message appears on your screen giving you the drive letter that Windows NT used for the connection and indicating whether the command was successful.

7. Now enter the following command:

    net view \\computername

    where computername is the name of the computer you chose in Step 1. The drive letter you mapped to the share should appear beside the share name, and the share type in the column should be titled Used as.

8. Enter the drive letter assigned in Step 6 at the command prompt, followed by a colon. For instance, enter **I:**.

> **NOTE**
>
> **Privileges**   You must have the necessary privileges to access the shared directory. Check with your network administrator for details.

9. Type the command **dir** and press the Enter key. A directory listing of the shared directory should appear on your screen. You now have accessed the shared directory through the mapped drive letter.

10. To delete the network drive mapping, enter the following command:

    net use drive_letter: /delete

    where drive_letter is the drive letter assigned in Step 6.

You also can map drive letters through Windows NT Explorer. To do so, pull down the Tools menu and select Map Network Drive. In the Drive property box, select the drive letter you wish to use. In the Path box, type in **\\Computer_Name\Share_Name**, where Computer_Name is the NetBIOS name of the computer to which you are connecting, and Share_Name is the name of the shared directory on the other computer.

Review Questions

1. Name three transport protocols that can be used to transfer SMBs and the only transport protocol that can transfer NCP packets.

2. Which protocol suite cannot be used for PC-to-PC communication when Microsoft operating systems are running on both PCs?

3. How many characters can you have in a NetBIOS name?

APPLY YOUR LEARNING

Exam Questions

1. Which three of the following are Transport layer protocols?

   A. ALP

   B. PPX

   C. TCP

   D. SPX

2. Which three of the following operate within the Network layer?

   A. Telnet

   B. WINS

   C. FTP

   D. IP

3. At which OSI layer does SMB operates?

   A. Application

   B. Transport

   C. Network

   D. Physical

4. Which three of the following protocols are available with Windows NT?

   A. AppleTalk

   B. IPX/SPX

   C. NetBEUI

   D. DLC

5. What is the simplest protocol to use for an isolated LAN with several DOS-based clients and Windows NT Server?

   A. NWLink

   B. TCP/IP

   C. DLC

   D. NetBEUI

6. What is the best protocol for a remote PC that interacts with the network via the Internet?

   A. NWLink

   B. TCP/IP

   C. DLC

   D. NetBEUI

7. At which OSI layer does NCP operate?

   A. Application and Presentation

   B. Transport and Network

   C. Network only

   D. Transport only

   E. Session and Transport

8. UDP is part of which protocol suite?

   A. TCP/IP

   B. IPX/SPX

   C. AppleTalk

   D. NetBEUI

9. How does TCP/IP compare to NetBEUI on a small network?

   A. Faster

   B. Slower

   C. Easier to install and configure

   D. None of the above

APPLY YOUR LEARNING

10. NetBIOS is an abbreviation for what?

    A. Network Basic Input/Output System

    B. Network Bilateral Operating System

    C. Network Binary Interchange Operating System

    D. Network Bus Input/Output System

11. Which of the following is a legal and recommended NetBIOS computer name?

    A. EAGLES_LODGE_PENT

    B. EAGLES!@#*_PC

    C. 486!!EAGLES_PC

    D. EAGLES LODGE

12. Which of the following UNC paths lead you to a file called DOUGHNUTS on a PC called FOOD located in the SWEETS directory of the JUNKFOOD share?

    A. \\DOUGHNUTS\FOOD\SWEETS\JUNK-FOOD

    B. \\FOOD\JUNKFOOD\SWEETS\DOUGH-NUTS

    C. \\FOOD\JUNKFOOD\DOUGHNUTS

    D. \\JUNKFOOD\DOUGHNUTS

13. Which of the following commands produces a list of shared resources on the computer described in Question 12?

    A. Net share \\FOOD

    B. Net view

    C. Net view \\FOOD

    D. Net view \\FOOD /shares

14. Which 802 category defines the Ethernet Standard?

    A. 802.10

    B. 802.3

    C. 802.12

    D. 802.5

15. You wish to connect a Windows NT computer to a Windows 95 computer to share files back and forth.

    Primary objective: You need to establish network connectivity by using a compatible protocol.

    Secondary objective: The Windows 95 computer needs to connect directly to the Internet.

    Secondary objective: You wish to administer HP JetDirect printers from the Windows NT computer.

    Suggested Solution: You install DLC and NetBEUI on the Windows NT computer. You install NetBEUI, DLC, NWLINK, and TCP/IP on the Windows 95 computers. Make sure that the NetBIOS names on both the Windows NT and Windows 95 computers are the same.

    A. This solution meets the primary objective and both secondary objectives.

    B. This solution meets the primary objective and one secondary objective.

    C. This solution meets the primary objective.

    D. This solution does not meet the primary objective.

16. You wish to connect a Windows NT computer to a Windows 95 computer to share files back and forth.

Primary objective: You need to establish network connectivity by using a compatible protocol.

Secondary objective: The Windows 95 computer needs to connect directly to the Internet.

Secondary objective: You wish to administer HP JetDirect printers from the Windows NT computer.

Suggested Solution: You install DLC and NetBEUI on the Windows NT computer. You install DLC, NWLINK, and TCP/IP on the Windows 95 computers. Make sure that the NetBIOS names on both the Windows NT and Windows 95 computers are different, and conform to the NetBIOS naming rules and recommendations.

A. This solution meets the primary objective and both secondary objectives.

B. This solution meets the primary objective and one secondary objective.

C. This solution meets the primary objective.

D. This solution does not satisfy the primary objective.

17. You wish to connect a Windows NT computer to a Windows 95 computer to share files back and forth.

Primary objective: You need to establish network connectivity by using a compatible protocol.

Secondary objective: The Windows 95 computer needs to connect directly to the Internet.

Secondary objective: You wish to administer HP JetDirect printers from the Windows NT computer.

Suggested Solution: You install DLC and NetBEUI on the Windows NT computer. You install NetBEUI, DLC, and NWLINK on the Windows 95 computers. Make sure that the NetBIOS names on both the Windows NT and Windows 95 computers are different, and conform to the NetBIOS naming rules and recommendations.

A. This solution meets the primary objective and both secondary objectives.

B. This solution meets the primary objective and one secondary objective.

C. This solution meets the primary objective.

D. This solution does not meet the primary objective.

Answers to Review Questions

1. SMBs are transferred between computers using NWLink (IPX/SPX), TCP/IP, and NetBEUI. DLC and AppleTalk cannot be used for SMB transport.

   NCP packets can only be transported using IPX/SPX (NWLink). See the sections titled "Server Message Blocks (SMB)" and "IPX/SPX."

2. DLC and AppleTalk cannot be used for PC-to-PC communication when both PCs' operating systems are Microsoft products. See the sections titled "Data Link Control (DLC)" and "AppleTalk."

3. A NetBIOS name can have up to 15 characters. See the section titled "NetBIOS Names."

Answers to Exam Questions

1. **C, D.** Answers A and B do not exist. See the section titled "Transport Protocols." TCP is the TCP/IP connection-oriented transport protocol, whereas SPX is the IPX/SPX connection-oriented transport protocol.

2. **D.** TCP operates only in the Transport layer. Telnet, WINS, and FTP all operate at the layers above the Transport layer. See the section titled "Transmission Control Protocol" within the section titled "Transport Protocols."

3. **A.** SMB is an Application layer protocol. See the section titled "Server Message Blocks."

4. **A, C, D.** B is incorrect because Windows NT does not have true IPX/SPX, but instead a version of IPX/SPX known as NWLink. See the section titled "NetWare IPX/SPX."

5. **D.** D is correct because NetBEUI has really no management considerations. A and B could also work, but have more management issues involved than D. C is not an option to connect DOS-based clients to a Windows NT server. See the section titled "NetBEUI."

6. **B.** TCP/IP is the protocol that would have to be used, because it is the only protocol that can be used on the Internet. See the section titled "TCP/IP—The Internet Protocols."

7. **A.** NCP is an Application layer protocol used to communicate with Novell servers. See the section titled "NetWare Core Protocol" under the section titled "NetWare IPX/SPX."

8. **A.** UDP operates at the Transport layer of the TCP/IP protocol suite. See the section titled "User Datagram Protocol (UDP)" under the section titled "TCP/IP—The Internet Protocols."

9. **B.** TCP/IP is slower than NetBEUI. It is harder to configure because it requires knowledge of IP addresses. See the section titled "NetBEUI."

10. **A.** All the other answers are made-up answers. See the section titled "NetBIOS Names."

11. **C.** A is more than 15 characters, B contains a *, and D has a space, which is not recommended. See the section titled "NetBIOS Names."

12. **B.** UNC names are always based on the following:

    \\Computername\Sharename\filename

    See the section titled "NetBIOS Names."

13. **C.** To see the list of shared resources on a specific computer from the command prompt, type:

    net view\\Computername

    See the section titled "NetBIOS Names."

Suggested Readings and Resources

1. Heywood, Drew. *Networking with Microsoft TCP/IP, 2nd Edition.* New Riders, 1997.

2. Dulaney, Emmett. *MCSE Training Guide: TCP/IP.* New Riders, 1998.

3. Siyan, Karanjit S. *Windows NT Server 4 Professional Reference.* New Riders, 1996.

4. Heywood, Drew. *Inside Windows NT Server 4, Administrators Resource Edition.* New Riders, 1997.

Chapter 8 targets the following objective in the Planning section of the Networking Essentials exam:

List the characteristics, requirements, and appropriate situations for WAN connection services. WAN connection services include: X.25, ISDN, Frame Relay, and ATM

▶ This is an important topic because it not only applies the theory learned in Chapter 2, "Networking Standards," but when you face some form of WAN connectivity need or problem, one or more of these options will more than likely be your solution.

CHAPTER 8

Connection Services

STUDY STRATEGIES

▶ The way to study for this material is to know the characteristics of each of the various WAN technologies or services, including those crucial to making decisions about which to implement. These characteristics include such things as speed, cost, and availability.

INTRODUCTION

Communication must occur between distant points, but few organizations can justify the costs required to construct a private wide area network. Up to this point, all the chapters have focused primarily on issues that relate to a local area network. As defined earlier in Chapter 1, a LAN is characterized by high bandwidth and the fact that the company controls and maintains all the connectivity devices as well as the transmission media. This chapter discusses some of the WAN connectivity issues that a company may wish to address.

Chapter 3, "Transmission Media," discussed some of the possible transmission media that a company could use to establish WAN connectivity. These include spread-spectrum, infrared, and satellite communications. Another possibility is fiber-optic cable, but often a company does not have access to the property to lay down any form of physical medium. All these options are expensive to undertake.

Fortunately, a variety of commercial options are available that enable organizations to pay for only the level of service they require. These commercial options take advantage of existing infrastructures supplied by the telephone companies, cable companies, and Internet Service Providers (ISPs). This chapter discusses some wide area network (WAN) service options. You will also learn about dial-up versus dedicated service. This chapter describes some of the available types of digital communication lines and examines some standards for WAN connection services.

THE PUBLIC TELEPHONE NETWORK

A major issue with WAN connectivity is whether the level of service you wish to employ exists at all points of communication. For example, if you are requiring a dedicated connection between Moscow, Russia, and Santiago, Chile, there would have to be the same level of service between both points of access. One WAN connectivity service that exists almost worldwide is the public telephone system.

Although recently cable television companies have begun to provide WAN connectivity service, almost all public carrier services to this point have been offered by the telephone companies. Thus in this chapter, almost all the technologies discussed will address the public telephone system.

Public telephone networks offer two general types of service:

◆ *Leased dedicated services.* The customer is granted exclusive access.

◆ *Dial-up services.* The customer pays on a per-use basis.

Switched services operate the Public Switched Telephone Network (PSTN), which you know as the telephone system. Voice-grade services have evolved to high levels of sophistication and can be adapted to provide many data services with devices such as modems. Newer switched options provide higher levels of service while retaining the advantages of switched access.

With dial-up service, subscribers don't have exclusive access to a particular data path. The PSTN maintains large numbers of paths but not nearly enough to service all customers simultaneously. The most obvious illustration of this is when you try to use the telephone and a recorded message says "all lines are busy." When a customer requests service, a dedicated path is switched into service to meet the customer's needs. When the customer hangs up, the path is dissolved, and the circuits are available for use by other customers. In situations in which the customer doesn't need full-time network access, switched service is extremely cost-effective.

The cost for this service can be either a flat monthly fee, or a time used/distance (traveled fee long distance charges). These costs vary considerably depending on where in the world you are located.

The workings of the public telephone system are seen in Figure 8.1.

Essentially any telephone or modem that uses a telephone jack connects into the wall. From the wall, lines (in most cases UTP lines) run to a *demarc* unit within the building. A demarc unit is the connection point between all the telephone lines in a building and the *local loop* line that leaves the building.

The local loop lines are usually higher-grade UTP or fiber-optic wires that are owned and maintained by the telephone company. These local loop lines connect the building with the *Central Office (CO)*. The central office is the local telephone station point that switches calls from one local loop line to another, to a trunk line, or

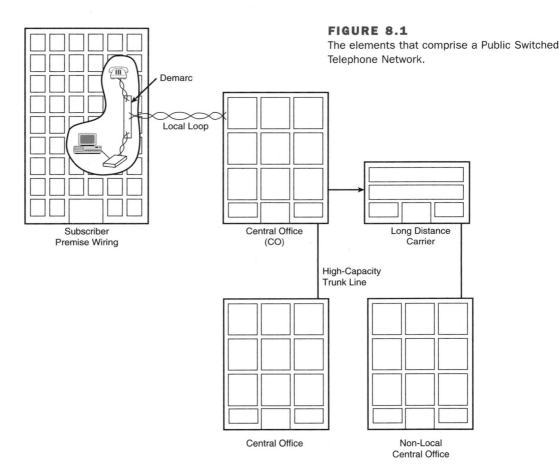

to a long distance carrier. Trunk lines connect COs together. Local
loop lines are higher in bandwidth than the wires running within a
building. Trunk lines are even higher in bandwidth than local loop
lines.

It is due to all this switching that the telephone system is referred to
as the Public Switched Telephone Network. You must remember,
however, that a telephone line connection is a *circuit switching* (refer
to Chapter 2) technology. That is, a constant path is established
between the two devices on the network.

When you use a modem over the telephone system, the modem
converts the computer's digital signal to an analog signal. This analog signal is then passed over an established pathway to the device

on the other end. You are charged for data transfer, if dialing long distance, whether or not data throughput is happening. This is because the telephone system is renting you constant line access.

Leased Line Types

When customers require full-time access to a communication path, a dedicated, leased line serves as one option. Several levels of digital lines are available. Digital lines are superior to analog lines because they tend to be more error-free. Following are some examples of digital line services:

◆ T1 and T3

◆ Digital data service

◆ Switched 56

T1 and T3

A very popular digital line is the *T1 leased line.* This leased line provides point-to-point connections and transmits a total of 24 channels across two wire pairs—one pair for sending and one for receiving—for a transmission rate of 1.544Mbps. A T1 is known as an E1 line in Europe.

Very few private networks require the capacity of a T1 line. The channels of a T1 line are often leased out on a fractional basis. Each T1 channel can transmit up to 64Kbps of data. All 24 channels at once equal 1.544Mbps. Fractional T1s are often guaranteed at 56Kbps, with 8Kbps being set aside for management purposes.

T3 (E3 in Europe) is similar to T1, but T3 has an even higher capacity. In fact, a T3 line can transmit at up to 45Mbps. This is because a T3 line is made up of 672 64Kbps channels.

A single-channel service on a T1 is called *DS-0. DS-1* service is a full T1 line. *DS-1C* is two T1 lines, *DS-2* is four T1 lines, and *DS-3* is a full T3 line (equivalent to 28 T1s). A level of service called *T4* is equal to 168 T1 lines.

Digital Data Service (DDS)

Digital Data Service (DDS) is a very basic form of digital service. DDS transmits from point to point at 2.4, 4.8, 9.6, or 56Kbps. In its most basic form, DDS provides a dedicated line.

Switched 56

A special service related to DDS, *Switched 56* offers a dial-up version of the 56Kbps DDS. With Switched 56, users can dial other Switched 56 sites and pay for only the connect time.

PACKET ROUTING SERVICES

Many organizations must communicate among several points. Leasing a line between each pair of points can prove too costly. Many services now are available that route packets between different sites. Some of the packet-routing services discussed in this chapter are as follows:

- ◆ ISDN
- ◆ X.25
- ◆ Frame Relay
- ◆ ATM
- ◆ SONET
- ◆ SMDS
- ◆ ADSL
- ◆ Cable Modem

Each of these services has characteristics that suit it to particular uses, and all these services are available on a leased basis from service providers, yet these services are not available in all locations. An organization that must communicate among many sites simply pays to connect each site to the service, and the service assumes the responsibility of routing packets. The expense of operating the network is then shared among all network subscribers. Because the exact switching process is concealed from the subscriber, these networks frequently are depicted as a communication cloud, as shown in Figure 8.2.

FIGURE 8.2
How a public network service is often represented.

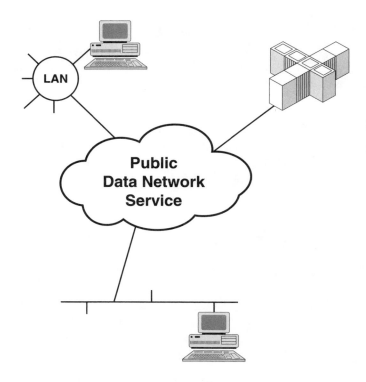

N O T E

Multiplexing Many digital transmission methods use a technique called multiplexing. *Multiplexing*, described in Chapter 3 enables broadband media to support multiple data channels.

The data rates of public network services can be compared to common LAN services such as Ethernet (10–100Mbps) and Token Ring (4–16Mbps) to give you an idea of how the public services' speed affects performance of the network's communications.

Before going into detail on the following WAN connectivity services, a recap of packet routing concepts is warranted. In Chapter 2, you were introduced to packet switching and other routing-related techniques used to send data over WAN links. Packet-switching networks often use virtual circuits to route data from the source to the destination. A *virtual circuit* is a specific path through the network—a chain of communication links leading from the source to the destination (as opposed to a scheme in which each packet finds its own path). Virtual circuits enable the network to provide better error-checking and flow control.

The two main forms of virtual circuits are the following:

◆ A *switched virtual circuit (SVC)* is created for a specific communication session and then disappears after the session. The next time the computers communicate, a different virtual circuit might be used.

◆ A *permanent virtual circuit (PVC)* is a permanent route through the network that is always available to the customer. With a PVC, charges are still billed on a per-use basis.

ISDN and B-ISDN

Integrated Services Digital Network (ISDN) is a group of ITU (CCITT) standards designed to provide voice, video, and data transmission services on digital telephone networks. ISDN uses multiplexing to support multiple channels on high-bandwidth circuits. The relationship of the ISDN protocols to the OSI reference model is shown in Figure 8.3.

The original idea behind ISDN was to enable existing phone lines to carry digital communications, and was at one time touted as a replacement to traditional analog lines. Thus, ISDN is more like traditional telephone service than some of the other WAN services discussed further on in this chapter. ISDN is intended as a dial-up service and not as a permanent, 24-hour connection.

ISDN separates the bandwidth into channels (see the following "In-depth" for more information). Based upon how these channels are used, ISDN can be separated into two classes of service.

◆ *Basic Rate (BRI)*. Basic Rate ISDN uses three channels. Two channels (called *B channels*) carry the digital data at 64Kbps. A third channel (called the *D channel*) provides link and signaling information at 16Kbps. *Basic Rate ISDN* thus is referred to as *2B+D*. A single PC transmitting through ISDN can use both B channels simultaneously, providing a maximum data rate of 128Kbps (or higher with compression).

◆ *Primary Rate (PRI)*. Primary Rate supports 23 64Kbps B channels and one 64Kbps D channel. The D channel is used for signaling and management, whereas the B channels provide the data throughput.

With a BRI line, if the line is currently being used for voice, only one B channel is available for data. This effectively reduces the throughput of the BRI down to 64Kbps.

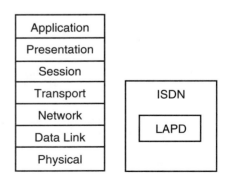

FIGURE 8.3
The relationship between ISDN and the OSI reference model.

ISDN CHANNEL TYPES

A variety of ISDN channel types are defined. These channel types, often called *bit pipes*, provide different types and levels of service. The following list details the various channels:

◆ *A channels.* Provide 4KHz analog telephone service.

◆ *B channels.* Support 64Kbps digital data.

◆ *C channels.* Support 8 or 16Kbps digital data, generally for out-of-band signaling.

◆ *D channels.* Support 16 or 64Kbps digital data, also for out-of-band signaling. D channels support the following subchannels:

  • *p subchannels* support low-bandwidth packet data.

  • *s subchannels* are used for signaling (such as call setup).

  • *t subchannels* support telemetry data (such as utility meters).

◆ *E channels.* Provide 64Kbps service used for internal ISDN signaling.

◆ *H channels.* Provide 384, 1,536, or 1,920Kbps digital service.

ISDN functions as the data-transmission service only. The LAPD protocol, which operates on the D channel, provides the acknowledged, connectionless, full-duplex service, as well as the physical addressing service.

Broadband ISDN (B-ISDN) is a refinement of ISDN that is defined to support higher-bandwidth applications, such as video, imaging, and multimedia. Physical layer support for B-ISDN is provided by *Asynchronous Transfer Mode (ATM)* and the *Synchronous Optical Network (SONET),* both discussed later in this chapter. Typical B-ISDN data rates are 51Mbps, 155Mbps, and 622Mbps over fiber-optic media.

X.25

X.25 is a packet-switching network standard developed by the International Telegraph and Telephone Consultative Committee

(CCITT, abbreviated from the French), which has been renamed the International Telecommunications Union (ITU). The standard, referred to as *Recommendation X.25*, was introduced in 1974 and is now implemented most commonly in WANs.

As shown in Figure 8.4, X.25 is one level of a three-level stack that spans the Network, Data Link, and Physical layers. The middle layer, *Link Access Procedures-Balanced (LAPB),* is a bit-oriented, full-duplex, synchronous Data Link layer LLC protocol. Physical layer connectivity is provided by a variety of standards, including X.21, X.21bis, and V.32.

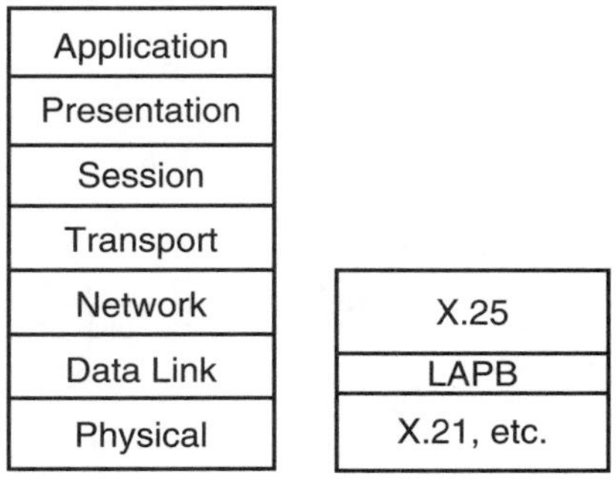

X.25 packet-switching networks provide the options of permanent or switched virtual circuits. Although a datagram (unreliable) protocol was supported until 1984, X.25 is now required to provide reliable service and end-to-end flow control. Because each device on a network can operate more than one virtual circuit, X.25 must provide error and flow control for each virtual circuit.

At the time X.25 was developed, this flow control and error checking was essential because X.25 was developed around relatively unreliable telephone line communications. The drawback is that error checking and flow control slow down X.25. Generally, X.25 networks are implemented with line speeds of up to 64Kbps, although actual throughput seems slower due to the error correction controls in place. These speeds are suitable for the file transfer and terminal activity that comprised the bulk of network traffic when X.25 was defined, most of this traffic being terminal connections to mainframes. Such speeds, however, are inadequate to provide LAN-speed services, which typically require speeds of 1Mbps or better. X.25 networks, therefore, are poor choices for providing LAN application services in a WAN environment. One advantage of X.25, however, is that it is an established standard that is used internationally. This, as well as lack of other services throughout the world, means that X.25 is more of a connection service to Africa, South America, and Asia, where lack of other services prevail.

Figure 8.5 shows a typical X.25 configuration. In X.25 parlance, a computer or terminal is called *data terminal equipment (DTE)*. A DTE can also be a gateway providing access to a local network. *Data communications equipment (DCE)* provides access to the *packet-switched network* (*PSN*). A *PSE* is a *packet-switching exchange,* also called a *switch* or *switching node.*

Application
Presentation
Session
Transport

Network	X.25
Data Link	LAPB
Physical	X.21, etc.

FIGURE 8.4
The relationship between X.25 and the OSI reference model.

FIGURE 8.5
A sample X.25 network.

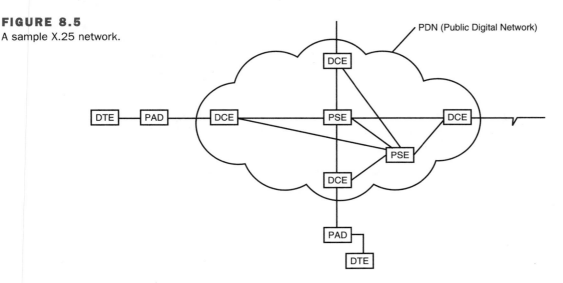

The X.25 protocol oversees the communication between the DTE and the DCE. A device called a *packet assembler/disassembler (PAD)* translates asynchronous input from the DTE into packets suitable for the PDN.

Frame Relay

Frame relay was designed to support the *Broadband Integrated Services Digital Network (B-ISDN)*, which was discussed in the preceding section. The specifications for frame relay address some of the limitations of X.25. As with X.25, frame relay is a packet-switching network service, but frame relay was designed around newer, faster fiber-optic networks.

Unlike X.25, frame relay assumes a more reliable network. This enables frame relay to eliminate much of the X.25 overhead required to provide reliable service on less reliable networks. Frame relay relies on higher-level protocol layers to provide flow and error control.

Frame relay is typically implemented as a public data network and, therefore, is regarded as a WAN protocol. The relationship of Frame Relay to the OSI model is shown in Figure 8.6. Notice that the scope of Frame Relay is limited to the Physical and Data Link layers.

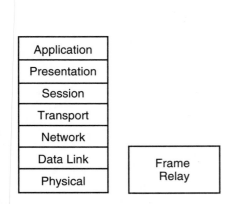

Frame relay provides permanent virtual circuits that supply permanent virtual pathways for WAN connections. Frame relay services are typically implemented at line speeds from 56Kbps up to 1.544Mbps (T1).

Customers typically purchase access to a specific amount of bandwidth on a frame relay service. This bandwidth is called the *committed information rate (CIR)*, a data rate for which the customer is guaranteed access, and is available in increments of 64Kbps. Customers might be permitted to access higher data rates on a pay-per-use, temporary basis. This arrangement enables customers to tailor their network access costs based on their bandwidth requirements.

To use frame relay, you must have special, frame-relay-compatible connectivity devices (such as frame-relay-compatible routers and bridges).

Asynchronous Transfer Mode (ATM)

Asynchronous Transfer Mode (ATM) is a high-bandwidth switching technology developed by the ITU Telecommunications Standards Sector (ITU-TSS). An organization called the ATM Forum is responsible for defining ATM implementation characteristics. ATM can be layered on other Physical layer technologies, such as *Fiber Distributed Data Interface* (FDDI) and SONET. The relationships of these protocols to the OSI model are shown in Figure 8.7.

Several characteristics distinguish ATM from other switching technologies. ATM is based on fixed-length, 53-byte cells, whereas other technologies employ frames that vary in length to accommodate different amounts of data. Because ATM cells are uniform in length, switching mechanisms can operate with a high level of efficiency. This high efficiency results in high data transfer rates. Some ATM systems can operate at an incredible rate of 622Mbps; a typical working speed for an ATM is around 155Mbps.

The unit of transmission for ATM is called a *cell*. All cells are 53 bytes long and consist of a 5-byte header and 48 bytes of data. The 48-byte data size was selected by the standards committee as a compromise to suit both audio- and data-transmission needs. Audio information, for instance, must be delivered with little *latency* (delay) to maintain a smooth flow of sound. Audio engineers therefore preferred a small cell so that cells would be more readily

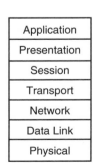

FIGURE 8.7

The relationship of ATM to the OSI reference model.

available when needed. For data, however, large cells reduce the overhead required to deliver a byte of information.

Asynchronous delivery is another distinguishing feature of ATM. *Asynchronous* refers to the characteristic of ATM in which transmission time slots don't occur periodically but are granted at irregular intervals. ATM uses a technique called *label multiplexing*, which allocates time slots on demand. Traffic that is time-critical, such as voice or video, can be given priority over data traffic that can be delayed slightly with no ill effect. Channels are identified by cell labels, not by specific time slots. A high-priority transmission need not be held until its next time slot allocation. Instead, it might be required to wait only until the current 53-byte cell has been transmitted.

TIME-DIVISION MULTIPLEXING

Other multichannel technologies utilize *time-division* techniques to allocate bandwidth to channels. A T1 (1.544Mbps) line, for example, might be time-division multiplexed to provide 24 voice channels. With this technique, each channel is assigned a specific time slot in the transmission schedule. The disadvantage of this technique is that an idle channel doesn't yield its bandwidth for the creation of other channels.

Devices communicate on ATM networks by establishing a virtual path, which is identified by a *virtual path identifier (VPI)*. Within this virtual path, virtual circuits can be established, which are in turn associated with *virtual circuit identifiers (VCIs)*. The VPI and VCI together make up a 3-byte field included in the cell header.

ATM is relatively new technology, and only a few suppliers provide the equipment necessary to support it. (ATM networks must use ATM-compatible switches, routers, and other connectivity devices.)

Other networks, such as a routed ethernet, require a 6-byte physical address as well as a network address to uniquely identify each device on an internetwork. An ATM can switch cells with 3-byte identifiers because VPIs and VCIs apply to only a given device-to-device link. Each ATM switch can assign different VPIs and VCIs for each link, and up to 16 million circuits can be configured for any given device-to-device link.

Although ATM was developed primarily as a WAN technology, it has many characteristics of value for high-performance LANs. An interesting advantage of ATM is that ATM makes it possible to use the same technology for both LANs and WANs. Some disadvantages, however, include the cost, the limited availability of the equipment, and the present lack of expertise regarding ATM due to its relatively recent arrival.

Synchronous Optical Network (SONET)

Bell Communications Research developed SONET, which has been accepted as an ANSI standard. As the "optical" in the name implies, SONET is a standard for communication over fiber-optic networks. Data rates for SONET are organized in a hierarchy based on the *Optical Carrier* (OC) speed and the corresponding *Synchronous Transport Signals* (STS) employed. The basic OC and STS data rate is 51.84Mbps, but higher data rates are provided in multiples of the basic rate. Thus OC-48 is 48×51.84Mbps or 2488.32 Mbps.

Switched Multimegabit Digital Service (SMDS)

Developed by Bell Communications Research in 1991, SMDS technology is related to ATM in that it transports data in 53-byte cells. SMDS (see Figure 8.8) is a connectionless Data Link layer service that supports cell switching at data rates of 1.544 to 45Mbps. IEEE 802.6 (DQDB metropolitan area network) is the primary Physical layer standard employed with SMDS, although other Physical layer standards are supported.

Asymmetric Digital Subscriber Line (ADSL)

One new type of broadband WAN connectivity being tested by the telephone companies is ADSL. Available since only 1997, ADSL is a Physical layer standard of sending data across existing telephone wires. By using a special ADSL modem, users can receive data at

FIGURE 8.8
The relationship of SMDS to the OSI Reference model.

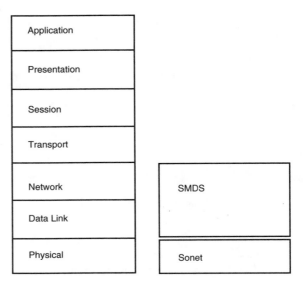

rates over 8Mbps, and send data at rates of up to 640Kbps. This is accomplished through the use of Frequency Division Multiplexing across the existing telephone lines. There is supposed to be support for ATM and IP protocols.

Cable Modems

Another new area of expansion into WAN connectivity services is the advent of the cable modem. This device enables networks to interconnect through existing cable TV lines. Some areas that offer this service have a full-duplex version that is capable of transmitting data at rates of 4–10Mbps. Other areas have cable standards in place that enable the coaxial TV cable to only receive data, relying upon an analog dial-up connection to be used to send data. This is definitely another area of technology that should be watched closely over the next few years.

CASE STUDY: MAKING DECISIONS ON CONNECTIVITY SERVICES OPTIONS

ESSENCE OF THE CASE

The essence of the case is as follows:

- Berg Industries has three locations.

- They wish to have bandwidth support for large data transfers.

- They wish to have WAN bandwidth support for email.

SCENARIO

Berg Industries (BI), a major gold explorer, has called you in to consult on their network connectivity. BI currently has three locations: one in Vancouver, Canada, another in San Francisco, and a third in Lima, Peru.

BI is heavily involved in surveying and mapping gold reserves found in Canada, the United States, and Peru. Each of these offices has its own LAN. Each local LAN has two main servers. One server houses the geological exploration data while the other server is the email server.

BI would like all geological data to be stored on the Vancouver server, for archival purposes. This data usually amounts to over a hundred megabytes of data every week.

BI would also like to have connectivity with the email systems. Email does not typically use a lot of bandwidth. You did, however, notice that all the local desktop PCs were fully multimedia equipped, and learned after talking to a few of the staff that small avi files are often sent around by staff members.

Your job is to present to BI the various commercial connectivity options that it could pursue to meet its needs.

ANALYSIS

The first two areas of analysis should be to decide whether Berg Industries needs point-to-point support or some form of multipoint support and what type of service is available in each of the three areas.

Because BI has only three locations, and theoretically only Vancouver needs to connect to San Francisco and Lima, point-to-point connections are an option. This would mean that all email would be routed through Vancouver, so if Vancouver's link goes down, email cannot go between Lima and San Francisco. In any case, a multipoint or a point-to-point system can both perform the function. Often when a company has multiple locations, or multiple nodes per location that must be connected, a multipoint option wins out over a point-to-point connection option.

The second area of concern is what services are available in what areas. Further investigation reveals that between San Francisco and Vancouver, PSTN, ISDN, X.25, and T1 are all available. Between Lima and Vancouver, as well as Lima and San Francisco, only the PSTN and X.25 systems are available.

The next area of concern is to break the data transmissions down into major types or categories. The two main types of data transfer BI engages in are those of email and geological data transfers.

As mentioned earlier, the geological data files are quite large. In fact, they are often over 100 megabytes or greater. This type of daily data transfer definitely requires a lot of bandwidth. Given the options, a T1 line would work the best,

continues

CASE STUDY: MAKING DECISIONS ON CONNECTIVITY SERVICES OPTIONS

continued

given that it can transfer at up to 1.544Mbps. The problem is that no T1 service runs down to Lima.

As for the email, the X.25 and the PSTN would suffice. Both of these services are available. The main difference between the two options is that the PSTN is based on a dialup connection. Thus email would probably be delayed, because most email systems wait to dial up every few hours, or dial up only after a certain number of messages has been queued. With X.25, you have a constant connection, so email gets delivered almost as soon as it is sent.

Before any final answer can be determined, the following three issues would need to be discussed with Berg Industries management:

- How quickly the geological data needs to be sent to Vancouver. A T1 line is rather expensive. In fact, it would probably be cheaper to dump the data onto a CD or tape backup, and courier a copy to Vancouver every week.

- The cost of the PSTN versus the X.25 service. A PSTN is on timed intervals, and long

distance rates apply. A company that communicates a lot may find that the speed of the X.25 service in delivering the emails justifies any small additional expense that X.25 may have over the PSTN.

- How quickly an X.25 link could be established in Peru. In North America, people often expect and receive very fast service. In many third world countries, it can take months (even years in some cases) to get services hooked up. Thus the time it would take to get an X.25 link established should also be considered.

This case study, like so many of the others, has shown that an obvious solution is not always that easy to find. Often you need to gather more information than the situation may lend itself to or you come to realize that tradeoffs must be made between costs and efficiency. You present the client with the possibilities and then help them make the decision that works best for them, even if it is not the "perfect" solution. The perfect solution can be beyond most corporate budgets or the available technology.

CHAPTER SUMMARY

KEY TERMS

- PSTN
- leased lines
- T1
- T3

This chapter examined some basic WAN connectivity concepts, such as dial-up and dedicated service lines. You learned about some types of digital lines, such as the following:

- ◆ T1 and T3
- ◆ DDS
- ◆ Switched 56

CHAPTER SUMMARY

This chapter also described the characteristics of some important WAN connectivity service standards and appropriate situations for utilizing them. The services included the following:

- ISDN
- X.25
- Frame Relay
- ATM
- SMDS
- SONET

The services also included the following two new technologies emerging on the WAN horizon:

- ADSL
- Cable Modems

For more information on packet switching and virtual circuits, refer to Chapter 2.

The WAN connection services are summarized in Table 8.1.

- Digital Data Service (DDS)
- Switched 56
- switched virtual circuit (SVC)
- Permanent Virtual Circuit (PVC)
- Integrated Services Digital Network (ISDN)
- Basic Rate ISDN (BRI)
- Primary Rate ISDN (PRI)
- Broadband ISDN (B-ISDN)
- X.25
- Frame Relay
- Asynchronous Transfer Mode (ATM)
- Synchronous Optical Network (SONET)
- Switched Multimegabit Digital Service (SMDS)
- Asymmetric Digital Subscriber Line (ADSL)
- cable modem

TABLE 8.1
WAN CONNECTION COMPARISON

Service	Speed	Connection Type	Connection Format
PSTN	up to 56Kbps	Dial-up	Point to Point
T1	1.544Mbps	Permanent	Point to Point
T3	45Mbps	Permanent	Point to Point
DDS	up to 56Kbps	Permanent	Point to Point
Switched 56	up to 56Kbps	Permanent	Point to Point
ISDN	128Kbps	Dial-up	Point to Point
B-ISDN	51–622Mbps	Dial-up	Point to Point
X.25	56Kbps	Permanent	Multipoint
Frame Relay	1.544Mbps	Permanent	Multipoint
ATM	up to 622Mbps	Permanent	Multipoint
SMDS	45Mbps	Permanent	Multipoint
SONET	2488Mbps	Permanent	Multipoint
ADSL	8Mbps	Permanent	Multipoint
Cable Modem	10Mbps	Permanent	Multipoint

APPLY YOUR LEARNING

Exercises

8.1 Accessing an X.25 Network Through Windows NT Dial-Up Networking

Objective: Learn how to configure Windows NT Dial-Up Networking to connect to an X.25 network provider.

Estimated time: 15 minutes

Windows NT Remote Access Service (RAS) is usually used for modem connections to remote PCs, but you can also use RAS to access an X.25 packet-switching network. RAS supports Packet Assembler/Disassembler (PAD) devices and X.25 smart cards. Alternatively, you can use Windows NT's Dial-Up Networking to connect to a commercial X.25 provider. This exercise assumes that any modems or RAS are not already installed. The purpose of this exercise is to simply show how you would go about selecting an X.25 PAD device in RAS.

1. Click the Start menu and choose Settings/Control Panel. Double-click the Windows NT Control Panel Network application.

2. Choose the Network application's Services tab. Click on the Add button. Choose Remote Access Service from the Network Services list and click the OK button. You are prompted for the location of the installation files. Type in the location and click on the Continue button.

3. A dialog box appears telling you that there are no RAS-compatible devices to add, and asking whether you wish to enable the Modem installer program to add a modem. Click on the No button.

4. The Add RAS Device dialog box appears. Click on the Install X.25 Pad button.

5. The Install X25 PAD dialog box appears. Here you need to select the port to which the PAD is to be connected, and the X.25 PAD name. This PAD name must correspond to the PAD supplied to you by your service provider. Select a PAD device and click on OK.

6. Click on OK again, and then in the Remote Access Setup click on Cancel. This stops the RAS install. You do not wish to actually install the PAD device because you do not have one connected to your machine. You are prompted that your changes will not be saved. Click on the Yes button.

7. Click on the Cancel button to close the Network applet.

Review Questions

1. What are the main differences between dial-up and leased lines?

2. X.25 has one main benefit over other WAN connectivity options. What is it?

3. ATM is fast. What are its drawbacks?

Exam Questions

1. To what does the D channel refer in ISDN?

   A. Data rate

   B. Degradation signaling

   C. 16Kbps control channel

   D. 144Kbps combination channel

APPLY YOUR LEARNING

2. The DS-0 service level provides a transmission rate of what speed?

    A. 64Kbps

    B. 128Kbps

    C. 1.544Mbps

    D. 45Mbps

3. A T3 line provides a transmission rate of what speed?

    A. 64Kbps

    B. 128Kbps

    C. 1.544Mbps

    D. 45Mbps

4. What is an SVC?

    A. It is a permanent path. Charges are billed on a monthly basis.

    B. It is a permanent path. Charges are billed on a per-use basis.

    C. It is a temporary path created for a specific communication session.

    D. It is none of the above.

5. How does X.25 compare to Frame Relay?

    A. Faster than

    B. Slower than

    C. About the same speed as

    D. Nearly identical to

6. What was designed to provide digital communications over existing phone lines?

    A. X.25

    B. ISDN

    C. ATM

    D. Frame relay

7. What is sometimes called 2B+D?

    A. Primary rate ISDN

    B. Basic rate X.25

    C. Primary rate frame relay

    D. Basic rate ISDN

8. What is a typical working speed for ATM?

    A. 1.544Mbps

    B. 45Mbps

    C. 155Mbps

    D. 622Mbps

9. What is the size and name of the byte-size blocks in which ATM divides data?

    A. 53, packets

    B. 53, cells

    C. 56, frames

    D. 128, cells

10. A modem uses what type of signaling?

    A. Digital

    B. Analog

    C. Dedicated

    D. None of the above

APPLY YOUR LEARNING

11. Which three of the following are digital line options?

    A. Switched 16

    B. T1

    C. DDS

    D. Switched 56

12. What service uses a PAD?

    A. X.25

    B. Frame relay

    C. ATM

    D. ISDN

13. What service transfers data in fixed-length units called cells?

    A. X.25

    B. Frame relay

    C. ATM

    D. ISDN

14. The corporate network needs to expand and connect over a WAN to many different international locations. You need to come up with a solution that will enable the corporation to communicate.

    Primary objective: You need constant connectivity.

    Secondary objective: Data transfer speeds of 56Mbps are desired.

    Secondary objective: You need to utilize a standard that is available worldwide.

    Suggested Solution: You utilize an X.25 connection service.

    A. This solution meets the primary objective and both secondary objectives.

    B. This solution meets the primary objective and one secondary objective.

    C. This solution meets the primary objective.

    D. This solution does not satisfy the primary objective.

Answers to Review Questions

1. Dial-up lines are used and accessed only when the subscriber initializes them. They tend to be cheaper, because a circuit is established only when the subscriber initializes the call. When a subscriber is not using the service, the lines are available for other subscribers. PSTN and ISDN lines are examples of this.

   A leased line is a constant connection that is dedicated to a subscriber. You are paying for the 24-hour-a-day service, as well as a possible data throughput usage. A T1 line is an example of this.

   See the sections titled "ISDN and B-ISDN" and "The Public Telephone Network."

2. The main advantage of X.25 is that it is an accepted standard utilized by almost all telephone companies worldwide. Thus its global availability is its main benefit. See the section titled "X.25."

3. ATM is very fast—up to 622Mbps. Its drawbacks are its price and limited availability. See the section titled "ATM."

APPLY YOUR LEARNING

Answers to Exam Questions

1. **C.** The D channel on an ISDN line is used for controlling and signaling the transmission. See the section titled "ISDN."

2. **A.** A DS-0 is a single channel on a T1 line. Each channel on a T1 line has a speed of 64Kbps. See the section titled "T1 and T3."

3. **D.** A single channel in a T1 and T3 line provides 64Kbps. A T1's total capacity is 1.544Mbps. See the section titled "T1 and T3."

4. **C.** SVC stands for Switched Virtual Circuit. See the section titled "X.25."

5. **B.** X.25 is slower than frame relay. X.25 has speeds of up to 56Kbps, whereas frame relay's speeds approach 1.544Mbps. See the sections titled "X.25" and "Frame Relay."

6. **B.** ISDN was designed to provide digital communications over existing phone lines. X.25 is a packet-switching standard. ATM and frame relay are not designed to go over existing phone lines. See the section titled "ISDN."

7. **D.** 2B+D is BRI or Basic Rate ISDN. See the section titled "ISDN."

8. **C.** ATM typically operates at 155Mbps, but can reach speeds of up to 622Mbps. See the section titled "ATM."

9. **B.** ATM's speed is due to the uniform size of its data cells. Each cell is 53 bytes in length. See the section titled "ATM."

10. **B.** A modem uses analog signals. Modem stands for MODulator/DEModulator. See the section titled "Digital and Analog Signaling" in Chapter 5, "Network Adapter Cards."

11. **B, C, D.** All options except A are digital line options. There is nothing called "Switched 16." See the section titled "Leased Line Types."

12. **A.** A PAD is a Packet Assembly Device. This is the connecting unit for an X.25 network. Frame Relay, ATM, and ISDN do not use a PAD. See the section titled "X.25."

13. **C.** ATM uses 53-byte packets of data called cells. See the section titled "Asynchronous Transfer Mode (ATM)."

14. **B.** X.25 allows for constant connectivity and is also available worldwide. The first secondary objective cannot be met, however, because X.25 supports only up to 56Kbps, not 56Mbps. See the section titled "X.25."

Suggested Readings and Resources

1. Black, Ulysses. *Computer Networks: Protocols, Standards and Interfaces—The Professionals Guide.* Prentice Hall, 1993.

2. Horak, Ray, and Mark Miller. *Communication Systems and Networks: Voice, Data and Broadband Technologies.* IDG, 1993.

Chapter 9 targets the following objective in the Implementation section of the Networking Essentials exam:

Choose a disaster recovery plan for various situations.

▶ This exam topic deals with proactive measures that you can take to prevent lost data and server downtime.

CHAPTER 9

Disaster Recovery

STUDY STRATEGIES

▶ When reading this chapter, pay particular attention to what type of options are available to protect data. Be especially aware of those options that have to do with hard drive failures.

▶ Also be aware of the differences between the different RAID levels of fault tolerance.

INTRODUCTION

One of the major issues that a network administrator must address is the possibility of system failure and associated downtime. The administrator must handle two major issues to guard against the danger of a failed server:

◆ Protecting data

◆ Reducing downtime

This chapter discusses both issues and examines how the use of fault-tolerant disk configurations and a backup strategy can help reduce the danger of lost time and data.

PROTECTING DATA

Natural disasters, equipment failures, power surges, and deliberate vandalism can cause the catastrophic loss of precious network data. Protecting the data is a primary responsibility of the network administrator. Microsoft highlights these important strategies for preventing data loss:

◆ Backup

◆ Uninterruptible Power Supply (UPS)

Both strategies are discussed in the following sections.

Backup

A backup schedule is an essential part of any data-protection strategy. You should design a backup system that is right for your situation and the data on your network.

A number of different strategies can be used in backing up files. One way is simply to copy a file to another drive. Operating systems, however, typically have special backup commands that help you with some of the bookkeeping required for maintaining a systematic backup schedule. Most backup commands mark the file with the date and time of the backup so that you (and the backup utility) can know when a copy of the file was last saved. This is the purpose of the FAT file system's Archive attribute. To determine whether this attribute exists, check the properties of any file on a FAT partition. If the Archive attribute is enabled, the file has changed since the last time a backup was done. In this chapter, you will see that some backup techniques reset this attribute, whereas others do not.

Although backups can be accomplished by saving files to a different drive, they typically are performed with some form of tape drive. Commonly called *DAT drives*, these devices are capable of storing many gigabytes of information quickly and economically. Moreover, the tapes are small and portable and cheaper on a per-megabyte basis than a hard drive. Another important step in your backup plan, therefore, is deciding where to store these backup tapes. Many companies choose to make two copies of each backup tape and store one of the copies off-site, thereby guarding against a catastrophic event such as a fire.

In addition to two types of copy commands, Microsoft identifies the following backup types:

◆ *Full backup.* Backs up all specified files.

◆ *Incremental backup.* Backs up only those files that have changed since the last full or incremental backup.

◆ *Differential backup.* Backs up the specified files if the files have changed since the last backup. This type doesn't mark the files as having been backed up, however. (A differential backup is somewhat like a copy command. Because the file is not marked as having been backed up, a later differential or incremental backup backs up the file again.)

◆ *Daily Copy.* This is a Microsoft Windows NT NTBACKUP utility specific command. This command backs up only those files that were changed the day that this option was selected when doing a Daily Copy backup and does not modify the archive bit of the files being backed up. This is a useful option if you wish to do a backup outside the regular backup schedule and do not wish to alter or affect the normal backup routine.

◆ *Copy.* This is the other Microsoft Windows NT NTBACKUP utility specific command. This command backs up all selected files, but does not modify the archive bit of those files being backed up. Again, this is a useful option if you wish to do a backup outside the regular backup schedule and do not wish to alter or affect the normal backup routine.

A typical backup plan includes some combination of these backup types performed at regular intervals. One common practice is to perform an incremental or differential backup each day and a full backup every week. Full backups make the restoration process easier because there is theoretically only one set of tapes from which to restore; however, they also require a lengthy backup process each night. This could mean that if the backup tape media is not large enough, someone must physically change the tapes, or there simply may not be enough time in the night to perform a full backup of all the data. Companies therefore try to purchase backup media and create a schedule to automate of the backup process, thus not requiring anyone to be physically present to change the tape media.

Incremental backups are much faster because they back up only those files that have been changed since the last backup. The Archive attribute switches on when a file is modified. An incremental backup backs up the file and then removes the attribute so that the file will not be backed up again unless it is changed the next day. A combination of incremental and full backups usually results in four to six incremental tape sets and one full tape set each week. If the drives fail, the administrator must restore the last full backup set, as well as all the incremental backups performed since the drive failure. This process obviously is considerably slower than a backup scheme in which a full backup is performed every night.

Differential backups are similar to incremental backups except that they do not reset the Archive attribute, which means that each backup during the week backs up all files changed since the last full backup. A full backup once a week (generally Friday or Saturday) and differentials every other day means that theoretically only two tapes are needed in case of failure: the last full backup and the last differential (see Figure 9.1).

Keeping a log of all backups is important. Most backup utilities can generate a backup log. Microsoft recommends that you make two copies of the backup log—store one with the backup tapes and keep one at the computer site. Always test your backup system before you trust it. Perform a sample backup, restore the data, and check the data to be sure it is identical to the original.

FIGURE 9.1
An ideal backup scheme implements a schedule of different backup types.

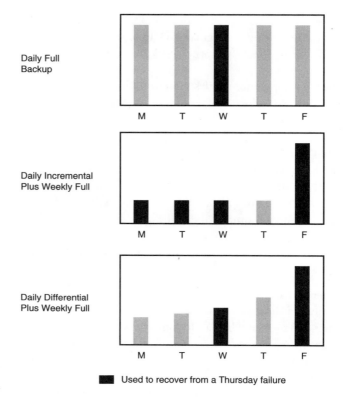

Daily Full
Backup

M   T   W   T   F

Daily Incremental
Plus Weekly Full

M   T   W   T   F

Daily Differential
Plus Weekly Full

M   T   W   T   F

▓ Used to recover from a Thursday failure

You can attach a tape drive directly to a single server, or you can back up several servers across the network at once. Backups over the network are convenient for the administrator, but they can produce considerable network traffic. You can reduce the effects of this extra traffic if you place the computer attached to the tape drive on an isolated network segment and connect it directly to secondary network interface cards on each of the servers.

A final point has to do with how long you wish to keep your stored data on the tape media. There is no correct time length. Some companies overwrite old tapes on a weekly basis, while others can keep their tape backups indefinitely. The correct time length depends on how important old data is to your firm. There is no simple answer to this question.

Uninterruptible Power Supply

An Uninterruptible Power Supply (UPS) is a special battery (or sometimes a generator) that supplies power to an electronic device in the event of a power failure. UPSs are commonly used with network servers to prevent a disorderly shutdown by warning users to log out. After a predetermined waiting period, the UPS software performs an orderly shutdown of the server. Many UPS units also regulate power distribution and serve as protection against power surges. Remember that in most cases a UPS generally does not provide for continued network functionality for longer than a few minutes. A UPS is not intended to keep the server running through a long power outage, but rather is designed to give the server time to do what it needs to before shutting down. This can prevent the data loss and system corruption that sometimes results from sudden shutdown. Some networks also have UPSs connected to their hubs and routers as well, giving administrators remote access to the servers so they can perform shutdown tasks in the event of a power outage.

When purchasing a UPS for a server, note that they come in many varieties (see Figure 9.2). As noted earlier, the UPS is really just a battery backup. Just like a car battery, the more powerful it is, the more expensive it is. Prices run from the hundreds to many thousands of dollars. Before you buy, know how many servers you will be running off the UPS and how much time they need to shut down properly. One of the most popular UPS manufacturers is APC (American Power Conversion), a company that offers a full line of power supply and UPS products.

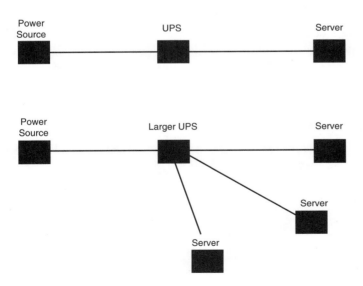

FIGURE 9.2
A large UPS can service numerous components at once.

In summary, a UPS enables a server to shut down gracefully. This in turn allows time for files to be saved, and corruption of data to be kept to a minimum. Backups mainly provide a quick method for system recovery. They require a long and tedious restoration process that can cost your company dearly in lost revenue and productivity. The following sections therefore examine some methods of minimizing—or even preventing—downtime in the event of a drive failure.

RECOVERING FROM SYSTEM FAILURE

Next to data security, keeping the network up and running properly is the most crucial day-to-day task of an administrator. The loss of a hard drive, even if not disastrous, can be a major inconvenience to your network users and may cost your organization in lost time and money. Procedures for lessening or preventing downtime from single hardware failures should be implemented. Disk configurations that enable this sort of protection are called *fault-tolerant* configurations. It should be noted that fault-tolerant configurations are not designed as a replacement for system tape backups.

Implementing a Fault-Tolerant Design

> **NOTE**
>
> **Balancing Needs and Costs** When developing a fault-tolerance scheme, remember that you must balance the need for rapid recovery from a failure against cost. The basic theory behind fault-tolerant design is hardware redundancy, which translates into additional hardware expenses. Also, remember that the greater the level of redundancy, the greater the complexity involved in the implementation.

Connecting network components into a fault-tolerant configuration ensures that one hardware failure doesn't halt the network. You can achieve network fault tolerance by providing redundant data paths, redundant hubs, and other such features. Generally, however, the data on the server itself—its hard drives—is the most crucial.

Using RAID

A vital tool for protecting a network's data is the use of a Redundant Array of Inexpensive Disks (RAID). Using a RAID system enables you to set up the best disk array design to protect your system. A RAID system combines two or more disks to create a large virtual disk structure that enables you to store redundant copies of the data. In a disk array, the drives are coordinated into different levels of RAID, to which the controller card distributes the data.

RAID uses a format of splitting data among drives at the bit, byte, or block level. The term *data striping* refers to the capability of arranging data in different sequences across drives. Demonstration of data stripping are shown in Figure 9.3. Microsoft calls this *disk stripping*.

Your input in designing the most reliable drive setup for your network is an important responsibility. You must choose the best RAID implementation level to meet your users' requirements in data integrity and cost. Seven levels of RAID are available on the market today: 0, 1, 2, 3, 4, 5, 6, and 10. A higher number isn't necessarily indicative of a better choice, so you must select the best level for

WARNING

Fault-Tolerance Does Not Replace Backups!   A fault-tolerant disk scheme is used only to speed recovery time from a hardware fault. None of these RAID levels is intended to be a replacement for regular tape backups.

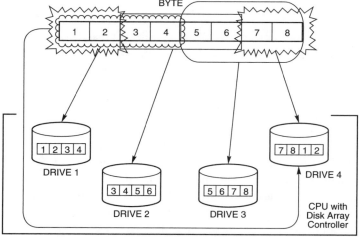

FIGURE 9.3
Data striping arranges data in different sequences across drives.

your environment. The following paragraphs present a brief discussion of some of these available levels, notably RAID 0, 1, and 5, which Windows NT Server supports. Windows NT Workstation supports only RAID 0, and Windows 95 is not able to use any RAID levels at all.

RAID 0

RAID 0 uses data striping and *block interleaving*, a process that involves distributing the data block by block across the disk array in the same location across each disk. Data can be read or written to these same sectors from either disk, thus improving performance. RAID 0 requires at least two disks, and the striped partitions must be of the same size. Note that redundancy of data is *not* provided in RAID 0, which means that the failure of any single drive in the array can bring down the entire system and result in the loss of all data contained in the array. RAID 0 is supported in Windows NT Server and Windows NT Workstation, but not in Windows 95. In short, RAID 0 does not provide any fault tolerance, just faster disk drive performance.

RAID 1

In RAID 1, drives are paired or mirrored: Each byte of information is written to two identical drives. *Disk mirroring* is defined as two hard drives—one primary, one secondary—that use the same disk channel (controller cards and cable), as shown in Figure 9.4. Disk mirroring is most commonly configured by using disk drives contained in the server.

Disk mirroring is called *disk duplexing* when a separate drive controller is added for each drive. Duplexing, which is covered later in this chapter, is a form of mirroring that enables you to configure a more robust hardware environment.

Mirroring does not provide a performance benefit such as RAID 0 provides. You can use mirroring, however, to create two copies of the server's data and operating system, which enables either disk to boot and run the server. If one drive in the pair fails, for instance, the other drive can continue to operate. Disk mirroring can be expensive, though, because it requires 2GB of disk space for every 1GB you want to mirror. You also must make sure that your power source has enough wattage to handle the additional devices. Mirroring requires two drives, and the mirrored partitions must be of the same

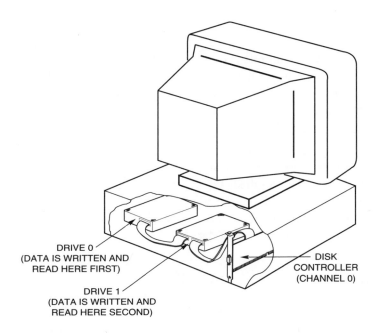

DRIVE 0
(DATA IS WRITTEN AND
READ HERE FIRST)

DRIVE 1
(DATA IS WRITTEN AND
READ HERE SECOND)

DISK
CONTROLLER
(CHANNEL 0)

size. Windows NT Server supports mirroring, but Windows NT Workstation and Windows 95 do not.

Remember that mirroring is done for fault-tolerant, not performance reasons. With this said, it should be noted that a Windows NT machine running a mirror set runs at about normal speed. It may exhibit a degradation if only one controller card is shared by the two hard drives. The controller must make each write twice, once for each drive. On the other hand, a mirrored hard drive set can produce marginal performance gains reading from the set because either drive can satisfy the read. For the best of both worlds, though, consider RAID 5.

RAID LEVEL 5 MOST POPULAR SCHEME

RAID Levels Supported in Windows NTRAID 2, 3, 4, and 5 are all versions of striping that incorporate similar fault-tolerant designs. Microsoft chose to support only RAID 5 striping in Windows NT Server. As the numbering scheme would imply, this is the newest revision of the four and is the most popular fault-tolerance scheme in use today. Level 5 requires less disk space than mirroring and has performance gains over other striping methods. As with mirroring, RAID level 5 is not available in Windows NT Workstation or Windows 95.

RAID 5

RAID 5 uses striping with parity information written across multiple drives to enable fault tolerance with a minimum of wasted disk space. This level also offers the advantage of enabling relatively efficient performance on writes to the drives, as well as excellent read performance.

Striping with parity is based on the principle that all data is written to the hard drive in binary code (ones and zeros). RAID 5 requires at least three drives because this version writes data across two of them and then creates the parity block on the third. This writing of data and the parity bit is spanned across all drives being used. If the first byte is 00111000 and the second is 10101001, then the system computes the third by adding the digits together using this system:

1+1=0, 0+0=0, 0+1=1, 1+0=1

The sum of 00111000 and 10101001 is 10010001, which is written to the third disk. This process would continues as the next parity bit is written to the first drive, and the data to the second and third. On the third round, the parity bit is written to the second drive and the data to the first and third drive. Then this cycle repeats itself.

If any of the disks fail, the process can be reversed and any disk can be reconstructed from the data and parity bits on the other two. See Figure 9.5 for an illustration of the process. Recovery includes replacing the bad disk and then regenerating its data through the Disk Administrator. A maximum of 32 disks can be connected in a RAID 5 array under Windows NT.

Choosing a RAID Level

When implementing a disk scheme, you have some options to consider. First, you must decide whether you are interested in performance gains (RAID 0), often used by read-only databases loaded from a CD-ROM, or data redundancy (RAID 1 or 5), often required by systems that need real-time access to continually changing data, such as a scheduling system. Mirroring (RAID 1), for instance, enables the fastest recovery but results in a 50% loss of disk space. Likewise, striping with parity (RAID 5) is more economical but requires at least three physical disks and therefore provides more points of potential hardware failure. RAID 0 makes sense when the data change little or not at all and are available from CD-ROM or

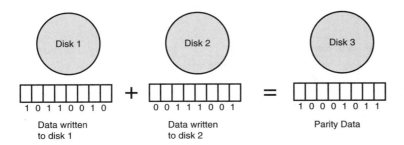

FIGURE 9.5
In this example, if Disk 2 fails, the system can reconstruct the information on it using the parity data.

If disk 2 fails, the system is able to reconstruct the information on it by using the parity data...

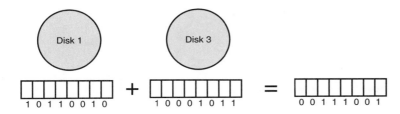

other types of backup storage. In Windows NT, all the RAID levels are supported as software implementations of RAID, but you can implement hardware versions as well.

Most network administrators prefer the RAID 5 solution, at least on larger servers with multiple drive bays. Because this level is a hybrid of striping and mirroring, it enables greater speed and more redundancy. Mirroring, however, offers the advantage of working well with non-SCSI hardware, because some older machines accommodate two IDE drives only, and is common as a fault-tolerant option on smaller, non-dedicated servers. Striping *without* parity should be reserved for workstations and servers on which speed considerations are paramount and possible downtime is an acceptable risk. See Figure 9.6 for a graphical comparison.

Disk Duplexing

In the event of disk channel failure (by a controller card or cable), access to all data on the channel stops and a message appears on the file server console screen (if your users don't let you know about it first). Even though drives can be mirrored, all disk activity on the mirrored pair ceases if the mirrored drives are connected to the same disk controller.

FIGURE 9.6
Different RAID levels offer their own unique
capabilities.

RAID 0 - Disk Striping

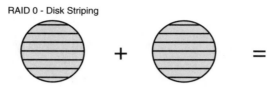

Requires at least two disks
Configured for performance gain, NOT FAULT TOLERANT

RAID 1 - Disk Mirroring

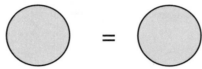

Fault Tolerant
Wastes 50% of disk space
Can slow down the system on extensive writes.

RAID 5 - Disk Striping with Parity

Fault Tolerant
More efficient in disk usage than mirroring
Performance aided by striping, slowed by writing parity
End result is moderate write performance, fast reads

Disk duplexing performs the function of simultaneously writing data
to disks located on different channels. As Figure 9.7 illustrates, each
hard disk in a duplexed pair connects to a separate hard disk controller. This figure shows a configuration in which the drives are
housed in separate disk subsystems. Each subsystem also has a separate power supply. Disk duplexing offers a more reliable setup than is
possible with mirroring because a failure of one disk drive's power
supply doesn't disable the server. Instead, the server continues to
work with the system that remains under power.

Working on the same channel is analogous to going to a baseball
game when only one gate into the stadium is open. You can enter
or exit through only one gate (channel) at the stadium (file server),
and the crowd (data) can get backed up on both sides. If more
than one gate (another channel) is open, though, the crowd (data)
doesn't become backed up on both sides of the fence (file server or
workstation). This is why disk duplexing, which uses a separate

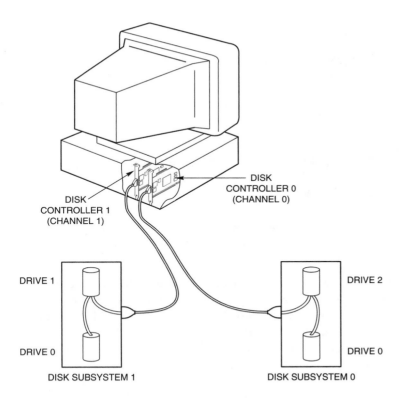

FIGURE 9.7
Disk duplexing simultaneously writes data to
two disks located on different controller cards.

adapter card for each disk, has faster reads and writes than disk mirroring.

Duplexing protects information at the hardware level with duplicate
channels (controller cards and cables) and duplicate hard drives.

Mirroring uses one controller card and two hard drives. The point
of failure for this setup is primarily the controller card or the cable
connecting the drives to the controller card. Disk duplexing uses
two controller cards and a minimum of one drive per controller
card. The point of failure is reduced with duplicate hardware.

THIRD-PARTY OPTIONS

A number of different vendors also offer RAID protection at the
hardware level on their server products. This protection is independent of the operating system, so if you really feel that RAID 5 on
your Windows 95 workstation is a necessity, these software vendors might have a solution for you.

The previous sections examined a number of different disk configurations. Exercise 9.1 shows how you implement these RAID levels and other disk configuration options in Windows NT. The primary program for managing disk storage resources is the Disk Administrator, a tool that is generally usable only by members of the Administrators or Server Operators groups.

OTHER FAULT-TOLERANCE MECHANISMS

Two other forms of fault tolerance exist on the market today. One of these is known as *server mirroring* while the other is a hardware solution known as a *super server*.

Server mirroring refers to having one server completely mirrored in all forms to another server. This means that if Server A goes down for any reason whatsoever, such as a failed hard drive, failed network card, or even a blown motherboard, the mirrored Server B takes over the duties of Server A. This type of fault tolerance is offered by Microsoft in their Microsoft Cluster Server product.

A second option on fault tolerance is a super server. A super server is a hardware solution offered by several different hardware manufacturers. The idea behind a super server is that almost any piece of equipment can be changed on the super server without shutting down the server. This can mean that the super server can have hot swappable components such as hard drives, CPUs, and even RAM.

CASE STUDY: IMPLEMENTING FAULT TOLERANCE FOR A CORPORATE NETWORK

ESSENCE OF THE CASE

The essence of the case is as follows:

- The company works on a small LAN with one server.
- A backup strategy is needed.
- Restore time should preferably not go over two hours.
- The insurance company wishes to be made aware of the costs and benefits of different fault-tolerance options.

SCENARIO

You are meeting with the branch manager of an insurance firm. This is a large insurance firm that employs fifty insurance brokers. They have just changed over from their old paper methods of filing insurance claims and contracts to using computers on a LAN.

The LAN is composed of 30 workstations and one file server. All data is stored on the file server which has a 3GB drive. Nothing of importance is stored on the workstations. Downtime should be kept to a 2 hour maximum, because brokers can still sell insurance using the software on their PCs, but if the server is down, they cannot retrieve any client information.

This insurance company is now very interested in designing a backup strategy and possibly installing some form of fault tolerance for the branch. Your job is to provide a backup solution and give a general cost analysis of different fault-tolerance methods.

ANALYSIS

This analysis is presented in two parts: Backup solutions and fault-tolerance options.

Backup Solutions

This company has a server with a very small hard drive of only three gigabytes in size. By today's standard this is not very large. Because a single backup tape can accommodate this size of a hard drive, a simple solution would be to do a full backup. No one needs to be around to switch tapes, and the backup process should not take more than a couple of hours. Also, restoring can be done much more quickly from a full backup than from a differential or incremental backup.

One could also make the argument that a differential backup should be done each night, with a full backup being done every week. This is often done when companies have such a large amount of data being backed up that one tape is not sufficient to do a full backup or when there are not enough hours during the night to accomplish a full backup. Because this company's data storage is not that large, and there is easily enough time in the evening to do a full backup, there is no reason why a full backup should not be done each night.

Fault Tolerance

This insurance company has several options for fault tolerance. These range from disk mirroring to clustered super servers. Almost all the fault-tolerance options can be done together.

continues

CASE STUDY: IMPLEMENTING FAULT TOLERANCE FOR A CORPORATE NETWORK

continued

UPS

A UPS should be purchased. The cost could be only a few hundred dollars, but the benefit of the UPS in preventing data corruption due to a power failure would more than offset this cost.

Disk Mirroring/Disk Duplexing

This option can be done. It would mean the purchase of an additional 3GB drive. If disk duplexing was done, it would also mean the purchase of a disk controller. If either of the drives failed (or controller cards if you were doing duplexing), the other drive could take over. This would prevent downtime for the company. This option would probably cost under $1000.

Disk Striping with Parity

This option is feasible. It would mean purchasing at least two more drives. If any of the drives failed, the data could be regenerated from the striped parity bit. This option would also cost probably under $1000. One thing to be aware of is that because the costs of hard drives are relatively low nowadays, disk striping with parity, in the case of the 3GB of storage, is really not much more expensive than disk mirroring, but would also provide an extra 3GB of disk storage space (original 3GB + 2 more 3GB drives equals 9GB, with 1/3 of the drive space used for the parity bit).

Server Clustering

Server clustering is also an option. This option would cost the equivalent of the price of all the hardware and software of the original server, plus the price of the clustering software. The benefit is that if any component fails in either server, the other clustered server can take over the functions of the downed server.

Super Server

This option would be the most expensive. It would cost well into the tens of thousands of dollars. The benefit is that if any component fails, a backup component can take over. In addition, faulty components can be replaced without downing the server.

Based on the fact that the company can afford several hours of downtime, the options for the super server and clustering would more than likely be voted down, because they exceed the requirements of the insurance company. The options of disk mirroring and disk striping/duplexing with parity are both contenders, and probably should be recommended based upon whichever option is cheapest.

CHAPTER SUMMARY

This chapter examined a number of options open to an administrator looking to provide data security and hardware redundancy for the network. Through the use of a regular backup plan, the installation of a UPS, and the implementation of a fault-tolerant disk scheme, you can help to ensure that your network will run as efficiently and safely as possible. Remember that there is no particular formula to use here; rather, you should follow a process of weighing costs against benefits. In the end, you want to provide the highest degree of safety for your critical data that you can achieve given your budget.

KEY TERMS

- Full backup
- Incremental backup
- Differential backup
- Daily copy
- Copy
- Uninterruptible Power Supply (UPS)
- RAID
- Data striping
- Disk striping
- Block interleaving
- Disk mirroring
- Disk duplexing
- Disk striping with parity
- Server mirroring
- Super server

APPLY YOUR LEARNING

Exercises

9.1   Exploring Windows NT's Disk Administrator

Objective: Explore the options available through Disk Administrator, such as establishing and breaking mirrored drives and creating or regenerating stripe sets with parity.

Estimated time: 10 minutes

To complete exercise 9.1, log on to a Windows NT 4.0 server or workstation with an account that has administrative authority. The server or workstation used can be a production machine—no changes will actually be made to the computer's configuration during this exercise if the steps in this exercise are followed.

1. Click Start, Programs, Administrative Tools. Then choose Disk Administrator. If this is the first time the application is run, or if disks have been added to the system, you will be asked for permission to write a signature block to the disk. If this message appears, click on Yes.

2. Observe the Disk Administrator window and maximize it if it is not already in this state. The configuration of the disk or disks on your machine is displayed.

3. Click one of the partitions on your screen. A dark black line appears around the partition, indicating that the partition is selected. Right-click on the partition and observe the available menu choices in the context-sensitive menu. Note that you can format the partition, delete the partition, change its logical drive letter, or examine its properties. If the disk is removable, the Eject option is also available.

4. Click Partition in the Menu bar and examine the choices. Most of the choices are unavailable, but they include Create Volume Set and Create Stripe Set. You also can change your active partition in this Menu bar.

5. Click Fault-tolerance on the Menu bar (Windows NT Server only) and observe that this menu enables you to establish and break mirrored drives, as well as to create or regenerate stripe sets with parity.

6. Feel free to explore further, and when you are finished examining the menus and options, close out of the Disk Administrator by clicking Partition, Exit. If you are asked to commit or save your changes, click Cancel.

Review Questions

1. What method of fault tolerance uses two controller cards on two separate hard drives?

2. What are the three backup methods that are not Microsoft NT NTBACKUP-specific?

APPLY YOUR LEARNING

Exam Questions

1. What is an incremental backup?

   A. Backs up parts of the specified file that have changed since the last backup

   B. Backs up and marks only those files that have changed since they were last backed up

   C. Backs up the files that have changed since they were last backed up but doesn't mark them as being backed up

   D. Backs up the files that have changed over the course of a specified time period

2. What is a differential backup?

   A. Backs up files that have changed since the last backup and doesn't mark the files as having been backed up

   B. Backs up files that have changed since the last backup and marks the files as having been backed up

   C. Copies all files that have been modified within a specific time period and marks them as having been backed up

   D. Copies all files that have been modified within a specified time period and doesn't mark them as having been backed up

3. What is the best way to reduce the effects of extra traffic caused by a network backup?

   A. Attach the tape drive directly to one of the servers

   B. Back up each server to a nearby server

   C. Place the computer attached to the tape drive on an isolated network segment

   D. Back up the servers in ascending order of the size of the backup

4. What does UPS stands for?

   A. Unintentional Packet Switch

   B. Unfamiliar Password Sequence

   C. Unknown Polling Sequence

   D. Uninterruptible Power Supply

5. How does RAID Level 5 operate?

   A. Uses bit interleave data striping

   B. Uses block interleave data striping

   C. Doesn't use data striping

   D. Provides parity-checking capabilities

6. How does RAID Level 1 operate?

   A. Uses bit interleave data striping

   B. Uses block interleave data striping

   C. Doesn't use data striping

   D. Provides parity-checking capabilities

7. What is the difference between disk mirroring and disk duplexing?

   A. Disk mirroring is more reliable.

   B. Mirrored disks share the same disk channels.

   C. Duplexed disks share the same disk channels.

   D. There is no difference.

APPLY YOUR LEARNING

8. True or False: Implementing a RAID system eliminates the need for tape backup.

   A. True

   B. False

9. What is the minimum number of disks needed to configure a stripe set with parity on Windows NT Server?

   A. Two

   B. Three

   C. Four

   D. Seven

10. RAID 5 is a term that describes which of the following?

    A. A weekday backup strategy for enterprise networks

    B. A fault-tolerant disk configuration

    C. An NDIS-compatible SCSI controller

    D. Data backup through directory replication

11. What is the maximum number of disks in a stripe set for NT?

    A. 2

    B. 16

    C. 32

    D. Limited only by hardware

12. What is the maximum number of drives supported in a mirror set?

    A. 2

    B. 4

C. 16

D. None of the above

13. A corporate network running Windows NT would like to increase the fault tolerance on its systems.

    Primary objective: The system cannot have a drive failure cause the system to become inaccessible.

    Secondary objective: The server on the network needs to be able to shut down properly in the event of a power failure.

    Secondary objective: Data access speed is not critical.

    Suggested Solution: You install three hard drives, set up disk striping, and add a UPS to the server.

    A. This solution meets the primary objective and both secondary objectives.

    B. This solution meets the primary objective and one secondary objective.

    C. This solution meets the primary objective.

    D. This solution does not meet the primary objective.

14. A corporate network running Windows NT would like to increase the fault tolerance on its systems.

    Primary objective: The system cannot have a drive failure cause the system to become inaccessible.

    Secondary objective: The server on the network needs to be able to shut down properly in the event of a power failure.

APPLY YOUR LEARNING

Secondary objective: Data access speed is not critical.

Suggested Solution: You install three hard drives and set up Disk Striping with Parity.

A. This solution meets the primary objective and both secondary objectives.

B. This solution meets the primary objective and one secondary objectives.

C. This solution meets the primary objective.

D. This solution does not satisfy the primary objective.

15. A corporate network running Windows NT would like to increase the fault tolerance on its systems.

Primary objective: The system cannot have a drive failure cause the system to become inaccessible.

Secondary objective: The server on the network needs to be able to shut down properly in the event of a power failure.

Secondary objective: Data access speed is not critical.

Suggested Solution: You install two hard drives, set up disk duplexing, and add a UPS to the server.

A. This solution meets the primary objective and both secondary objectives.

B. This solution meets the primary objective and one secondary objectives.

C. This solution meets the primary objective.

D. This solution does not satisfy the primary objective.

Answers to Review Questions

1. Disk duplexing uses two controller cards, one for each disk. Disk duplexing is the same as disk mirroring, but disk mirroring uses only one controller card. See the section titled "Disk Duplexing."

2. The three methods of backup are full, incremental, and differential backups. Full back up backs up all data. An incremental backup backs up only the data that has changed since the last incremental backup. Incremental backups remove the archive bit on a file. The third option is differential backup. A differential backup does not remove the archive bit on a file, and backs up all data since the last full backup. See the section titled "Backup."

Answers to Exam Questions

1. **B.** A is incorrect because the entire file is always backed up. C is incorrect because this is a differential backup. D is incorrect because files are not backed up over "the course of a specified time." See the section titled "Backup."

2. **A.** B is incorrect because the files are not marked in a differential backup. C is incorrect because no files are copied, and nothing is marked as "backed up." D is incorrect because files are not backed up due to a time interval. See the section titled "Backup."

3. **C.** A is incorrect because a tape drive attached to the computer to back up that computer is not a network backup. B is incorrect because it does not reduce network traffic. D is incorrect because backing up according to server size does not

APPLY YOUR LEARNING

reduce the network traffic. See the section titled "Backup."

4. **D**. All answers but D are made up. See the section titled "Uninterruptible Power Supply."

5. **D**. All answers but D do not apply to RAID 5. See the section titled "RAID5."

6. **C**. A and B have nothing to do with RAID 1. D is a function of RAID 5. See the section titled "RAID 1."

7. **B**. Disk duplexing is disk mirroring, but with each hard drive on a separate controller card. See the section titled "Disk Duplexing."

8. **B**. RAID systems never replace the need for a backup. RAID systems provide a short term solution for drive failures. See the section titled "Implementing a Fault-Tolerant Design."

9. **B**. Stripe sets with parity need a minimum of three disks. Disk mirroring requires only two disks. See the section titled "RAID 5."

10. **B**. RAID 5 is a fault-tolerant "Redundant Array of Inexpensive Disks." See the section titled "RAID 5."

11. **C**. 32 is the maximum disks handled in a stripe set for NT. See the section titled "RAID 5."

12. **A**. Mirror sets contain only 2 disks. See the section titled "Disk Duplexing."

13. **D**. Disk Striping does not provide any fault tolerance. It yields faster reads when accessing the data. Adding a UPS does meet both secondary objectives. The primary objective is not met by implementing Disk Striping (RAID 0). Disk striping with parity and disk duplexing would meet the required solution. See the sections titled "Implementing a Fault-Tolerant Design" and "Uninterruptible Power Supply."

14. **B**. Disk striping with parity meets the primary objective and second secondary objective. Because the proposed solution contains nothing about power outages, the first secondary objective is not met. See the sections titled "Implementing a Fault-Tolerant Design" and "Uninterruptible Power Supply."

15. **A**. All objectives are met with this solution. See the sections titled "Implementing a Fault-Tolerant Design" and "Uninterruptible Power Supply."

Suggested Readings and Resources

1. Siyan, Karanjit S. *Windows NT Server 4 Professional Reference*. New Riders, 1996.

2. Heywood, Drew. *Inside Windows NT Server 4.* New Riders, 1997.

3. Casad, Joe. *MCSE Training Guide: Windows NT Server 4*. New Riders, 1997.

4. Sirockman, Jason. *MCSE Training Guide: Windows NT Server 4 Enterprise*. New Riders, 1997.

PART III

IMPLEMENTATION

Chapter 10 targets the following objectives in the "Implementation" and the "Standards and Terminology" sections of the Networking Essentials exam:

Choose an administrative plan to meet specified needs, including performance management, account management, and security

▶ Network security can vary depending on the network operating system being used. Because of the existence of different security models, it is important to understand the different administrative models that exist. One model may be ideal for one situation, but impractical for another. This chapter analyzes these issues and explains the various administrative models in order to address the issues of performance, account management, and security. To master this exam topic, pay particular attention to the differences between Workgroup and Domain administrative models. This objective is addressed throughout the entire chapter.

Compare user-level security with access permission assigned to a shared directory on a server

▶ This exam objective is designed to encourage you to know the different permissions available to assign to users or groups on a shared directory.

CHAPTER 10

Managing and Securing a Microsoft Network

OUTLINE

▶ This chapter addresses two exam topics. In order to study for these topics, pay particular attention to the differences in what Windows 95 and Windows NT computers offer in terms of security. Be aware that Windows NT security is much more complex than that offered by Windows 95.

▶ Both Windows 95 and Windows NT offer share level security. Be aware of the differences between share level security on Windows NT and Windows 95, as well as the difference between file level and share level security that is offered by Windows NT.

INTRODUCTION

In the preceding chapters, the process of establishing a physical connection between the machines on your network and installing the drivers and services necessary to enable network communication was examined. With these initial considerations out of the way, the next step is to begin organizing and controlling the manner and scope of network usage. This chapter deals with the process of implementing resource sharing, with the main focus being the administration of a Microsoft network.

The process of implementing resource sharing will be presented in the following order: First, a general overview of some key resource terms is presented. From this perspective, several different administrative models will be presented and contrasted. You should focus on the administrative models supported by Windows NT and Windows 95. After you have this background, file security and then print security will be analyzed from both Windows NT and Windows 95 perspectives. The final area of discussion will focus on some additional administrative tasks that should be performed on a network

EXAM TIP

Resource Security in Windows NT and Windows 95   Pay particular attention to how Windows NT and Windows 95 perform resource security. Be prepared to explain the differences between these two major models.

RESOURCE SHARING BASICS

Microsoft uses very specific terms to describe elements of its networking structure, and as such, a good understanding of these terms is essential. The five most basic terms that you must understand are *resources*, *sharing*, *users*, *groups*, and *security*.

Resources

The first concept to be discussed is a *resource*. A resource is essentially any component that you would like to use on the network. This could be as simple as a file on another machine, to a printer located at the end of the hall, to even a certain task available by a specific program. The two key resources detailed in this chapter are data files and printers, but in theory, a resource can be any information or device relating to the network. Without networking, a resource can be accessed only by physically sitting at the machine on which the resource is installed. This would mean that you could only access a local file or a local printer. The creation of a networking structure grants you the capability to use a server computer to share resources with others at remote client machines.

Sharing

This brings us to the second important concept: sharing. Only by specifying that you want to grant others access to a resource—be it a directory, a CD-ROM drive, or a printer—do you make the resource available for use from remote computers and devices. A shared resource is simply a resource whose owner has leveraged networking to make it available for use by others. Some resources are not available until an administrator actually manually shares out the resource. Some examples of these resources are files and printers. Other resources are automatically shared out when installed. An example of this is the ability to see a computer on the network when browsing the network.

Users

A *user* is anyone who requests network resources. In most cases, you assign a unique username and password to every individual on your network. Users can be created on a number of operating systems, including Windows NT, NetWare, and UNIX. Users cannot be created on Windows 95 or Windows for Workgroups because neither of these operating systems have the capability of establishing a user database. Both Windows 95 and Windows for Workgroups do enable the creation of individualized profiles, but as you will see later in the chapter, they must rely on another machine's database to provide true user authentication, such as an Windows NT domain controller.

Groups

Groups are administrative units that are comprised of one or more users with similar needs for network resources. Often users are placed into groups, and resource access is managed on a group basis, as opposed to an individual user basis. It is much easier to manage five groups than five hundred users. Two types of groups exist on Windows NT—local and global. These groups are key to efficient security in the Microsoft model.

Security

The issue of *security* is one of the main focuses of this chapter. Security is the process of giving "Rights" or "Permissions" to groups or users, such that they can access resources on the network. Different Network operating systems use different terms to describe these types of security issues. Windows NT makes a distinction between "Rights" and "Permissions." The details of these differences between these "Rights" and "Permissions" will be addressed in greater detail later on in this chapter.

GENERAL NETWORK ADMINISTRATIVE MODELS

Choose an administrative plan to meet specified needs, including performance management, account management, and security.

There are numerous networking administrative models that perform security to choose from. Most network operating systems follow or include only one model, yet others allow you to pick from several models. This section will discuss four commonly used network security models that are commonly used in networking today. These are:

- ◆ Workgroups
- ◆ Bindery-based
- ◆ Domains
- ◆ Directory services

These four classifications are not etched in stone, and are by no means the only four options in existence. They do, however, represent the majority of the network security models found on the market today. When comparing these models, pay particular attention to the sections on workgroups and domains, as these are the two current models used by Microsoft networks.

Workgroup Model

One common security model used on small networks is the workgroup model. This administrative model is built into network operating systems such as Windows 95, Windows for Workgroups, and Windows NT.

In a workgroup model, there is no centralized database or server that stores user account information (see Figure 10.1). This type of security model is found on a peer-to-peer type network. In a workgroup model, there are one or more machines that have a resource to share. Assume this resource is a directory containing some files. In order to allow other computers to access these files, the computers containing these files in the directory must have a service running that allows them advertise this sharing of resources.

A workgroup is just a name associated with a group of computers. Any computer, when installed, can be part of any workgroup they wish. If none exists, you can install a computer to be part of a new workgroup. The name of a workgroup is simply for organizational purposes, such that when one uses a network browser, computers that are part of the same workgroup will be clustered together. Often workgroup names will be descriptive, such as ENGINEERING or ACCOUNTING.

N O T E

The Apple Version of Workgroups
Apple computers also follow a model similar to a workgroup model, but the terminology used by Apple computers is a "zone" as opposed to a "workgroup." Multiple network segments can be joined to form a single zone, and a single segment can have multiple zones.

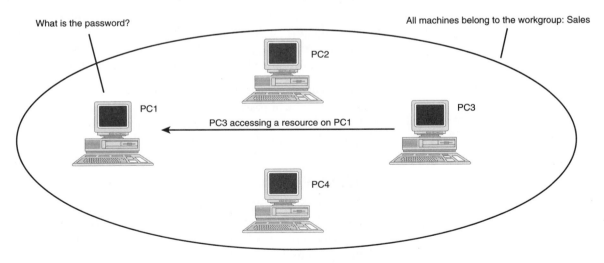

FIGURE 10.1
A workgroup does not rely on a centralized user account database.

There are two variations found within the Workgroup model. One is a Windows 95 and Windows for Workgroups variation, while the other is a Windows NT variation.

Windows 95

In order for users on other computers to access files or printers on other computers, their computers must have a redirector (see Chapter 1) installed that will allow them to connect to the advertising service. In Windows 95, the redirector is called "Client for Microsoft Networks," and the service that allows shared files to be accessed over the network is called "File and printer sharing for Microsoft networks." Exercise 10.5 will give you hands-on practice in installing and using these services.

When a resource is shared out on the network, this provides the capability to allow users access to the resource, but there is no capability to give this access to the resource on a user-by-user, or group-by-group basis. This is because when sharing out a resource, you can only specify a password to protect the resource. When anyone tries to connect to this shared resource, they will be prompted for a password. If they type in the correct password, when prompted, they will get access to the resource. If they do not know the password, they will be denied access. This is very similar to "Ali Babba and the 40 thieves." In order to get into the secret cave, Ali Babba needed to know the password, which was "Open Sesame." The workgroup works on the same principle. Anyone who does know the password will be allowed access; anyone who doesn't will be denied.

This security model works well in small networks. As a network grows, the use of passwords on every shared resource becomes cumbersome. There is also no method of controlling anyone from telling others the password to your shared resources.

Windows NT

Windows NT Workstation and Server both have the ability to be installed within a workgroup. This option is selected during the installation of the software, but can, in most cases, also be done after the computer is installed.

The Windows NT workgroup model works in a fashion similar to that used by Windows 95, yet there is a major exception. Each

Windows NT computer does contain a local database of user accounts. In order to access a local Windows NT computer, you would need to log on to the computer using a name and password found in the local user account database. The contents of this local user account database are not used with any other computers.

WHEN WINDOWS 95 CAN OFFER USER-LEVEL SECURITY

Windows 95 does have the ability to reference accounts on a Windows NT server (in a workgroup or a domain) or Novell server offering bindery services. This is known as implementing user level security in Windows 95.

The ability for Windows 95 to provide this service does rely on the presence of either a Windows NT domain controller, Windows NT computer as part of a workgroup, or a Novell server with bindery services being present. The user, when logging on to the Windows 95 computer, will have their logon credentials passed onto the respective server for authentication.

In conclusion, when mixing Windows 95 and Windows NT (or Novell) servers, it is possible for Windows 95 to offer user level security and for Windows NT computers, as part of a workgroup, to share their account databases.

Windows NT in a workgroup model has the capability to reference users on a user-by-user basis when assigning security to shared resources. The users a Windows NT computer can reference are only the ones found within its own user account database. To have a security model, you would need to create all of the users on your network in each of the Windows NT local databases. If your network had ten users and ten Windows NT computers, if you added one new computer, you would have to recreate all of your ten users within that new computer's local user account database. Likewise, if a new user is added to the network, their name would have to be added to all of the local databases on each of the existing Windows NT computers. The same would go if a user changed their password; each Windows NT computer would need to be updated with the new password of the user.

The workgroup networking model is highly decentralized, and requires an administrator to perform many repetitive tasks, such as adding user accounts or having users create many different shares and assigning passwords to these shares. The workgroup model for Windows NT is similar to the Windows 95 workgroup model, in that it is often only found on very small networks.

Bindery-Based Model

The bindery-based model is one that is used by Novell NetWare versions up to NetWare 3.2 (all Novell servers that are version 4 or higher use Directory Services). Bindery-based networks follow the client/server model of networking. Novell bindery-based servers still have a large presence in many networks to this day.

In a bindery model, there is one server and many clients. The server contains a flat user account database (see Figure 10.2). A flat user account database is one that contains the names of users, in one single list from A to Z, who are allowed to log onto the system. Also, this database of user accounts is used to assign who has rights or privileges to use different resources on the network. These rights are either assigned on a user-by-user basis or a group-by-group basis.

The server is also responsible for containing all of the services on the network. The client machines are not designed to provide any

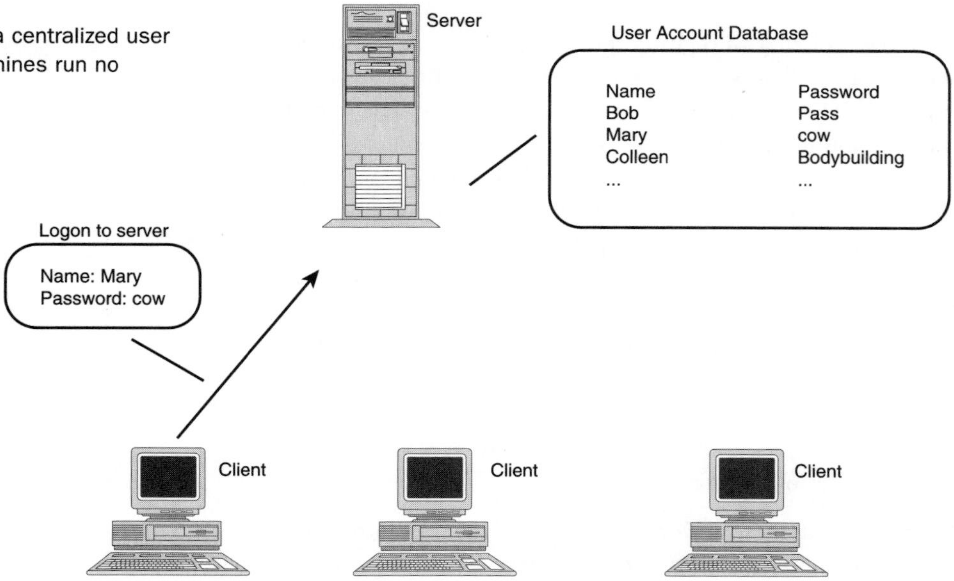

FIGURE 10.2

A Bindery-based network has a centralized user account database. Client machines run no services.

Server

User Account Database

Name	Password
Bob	Pass
Mary	cow
Colleen	Bodybuilding
...	...

Logon to server

Name: Mary
Password: cow

Client   Client   Client

services at all. This allows for a more centralized method of management of the network.

A client machine on this system is one that has a redirector installed on it, such that it will connect to a central server, and try to authenticate against that server's user account database. The user will supply a valid name that exists within the user account database (logon name) and an associated password.

If the name and password exist within the server's user account database, the user is granted permission to use the network, and in turn, the user's computer is given a "key" by the authenticating server. This key is similar to a security badge that you may wear when touring a secured facility. The key essentially identifies who you are as an individual and what groups you belong to. Based upon this key, you as a user will be granted access to shared resources or denied shared resources. This granting of the key is transparent to the user; they will in most cases "see" those resources available to them and not see the resources that are not available to them.

In a bindery model, there is a benefit of having one centralized database from which to perform all of the management tasks. This is preferred in a larger network for managing resources, as it simplifies and centralizes the management of these resources. There is also the benefit of having the capability to give access to shared resources on a user-by-user or group-by-group basis as security can be done on a more specific basis. Also, users will not have to remember a whole host of passwords to access different resources, but instead get seamless access or denial of resources that they wish to use.

A problem with the bindery model is when you have many servers on the network. Bindery models do not allow for the sharing of database lists between servers, as each server maintains its own user account database. Because of this limitation, as more servers are added to the network, every time a new user account is created, it would have to be added to the user account database on each server that would contain a resource being shared out to that user. Thus, as a network grows, an administrator would need to do repetitive tasks in order to maintain the security of the network.

A second issue with a bindery-based network system is that this administrative model uses different utilities to perform different functions. Thus, one utility is used to manage the file system, another to manage the users, and even another to manage the printers.

Every time a new service or resource is added, a new administrative utility often must be learned to manage that resource or service.

Domain Model

The domain model is another client/server model that is used in Windows NT Server and OS/2 networks. It is similar to the bindery security model, in its centralized administration of user accounts and flat list of user accounts, but scales better for larger networks.

The domain model is a security model that uses a flat user account database similar to the bindery model. The main difference is that this database is stored on one or more computers known as domain controllers (see Figure 10.3).

When a Windows NT server is installed, one of the parameters that must be configured is what role the server should assume. There are three possibilities:

◆ Primary domain controller (PDC)

◆ Backup domain controller (BDC)

◆ Member server

FIGURE 10.3
A domain contains Domain Controllers that store the user account database.

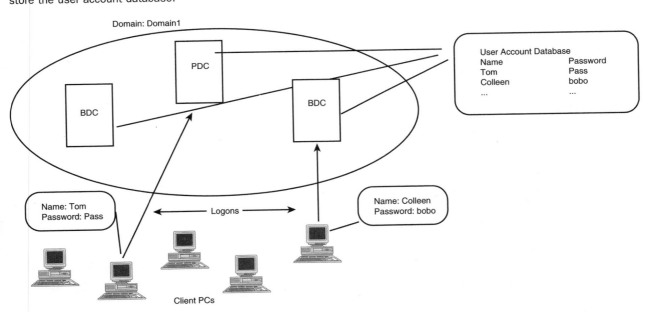

Primary and backup domain controllers perform essentially the same function. It is their role to store the user account database. The difference is that a PDC stores the master copy of this database. It is in this master copy that changes can occur. If a new user was added, the PDC's database would be affected. The backup domain controller's user account database is a replicated copy of that from the PDC.

There can only exist one PDC in a domain, yet you can specify as many BDCs as you wish. At any time a BDC can be promoted to a PDC, and thus a PDC demoted to a BDC. Issues that involve the number of BDC's, the placement of the domain controllers, and so on are covered in books and courses relating to the Windows NT Server and the Windows NT Enterprise exams.

The role of a member server is that it contains resources such as files, printers, and applications that users may wish to access on the network. It in itself does not store a domain user account database, but instead gives access to resources to users based upon the users drawn from the list of user accounts on the domain controllers. The member servers are also not involved with processing logon request for client machines, as this is a function that is only performed by domain controllers.

By placing the shared resources out on the network on member servers, you are placing these resources on computers that are not allocating their system resources such as RAM, CPU power, and disk space to process and maintain the user account database and the user's logon requests.

Some drawbacks to the domain model are that there is a separate utility to perform different administrative functions, depending on the resource being administered. That is, similar to the bindery model, there is one utility to create users in and another to manage printers with. If, for example, you were to install a fax server, there would be a new utility to manage this fax server. Another important issue with the domain model is that a domain is not designed scale to more than 40,000 accounts. An account is every registered user, group, and computer within the domain. Thus in some larger networks, multiple domains would need to be created.

NTDS versus x.500 Directory Services Microsoft has recently begun calling its domain model "Windows NT Directory Services" or "NTDS." This is simply a naming convention. The domain model, or NTDS, does not provide the features and functionality of true x.500 Directory Services. This will be part of Microsoft Windows NT 5.0 Active Directory Services. For more information on Directory Services, see the following section.

Directory Services Model

Directory Services, also known as the X.500 standard, is the latest in security management to be offered for networking security. It currently is used by Banyan Vines, Novell NetWare 4.x and higher, and is to be incorporated into the release of Windows NT 5.

Directory Services is a powerful security management system for a network, as it can accommodate a small to extremely large network. It solves many of the limitations found in the workgroup, bindery, and domain security models.

Directory Services is based upon a hierarchical distributed database model (see Figure 10.4). This model allows for the management of all resources through one utility, as well as providing a high level of fault tolerance within the system.

Management on a Directory Service security system is based on a hierarchical user account database. The idea behind this is similar to a file system database. No one stores all of their files in one directory on their hard drive. Files are grouped together into directories such that files that go together or are related to one another are placed together for management purposes and ease of reference. The same

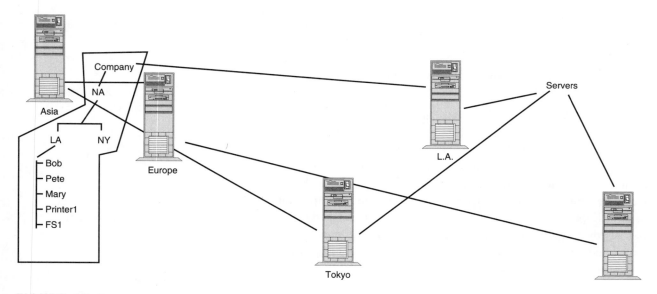

FIGURE 10.4
Directory Services has a distributed hierarchical database.

can be said for a Directory Service user account database. Instead of directories, containers store users together that work together or access the same resources together. In fact, many Directory Services databases are organized in a manner that is similar to their corporate organizational charts.

The management of resources is not limited to users and groups within a Directory Services database. Other resources on the network also have objects within the database. Thus when a printer is installed, its object is placed into the database as well. Management of this printer can also be done from the Directory Services database. So could the management of a fax server or any other device on the network. This functionality allows administrators to use one utility to do most of their network management.

The third main benefit of Directory Services is that it allows the partitioning of the database such that portions of it, partitioned around the containers, can be placed on different servers. This would mean that if a user is added in Los Angeles, the server in London, England does not need to be updated. This feature allows for the minimization of network traffic over slow WAN links. In a domain model, all user accounts are copied to all BDCs whenever a user account is added.

In short, the Directory Services model is the standard that all operating systems are migrating toward, as this model has features that can ease administration of the network, as well as allow a network to scale to any size desired.

In summary, here are the following features of the four administrative models:

REVIEW BREAK

♦ There are two derivatives of workgroup models—one used by Windows 95, the other by Windows NT.

♦ Windows 95 workgroup models have no user account databases; all security is done with the use of passwords.

♦ Windows NT workgroups have a decentralized user account database requiring administrators to perform repetitive administrative tasks such as creating users multiple times.

♦ Bindery-based systems use a flat user account database. This user account database is not shared with other servers. You must use different utilities to manage different resources.

◆ Domain-based systems are similar to bindery-based systems, with the exception that more than one server shares the same user account database.

◆ Directory Services allows for a distributed hierarchical database shared by all servers, from which all resources can be managed.

MANAGING USER ACCOUNTS AND GROUPS USING WINDOWS NT

As seen earlier in this chapter, when looking at the Networking security models, the Windows NT domain model is designed to provide far greater security than Windows 95. As such, Windows NT, using the domain administrative model, is the centerpiece of any Microsoft network where security is a major issue. An organization might not feel that its everyday documents require security, but most companies have payroll information or other data that they want to guard from access by unauthorized individuals. This section will focus on the Windows NT domain administrative model in describing how a domain is managed and how security for files and printers is accomplished.

User Accounts

In most instances, a user account is created for each individual on the network and is meant for use only by that one person. This is done through the "User Manager for Domains" utility (as seen in Figure 10.6 in Exercise 10.1). This account generally is a contracted form of the person's name or some other unique value, and no two users can have the same username in a single user account database. At their most basic level, a user account usually contains values for the following three properties:

◆ A username. This element distinguishes one account from another. This property requires a value.

◆ A password. This element confirms the user's identity. Individual passwords should be kept private to avoid unauthorized access. This property may be optional, depending upon security restrictions.

◆ The groups of which the user is a member. These groups determine the user's rights and permissions on the network. This is an optional property.

A number of other optional properties, such as a home directory (a place where a user can store personal files on the network) or specific information about the user such as their full name or description, also exist. None of these properties are crucial to the functioning of the account in the way that the elements enumerated above are. In Exercise 10.1, you create a very basic user account and observe some of the available options.

DEFAULT ACCOUNTS IN WINDOWS NT

When Windows NT is first installed, there are only two user accounts that are created. The first one is named Administrator, and you are prompted to supply a password for this account during the installation process. The second account is called Guest. This account is disabled by default.

There can be a third account created, depending on whether or not you install Internet Information Server (IIS) during the Windows NT install. The name of this account is IUSER_Computername, where Computername is the NetBIOS name of the computer that IIS is installed upon.

In the creation of user accounts and their passwords, you must strike a balance between security and user friendliness. Passwords have settings such as expiration dates, uniqueness, and how often they must be changed. Setting these options such that a password must be changed on a basis that is that is too frequent or one that requires too many long, unique passwords is almost certain to result in a less, rather than more, secure environment. If users are unable to remember such a password, they often simply will stick a note to their monitor with their password on it or come up with some other highly insecure way of jogging their memory. If this starts happening, you know that your policies are probably too stringent.

Groups

Now that a user has been established, the next step in granting that individual access to resources is to assign proper permissions. To ease the management of all users in the system, this should be done by creating a group or a set of groups, assigning permissions to the groups, and then placing the user inside the appropriate groups. As mentioned before, it is easier to manage five groups than five hundred users.

By default, Windows NT creates a number of built-in groups that are defined with the rights necessary to perform particular tasks. These groups are task-specific and are inherently different from the type of groups you normally create, which are resource-specific. These kinds of groups are discussed in more detail in the next In-depth.

Windows networks can include two types of the resource specific groups: global and local. Each of these has very specific functions.

Global

Global groups, like user accounts, are created only on the primary domain controller of a Microsoft domain. Backup domain controllers receive a copy of this database; thus, they also contain global groups. These groups function primarily as containers for user accounts. Global groups are designed to contain general groupings of people, such as Sales, Accounting, or the IS department. Global groups cannot contain other groups—only users from the domain in which the global group is created are permitted to be part of a global group.

Local

Local groups, on the other hand, can be created on Windows NT Server or Workstation and can include both user accounts and global groups. Moreover, these groups are assigned permissions (see next section for more on permissions).

The premise behind local groups is that an administrator—who is in charge of a server, such as the accounting server—can create a local group for this server's specific management needs. An example might be that the local server has two directories shared out. One directory is called Bonuses and the other is called Corporate Policies. This

> **NOTE**
>
> **Local Users in Windows NT**
> Windows NT does give you the ability to create local user accounts that cannot be added to a global group. For more information on this and other Windows NT issues, consult a book that focuses on Windows NT Server, like those mentioned in the "Suggested Readings and Resources" section of this book.

administrator could create two local groups, one called Restricted and one called General.

For the local group Restricted, this group may contain only the global groups of Sales Managers, Accounting Managers, and Human Resource Managers. The local administrator then would assign permissions to the Bonuses directory by using this local group called Restricted.

For the local group General, this group may contain all global groups, and this local group called General may be given the permissions to the Corporate Policies directory.

In Exercise 10.2, you create both types of groups and explore how they interact with users and resources. Note that this exercise assumes you are using a Windows NT domain controller. If this is not the case, you will be unable to complete the steps as written. In that case, you can participate in the creation of the local group and ignore instructions that deal with global groups.

BUILT-IN GLOBAL AND LOCAL GROUPS IN WINDOWS NT

Windows NT also contains some built-in global and local groups. These groups are given permissions and rights to various components on the network in order to provide some general functionality on the system. Users can be added to or removed from these groups.

These global groups only exist on domain controllers.

◆ *Domain Users*. All users created within a domain are placed into this group.

◆ *Domain Admins*. The Administrator account is placed within this group. All domain-wide administrators should also be placed in this group.

These local groups are found on domain controllers, member servers, and Windows NT workstations that are part of a domain.

◆ *Administrators*. Contains the Domain Admin global group. This group can manage all security and resources on the computer.

◆ *Users*. This group contains the global Users group.

continues

continued

◆ Guest. This group contains the guest account.

◆ *Account Operators*. Members of this group have the ability to create users and groups, both global and local. This group cannot manipulate the Administrator, the Administrators group, the Domain Admins group, or the Server operators group. This group is only found on domain controllers.

◆ *Backup Operators*. Members of this group have the rights needed to backup and restore files on the computer.

◆ *Print Operators*. Members of this group can manage all printers on the computer. This group is only found on domain controllers.

◆ *Server Operators*. Members of this group can share and stop sharing resources on the server, backup and restore files on the server, and shut down the server. This group is only found on domain controllers.

◆ *Replicator*. This group is used with the Directory Replicator Service.

Usually, the default rights associated with these built-in groups will be fine to perform the functions for which they are intended. The Administrators, Server Operators, Backup Operators, Print Operators, and Account Operators groups all have the right to log on to Windows NT Server interactively. This feature is not granted to other users by default on Windows NT Server.

For managing resources, you create the group and add users to it, at which time the group is ready to be given permissions in the file system, such as Read permissions to a directory or Print permissions to a printer.

Windows NT also creates four special groups, each of which has special uses and access privileges. You cannot delete or rename these groups. You cannot add or remove users from these groups. Because of this, these groups do not appear in User Manager for Domains. Based upon where you are or what you are doing, the system will associate you with one or more of these groups. You can give or deny these special groups permissions to resources. The following list details these four groups:

◆ *Everyone*. This umbrella group includes all users on the network.

◆ *Creator-owner*. If a user creates or owns a directory, he gains whatever rights are given to this group, as each file and directory is always associated with an owner.

◆ *Interactive*. This group is fluid, in that a user becomes a part of it when they access a local resource, and they are excluded from it when accessing a resource over a network connection.

◆ *Network*. This group is exactly the opposite of an interactive user group. This is another fluid group that includes any user that is accessing a resource over a network connection.

Creating groups and users provides the base upon which the rest of your security is built. You should now know what a user is, and how users and groups interact. Do not get overly caught up on the different groups and their abilities. That is the purpose of the Windows NT Server exam. The next section explores using these groups and users to give or restrict access to network resources.

Permissions

Permissions refers specifically to the level of trust that the owner of a resource has in the people with which he or she shares the resource. Although very subtle permissions structures can be constructed using Windows NT and Windows 95, a resource generally will either be shared as read-only or full-control. By default, both Windows NT and Windows 95 share resources with full control, which means that others cannot only view your shared resources but also can append, modify, and even delete them. For the less-trusting owner, a good compromise is to grant read-only permissions, which enable others to view your files or print to your printer, but not to modify those files or change the printer's settings.

Rights

The difference between having rights and receiving permissions might seem like nothing more than a matter of semantics, but this is not the case. In Microsoft terminology, *rights* are general attributes that particular users or groups have. These rights include the capability to log on locally or to load and unload device drivers. These particular user rights make administrators more powerful than users. Permissions refer to the level of control a particular user or group has over a specific resource. Examples of resource control would be the "Read" permission to a file or directory, or the ability to "Print" to a shared printer.

MORE ON RIGHTS

If a user and an administrator have full-control access to a directory, either of them can read, modify, or even delete that resource. If the directory must be restored from tape, however, only a member of the Administrators, Server Operators, or Backup Operators groups can accomplish this task. By default, only these groups have the right to restore files and directories. To see the different rights available to Windows NT users, select the Policies menu in User Manager for Domains and then select User Rights. Choose the check box in the lower left to view additional Advanced Rights.

All these terms might make network security seem a bit daunting, but this is not necessarily so. Perhaps it is easiest to think of server or workstation resources just as you would think of anything else that you must care for and protect.

For instance, imagine that you have a house. If you want, you can just keep the house to yourself and not admit entrance to anyone else, thus preventing damage to your possessions. Of course, you also can allow others to enter, but then you take the chance that someone might damage your possessions, either maliciously or inadvertently. Because of this, it's a good idea to take some precautions about who you invite to your house. Moreover, you almost certainly will be more watchful of some guests than others, and you will seek to protect certain rooms or possessions more than others. Lastly, because you can't watch everyone all the time, you probably will want to have some good locks on the doors and sufficient insurance against theft or disaster.

IMPLEMENTING SECURITY ON WINDOWS NT

Compare user-level security with access permission assigned to a shared directory on a server.

The previous section discussed security issues on a Windows NT network; this section will look at how to implement security on a Windows NT network. The main areas of focus will be on how to implement security on shared directories, on NTFS partitions, and on printers being shared by a Windows NT computer.

Creating and Assigning Permissions to a Shared Folder in Windows NT

In Exercise 10.3, you create and share a directory called Public. The group Everyone is given Read permissions to the directory, and the group Local Training is given Full Control. Remember that only directories can be shared, and all files and subdirectories within that directory are available over the network through the share. Exercise 10.3 assumes a FAT partition with no NTFS file-level security, or an NTFS partition on which no restrictions have been set. Remember that NTFS is the native Windows NT file system, and that it allows for additional security beyond what the FAT file system can offer.

GENERAL ADMINISTRATIVE RULES

Rights and permissions also can be given directly to user accounts themselves, but this is not recommended. Not only is such security cumbersome, but it is also difficult to administrate and troubleshoot.

If you have a user who has specific resources that are different than those of anyone else on the network, resist the urge to simply assign that user the needed permissions directly. Rather, create a new set of groups (local and, if needed, global), place the user into the proper group or groups, and then assign permissions and rights through the local groups as needed.

This might seem unnecessarily redundant, but it can be very useful later on, especially if the user leaves your organization and is replaced by a new user who now needs the same permissions. The new user simply can be placed into the needed group(s), and the old account can be removed from them. If, on the other hand, you have assigned file system permissions directly, you then must hunt down all the directories to which the original user had access, remove the old user from each one, and then insert the new user.

Assigning File-Level Permissions on an NTFS Partition

If you are using the standard FAT file system native to DOS, Windows, and Windows 95, your Windows NT security structure will be complete after you assign share-level permissions to your files. In Exercise 10.4, however, assume that the partition on which the share is located is formatted with NTFS, Windows NT's native file system. In this case, you can assign additional rights within the share on a per-directory and even per-file basis. The strength of NTFS security is two-fold:

◆ NTFS security gives the administrator a wider range of flexibility in assigning rights to files and directories.

◆ NTFS security provides security even at the local level, something that a FAT partition does not support. Interactive users are unaffected by share-level security options, but still are limited by NTFS file-level security.

In the Public folder shared in Exercise 10.3, you see that two share-level permissions exist for this directory:

◆ Everyone: Read

◆ Administrators: Full Control

In Exercise 10.4, you will assign a new permission to this directory, this time through NTFS security. The permission to be assigned will be:

◆ Everyone: Change

You should always consider how this change will affect the permissions of the Everyone and Administrators groups before altering your permissions structure. Remember that Read permissions allow Read (R) and Execute (X) permissions, while Change grants these permissions plus Write (W) and Delete (D). Likewise, Full control offers these permissions plus Take Ownership (O) and Change Permissions (P). Share-level rights and file-level rights are both cumulative within themselves. For instance, an administrator on a Windows NT network will be a member of both Administrators and Everyone—and possibly a number of other groups as well.

WARNING

No Access   The exception to the principle of additive privilege is the No Access permission, which immediately blocks all other rights. Because of this, the No Access option should be used sparingly and very carefully. Numerous No Access permissions on the network usually point to a poorly implemented security structure. If you don't want users to access a resource, it is sufficient simply to not give them permission—explicitly banning the users access generally is overkill. Also, never implement No Access for the Everyone group—this group includes you, as well as all other administrators and users, none of whom will be able to get to the resource until the No Access is removed, even if they belong to other groups that do have sufficient permissions.

In your Public share, the user would gain RX from the Everyone group and RXWDOP from the Administrator group. The user then would have RXWDOP over the share. On the other hand, if you include the NTFS permissions for Everyone, the user has RXW-DOP over the share and only RXWD at the file level. Under NTFS, only permissions granted at *both* the share level and the file level will be applied, and the administrative user will have only Change (RXWD) permissions over the share.

Generally, you will try to use a Windows NT domain model to provide resource access on your network. In some situations, though, you may need to implement a workgroup sharing model or use a Windows 95 machine as a server. The main reasons for this is because the size of the network is not large enough or the security of the data is not critical enough to justify the expense of Windows NT.

Printer Sharing with Windows NT

The second major resource with which you will be expected to be familiar is the printer. For many administrators, printers have been a constant trouble spot, and it seems that a disproportionate percentage of network problems are caused by these devices. Because many of these problems are due to improper or modified printer configurations, careful setup and effective security structures can save an administrator considerable time in this area.

To connect to a network printer, you first must install and configure the printer on a server. Every network printer, in other words, is just a local printer that has been shared by its owner.

Windows NT has the capability to enable remote users to dynamically download print drivers specific to their own system into RAM each time the users print. This allows for easy driver updates and also enables users to connect to a new printer without having rights to install drivers on their local system. This process is called connecting to a printer.

> **NOTE**
>
> **Drivers**   Remember that a driver is a piece of software that allows a piece of hardware, in this case a printer, to communicate to the operating system, in this case Windows NT or Windows 95.

As you install and assign permissions to the printer in Exercise 10.7, observe that many of the processes are very similar to the steps you took in creating, sharing, and securing files and folders. The groups and users that you can draw from are the same in granting Printer permissions as they are when granting File permissions.

IMPLEMENTING SECURITY ON WINDOWS 95

As noted earlier, Windows 95 also can act as a server, albeit in a less robust capacity. Windows 95, under the workgroup model, was shown to have one type of security. Windows 95 can actually support two types of security: share-level and user-level. Share-level security is supported in a workgroup model or when a Windows 95 machine is part of a Windows NT domain. User-level security is only supported when Windows 95 is part of a Windows NT domain, or in the presence of a Windows NT server or workstation, or as a client in a Novell bindery-based security model.

As you read about the different security models, notice that Windows 95's user-level security is nearly identical to Windows NT's share-level authentication. Moreover, notice that Windows 95 does not support file-level local security as provided by Windows NT NTFS partitions, nor does Windows NT have the ability to provide Windows 95's low-security, password-only share-level option.

Share-Level Security on Windows 95

Under Windows 95's simple share-level security, passwords are assigned to permit access to each directory or printer share. To access the share, a user must supply the correct password.

When creating a shared directory using share-level security, you can grant one of three types of access:

◆ *Read-only access.* After entering the correct password, a remote user can access a directory, its subdirectories, and its files. However, the user cannot delete files or write files to that directory.

◆ *Full access.* A remote user who supplies the correct password has read and write privileges to that directory and all its files and subdirectories.

◆ *Depends on password.* Two different passwords can be created: one allowing read-only access, and one allowing full access.

No Password If no password is entered, all users have full or read-only access to the directory, depending on which option was specified when the shared directory was created.

The type of access granted to a user depends on the password that the user has supplied.

In Exercise 10.5, you create a directory share using share-level security. Remember that a share is an entry point on your computer from which you can give others access to your local resources.

Print queues also can be shared with other network users using share-level security. If a password is specified for the share, a network user must enter that password to access the print queue and connect to that printer. If a printer is shared with a blank password field—meaning no password was entered—any user can connect to and print to that printer.

Because share-level security relies on access passwords, this form of security has the following disadvantages:

◆ To access different shares, a network user must know numerous passwords.

◆ Passwords can easily be forgotten. Windows 95 can cache passwords so a user does not need to enter them each time. However, if the creator of the share forgets the password, then the password must be changed to enable another user to access the share.

◆ Nothing prevents a user from disclosing the password to an unauthorized user.

User-Level Security on Windows 95

User-level security can be used to overcome the shortcomings of share-level security, and where it is available, this type of security is generally the preferred security structure. With user-level security, you can grant specific user accounts or group accounts to a shared directory or printer. Instead of relying on a password that could be used by anyone, the user account accessing a shared resource must be authenticated to ensure that that account has been granted access. User-level security, therefore, provides a level of personal flexibility and accountability that is not available with share-level security.

Windows 95 cannot manage user accounts by itself as it does not have the ability to house and manage a user account database.

Instead, the application must use another authentication database, such as that of a Windows NT or a NetWare server, which can authenticate the user trying to access the resource. In user-level security, Windows 95 must defer to a machine with a user database and present all requests for access to that machine for authentication.

USER-LEVEL SECURITY

Windows 95 ships with the ability to perform user-level security with Novell NetWare and Windows NT. Other developers can write their own services to perform user-level security as well.

To initiate user-level security, the Windows 95 computer must obtain a copy of the accounts list from one of the following sources:

◆ Windows NT Server 3.5 (or later) computer

◆ Windows NT Workstation 3.5 (or later) computer

◆ Windows NT 3.5 (or later) domain controller

◆ NetWare 3.x server

◆ NetWare 4.x server with bindery emulation enabled

When a directory is shared with user-level security, the users or groups to be granted access to the share are assigned privileges. You can grant each user or group one of the following privileges:

◆ *Read-only*. Users can access files and subdirectories in a directory, but cannot delete or save files to that share.

◆ *Full access*. Users can read, write, and delete files in the directory.

◆ *Custom*. Any number of the following privileges can be granted:

  • Read Files

  • Write to Files

  • Create Files

  • List Files

  • Delete Files

  • Change File Attributes

  • Change Permissions

Exercise 10.6 demonstrates how to grant a network user access to a directory share. For this exercise, you must be part of a domain that contains a server with a user accounts database or a stand-alone Windows NT Server or Workstation account database that could be used. If the user accounts exist on a NetWare server, you will need to install the Client for NetWare Networks, the IPX/SPX-compatible protocol, and File and Printer Sharing for NetWare Networks, and make your selections accordingly throughout the exercise.

You now have learned what a user and a group are, and how they can be used to provide network access and file security. You have seen the way that both Windows 95 and Windows NT handle security issues, and should be able to see some of their major differences. Remember that the same principles that guide file sharing also work for the other major network resource printers that you will examine.

Printer Sharing with Windows 95

To use Windows 95 as a network print server, the printer must be attached to the Windows 95 machine locally and configured with the proper driver, just as it would be if it were serving only local users. The printer then must be shared to enable other users to access it. To share a printer in Windows 95, a 32-bit, protected-mode client, and the "file and printer sharing" service must be enabled.

Exercise 10.8 demonstrates how to share a network printer from a Windows 95 machine. This exercise assumes that you already have installed and configured a printer.

When the printer has been configured and shared on the network print server, a Windows 95 client can be configured to connect to the print server and print to the printer over the network. This configuration can be established either manually with the Add Printer Wizard or by configuring the network printer for Point and Print setup.

Printer security can support either share-level or user-level security, depending on the security role the computer is part of, as described in the previous sections. Share-level security requires that the user of a printer be able to provide a password in order to print to the shared printer. User-level security will allow the administrator to select, on a user-by-user or group-by-group basis, who can or cannot print to the shared printer.

ADDITIONAL ADMINISTRATIVE TASKS

Besides setting up the network and making sure that your users have access to what they need (and can't get to things they don't), an administrator also has a number of other important day-to-day tasks to fulfill. The remainder of this chapter gives you a brief introduction to the following responsibilities:

◆ Auditing

◆ Handling data encryption

◆ Handling virus protection

◆ Securing equipment

Auditing

Another option you might need to consider is auditing, which is the process of creating a database that records particular events that occur on your network. Generally, you can decide what events to audit, from application information to security options. Figure 10.1 shows one of many different auditing windows in Windows NT.

The utilities to perform auditing come with Windows NT and Windows 95. These tools are known as Event Viewer and Performance Monitor in NT, and both are discussed in greater detail within Chapter 11, "Monitoring the Network." Windows 95 does come with a utility called System Monitor. There are also a variety of third-party auditing tools available on the market.

Handling Data Encryption

Usually, the file and share security discussed previously is more than adequate. However, if your network is used for especially sensitive data and you want to prevent anyone from stealing information, you

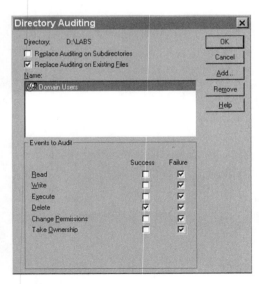

FIGURE 10.5
A directory auditing window in Windows NT.

can take an additional security measure by forcing data encryption. Encryption codes the information sent on the network using a special algorithm and then decodes it on the other end. This technique offers varying degrees of safety, largely based on the length and complexity of the code used to encrypt the data. With the advent of the Internet, encryption technology is becoming more important and is key in the new "secure transactions" toward which companies on the World Wide Web are now working.

Handling Virus Protection

Much like humans, computers are susceptible to certain types of viruses. Unlike those that strike us, though, computer viruses are created intentionally with the aim of injuring or altering your machines. Viruses can be spread through computer systems in many ways, but the most common is through an executable file. Having a good virus scanning program—none come with any Microsoft program—is a necessity for an administrator. Numerous third-party companies make virus-scanning software, including Norton and MacAfee, to name just two.

> **NOTE**
>
> **Anti-Virus Software**   Anti-virus software cannot simply detect any virus; rather, this software generally is designed to look for particular infections. Because of this, scanning software is updated regularly, often at no extra charge. Even if it does cost a bit, though, always keep your virus-checking software as new as possible.

Securing Equipment

You might think that if you have taken care of backup, RAID, shares, NTFS permissions, virus scanning, and encryption, your data is completely safe. There is, however, one more thing of which you should be sure. Any computer is far more insecure if people can get to its server, so you always should lock your server in a room that only authorized personnel have access to. Having the server out in the open provides a security risk, such that it is open to anyone to tamper with it. Most companies have a "server room"—often a large wiring closet—where all server machines are stored. Make sure this location is neither too cold nor too hot, that it has adequate ventilation, and that only authorized individuals have access to it.

Additionally, whenever you make a change to the network, be certain to document the changes you have made. This can make troubleshooting and maintenance far easier and can save you valuable time. See Chapter 11 for more information.

CASE STUDY: WHICH MODEL FOR SECURITY?

ESSENCE OF THE CASE

The essence of the case is as follows:

- There will be eleven users sharing files on the system.

- A Windows 95 workgroup and Windows NT domain model are to be compared.

- The company plans on expanding in the future.

- There is some very confidential information within the law firm.

SCENARIO

You have been called in to a small law office. This law office has five lawyers, five legal secretaries, and a receptionist. The law office has done everything the old-fashioned way; that is, using the old typewriter, pens, and paper. They feel that they will be more productive if they could put all of their documents on the network, thus allowing them to find old cases faster, as well as letting them produce legal documentation faster.

This law firm wants all to share files back and forth, yet they do want to have some degree of security in who can access which files. Some of the documents that they hold contain very confidential information. It is a small firm, yet they are intent on expanding in the future.

The firm has decided to use a Microsoft networking solution, but are not sure of whether to use a workgroup model based on Windows 95 or a Windows NT domain model. Your job is to present the issues of choosing one system versus another, so that the two senior partners can decide which option they would like to pursue.

ANALYSIS

This analysis will be presented by comparing a Windows 95 workgroup to a Windows NT domain model. It will conclude with a table contrasting the two solutions.

Windows 95 Workgroup

A Windows 95 workgroup solution would definitely be a cheaper option in terms of software costs. All computers would have Windows 95 installed on them. Each user would be in charge of maintaining share level security themselves.

The Windows 95 workgroup solution would require that each user be trained and become proficient in the management of their computer, in order to have an effective security system in place. Also, passwords for each shared resource would need to be maintained by each user.

As this network grows, the ability to manage all the files on this type of distributed network would come under pressure. As people are added to the system, the number of passwords for each shared resource would increase.

The ability to fully secure information would be in jeopardy. Because Windows 95 only supports share-level security and not file system security, anyone can go up to any computer and interactively obtain any document they want.

Windows NT Domain Model

The Windows NT domain model would cost more than the workgroup model, as you would need to purchase Windows 95 for each desktop, yet you would still need to purchase a Windows NT server.

CASE STUDY: WHICH MODEL FOR SECURITY?

One benefit of having a Windows NT server running a domain is that all security and user accounts could be centrally managed. A policy on password changes could be enforced, and this model would allow for growth over time.

Because users are granted access on a user-by-user or group-by-group basis, passwords for resource access would not be required. Instead, each user would only need to remember one password, the one to log in to the system.

Since Windows NT provides file system security, sensitive documents could be placed on the server, without fear of unauthorized access from other users. Still, a secure room should be created in which to store the Windows NT server.

Windows NT also supports auditing, and has an auditing program built into the system. This would also allow for a degree of security, as it would allow an administrator to be able to see when and who is accessing what documents.

To manage the system, only one (or perhaps two) user would need to be trained as system manager.

Comparing the Two Systems

Table 10.1 compares both systems.

TABLE 10.1
WORKGROUP VERSUS DOMAIN-BASED NETWORKS

Feature	Workgroup	Domain
Cost of software	Lower	Higher
Cost of hardware	Lower	Higher
Number of people that would need training	More	Less
File system security	No	Yes
Share-level security	Yes	Yes
Requires a secure server room	No	Yes
Provides better security	No	Yes
Provide auditing	No	Yes

As usual, there is no right or wrong answer or option here. If this law office feels that the security of the documents is not that great, they can opt for the workgroup model and save some money.

If this law firm feels that security of the data is important, they would more than likely go for the domain model supplied by Windows NT. They could justify the higher cost of the domain model by citing their security requirements.

CHAPTER SUMMARY

KEY TERMS

- Resource
- Sharing
- User
- Groups
- Security
- Zone
- Workgroup
- Bindery
- Domain
- Primary domain controller (PDC)
- Backup domain controller (BDC)
- Directory Services
- Global groups
- Local groups
- File-level security
- Share-level security
- Auditing
- Encryption
- Viruses

You now have learned to create users and groups and to configure sharing and security for Microsoft resources using either Windows NT or Windows 95. You also can connect to either of these machines to gain access to their shared files and printers. Furthermore, this chapter introduced you to a few optional security measures available for sensitive data.

Knowing how to create network resources through sharing is crucial not only for the Networking Essentials exam, but for an understanding of practical Microsoft networking as well. Make sure that you can implement each of these structures and understand how they work. Experiment with permissions and user rights and make sure that the relationship between groups and users is clear.

APPLY YOUR LEARNING

Exercises

10.1 Creating a User Account in Windows NT

Objective: Create a new NT user account.

Estimated time: 10 minutes

1. Click Start, Programs, Administrative Tools. Choose either User Manager (Windows NT Workstation) or User Manager for Domains (Windows NT Server).

2. User Manager opens (see Figure 10.6). If this is a new install, only two users appear in the top window. As you might expect, Administrator is the default administrative account for the machine, and Guest is the default account for anonymous access by users who do not have a username and password of their own. The Guest account is disabled by default and must be manually enabled before it is usable. If IIS is installed as well, a user account with the name of IUSER_<computername> (<computername> is the NetBIOS name of your computer) is also present.

3. Click Policies, Account to prompt the Account Policy dialog box to appear (see Figure 10.7). Observe that, by default, passwords must be changed every 42 days. In addition, no restrictions are made as to password length or uniqueness. Account Lockout is turned off. Here, you can set some of the default security information for your network. If you are concerned that someone might try to break into your network by stealing or guessing a user's password, these settings should be set to restrictive levels. Leave the defaults as they are and click Close to return to the User Manager.

4. Click User, New User. The New User dialog box appears (see Figure 10.8).

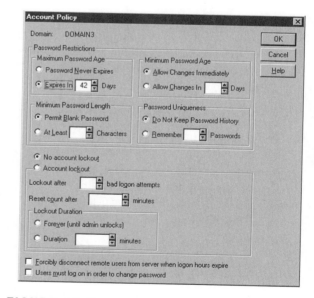

FIGURE 10.7
The Windows NT Accounts Policy window enables you to set password characteristics.

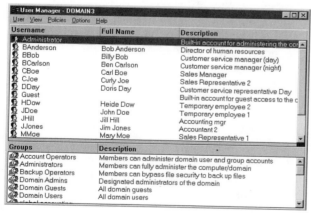

FIGURE 10.6
Account administration is done through the Windows NT User Manager for Domains program.

APPLY YOUR LEARNING

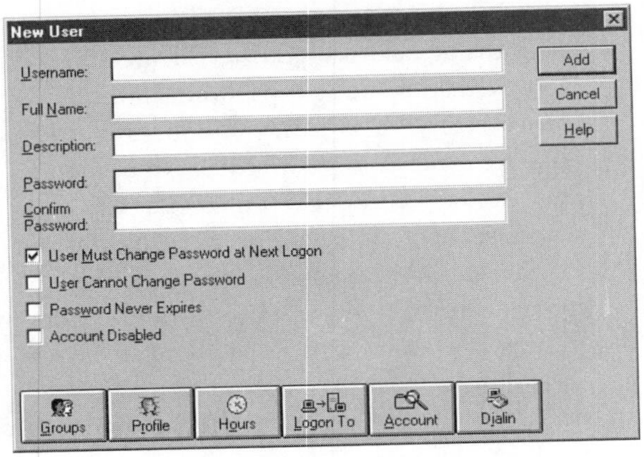

FIGURE 10.8
The Windows NT New User dialog box enables you to record information about a new user.

5. In the top field, type in a unique username (in this case, **TestUser**) for the new account. This name can be between 1 and 20 characters and cannot include spaces or any of the following characters:

   " / \ [ ] : ; | = , + * ? < >

6. Two text fields enable you to identify the user for which the account is being created. The Full Name field generally defines the person, and the Description field defines the role they fill in the organization. Fill both of these fields with the values **Test User** and **Training Department Manager.**

7. In the password field, you may enter any combination of 1 to 14 characters of your choice, with the same exceptions that apply to the creation of user accounts. Enter **PASSWORD** in both the Password and Confirm Password fields. (Remember that all passwords are case-sensitive, so it matters whether you type PASSWORD or password.)

8. Examine the check boxes below the Confirm Password field. By default, the User Must Change Password at Next Logon field is checked. The first time that a new user logs on, he is asked to provide a new password. This enables you to set an initial password but then transfer security over to the user by having him define his own access password.

9. The User Cannot Change Password option generally is used only for guest or multi-user accounts, thereby keeping one guest from changing the password and locking all other guest users out. Leave this box unchecked.

10. The Password Never Expires option is intended for system or guest accounts that require a static password. As you will see, system policies can be set by requiring occasional password changes by network users. This setting overrides such policies. Leave this box unchecked.

11. The Account Disabled option enables you to disable an account temporarily while a user is on vacation or after he no longer is allowed access to the network. Generally, this option is preferable to simply deleting the account, at least until it has been determined that the user definitely will not use the account again. Leave this box unchecked.

12. The row of buttons at the bottom of the window contains additional configuration options. You use the Groups button in the next exercise, but the other buttons contain options beyond the scope of this book. Ignore them for now, but it would be a good idea to return later to click on each of them in turn and investigate the windows they spawn. Close each without making modifications. This idea is good to follow in all exercises because the key to mastering any Windows-based

APPLY YOUR LEARNING

product is to know where to click to find the option you need. You should get used to exploring all the tabs and buttons available, but don't change anything unless you know what will happen.

13. Click the Add button. Notice that although all the fields clear, the Add User window remains open. This enables faster creation of multiple users.

14. Click Close to return to User Manager. You now see a third user, which is the TestUser account you just created.

15. Click User, Exit.

10.2 Creating Groups on Windows NT

Objective: Create new global and local groups and assign accounts to them.

This lab can only be completed if you are on a Windows NT domain controller, and the primary domain controller is online.

Estimated time: 10 minutes

1. Open User Manager for Domains. Observe the groups in the bottom window pane. Some groups have globe icons, such as the Domain Admins group. Others, such as the Administrators group, have a computer icon. As you might suspect, Domain Admins is a global group, while Administrators is a local group.

2. Click the User menu choice and choose New Global Group. The New Global Group dialog box appears (see Figure 10.9).

3. Type **Global Training** in the Group Name field. In the Description field, type **Training Department Members**.

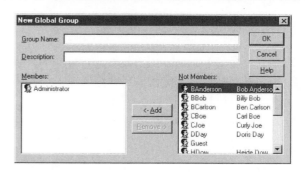

FIGURE 10.9
The New Global Group dialog box enables you to enter members and a description for a global group.

4. Note the two boxes at the bottom of the screen. Administrator, Guest, and TestUser are displayed in the Not Members box. Choose TestUser and click the Add button. TestUser moves into the Members box. It should be also noted that if any users were selected at the time you created the group, they will also be members of this group.

5. Click Close to return to User Manager for Domains.

6. Click User and select New Local Group.

7. The New Local Group dialog box appears (see Figure 10.10).

FIGURE 10.10
The New Local Group dialog box enables you to add users and global groups.

APPLY YOUR LEARNING

8. Enter **Local Training** in the Group Name field and leave the Description field blank.

9. Observe the members list box, which is empty. Click on Add.

10. The Add Users and Groups dialog box appears. Choose the Global Training group and click Add. Note that you also could have added TestUser to the group directly. In Windows NT Workstation—which does not support the creation of global groups—this would have been your only choice. Click Close to return to User Manager for Domains. Click OK to return to the New Local Group dialog box. The members list now includes the Global Training group. Click OK to return to User Manager for Domains.

11. Click User, Exit.

10.3 Sharing a Directory on a Windows NT FAT Partition

Objective: Share a Windows NT directory and assign share-level security to it.

Estimated time: 15 minutes

1. Click on Start, Programs. Then click on the Windows NT Explorer icon to bring up the Explorer window. Double-click on the icon representing your C: drive.

2. Select the root of the C: drive and then right-click on it to call a context-sensitive menu.

3. Select New, Folder. A folder appears under C:, and you are prompted to enter the name of the folder. Type **Public** and press Enter.

4. Click on the new Public folder (in the left window). The folder is highlighted, and the right window is now empty.

5. Right-click in the right window to make a context-sensitive menu appear. Select New, Text Document. Name the document My Shared Doc.

6. Select the Public folder again. Click File, Properties (or use the quick menu and select Sharing from there) to call the Properties dialog box.

7. Click on the Sharing tab. Note that the directory currently is not shared.

8. Click the Shared As option. The Share Name box fills with "Public." You can change or leave this initial name. In this case, change the share. Replace Public with **My Share** to illustrate the difference between a directory name and a share name.

9. Observe the Maximum Connections option. This option enables you to control the number of concurrent users accessing the folder. Leave the default, which enables unlimited concurrent connections to the share.

10. Click on the Permissions button to call the Access Through Share Permissions dialog box (see Figure 10.11). Observe that, by default, Everyone has Full Control over the new share.

11. Select the Everyone group and click the down arrow in the Type of Access box. The following four selections appear:

    • *No Access.* A member of any group with this permission is banned from the shared resource.

    • *Read.* Members can list, read, and execute files, but cannot modify or delete them.

    • *Change.* Members can read, list, execute, and delete files, but are not able to change file permissions or assume ownership of the files.

APPLY YOUR LEARNING

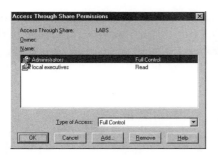

FIGURE 10.11
The Access Through Share
Permissions dialog box enables you
to determine the type of access for a
particular group.

- *Full Control.* Members have complete control
  of the resources, assuming that they have sufficient rights to match their permissions.

12. Click on Read in the Type of Access window.
    Observe that the permissions level for Everyone
    in the main window reflects the change.

13. Click on Add to call the Add Users and Groups
    window. Select the Local Training group and
    click the Add button. The Local Training group
    appears in the lower window. Click the Type of
    Access down arrow and select Full Control.

14. Click the OK button and observe that Local
    Training has been added to the list of groups
    with permissions to the share.

15. Click OK to close the window and then click
    OK on the Public Properties application.

16. In a few seconds, a hand appears under the
    Public folder, indicating that the folder has been
    shared.

17. Test the share by connecting to it from a
    Windows 95 or a Windows NT client.

10.4 Setting NTFS Permissions on a Shared Folder

Objective: Add NTFS security to the Public share.

Estimated time: 15 minutes

1. Click Start, Programs. Select Windows NT
   Explorer to open the Explorer window. Choose a
   directory on an NTFS partition. If you do not
   have an NTFS partition, you cannot complete
   this lab.

2. Create a directory called TestNTFS and then
   right-click on it. Select the Properties option
   from the menu to open the TestNTFS Properties
   window.

3. In the TestNTFS Properties window, click on the
   Security tab and then click the Permissions button to open the Directory Permissions dialog box
   (see Figure 10.12).

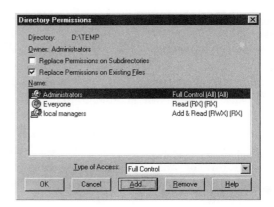

FIGURE 10.12
The Directory Permissions dialog box enables
you to update or replace permissions for a
group.

APPLY YOUR LEARNING

4. Observe that the directory currently has its default permissions list with Everyone—Full Control as the only entry.

5. Select Everyone. Click the down arrow on the Type of Access field and choose Read.

6. Take note of the check boxes near the top of the window. The Replace Permissions on Files option is checked, while the Replace Permissions on Subdirectories option is cleared. If you have subdirectories and want the new access permissions to filter down through them, you must check this box. Because no subdirectories exist in this instance, the point is currently moot, so leave the defaults as they are.

7. If you need to enter additional groups into the list, you can do so by using the Add button. Click this button and observe the Add Users and Groups window. Select the Administrators Local group and then click on the down arrow next to the Type of Access drop-down list and observe the expanded choices. Permissions are broken down to more specific levels, and Special File Access and Special Directory Access enable you to mix and match permissions to suit your needs. In reality, you rarely will grant a group only the List and Delete permissions, but you can if you need to. If, for instance, a user needs to be able to write to a directory, but should not be able to view, read, or modify files in that directory, only Write permission would be given to him. Give Administrators Full Control permissions.

8. Click OK to return to the Directory Permissions window. Then click OK to set the new permissions and return to Explorer.

9. Click File, Exit to close Explorer.

10. Share the TestNTFS directory with Everyone—Full Control permissions and log on to the share from a remote machine and observe the permissions available when you log on as an Administrator as opposed to a TestUser. You should be able to modify, create, and delete files across the share if you are logged on as an Administrator, but you should be able to only read and execute while logged on as a TestUser.

10.5 Sharing a Directory Using Share-Level Security

Objective: Share a Windows 95 directory using share-level security.

Estimated time: 10 minutes

1. From the Start menu, choose Settings, Control Panel to display the Control Panel.

2. Double-click on the Network icon to display the Network dialog box (see Figure 10.13).

3. Choose the Access Control tab and then choose share-level access control.

4. Select the Configuration tab and choose File, Print Sharing to display the File and Print Sharing dialog box (see Figure 10.14).

5. Select both the I want to be able to give others access to my files check box and the I want to be able to allow others to print to my printer(s) check box to enable others to access your printers and files. Then choose OK to automatically install File and Printer Sharing for Microsoft Networks. You may be prompted for the location of the source files. If so, type in the location and click on OK.

APPLY YOUR LEARNING

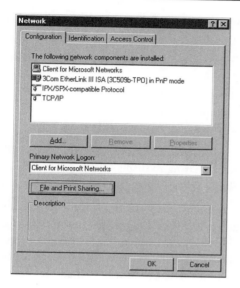

FIGURE 10.13
Use the Windows 95 Network Application to add and configure networking components.

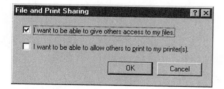

FIGURE 10.14
Windows 95 File and Printer Sharing options offer you the chance to grant access to your files and printer.

6. Choose OK and restart the computer.

7. After Windows 95 has restarted, click Start, Windows Explorer and make a new folder on your C: drive named Password. Choose the Password directory and make a text file within it called Password Test.

8. Right-click on the Password directory to display the context-sensitive menu.

> **NOTE** **Share-Level versus User-Level Security** Share-level security is used by default when File and Printer Sharing for Microsoft Networks is installed. The next exercise demonstrates how this can be changed. Conversely, File and Printer Sharing for NetWare Networks must use user-level security. The share-level security option is unavailable if File and Printer Sharing for NetWare Networks is installed.

9. Choose Sharing from the context-sensitive menu to open the Sharing tab of the Properties application, as shown in Figure 10.15.

10. Accept Password as the share name and choose Access Type: Read-Only. Enter a password for Read-only access of **read** and choose OK. The

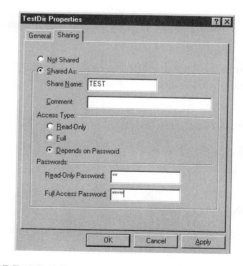

FIGURE 10.15
This Properties application for a shared directory uses share-level security.

APPLY YOUR LEARNING

sharing hand symbol replaces the folder symbol for the shared directory.

11. If you have another computer on the network, browse the first computer in Network Neighborhood to display the share name. The share name Password is displayed under the appropriate computer name.

12. Double-click on the share name Password. You are prompted for the password.

13. Enter **read** at the password prompt and choose OK to display the directory contents.

14. Copy the Password Test file from the share to your local hard drive. The file read will be successful.

15. Modify the file and try to copy it back. Then try to delete the original in the shared directory. Neither the file write nor the file delete will be allowed.

10.6 Sharing a Directory Using User-Level Security

Objective: Allow Windows 95 to access another machine's user accounts list and share a directory using user-level security.

Estimated time: 15 minutes

1. From the Start menu, choose Settings, Control Panels to display the Control Panels window.

2. Double-click on the Network icon to display the Network dialog box.

3. Choose the Access Control tab and select User-level access control, as shown in Figure 10.16. If sharing is already installed, you will be notified in a dialog box that all of your shares will be lost, a dialog box that all of your shares will be lost,

and that you will have to re-share all of your folders again. If this is the case, click OK.

4. Type the name of the server with the user accounts or the domain name into the Obtain list of users and groups from field. Windows 95 attempts to access the Windows NT or NetWare server to obtain the users list.

5. Select the Configuration tab and choose File, Print Sharing to display the File and Print Sharing dialog box.

6. Select both the I want to be able to give others access to my files check box and the I want to be able to allow others to print to my printer(s) check box to enable others to access your printers and files. Then choose OK to automatically install File and Printer Sharing for Microsoft Networks. You may be prompted for the location

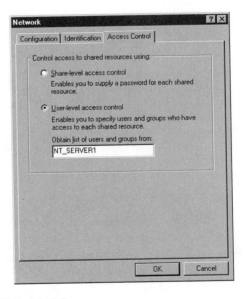

FIGURE 10.16
The User-level access control option enables advanced Windows 95 networking security.

APPLY YOUR LEARNING

of the source files; if this is the case, type in the location and click on OK.

7. Choose OK and restart the computer. Until you have restarted, the new settings will not take effect, and you will not be able to complete the exercise.

8. After Windows 95 restarts, click Start, Windows Explorer. Create a new directory called UserLevel and then create a new text file in the folder named UserTest. Now choose the directory. Observe that the Password folder is no longer shared, as the change to user-level security results in the loss of all existing shares. (This doesn't wipe out the files or folders, but it does eliminate the logical network path to them.)

9. Right-click on the UserLevel directory to display its context-sensitive menu.

10. Select Sharing from the context-sensitive menu to display the Sharing tab of the Properties application.

11. Type **UserLevl** for the share name and give the Local Training group full-access privileges by selecting the group and choosing Full Access. Choose OK. Then choose OK again. The folder symbol for the shared directory is replaced with an icon of a folder held by a hand.

12. Log on to another computer on the network using the username to which you gave full-access permissions. Locate the share name UserLevl in the Explorer by browsing the entire network. The share name UserLevl is displayed under the appropriate computer name.

13. Double-click on the share name UserLevl to display the directory contents.

> **NOTE** **Share Names** Sharing the folder UserLevel with the 8.3 compatible name UserLevl enables DOS workstations on the network to properly understand the name of the share. Remember that if all machines on your network are not capable of long filename support, you should continue to use network file-naming conventions that correspond to your network's lowest common denominator.

14. Try to copy a file to the shared directory. The file write is allowed.

10.7 Creating a Local Printer with Windows NT

Objective: Create a locally installed printer on NT.

Estimated time: 20 minutes

1. Click Start, Settings. Then choose Printers to open the Printers window.

2. Double-click on Add Printer to display the Add Printer Wizard. As with many other administrative tasks, the process of creating and sharing a printer has been streamlined and simplified by the use of a "wizard," a small program that leads you through a particular task. Choose My Computer and click Next.

3. The wizard asks you to specify the port or ports to which the new printer should print. Choose lpt1: and click Next.

APPLY YOUR LEARNING

PORTS

You can define multiple ports because printers in Windows NT and Windows 95 are virtualized. This refers to the fact that a printer in these environments is not a physical machine, but rather a collection of settings and configuration information about a particular machine. You can test this by installing a printer—or a modem or a network card—that is not actually physically present in your machine. The device will install perfectly, but you will receive an error if an application attempts to access it, because this device doesn't exist. When a matching physical device is attached, the virtual device will recognize it and forward information as needed. For those of you who have used print queues, it might be easier to think of a printer as a new name for a print queue. The machine itself is referred to as a printing device.

4. The wizard now asks you to specify the type of physical device to which you are printing or the device type that your printer emulates. Click HP in the left pane and then find and select HP Color LaserJet. Then click Next.

5. Now you are asked to name your new printer. Remember that each printer on your machine must have a unique name, and that name should be descriptive of its type or function. Type **Color Printer** and click Next.

6. Now you are asked whether the printer will be shared, and if so, what other operating systems will access it. Click Shared, call the new share **MyLaser**, and select Windows 95 from the list of additional operating systems. Note that each supported Windows NT platform requires a different driver. Click Next.

7. The wizard now has all the information it needs. Leave the Print Test Page option on and click

Finish. You will need the source files for both Windows NT Server or Workstation and for Windows 95. You are prompted for the location of the source files, and the necessary drivers are loaded.

8. The Printer icon for Color Printer is created in the Printers window. Select it, and the queue appears. Print a document to the new printer and check the queue again. The document should be waiting to print.

10.8 Sharing a Printer on the Network with Windows 95

Objective: To share a printer on the network from Windows 95.

Estimated Time: 5 minutes

This lab assumes that a printer is already installed.

1. Click My Computer and double-click on the Printers folder. Right-click on the Printer icon and choose Properties to display the Properties sheet.

2. Choose the Sharing tab to display the Sharing configuration settings.

3. Select Shared As and enter a share name and an optional descriptive comment for the printer. Windows 95 does not allow a share name to contain invalid characters, including spaces. In addition, the share name must not exceed 12 characters.

4. You also must grant permissions to access this printer. If share-level permissions are used, you must assign a password to the printer. To access the print queue, users must supply the correct password. If user-level permissions are used, you

APPLY YOUR LEARNING

must add the users who will be granted access to this print queue. For example, to enable everyone to print to the print queue, you would add the Everyone group and grant it the print access right. If you can, assign these permissions from what you have learned. If you have problems, refer back to previous exercises for instructions on setting permissions. Remember that files and printers are shared through the same process with just a few twists.

5. Choose OK to share the printer. The Printer icon now appears as a hand holding or sharing the printer with others. Remote users with the correct permissions now can access the print queue after setting up the correct printer driver on their computers.

Review Questions

1. What are the two types of security Windows 95 offers?

2. What is the difference between a primary domain controller (PDC) and a backup domain controller (BDC)?

3. What is the difference between share-level security and file system security in Windows NT?

Exam Questions

1. Which type of account is only available on Windows NT domain controllers?

   A. User

   B. Global group

   C. Local group

   D. Container user

2. This group usually is used to assign permissions.

   A. Global

   B. LAN

   C. Local

   D. Either global or local

3. Share-level permissions enable which of the following actions?

   A. Defining access levels by user

   B. Controlling file-level access

   C. Providing no access security at all

   D. Defining access levels by password

4. True or false: User-level access is less secure than share-level access.

   A. True

   B. False

5. Which of the following does not add additional security to your network?

   A. Auditing

   B. Virus scanning

   C. Data compression

   D. Data encryption

APPLY YOUR LEARNING

6. "Log on Locally" is one example of which of the following?

   A. Permissions

   B. Rights

   C. Privileges

   D. Attributes

7. Read and Change are two types of which of the following?

   A. Permissions

   B. Rights

   C. Privileges

   D. Attributes

8. A shared printer is available to whom?

   A. Everyone on the network

   B. Only the person who shared it

   C. Anyone with rights to the share

   D. Anyone with permissions to the share

9. Which group includes everyone who uses a resource locally?

   A. Everyone

   B. Interactive

   C. Creator-Owner

   D. Network

10. How many times should each user be created in a single domain?

    A. Once

    B. Once on each domain controller

C. Once on every Windows NT-based machine

D. You should avoid creating users and use global groups instead.

11. This is required for local file-level security.

    A. NTFS

    B. Share-level security

    C. User-level security

    D. FAT

12. What two types of general groups can Windows NT domains include?

    A. Local

    B. Domain

    C. Global

    D. Everyone

13. True or false: A single user can be placed in more than one group.

    A. True

    B. False

14. You want to centralize the management of your network.

    Required result: You want to have passwords and user accounts as part of your security.

    Optional result 1: You want to have file system security on your hard drive.

    Optional result 2: You want to implement share-level security on your shared directories and printers.

APPLY YOUR LEARNING

Suggested solution: You install Windows 95 and implement share-level security. You make sure that the hard drives have NTFS partitions.

A. This solution will obtain the required result and both optional results.

B. This solution will obtain the required result and one optional result.

C. This solution will obtain the required result.

D. This solution does not satisfy the required result.

15. You want to centralize the management of your network.

Required result: You want to have passwords and user accounts as part of your security.

Optional result 1: You want to have file system security on your hard drive.

Optional result 2: You want to implement share level security on your shared directories and printers.

Suggested solution: You install Windows NT and implement share-level security. You make sure that the hard drives have FAT partitions.

A. This solution will obtain the required result and both optional results.

B. This solution will obtain the required result and one optional result.

C. This solution will obtain the required result.

D. This solution does not satisfy the required result.

16. You want to centralize the management of your network.

Required result: You want to have passwords and user accounts as part of your security.

Optional result 1: You want to have file system security on your hard drive.

Optional result 2: You want to implement share level security on your shared directories and printers.

Suggested solution: You install Windows NT and implement share-level security. You make sure that the hard drives have NTFS partitions.

A. This solution will obtain the required result and both optional results.

B. This solution will obtain the required result and one optional result.

C. This solution will obtain the required result.

D. This solution does not satisfy the required result.

Answers to Review Questions

1. Windows 95 offers two types of security: share-level and user-level.

Share-level security is available at all times to Windows 95 to allow peer-to-peer networking. Share-level security relies on the use of passwords to protect individual shared resources. Each resource would have its own password.

User-level security relies on the presence of a Windows NT Workstation, Windows NT Server,

APPLY YOUR LEARNING

or a Novell server to supply a database of user accounts. User-level security provides security on a user-by-user or group-by-group basis.

See the section titled "Implementing Security on Windows 95."

2. A primary domain controller (PDC) and a back-up domain controller (BDC) provide essentially the same functions. They both maintain a User Account database as well as process logon requests for users on client machines. The main difference between a PDC and a BDC is that a PDC contains the master copy of the user account database. The BDCs contain a replica copy of this master database. All changes to the database—that is, the addition and deletion of user accounts—are done on the PDC's user account database.

See the section titled "Implementing Security on Windows NT."

3. Share-level security is the ability to share a directory out on the network and assign this share permissions. The permissions available for this are Full Control, Read, Change, and No Access. These permissions only apply to users accessing the share from a remote machine. Share-level security can be applied to FAT and NTFS partitions.

File system security is a level of security that can be applied on an NTFS partition. This level of security applies to directories and files. File system security applies to people accessing these files over the network, or if the user is interactive to the PC.

See the section titled "Implementing Security on Windows NT" and "Implementing Security on Windows 95."

Answers to Exam Questions

1. **B**. User accounts and local groups exist on all Windows NT computers. A container user is a fictitious term. See the section titled "Managing User Accounts and Groups Using Windows NT."

2. **C**. Local groups are normally used to assign permissions. The general practice is to place users into global groups, and then place the global groups into local groups. The local groups are then assigned permissions. See the section titled "Managing User Accounts and Groups Using Windows NT."

3. **D**. Share-level permissions are applied to files and printers on Windows 95 computers. This level of security does not allow for a user-by-user level of security. Because of this, A and B are both incorrect. C is incorrect, as share-level security does provide access security. See the section titled "Share-level Security on Windows 95."

4. **B**. This answer is false because share-level security does not control access based upon who is accessing the share, but instead controls on whether a person knows the password. See the section titled "Implementing Security on Windows 95."

5. **C**. Data compression allows you to obtain more disk space on a hard drive. See the section titled "Additional Administrative Tasks" in Chapter 9, "Disaster Recovery."

6. **B**. The ability to log on locally is a right. Permissions deals with resource shares. Privileges is just another word in the English language. Attributes are what files and directories will allow to be performed on them. See the section titled "Managing User Accounts and Groups Using Windows NT."

APPLY YOUR LEARNING

7. **A.** Read and Change are two types of Permissions. Rights are what the system will allow you to do to it, such as "log on locally" or "back up files and directories." Privileges is another word in the English language that sounds good. Attributes are what files and directories will allow to be performed on them. See the section titled "Managing User Accounts and Groups Using Windows NT."

8. **D.** Resource shares are based upon permissions. See the answers for question 7, 8, and 9 for why C is incorrect. A and B are incorrect, as these would be dependent upon what permissions were assigned to the share. See the section titled "Permissions."

9. **B.** The Interactive group is that special group that applies to anyone locally on a machine. Network group is anyone on a remote machine from the resource. Creator-Owner is a file permission. Everyone is all people in the domain. See the section titled "Groups."

10. **A.** A user can only be created once in a single domain. See the section titled "User Accounts."

11. **A.** File-level security is only applied on Windows NT computers that have an NTFS partition. D is incorrect, as FAT does not support file-level security. B and C are incorrect, as they are Windows 95 security models. See the section titled

"Assigning File-Level Permissions on an NTFS Partition."

12. **A, C.** Windows NT domains have two general types of groups, local and global. C is incorrect because it is a specific group. B is incorrect because there does not exist a domain group. See the section titled "Groups."

13. **A.** A user can be placed in as many groups as the administrator wishes. See the section titled "Groups."

14. **D.** Windows 95 does not have the ability to create a user account database, nor can it provide file system security with an NTFS partition. It can, however, offer share-level security. The only possible result that could be correct would be optional result 2. See the sections titled "Implementing Security on Windows NT" and "Implementing Security on Windows 95."

15. **B.** Both the required result and the second optional result are met with the proposed solution. The first optional result cannot be met, as only NTFS partitions can offer file system security. See the section titled "Implementing Security on Windows NT."

16. **A.** All results are met with the installation of Windows NT using NTFS partitions. See the section titled "Implementing Security on Windows NT."

Suggested Readings and Resources

1. Siyan, Karanjit S. *Windows NT Server 4 Professional Reference*. New Riders, 1996.

2. Heywood, Drew. *Inside Windows NT Server 4.* New Riders, 1997.

3. Casad, Joe. *MCSE Training Guide: Windows NT Server 4*. New Riders, 1997.

4. Sirockman, Jason. *MCSE Training Guide: Windows NT Server 4 Enterprise*. New Riders, 1997.

5. Boyce, Jim. *Inside Windows 95, Deluxe Edition*. New Riders, 1996.

Chapter 11 targets the following objective in the Implementation section of the Networking Essentials exam:

Select the appropriate hardware and software tools to monitor trends on a given network.

▶ One of the most important things an administrator can do is monitor the network. By monitoring the network, the administrator is able to determine the demand placed upon the system and the usage of resources. This exam objective is designed to encourage you to develop your ability to determine what tools you should use in monitoring the network for trends.

CHAPTER 11

Monitoring the Network

STUDY STRATEGIES

▶ When you read this chapter, be very aware of the role that different devices and programs play in monitoring the network. Pay particular attention to the following Microsoft programs: Performance Monitor, Network Monitor, System Monitor, and Event Viewer. Be aware of what each of these programs can monitor. Each of these programs resides either on a Windows 95 or Windows NT computer, or both. Each of these programs also has a particular set of component of information that it records. By becoming proficient in recognizing when you should use which program, you should have no difficulty in meeting the exam objective.

INTRODUCTION

An important part of network management involves monitoring trends on the network. By effectively monitoring network behavior, you can anticipate problems and correct them before they disrupt the network. Monitoring the network also provides you with a *baseline*, a sampling of how the network functions in its equilibrium state. By establishing a baseline on your system, you can determine whether your network can handle the current resource usage or whether additional resources are needed.

This chapter presents various programs or mechanisms that can be used to monitor and record information about the network. The explanation of what these different mechanisms are and when you would utilize them is addressed in this chapter.

MONITORING NETWORK TRENDS

Monitoring the network is an ongoing task that requires data from several different areas. Some of the monitoring tools that keep watch on the network are discussed in other chapters. The purpose of this chapter is to bring these tools together so that you can view them in the context of an overall network monitoring strategy. The following list details some tools you can use to document network activities:

- ◆ Written documentation

- ◆ A statistics-gathering or performance-monitoring tool, such as Windows NT's Performance Monitor

- ◆ A network-monitoring and protocol-analysis program—such as Windows NT's Network Monitor or the more powerful Network Monitor tool included with Microsoft's BackOffice System Management Server (SMS) package—or a hardware-based protocol analyzer

- ◆ A system event log, such as the Windows NT event log, which you can access through Windows NT's Event Viewer application

KEEPING RECORDS

A detailed history of changes to the network serves as a tremendous aid in troubleshooting. When a problem occurs, the first thing you want to know is *what* has changed and *when* it was changed. This information can be gathered from written documentation.

Your documentation of the network should begin from the day the network is installed. The layout, design, components, and software should all be recorded within your network documentation. Contact names, service contracts, as well as important support telephone numbers should also be part of your network's documentation.

This documentation can be as simple as sketched designs and information written on a piece of paper, or as elaborate as an electronic schematic and database stored on a computer.

The following list details some items your configuration records should include:

- ◆ Descriptions of all hardware, including installation dates, repair histories, configuration details (such as interrupts and addresses), and backup records for each server

- ◆ A map of the network showing locations of hardware components and cabling details

- ◆ Documentation describing why certain layouts or naming conventions were chosen, so that these conventions can be followed in the future

- ◆ Current copies of workstation configuration files, such as CONFIG.SYS and AUTOEXEC.BAT files for DOS and Windows 3.1 machines, or backup copies of the registry files for Windows 95 and NT

- ◆ Service agreements and important telephone numbers, such as the numbers of vendors, contractors, and software support lines

- ◆ Software licenses to ensure that your network operates within the bounds of the license terms

- ◆ A history of past problems and related solutions

Records of the network are used for more than just troubleshooting. They also supply a wealth of information for future planning. Records can help you maintain consistency within the hardware and software. Detailed records also save a lot of time when software and hardware audits are performed—a common event within medium- and large-sized organizations.

MONITORING PERFORMANCE

One of the most important tasks that should be performed on the network is some form of statistical collecting. These statistics can range from the performance of servers, workstations, and other devices on the network to the performance of individual components within a program or service itself. This section looks at three types of performance monitoring tools: Simple Network Management Protocol (SNMP), Windows NT Performance Monitor, and Windows 95's System Monitor.

Simple Network Management Protocol (SNMP)

Many types of software and hardware on the market enable you to collect statistics on the network. One important protocol used within the TCP/IP protocol suite that assists in statistic collecting is the *Simple Network Management Protocol (SNMP)*.

SNMP is a protocol that is supported by most pieces of hardware and software that support the TCP/IP protocol stack. This protocol allows for the collection of statistics of various resources on the network. For this information to be collected about a resource, the resource must run an SNMP service, or have some other device run the SNMP service on its behalf.

The SNMP service collects predefined information. This information is stored in a *Management Information Base (MIB)*. An MIB is a database of information that can be read by management software designed to work with SNMP. An example of this management software is IBM's OpenView.

Management software issues one of the following three main commands:

◆ The *get* command gathers information within an MIB.

◆ The *get next* command gets the next piece of information within the MIB.

◆ The *set* command places information within the MIB.

These devices that have an SNMP service monitoring them can also be configured to issue *traps*, or system messages, when certain parameters are reached or exceeded.

Windows NT Performance Monitor

Windows NT's Performance Monitor tool lets you monitor important system parameters for the computers on your network in real time. Performance Monitor can keep an eye on a large number of system parameters, providing a graphical or tabular profile of system and network trends. Performance Monitor also can save performance data in a log for later reference. You can use Performance Monitor to track statistical measurements (called *counters*) for any of several hardware or software components (called *objects*). An example of these counters for an object being displayed in a chart format can be seen in Figure 11.1.

Some Performance Monitor objects that relate to network behavior are as follows:

◆ Network segment

◆ Server

◆ Server work queues

◆ Workstation or other Redirectors

◆ Protocol-related objects, such as TCP, UDP IP, NetBEUI, NWLink, and NetBIOS

◆ Service-related objects, such as Browser and Gateway Services for NetWare

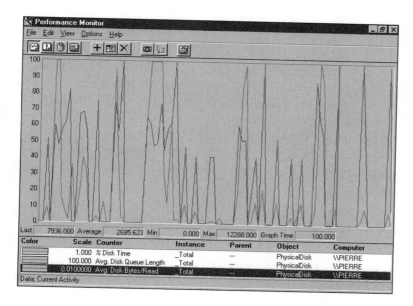

FIGURE 11.1
A Windows NT Performance Monitor chart.

Some Performance Monitor counters that relate to the performance of components or resources on a computer are as follows:

◆ Processor

◆ Memory

◆ PhysicalDisk

Software installed on Windows NT can, in some cases, also create its own Performance Monitor counters. Microsoft's BackOffice products create a vast number of objects and counters for you to monitor. Third-party products can also create objects and counters to monitor.

You should use Performance Monitor if you are experiencing problems, but you should also use Performance Monitor to log network activity when things are running smoothly. Logging normal network activity, especially after the network has been installed or a new resource has been added or changed helps you establish a baseline. It is this baseline to which later measurements can be compared.

Exercises 11.2 and 11.3 at the end of this chapter provide you with a guided tour of Windows NT's Performance Monitor application. More information about Performance Monitor is covered within courses dealing with Windows NT Server, Workstation, and the Windows NT Enterprise books and courses.

One final thing to note is that Performance Monitor does not gather information relating to the hard drive of a computer unless the command *diskperf –y* is run from the command prompt. Use *diskperf –ye* if the hard drive is part of a stripe set. After these commands are run, monitoring of the hard drives will continue until *diskperf – n* is issued at the command prompt. If you issue any of these commands, the computer must be rebooted for them to take effect.

Windows 95 System Monitor

Windows 95 includes a program called System Monitor that also enables you to collect information on the Windows 95 machine in real time. System Manager collects information on different *Categories* of *Items* on the system (see Figure 11.2).

The main categories within System Monitor are as follows:

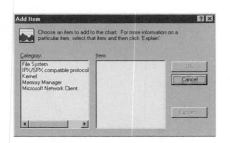

FIGURE 11.2
Windows 95's System Monitor.

- ◆ *File System.* Information written to or read from the hard drive

- ◆ *IPX/SPX compatible protocol.* Information on the number of IPX and SPX packets sent out from and received by the computer

- ◆ *Kernel.* Processor usage, number of threads being processed, and the number of virtual machines running on the computer

- ◆ *Memory Manager.* Various memory items that can be tracked on the computer

- ◆ *Microsoft Network Client.* The number of files, sessions, resources, and bytes sent or received by the network client

Although Windows 95's System Monitor is not as elaborate or extensive in the collection of information and statistics as Windows NT's Performance Monitor, nor can System Monitor collect information to a log file, it is a useful tool for baselining a Windows 95 computer.

In most cases a constant recording of system information by Performance Monitor or System Monitor is not needed. The continuous use of these programs consumes computer resources that are best left for other programs. Also, after a baseline is established, the collection of redundant information is often not warranted.

MONITORING NETWORK TRAFFIC

Protocol analysis tools monitor network traffic by intercepting and decoding frames. Software-based tools, such as Windows NT Server's Network Monitor (see Figure 11.3), analyze frames coming and going, in real time, from the computer on which they run. Network Monitor records a number of statistics, including the percent of network utilization and the broadcasts per second. In addition, Network Monitor tabulates frame statistics (such as frames sent and received) for each network address.

An enhanced version of Network Monitor, which is included with the Microsoft BackOffice System Management Server (SMS) package, monitors traffic on more than just the traffic between the local computer and other devices. It will also monitor traffic that is just between other devices, and also traffic on remote networks, provided a monitor agent is installed on the remote network segment.

For large networks, or for networks with complex traffic patterns, you might want to use a hardware-based protocol-analysis tool. A hardware-based protocol analyzer is a portable device that can be as small as a palmtop PC or as large as a suitcase. The advantage of a hardware-based protocol analyzer is that you can carry it to strategic places around the network (such as a network node or a busy cabling intersection) and monitor the traffic at that point.

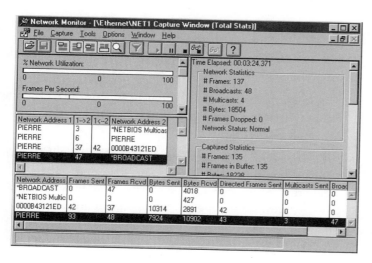

FIGURE 11.3
Windows NT Server's Network Monitor main screen.

Some protocol analyzers are quite sophisticated. In addition to keeping network traffic statistics, they can capture bad frames and often isolate the source. They also can help determine the cause of bottlenecks, protocol problems, and connection errors. A hardware-based protocol analyzer is often a good investment for a large network because it concentrates a considerable amount of monitoring and troubleshooting power into a single, portable unit. For a smaller network, however, a hardware-based analyzer might not be worth the initial five-figure expense because less expensive software-based products perform many of the same functions.

LOGGING EVENTS

Some operating systems, such as Windows NT, have the capability to keep a running log of system events. That log serves as a record of previous errors, warnings, and other messages from the system. Studying the event log can help you find recurring errors and discover when a problem first appeared. The event log should also be scanned on a regular basis to look for any indications of potential problems.

Windows NT's Event Viewer application provides you with access to the event log. You can use Event Viewer to monitor the following types of events:

- *System events.* Warnings, error messages, and other notices describing significant system events. Examples of system log entries include browser elections, service failures, and network connection failures.

- *Security events.* Events tracked through Windows NT's auditing features. Refer to Chapter 10, "Managing and Securing a Microsoft Network."

- *Application events.* Messages from Win32 applications. If you're having a problem with an application, you can check the application log for an application-related error or warning message, provided the application is programmed to write to the event log. Some NT services such as the JET database engine used by WINS record their information in the application events log rather than the system log.

Event Viewer is part of the Windows NT Server Administrative Tools group. To start Event Viewer, click on the Start button and choose Programs, Administrative Tools, Event Viewer. Figure 11.4 shows the Event Viewer main screen. Click on the Log menu to select the System, Security, or Application log.

If you double-click on a log entry in Event Viewer, an Event Detail dialog box appears on your screen (see Figure 11.5). An Event Detail provides a detailed description of the event.

The Windows NT Event Viewer utility contains the following five types of events:

◆ *Information.* These events simply state that something of importance has been done, such as the loading of a protocol. These events are recorded for a matter of information only.

◆ *Warning.* These events serve as a warning that some event that may be important has occurred. Often when services are stopped, a warning event is generated.

◆ *Stop.* These events occur when something of significance, such as a detrimental event, has occurred. Often when services or hardware fail, a Stop event is generated.

◆ *Success.* This event is generated within the auditing log. Success events are generated when an object that was audited as successful has occurred. You might, for example, audit the successful logon of users.

◆ *Failure.* This event is generated within the auditing log. Failure events are generated when an object that was audited as a Failure has occurred, such as the failure of users to log on.

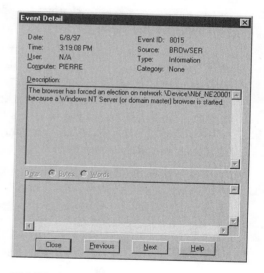

FIGURE 11.5
Event detail describing a system event.

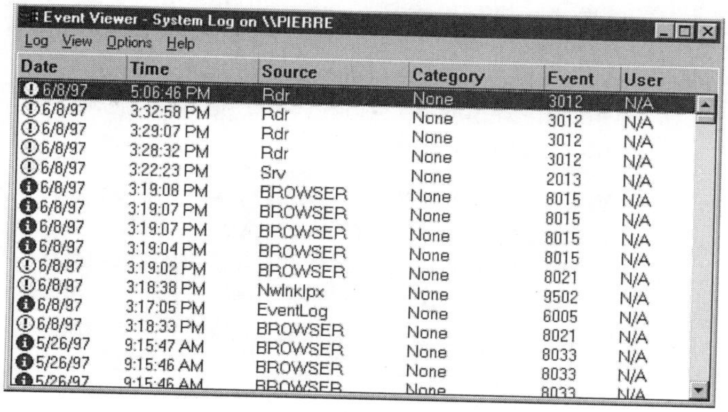

FIGURE 11.4
The Event Viewer main screen.

CASE STUDY: MONITORING THE NETWORK

ESSENCE OF THE CASE

The essence of the case is as follows:

- What documentation will be required?

- What baselining will be done?

- What preventive monitoring will be performed?

SCENARIO

Books Unlimited, a major up-and-coming retail book chain, has decided to implement a network. You have been called in to set up the network, as well as tune the network, so that problems can be avoided and a preventive maintenance program can be implemented.

Books Unlimited requires a general list of what steps and measures you wish to implement on the network for monitoring purposes. This information will be collected before and after the network is installed. This list will act as a guideline for the eventual monitoring and maintenance program that will be implemented.

The Books Unlimited network will be a Windows NT network, with Exchange, SQL, and SMS BackOffice products being installed. The transport protocol to be used is TCP/IP. When possible, Books Unlimited would like to use resources that come with NT, and SMS to monitor resources in the network.

ANALYSIS

To address the needs of Books Unlimited, the three primary issues are addressed in the following order: records and documentation, baselining, and monitoring.

Records and Documentation

One of the things that should be performed on any network, right from the beginning, is the collection of documentation and the keeping of records. The Books Unlimited network should be no exception.

Records and documentation begin before the first components of a network are put into place. A design of the Books Unlimited network physical layout, file system structures, naming conventions, and hardware types should be put down on paper. In most cases, hardware and software are listed for cost purposes, but a proper design shows how and why the design being implemented was used. A completely documented design includes details such as why one cable type versus another was chosen, why one network card versus another was selected, and even the reasons why the naming conventions being put into place were chosen.

In addition to the paper information of the design, components, and reasoning, all documentation that came with any piece of hardware should also be kept. This includes items such as warranties, licenses, and configuration information. Documentation for any software shipped with the hardware should also be filed away for future use.

All service contracts, licenses, warranties, purchase receipts, and contact numbers for the Books Unlimited network should also be documented. This information is beneficial if the company ever needs to contact key people in the

CASE STUDY: MONITORING THE NETWORK

event of an emergency, or if a corporate audit is performed on the software and hardware of this Books Unlimited location.

This collection of documentation and recordkeeping is something that will be continued for the life of the network. As a network grows, new components are being added all the time. The addition of new components means new software and documentation; therefore, keeping up-to-date records is always important.

Baselining

Baselining of the Books Unlimited network is an important first step, after hardware components are put into place. In an ideal world, a person would be able to develop a model of the future network within a laboratory. But many companies do not have the resources or time to perform such research. Often, network designers need to draw upon their experience and knowledge of networks to come up with the optimal solution.

In either case, after the network is actually installed for use, it is very important to begin baselining the network. Baselining is the recording of the resource usage on the network. Baselining is done on a continual basis over several weeks, after a network is put into place. Statistics such as processor usage or the speed of the network can be recorded. Based upon the information gathered, adjustments to the network can be made. These adjustments could be as simple as changing some parameters on some of the computers to optimize resource usage, or as involved as reevaluating the initial decisions made on components such as cable types or servers.

Microsoft's Performance Monitor and Network Monitor are good tools to monitor resources on Books Unlimited's network. Performance Monitor basically tracks the components within a Microsoft NT computer (System Monitor is used for Windows 95), whereas Network Monitor enables a person to see how well the usage of the network is performing.

Microsoft Exchange, SQL, and SMS servers all add objects and counters that can be monitored with Performance Monitor. Careful research should be done on each of these products to see what boundaries or thresholds should be established by the resources being monitored. Also, if you wish to monitor the TCP/IP protocol in Performance Monitor, the SNMP service must be loaded on the Windows NT computer.

After any new resource is added to Books Unlimited's network, a baseline of the usage or performance of that resource should be undertaken. This ensures that the resource in question is being used, or is configured, in its optimal capacity.

Monitoring

In many ways, baselining is monitoring. The main difference is that baselining is done after a new network has been installed or a new resource has been introduced to the network. Based upon the information generated by the baseline and saved by the network administrator, adjustments, if needed, can be made to the new network or added resource. This information on the network that is saved is the baseline against which any monitoring events in the future will be compared. Monitoring, on the other hand, is the ongoing

continues

CASE STUDY: MONITORING THE NETWORK

continued

process of measuring the network's performance. Monitored events should be compared periodically to the baseline to see whether any abnormal events are occurring.

As time goes on, resources may be used in ways not previously thought of by Books Unlimited. Equipment begins to fail over time. Monitoring the Books Unlimited network on a continual basis enables administrators to detect resources about to fail or the unexpected use of certain resources.

Performance Monitor can be used under these situations, but is often not ideal for continual monitoring because it does place a load on resources of the computer that is running Performance Monitor. For continual monitoring, one should run Performance Monitor on a computer that is not going to be part of the monitored set of resources. Also, Performance Monitor tends to generate too much detailed information that is very similar to that collected through the baseline. More commonly used tools to perform ongoing monitoring are the Event Viewer, and SNMP in a TCP/IP network. Both of these utilities allow for the collection of events on an ongoing basis. The information generated

from these utilities should be examined on a daily basis. Often, a few minutes several times a day is all that is needed to verify that all is well on the network.

A protocol analyzer is also a good tool to use for analyzing the amount of network traffic being generated on the network. A protocol analyzer is also a great tool to be used when there is some form of connectivity issue. For example, if a person is running an application on the server, and this application is always failing at a certain point of use, a protocol analyzer can detect and display the actual file that is causing the application to hang. In the case of Books Unlimited, they have a small LAN only, and hence a software protocol analyzer, as opposed to a hardware protocol analyzer, is probably a more cost-efficient alternative.

In summary, recordkeeping, baselining, and monitoring of the network should always be done by Books Unlimited. If all these tasks are done, the network can be properly adjusted and perform at its optimum. Also if a problem does arise, it can, in most cases, be detected early by monitoring and resolved quickly with the information contained in the network records and documentation.

CHAPTER SUMMARY

This chapter reviewed some of the tools and resources that can be used to monitor network trends and information. These tools and resources include the following:

◆ Documentation of the components placed on the network as well as the network's design

◆ Performance monitoring devices

◆ Hardware- and software-based network monitoring and protocol analysis tools

◆ Event logs

No single monitoring or recording method on its own is sufficient on a network. You should instead use all the methods listed here.

KEY TERMS

• Baseline

• Management Information Base (MIB)

• Performance Monitor

• System Monitor

• Network Monitor

• Event Viewer

• SNMP

APPLY YOUR LEARNING

Exercises

11.1 Using Network Monitor

Objective: Examine the main window display of Windows NT Server 4.0's Network Monitor application.

Estimated time: 15 minutes

1. If Network Monitor has been installed on your system, click the Start menu and choose Programs, Administrative Tools. Then choose the Network Monitor application from the Administrative Tools group and proceed to Step 4.

2. If Network Monitor hasn't been installed on your system, you must install it, along with a component called the Network Monitor Agent. Network Monitor and the Network Monitor Agent can be installed together with the Control Panel Network application. Click the Start menu and choose Settings, Control Panel. Double-click the Network application and choose the Services tab.

3. In the Network application Services tab, click on the Add button. Choose Network Monitor and Agent from the Network Service list and click OK. Windows NT prompts you for the Windows NT installation disk. When the installation is complete, click OK and then Yes to shut down your system and restart Windows NT. Then start the Network Monitor application, as described in Step 1.

4. Examine the four panes of the Network Monitor main screen. The following list describes the four panes:

    • The Graph pane is located in the upper-left corner of the display. The Graph section includes five bar graphs describing network activity. Only two of the graphs are visible; use the scroll bar to view the other three graphs.

    • The Session Statistics pane, which appears below the Graph pane, tracks network activity by session, showing the two computers in the session and the frames sent each way.

    • The Total Statistics pane, which appears to the right of the Graph pane, lists such important statistics as the number of frames and the number of broadcasts. You can use the scroll bar to reach other entries that are not visible.

    • The Station Statistics pane, which sits at the bottom of the window, shows statistics for frames listed by network address.

5. Pull down the Capture menu and choose Start. Network Monitor then starts monitoring the network.

6. Ping the Network Monitor PC from another computer on the network. (Go to the command prompt and type **ping**, followed by the IP address on the Network Monitor computer—for example, ping 111.121.131.141.) Watch the Station Statistics pane at the bottom of the screen to see any new information.

7. Experiment with sending files or other requests to or from the Network Monitor PC. Study the effect of network activity on the values displayed in the four panes of the Network Monitor main window.

8. When you are finished, pull down the Capture menu and click Stop to stop capturing data. Then exit Network Monitor. When prompted to save your captured data, click on No.

APPLY YOUR LEARNING	

11.2 Creating a Chart in Performance Monitor

Objectives: Become familiar with the process of creating and reading a Performance Monitor chart. Understand the basic components of the Performance Monitor main window and the Add to Chart dialog box. Learn how to turn on disk performance counters by using the *diskperf* command.

Estimated time: 25 minutes

1. From the Start menu, select Programs. Choose the Administrative Tools group and click Performance Monitor. The Performance Monitor main window appears on your screen.

2. Pull down the Edit menu and choose Add to Chart (see Figure 11.6). The Add to Chart dialog box appears (see Figure 11.7). You can also invoke the Add to Chart dialog box by clicking the plus sign in the tool bar of the Performance Monitor main window.

3. The box labeled Computer at the top of the Add to Chart dialog box tells Performance Monitor

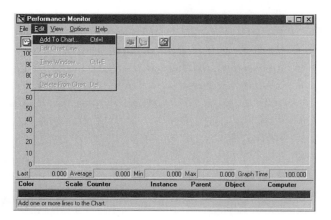

FIGURE 11.6
The Performance Monitor main window.

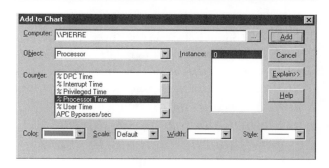

FIGURE 11.7
The Add to Chart dialog box.

which computer you want to monitor. The default is the local system. Click the ellipsis button to the right of the box for a list of computers on the network.

4. The box labeled Object tells Performance Monitor which object you want to monitor. As you learned earlier in this chapter, an object is a hardware or software component of your system. You can think of an object as a category of system statistics. Pull down the Object menu. Scroll through the list of objects and look for the Processor, Memory, PhysicalDisk, LogicalDisk, Server, and Network Segment objects described earlier in this chapter. Choose the PhysicalDisk object. If you have more than one physical disk on your system, a list of your physical disks appears in the Instance box to the right of the Object box. The Instance box lists all instances of the object selected in the Object box. If necessary, choose a physical disk instance.

5. The box labeled Counter displays the counters (the statistical measurements) that are available for the object displayed in the Object box. Scroll through the list of counters for the PhysicalDisk object. If you feel like experimenting, select a

APPLY YOUR LEARNING

different object in the Object box. Notice that the new object is accompanied by a different set of counters. Switch back to the PhysicalDisk object and choose the %Disk Time counter. Click the Explain button on the right side of the Add to Chart dialog box. Notice that a description of the %Disk Time counter appears at the bottom of the dialog box. To add this to your chart, click on the Add button.

6. Click the Done button in the Add to Chart dialog box. The dialog box disappears, and you see the Performance Monitor main window.

7. In the Performance Monitor main window, a vertical line sweeps across the chart from left to right. You may also see a faint colored line at the bottom of the chart recording a %Disk Time value of 0. If so, you haven't enabled the disk performance counters for your system. (If the disk performance monitors are enabled on your system, you should see a spikey line that looks like the readout from an electrocardiogram. You're done with this step. Go on to Step 8. If you still have no disk activity, activate the help on the start menu, and perform a maximum search. This should generate a lot of disk activity.)

If you need to enable the disk performance counters, click the Start button and go to the command prompt. Enter the command **diskperf -y**. Then reboot your system and repeat Steps 1–7. (You don't have to browse through the object and counter menus this time.)

8. You should now see a spikey line representing the percent of time that the physical disk is busy reading or writing. Select Add to Chart from the Edit menu. Select the PhysicalDisk object and choose the counter Avg. Disk Queue Length. Click the Add button. Then choose the counter

Avg. Disk Bytes/Read. Click the Add button and then click the Done button.

9. Examine the Performance Monitor main window. All three of the counters you selected should be tracing out spikey lines on the chart. Each line is a different color. At the bottom of the window is a table showing which counter corresponds with which color. The table also gives the scale of the output, the instance, the object, and the computer.

10. Below the chart (but above the table of counters) is a row of statistical parameters labeled: Last, Average, Min, Max, and Graph Time. These parameters pertain to the counter that is selected in the table at the bottom of the window. Select a different counter and you see that some of these values change. The Last value is the counter value over the last reading. Graph time is the time it takes (in seconds) for the vertical line that draws the chart to sweep across the window. If you have several lines on the chart, **Ctrl + H** highlights different lines on the chart.

11. Start Windows Explorer. Select a file (a graphics file or a word processing document) and choose Copy from Explorer's Edit menu. (This copies the file you selected to the clipboard.) Go to another directory and select Paste from the Edit menu. (This creates a copy of the file in the second directory.) Minimize Explorer and return to the Performance Monitor main screen. The disk activity caused by your Explorer session is now reflected in the spikes of the counter lines.

12. Pull down the Options menu and select Chart. The Chart Options dialog box appears on your screen (see Figure 11.8). The Chart Options dialog box provides a number of options governing the chart display. The Update Time section

APPLY YOUR LEARNING

enables you to choose an update interval. The update interval tells Performance Monitor how frequently it should update the chart with new values. (If you choose the Manual Update option, the chart updates only when you press **Ctrl + U** or click Update Now in the Options menu.) Experiment with the Chart Options or click the Cancel button to return to the main window.

13. Pull down the File menu. Choose Exit to exit Performance Monitor. Note that the Save Chart Settings and Save Chart Settings As options in the File menu enable you to save the collection of objects and counters you're using now so you can monitor the same counters later and avoid setting them up again. The Export Chart option enables you to export the data to a file that you can then open with a spreadsheet or database application. The Save Workspace option saves the settings for your chart, as well as any settings for alerts, logs, or reports specified in this session. Learn more about alerts, logs, and reports in Exercise 11.3.

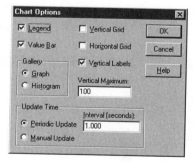

FIGURE 11.8
The Chart Options dialog box.

11.3 Performance Monitor Alerts, Logs, and Reports

Objectives: Become familiar with the alternative views (Alert view, Log view, and Report view) available through the Performance Monitor View menu. Log performance data to a log file.

Estimated time: 25 minutes

1. Click Programs in the Start menu and choose Performance Monitor from the Administrative Tools group. The Performance Monitor main window appears onscreen.

2. Pull down the View menu. You see four options, as follows:

   • The Chart option plots the counters you select in a continuous chart (refer to Exercise 11.1).

   • The Alert option automatically alerts a network official or executes an application if the predetermined counter threshold is surpassed.

   • The Log option saves your system performance data to a log file.

   • The Report option displays system performance data in a report format.

   The setup is similar for each of these view formats. All use some form of the Add to Chart dialog box (refer to Exercise 11.2). All have options that are configured through the first command at the top of the Options menu. (The first command at the top of the Options menu changes its name depending on the active view. It was the Chart option in Exercise 11.2.)

3. Click the Alert option in the View menu.

APPLY YOUR LEARNING

4. Click the plus sign in the toolbar or choose Add to Alert from the Edit menu. The Add to Alert dialog box (see Figure 11.9) is similar to the Add to Chart dialog box except for two additional items at the bottom of the screen. The Alert If box enables you to type in a threshold for the counter. The Over/Under option buttons specify whether you want to receive an alert if the counter value is over or under the threshold value. The Run Program on Alert box lets you specify a command line that executes if the counter value reaches the threshold you specify in the Alert If box. You can ask Performance Monitor to send a message to your beeper, to send you an email message, or to notify your paging service.

Don't specify a batch file in the Run Program on Alert box. Performance Monitor uses Unicode format, which can confuse the command-prompt interpreter. (The < and > symbols, which are used in Unicode format, are interpreted as a redirection of input or output.)

5. The default object in the Add to Alert dialog box should be the Processor object. The default counter should be %Processor Time. Enter the value **5%** in the Alert If box and make sure the Alert If option button is set to Over. In the Run Program on Alert box, type **SOL**. Set the Run Program on Alert option button to First Time. This configuration tells Performance Monitor to execute Windows NT's Solitaire program when the %Processor Time exceeds 5%.

If the Run Program on Alert option button is not set to First Time, Performance Monitor executes a new instance of Solitaire every time the %Processor Time exceeds 5%, which happens every time it executes a new instance of Solitaire. You'll probably have to close Performance Monitor using the X button or reboot to stop the incessant shuffling and dealing.

6. Click the Add button and then click the Done button. The Alert Legend at the bottom of the Alert window describes the active alert parameters. The Alert Log shows every instance of an alert (see Figure 11.10).

7. Make some changes to your desktop. (Hide or reveal the task bar, change the size of the Performance Monitor window—anything that causes a 5% utilization of the processor.) The

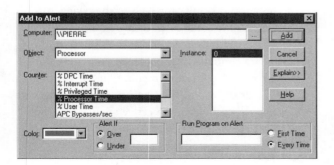

FIGURE 11.9
The Add to Alert dialog box.

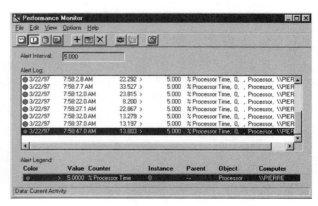

FIGURE 11.10
The Performance Monitor alert log.

APPLY YOUR LEARNING

Solitaire program should miraculously appear on your screen. In a real alert situation, Performance Monitor executes an alert application rather than starting a card game.

8. Pull down the Edit menu and select Delete Alert.

9. Pull down the View menu and select Log. Performance Monitor's Log view saves performance data to a log file rather than displaying it on the screen.

10. Pull down the Edit menu and select Add to Log. Notice that only the objects appear in the Add to Log dialog box. The counters and instances boxes don't appear because Performance Monitor automatically logs all counters and all instances of the object to the log file. Select the Memory Object and click Add. If you want, you can select another object, such as the Paging File object, and click Add again. When you are finished adding objects, click Done.

11. Pull down the Options menu and select Log. The Log Options dialog box appears on your screen (see Figure 11.11). The Log Options dialog box enables you to designate a log file that Performance Monitor is to use to log the data. In the File name box, enter the name exer2.log. You also can specify an update interval. The update interval is the interval at which Performance Monitor records performance data to the log. The Manual Update option button specifies that the file won't be updated unless you press **Ctrl + U** or select Update Now from the Options menu. Click the Start Log button to start saving data to the log. Wait a few minutes and then return to the Log Options dialog box and click the Stop Log button.

12. Pull down the View menu and switch to Chart view.

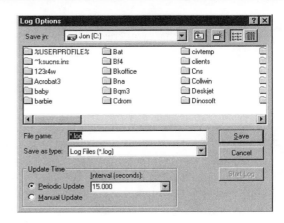

FIGURE 11.11
The Log Options dialog box.

13. Pull down the Options menu and select Data From. The Data From dialog box enables you to specify a source for the performance data that appears in the Chart. Note that the default source is Current Activity. (That is why the chart you created in Exercise 11.2 took its data from current system activity.) The alternative to the Current Activity option is to use data from a log file. Click the Log File option button. Click the ellipsis button to the right of the log file window and select the exer2 file you created in Step 11. Click OK.

14. Pull down the Edit menu and click Add to Chart. Click the down arrow to the right of the Object menu. Notice that your only object choices are the Memory object and any other objects you selected in Step 10. Select the Memory object. Browse through the counter list and select Pages/sec. Click the Add button. Select any other memory counters you want to display and click the Add button. Click Done.

15. The log file's record of the counters you selected in Step 14 appears in the chart in the

APPLY YOUR LEARNING

Performance Monitor's main window. Notice that, unlike the chart you created in Exercise 11.1, this chart does not continuously sweep out new data. That is because this chart represents static data from a previous, finite monitoring session.

16. Pull down the Edit menu and select Time Window. The Time Window enables you to focus on a particular time interval within the log file (see Figure 11.12). In this example (because you collected data for only a few minutes), the Time Window may seem unnecessary. If you collected data for a longer period, however, and you want to zero in on a particular event, the Time Window can be very useful. Set the beginning and end points of your time window by adjusting the gray start and stop sliders on the Time Window slide bar. The Bookmark section at the bottom of the dialog box enables you to specify a log file bookmark as a start or stop point. (You can create a bookmark by selecting the Bookmark option from the Options menu while you are collecting data to the log file or by clicking the book in the Performance Monitor tool bar.) Click OK to view the data for the time interval.

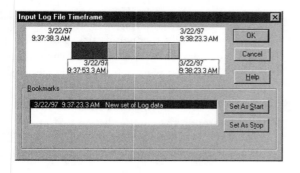

FIGURE 11.12
The Performance Monitor Input Log File Timeframe dialog box.

17. Pull down the View menu and switch to Report view. Pull down the Options menu and select Data From. Switch the Data From setting back to Current Activity. Report view displays the performance data in a text report rather than in a graphics format.

18. Select Add to Report from the Edit menu. Select the processor object and choose the %Processor Time, %Interrupt Time, and Interrupts/sec counters. (Hold down the Ctrl key to select all three and then click Add.) Select the PhysicalDisk object and choose the %Disk Time, Avg. Disk Queue Length, and Current Disk Queue Length counters. Click the Add button. Select the Memory object and choose the Pages/sec, Page Faults/sec, and Available Bytes counters. Click the Add button. Click Done.

19. Examine the main report window. Performance Monitor displays a report of the performance data you specified in a hierarchical format, with counters listed under the appropriate object.

20. Select Exit in the File menu to exit Performance Monitor.

Review Questions

1. What is the purpose of Simple Network Management Protocol (SNMP)?

2. What is a protocol analyzer, and what are the two main types?

3. What is the purpose of creating a baseline?

4. What tools does Microsoft Windows NT and Windows 95 offer to enable you to monitor the network?

APPLY YOUR LEARNING

Exam Questions

1. What is an advantage of hardware-based network monitoring tools over software-based tools?

   A. They are less expensive.

   B. They are easier to use.

   C. A hardware-based tool can also serve as a PC.

   D. None of the above.

2. Which tool would you use to determine whether a Windows NT Server system displayed the same error message at the same time every day?

   A. Network Monitor

   B. Performance Monitor

   C. Event Viewer

   D. None of the above

3. Which tool would you use to determine whether a Windows NT Server machine has enough RAM?

   A. Network Monitor

   B. Performance Monitor

   C. Event Viewer

   D. None of the above

4. An enhanced version of Network Monitor is included with which product?

   A. Windows NT

   B. Windows 95

   C. SMS

   D. SNMP

5. Which utility keeps a record of the repair histories of network hardware?

   A. Network Monitor

   B. Event log

   C. Client Manager

   D. Nothing—you must do it yourself

6. What does an MIB stand for?

   A. Management Information Base

   B. Message Information Base

   C. Managed Information BIOS

   D. Motherboards Information Board

7. Which program comes only with Windows 95?

   A. Network Monitor

   B. Performance Monitor

   C. SNMP

   D. System Monitor

8. You wish to use the correct utility to monitor the network. All your computers are either Windows NT or Windows 95.

   Primary objective: You need to see the network traffic that is generated between computers.

   Secondary objective: You need to be able to log performance information on your Windows NT servers.

   Secondary objective: You need to plot Windows NT Performance information to charts.

   Suggested Solution: You install Network Monitor to trace the network traffic, and System Monitor on the Windows NT computers to log and chart performance information.

A. This solution meets the primary objective and both secondary objectives.

B. This solution meets the primary objective and one secondary objective.

C. This solution meets the primary objective.

D. This solution does not meet the primary objective.

9. You wish to use the correct utility to monitor the network. All your computers are either Windows NT or Windows 95.

Primary objective: You need to see the network traffic that is generated between computers.

Secondary objective: You need to be able to log performance information on your Windows NT servers.

Secondary objective: You need to plot Windows NT Performance information to charts.

Suggested Solution: You install Performance Monitor on all Windows NT machines to track the network traffic and log and chart performance information.

A. This solution meets the primary objective and both secondary objectives.

B. This solution meets the primary objective and one secondary objective.

C. This solution meets the primary objective.

D. This solution does not meet the primary objective.

10. You wish to use the correct utility to monitor the network. All your computers are either Windows NT or Windows 95.

Primary objective: You need to see the network traffic that is generated between computers.

Secondary objective: You need to be able to log performance information on your Windows NT servers.

Secondary objective: You need to plot Windows NT Performance information to charts.

Suggested Solution: You install Network Monitor on a Windows 95 machine to trace the network traffic, and Performance Monitor on the Windows 95 computers to log and chart performance information on the Windows NT computers.

A. This solution meets the primary objective and both secondary objectives.

B. This solution meets the primary objective and one secondary objective.

C. This solution meets the primary objective.

D. This solution does not satisfy the primary objective.

Answers to Review Questions

1. The purpose of SNMP is to record and deliver statistics on various network parameters. This can be information such as whether a buffer is becoming too full, the IP address of a computer, or the routing table within a router.

   SNMP information is delivered to a management utility such as SMS in a process known as a *trap*. Information can also be obtained by a management utility, with the issuance of a *get* or *get next* command. Information can be set with the issuance of a *set* command.

   See the section titled "Simple Network Management Protocol (SNMP)" for more information.

APPLY YOUR LEARNING

2. The purpose of a protocol analyzer is to capture and record network traffic being sent across the transmission media.

   Protocol analyzers are of two types: software and hardware. Software programs are installed into computers. They use the computer's network connectivity to collect the data on the transmission media. A hardware protocol analyzer is a dedicated, portable device used for the collection of network information. It uses a built-in adapter to connect to the transmission media.

   See the section titled "Monitoring Network Traffic" for more information.

3. The purpose of creating a baseline is to establish a historic record of how a network and its resources operate in equilibrium.

   See the section titled "Introduction" for more information.

4. Microsoft Windows NT comes with the following tools to collect and monitor information:

   • *Performance Monitor.* This utility is used to collect information about different objects and counters on a Windows NT computer. It collects information on a real-time basis.

   • *Event Viewer.* This utility is used to collect information on any events that have happened on a Windows NT system. It collects information on events as they occur.

   • *Network Monitor.* This utility is used to collect information that is going across the transmission media. It collects information in real time.

   See the sections titled "Windows NT Performance Monitor," "Monitoring Network Traffic," and "Logging Events" for more information.

Microsoft Windows 95 comes with the following utility:

   • *System Monitor.* This collects information on various resources installed on a Windows 95 computer. This utility collects information in real time.

Answers to Exam Questions

1. **D.** Hardware-based network monitoring tools are almost always more expensive and more complex to use than software tools. These hardware tools do not serve as PCs. They do, however, provide more information for analysis and tend to be portable. See the section titled "Monitoring Network Traffic."

2. **C.** Event Viewer logs error messages and the times that they occurred. Network Monitor captures the message, if it is a network error, but not the time. Performance Monitor does not track messages. See the section titled "Logging Events."

3. **B.** Performance Monitor monitors components of an NT machine, such as RAM. Network Monitor does not monitor RAM, and Event Viewer tracks system messages, not hardware. See the section titled "Monitoring Performance."

4. **C.** The enhanced version comes with SMS. See the section titled "Keeping Records."

5. **D.** Repair histories are kept only if you document them. See the section titled "Monitoring Network Traffic."

6. **A.** An MIB is a Management Information Base. See the section titled "Simple Network Management Protocol (SNMP)."

APPLY YOUR LEARNING

7. **D**. Network Monitor and SNMP can be installed on Windows 95 and NT; Performance Monitor can be installed on only Windows NT. Only System Monitor comes with Windows 95. See the section titled "Monitoring Network Traffic" and "Simple Network Management Protocol (SNMP)."

8. **C**. The primary objective is met because Network Monitor shows the network traffic generated between two computers. Neither secondary objective is met, because System Monitor can be installed only on Windows 95 computers. See the sections titled "Windows NT Performance Monitor," "Windows 95 System Monitor," and "Monitoring Network Traffic."

9. **D**. Both secondary objectives are met because Performance Monitor allows for the logging and charting of performance information on a Windows NT computer. The primary objective is not met because you would need Network Monitor to see the network traffic generated by two computers. See the sections titled "Windows NT Performance Monitor," "Windows 95 System Monitor," and "Monitoring Network Traffic."

10. **C**. The primary objective is met because Network Monitor shows network traffic between computers. Neither optional result can be met, because Performance Monitor cannot be run on Windows 95 computers. See the sections titled "Windows NT Performance Monitor," "Windows 95 System Monitor," and "Monitoring Network Traffic."

Suggested Readings and Resources

1. Siyan, Karanjit S. *Windows NT Server 4 Professional Reference*. New Riders, 1996.

2. Heywood, Drew. *Inside Windows NT Server 4*. New Riders, 1997.

3. Casad, Joe. *MCSE Training Guide: Windows NT Server 4*. New Riders, 1997.

4. Sirockman, Jason. *MCSE Training Guide: Windows NT Server 4 Enterprise*. New Riders, 1997.

5. Boyce, Jim. *Inside Windows 95, Deluxe Edition*. New Riders, 1996.

TROUBLESHOOTING

Chapter 12 targets the following objectives in the Troubleshooting section of the Networking Essentials exam:

Identify common errors associated with components required for communications

▶ The purpose of this test objective is to make sure you are able to isolate what problems are associated with what components on the network.

Diagnose and resolve common connectivity problems with cards, cables, and related hardware

▶ This exam objective reflects the need for you to be able to not only diagnose common connectivity problems with cards, cables, and other related hardware, but also to be able to resolve these problems in order to reestablish connectivity on the network.

Resolve broadcast storms

▶ This exam objective is designed to ensure that you understand what causes a broadcast storm and methods of resolving these broadcast storms.

Identify and resolve network performance problems

▶ This exam objective addresses your ability to use tools and understand issues relating to identifying and resolving poor performance on a network.

CHAPTER 12

Troubleshooting

STUDY STRATEGIES

▶ There is a lot of information in this chapter. One method of studying this information would be to memorize everything. This can be time consuming and may not help when you encounter novel situations. Instead, take time to try to relate the information on troubleshooting to all of the previous chapters.

▶ Pay attention to the devices that can be used to troubleshoot network problems, particularly when you would use a particular device.

INTRODUCTION

Troubleshooting is the art of seeking out the cause of a problem and eliminating the problem by managing or eliminating the cause. With something as complex as a computer network, the list of possible problems and causes is nearly endless. In real life, however, a large number of network problems fall into a few well-defined categories. One thing to be aware of is that no matter what the problem is on your network, the OSI model serves as an excellent reference tool to help you isolate the area of trouble. In this chapter, you learn these categories. You will also learn about some of the strategies and tools you can use to troubleshoot network problems.

Of course, no matter how effective you are at problem solving, it almost always is better to avoid problems than to solve them. Chapter 10, "Managing and Securing a Microsoft Network," discusses administration strategies that minimize the need for troubleshooting. Chapter 11, "Monitoring the Network," discusses monitoring and record-keeping strategies that can help you identify problems when they appear. This chapter looks specifically at troubleshooting techniques for solving problems related to network cabling, adapter cards, modems, and other important connectivity components. In addition, you learn some guidelines for troubleshooting network performance problems and are provided with some important sources for finding troubleshooting information.

INITIATING THE TROUBLESHOOTING PROCESS

Microsoft recommends the following five-step approach to network troubleshooting:

1. Set the problem's priority. Ask yourself a few questions: How serious is this problem? Will the network still function if I attend to other matters first? Can I quantify the loss of work time or productivity the problem is causing? These will help you determine the severity of the problem relative to the other pressing problems you might face.

2. Collect information to identify the symptoms. Collecting information can be as simple as asking users to describe the problem in detail. A user's description of the problem can lead to further questions, which can lead to a deeper description. If you keep a documented history of your network (see Chapter 11), you can compare the present behavior of the network with the baseline behavior. You also can look for possible previous occurrences of the problem, and their documented solutions.

3. Develop a list of possible causes. Again, ask yourself a few questions: Could the problem be related to connectivity devices? Cabling? Protocols? A faltering workstation? What do past occurrences have in common with the present occurrence? List all possibilities.

4. Test to isolate the cause. Develop tests that will prove or disprove each of the possible causes. The tests could be as simple as checking a setup parameter or as complicated as studying network traffic with a protocol analyzer. You learn about some of the hardware and software network testing tools in the section titled "Using Troubleshooting Tools" later in this chapter.

5. Study the results of the test to identify a solution. Your tests will (ideally) point you to the real problem; after you know the problem, you can determine a solution. Make sure that when testing, you perform only one change at a time, thereby eliminating the problem of determining what change provided the solution.

> **NOTE**
>
> **Users in the Troubleshooting Equation** Also remember that if the user is the problem, education and training for the user is the fix.

These five steps are sufficient to guide you through a myriad of network problems. Similar approaches appear in the documentation of other network vendors.

Part of the challenge of network troubleshooting is to determine how you can apply these five troubleshooting steps to your own situation.

USING TROUBLESHOOTING TOOLS

Network administrators use a number of tools for searching out network problems. The following list details some of these tools. The tools most commonly employed are Protocol Analyzers, Digital Voltmeters, Time Domain Reflectometers, and Oscilloscopes.

Protocol Analyzers

Protocol analyzers are hardware or software products that are used to monitor network traffic, track network performance, and analyze packets. Protocol analyzers can identify bottlenecks, protocol problems, and malfunctioning network components (see Chapter 11).

> **EXAM TIP**
>
> **Troubleshooting Tools** Although these tools do not fall nicely into any exam objective category, you will be tested in your understanding of what each of these tools does.

Digital Volt Meter (DVM)

Digital voltmeters are hand-held electronic measuring tools that enable you to check the voltage of network cables. They also can be used to check the resistance of terminators.

You can use a DVM to help you find a break or a short in a network cable.

DVMs are usually inexpensive battery operated devices that have either a digital or needle read out, and two metal prongs attached to the DVM by some wires a foot or more in length. By sending a small current through the wires and out through the metal prongs, resistance and voltages of terminators and wires can be measured.

> **NOTE**
>
> **Meters** Voltmeters that test voltage and resistance sometimes are called Multimeters. There are also devices called Ohmmeters used to test resistance only.

Time-Domain Reflectometers

A *Time-Domain Reflectometer (TDM)* sends sound waves along a cable and look for imperfections that might be caused by a break or a short in the line. A good TDR will often be able to detect faults on a cable to within a few feet.

Oscilloscope

An oscilloscope measures fluctuations in signal voltage and can help find faulty or damaged cabling. Oscilloscopes are often more expensive electronic devices that show the signal fluctuations on a monitor.

Other Tools

Several diagnostic software tools provide information on virtually any type of network hardware, as well. A considerable number of diagnostic software packages are available at a variety of prices.

A common software tool distributed with most network cards is a Send/Receive package. This software tool allows two computers, with network cards and cables, to connect to each other. This tool does not rely on a networked operating system, nor can it be used to send data. It will simply send packets from one computer to the other, establishing that the network cards and underlying transmission media are connected and configured properly.

TROUBLESHOOTING TRANSMISSION MEDIA AND OTHER NETWORK COMPONENTS

Identify common errors associated with components required for communications

Diagnose and resolve common connectivity problems with cards, cables, and related hardware

Most network problems occur on the transmission media or with the components that attach devices to the transmission media. All of these components operate at the Physical, Datalink, and Network levels of the OSI model. The components that connect PCs and enable them to communicate are susceptible to many kinds of problems. The following sections discuss these important connectivity and communication components and some of the problems associated with them:

◆ Cables and connectors

◆ Network adapter cards

◆ Modems

◆ Hubs and MSAUs

◆ Repeaters, Bridges, Gateways, and Routers

These components were introduced in previous chapters of this book. (See Chapter 3, "Transmission Media," Chapter 5, "Network Adapter Cards," and Chapter 6, "Connectivity Devices and Transfer Mechanisms") This chapter concentrates on troubleshooting guidelines.

Troubleshooting Cables and Connectors

Most network problems occur at the OSI Physical layer, and cabling is one of the most common causes. A cable might have a short or a break, or it might be attached to a faulty connector. Tools such as DVMs and TDRs help search out cabling problems.

Cabling problems can cause one of three major problems:

◆ An individual computer cannot access the network

◆ A group of computers cannot access the network

◆ None of the computers can access the network

When networks are configured using a star topology, an individual cable break between the computer and hub or MASU will cause a failure in communication between that individual computer and the rest of the network. This type of cable break will not cause problems for all of the other computers on the network.

A break in cables connecting multiple hubs together will cause a communications outage between the computers on one side of the cable and the computers on the other side of the cable break. In most cases the communications between computers within the broken segment can continue.

In the case of a MSAU, if a cable connecting MSAUs together is broken, this will often cause all computers on the ring to fail, because the ring is not complete. A break in the cable on a Bus topology will also cause all computers on the network segment to be unable to communicate with any other computers on the network.

When troubleshooting any network, begin with the more obvious physical problems. Make sure that all connectors are tight and properly connected, that ground wires and terminators with the proper resistance are used when required, and that manufacturer's specifications (such as cable grade, cable lengths, and maximum number of nodes) are met and are consistent with the specifications for the transmission medium.

Try the following checks when troubleshooting network cabling problems:

◆ With 10BASE-T, make sure the cable used has the correct number of twists to meet the data-grade specifications.

◆ Look for electrical interference, which can be caused by tying the network cable together with monitor and power cords. Fluorescent lights, electric motors, and other electrical devices can cause interference if they are located too close to cables. These problems can often be alleviated by placing the cable away from these devices that generate electromagnetic interference or by upgrading the cable to one that has better shielding.

◆ Make sure that connectors are pinned properly and crimped tightly.

◆ If excess shielding on coaxial cable is exposed, make sure it doesn't ground out the connector.

◆ Ensure that coaxial cables are not coiled tightly together. This can generate a magnetic field around the cable, causing electromagnetic interference.

◆ On coaxial Ethernet LANs, look for missing terminators or terminators with improper resistance ratings or resistance readings.

◆ Watch out for malfunctioning transceivers, concentrators, or T-connectors. All of these components can be checked by replacing the suspect devices.

◆ Test the continuity of the cable by using the various physical testing devices discussed in the previous section, or by using a software-based cable testing utility.

◆ Make sure that all the component cables in a segment are connected. A user who moves his client and removes the T-connector incorrectly can cause a broken segment.

◆ Examine cable connectors for bent or broken pins.

◆ On Token Ring networks, inspect the attachment of patch cables and adapter cables. Remember, patch cables connect MSAUs, and adapter cables connect the network adapter to the MSAU.

One advantage of a Token Ring network is its built-in capability to monitor itself. Token Ring networks provide electronic troubleshooting and, when possible, actually make repairs. When the Token Ring network can't make its own repairs, a process called beaconing narrows down the portion of the ring in which the problem is most likely to exist. (See Chapter 4, "Network Topologies and Architectures," for more information on beaconing.)

Troubleshooting Network Adapter Cards

Network problems often result from malfunctioning network adapter cards. The process of troubleshooting the network adapter works like any other kind of troubleshooting process: Start with the simple. The following list details some aspects you can check if you think your network adapter card might be malfunctioning:

◆ Make sure the cable is properly connected to the card.

◆ Confirm that you have the correct network adapter card driver and that the driver is installed properly (see Chapter 5). Be sure the card is properly bound to the appropriate transport protocol (see Chapter 7, "Transport Protocols").

◆ Make sure the network adapter card and the network adapter card driver are compatible with your operating system. If you use Windows NT, consult the Windows NT hardware compatibility list. If you use Windows 95 or another operating system, rely on the adapter card vendor specifications.

◆ Test for resource conflicts. Make sure another device isn't attempting to use the same resources (see Chapter 5). If you think a resource conflict might be the problem, but you can't pinpoint the conflict using Windows NT Diagnostics, Windows 95's Device Manager, or some other diagnostic program, try removing all the cards except the network adapter and then replacing the cards one by one. Check the network with each addition to determine which device is causing the conflict.

◆ Run the network adapter card's diagnostic software. This will often indicate which resource on the network card is failing.

◆ Examine the jumper and DIP switch settings on the card. Make sure the resource settings are consistent with the settings configured through the operating system.

◆ Make sure the card is inserted properly in the slot. Remove and reseat the card.

◆ If necessary, remove the card and clean the connector fingers (don't use an eraser because it leaves grit on the card).

◆ Replace the card with one that you know works. If the connection works with a different card, you know the card is the problem.

Token Ring network adapters with failure rates that exceed a preset tolerance level might actually remove themselves from the network. Try replacing the card. Some Token Ring networks also can experience problems if a Token Ring card set at a ring speed of 16 Mbps is inserted into a ring using a 4 Mbps ring speed and vise versa.

Broadcast storms (discussed later in this chapter) are often caused by faulty network adapters as well.

Troubleshooting HUBs and MSAUs

If you experience problems with a hub-based LAN, such as a 10BASE-T network, you often can isolate the problem by disconnecting the attached workstations one at a time. If removing one of the workstations eliminates the problem, the trouble may be caused by that workstation or its associated cable length. If removing each of the workstations doesn't solve the problem, the fault may lie with the hub. Check the easy components first, such as ports, switches, and connectors. Then use a different hub (if you have it) and see whether the problem persists. If your hub doesn't work properly, call the manufacturer.

If you're troubleshooting a Token Ring network, make sure the cables are connected properly to the MSAUs, with ring-out ports connecting to the ring-in ports throughout the ring. If you suspect the MSAU, isolate it by changing the ring-in and ring-out cables to bypass the MSAU. If the ring is now functional again, consider replacing the MSAU. In addition, you might find that if your network has MSAUs from more than one manufacturer, they may not be wholly compatible. Impedance and other electrical characteristics can show slight differences between manufacturers, causing intermittent network problems. Some MSAUs (other than the 8228) are active and require a power supply. These MSAUs fail if they have a blown fuse or a bad power source. Your problem also might result from a misconfigured MSAU port. MSAU ports using the hermaphrodite connector need to be reinitialized with the setup tool. Removing drop cables and reinitializing each MSAU port is a quick fix that is useful on relatively small Token Ring networks.

Isolating problems with patch cables, adapter cables, and MSAUs is easier to do if you have a current log of your network's physical design. After you narrow down the problem, you can isolate potential problem areas from the rest of the network and then use a cable tester to find the actual problem.

Troubleshooting Modems

A modem presents all the potential problems you find with any other device. You must make sure that the modem is properly installed, that the driver is properly installed, and that the resource settings do not conflict with other devices. Modems also pose some unique problems because they must connect directly to the phone system, they operate using analog communications, and they must make a point-to-point connection with a remote machine.

The online help files for both Windows NT and Windows 95 include a topic called the Modem Troubleshooter (see Figure 12.1). The Modem Troubleshooter leads you to possible solutions for a modem problem by asking questions about the symptoms. As you answer the questions (by clicking the gray box beside your answer), the Modem Troubleshooter zeroes in on more specific questions until (ideally) it leads you to a solution. See Exercise 12.1 at the end of this chapter for more on the Modem Troubleshooter.

FIGURE 12.1
Windows NT Help showing topics on troubleshooting modems.

Some common modem problems (in addition to the basic device problems discussed earlier in this chapter, such as connectivity and resource settings) are as follows:

◆ *Dialing problems.* The dialing feature is improperly configured. For instance, the modem isn't dialing 9 to bypass your office switchboard, or it *is* dialing 9 when you're away from your office. The computer also could be dialing an area code or an international code when it shouldn't. Check the dialing properties for the connection.

◆ *Connection problems.* You cannot connect to another modem. Your modem and the other modem might be operating at different speeds. Verify that the maximum speed setting for your modem is the highest speed that both your modem and the other modem can use. Also make sure the Data Bits, Parity, and Stop Bits settings are consistent with the remote computer.

◆ *Digital Phone Systems.* You cannot plug a modem into a telephone line designed for use with digital phone systems. These digital phone systems are commonplace in most office environments.

◆ *Protocol problems.* The communicating devices are using incompatible line protocols. Verify that the devices are configured for the same or compatible protocols. If one computer initiates a connection using PPP, the other computer must be capable of using PPP.

Repeaters, Bridges, and Routers

Issues dealing with repeaters, bridges and routers are often more technically advanced, than those covered in a book such as *Networking Essentials.* Companies such as Cisco, Bay Networks, and 3Com have their own dedicated books and courses on dealing with the installation, configuration and troubleshooting of repeaters, bridges and routers. In general, there are some basic troubleshooting steps you can do when working with these three devices.

As mentioned in Chapter 2, "Networking Standards," and Chapter 6, repeaters are responsible for regenerating a signal sent down the transmission media. Problems with repeaters are that they do not work—that is, the signal is not being regenerated. If this is the case, the signal being sent to devices on the other side of the repeater from the sending device will not receive the signal.

Problems with bridges are almost identical to that of a repeater. The signal being sent to devices on the other side of the bridge from the sending device will not receive the signal. Other issues with bridges are that the table of what devices are on what interface of the bridge can get corrupt. This can lead from one to all machines not receiving packets on the network. Diagnostic utilities provided by the bridge's manufacturer can resolve this type of problem.

Problems with routers can be complex, and troubleshooting them often involves a high level of understanding of the different protocols in use on the network, as well as the software and commands used to program a router. There are generally two types of router problems.

The first router problem that is commonly found is that packets are just not being passed through, because the router is "dead," or simply not functioning. The second common problem with routers is that the routing tables, within the routers, are corrupted or incorrectly programmed. This problem will either lead to computers on different networks being unable to communicate with each other or to the fact that certain protocols simply do not work.

HANDLING BROADCAST STORMS

Resolve broadcast storms.

A *broadcast storm* is a sudden flood of broadcast messages that clogs the transmission medium, approaching use of 100 percent of the bandwidth. Broadcast storms cause performance to decline and, in the worst case, computers cannot even access the network. The cause of a broadcast storm is often a malfunctioning network adapter, but a broadcast storm also can be caused when a device on the network attempts to contact another device that either doesn't exist or for some reason doesn't respond to the broadcast.

If the broadcast messages are viable packets (or even error-filled but partially legible packets), a network-monitoring or protocol-analysis tool often can determine the source of the storm (see Chapter 11). If the broadcast storm is caused by a malfunctioning adapter throwing illegible packets onto the line, and a protocol analyzer can't find the source, try to isolate the offending PC by removing computers from the network one at a time until the line returns to normal. (For more information, see "Troubleshooting Network Adapter Cards," earlier in this chapter.)

TROUBLESHOOTING PROTOCOLS

When discussing troubleshooting protocols, three protocol stacks are at issue: NetBEUI, NWLink, and TCP/IP. It is these three protocol stacks that can be used by Microsoft networks to communicate over the network. It is important that computers wishing to communicate with one another run the same transport protocol, or else communication will not occur.

NetBEUI

NetBEUI is a relatively simple protocol to troubleshoot. The most important thing to remember is that NetBEUI is a non-routable protocol, and will not pass through routers. The other important issue concerning NetBEUI is that the computers address each other by their NetBIOS names. Thus each NetBIOS name must be unique (this holds true for all protocols on computers utilizing Microsoft operating systems). This latter issue is detected by Microsoft operating systems (DOS, Windows 95, Windows NT), when a computer first initializes on the network.

NWLink (IPX/SPX)

NWLink (IPX/SPX) will generate communication problems if the incorrect frame type is chosen. Two computers running different frame types will not communicate with one another. A computer can run more than one frame type, and this is often the case when running an Ethernet network, as an Ethernet network has the greatest selection of frame types. Frame types are discussed in detail in Chapter 2.

Older Novell systems (systems prior to NetWare 3.12) had a default frame type of 802.3. All new systems use a frame type of 802.2. Both systems can use both frame types. Windows 95 and Windows

NT will install the 802.2 frame type if it is detected but not 802.3. If your network is running both the 802.2 and 802.3 frame types, you will need to manually add the 802.3 frame type to your Windows 95 and Windows NT computers.

TCP/IP

TCP/IP relies on a strong knowledge of the protocol stack in order to troubleshoot it. Basic configuration of the protocol includes the correct IP address information being set on the computer. If you wish to communicate to other network segments, then a proper default gateway will need to be set.

Other issues involving TCP/IP are that services are running correctly. If you are using a DHCP server to hand out IP addressing information to the computers, make sure that the DHCP server is running correctly. Also, make sure that the server has not run out of addresses, or is not giving out addresses that exist on another DHCP computer.

If name-to-address resolution is at issue, make sure that the DNS server (used for non-Microsoft computers) and the WINS server (used to locate Microsoft NetBIOS names) are both running, or contain the name to IP address resolution being requested.

TROUBLESHOOTING NETWORK PERFORMANCE

Identify and resolve network performance problems.

If your network runs slower than it used to run (or slower than it ought to run), the problem might be that the present network traffic exceeds the level at which the network can operate efficiently. Some possible causes for increased traffic are new hardware (such as a new workstation) or new software (such as a network computer game or some other network application). A generator or another mechanical device operating near the network could cause a degradation of network performance. In addition, a malfunctioning network device could act as a bottleneck. Ask yourself what has changed since the last time the network operated efficiently, and begin there with your troubleshooting efforts.

Some of the techniques described in previous chapters can help you troubleshoot network performance. A performance monitoring tool, such as Windows NT's Performance Monitor, can help you look for bottlenecks that are adversely affecting your network. See Chapter 11 for more information on Performance Monitor.

The monitoring and record-keeping procedures discussed in Chapter 11 also can help you troubleshoot network performance by providing you with baseline performance data that you can use to gauge later fluctuations.

For instance, the increased traffic could be the result of increased usage. If usage exceeds the capacity of the network, you might want to consider expanding or redesigning your network. You also might want to divide the network into smaller segments by using a router or a bridge to reduce network traffic. A protocol analyzer can help you measure and monitor the traffic at various points on your network.

HANDLING OTHER NETWORK PROBLEMS

The following list details some other common problems that could affect your network:

- ◆ *Operating system conflicts.* Operating system upgrades sometimes can cause older programs to become incompatible with the operating system itself. This problem is compounded in network environments because, during the transition to a new network operating system, some servers will run the new version for a period of time while others are still running the previous version. Microsoft recommends that you perform a test upgrade on an isolated part of the network to ensure that all hardware and software systems function properly when the upgrade is made.

- ◆ *Server crashes.* A server disk crash can be disastrous if you aren't adequately prepared for it. You should devise a system of regular backups and, depending on the nature of your data, explore other safeguards such as a RAID fault tolerant system. (Refer to Chapter 9, "Disaster Recovery.")

◆ *Power fluctuations.* A small fluctuation in the power supply can make the network misbehave. If the power goes off completely—even for a moment—the whole network could shut down, causing users to lose their work in progress. A disorderly shutdown also can cause problems with file servers. The best solution is to prepare for a power outage before it happens. Connect each server to an Uninterruptible Power Supply (UPS), and encourage your users to perform occasional saves as they work.

If you implement all the measures discussed so far and you still experience problems, your next step may be to consult the experts. Or, even before you start your own troubleshooting, you may want to consult the available information to learn more about the problem. The next section discusses some online and offline sources of help.

GETTING SUPPORT

An important aspect of troubleshooting is knowing where to turn for critical information on your network environment. Many online and offline sources can provide troubleshooting information. Some of these sources (in addition to the online help provided with your operating system), include the following:

◆ *Vendor documentation and help lines.* Hardware and software vendors often provide troubleshooting tips with the owner's documentation. Vendors also often provide technical assistance by phone.

◆ *Bulletin board services.* A number of electronic bulletin boards supply networking information. See vendor documentation for more information on how to reach a particular vendor's official BBS.

◆ *The Internet.* The major network vendors all sponsor active forums and newsgroups on the Internet, CompuServe, and other online services. Most of this information is also supplied through the Web. Updated drivers, white papers, technical specifications, and knowledgebases can often be found at vendors' Web sites. Also refer to your vendors' documentation.

◆ *CD-ROMs.* Several vendors now market CD-ROMs with network and PC hardware information. Windows NT Server's Books Online (located on the Windows NT Installation CD-ROM) provides an additional layer of documentation that isn't found with online help. Microsoft's TechNet contains product information, technical information, articles, and announcements. TechNet is available on a subscription basis through Microsoft (call 800-344-2121). Novell's NSEPro CD-ROM is a NetWare oriented encyclopedia of network information. The Micro House Technical Library (MHTL) is another impressive database of technical information. The MHTL addresses such items as BIOS settings for IDE drives and jumper settings for popular peripheral boards. The MHTL comes with a rich collection of informative illustrations.

CASE STUDY: TROUBLESHOOTING A NETWORK

ESSENCE OF THE CASE

The essence of the case is as follows:

- The LAN runs a bus topology.

- There are two networked segments connected by a router.

- Network connectivity is not available for one segment.

- The computers on the affected segment can for a short time communicate.

SCENARIO

You are brought into XYZ company to help troubleshoot the network. The network is a small 60-user Ethernet network using a bus topology running Thinnet wire. There is a router placed in the middle of this bus topology, essentially dividing the LAN into two equally sized segments of 30 computers each.

At issue is that at certain times, none of the computers are able to communicate with each other on one of the network segments. The other network segment is able to communicate only with PCs on its own segment.

As noted, this situation is not always the case. At certain times, the network is fully functional. At a given point in the day the network becomes inoperable. When everyone on the affected segment shuts down their PCs and turns them back on again, the network is operable for a few minutes, but then returns to an inoperable state.

CASE STUDY: TROUBLESHOOTING A NETWORK

ANALYSIS

This case study is a nice example of a broadcast storm. As discussed earlier in the chapter, a broadcast storm is caused by a "chatty" or malfunctioning network card. This chatty card causes broadcast packets, or packets addressed to all devices on the network. The broadcast storm can saturate the bandwidth on a network and cause all of the computers to not be able to communicate with each other.

The problems experienced by the network in this case study are also commonly attributed to broken cables, terminators, or a malfunctioning router.

A broken Thinnet cable would have permanently affected all computers on the one network segment. The fact that the computers could transmit to one another after they were all shut down and restarted, negates the possibility of a broken cable being suspect.

A missing terminator would also cause all PCs on the network segment to not be able to communicate with each other. Just as with the issue with the broken cable, the PCs would not be able to communicate with one another even for a short period after they were shut down.

If the router were the problem, two things would happen. The first would be an absence of communication between the two network segments. Second, only certain computers would be able to communicate between the network segments. A faulty router would not cause one network segment to be unable to communicate with another.

The compelling reason for the broadcast storm being the culprit is the fact that the computers can communicate with each other once they are all rebooted. Shortly after they reboot, the network becomes inaccessible. This inaccessibility is due to the fact that the computer with the chatty network card has come on line.

You can track down the computer with the chatty network card in either of two ways. Run a protocol analyzer to see if the broadcasts are issuing a source address, and cross reference this source address with your documentation. Another method would be to systematically shut down each PC, one at a time, until the faulty network card is found.

CHAPTER SUMMARY

KEY TERMS

- Protocol analyzers
- Digital voltmeters
- Time-Domain Reflectometer (TDM)
- Oscilloscope
- Broadcast storm
- Network adapter card
- Modem
- Hub
- MSAU
- Repeater
- Bridge
- Router
- NetBEUI
- NWLink
- TCP/IP

Troubleshooting is an essential part of network operations. The best kind of troubleshooting is, of course, anticipating problems before they occur; however, in spite of all your efforts, you'll eventually need to track down a problem that is stopping or slowing your network. This chapter looked at general troubleshooting strategies and at solutions for each of the problem areas identified by Microsoft in the Networking Essentials test objectives, as follows:

- Problems with communication components
- Connectivity problems
- Broadcast storms
- Network performance problems

This chapter also looked at online and offline sources of troubleshooting information.

APPLY YOUR LEARNING

Exercises

12.1 Modem Troubleshooter

Objective: Learn how to access Windows NT's or Windows 95's Modem Troubleshooter. This exercise addresses Microsoft's exam objective: Identify common problems associated with components required for communications.

Estimated time: 10 minutes

Modem Troubleshooter is part of Windows NT's online help system. The easiest way to access it is to start Help and search for modems in the index.

1. Click the Start button and choose Help.

2. In the Help Topics dialog box, click the Index tab. Enter **modem** in the search box at the top of the screen.

3. Look for the troubleshooting subtopic under the modems topic in the index. Double-click Troubleshooting. The Modem Troubleshooter will appear (refer to Figure 12.1).

4. Browse through the Modem Troubleshooter's topics. Click the gray box to the left of each symptom for a look at possible causes or more diagnostic questions.

5. When you're finished, close the Help window.

12.2 Windows NT Books Online

Objective: Access Windows NT's Books Online, a CD-ROM-based source of configuration and troubleshooting information.

Estimated time: 10 minutes

1. Click the Start menu and choose Programs/Books Online.

2. Windows NT prompts you for the location of the Books Online files. The files are located on the Windows NT Installation CD-ROM in the Support directory's Books subdirectory.

3. In the Books Online main dialog box, click the Contents tab. Double-click the book icon to reveal the major subcategories for Books Online (see Figure 12.2).

4. Browse through the topics in Books Online. Notice the extensive Networking Supplement section devoted to networking issues. Try to get a feeling for the kinds of questions that are best answered by Books Online.

5. When you are finished, close the Books Online dialog box.

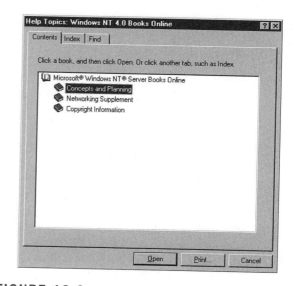

FIGURE 12.2

Windows NT's Books Online contains information not found in online help.

APPLY YOUR LEARNING

Review Questions

1. What are four tools that can be used to troubleshoot network problems? Briefly define each.

2. What will a broken or improperly terminated cable in a BUS topology cause?

3. What is a broadcast storm and what causes it?

4. What Microsoft utility can be used to detect bottlenecks within a computer? What Microsoft program can be used to detect bottlenecks on the network?

Exam Questions

1. Which three of the following are troubleshooting steps in Microsoft's five-step troubleshooting process?

   A. Collect information to identify the symptoms.

   B. Develop a list of possible causes.

   C. Reboot the server.

   D. Set the problem's priority.

2. What does MSDL stands for?

   A. Minor Switching Delay Log

   B. Microsoft Storage Device Language

   C. Microsoft Domain License

   D. Microsoft Download Library

3. What can you use to look for breaks in network cables by measuring cable voltage?

   A. Protocol analyzer

   B. DVM

   C. TDR

   D. MSDL

4. Most network problems occur at what OSI layer?

   A. Physical

   B. Data Link

   C. Network

   D. Session

5. What is a sudden, unexpected flood of broadcast messages on the network is known as?

   A. Net frenzy

   B. Tornado

   C. Broadcast storm

   D. Electric shower

6. What device sends sound waves down the cable to look for imperfections?

   A. DVMs

   B. Oscilloscopes

   C. TDRs

   D. None of the above

7. Which of the following would degrade network performance? Choose three.

   A. A generator or electrical device near the network

   B. A networked computer game

   C. A sudden, disorderly shutdown of a workstation

   D. New hardware

APPLY YOUR LEARNING

8. Which two of the following are possible problems with Token Ring network adapters?

   A. Broadcast messages from the card are not timed right.

   B. The card is not bound to a network service.

   C. The card removed itself from the network.

   D. A 16Mbps card is placed on a 4Mbps ring.

9. You want to have a set of tools to be able to isolate problems with your transmission media. The object is to have the tools to analyze and troubleshoot problems on your Thinnet Ethernet network.

   Required Result: You need to be able to test for breaks in the cables on the network

   Optional result 1: You wish to be able to test for the resistance of terminators attached to the ends of your cables.

   Optional result 2: You wish to be able to track network traffic on your cables.

   Suggested solution: You purchase an oscilloscope and a Time Domain Reflectometer.

   A. This solution will obtain the required result and both optional results.

   B. This solution will obtain the required result and one of optional results.

   C. This solution will obtain the required result.

   D. This solution does not satisfy the required result.

10. You wish to analyze the performance of your network. You would like to see what systems are generating the most network traffic.

Required result: You need to see which systems are generating the most traffic on the network cable segments.

Optional result 1: You wish to see which resources are being used on the workstation.

Optional result 2: You wish to log the information about system resource usage for analysis at a later time.

Suggested Solution: You load Performance Monitor on the computers you wish to analyze and select the objects you wish to monitor.

A. This solution will obtain the required result and both optional results.

B. This solution will obtain the required result and one of the optional results.

C. This solution will obtain the required result.

D. This solution does not satisfy the required result.

Answers to Review Questions

1. Four tools can be used to troubleshoot a network:

   • *Protocol analyzer.* This hardware or software tool can capture and analyze traffic and packets on a network. The Microsoft software version of this tool is called Network Monitor.

   • *Digital Volt Meter (DVM).* This electronic measuring device can be used to check the voltage of cable segments, allowing you to see if there are breaks on a cable, and the resistance of terminators on cable segments.

   • *Time-Domain Reflectometer (TDR).* A TDR sends sound waves along a cable to look for imperfections that may be caused by a break or short in the line.

- Oscilloscope. This device measures the fluctuation in signal voltage to help find faulty or damaged cables.

See the section titled "Using Troubleshooting Tools."

2. On a BUS topology, a broken cable segment or an improperly terminated cable segment will cause all devices on that cable segment to not be able to communicate with one another. See the section titled "Troubleshooting Cables and Connectors."

3. A broadcast storm is a network segment that is being saturated by broadcast packets. Packets that are broadcast are intended for all recipients. A broadcast storm will cause network traffic to slow or even halt traffic on the network segment.

A faulty or "chatty" network card is often the cause of a broadcast storm. See the section titled "Handling Broadcast Storms."

4. Microsoft's Performance Monitor is used to track objects and counters within a computer. Microsoft's Network Monitor is designed to track packets and traffic outside a computer. See the section titled "Troubleshooting Network Performance."

Answers to Exam Questions

1. **A, B, D.** Rebooting a server is a task in troubleshooting problems, but is not part of Microsoft's five-step troubleshooting process. Many problems on a network do not involve a server, thus rebooting a server will be of no avail.

See the section titled "Initiating the Troubleshooting Process."

2. **D.** MSDL is the official acronym for the Microsoft Download Library. See the section titled "Getting Support."

3. **B.** A Digital Voltmeter uses electrical signals to look for breaks in a cable. A TDR uses sound signals. MSDL is a reference tool for information. A protocol analyzer analyzes packets on a network. See the section titled "Using Troubleshooting Tools."

4. **A.** Most network problems occur at the OSI Physical layer, or in other words, involve the transmission media. See the section titled "Establishing Troubleshooting Connectivity and Communication."

5. **C.** A broadcast storm is the official definition of a sudden broadcast of network messages. See the section titled "Handling Broadcast Storms."

6. **C.** Time Domain Reflectometers use sound waves to test for imperfections. DVMs use electrical signals. Oscilloscopes do not look for cable imperfections, but instead measure electrical signals. See the section titled "Using Troubleshooting Tools."

7. **A, B, D.** C is not correct because the shutting down of a PC on the network causes one fewer PC to generate traffic on the network. See the section titled "Troubleshooting Network Performance."

8. **C, D.** A is incorrect because Token Ring networks can transfer information on the transmission media only when they have the token. B is incorrect because cards do not bind to services, but to transport protocols. See the section titled "Troubleshooting Network Adapter Cards."

APPLY YOUR LEARNING

9. **C.** A TDR will test for cable breaks, but does not test for the resistance of a terminator. This is done by a Digital Volt Meter. An oscilloscope checks the flow of a current. Neither a TDR or an oscilloscope will analyze network traffic.

10. **D.** Performance Monitor will do both of the optional results but will not achieve the required result, because Performance Monitor does not trace traffic on the network transmission media. To analyze network traffic on the transmission media, you would need to use a protocol analyzer such as Network Monitor.

Suggested Readings and Resources

For all Web sites, do searches on the key words of "troubleshooting" and the name of the component you wish to troubleshoot.

1. Sirockman, Jason. *MCSE Training Guide: Windows NT 4 Enterprise, 2nd Edition.* New Riders, 1998.

2. Microsoft Technet CD. For more information, go to www.microsoft.com/technet

3. www.microsoft.com/support

4. www.cisco.com

5. www.novell.com

6. Brooks, Charles, and Marcraft International. *A+ Certification Training Guide.* New Riders, 1998.

7. Mueller, Scott. *Upgrading and Repairing PCs, Eighth Edition.* Que, 1997.

FINAL REVIEW

Fast Facts: Networking Essentials

Fast Facts: Windows NT Server 4

Fast Facts: Windows NT Server 4 Enterprise

Fast Facts: Windows NT Workstation 4

Study and Exam Prep Tips

Practice Exam

Twelve chapters of this book have looked at objectives and components of the Microsoft Networking Essentials exam. After reading all of that, what is it that you must really know? What should you read as you sit and wait in the parking lot of the testing center—right up until the hour before going in to gamble your $100 and pride?

The following material covers the salient points of the 12 previous chapters and the points that make excellent test fodder. Although there is no substitute for real-world, hands-on experience, knowing what to expect on the exam can be equally meaningful. The information that follows is the networking equivalent of *Cliffs Notes*, providing the information you must know in each of the four sections to pass the exam. Don't just memorize the concepts given; attempt to understand the reason why they are so, and you will have no difficulties passing the exam.

STANDARDS AND TERMINOLOGY

The Standards and Terminology section is designed to test your understanding and knowledge of terms used in networking, as well as some of the more common standards that have been implemented in the industry.

Define Common Networking Terms for LANs and WANs

The Networking Essentials exam does not really test on definitions of terms. You are asked questions though, and, based on these questions, you need to understand the definitions of the terms used in order to successfully answer the questions.

Fast Facts: Networking Essentials Exam

The best mechanism to study for this area would be to be able to review the key terms found in every chapter and provide the correct definition for each term. Below is a list of some of the more general networking terms you should be aware of.

◆ **peer-to-peer networking**. A networking model where both the services and the client are performed by the same computer.

◆ **client/server networking**. A networking model where a specific role of providing services or acting as a client (not both) is performed by a computer.

◆ **centralized computing**. A form of computing where all the processing is done by one central computer.

◆ **distributed computing**. A form of computing where all the processing is shared by many different computers.

◆ **file services**. Services allowing for the storage and access of files.

◆ **print services**. Services that allow the sharing of a printer.

◆ **file and print server**. A server that provides file and print services.

◆ **application server**. A server that provides some high-end application used by many different computers.

◆ **token-ring network**. A network that follows a logical topology of a ring, but a physical topology of a star. The computers are connected to a concentrator known as an MSAU or MAU. Computers rely on the possession of a token before the transmission of data on the network. This type of network is known as a deterministic network.

◆ **ethernet network**. This type of a network is run as a logical bus, but can take on the physical topology of a bus or a star. The concentrator used by these computers, when in a star topology, is called a hub. This type of network is known as a contention-based network because each device contends with every other device for network access.

◆ **LAN**. Also known as a Local Area Network. Often characterized by fast transmission speeds and short distances between devices, and by the fact that the company running the network has control over all devices and transmission media.

◆ **WAN**. Also known as a Wide Area Network. When compared to a LAN, a WAN is often characterized by lower data transmission rates and the coverage of long distances, and by the fact that a third party is involved with the supply and maintenance of the transmission media.

Compare a File and Print Server with an Application Server

A file server is a service that is involved with giving access to files and directories on the network. The purpose of the file server is to give large numbers of users access to a centrally stored set of files and directories.

A print server is a computer or device that gives large number of users access to a centrally maintained printing device. A computer that is a file server often acts as print server, too. These types of computers are known as file and print servers.

An application server is responsible for running applications such as Exchange Server or SQL Server on the network. Application servers perform services that often require a more advanced level of processing than a user's personal computer is able to provide.

Compare User-Level Security with Access Permission Assigned to a Shared Directory on a Server

User-level security is a security model in which access to resources is given on a user-by-user basis, a group-by-group basis, or both. This type of access restriction allows an administrator to grant access to resources and affords users seamless access to those resources. User-level security is offered by Windows NT in both the workgroup and domain models.

The permissions to a shared directory are:

◆ **Read**. The user is allowed to read files within a share. He can also see all files and subdirectories.

◆ **Change**. The user can modify existing files and directories and create new files and directories within the share.

◆ **Full Control**. The user can see, modify, delete, and take ownership of all files and directories within the share.

◆ **No Access**. The user cannot access any files or directories within the share.

Share-level permissions apply to anyone accessing the share over the network and do not apply to users who are interactive on the computer where the share resides. Share-level permissions can be set on both FAT and NTFS partitions.

Compare a Client/Server Network with a Peer-to-Peer Network

A client/server network is one in which a computer has a specific role. A server is a computer, often with more

RAM, more hard drive space, and a faster CPU than the other machines. A server services requests from clients. These requests could be for the use of files and printers, application services, communication services, and database services.

Clients are the computers on which users work. These computers typically are not as powerful as servers. Client computers are designed to submit requests to the server.

Peer-to-peer networks are made up of several computers that play the roles of both a client and a server; thus there is no dedicated computer running file and printer services, application services, communication services, or database services.

Compare the Implications of Using Connection-Oriented Communications with Connectionless Communications

In general, connection-oriented communication differs from connectionless communication as follows:

◆ **Connection-oriented mode**. Error correction and flow control are provided at internal nodes along the message path.

◆ **Connectionless mode**. Internal nodes along the message path do not participate in error correction and flow control.

In connection-oriented mode, the chain of links between the source and destination nodes forms a kind of logical pathway connection. The nodes forwarding the data packet can track which packet is part of which connection. This enables the internal nodes to provide flow control as the data moves along the path. For example, if an internal node determines that a link is malfunctioning, the node can send a notification message backward through the path to the source computer. Furthermore, because the internal node distinguishes among individual, concurrent connections in which it participates, this node can transmit (or forward) a "stop sending" message for one of its connections without stopping all communications through the node. Another feature of connection-oriented communication is that internal nodes provide error correction at each link in the chain. Therefore, if a node detects an error, it asks the preceding node to retransmit.

SPX and TCP are two major examples of connection-oriented protocols.

Connectionless mode does not provide these elaborate internal control mechanisms; instead, connectionless mode relegates all error-correcting and retransmitting processes to the source and destination nodes. The end nodes acknowledge the receipt of packets and retransmit if necessary, but internal nodes do not participate in flow control and error correction (other than simply forwarding messages between the end nodes).

IPX and UDP are two major examples of connection-oriented protocols.

The advantage of connectionless mode is that connectionless communications can be processed more quickly and more simply because the internal nodes only forward data and thus don't have to track connections or provide retransmission or flow control.

Distinguish Whether SLIP or PPP Is Used as the Communications Protocol for Various Situations

Two other standards vital to network communication are Serial Line Internet Protocol (SLIP) and Point-to-Point Protocol (PPP). SLIP and PPP were designed to support dial-up access to networks based on the Internet transport protocols. SLIP is a simple protocol that functions at the Physical layer, whereas PPP is a considerably enhanced protocol that provides Physical layer and Data Link layer functionality.

Windows NT supports both SLIP and PPP from the client end using the Dial-Up Networking application. On the server end, Windows NT RAS (Remote Access Service) supports PPP but doesn't support SLIP. In other words, Windows NT can act as a PPP server but not as a SLIP server.

PPP

PPP was defined by the Internet Engineering Task Force (IETF) to improve on SLIP by providing the following features:

◆ Security using password logon

◆ Simultaneous support for multiple protocols on the same link

◆ Dynamic IP addressing

◆ Improved error control

Different PPP implementations might offer different levels of service and negotiate service levels when connections are made. Because of its versatility, interoperability, and additional features, PPP has surpassed SLIP as the most popular serial-line protocol.

SLIP

Developed to provide dial-up TCP/IP connections, SLIP is an extremely rudimentary protocol that suffers from a lack of rigid standardization in the industry, which sometimes hinders different vendor implementations of SLIP from operating with each other.

SLIP is most commonly used on older systems or for dial-up connections to the Internet via SLIP-server Internet hosts.

Certain dial-up configurations cannot use SLIP for the following reasons:

- SLIP supports the TCP/IP transport protocol only. PPP, however, supports TCP/IP, as well as a number of other transport protocols, such as NetBEUI, IPX, AppleTalk, and DECnet. In addition, PPP can support multiple protocols over the same link.

- SLIP requires static IP addresses. Because SLIP requires static, or preconfigured, IP addresses, SLIP servers do not support the Dynamic Host Configuration Protocol (DHCP), which assigns IP addresses dynamically or when requested. (DHCP enables clients to share IP addresses so that a relatively small number of IP addresses can serve a larger user base.) If the dial-up server uses DHCP to assign an IP address to the client, the dial-up connection won't use SLIP.

- SLIP does not support dynamic addressing through DHCP so SLIP connections cannot dynamically assign a WINS or DNS server.

Define the Communication Devices that Communicate at Each Level of the OSI Model

- **Repeater**. Operates at the Physical layer of the OSI model. The purpose of a repeater is to regenerate a signal, allowing a signal to travel beyond the maximum distance specified by the transmission media.

- **Hub**. Operates at the Physical layer. A hub is a concentrator that connects 10BASE-T cabling together on an Ethernet network. Some hubs also have the capability to act as a repeater.

- **MSAU**. Operates at the Physical layer. An MSAU performs the same purpose of a hub, but is used on token-ring networks.

- **Network Interface Card (NIC)**. Operates at the Data Link layer. A NIC is responsible for converting information in a computer to a signal that will be sent on the transmission media.

- **Bridge**. Operates at the Data Link layer of the OSI mode. A bridge is responsible for isolating network traffic on a cable segment. It performs this task by building address tables that contain the MAC address or hardware addresses of devices on ether side of it.

- **Router**. Operates at the Network layer of the OSI model. It is responsible for connecting different segments that have dissimilar logical network addresses.

- **Gateway**. Can appear at any level of the OSI model but is primarily seen at the Network layer and higher. The purpose of a gateway is to convert one network protocol to another.

Describe the Characteristics and Purpose of the Media Used in IEEE 802.3 and IEEE 802.5 Standards

The various media types used by the IEEE 802.3 and 802.5 are discussed below.

IEEE 802.3

This standard defines characteristics related to the MAC sublayer of the Data Link layer and the OSI Physical layer. Except for one minor distinction—frame type—IEEE 802.3 Ethernet functions identically to DIX Ethernet v.2.

The MAC sublayer uses a type of contention access called *Carrier Sense Multiple Access with Collision Detection (CSMA/CD)*. This technique reduces the incidence of collision by having each device listen to the network to determine whether it's quiet ("carrier sensing"); a device attempts to transmit only when the network is quiescent. This reduces but does not eliminate collisions because signals take some time to propagate through the network. As devices transmit, they continue to listen so they can detect a collision should it occur. When a collision occurs, all devices cease transmitting and send a "jamming" signal that notifies all stations of the collision. Each device then waits a random amount of time before attempting to transmit again. This combination of safeguards significantly reduces collisions on all but the busiest networks.

The IEEE 802.3 Physical layer definition describes signaling methods (both baseband and broadband), data rates, media, and topologies. Several Physical layer variants also have been defined. Each variant is named following a convention that states the signaling rate (1 or 10) in Mbps, baseband (BASE) or broadband (BROAD) mode, and a designation of the media characteristics.

The following list details the IEEE 802.3 variants of transmission media:

◆ **1BASE5**. This 1-Mbps network utilizes UTP cable with a signal range up to 500 meters (250 meters per segment). A star physical topology is used.

◆ **10BASE5**. Typically called Thick Ethernet, or Thicknet, this variant uses a large diameter (10 mm) "thick" coaxial cable with a 50-ohm impedance. A data rate of 10 Mbps is supported with a signaling range of 500 meters per cable segment on a physical bus topology.

◆ **10BASE2**. Similar to Thicknet, this variant uses a thinner coaxial cable that can support cable runs of 185 meters. (In this case, the "2" only indicates an approximate cable range.) The transmission rate remains at 10 Mbps, and the physical topology is a bus. This variant typically is called Thin Ethernet, or Thinnet.

◆ **10BASE-F**. This variant uses fiber-optic cables to support 10-Mbps signaling with a range of four kilometers. Three subcategories include *10BASE-FL* (fiber link), *10BASE-FB* (fiber backbone), and *10BASE-FP* (fiber passive).

◆ **10BROAD36**. This broadband standard supports channel signal rates of 10 Mbps. A 75-ohm coaxial cable supports cable runs of 1,800 meters (up to 3,600 meters in a dual-cable configuration) using a physical bus topology.

◆ **10BASE-T**. This variant uses UTP cable in a star physical topology. The signaling rate remains at 10 Mbps, and devices can be up to 100 meters from a wiring hub.

◆ **100BASE-X**. This proposed standard is similar to 10BASE-T but supports 100 Mbps data rates.

IEEE 802.5

The IEEE 802.5 standard was derived from IBM's Token Ring network, which employs a ring logical topology and token-based media-access control. Data rates of 1, 4, and 16 Mbps have been defined for this standard.

Explain the Purpose of NDIS and Novell ODI Network Standards

The *Network Driver Interface Specification (NDIS)*, a standard developed by Microsoft and the 3Com Corporation, describes the interface between the network transport protocol and the Data Link layer network adapter driver. The following list details the goals of NDIS:

◆ To provide a vendor-neutral boundary between the transport protocol and the network adapter card driver so that an NDIS-compliant protocol stack can operate with an NDIS-compliant adapter driver.

◆ To define a method for binding multiple protocols to a single driver so that the adapter can simultaneously support communications under multiple protocols. In addition, the method enables you to bind one protocol to more than one adapter.

The *Open Data-Link Interface (ODI)*, developed by Apple and Novell, serves the same function as NDIS. Originally, ODI was written for NetWare and Macintosh environments. Like NDIS, ODI provides rules that establish a vendor-neutral interface between the protocol stack and the adapter driver. This interface also enables one or more network drivers to support one or more protocol stacks.

PLANNING

The planning section on the exam tests your ability to apply networking components and standards when designing a network.

Select the Appropriate Media for Various Situations

Media choices include:

◆ Twisted-pair cable

◆ Coaxial cable

◆ Fiber-optic cable

◆ Wireless

Situational elements include:

◆ Cost

◆ Distance limitations

◆ Number of nodes

Summary Table 1 outlines the characteristics of the cable types discussed in this section.

Summary Table 2 compares the different types of wireless communication media in terms of cost, ease of installation, distance, and other issues.

SUMMARY TABLE 1
COMPARISON OF CABLE MEDIA

Cable Type	Cost	Installation	Capacity	Range	EMI
Coaxial Thinnet	Less than STP	Inexpensive/easy	10 Mbps typical	185 m	Less sensitive than UTP
Coaxial Thicknet	Greater than STP Less than Fiber	Easy	10 Mbps typical	500 m	Less sensitive than UTP
Shielded Twisted-Pair (STP)	Greater than UTP Less than Thicknet	Fairly easy	16 Mbps typical up to 500 Mbps	100 m typical	Less sensitive than UTP
Unshielded twisted-pair (UTP)	Lowest	Inexpensive/easy	10 Mbps typical up to 100 Mbps	100 m typical	Most sensitive
Fiber-optic	Highest	Expensive/Difficult	100 Mbps typical	Tens of Kilometers	Insensitive

SUMMARY TABLE 2
COMPARISON OF WIRELESS MEDIA

Cable Type	Cost	Installation	Distance	Other Issues
Infrared	Cheapest of all the wireless	Fairly easy; may require line of sight	Under a kilometer	Can attenuate due to fog and rain
Laser	Similar to infrared	Requires line of site	Can span several kilometers	Can attenuate due to fog and rain
Narrow band radio	More expensive than infrared and laser; may need FCC license	Requires trained technicians and can involve tall radio towers	Can span hundreds of kilometers	Low power devices can attenuate; can be eavesdropped upon; can also attenuate due to fog, rain, and solar flares
Spread spectrum radio	More advanced technology than narrow band radio, thus more expensive	Requires trained technicians and can involve tall radio towers	Can span hundreds of kilometers	Low power devices can attenuate; can also attenuate due to fog, rain, and solar flares
Microwave	Very expensive as it requires link to satellites often	Requires trained technicians and can involve satellite dishes	Can span thousands of kilometers	Can be eavesdropped upon; can also attenuate due to fog, rain, and solar flares

Select the Appropriate Topology for Various Token-Ring and Ethernet Networks

The following four topologies are implemented by Ethernet and token-ring networks:

- **Ring**. Ring topologies are wired in a circle. Each node is connected to its neighbors on either side, and data passes around the ring in one direction only. Each device incorporates a receiver and a transmitter and serves as a repeater that passes the signal to the next device in the ring. Because the signal is regenerated at each device, signal degeneration is low. Most ring topologies are logical, and implemented as physical stars. Token-ring networks follow a ring topology.

- **Bus**. Star topologies require that all devices connect to a central hub. The hub receives signals from other network devices and routes the signals

to the proper destinations. Star hubs can be interconnected to form tree or hierarchical network topologies. A star physical topology is often used to physically implement a bus or ring logical topology that is used by both Ethernet and token-ring networks.

- **Star**. Star topologies require that all devices connect to a central hub. The hub receives signals from other network devices and routes the signals to the proper destinations. Star hubs can be interconnected to form tree or hierarchical network topologies. A star physical topology is often used to physically implement a bus or ring logical topology that is used by both Ethernet and token-ring networks.

- **Mesh**. A mesh topology is really a hybrid model representing a physical topology because a mesh topology can incorporate all of the previous topologies. The difference is that in a mesh topology every device is connected to every other device on the network. When a new device is added, a connection to all existing devices must be made. Mesh topologies can be used by both Ethernet and token-ring networks.

Select the Appropriate Network and Transport Protocol or Protocols for Various Token-Ring and Ethernet Networks

Protocol choices include:

- ◆ DLC
- ◆ AppleTalk
- ◆ IPX
- ◆ TCP/IP
- ◆ NFS
- ◆ SMB

Data Link Control (DLC)

The Data Link Control (DLC) protocol does not provide a fully functioning protocol stack. In Windows NT systems, DLC is used primarily to access to Hewlett-Packard JetDirect network-interface printers. DLC also provides some connectivity with IBM mainframes. It is not a protocol that can be used to connect Windows NT or 95 computers together.

AppleTalk

AppleTalk is the computing architecture developed by Apple Computer for the Macintosh family of personal computers. Although AppleTalk originally supported only Apple's proprietary LocalTalk cabling system, the suite has been expanded to incorporate both Ethernet and token-ring Physical layers. Within Microsoft operating systems, AppleTalk is only supported by Windows NT Server. Windows NT Workstation and Windows 95 do not support AppleTalk. AppleTalk cannot be used for Microsoft to Microsoft operating system communication, only by NT servers supporting Apple clients.

The LocalTalk, EtherTalk, and TokenTalk Link Access Protocols (LLAP, ELAP, and TLAP) integrate AppleTalk upper-layer protocols with the LocalTalk, Ethernet, and token-ring environments.

Apple's *Datagram Deliver Protocol (DDP)* is a Network layer protocol that provides connectionless service between two sockets. The AppleTalk Transaction Protocol (ATP) is a connectionless Transport layer protocol. Reliable service is provided through a system of acknowledgments and retransmissions. The *AppleTalk File Protocol (AFP)* provides file services and is responsible for translating local file service requests into formats required for network file services. AFP directly translates command syntax and enables applications to perform file format translations. AFP is responsible for file system security and verifies and encrypts logon names and passwords during connection setup.

IPX

The *Internetwork Packet Exchange Protocol (IPX)* is a Network layer protocol that provides connectionless (datagram) service. (IPX was developed from the XNS protocol originated by Xerox.) As a Network layer protocol, IPX is responsible for internetwork routing and maintaining network logical addresses. Routing uses the RIP protocol (described later in this section) to make route selections. IPX provides similar functionality as UDP does in the TCP/IP protocol suite.

IPX relies on hardware physical addresses found at lower layers to provide network device addressing. IPX also uses sockets, or upper-layer service addresses, to deliver packets to their ultimate destinations. On the client, IPX support is provided as a component of the older DOS shell and the current DOS NetWare requester.

TCP/IP

TCP/IP is a broad protocol that covers many different areas. This summary presents some of the most important protocols within the TCP/IP protocol suite.

Internet Protocol (IP)

The *Internet Protocol (IP)* is a connectionless protocol that provides datagram service, and IP packets are most commonly referred to as IP datagrams. IP is a packet-switching protocol that performs the addressing and route selection.

IP performs packet disassembly and reassembly as required by packet size limitations defined for the Data Link and Physical layers being implemented. IP also performs error checking on the header data using a checksum, although data from upper layers is not error-checked.

Transmission Control Protocol (TCP)

The *Transmission Control Protocol (TCP)* is an internetwork connection-oriented protocol that corresponds to the OSI Transport layer. TCP provides full-duplex, end-to-end connections. When the overhead of end-to-end communication acknowledgment isn't required, the User Datagram Protocol (UDP) can be substituted for TCP at the Transport (host-to-host) level. TCP and UDP operate at the same layer.

TCP corresponds to SPX in the NetWare environment (see the NetWare IPX/SPX section). TCP maintains a logical connection between the sending and receiving computer systems. In this way, the integrity of the transmission is maintained. TCP detects any problems in the transmission quickly and takes action to correct them. The tradeoff is that TCP isn't as fast as UDP, due to the number of acknowledgments received by the sending host.

TCP also provides message fragmentation and reassembly and can accept messages of any length from upper-layer protocols. TCP fragments message streams into segments that can be handled by IP. When used with IP, TCP adds connection-oriented service and performs segment synchronization, adding sequence numbers at the byte level.

Windows Internet Naming Services (WINS)

Windows Internet Naming Service (WINS) provides a function similar to that of DNS, with the exception that it provides a NetBIOS name to IP address resolution. This is important because all of Microsoft's networking requires the capability to reference NetBIOS names. Normally NetBIOS names are obtained with the issuance of broadcasts, but because routers normally do not forward broadcasts, a WINS server is one alternative that can be used to issue IP addresses to NetBIOS name requests. WINS servers replace the need for LMHOSTS files on a computer.

Domain Name System (DNS)

The Domain Name System (DNS) protocol provides host name and IP address resolution as a service to client applications. DNS servers enable humans to use logical node names, utilizing a fully qualified domain name structure to access network resources. Host names can be up to 260 characters long. DNS servers replace the need for HOSTS files on a computer.

Network File System (NFS)

Network File System (NFS), developed by Sun Microsystems, is a family of file-access protocols that are a considerable advancement over FTP and Telnet. Since Sun made the NFS specifications available for public use, NFS has achieved a high level of popularity.

Server Messaging Blocks (SMB)

One protocol that is slightly independent is Microsoft's Server Messaging Blocks (SMB). SMBs are Microsoft's equivalent to NCP packets. Like NCP packets, SMBs operate at the Application layer of the OSI model.

SMBs allow machines on a Microsoft network to communicate with one another. Through the use of SMBs, file and print services can be shared. SMBs can use TCP/IP, NWLink (IPX/SPX), and NetBEUI because SMBs utilize a NetBIOS interface when communicating. For more information on NetBIOS names, see the following section.

Select the Appropriate Connectivity Devices for Various Token-Ring and Ethernet Networks

Connectivity devices include:

◆ **Repeaters**. Repeaters regenerate a signal and are used to expand LANs beyond cabling limits.

◆ **Bridges**. Bridges know the side of the bridge on which a node is located. A bridge passes only packets addressed to computers across the bridge, so a bridge can thus filter traffic, reducing the load on the transmission medium.

◆ **Routers**. Routers forward packets based on a logical (as opposed to a physical) address. Some

routers can determine the best path for a packet based on routing algorithms.

◆ **Brouters**. A brouter is a device that is a combination of a bridge and a router, providing both types of services.

◆ **Gateways**. Gateways function under a process similar to routers except that gateways can connect dissimilar network environments. A gateway replaces the necessary protocol layers of a packet so that the packet can circulate in the destination environment.

List the Characteristics, Requirements, and Appropriate Situations for WAN Connection Services

WAN connection services include:

◆ X.25

◆ ISDN

◆ Frame relay

◆ ATM

X.25

X.25 is a packet-switching network standard developed by the International Telegraph and Telephone Consultative Committee (CCITT), which has been renamed the International Telecommunications Union (ITU). The standard, referred to as *Recommendation X.25*, was introduced in 1974 and is now implemented most commonly in WANs.

At the time X.25 was developed, this flow control and error checking was essential because X.25 was developed around relatively unreliable telephone line communications. The drawback is that error checking and flow control slow down X.25. Generally, X.25 networks are implemented with line speeds up to 64 Kbps, although actual throughput seems slower due to the error correction controls in place. These speeds are suitable for the file transfer and terminal activity that comprised the bulk of network traffic when X.25 was defined, most of this traffic being terminal connections to mainframes. Such speeds, however, are inadequate to provide LAN-speed services, which typically require speeds of 1 Mbps or better. X.25 networks, therefore, are poor choices for providing LAN application services in a WAN environment. One advantage of X.25, however, is that it is an established standard that is used internationally. This, as well as lack of other services throughout the world, means that X.25 is more of a connection service to Africa, South America, and Asia, where a lack of other services prevails.

ISDN

The original idea behind ISDN was to enable existing phone lines to carry digital communications, and it was at one time touted as a replacement to traditional analog lines. Thus, ISDN is more like traditional telephone service than some of the other WAN services. ISDN is intended as a dial-up service and not as a permanent 24-hour connection.

ISDN separates the bandwidth into channels. Based upon how these channels are used, ISDN can be separated into two classes of service:

◆ **Basic Rate (BRI)**. Basic Rate ISDN uses three channels. Two channels (called B channels) carry the digital data at 64 Kbps. A third channel (called the D channel) provides link and signaling information at 16 Kbps. Basic Rate ISDN thus is referred to as 2B+D. A single PC transmitting

through ISDN can use both B channels simultaneously, providing a maximum data rate of 128 Kbps (or higher with compression).

◆ **Primary Rate (PRI)**. Primary Rate supports 23 64 Kbps B channels and one 64 Kbps D channel. The D channel is used for signaling and management, whereas the B channels provide the data throughput.

In a BRI line, if the line was currently being used for voice, this would only allow one of the B channels to be available for data. This effectively reduces the throughput of the BRI to 64 Kbps.

Frame Relay

Frame Relay was designed to support the *Broadband Integrated Services Digital Network (B-ISDN)*, which was discussed in the previous section. The specifications for Frame Relay address some of the limitations of X.25. As with X.25, Frame Relay is a packet-switching network service, but Frame Relay was designed around newer, faster fiber-optic networks.

Unlike X.25, Frame Relay assumes a more reliable network. This enables Frame Relay to eliminate much of the X.25 overhead required to provide reliable service on less reliable networks. Frame Relay relies on higher-level protocol layers to provide flow and error control.

Frame Relay typically is implemented as a public data network and, therefore, is regarded as a WAN protocol. The scope of Frame Relay, with respect to the OSI model, is limited to the Physical and Data Link layers.

Frame Relay provides permanent virtual circuits that supply permanent virtual pathways for WAN connections. Frame Relay services typically are implemented at line speeds from 56 Kbps up to 1.544 Mbps (T1).

Customers typically purchase access to a specific amount of bandwidth on a frame-relay service. This bandwidth is called the *committed information rate (CIR)*, a data rate for which the customer is guaranteed access. Customers might be permitted to access higher data rates on a pay-per-use temporary basis. This arrangement enables customers to tailor their network access costs based on their bandwidth requirements.

To use Frame Relay, you must have special Frame Relay-compatible connectivity devices (such as frame-relay-compatible routers and bridges).

Asynchronous Transfer Mode (ATM)

Asynchronous Transfer Mode (ATM) is a high-bandwidth switching technology developed by the ITU Telecommunications Standards Sector (ITU-TSS). An organization called the ATM Forum is responsible for defining ATM implementation characteristics. ATM can be layered on other Physical layer technologies, such as Fiber Distributed Data Interface (FDDI) and SONET.

Several characteristics distinguish ATM from other switching technologies. ATM is based on fixed-length 53-byte cells, whereas other technologies employ frames that vary in length to accommodate different amounts of data. Because ATM cells are uniform in length, switching mechanisms can operate with a high level of efficiency. This high efficiency results in high data transfer rates. Some ATM systems can operate at an incredible rate of 622 Mbps; a typical working speed for an ATM is around 155 Mbps.

The unit of transmission for ATM is called a cell. All cells are 53 bytes long and consist of a 5-byte header and 48 bytes of data. The 48-byte data size was selected by the standards committee as a compromise to suit both audio- and data-transmission needs. Audio information, for instance, must be delivered with little latency (delay) to maintain a smooth flow of sound. Audio engineers therefore preferred a small cell so that cells would be more readily available when needed. For data, however, large cells reduce the overhead required to deliver a byte of information.

Asynchronous delivery is another distinguishing feature of ATM. "Asynchronous" refers to the characteristic of ATM in which transmission time slots don't occur periodically but are granted at irregular intervals. ATM uses a technique called *label multiplexing*, which allocates time slots on demand. Traffic that is time-critical, such as voice or video, can be given priority over data traffic that can be delayed slightly with no ill effect. Channels are identified by cell labels, not by specific time slots. A high-priority transmission need not be held until its next time slot allocation. Instead, it might be required to wait only until the current 53-byte cell has been transmitted.

IMPLEMENTATION

The Implementation section of the exam tests your knowledge of how to implement, test, and manage an installed network.

Choosing an Administrative Plan to Meet Specified Needs, Including Performance Management, Account Management, and Security

Administrative plans can be broken down into three areas: performance management, account management, and security.

Performance Management

Performance management is best done through the establishment of a baseline of the network performance and a baseline of a computer's performance. Based upon the information in a baseline, the administrators of the network can establish when network or computer performance is abnormal.

Account Management

Account management within Windows NT is done through the use of groups. In a workgroup model, there exist local groups, or groups that are local to the computer. These groups are not seen on other machines in the network. Users are placed into these local groups and assigned permissions to resources, such as printers, shares, or files and directories.

Windows 95 computers do not have built-in groups. There also is no account database on a Windows 95 computer to provide user accounts.

Windows NT domain models do make use of user accounts and groups. Like the workgroup model, the domain model has user accounts and local groups. A domain model also has global groups. Global groups reside on a domain controller and can be referenced as a resource user by any Windows NT computer within the domain sharing resources.

Security

Windows 95 computers have the capability to provide share-level security, which involves password protecting resources.

Windows NT computers can provide user-level security, in which users are granted access to resources on a user or local group basis (workgroups and domains support this) and a global group basis (only domains support this).

Choosing a Disaster Recovery Plan for Various Situations

Disaster recovery applies to many different components on the network. The following sections describe the most common issues and solutions used in a disaster recovery program.

Uninterruptible Power Supply (UPS)

An uninterruptible power supply (UPS) is a special battery (or sometimes a generator) that supplies power to an electronic device in the event of a power failure. UPSs commonly are used with network servers to prevent a disorderly shutdown by warning users to log out. After a predetermined waiting period, the UPS software performs an orderly shutdown of the server. Many UPS units also regulate power distribution and serve as protection against power surges. Remember that in most cases, a UPS generally does not provide for continued network functionality for longer than a few minutes. A UPS is not intended to keep the server running through a long power outage, but rather to give the server time to do what it needs before shutting down. This can prevent the data loss and system corruption that sometimes result from sudden shutdown.

Tape Backup

Tape backups are done to store data offline in the event that the hard drive containing the data fails. There are three types of tape backups:

◆ **Full backup**. Backs up all specified files.

◆ **Incremental backup**. Backs up only those files that have changed since the last backup.

◆ **Differential backup**. Backs up the specified files if the files have changed since the last backup. This type doesn't mark the files as having been backed up, however. (A differential backup is somewhat like a copy command. Because the file is not marked as having been backed up, a later differential or incremental backup will back up the file again.)

RAID 1

In level 1, drives are paired or mirrored with each byte of information being written to each identical drive. You can duplex these devices by adding a separate drive controller for each drive. Disk mirroring is defined as two hard drives (one primary, one secondary) that use the same disk channel or controller cards and cable. Disk mirroring is most commonly configured by using disk drives contained in the server. Duplexing is a form of mirroring that involves the use of a second controller and that enables you to configure a more robust hardware environment.

RAID 5

RAID 5 uses striping with parity information written across multiple drives to enable fault-tolerance with a minimum of wasted disk space. This level also offers the advantage of enabling relatively efficient performance on writes to the drives, as well as excellent read performance.

Striping with parity is based on the principle that all data is written to the hard drive in binary code (ones and zeros). RAID 5 requires at least three drives because this version writes data across two of them and then creates the parity block on the third. If the first byte is 00111000 and the second is 10101001, the system computes the third by adding the digits together using this system:

1+1=0, 0+0=0, 0+1=1, 1+0=1

The sum of 00111000 and 10101001 is 10010001, which would be written to the third disk. If any of the

disks fail, the process can be reversed and any disk can be reconstructed from the data on the other two. Recovery includes replacing the bad disk and then regenerating its data through the Disk Administrator. A maximum of 32 disks can be connected in a RAID 5 array under Windows NT.

Given the Manufacturer's Documentation for the Network Adapter, Install, Configure, and Resolve Hardware Conflicts for Multiple Network Adapters in a Token-Ring or Ethernet Network

The following resources are configurable on network adapter cards:

- IRQ
- Base I/O port address
- Base memory address
- DMA channel
- Boot PROM
- MAC address
- Ring speed (token-ring cards)
- Connector type

Not all network adapter cards have all of these resources available for configuration. These resource settings on the network adapter card must be different than the settings found on other components used within the computer.

Some network adapter cards use jumper settings to configure these settings, others use software, and others can have this done through the operating system software, such as Windows 95 and Windows NT. The method of configuration is dependent upon the manufacturer.

Implementing a NetBIOS Naming Scheme for All Computers on a Given Network

NetBIOS is an interface that provides NetBIOS-based applications with access to network resources. Every computer on a Windows NT network must have a unique name for it to be accessible through the NetBIOS interface. This unique name is called a computer name or a NetBIOS name.

On a NetBIOS network, every computer must have a unique name. The computer name can be up to 15 characters long. A NetBIOS name can include alphanumeric characters and any of the following special characters:

    ! @ # $ % ^ & ( ) - _ ' { } . ~

Note that you cannot use a space or an asterisk in a NetBIOS name. Also, NetBIOS names are not case sensitive.

Selecting the Appropriate Hardware and Software Tools to Monitor Trends in the Network

The hardware and software tools described in the next five sections are used to monitor trends in a network.

Protocol Analyzer

This can be a hardware or software tool to analyze the traffic in a network. Protocol analyzers capture packets on a network and display their contents. The software version of this tool supplied by Microsoft is Network Monitor. Network Monitor ships with Windows NT as a scaled-down version that can only capture data between the host computer and those to which the host talks.

Event Viewer

This software tool is found on Windows NT. It reports one of three event types:

- **System Events**. Those generated by the operating system.

- **Application Events**. Those generated by any application that is programmed to make event calls to the Event Viewer.

- **Auditing**. Any auditing being performed on NTFS partitions or by users interacting with the network.

Performance Monitor

Windows NT's Performance Monitor tool lets you monitor important system parameters for the computers on your network in real time. Performance Monitor can keep an eye on a large number of system parameters, providing a graphical or tabular profile of system and network trends. Performance Monitor also can save performance data in a log for later reference. You can use Performance Monitor to track statistical measurements (called *counters*) for any of several hardware or software components (called *objects*).

System Monitor

Windows 95 includes a program called System Monitor that also allows information to be collected on the Windows 95 machine in real time. System Monitor collects information on different categories of items on the system. System Monitor is not as detailed as Windows NT's Performance Monitor.

Simple Network Management Protocol (SNMP)

SNMP is a TCP/IP protocol used to perform management operations on a TCP/IP network. SNMP-enabled devices allow for information to be sent to a management utility (this is called a *trap*). SNMP devices also allow for the setting and extraction of information (this is done by the issuance of a set or get command) found in their Management Information Base (MIB).

TROUBLESHOOTING

The Troubleshooting section of the exam covers many of the topics covered in previous sections. Emphasis of this section is to test your understanding of what can cause problems, and how to fix them.

Identifying Common Errors Associated with Components Required for Communications

The utilities described in the next four sections can be used to diagnose errors associated with components required for communications.

Protocol Analyzers

Protocol analyzers are either hardware or software products used to monitor network traffic, track network performance, and analyze packets. Protocol analyzers can identify bottlenecks, protocol problems, and malfunctioning network components.

Digital Volt Meter (DVM)

Digital volt meters are handheld electronic measuring tools that enable you to check the voltage of network cables. They also can be used to check the resistance of terminators. You can use a DVM to help you find a break or a short in a network cable.

DVMs are usually inexpensive battery-operated devices that have either a digital or needle readout and two metal prongs attached to the DVM by some wires a foot or more in length. By sending a small current through the wires and out through the metal prongs, resistance and voltages of terminators and wires can be measured.

Time-Domain Reflectometers (TDR)

Time-domain reflectometers send sound waves along a cable and look for imperfections that might be caused by a break or a short in the line. A good TDR can detect faults on a cable to within a few feet.

Oscilloscope

An oscilloscope measures fluctuations in signal voltage and can help find faulty or damaged cabling. Oscilloscopes are often more expensive electronic devices that show the signal fluctuations on a monitor.

Several diagnostic software tools provide information on virtually any type of network hardware, as well. A considerable number of diagnostic software packages are available for a variety of prices.

A common software tool distributed with most network cards is a Send/Receive package. This software tool allows two computers with network cards and cables to connect to each other. This tool does not rely on a networked operating system, nor can it be used to send data. It simply sends packets from one computer to the other, establishing that the network cards and underlying transmission media are connected and configured properly.

Diagnosing and Resolving Common Connectivity Problems with Cards, Cables, and Related Hardware

Most network problems occur on the transmission media or with the components that attach devices to the transmission media. All of these components operate at the Physical, DataLink, or Network levels of the OSI model. The components that connect PCs and enable them to communicate are susceptible to many kinds of problems.

Troubleshooting Cables and Connectors

Most network problems occur at the OSI Physical layer, and cabling is one of the most common causes. A cable might have a short or a break, or it might be attached to a faulty connector. Tools such as DVMs and TDRs help search out cabling problems.

Cabling problems can cause three major problems: An individual computer cannot access the network, a group of computers cannot access the network, or none of the computers can access the network.

On networks that are configured in a star topology, an individual cable break between the computer and hub or MSAU causes a failure in communication between

that individual computer and the rest of the network. This type of cable break does not cause problems between all of the other computers on the network.

A cable break in cables connecting multiple hubs causes a break in communications between the computers on one side of the cable break and the computers on the other side of the cable break. In most cases, the communications between computers within the broken segment can continue.

In the case of MSAU, the breakage of a cable connecting MSAUs often causes all computers on the ring to fail because the ring is not complete. A break in the cable on a bus topology also causes all computers on the network segment to be unable to communicate with any other computers on the network.

Try the following checks when troubleshooting network cabling problems:

- ◆ With 10BASE-T, make sure the cable used has the correct number of twists to meet the data-grade specifications.

- ◆ Look for electrical interference, which can be caused by tying the network cable together with monitor and power cords. Fluorescent lights, electric motors, and other electrical devices can cause interference if they are located too close to cables. These problems often can be alleviated by placing the cable away from devices that generate electromagnetic interference or by upgrading the cable to one that has better shielding.

- ◆ Make sure that connectors are pinned properly and crimped tightly.

- ◆ If excess shielding on coaxial cable is exposed, make sure it doesn't ground out the connector.

- ◆ Ensure that coaxial cables are not coiled tightly together. This can generate a magnetic field around the cable, causing electromagnetic interference.

◆ On coaxial Ethernet LANs, look for missing terminators or terminators with improper resistance ratings.

◆ Watch out for malfunctioning transceivers, concentrators, or T-connectors. All of these components can be checked by replacing the suspect devices.

◆ Test the continuity of the cable by using the various physical testing devices discussed in the previous section or by using a software-based cable testing utility.

◆ Make sure that all the component cables in a segment are connected. A user who moves his client and removes the T-connector incorrectly can cause a broken segment.

◆ Examine cable connectors for bent or broken pins.

◆ On token-ring networks, inspect the attachment of patch cables and adapter cables. Remember, patch cables connect MSAUs, and adapter cables connect the network adapter to the MSAU.

One advantage of a token-ring network is its built-in capability to monitor itself. token-ring networks provide electronic troubleshooting and, when possible, actually make repairs. When the token-ring network can't make its own repairs, a process called *beaconing* narrows down the portion of the ring in which the problem is most likely to exist.

Troubleshooting Network Adapter Cards

Network problems often result from malfunctioning network adapter cards. The process of troubleshooting the network adapter works like any other kind of troubleshooting process: Start with the simple. The following list details some aspects you can check if you think your network adapter card might be malfunctioning:

◆ Make sure the cable is properly connected to the card.

◆ Confirm that you have the correct network adapter card driver and that the driver is installed properly. Be sure the card is properly bound to the appropriate transport protocol.

◆ Make sure the network adapter card and the network adapter card driver are compatible with your operating system. If you use Windows NT, consult the Windows NT hardware compatibility list. If you use Windows 95 or another operating system, rely on the adapter card vendor specifications.

◆ Test for resource conflicts. Make sure another device isn't attempting to use the same resources. If you think a resource conflict might be the problem, but you can't pinpoint the conflict using Windows NT Diagnostics, Windows 95's Device Manager, or some other diagnostic program, try removing all the cards except the network adapter and then replacing the cards one by one. Check the network with each addition to determine which device is causing the conflict.

◆ Run the network adapter card's diagnostic software. This will often indicate which resource on the network card is failing.

◆ Examine the jumper and DIP switch settings on the card. Make sure the resource settings are consistent with the settings configured through the operating system.

◆ Make sure the card is inserted properly in the slot. Reseat if necessary.

◆ If necessary, remove the card and clean the connector fingers (don't use an eraser because it leaves grit on the card).

◆ Replace the card with one that you know works. If the connection works with a different card, you know the card is the problem.

Token-ring network adapters with failure rates that exceed a preset tolerance level might actually remove themselves from the network. Try replacing the card. Some token-ring networks also can experience problems if a token-ring card set at a ring speed of 16 Mbps is inserted into a ring using a 4 Mbps ring speed, and vice versa.

Troubleshooting Hubs and MSAUs

If you experience problems with a hub-based LAN, such as a 10BASE-T network, you often can isolate the problem by disconnecting the attached workstations one at a time. If removing one of the workstations eliminates the problem, the trouble may be caused by that workstation or its associated cable length. If removing each of the workstations doesn't solve the problem, the fault may lie with the hub. Check the easy components first, such as ports, switches, and connectors, and then use a different hub (if you have it) to see if the problem persists. If your hub doesn't work properly, call the manufacturer.

If you're troubleshooting a token-ring network, make sure the cables are connected properly to the MSAUs, with ring-out ports connecting to the ring-in ports throughout the ring. If you suspect the MSAU, isolate it by changing the ring-in and ring-out cables to bypass the MSAU. If the ring is now functional again, consider replacing the MSAU. In addition, you might find that if your network has MSAUs from more than one manufacturer, they are not wholly compatible. Impedance and other electrical characteristics can show slight differences between manufacturers, causing intermittent network problems. Some MSAUs (other than the 8228) are active and require a power supply. These MSAUs fail if they have a blown fuse or a bad power source. Your problem also might result from a misconfigured MSAU port. MSAU ports using the hermaphrodite connector need to be reinitialized with the setup tool. Removing drop cables and reinitializing each

MSAU port is a quick fix that is useful on relatively small token-ring networks.

Isolating problems with patch cables, adapter cables, and MSAUs is easier to do if you have a current log of your network's physical design. After you narrow down the problem, you can isolate potential problem areas from the rest of the network and then use a cable tester to find the actual problem.

Troubleshooting Modems

A modem presents all the potential problems you find with any other device. You must make sure that the modem is properly installed, that the driver is properly installed, and that the resource settings do not conflict with other devices. Modems also pose some unique problems because they must connect directly to the phone system, they operate using analog communications, and they must make a point-to-point connection with a remote machine.

The online help files for both Windows NT and Windows 95 include a topic called the Modem Troubleshooter. The Modem Troubleshooter leads you to possible solutions for a modem problem by asking questions about the symptoms. As you answer the questions (by clicking the gray box beside your answer), the Modem Troubleshooter zeroes in on more specific questions until (ideally) it leads you to a solution.

Some common modem problems are as follows:

◆ **Dialing problems**. The dialing feature is improperly configured. For instance, the modem isn't dialing 9 to bypass your office switchboard, or it is dialing 9 when you're away from your office. The computer also could be dialing an area code or an international code when it shouldn't. Check the dialing properties for the connection.

◆ **Connection problems**. You cannot connect to another modem. Your modem and the other modem might be operating at different speeds.

Verify that the maximum speed setting for your modem is the highest speed that both your modem and the other modem can use. Also make sure the Data Bits, Parity, and Stop Bits settings are consistent with the remote computer.

◆ **Digital phone systems**. You cannot plug a modem into a telephone line designed for use with digital phone systems. These digital phone systems are commonplace in most office environments.

◆ **Protocol problems**. The communicating devices are using incompatible line protocols. Verify that the devices are configured for the same or compatible protocols. If one computer initiates a connection using PPP, the other computer must be capable of using PPP.

Repeaters, Bridges, and Routers

Issues dealing with repeaters, bridges, and routers are often more technically advanced than those covered in a book such as Networking Essentials. Companies such as Cisco, Bay Networks, and 3Com have their own dedicated books and courses on dealing with the installation, configuration, and troubleshooting of repeaters, bridges, and routers. In general, there are some basic troubleshooting steps you can do when working with these three devices.

Repeaters are responsible for regenerating a signal sent down the transmission media. The typical problem with repeaters is that they do not work—that is, the signal is not being regenerated. If this is the case, the signal being sent to devices on the other side of the repeater from the sending device will not receive the signal.

Problems with bridges are almost identical to that of a repeater. The signal being sent to devices on the other side of the bridge from the sending device will be received. Other issues with bridges are that the table of

which devices are on which interface of the bridge can get corrupt. This can lead from one to all machines not receiving packets on the network. Diagnostic utilities provided by the bridge's manufacturer can resolve this type of problem.

Problems with routers can be complex, and troubleshooting them often involves a high level of understanding of the different protocols in use on the network, as well as the software and commands used to program a router. There are generally two types of router problems.

The first router problem that is commonly found is that packets are just not being passed through because the router is 'dead' or simply not functioning. The second common problem with routers is that the routing tables within the routers are corrupted or incorrectly programmed. This problem either leads to computers on different networks being unable to communicate with each other or to the fact that certain protocols simply do not work.

Resolve Broadcast Storms

A *broadcast storm* is a sudden flood of broadcast messages that clogs the transmission medium, approaching 100 percent of the bandwidth. Broadcast storms cause performance to decline and, in the worst case, computers cannot even access the network. The cause of a broadcast storm is often a malfunctioning network adapter, but a broadcast storm also can be caused when a device on the network attempts to contact another device that either doesn't exist or for some reason doesn't respond to the broadcast.

If the broadcast messages are viable, a network-monitoring or protocol-analysis tool often can determine the source of the storm. If the broadcast storm is caused by a malfunctioning adapter throwing illegible packets onto the line, and a protocol analyzer can't find the source, try to isolate the offending PC by removing computers from the network one at a time until the line returns to normal.

Identify and Resolve Network Performance Problems

If your network runs slower than it used to run (or slower than it ought to run), the problem might be that the present network traffic exceeds the level at which the network can operate efficiently. Some possible causes for increased traffic are new hardware (such as a new workstation) or new software (such as a network computer game or some other network application). A generator or another mechanical device operating near the network could cause a degradation of network performance. In addition, a malfunctioning network device could act as a bottleneck. Ask yourself what has changed since the last time the network operated efficiently, and begin there with your troubleshooting efforts.

A performance monitoring tool, such as Windows NT's Performance Monitor or Network Monitor, can help you look for bottlenecks that are adversely affecting your network. For instance, the increased traffic could be the result of increased usage. If usage exceeds the capacity of the network, you might want to consider expanding or redesigning your network. You also might want to divide the network into smaller segments by using a router or a bridge to reduce network traffic. A protocol analyzer can help you measure and monitor the traffic at various points on your network.

Now that you have thoroughly read through this book, worked through the exercises and got as much hands on exposure to NT Server as you could, you've now booked your exam. This chapter is designed as a last minute cram for you as you walk out the door on your way to the exam. You can't re-read the whole book in an hour, but you will be able to read this chapter in that time.

This chapter is organized by objective category, giving you not just a summary, but a rehash of the most important point form facts that you need to know. Remember that this is meant to be a review of concepts and a trigger for you to remember wider definitions. In addition to what is in this chapter, make sure you know what is in the glossary because this chapter does not define terms. If you know what is in here and the concepts that stand behind it, chances are the exam will be a snap.

Fast Facts

WINDOWS NT SERVER 4 EXAM

PLANNING

Remember: Here are the elements that Microsoft says they test on for the "Planning" section of the exam.

◆ Plan the disk drive configuration for various requirements. Requirements include: choosing a file system and fault tolerance method

◆ Choose a protocol for various situations. Protocols include: TCP/IP, NWLink IPX/SPX Compatible Transport, and NetBEUI

Minimum requirement for installing NT Server on an Intel machine is 468DX/33, 16MB of RAM, and 130MB of free disk space.

The login process on an NT Domain is as follows:

1. WinLogon sends the user name and password to the Local Security Authority (LSA).

2. The LSA passes the request to the local NetLogon service.

3. The local NetLogon service sends the logon information to the NetLogon service on the domain controller.

4. The NetLogon service on the domain controller passes the information to the domain controller's Security Accounts Manager (SAM).

5. The SAM asks the domain directory database for approval of the user name and password.

6. The SAM passes the result of the approval request to the domain controller's NetLogon service.

7. The domain controller's NetLogon service passes the result of the approval request to the client's NetLogon service.

8. The client's NetLogon service passes the result of the approval request to the LSA.

9. If the logon is approved, the LSA creates an access token and passes it to the WinLogon process.

10. WinLogon completes the logon, thus creating a new process for the user and attaching the access token to the new process.

The system partition is where your computer boots and it must be on an active partition.

The boot partition is where the WINNT folder is found and it contains the NT program files. It can be on any partition (not on a volume set, though).

NT supports two forms of software-based fault tolerance: Disk Mirroring (RAID 1) and Stripe Sets with Paritiy (RAID 5).

Disk Mirroring uses 2 hard drives and provides 50% disk space utilization.

Stripe sets with Parity use between 3 and 32 hard drives and provides a (n-1)/n*100% utilization (n = number of disks in the set).

Disk duplexing provides better tolerance than mirroring because it does mirroring with separate controllers on each disk.

NT Supports 3 file systems: NTFS, FAT, and CDFS (it no longer supports HPFS, the OS/2 file system nor does it support FAT32, a file system used by Windows 95).

The following table is a comparison of NTFS and FAT features:

Table 1.1 shows a quick summary of the differences between file systems:

SUMMARY TABLE 1
FAT VERSUS NTFS COMPARISON

Feature	FAT	NTFS
File name length	255	255
8.3 file name compatibility	Yes	Yes
File size	4 GB	16 EB
Partition size	4 GB	16 EB
Directory structure	Linked list	B-tree
Local security	No	Yes
Transaction tracking	No	Yes
Hot fixing	No	Yes
Overhead	1 MB	>4 MB
Required on system partition for RISC-based computers	Yes	No
Accessible from MS-DOS/ Windows 95	Yes	No
Accessible from OS/2	Yes	No
Case-sensitive	No	POSIX only
Case preserving	Yes	Yes

Feature	FAT	NTFS
Compression	No	Yes
Efficiency	200 MB	400 MB
Windows NT formattable	Yes	Yes
Fragmentation level	High	Low
Floppy disk formattable	Yes	No

The following is a table to summarize the protocols commonly used by NT for network communication:

SUMMARY TABLE 2
PRIMARY PROTOCOL USES

Protocol	Primary Use
TCP/IP	Internet and WAN connectivity
NWLink	Interoperability with NetWare
NetBEUI	Interoperability with old Lan Man networks

The main points regarding TCP/IP are as follows:

- ◆ Requires IP Address, and Subnet Mask to function (default Gateway if being routed)

- ◆ Can be configured manually or automatically using DHCP server running on NT

- ◆ Common address resolution methods are WINS and DNS

INSTALLATION AND CONFIGURATION

Remember: Here are the elements that Microsoft says they test on for the "Installation and Configuration" section of the exam.

- ◆ Install Windows NT Server on Intel-based platforms.

- ◆ Install Windows NT Server to perform various server roles. Server roles include: Primary domain controller, Backup domain controller, and Member server.

- ◆ Install Windows NT Server by using various methods. Installation methods include: CD-ROM, Over-the-network, Network Client Administrator, and Express versus custom.

- ◆ Configure protocols and protocol bindings. Protocols include: TCP/IP, NWLink IPX/SPX Compatible Transport, and NetBEUI.

- ◆ Configure network adapters. Considerations include: changing IRQ, IObase, and memory addresses and configuring multiple adapters.

- ◆ Configure Windows NT server core services. Services include: Directory Replicator, License Manager, and Other services.

- ◆ Configure peripherals and devices. Peripherals and devices include: communication devices, SCSI devices, tape devices drivers, UPS devices and UPS service, mouse drivers, display drivers, and keyboard drivers.

- ◆ Configure hard disks to meet various requirements. Requirements include: allocating disk space capacity, providing redundancy, improving security, and formatting.

- ◆ Configure printers. Tasks include: adding and configuring a printer, implementing a printer pool, and setting print priorities.

- ◆ Configure a Windows NT Server computer for various types of client computers. Client computer types include: Windows NT Workstation, Microsoft Windows 95, and Microsoft MS-DOS-based.

The Hardware Compatibility list is used to ensure that NT supports all computer components.

NT can be installed in 3 different configurations in a domain: Primary Domain Controller, Backup Domain Controller, and Member Server.

Two sources can be used for installation files: CD-ROM or network share (which is the hardware specific files from the CD copied onto a server and shared).

Three Setup diskettes are required for all installations when a CD-ROM is not supported by the operating system present on the computer at installation time (or if no operating system exists and the computer will not boot from the CD-ROM.)

WINNT and WINNT32 are used for network installation; WINNT32 for installations when NT is currently present on the machine you are installing to and WINNT when it is not.

The following table is a summary of the WINNT and WINNT32 switches:

SUMMARY TABLE 3
WINNT AND WINNT32 SWITCH FUNCTIONS

Switch	Function
/B	Prevents creation of the three setup disks during the installation process
/S	Indicates the location of the source files for NT installation (e.g., /S:D:\NTFiles)
/U	Indicates the script file to use for an unattended installation (e.g., /U:C:\Answer.txt)
/UDF	Indicates the location of the uniqueness database file which defines unique configuration for each NT machine being installed (e.g., /UDF:D:\Answer.UDF)
/T	Indicates the place to put the temporary installation files
/OX	Initiates only the creation of the three setup disks

Switch	Function
/F	Indicates not to verify the files copied to the setup diskettes
/C	Indicates not to check for free space on the setup diskettes before creating them

To remove NT from a computer you must do the following:

1. Remove all the NTFS partitions from within Windows NT and reformat them with FAT (this ensures that these disk areas will be accessible by non-NT operating systems).

2. Boot to another operating system, such as Windows 95 or MS-DOS.

3. Delete the Windows NT installation directory tree (usually WINNT).

4. Delete pagefile.sys.

5. Turn off the hidden, system, and read-only attributes for NTBOOTDD.SYS, BOOT.INI, NTLDR, and NTDETECT.COM and then delete them. You might not have all of these on your computer, but if so, you can find them all in the root directory of your drive C.

6. Make the hard drive bootable by placing another operating system on it (or SYS it with DOS or Windows 95 to allow the operating system with does exist to boot).

The Client Administrator allows you to do the following:

◆ Make Network Installation Startup disk: shares files and creates bootable diskette for initiating client installation.

◆ Make Installation Disk Set: copies installation files to diskette for installing simple clients like MS-DOS network client 3.0.

◆ Copy Client-Based Network Administration Tools: creates a folder which can be attached to from Windows NT Workstation and Windows 95 clients to install tools for administering an NT Server from a workstation.

MANAGING RESOURCES

Remember: Here are the elements that Microsoft says they test on for the "Managing Resources" section of the exam.

◆ Manage user and group accounts. Considerations include: managing Windows NT groups, managing Windows NT user rights, administering account policies, and auditing changes to the user account database.

◆ Create and manage policies and profiles for various situations. Policies and profiles include: local user profiles, roaming user profiles, and system policies.

◆ Administer remote servers from various types of client computers. Client computer types include: Windows 95 and Windows NT Workstation.

◆ Manage disk resources. Tasks include: copying and moving files between file systems, creating and sharing resources, implementing permissions and security, and establishing file auditing.

Network properties dialog box lets you install and configure the following:

◆ Computer and Domain names

◆ Services

◆ Protocols

◆ Adapters

◆ Bindings

When configuring NWLink ensure that if more than one frame type exists on your network that you don't use AutoDetect or only the first frame type encountered will be detected from then on.

The following table shows you three TCP/IP command-line diagnostic tools and what they do:

SUMMARY TABLE 4
TCP/IP COMMAND LINE DIAGNOSTIC TOOLS

Tool	Function
IPConfig	Displays the basic TCP/IP configuration of each adapter card on a computer (with/all displays detailed configuration information)
Ping	Determines connectivity with another TCP/IP host by sending a message that is echoed by the recipient if received
Tracert	Traces each hop on the way to a TCP/IP host and indicates points of failure if they exist

Network adapter card configuration of IRQ and I/O port address may or may not be configurable from the Network Properties dialog box; it depends on the card.

To allow NT computers to participate in a domain, a computer account must be created for each one.

Windows 95 clients need special profiles and policies created on a Windows 95 machine and then copied onto an NT Server to participate in domain profile and policy configuration.

Windows 95 clients need printer drivers installed on an NT Server acting as a print controller to print to an NT controller printer.

Typical services tested for NT Server are listed and described in the following table:

SUMMARY TABLE 5
NT SERVER SERVICES AND THEIR FUNCTIONS

Service	Function
DNS	Provides TCP/IP address resolution using a static table and can be use for non-Microsoft hosts
WINS	Provides TP/IP address resolution using a dynamic table and can be used for Microsoft hosts
DHCP	Provides automatic configuration of TCP/IP clients for Microsoft clients
Browser	Provides a list of domain resources to Network Neighborhood and Server Manager
Replicator	Provides import and export services for automated file distribution between NT computers (Servers can be export and import, Workstations can only be import)

REGEDT32.EXE and REGEDIT are used to view and modify registry settings in NT.

The five registry subtrees are:

◆ **HKEY_LOCAL_MACHINE.** Stores all the computer-specific configuration data.

◆ **HKEY_USERS.** Stores all the user-specific configuration data.

◆ **HKEY_CURRENT_USER.** Stores all configuration data for the currently logged on user.

◆ **HKEY_CLASSES_ROOT.** Stores all OLE and file association information.

◆ **HKEY_CURRENT_CONFIG.** Stores information about the hardware profile specified at start-up.

REGEDT32.EXE allows you to see and set security on the registry and allows you to open the registry in read-only mode, but does not allow you to search by key value.

NT checking for serial mice at boot may disable a UPS. To disable that check, place the /noserialmice in the boot line in the BOOT.INI file.

The SCSI adapters icon in the Control Panel lets you add and configure SCSI devices as well as CD-ROM drives.

Many changes made in the disk administrator require that you choose the menu Partition, Commit Changes for them to take effect.

Although you can set drive letters manually, the following is how NT assigns letters to partitions and volumes:

1. Beginning from the letter C:, assign consecutive letters to the first primary partition on each physical disk.

2. Assign consecutive letters to each logical drive, completing all on one physical disk before moving on to the next.

3. Assign consecutive letters to the additional primary partitions, completing all on one physical disk before moving on to the next.

Disk Administrator allows for the creation of two kinds of partitions (primary and extended) and four kinds of volumes (volume set, stripe set, mirror set, and stripe set with parity). The following table is a summary of their characteristics:

SUMMARY TABLE 6
PARTITION CHARACTERISTICS

Object	Characteristics
Primary partition	Non-divisible disk unit which can be marked active and can be made bootable.
	Can have up to four on a physical drive.
	NT system partition must be on a primary.
Extended partition	Divisible disk unit which must be divided into logical disks (or have free space used in a volume) in order to function as space storage tool.
	Can have only one on a physical drive.
	Logical drive within can be the NT boot partition.
Volume Set	Made up of 2-32 portions of free space which do not have to be the same size and which can be spread out over between 1 and 32 disks of many types (IDE, SCSI, etc.).
	Can be added to if formatted NTFS.
	Cannot contain NT boot or system partition.
	Removing one portion of the set destroys the volume and the data is lost.
	Is not fault tolerant.
Stripe Set	Made up of 2-32 portions of free space which have to be the same size and which can be spread out over between 2 and 32 disks of many types (IDE, SCSI, etc.).
	Cannot be added to and removing one portion of the set destroys the volume and the data is lost.
	Is not fault tolerant.
Mirror Set	Made up of 2 portions of free space which have to be the same size and which must be on 2 physical disks.
	Identical data is written to both mirror partitions and they are treated as one disk.
	If one disk stops functioning the other will continue to operate.
	The NT Boot and System partitions can be held on a mirror set.
	Has a 50% disk utilization rate.
	Is fault tolerant.
Stripe Set with Parity	Made up of 3-32 portions of free space which have to be the same size and must be spread out over the same number of physical disks.
	Maintains fault tolerance by creating parity information across a stripe.
	If one disk fails, the stripe set will continue to function, albeit with a loss of performance.
	The NT Boot and System partitions cannot be held on a Stripe Set with Parity.
	Is fault tolerant.

Disk Administrator can be used to format partitions and volumes either FAT or NTFS.

If you have any clients who access a shared printer that are not using NT or are not using the same hardware platform as your printer server then you must install those drivers when you share the printer.

By assigning different priorities for printers associated with the same print device you can create a hierarchy among users' print jobs, thus ensuring that the print jobs of some users print sooner than others.

By adjusting the printer schedule you can ensure that jobs sent to particular printers are only printed at certain hours of the day.

A printer has permissions assigned to it. The following is a list of the permissions for printers.

- **No Access.** Completely restricts access to the printer.

- **Print.** Allows a user or group to submit a print job, and to control the settings and print status for that job.

- **Manage Documents.** Allows a user or group to submit a print job, and to control the settings and print status for all print jobs.

- **Full Control.** Allows a user to submit a print job, and to control the settings and print status for all documents as well as for the printer itself. In addition, the user or group may share, stop sharing, change permissions for, and even delete the printer.

Printer pools consist of one or more print devices that can use the same print driver controlled by a single printer.

MS-DOS users must have print drivers installed locally on their computers.

The assignment of permissions to resources should use the following procedure:

1. Create user accounts.

2. Create global groups for the domain and populate the groups with user accounts.

3. Create local groups and assign them rights and permissions to resources and programs in the domain.

4. Place global groups into the local groups you have created, thereby giving the users who are members of the global groups access to the system and its resources.

The built-in local groups in a Windows NT Domain are as follows:

- Administrators
- Users
- Guests
- Backup Operators
- Replicator
- Print Operators
- Server Operators
- Account Operators

The built-in global groups in an NT Domain are as follows:

- Domain Admins
- Domain Users
- Domain Guests

The system groups on an NT server are as follows:

- Everyone
- Creator Owner

◆ Network

◆ Interactive

The built-in users on an NT server are as follows:

◆ Administrator

◆ Guest

The following table describes the buttons on the User Properties dialog box and their functions:

SUMMARY TABLE 7
BUTTONS ON THE USER PROPERTIES DIALOG BOX

Button	Function
Groups	Enables you to add and remove group memberships for the account. The easiest way to grant rights to a user account is to add it to a group that possesses those rights.
Profile	Enables you to add a user profile path, a logon script name, and a home directory path to the user's environment profile. You learn more about the Profile button in the following section.
Hours	Enables you to define specific times when the users can access the account. (The default is always.)
Logon To	Enables you to specify up to 8 workstations from which the user can log on. (The default is all workstations.)
Account	Enables you to provide an expiration date for the account. (The default is never.) You also can specify the account as global (for regular users in this domain) or domain local.

The following table is a summary of the account policy fields:

SUMMARY TABLE 8
ACCOUNT POLICY FIELDS

Button	Function
Maximum Password Age	The maximum number of days a password can be in effect until it must be changed.
Minimum Password Age	The minimum number of days a password must stay in effect before it can be changed.
Minimum Password Length	The minimum number of characters a password must include.
Password Uniqueness	The number of passwords that NT remembers for a user; these passwords cannot be reused until they are no longer remembered.
Account Lockout	The number of incorrect passwords that can be input by a user before the account becomes locked. Reset will automatically set the count back to 0 after a specified length of time. In addition the duration of lockout is either a number of minutes or forever (until an administrator unlocks it).
Forcibly disconnect remote users from server when logon hours expire	In conjunction with logon hours, this checkbox enables forcible disconnection of a user when authorized hours come to a close.
Users must log on in order to change password	Ensures that a user whose password has expired cannot change his or her password but has to have it reset by an administrator.

Account SIDs are unique; therefore, if an account is deleted, the permissions cannot be restored by recreating an account with the same name.

Local profiles are only available from the machine on which they were created, whereas roaming profiles can be accessed from any machine on the network.

A mandatory profile is a roaming profile that users cannot change. They have the extension .MAN.

Hardware profiles can be used with machines that have more than one hardware configuration (such as laptops).

The System Policy editor (POLEDIT) has two modes, Policy File mode and Registry Mode.

The application of system policies is as follows:

1. When you log in, the NT Config.pol is checked. If there is an entry for the specific user, then any registry settings indicated will be merged with, and overwrite if necessary, the users registry.

2. If there is no specific user entry, any settings for groups that the user is a member of will be applied to the user.

3. If the user is not present in any groups and not listed explicitly then the Default settings will be applied.

4. If the computer that the user is logging in on has an entry, then the computer settings are applied.

5. If there is not a computer entry for the user then the default computer policy is applied.

Windows 95 policies are not compatible with NT and therefore Windows 95 users must access a Windows 95 policy created on an Windows 95 machine and copied to an NT machine and named Config.Pol.

The Net Use command line can be used to map a drive letter to a network share; using the /persistent switch ensures that it is reconnected at next logon.

FAT long file names under NT have 8.3 aliases created to ensure backward compatibility. The following is an example of how aliases are generated from 5 files that all have the same initial characters:

Team meeting Report #3.doc	TEAMME~1.DOC
Team meeting Report #4.doc	TEAMME~2.DOC
Team meeting Report #5.doc	TEAMME~3.DOC
Team meeting Report #6.doc	TEAMME~4.DOC
Team meeting Report #7.doc	TE12B4~1.DOC

A long file name on a FAT partition uses one file name for the 8.3 alias and then one more FAT entry for every 13 characters in the name.

A FAT partition can be converted to NTFS without loss of data through the command line

CONVERT <drive>: /FS:NTFS

NTFS supports compression as a file attribute that can be set in the file properties.

Compression can be applied to a folder or a drive and the effect is that the files within are compressed and any file copied into it will also become compressed.

Compression can be applied through the use of the COMPACT.EXE program through the syntax

COMPACT <file or directory path> [/switch]

The available switches for COMPACT are as follows:

SUMMARY TABLE 9
COMPACT Switches

Switch	Function
/C	Compress
/U	Uncompress
/S	Compress an entire directory tree
/A	Compress hidden and system files
/I	Ignore errors and continue compressing
/F	Force compression even if the objects are already compressed
/Q	Display only summary information

Share-level permissions apply only when users access a resource over the network, not locally. The share-level permissions are:

- **No Access.** Users with No Access to a share can still connect to the share, but nothing appears in File Manager except the message You do not have permission to access this directory.

- **Read.** Allows you to display folder and file names, display file content and attributes, run programs, open folders inside the shared folder.

- **Change.** Allows you to create folders and files, change file content, change file attributes, delete files and folders, do everything READ permission allows.

- **Full Control.** Allows you to change file permissions and do everything change allows for.

Share-level permissions apply to the folder that is shared and apply equally to all the contents of that share.

Share-level permissions apply to any shared folder, whether on FAT or NTFS.

NTFS permissions can only be applied to any file or folder on an NTFS partition.

The actions that can be performed against an NTFS object are as follows:

- Read (R)
- Write (W)
- Execute (X)
- Delete (D)
- Change Permissions (P)
- Take Ownership (O)

The NTFS permissions available for folders are summarized in the following table:

SUMMARY TABLE 10
NTFS Folder Permissions

Permission	Action permitted
No Access	none
List	RX
Read	RX
Add	WX
Add & Read	RXWD
Change	RXWD
Full Control	RXWDPO

The NTFS permissions available for files are summarized in the following table:

SUMMARY TABLE 11
NTFS FILE PERMISSIONS

Permission	Action permitted
No Access	none
Read	RX
Add & Read	RX
Change	RXWD
Full Control	RXWDPO

If a user is given permission to a resource and a group or groups that the user is a member is also given access then the effective permission the user has is the cumulation of all of the user permissions. This applies unless any of the permissions are set to No Access in which case the user has no access to the resource.

If a user is given permission to a shared resource and is also given permission to that resource through NTFS permissions then the effective permission is the most restrictive permission.

The File Child Delete scenario manifests itself when someone has full control to a folder but is granted a permission which does not enable deletion (Read or No Access, for example). The effect is that a user will be able to delete files inside the folder even though sufficient access does not appear to be present.

To close the File Child Delete loophole, do not grant a user Full Control access to a folder but instead, use special Directory permissions to assign RXWDPO access, this eliminates the File Child Delete permission.

Access Tokens do not refresh and a user needs to log off and log back on if changed permissions are to take effect.

MONITORING AND OPTIMIZATION

Remember: Here are the elements that Microsoft says they test on for the "Monitoring and Optimization" section of the exam.

◆ Monitor performance of various functions by using Performance Monitor. Functions include: processor, memory, disk, and network.

◆ Identify performance bottlenecks.

Performance monitor has 4 views: chart, alert, log, and report.

The subsystems that are routinely monitored are: Memory, Disk, Network, and Processor.

Disk counters can be enabled through the command line:

Diskperf –y

Or

Diskperf –ye (for RAID disks and volumes)

TROUBLESHOOTING

Remember: Here are the elements that Microsoft says they test on for the "Troubleshooting" section of the exam.

◆ Choose the appropriate course of action to take to resolve installation failures.

◆ Choose the appropriate course of action to take to resolve boot failures.

- ◆ Choose the appropriate course of action to take to resolve configuration errors.

- ◆ Choose the appropriate course of action to take to resolve printer problems.

- ◆ Choose the appropriate course of action to take to resolve RAS problems.

- ◆ Choose the appropriate course of action to take to resolve connectivity problems.

- ◆ Choose the appropriate course of action to take to resolve fault tolerance problems. Fault-tolerance methods include: tape backup, mirroring, stripe set with parity, and disk duplexing.

The acronym DETECT can be used to define the troubleshooting process and stands for:

- ◆ Discover the problem.

- ◆ Explore the boundaries.

- ◆ Track the possible approaches.

- ◆ Execute an Approach.

- ◆ Check for success.

- ◆ Tie up loose ends.

An NTHQ diskette can test a computer to ensure that NT will successfully install on it.

The following list identifies possible sources of installation problems:

- ◆ Media errors

- ◆ Insufficient disk space

- ◆ Non-supported SCSI adapter

- ◆ Failure of dependancy service to start

- ◆ Inability to connect to the domain controller

- ◆ Error in assigning domain name

The files involved in the boot process are identified in the following table for both Intel and RISC machines:

SUMMARY TABLE 12
FILES INVOLVED IN THE BOOT PROCESS

Intel	RISC
NTLDR	OSLOADER.EXE
BOOT.INI	NTOSKRNL.EXE
NTDETECT.COM	
NTOSKRNL.EXE	

In the NT boot process (in BOOT.INI) ARC paths define the physical position of the NT operating system files and come in two forms:

Scsi(0)disk(0)rdisk(0)partition(1)\WINNT

Multi(0)disk(0)rdisk(0)partition(1)\WINNT

SCSI arc paths define hard drives which are SCSI and which have their bios disabled. The relevant parameters are:

- ◆ SCSI: the SCSI controller starting from 0

- ◆ DISK: the physical disk starting from 0

- ◆ PARTITION: the partition on the disk stating from 1

- ◆ \folder: the folder in which the NT files are located

MULTI arc paths define hard drives which are non-SCSI or SCSI with their bios enabled. The relevant parameters are:

- ◆ MULTI: the controller starting from 0

- ◆ RDISK: the physical disk starting from 0

◆ PARTITION: the partition on the disk stating from 1

◆ \folder: the folder in which the NT files are located

Partitions are numbered as follows:

1. The first primary partition on each disk gets the number 0.

2. Each additional primary partition then is given a number, incrementing up from 0.

3. Each logical drive is then given a number in the order they appear in the Disk Administrator.

Switches on boot lines in the boot.ini file define additional boot parameters. The following table lists the switches you need to know about and their function:

SUMMARY TABLE 13
BOOT.INI FILE SWITCHES

Switch	Function
/basevideo	Loads standard VGA video driver (640x480, 16 color)
/sos	Displays each driver as it is loaded
/noserialmice	Prevents autodetection of serial mice on COM ports which may disable a UPS connected to the port

A recovery disk can be used to bypass problems with system partition. Such a disk contains the following files (broken down by hardware platform):

SUMMARY TABLE 14
FILES ON A FAULT-TOLERANT BOOT DISKETTE

Intel	RISC
NTLDR	OSLOADER.EXE
NTDETECT.COM	HAL.DLL

Intel	RISC
BOOT.INI	*.PAL (for Alpha machines)
BOOTSECT.DOS (allows you to boot to DOS)	
NTBOOTDD.SYS (the SCSI driver for a hard drive with SCSI bios not enabled)	

An Emergency repair disk can be used to recover an NT system if the registry becomes corrupted and must be used in conjunction with the three setup diskettes used to install NT.

The RDISK programs allows you to update the \REPAIR folder which in turn is used to update your repair diskette.

The Event Viewer allows you to see three log files: System Log, Security Log, and Application Log.

The Windows NT Diagnostics program allows you to see (but not modify) configuration settings for much of your hardware and environment.

The course of action to take when a stop error occurs (blue screen) can be configured from the System Properties dialog box (in the Control Panel) on the Startup/Shutdown tab.

To move the spool file from one partition to another, use the Advanced Tab on the Server Properties dialog box; this can be located from the File, Server Properties menu in the printers dialog box.

Common RAS problems include the following:

◆ User Permission: user not enabled to use RAS in User Manager for Domains.

◆ Authentication: often caused by incompatible encryption methods (client using different encryption than server is configured to receive).

◆ Callback with Multilink: Client configured for callback but is using multilink; server will only call back to a single number, thereby removing multilink functionality.

◆ Autodial at Logon: Shortcuts on desktop referencing server-based applications or files causes autodial to kick in when logon is complete.

User can't login may be caused by a number of factors including:

◆ Incorrect user name or password

◆ Incorrect domain name

◆ Incorrect user rights (inability to log on locally to an NT machine, for example)

◆ Netlogon service on server is stopped or paused

◆ Domain controllers are down

◆ User is restricted in system policies from logging on at a specific computer

The right to create backups and restore from backups using NT Backup is granted to the groups Administrators, Backup Operators, and Server Operators by default.

NT Backup will only backup files to tape, no other media is supported.

The following table summarizes the backup types available in NT backup:

SUMMARY TABLE 15
BACKUP TYPES AVAILABLE IN NTBACKUP

Type	Backs Up	Marks?
Normal	All selected files and folders	Yes
Copy	All selected files and folders	No
Incremental	Selected files and folders not marked as backed up	Yes
Differential	Selected files and folders not marked as backed up	No
Daily Copy	Selected files and folders changed that day	No

The local registry of a computer can be backed up by selecting the Backup Local Registry checkbox in the Backup Information dialog box.

Data from tape can be restored to the original location or to an alternate location and NTFS permissions can be restored or not, however, you cannot change the names of the objects being restored until the restore is complete.

Backup can be run from a command line using the NTBACKUP command in the syntax:

Ntbackup backup path [switches]

Some command line backup switches are shown in the following table:

SUMMARY TABLE 16
NTBACKUP COMMAND LINE SWITCHES

Switch	Function
/a	Append the current backup to the backup already on the tape
/v	verify the backed up files when complete
/d "text"	Add an identifying description to the backup tape
/t option	specify the backup type. Valid options are: normal, copy, incremental, differential, and daily

To recover from a failed mirror set you must do the following:

1. Shut down your NT server and physically replace the failed drive.

2. If required, boot NT using a recovery disk.

3. Start the Disk Administrator using the menu Start, Programs, Administrative Tools (Common), Disk Administrator.

4. Select the mirror set by clicking on it.

5. From the Fault Tolerance menu choose Break Mirror. This action exposes the remaining partition as a volume separate from the failed one.

6. Reestablish the mirror set if desired by selecting the partition you desire to mirror and a portion of free space equal in size and choosing the menu Fault Tolerance, Establish Mirror.

To regenerate a stripe set with parity do the following:

1. Shut down your NT server and physically replace the failed drive.

2. Start the Disk Administrator using the menu Start, Programs, Administrative Tools (Common), Disk Administrator.

3. Select the stripe set with parity by clicking on it.

4. Select an area of free space as large or larger than the portion of the stripe set that was lost when the disk failed.

5. Choose Fault Tolerance, Regenerate.

Hopefully, this has been a helpful tool in your final review before the exam. You might find after reading this that there are some places in the book you need to revisit. Just remember to stay focused and answer all the questions. You can always go back and check the answers for the questions you are unsure of. Good luck!

The fast facts listed in this section are designed as a refresher of key points and topics that are required to succeed on the Windows NT server 4.0 in the Enterprise exam. By using these summaries of key points, you can spend an hour prior to your exam to refresh key topics, and ensure that you have a solid understanding of the objectives and information required for you to succeed in each major area of the exam.

The following are the main categories Microsoft uses to arrange the objectives:

◆ Planning

◆ Installation and configuration

◆ Managing resources

◆ Connectivity

◆ Monitoring and optimization

◆ Troubleshooting

For each of these main sections, or categories, the assigned objectives are reviewed, and following each objective, review material is offered.

Fast Facts

WINDOWS NT SERVER 4 ENTERPRISE EXAM

PLANNING

Plan the implementation of a directory services architecture. Considerations include the following:

◆ Selecting the appropriate domain model

◆ Supporting a single logon account

◆ Enabling users to access resources in different domains

The main goals of directory services are the following:

◆ One user, one account

◆ Universal resource access

◆ Centralized administration

◆ Directory synchronization

To ensure that you are selecting the best plan for your network, always address each of the goals of directory services.

The requirements for setting up a trust are as follows:

◆ The trust relationship can be established only between Windows NT Server domains.

◆ The domains must be able to make an RPC connection. To establish an RPC connection, you must ensure that a network connection exists between the domain controllers of all participating domains.

◆ The trust relationship must be set up by a user with administrator access.

◆ You should determine the number and type of trusts prior to the implementation.

◆ You must decide where to place the user accounts, as that is the trusted domain.

Trust relationships enable communication between domains. The trusts must be organized, however, to achieve the original goal of directory services. Windows NT domains can be organized into one of four different domain models:

◆ The single-domain model

◆ The single-master domain model

◆ The multiple-master domain model

◆ The complete-trust model

Table 1 summarizes the advantages and disadvantages of the domain models.

TABLE 1
PROFILING THE DOMAIN MODELS

Domain Model	Advantages	Disadvantages
Single-domain model	Centralized administration.	Limited to 40,000 user accounts. No trust relationships. No distribution of resources.
Single-master domain model	Centralized administration. Distributed resources.	Limited to 40,000 user accounts.
Multiple-master domain model	Unlimited number of user accounts; each master domain can host 40,000 user accounts. Distributed resources. Complex trust relationships.	No centralized administration of user accounts.
Complete-trust model	Unlimited number of user accounts; each domain can host 40,000 user accounts. Complex trust relationships.	No centralized administration of user accounts.

Plan the disk drive configuration for various require- ments. Requirements include choosing a fault-tolerance method.

Windows NT Server 4 supports the following fault- tolerant solutions:

◆ RAID Level 0 (disk striping)

◆ RAID Level 1 (disk mirroring)

◆ RAID Level 5 (disk striping with parity)

A comparison of the three fault-tolerance options might help to summarize the information and to ensure that you have a strong understanding of the options available in Windows NT Server 4 (see Table 2).

Choose a protocol for various situations. The protocols include the following:

◆ TCP/IP

◆ TCP/IP with DHCP and WINS

◆ NWLink IPX/SPX Compatible Transport Protocol

◆ Data Link Control (DLC)

◆ AppleTalk

Windows NT Server 4 comes bundled with several pro- tocols that can be used for interconnectivity with other systems and for use within a Windows NT environ- ment. You examine the various protocols, then try to define when each protocol best fits your network needs. The protocols discussed to prepare you for the enter- prise exam are the following:

◆ **NetBEUI.** The NetBEUI protocol is the easiest to implement and has wide support across plat- forms. The protocol uses NetBIOS broadcasts to locate other computers on the network. This process of locating other computers requires addi- tional network traffic and can slow down your entire network. Because NetBEUI uses broadcasts to locate computers, it is not routable; in other words, you cannot access computers that are not on your physical network. Most Microsoft and IBM OS/2 clients support this protocol. NetBEUI is best suited to small networks with no

TABLE 2
SUMMARY OF FAULT-TOLERANCE OPTIONS IN WINDOWS NT SERVER 4

Disk Striping	Disk Mirroring/ Disk Duplexing	Disk Striping with Parity
No fault tolerance.	Complete disk duplication.	Data regeneration from stored parity information.
Minimum of two physical disks, maximum of 32 disks.	Two physical disks	Minimum of three physical disks, maximum of 32 disks.
100 percent available disk utilization.	50 percent available disk utilization.	Dedicates the equivalent of one disk's space in the set for parity information. The more disks, the higher the utilization.
Cannot include a system/boot partition.	Includes all partition types.	Cannot include a system/boot partition.
Excellent read/write performance.	Moderate read/write performance.	Excellent read and moderate write performance.

requirements for routing the information to remote networks or to the Internet.

◆ **TCP/IP.** Transmission Control Protocol/Internet Protocol, or TCP/IP, is the most common protocol—more specifically, it is the most common suite of protocols. TCP/IP is an industry-standard protocol that is supported by most network operating systems. Because of this acceptance throughout the industry, TCP/IP enables your Windows NT system to connect to other systems with a common communication protocol.

The following are advantages of using TCP/IP in a Windows NT environment:

- The capability to connect dissimilar systems

- The capability to use numerous standard connectivity utilities, including File Transfer Protocol (FTP), Telnet, and PING

- Access to the Internet

If your Windows NT system is using TCP/IP as a connection protocol, it can communicate with many non-Microsoft systems. Some of the systems it can communicate with are the following:

- Any Internet-connected system

- UNIX systems

- IBM mainframe systems

- DEC Pathworks

- TCP/IP-supported printers directly connected to the network

◆ **NWLink IPX/SPX Compatible.** The IPX protocol has been used within the NetWare environment for years. By developing an IPX-compatible protocol, Microsoft enables Windows NT systems to communicate with NetWare systems.

NWLink is best suited to networks requiring communication with existing NetWare servers and for existing NetWare clients.

Other utilities must be installed, however, to enable the Windows NT Server system to gain access into the NetWare security. Gateway Services for NetWare/Client Services for NetWare (GSNW/CSNW) must be installed on the Windows NT server to enable the computer to be logged on to a NetWare system. GSNW functions as a NetWare client, but it also can share the connection to the Novell box with users from the Windows NT system. This capability enables a controlled NetWare connection for file and print sharing on the NetWare box, without requiring the configuration of each NT client with a duplicate network redirector or client.

◆ **DataLink Control.** The DLC protocol was originally used for connectivity in an IBM mainframe environment, and maintains support for existing legacy systems and mainframes. The DLC protocol is also used for connections to some network printers.

◆ **AppleTalk.** Windows NT Server can configure the AppleTalk protocol to enable connectivity with Apple Macintosh systems. This protocol is installed with the Services for the Macintosh included with your Windows NT Server CD-ROM. The AppleTalk protocol enables Macintosh computers on your network to access files and printers set up on the Windows NT server. It also enables your Windows NT clients to print to Apple Macintosh printers.

The AppleTalk protocol is best suited to connectivity with the Apple Macintosh.

INSTALLATION AND CONFIGURATION

Install Windows NT Server to perform various server roles. Server roles include the following:

◆ Primary domain controller

◆ Backup domain controller

◆ Member server

The following are different server roles into which Windows NT Server can be installed:

◆ **Primary Domain Controller.** The Primary Domain Controller (PDC) is the first domain controller installed into a domain. As the first computer in the domain, the PDC creates the domain. This fact is important to understand because it establishes the rationale for needing a PDC in the environment. Each domain can contain only one PDC. All other domain controllers in the domain are installed as Backup Domain Controllers. The PDC handles user requests and logon validation, and it offers all the standard Windows NT Server functionality. The PDC contains the original copy of the Security Accounts Manager (SAM), which contains all user accounts and security permissions for your domain.

◆ **Backup Domain Controller.** The Backup Domain Controller (BDC) is an additional domain controller used to handle logon requests by users in the network. To handle the logon requests, the BDC must have a complete copy of the domain database, or SAM. The BDC also runs the Netlogon service; however, the Netlogon service in a BDC functions a little differently than in a PDC. In the PDC, the Netlogon

service handles synchronization of the SAM database to all the BDCs.

◆ **Member server.** In both of the domain controllers, PDC or BDC, the computer has an additional function: The domain controllers handle logon requests and ensure that the SAM is synchronized throughout the domain. These functions add overhead to the system. A computer that handles the server functionality you require without the overhead of handling logon validation is called a *member server*. A member server is a part of the domain, but it does not need a copy of the SAM database and does not handle logon requests. The main function of a member server is to share resources.

After you have installed your computer into a specific server role, you might decide to change the role of the server. This can be a relatively easy task if you are changing a PDC to a BDC or vice versa. If you want to change a domain controller to a member server or member server to a domain controller, however, you must reinstall into the required server role. A member server has a local database that does not participate in domain synchronization. In changing roles, a member server must be reinstalled to ensure that the account database and the appropriate services are installed.

Configure protocols and protocol bindings. Protocols include the following:

◆ TCP/IP

◆ TCP/IP with DHCP and WINS

◆ NWLink IPX/SPX Compatible Transport Protocol

◆ DLC

◆ AppleTalk

You install a new protocol in Windows NT Server through the Network Properties dialog box.

Following are the protocols, and the configuration options available with each:

◆ **TCP/IP.** The following tabs are available for configuration in the Microsoft TCP/IP Properties dialog box:

• **IP Address.** The IP Address tab enables you to configure the IP address, the subnet mask, and the default gateway. You also can enable the system to allocate IP address information automatically through the use of the DHCP server.

An IP address is a 32-bit address that is broken into four octets and used to identify your network adapter card as a TCP/IP host. Each IP address must be a unique address. If you have any IP address conflicts on your computer, you cannot use the TCP/IP protocol.

Your IP address is then grouped into a subnet. The process you use to subnet your network is to assign a subnet mask. A *subnet mask* is used to identify the computers local to your network. Any address outside your subnet is accessed through the default gateway, also called the *router*. The default gateway is the address of the router that handles all routing of your TCP/IP information to computers, or hosts, outside your subnet.

• **DNS.** The DNS tab shows you the options available for configuring your TCP/IP protocol to use a DNS server. The Domain Name System (DNS) server translates TCP/IP host names of remote computers into IP addresses. Remember that an IP address is a unique address for each computer. The DNS server contains a database of all the computers you can access by host name. This database is used when you access a Web page on the Internet. Working with the naming scheme is easier than using the IP address of the computer.

• **WINS Address.** The WINS Address tab enables you to configure your primary and secondary Windows Internet Names Services (WINS) server addresses. WINS is used to reduce the number of NetBIOS broadcast messages sent across the network to locate a computer. By using a WINS server, you keep the names of computers on your network in a WINS database. The WINS database is dynamic.

In configuring your WINS servers, you can enter your primary WINS server and a secondary WINS server. Your system searches the primary WINS server database first, then the secondary database if no match was found in the primary one.

• **DHCP Relay.** The DHCP relay agent is used to find your DHCP servers across routers. DHCP addresses are handed out by the DHCP servers. The client request, however, is made with a broadcast message. Broadcast messages do not cross routers; therefore, this protocol might place some restrictions on your systems. The solution is to use a DHCP relay agent to assist the clients in finding the DHCP server across a router.

In configuring your DHCP relay agent, you can specify the seconds threshold and the maximum number of hops to use in searching for the DHCP servers. At the bottom of the tab, you can enter the IP addresses of the DHCP servers you want to use.

- **Routing.** In an environment in which multiple subnets are used, you can configure your Windows NT Server as a multihomed system. In other words, you can install multiple network adapters, each connecting to a different subnet. If you enable the Enable IP Forwarding option, your computer acts as a router, forwarding the packets through the network cards in the multihomed system to the other subnet.

◆ **NWLINK IPX/SPX Compatible.** The configuration of the NWLink protocol is simple in comparison to the TCP/IP protocol. It is this simplicity that makes it a popular protocol to use.

The NWLink IPX/SPX Properties dialog box has two tabs:

- **General.** On the General tab, you have the option to assign an internal network number. This eight-digit hexadecimal number format is used by some programs with services that can be accessed by NetWare clients.

  You also have the option to select a frame type for your NWLink protocol. The frame type you select must match the frame type of the remote computer with which you need to communicate. By default, Windows NT Server uses the Auto Frame Type Detection setting, which scans the network and loads the first frame type it encounters.

- **Routing.** The Routing tab of the NWLink IPX/SPX Properties dialog box is used to enable or disable the Routing Information Protocol (RIP). If you enable RIP routing over IPX, your Windows NT Server can act as an IPX router.

◆ **DLC.** The configuration of DLC is done through Registry parameters. The DLC protocol is configured based on three timers:

- **T1.** The response timer
- **T2.** The acknowledgment delay timer
- **Ti.** The inactivity timer

The Registry contains the entries that can be modified to configure DLC. You can find the entries at

HKEY_LOCAL_MACHINE\SYSTEM\Current ControlSet\Services\DLC\Parameters\ELNKIII *adapter name*

◆ **AppleTalk.** To install the AppleTalk protocol, you install Services for Macintosh.

Table 3 reviews the protocols that you can configure for your NT enterprise (including the subcomponents—tabs—of each protocol).

TABLE 3
PROTOCOLS TO CONFIGURE

Protocol	Subcomponent (Tab)
TCP/IP	IP Address
	DNS
	WINS Address
	DHCP Relay
	Routing
NWLink IPX/SPX Compatible	General
	Routing
AppleTalk	General
	Routing

The binding order is the sequence your computer uses to select which protocol to use for network communications. Each protocol is listed for each network-based service, protocol, and adapter available.

The Bindings tab contains an option, Show Bindings for, that can be used to select the service, adapter, or protocol you want to modify in the binding order. By clicking the appropriate button, you can enable or disable each binding, or move up or down in the binding order.

Configure Windows NT Server core services. Services include the following:

◆ Directory Replicator

◆ Computer Browser

In this objective, you look at configuring some of the core services in the Windows NT Server. These services are the following:

◆ **Server service.** The Server service answers network requests. By configuring Server service, you can change the way your server responds and, in a sense, the role it plays in your network environment. To configure Server service, you must open the Network dialog box. To do this, double-click the Network icon in the Control Panel. Select the Services tab. In the Server dialog box, you have four optimization settings. Each of these settings modifies memory management based on the role the server is playing. These options are the following:

 • **Minimize Memory Used.** The Minimize Memory Used setting is used when your Windows NT Server system is accessed by less than 10 users.

 This setting allocates memory so a maximum of 10 network connections can be properly maintained. By restricting the memory for network connections, you make more memory available at the local or desktop level.

 • **Balance.** The Balance setting can be used for a maximum of 64 network connections. This setting is the default when using NetBEUI software. Like the Minimize setting, Balance is best used for a relatively low number of users connecting to a server that also can be used as a desktop computer.

 • **Maximize Throughput for File Sharing.** The Maximize Throughput for File Sharing setting allocates the maximum amount of memory available for network connections. This setting is excellent for large networks in which the server is being accessed for file and print sharing.

 • **Maximize Throughput for Network Applications.** If you are running distributed applications, such as SQL Server or Exchange Server, the network applications do their own memory caching. Therefore, you want your system to enable the applications to manage the memory. You accomplish this by using the Maximize Throughput for Network Applications setting. This setting also is used for very large networks.

◆ **Computer Browser service.** The Computer Browser service is responsible for maintaining the list of computers on the network. The browse list contains all the computers located on the physical network. As a Windows NT Server, your system plays a big role in the browsing of a network. The Windows NT Server acts as a master browser or backup browser.

The selection of browsers is through an election. The election is called by any client computer or when a preferred master browser computer starts up. The election is based on broadcast messages.

Every computer has the opportunity to nominate itself, and the computer with the highest settings wins the election.

The election criteria are based on three things:

- The operating system (Windows NT Server, Windows NT Workstation, Windows 95, Windows for Workgroups)

- The version of the operating system (NT 4.0, NT 3.51, NT 3.5)

- The current role of the computer (master browser, backup browser, potential browser)

◆ **Directory Replicator service.** You can configure the Directory Replicator service to synchronize an entire directory structure across multiple servers.

In configuring the directory service, you must select the export server and all the import servers. The export server is the computer that holds the original copy of the directory structure and files. Each import server receives a complete copy of the export server's directory structure. The Directory Replicator service monitors the directory structure on the export server. If the contents of the directory change, the changes are copied to all the import servers. The file copying and directory monitoring is completed by a special service account you create. You must configure the Directory Replicator service to use this service account. The following access is required for your Directory Replicator service account:

- The account should be a member of the Backup Operators and Replicators groups.

- There should be no time or logon restrictions for the account.

- The Password Never Expires option should be selected.

- The User Must Change Password At Next Logon option should be turned off.

When configuring the export server, you have the option to specify the export directory. The default export directory is C:\WINNT\system32\repl\export\.

In the Import Directories section of the Directory Replication dialog box, you can select the import directory. The default import directory is C:\WINNT\system32\repl\import.

Remember that the default directory for executing logon scripts in a Windows NT system is C:\WINNT\system32\repl\import\scripts.

Configure hard disks to meet various requirements. Requirements include the following:

◆ Providing duplication

◆ Improving performance

All hard disk configuration can be done using the Disk Administrator tool. The different disk configurations you need to understand for the enterprise exam are the following:

◆ **Stripe set.** A stripe set gives you improved disk read and write performance; however, it supplies no fault tolerance. A minimum of two disks is required, and the configuration can stripe up to 32 physical disks. A stripe set cannot include the system partition.

◆ **Volume set.** A volume set enables you to extend partitions beyond one physical disk; however, it supplies no fault tolerance. To extend a volume set, you must use the NTFS file system.

◆ **Disk mirroring.** A mirror set uses two physical disks and provides full data duplication. Often referred to as RAID level 1, disk mirroring is a useful solution to assigning duplication to the system partition, as well as any other disks that might be in the system.

◆ **Stripe set with parity.** A stripe set with parity enables fault tolerance in your system. A minimum of three physical disks is required, and a maximum of 32 physical disks can be included in a stripe set with parity. A stripe set with parity cannot include the system partition of your Windows NT system.

The solution that supplies the best duplication and optimization mix is the stripe set with parity.

Configure printers. Tasks include the following:

◆ Adding and configuring a printer

◆ Implementing a printer pool

◆ Setting print priorities

The installation of a printer is a fairly simplistic procedure and is not tested heavily on the exam; however, the printer pool is a key point. The items to remember about printer pools are as follows:

◆ All printers in a printer pool must be able to function using the same printer driver.

◆ A printer pool can have a maximum of eight printers in the pool.

Configure a Windows NT Server computer for various types of client computers. Client computer types include the following:

◆ Windows NT Workstation

◆ Windows 95

◆ Macintosh

The Network Client Administrator is found in the Administrative Tools group. You can use the Network Client Administrator program to do the following:

◆ **Make a Network Installation Startup Disk.** This option creates an MS-DOS boot disk that contains commands required to connect to a network server and that automatically installs Windows NT Workstation, Windows 95, or the DOS network clients.

◆ **Make an Installation Disk Set.** This option enables the creation of installation disks for the DOS network client, LAN Manager 2.2c for DOS, or LAN Manager 2.2c for OS/2.

◆ **Copy Client-Based Network Administration Tools.** This option enables you to share the network administration tools with client computers. The client computers that can use the network administration tools are Windows NT Workstation and Windows 95 computers.

◆ **View Remoteboot Client Information.** This option enables you to view the remoteboot client information. To install remoteboot, go to the Services tab of the Network dialog box.

When installing a client computer, you must ensure that your Windows NT system is prepared for and configured for the client. The Windows clients can connect to the Windows NT server without any configuration required on the server; however, some configuration is required on the client computers. For the Apple Macintosh client, the NT server must install the services for the Macintosh, which includes the AppleTalk protocol. This protocol enables the seamless connection between the Windows NT system and the Apple clients.

MANAGING RESOURCES

Manage user and group accounts. Considerations include the following:

◆ Managing Windows NT user accounts

◆ Managing Windows NT user rights

◆ Managing Windows NT groups

◆ Administering account policies

◆ Auditing changes to the user account database

AGLP stands for Accounts/Global Groups/Local Groups/Permissions. When you want to assign permissions to any resource, you should follow a few simple rules. All user accounts are placed into global groups, and global groups get assigned into local groups. The local groups have the resources and permissions assigned to them.

When you are working with groups across trust relationships, the following guidelines are useful:

◆ Always gather users into global groups. Remember that global groups can contain only user accounts from the same domain. You might have to create the same named global group in multiple domains.

◆ If you have multiple account domains, use the same name for a global group that has the same types of members. Remember that when multiple domains are involved, the group name is referred to as DOMAIN\GROUP.

◆ Before the global groups are created, determine whether an existing local group meets your needs. There is no sense in creating duplicate local groups.

◆ Remember that the local group must be created where the resource is located. If the resource is on

a Domain Controller, create the local group in the Domain Account Database. If the resource is on a Windows NT Workstation or Windows NT Member Server, you must create the group in that system's local account database.

◆ Be sure to set the permissions for a resource before you make the global groups a member of the local group assigned to the resource. That way, you set the security for the resource.

Create and manage policies and profiles for various situations. Policies and profiles include the following:

◆ Local user profiles

◆ Roaming user profiles

◆ System policies

You can configure system policies to do the following:

◆ Implement defaults for hardware configuration—for all computers using the profile or for a specific machine.

◆ Restrict the changing of specific parameters that affect the hardware configuration of the participating system.

◆ Set defaults for all users in the areas of their personal settings that the users can configure.

◆ Restrict users from changing specific areas of their configuration to prevent tampering with the system. An example is disabling all Registry editing tools for a specific user.

◆ Apply all defaults and restrictions on a group level rather than just a user level.

Some common implementations of user profiles are the following:

◆ Locking down display properties to prevent users from changing the resolution of their monitor. Display properties can be locked down as a whole or on each individual property page of display properties. You adjust this setting by clicking the Control Panel, Display, Restrict Display option of the Default User Properties dialog box.

◆ Setting a default color scheme or wallpaper. You can do this by clicking the Desktop option of the Default User Properties dialog box.

◆ If you want to restrict access to portions of the Start menu or desktop, you can do this by clicking the Shell, Restrictions option of the Default User Properties dialog box.

◆ If you need to limit the applications that the user can run at a workstation, you can do so by clicking the System, Restrictions option of the Default User Properties dialog box. You can also use this option to prevent the user from modifying the Registry.

◆ You can prevent users from mapping or disconnecting network drives by clicking the Windows NT Shell, Restrictions option of the Default User Properties dialog box.

Profiles and policies can be very powerful tools to assist in the administrative tasks in your environment. The following list reviews each of the main topics covered in this objective:

◆ **Roaming profiles.** The user portion of the Registry is downloaded from a central location, allowing the user settings to follow the user anywhere within the network environment.

◆ **Local profiles.** The user settings are stored at each workstation and are not copied to other computers. Each workstation that you use will have different desktop and user settings.

◆ **System policies.** System policies enable the administrator to restrict user configuration changes on systems. This enables the administrator to maintain the settings of the desktop of systems without the fear that a user can modify them.

◆ **Computer policies.** Computer policies allow the lockdown of common machine settings that affect all users of that computer.

Administer remote servers from various types of client computers. Client computer types include the following:

◆ Windows 95

◆ Windows NT Workstation

This objective focuses on the remote administration tools available for your Windows NT Server. The following list summarizes the key tools:

◆ **Remote Administration Tools for Windows 95.** Allows User Manager, Server Manager, Event Viewer, and NTFS file permissions to be executed from the Windows 95 computer.

◆ **Remote Administration for Windows NT.** Allows User Manager, Server Manager, DHCP Manager, System Policy Editor, Remote Access Admin, Remote Boot Manager, WINS Manager, and NTFS file permissions to be executed from a Windows NT machine.

◆ **Web Based Administration.** Allows for common tasks to be completed through an Internet connection into the Windows NT Server.

Manage disk resources. Tasks include the following:

◆ Creating and sharing resources

◆ Implementing permissions and security

◆ Establishing file auditing

Windows NT has two levels of security for protecting your disk resources:

- Share permissions
- NTFS permissions

NTFS permissions enable you to assign more comprehensive security to your computer system. NTFS permissions can protect you at the file level. Share permissions, on the other hand, can be applied only to the folder level. NTFS permissions can affect users logged on locally or across the network to the system where the NTFS permissions are applied. Share permissions are in effect only when the user connects to the resource through the network.

The combination of Windows NT share permissions and NTFS permissions determines the ultimate access a user has to a resource on the server's disk. When share permissions and NTFS permissions are combined, no preference is given to one or the other. The key factor is which of the two effective permissions is the most restrictive.

For the exam, remember the following tips relating to managing resources:

- Users can be assigned only to global groups in the same domain.
- Only global groups from trusted domains can become members of local groups in trusting domains.
- NTFS permissions are assigned only to local groups in all correct test answers.
- Only NTFS permissions give you file-level security.

CONNECTIVITY

Configure Windows NT Server for interoperability with NetWare servers by using various tools. The tools include the following:

- Gateway Service for NetWare
- Migration Tool for NetWare

Gateway Service for NetWare (GSNW) performs the following functions:

- GSNW enables Windows NT Servers to access NetWare file and print resources.
- GSNW enables the Windows NT Servers to act as a gateway to the NetWare file and print resources. The Windows NT Server enables users to borrow the connection to the NetWare server by setting it up as a shared connection.

The Migration Tool for NetWare (NWCONV) transfers file and folder information and user and group account information from a NetWare server to a Windows NT domain controller. The Migration Tool can preserve the folder and file permissions if it is being transferred to an NTFS partition.

Connectivity between Windows NT and a NetWare server requires the use of GSNW. If the user and file information from NetWare is to be transferred to a Windows NT Server, the NetWare Conversion utility, NWCONV, is used for this task. The following list summarizes the main points in this section on NetWare connectivity:

- GSNW can be used as a gateway between Windows NT clients and a NetWare server.
- GSNW acts as a NetWare client to the Windows NT Server, allowing the NT server to have a connection to the NetWare server.

◆ GSNW is a service in Windows NT, and is installed using the Control Panel.

◆ For GSNW to be used as a gateway into a NetWare server, a gateway user account must be created and placed in a NetWare group called NTGATEWAY.

◆ In configuring the GSNW as a gateway, you can assign permissions to the gateway share by accessing the GSNW icon in the Control Panel.

◆ For GSNW to be functional, the NWLINK IPX/SPX protocol must be installed and configured.

◆ To convert user and file information from a NetWare server to a Windows NT server, you can use the NWCONV.EXE utility.

◆ NWCONV requires that GSNW be installed prior to any conversion being carried out.

◆ To maintain the NetWare folder- and file-level permissions in the NWCONV utility, you must convert to an NTFS partition on the Windows NT system.

Install and configure multiprotocol routing to serve various functions. Functions include the following:

◆ Internet router

◆ BOOTP/DHCP Relay Agent

◆ IPX router

Multiprotocol routing gives you flexibility in the connection method used by your clients, and in maintaining security. Check out the following:

◆ **Internet router.** Setting up Windows NT as an Internet router is as simple as installing two network adapters in the system, then enabling IP routing in the TCP/IP protocol configuration. This option enables Windows NT to act as a

static router. Note that Windows NT cannot exchange Routing Information Protocol (RIP) routing packets with other IP RIP routers unless the RIP routing software is installed.

◆ **IPX router.** You enable the IPX router by installing the IPX RIP router software by choosing Control Panel, Networks, Services.

After installing the IPX RIP router, Windows NT can route IPX packets over the network adapters installed. Windows NT uses the RIP to exchange its routing table information with other RIP routers.

The inclusion of the industry-standard protocols, and tools to simplify the configuration and extension of your NT network into other environments, makes this operating system a very powerful piece of your heterogenous environment. The following are the main factors to focus on for this objective:

◆ A strong understanding of the functionality of each of the Windows NT protocols—with a strong slant toward TCP/IP and the configuration options available. Understanding and configuration of the DHCP server are also tested on this exam.

◆ The services used to resolve the IP addresses and names of hosts in a TCP/IP environment. DNS service, WINS Service, the Hosts file, and the LMHosts files are among the services tested.

◆ The routing mechanisms available in Windows NT. These mechanisms are powerful, and largely unknown to the vast majority of NT administrators. Ensure that you review the configuration and functionality of Internet or IP routing, as well as the IPX routing tools available.

Install and configure Internet Information Server, and install and configure Internet services. Services include the following:

◆ The World Wide Web

◆ DNS

◆ Intranets

Internet Information Server (IIS) uses Hypertext Transfer Protocol (HTTP), File Transfer Protocol (FTP), and the Gopher service to provide Internet publishing services to your Windows NT Server computer.

IIS provides a graphical administration tool called the Internet Service Manager. With this tool, you can centrally manage, control, and monitor the Internet services in your Windows NT network. The Internet Service Manager uses the built-in Windows NT security model, so it offers a secure method of remotely administering your Web sites and other Internet services.

IIS is an integrated component in Windows NT Server 4.0. The IIS services are installed using the Control Panel, Networks icon or during the installation phase. The following list summarizes the key points in installing and configuring IIS:

◆ The three Internet services included in IIS are HTTP, FTP, and Gopher.

◆ HTTP is used to host Web pages from your Windows NT server system.

◆ FTP is a protocol used for transferring files across the Internet using the TCP/IP protocol.

◆ Gopher is used to create a set of hierarchical links to other computers or to annotate files or folders.

◆ The Internet Service Manager is the utility used to manage and configure your Internet services in IIS.

◆ The Internet Service Manager has three views that you can use to view your services. The three views are Report View, Servers View, and Services View.

Install and configure Remote Access Service (RAS). Configuration options include the following:

◆ Configuring RAS communications

◆ Configuring RAS protocols

◆ Configuring RAS security

RAS supports the Serial Line Internet Protocol (SLIP) and Point-to-Point Protocol (PPP) line protocols, and the NetBEUI, TCP/IP, and IPX network protocols.

RAS can connect to a remote computer using any of the following media:

◆ **Public Switched Telephone Network (PSTN).** (PSTN is also known simply as the phone company.) RAS can connect using a modem through an ordinary phone line.

◆ **X.25.** A packet-switched network. Computers access the network through a Packet Assembler Disassembler (PAD) device. X.25 supports dial-up or direct connections.

◆ **Null modem cable.** A cable that connects two computers directly. The computers then communicate using their modems (rather than network adapter cards).

◆ **ISDN.** A digital line that provides faster communication and more bandwidth than a normal phone line. (It also costs more, which is why not everybody has it.) A computer must have a special ISDN card to access an ISDN line.

RAS is designed for security. The following are some of RAS's security features:

◆ **Auditing.** RAS can leave an audit trail, enabling you to see who logged on when and what authentication they provided.

- **Callback security.** You can enable the RAS server to use callback (hang up all incoming calls and call the caller back), and you can limit callback numbers to prearranged sites that you know are safe.

- **Encryption.** RAS can encrypt logon information, or it can encrypt all data crossing the connection.

- **Security hosts.** In case Windows NT is not safe enough, you can add an extra dose of security by using a third-party intermediary security host—a computer that stands between the RAS client and the RAS server and requires an extra round of authentication.

- **PPTP filtering.** You can tell Windows NT to filter out all packets except ultra safe Point-to-Point Tunneling Protocol (PPTP) packets.

RAS can be a very powerful and useful tool in enabling you to extend the reaches of your network to remote and traveling users. The following list summarizes main points for RAS in preparation for the exam:

- RAS supports SLIP and PPP line protocols.

- With PPP, RAS can support NetBEUI, NWLINK, and TCP/IP across the communication line.

- RAS uses the following media to communicate with remote systems: PSTN, X.25, Null Modem cable, and ISDN.

- The RAS security features available are auditing, callback security, encryption, and PPTP filtering.

- To install RAS, click the Network icon in the Control Panel.

MONITORING AND OPTIMIZATION

Establish a baseline for measuring system performance. Tasks include creating a database of measurement data.

You can use numerous database utilities to analyze the data collected. The following are some of the databases that Microsoft provides:

- Performance Monitor
- Microsoft Excel
- Microsoft Access
- Microsoft FoxPro
- Microsoft SQL Server

The following list summarizes the key items to focus on when you are analyzing your computer and network:

- Establish a baseline measurement of your system when functioning at its normal level. Later, you can use the baseline in comparative analysis.

- Establish a database to maintain the baseline results and any subsequent analysis results on the system, to compare trends and identify potential pitfalls in your system.

- The main resources to monitor are memory, the processor, the disks, and the network.

The following list summarizes the tools used to monitor your NT server that are available and are built into Windows NT Server 4.0:

- Server Manager
- Windows NT Diagnostics
- Response Probe

◆ Performance Monitor

◆ Network Monitor

Monitor performance of various functions by using Performance Monitor. Functions include the following:

◆ Processor

◆ Memory

◆ Disk

◆ Network

To summarize the main views used within Performance Monitor, review the following list:

◆ **Chart view.** This view is very useful for viewing the objects and counters in a real-time mode. This mode enables you to view the data in a graphical format. You can also use the chart view to view the contents of a log file.

◆ **Log view.** This view enables you to set all the options required for creating a log of your system resources or objects. After this log is created, you can view it by using the chart view.

◆ **Alert view.** Use the alert view to configure warnings or alerts of your system resources or objects. In this view, you can configure threshold levels for counters and can then launch an action based on the threshold values being exceeded.

◆ **Report view.** The report view enables you to view the object and counters as an averaged value. This view is useful for comparing the values of multiple systems that are configured similarly.

When monitoring the disk, remember to activate the disk counters using the command diskperf –y. If you do not enter this command, you can select counter but will not see any activity displayed. In the case of a software RAID system, start diskperf with the -ye option.

When you want to monitor TCP/IP counters, make sure that SNMP is installed. Without the SNMP service installed, the TCP/IP counters are not available.

Performance Monitor is a graphical utility that you can use for monitoring and analyzing your system resources within Windows NT. You can enable objects and counters within Performance Monitor; it is these elements that enable the logging and viewing of system data.

In preparing you for this objective, this section introduces numerous objects and counters that you use with Performance Monitor. To prepare for the exam, you need to understand the following key topics:

◆ The four views available in Performance Monitor are the report view, the log view, the chart view, and the alert view.

◆ The main resources to monitor in any system are the disk, the memory, the network, and the processor.

◆ Each of the main resources is grouped as a separate object, and within each object are counters. A counter is the type of data available from a type of resource or object. Each counter might also have multiple instances. An instance is available if multiple components in a counter are listed.

◆ To enable the disk counters to be active, you must run the DISKPERF utility.

Monitor network traffic by using Network Monitor. Tasks include the following:

◆ Collecting data

◆ Presenting data

◆ Filtering data

Network Monitor is a network packet analyzer that comes with Windows NT Server 4. Actually, two versions of Network Monitor are available from Microsoft.

The first version comes with Windows NT Server 4 (simple version). This version can monitor the packets (frames) sent or received by a Windows NT Server 4 computer. The second version comes with Microsoft Systems Management Server (full version). This version can monitor all traffic on the network.

By fully understanding the various components found while analyzing traffic, you will be more successful in locating potential network bottlenecks and offering relevant optimization recommendations. The main components that need to be monitored with your network traffic analysis are the following:

◆ Locate and classify each service. Analyze the amount of traffic generated from each individual service, the frequency of the traffic, and the overall effect the traffic has on the network segment.

◆ Understand the three different types of frames: broadcast, multicast, and directed.

◆ Review the contents of a frame and ensure that you can find the destination address, source address, and data located in each frame.

The following points summarize the key items to understand in building a strong level of knowledge in using Network Monitor as a monitoring tool:

◆ Two versions of Network Monitor are available: the scaled-down version that is built into the Windows NT Server operating system, and the full version that is a component of Microsoft Systems Management Server.

◆ The Network Monitor windows consist of four sections: Graph, Session Statistics, Station Statistics, and Total Statistics.

◆ After Network Monitor captures some data, you use the display window of Network Monitor to view the frames. The three sections of the display window are the Summary pane, the Detail pane, and the Hexadecimal pane.

Identify performance bottlenecks and optimize performance for various results. Results include the following:

◆ Controlling network traffic

◆ Controlling the server load

To optimize the logon traffic in your Windows NT network, you should consider four main points:

◆ Determine the hardware required to increase performance.

◆ Configure the domain controllers to increase the number of logon validations.

◆ Determine the number of domain controllers needed.

◆ Determine the best location for each of the domain controllers.

The following are a few good points to follow in optimizing file-session traffic:

◆ Remove any excess protocols that are loaded.

◆ Reduce the number of wide area network (WAN) links required for file transfer.

The following are three points to consider when attempting to optimize server browser traffic:

◆ Reduce the number of protocols.

◆ Reduce the number of entries in the browse list.

◆ Increase the amount of time between browser updates.

Trust relationships generate a large amount of network traffic. In optimizing your system, attempt to keep the number of trusts very low.

TROUBLESHOOTING

Choose the appropriate course of action to take to resolve installation failures.

Troubleshooting a Windows NT system requires that you have a strong understanding of the processes and tools available to you. To be an effective troubleshooter, first and foremost you must have experience. The following is a list of some common installation problems:

◆ Hard disk problems

◆ Unsupported CD-ROMs

◆ Network adapter problems and conflicts

◆ Naming problems (each computer must be uniquely named, following the NetBIOS naming conventions)

Always use the hardware compatibility list to ensure that your components are supported by Windows NT.

Choose the appropriate course of action to take to resolve boot failures.

For startup errors, try the following:

◆ Check for missing files that are involved in the boot process, including NTLDR, NTDE-TECT.COM, BOOT.INI, NTOSKRNL.EXE, and OSLOADER (RISC).

◆ Modify BOOT.INI for options.

◆ Create an NT boot disk for bypassing the boot process from the hard disk.

◆ Use the Last Known Good option to roll back to the last working set of your Registry settings.

Choose the appropriate course of action to take to resolve configuration errors. Tasks include the following:

◆ Backing up and restoring the Registry

◆ Editing the Registry

You can resolve many problems that you encounter within Windows NT by configuring the Registry. However, before you make any Registry configurations, you must have a strong understanding of the keys within the Registry and always back up the Registry prior to making any modifications to ensure a smooth rollback if additional problems occur. The following are the main tools used to modify the Registry:

◆ REGEDT32

◆ REGEDIT

For configuration problems, remember the following:

◆ Using the Registry for configuration and troubleshooting can cause additional problems if you do not maintain a full understanding of the Registry.

◆ Always back up the Registry prior to editing the contents.

◆ You can back up and restore the local Registry by using REGEDT32.

Choose the appropriate course of action to take to resolve printer problems.

For troubleshooting printers, you should do the following:

◆ Understand and review the overview of the printing process.

◆ Understand the files involved in the printing process.

◆ As a first step in troubleshooting a printer, always verify that the printer is turned on and online.

◆ Note that the most common errors associated with a printer are an invalid printer driver or incorrect resource permissions set for a user.

Choose the appropriate course of action to take to resolve RAS problems.

The following is a list of some of the problems that you might encounter with RAS:

◆ You must ensure that the protocol you are requesting from the RAS client is available on the RAS server. There must be at least one common protocol or the connection will fail.

◆ If you are using NetBEUI, ensure that the name you are using on the RAS client is not in use on the network to which you are attempting to connect.

◆ If you are attempting to connect using TCP/IP, you must configure the RAS server to provide you with an address.

You can use the Remote Access Admin tool to monitor the ports as well as the active connections of your RAS server.

Numerous RAS settings can cause some problems with your RAS connections. Ensure that you understand the installation process, as well as any configuration settings required to enable your RAS server. You can avoid some of the common problems that can occur by doing the following:

◆ Ensuring that the modem and communication medium are configured and functional prior to installing RAS. It can be very difficult to modify settings after the installation, so it is recommended to have all hardware tested and working first.

◆ Verifying that dial-in permissions have been enabled for the required users. This small task is commonly forgotten in your RAS configuration.

Choose the appropriate course of action to take to resolve connectivity problems.

To test and verify your TCP/IP settings, you can use the following utilities:

◆ IPCONFIG

◆ PING

The most effective method for troubleshooting connectivity is to understand thoroughly the installation and configuration options of each of the network protocols. If you understand the options available, you can narrow down the possible problem areas very quickly. Also ensure that you use utilities such as IPCONFIG and PING to test your connections.

Choose the appropriate course of action to take to resolve resource access and permission problems.

You should keep in mind two main issues about permissions:

◆ The default permissions for both share and NTFS give the Windows NT group Everyone full control over the files and folders. Whenever you format a drive as NTFS or first share a folder, you should remove these permissions. The Everyone group contains everyone, including guests and any other user who, for one reason or another, can connect to your system.

◆ The NTFS folder permission delete takes precedence over any file permissions. In all other cases, the file permissions take precedence over the folder permissions.

Choose the appropriate course of action to take to resolve fault-tolerance failures. Fault-tolerance methods include the following:

◆ Tape backup

◆ Mirroring

◆ Stripe set with parity

In using the NTBACKUP tool, the primary thing that you need to do is to determine the frequency and type of backup that you will do. There are three main types of backups that you might want to perform:

♦ **Full.** This backs up all the files that you mark, and marks the files as having been backed up. This is the longest of the backups because it transfers the most data.

♦ **Differential.** This backs up all the files that have changed since the last backup. A differential backup does not mark the files as being backed up. As time passes since the last full backup, the differentials become increasingly larger. However, you need only reload the full backup and the differential to return to the position of the last backup.

♦ **Incremental.** This backs up any files that have changed since the last backup, and then marks them as having been backed up. If your system crashes, you need to start by loading a full backup and then each incremental backup since that full backup.

If you are mirroring the system partition, the disks and partitions should be absolutely identical. Otherwise, the MBR/DBR (master boot record/disk boot record) that contains the driver information will not be correct.

Although ARC naming looks complicated, it is really rather simple. The name is in four parts, of which you use three. The syntax is as follows:

```
multi/scsi(#)disk(#)rdisk(#)partition(#)
```

The following list outlines the parts of the name:

♦ **multi/scsi.** You use either multi or scsi, not both. Use multi in all cases except when using a scsi controller that cannot handle int13 (hard disk access) BIOS routines. Such cases are uncommon. The number is the logical number of the controller with the first controller being 0, the second being 1, and so forth.

♦ **disk.** When you use a scsi disk, you use the disk parameter to indicate which of the drives on the controller is the drive you are talking about. Again, the numbers start at 0 for the first drive and then increase for each subsequent drive.

♦ **rdisk.** Use this parameter for the other controllers in the same way as you use the disk parameter for scsi.

♦ **partition.** This is the partition on the disk that you are pointing at. The first partition is 1, the second is 2, and so forth. Remember that you can have up to four primary partitions, or three primary and one extended. The extended partition is always the last one, and the first logical drive in the partition will have the partition's number. Other drives in the extended partition each continue to add one.

Breaking a mirror set. The boot floppy will get the operating system up and running. You should immediately back up the mirrored copy of the mirror set. To back up the drive, you must break your mirror set. To do this, perform the tasks outlined in Step by Step FF.1.

STEP BY STEP

FF.1 Breaking the Mirror Set

1. Run the Disk Administrator.

2. From the Disk Administrator, click the remaining fragment of the mirrored set.

3. Choose Fault Tolerance, Break Mirror set from the menu.

   At the end of these three steps, you should notice that the mirror set has been broken, and you can now back up the drive.

Regenerating a stripe set with parity. Fixing a stripe set with parity is simple. Perform the tasks outlined in Step by Step FF.2 to regenerate your stripe set with parity.

STEP BY STEP

FF.2 Regenerating the Stripe Set

1. Physically replace the faulty disk drive.

2. Start the Disk Administrator.

3. Select the stripe set with parity that you need to repair and then Ctrl+click the free space of the drive you added to fix the stripe set.

4. Choose Fault Tolerant, Regenerate. Note that this process can take some time, although the process takes less time than restoring from tape.

   The drives regenerate all the required data from the parity bits and the data bits, and upon completion your stripe set with parity is completely functional.

◆ **Share permissions.** A common problem when troubleshooting share resources is in the share permissions. Ensure that the minimum functional permissions have been assigned. Always remove the Everyone group from having full control of a share.

◆ **Combining NTFS and share permissions.** When combining these permissions, remember that NT uses the most restrictive of the permissions when combining. As a rule, use the NTFS permissions as the highest level of permissions, and use the share permissions mainly for access to the folder or share.

◆ **Tape backups.** In any system that you are using, ensure that you have a good backup strategy. Any component in your system can be faulty, and it is your responsibility to have a recovery plan in case of emergencies.

◆ **Disk mirroring.** If you are implementing disk mirroring in your system, ensure that you have created a fault-tolerant boot disk that you can use in case of drive failure. By having this disk pre-configured and handy, you can break the mirror set and replace the drive with very little downtime for your server.

◆ **Stripe set with parity.** This system automatically regenerates data if a drive is faulty. Although your system performance will dramatically decline, it is still a functional box and you risk no possibility of losing any data. If you find that a drive in your stripe set is faulty, replace the drive and use the regenerate command from the Disk Administrator.

Perform advanced problem resolution. Tasks include the following:

◆ Diagnosing and interpreting a blue screen

◆ Configuring a memory dump

◆ Using the event log service

Three utilities come with Windows NT that enable you to work with the memory dump files that are created. You can find all of these utilities on the Windows NT Server CD-ROM. Each utility can be a very helpful tool. The following list briefly describes these utilities:

◆ **DUMPCHK.** This utility checks that the dump file is in order by verifying all the addresses and listing the errors and system information.

◆ **DUMPEXAM.** This creates a text file that can provide the same information that was on the blue screen at the time the stop error occurred.

You need the symbol files and the kernel debugger extensions as well as IMAGEHLP.DLL to run DUMPEXAM.

◆ **DUMPFLOP.** This utility backs up the dump file to a series of floppies so that you can send them to Microsoft.

The following list summarizes the key points required for this objective:

◆ The Event Viewer is a very powerful troubleshooting tool. The three logs that can be viewed through the Event Viewer are the system log, the application log, and the security log.

◆ Cross-reference the events in the Event Viewer with knowledge base articles found on Microsoft TechNet for troubleshooting help.

◆ Interpreting blue screens can be very difficult. Use memory dump files and the following utilities to view your memory dumps to help you isolate the problem:

  • DUMPCHK

  • DUMPEXAM

  • DUMPFLOP

◆ If the problem persists, you might have to use the kernel debugger that is included on the NT Server CD-ROM in the \Support\debug folder.

◆ You can use the kernel debugger to monitor a remote machine through a null modem, or by using the RAS service into a machine that is connected to the problematic computer through a null modem.

Now that you have thoroughly read through this book, worked through the exercises, and picked up as much hands-on exposure to NT Workstation as possible, you're ready to take your exam. This chapter is designed to be a last-minute cram for you as you walk out the door on your way to the exam. You can't re-read the whole book in an hour, but you will be able to read this chapter in that time. This chapter is organized by objective category and summarizes the basic facts you need to know regarding each objective. If you know what is in here, chances are the exam will be a snap.

Fast Facts

WINDOWS NT WORKSTATION 4 EXAM

PLANNING

Remember: Here are the elements that Microsoft says they test on in the "Planning" section of the exam.

◆ Create unattended installation files.

◆ Plan strategies for sharing and securing resources.

◆ Choose the appropriate file system to use in a given situation. File systems and situations include: NTFS, FAT, HPFS, security, and dual-boot systems.

The files used for unattended installation are

◆ An unattended answer file (UNATTEND.TXT)

◆ A uniqueness database file (a .UDF file)

◆ SYSDIFF.EXE

◆ WINDIFF.EXE

Some switches available for WINNT32.EXE are useful for unattended installations:

◆ /u:answerfile (where *answerfile* might be UNATTEND.TXT, for example)

◆ /s:*sourcepath* (where *sourcepath* might be e:\i386, for example)

◆ /udf:*userid*,x:\udf.txt

The content of the OEM directory is copied to the destination machine before NT is installed to allow for additional file or application installation after NT has been installed.

SYSDIFF.EXE can be used to create a snapshot file, a difference file, and/or an .INF file.

.INF files are preferred over difference files because .INF files contain instructions on how to install the software, whereas the difference file contains the whole software package in one large file.

WINDIFF.EXE is used to compare one NT system to another.

The built-in groups in NT Workstation are

◆ Users

◆ Power Users

◆ Administrators

◆ Guests

◆ Backup Operators

◆ Replicator

Table 1 lists the default rights assigned to users or groups on an NT Workstation.

Table 2 lists the built-in capabilities of the built-in groups.

TABLE 1
ASSIGNMENT OF DEFAULT USER RIGHTS

Right	Administrators	Power Users	Users	Guests	Everyone	Backup Operators
Access This Computer from the Network	X	X				X
Back Up Files and Directories	X					X
Change the System Time	X	X				
Force Shutdown from a Remote System	X	X				
Load and Unload Device Drivers	X					
Log On Locally	X	X	X	X	X	X
Manage Auditing and Security Log	X					
Restore Files and Directories	X					X
Shut Down the System	X	X	X		X	X
Take Ownership of Files or Other Objects	X					

TABLE 2
BUILT-IN USER CAPABILITIES

Built-In Capability	Administrators	Power Users	Users	Guests	Everyone	Backup Operators
Create and Manage User Accounts	X	X				
Create and Manage Local Groups	X	X				
Lock the Workstation	X	X	X	X	X	X
Override the Lock of the Workstation	X					
Format the Hard Disk	X					
Create Common Groups	X	X				
Share and Stop Sharing Directories	X	X				
Share and Stop Sharing Printers	X	X				

The following special groups are maintained by NT:

◆ Network

◆ Interactive

◆ Everyone

◆ Creator Owner

Table 3 shows the advantages and disadvantages of storing home directories on a server and on a local computer.

Table 4 shows the advantages and disadvantages of running applications from a server and from a local machine.

TABLE 3
HOME DIRECTORIES ON THE SERVER VERSUS HOME DIRECTORIES ON THE LOCAL COMPUTER

Server-Based Home Directories	*Local Home Directories*
Centrally located so that users can access them from any location on the network.	Available only on the local machine. For roaming users (who log in from more than one computer on the network), the directory is not accessible from other systems.
During a regular backup of the server, information in users' home directories is also backed up.	Often users' local workstations are not backed up regularly as part of a scheduled backup process. If a user's machine fails, the user cannot recover the lost data.
Windows NT does not provide a way to limit the size of a user's directory. Thus, if a lot of information is being stored in home directories, the directories use up a lot of server disk space.	If a user stores a lot of information in his home directory, the space is taken up on his local hard drive instead of the server.
If the server is down, the user won't have access to her files.	The user has access to his files even when the network is down because the files are stored locally.
Some network bandwidth is consumed due to the over-the-network access of data or files.	No network traffic is generated by a user accessing his or her files.

TABLE 4
SHARED NETWORK APPLICATIONS VERSUS LOCALLY INSTALLED APPLICATIONS

Shared Network Applications	*Locally Installed Applications*
Take up less disk space on the local workstation.	Use more local disk space.
Easier to upgrade/control.	Upgrades must "touch" every machine locally.
Use network bandwidth.	Use no network bandwidth for running applications.
Slower response time because applications are accessed from the server.	Faster, more responsive.
If the server is down, users can't run applications.	Users can run applications regardless of server status.

NT Workstation supports the following file formats:

◆ FAT16 (a universal standard format)

◆ NTFS (an NT proprietary format)

◆ CDFS (CD-ROM format)

NT Workstation does not support these file formats:

◆ FAT32 (supported by Windows 95 OSR2 and Windows 98)

◆ HPFS (supported by OS/2)

Table 5 provides a comparison between FAT and NTFS.

TABLE 5

COMPARISON OF NTFS AND FAT FILE SYSTEMS USING WINDOWS NT WORKSTATION

Feature	FAT	NTFS
Support for long filenames (up to 255 characters)	Yes	Yes
Compression	No	Yes
Security	No	Yes
Dual-boot capabilities with non–Windows NT systems	Yes	No
Maximum file/partition size	4GB	16EB
Recommended partition size	0–400MB	400MB–16EB
Capability to format a floppy	Yes	No
Recoverability (transaction logging)	No	Yes

INSTALLATION AND CONFIGURATION

Remember: Here are the elements that Microsoft says they test on in the "Installation and Configuration" section of the exam.

- Install Windows NT Workstation on an Intel platform in a given situation.

- Set up a dual-boot system in a given situation.

- Remove Windows NT Workstation in a given situation.

- Install, configure, and remove hardware components for a given situation. Hardware components include: network adapter drivers, SCSI device drivers, tape device drivers, UPSs, multimedia devices, display drivers, keyboard drives, and mouse drivers.

- Use Control Panel applications to configure a Windows NT Workstation computer in a given situation.

- Upgrade to Windows NT Workstation 4.0 in a given situation.

- Configure server-based installation for wide-scale deployment in a given situation.

NTHQ.EXE (available on the Workstation CD-ROM) can be used to evaluate a computer for NT installation. It is used to verify hardware and produce a report indicating which components are and are not on the HCL.

Table 6 lists the minimum hardware requirements for NT Workstation installation.

NT Workstation supports four installation types. Table 7 lists the components installed with each of the four installation types.

TABLE 6
WINDOWS NT WORKSTATION 4.0 MINIMUM INSTALLATION REQUIREMENTS

Component	Minimum Requirement
CPU	32-bit Intel x86-based (80486/33 or higher) microprocessor or compatible (the 80386 microprocessor is no longer supported)
	Intel Pentium, Pentium Pro, or Pentium II microprocessor
	Digital Alpha AXP-based RISC microprocessor
	MIPS Rx400-based RISC microprocessor
	PowerPC-based RISC microprocessor
Memory	Intel x86-based computers: 12MB RAM
	RISC-based computers: 16MB RAM
Hard disk	Intel x86-based computers: 110MB
	RISC-based computers: 148MB
Display	VGA or better resolution
Other drives	Intel x86-based computers require a high-density 3 ½" floppy drive and a CD-ROM drive (unless you are planning to install Windows NT over a network)
Optional	Network adapter card
	Mouse or other pointing device, such as a trackball

TABLE 7
VARYING COMPONENTS IN FOUR SETUP OPTIONS

Component	Typical	Portable	Compact	Custom
Accessibility options	X	X	None	All options
Accessories	X	X	None	All options
Communications programs	X	X	None	All options
Games			None	All options
Windows Messaging			None	All options
Multimedia	X	X	None	All options

Windows NT Workstation can be installed using a variety of procedures given different circumstances:

◆ Locally, by using the three Setup floppy disks and a CD-ROM

◆ Locally, by using the CD-ROM and creating and using the three Setup floppy disks

◆ Locally, using the CD without Setup floppy disks, but by booting instead to an operating system that recognizes the CD-ROM

◆ Locally, by booting to the CD-ROM from a computer that recognizes the CD-ROM as a boot device

◆ Over the network, by creating and using the three Setup floppy disks

◆ Over the network, but without the Setup floppies

When you're installing NT on a computer with an existing operating system present, if the computer recognizes either the CD-ROM or a supported network adapter and connection to a network share on which the installation files are present, you can use one of two programs to install NT:

◆ **WINNT.EXE.** For installation from existing non-NT operating systems

◆ **WINNT32.EXE.** For installation or upgrade from existing NT installations

Table 8 describes the switches available for use with WINNT.EXE and WINNT32.EXE.

Dual booting is a method of installing two operating systems on a single machine and letting the user choose which will boot at startup time (only one can be booted at any time).

TABLE 8
SWITCHES FOR MODIFYING THE WINNT.EXE AND WINNT32.EXE INSTALLATION PROCESSES

Switch	Effect
/b	Prevents creation of the three Setup boot disks. Create a temporary folder named WIN_NT.~BT and copy to it the boot files that would normally be copied to the three floppies. The contents of the temporary folder are used instead of the Setup boot disks to boot the machine when the user is prompted to restart.
/c	Skips the step of checking for available free space. (This switch cannot be used with WINNT32.EXE.)
/I:*inf_file*	Specifies the name of the Setup information file. The default filename is DOSNET.INF.
/f	Prevents verification of files as they are copied. (This switch cannot be used with WINNT32.EXE.)
/l	Creates a log file called $WINNT.LOG, which lists all errors that occur as files are being copied to the temporary directory. (This switch cannot be used with WINNT32.EXE.)
/ox	Creates the three Setup boot disks and then stops.
/s:*server_path*	Specifies the location of the installation source files.
/u	Allows all or part of an installation to proceed unattended (as detailed in Chapter 1, "Planning"). The /b option for floppyless installation is automatically invoked, and the /s option for location of the source files must be used. The /u option can be followed with the name of an answer file to fully automate installation.
/udf	During an unattended installation, specifies settings unique to a specific computer, which are contained in a uniqueness database file (see Chapter 1).
/w	This *undocumented* flag enables the WINNT.EXE program to execute in Windows (normally, it must be executed from an MS-DOS command prompt).
/x	Prevents creation of the three Setup boot disks. You must already have the three boot disks.

NT Workstation can dual boot with any of the following operating systems:

- ◆ MS-DOS
- ◆ Microsoft Windows (3.1, 3.11, 95, 98)
- ◆ OS/2
- ◆ Microsoft Windows NT (Server or Workstation, any version)

Dual booting with an operating system other than NT (Server or Workstation) requires that at least the primary partition be formatted FAT.

If you remove NT Workstation from a machine, you must SYS (for the OS that remains) on the primary partition to remove the following:

- ◆ All paging files (C:\PAGEFILE.SYS)
- ◆ C:\BOOT.INI, C:\BOOTSECT.DOS, C:\NTDETECT.COM, C:\NTLDR (these are hidden, system, read only files)
- ◆ *.PAL (on Alpha computers)
- ◆ NTBOOTDD.SYS (on computers with SCSI drives with the BIOS disabled)
- ◆ The *winnt_root* folder
- ◆ The C:\Program files\Windows Windows NT folder

Most device drivers not written for NT 4.0 will not work with NT 4.0 (that includes network adapter drivers for NT 3.51 and Windows 95).

All mass storage device installation and settings (including those for tape drives and IDE hard drives) are configured from the SCSI icon in the Control Panel.

During boot, NT's automatic hardware detection process can cause a UPS to shut off because of a pulse that's sent through the COM port to detect a serial mouse. This can be prevented by including the /noserialmice switch in the boot line of the BOOT.INI file.

MANAGING RESOURCES

Remember: Here are the elements that Microsoft says they test on in the "Managing Resources" section of the exam.

- ◆ Create and manage local user accounts and local group accounts to meet given requirements.
- ◆ Set up and modify user profiles.
- ◆ Set up shared folders and permissions.
- ◆ Set permissions on NTFS partitions, folders, and files.
- ◆ Install and configure printers in a given environment.

Using local groups to assign rights and permissions on an NT Workstation can reduce administrative overhead.

The following account policies can be set from the User Manager:

- ◆ **Maximum Password Age.** This option enables you to specify how long a user's password is valid. The default is that passwords expire in 42 days.

- ◆ **Minimum Password Age.** This specifies how long a user must keep a particular password before she can change it again. If you force a user to change her password, and you leave this set to Allow Changes Immediately, after the user has changed her password once, she can change it right back to the old one. If you are requiring password changes for security reasons, this breaks down your security. For that reason, you may want to set a minimum password age.

- ◆ **Minimum Password Length.** The default on Windows NT is to allow blank passwords. Once again, for security reasons, you may not want to allow this. You can set a minimum password length of up to 14 characters, which is the maximum password length allowed under Windows NT.

◆ **Password Uniqueness.** If you want to force users to use a different password each time they change their passwords, you can set a value for password uniqueness. If you set the password uniqueness value to remember two passwords, when a user is prompted to change her password, she cannot use the same password again until she changes her password for the third time. The maximum password uniqueness value is 24.

◆ **Lockout After Bad Logon Attempts.** Setting a value for this option prevents the account from being used after this number is reached, even if the right password is finally entered. If you set this value to five, which is the default when Account Lockout is enabled, on the sixth attempt, a person cannot log on to Windows NT—even if the user (or hacker) types in the correct username and password.

◆ **Reset Counter After.** This value specifies when to refresh the counter for bad logon attempts. The default value is 30 minutes. That means if Account Lockout is set to five and a user tries to log on unsuccessfully four times, he can stop, wait 45 minutes, and then try again. The counter will have been reset by then, and he can try to log on five more times before the account will be locked out.

◆ **Lockout Duration.** This value specifies how long the account should remain locked if the lockout counter is exceeded. It is generally more secure to set Lockout Duration to forever so that the administrator must unlock the account. That way, the administrator is warned of the activity on that account.

◆ **Users Must Log On to Change Password.** This setting requires a user to log on successfully before changing his password. If a user's password expires, the user cannot log on until the administrator changes the password for the user.

Home directories can be created so that each user who logs on has a specific location on the local machine or the network where he or she can store personal information.

In order to use RAS, a user must be granted dial-in permission in the User Manager.

You create new accounts through User Manager. Two accounts are created automatically when NT is installed: Administrator and Guest.

The following password options can be configured for a user when the account is created:

◆ **User Must Change Password at Next Logon.** When this is selected (which is the default when creating new users), the user is prompted to change his password when he logs on to Windows NT. This setting is not compatible with the account policy that forces a user to log on to change his password. If both are selected, the user must contact the administrator to change the password.

◆ **User Cannot Change Password.** Setting this option prevents a user from changing her password. If both this setting and User Must Change Password are selected, you get an error message stating that you cannot check both options for the same user when you attempt to add the account.

◆ **Password Never Expires.** You can use this option to override the setting for password expiration in the Account Policy. This option tends to be used for accounts that will be assigned to services, but it can be granted to user accounts as well. If you have both this option and User Must Change Password at Next Logon selected, a warning tells you that the user will not be required to change her password.

◆ **Account Disabled.** Instead of deleting a user's account when he or she leaves the company, it is a good idea to disable the account. If the user will be replaced, it is likely that the new individual who's hired will need the same rights and permissions the previous user had. By disabling the account, you prevent the previous employee from accessing your Windows NT Workstation or domain. When the new individual is hired, however, you can rename the old account to the new name and have the user change the password.

◆ **Account Locked Out.** This option is visible only if you have Account Lockout enabled in the Account Policy. You, as an administrator, can never check this box; it will be grayed out. The only time this box is available is when a user's account has been locked out because it has exceeded the specified number of bad logon attempts. If the Lockout Duration is set to forever, the administrator must go into that user's account and uncheck the Account Locked Out check box.

Table 9 lists the buttons available from a user's Properties dialog box in User Manager.

TABLE 9
USER PROPERTY BUTTONS IN USER MANAGER

Button	Enables You to Modify...
Groups	The groups the user is a member of
Profile	The user's profile path, login script path, and home directory location
Account	The user's account expiration date and account type
Hours	The hours a user can log in to the computer
Dialin	Whether the user can dial in using RAS and what callback features (if any) are enabled

You can create account templates to reduce the amount of administration that's required to create groups of similar accounts. Accounts created from a template inherit the template's configuration for the following features:

◆ Account Description option

◆ User Must Change Password at Next Logon option

◆ User Cannot Change Password option

◆ Password Never Expires option

◆ Group memberships

◆ All user-environment profile properties

◆ All dial-in properties

In account configuration, the %UserName% variable can represent individual users' login names whenever they're needed to access or create a folder. (For example, you might use it when creating home folders called by the users' login names.)

When a user leaves the company, it is always better to disable his account than to delete it for the following reasons:

◆ A disabled account cannot be used to log in (rendering it unuseable).

◆ Deleting an account also deletes the SID associated with it, thus removing the permissions for that user from all locations on the network.

◆ A user whose account is deleted will have to have her permissions restored everywhere if she should return.

◆ Renaming an account grants the permissions of the former user to the new user.

Local groups can be created to grant access to Workstation resources and to assign users' rights on the system. The following local groups are created when NT Workstation is installed:

- **Administrators.** The Administrators group has full control over the Windows NT Workstation. This account has the most control on the computer. However, members of the Administrators group do not automatically have control over all files on the system. By using an NTFS partition, a user can configure a file's permissions to restrict access from the administrator. If the administrator needs to access the file, she can take ownership of the file and then access it. Administrative privilege is one of three levels of privilege you can assign to a user in Windows NT. It is the highest level of privilege that can be assigned.

- **Guests.** The Guests group is used to give someone limited access to the resources on the Windows NT Workstation. The Guest account is automatically added to this group. The Guests group is one of the three levels of privilege you can assign to a Windows NT user account.

- **Users.** The Users group provides a user with the necessary rights to use the computer. By default, all accounts created on Windows NT Workstation are put into the Users group, except for the built-in Administrator and Guest accounts. User privilege is one of the three levels of privilege you can assign in Windows NT.

- **Power Users.** The Power Users group gives members the ability to perform certain system tasks without giving them complete administrative control over the machine. One of the tasks a power user can perform is the sharing of directories. An ordinary user on Windows NT Workstation cannot share directories.

- **Backup Operators.** The Backup Operators group gives its members the ability to bypass the security placed on any file when using the NT Backup utility. This allows them complete resource access, but only for the specialized job of backing up files, not for general access.

- **Replicator.** The Replicator group is used only to enable directory replication. This process allows file transfer to take place between an export computer (which must be an NT Server) and an import computer (which can be NT Workstation or NT Server). You will not see questions regarding this group and its service on the NT Workstation exam; but if you want more information, you can consult the NT Server book in this MCSE series.

Group accounts cannot be renamed.

User profiles fall into two categories: local and roaming. In addition, roaming user profiles fall into two categories: mandatory and personal. A local profile is located on a specific machine and takes effect only when a user logs onto that machine. A roaming profile is available over the network and can be accessed from any machine that has network connectivity to the machine holding the profile. Mandatory profiles (which have the extension .MAN) are read only and, therefore, cannot be changed by a user.

Shared folders allow users to access Workstation resources from the network (by default, no resources are made generally accessible to users over the network).

The following permissions are available on shared folders:

- **No Access.** If a user or group is given the No Access permission to a shared folder, that user or group cannot open the shared folder even though he will see the shared folder on the network. The

No Access permission overrides all other permissions a user or group might have to the folder.

◆ **Read.** The Read permission allows a user or group to display files and subfolders within the shared folder. It also allows the user or group to execute programs that might be located within the shared folder.

◆ **Change.** The Change permission allows a user or group to add files or subfolders to the shared folder and to append or delete information from existing files and subfolders. The Change permission also encompasses everything included within the Read permission.

◆ **Full Control.** If a user or group is given the Full Control permission, that user or group has the ability to change the file permissions and to perform all tasks allowed by the Change permission.

In order to share a folder on an NT Workstation, you must have that right. It is given by default to the built-in Administrators and Power Users groups.

You can share a folder remotely by using the Server Manager. Shares can be created, modified, or removed from a folder through the folder share permissions (accessible by right-clicking the folder and choosing Sharing).

If a user is given individual permission to access a folder and is also a member of one or more groups which are given access, the user's effective permission is the combination of the permissions (the highest level). This is true unless one of the permissions is No Access, in which case the No Access permission prevails over all others.

The permission granted to a share is also the permission granted to the tree structure inside that share. Sharing one folder within another shared folder gives two points of access and, potentially, two levels of access to the same resource.

Shared permissions apply only to network access; NTFS permissions apply both over the network and locally.

Table 10 describes the access permissions available on NTFS.

TABLE 10
STANDARD NTFS PERMISSIONS

Permission	Folder	File
Read (R)	Enables the user to display the folder and subfolders, attributes, and permissions	Enables the user to display the file, its attributes, and its permissions
Write (W)	Enables the user to add files or folders, change attributes for the folder, and display permissions	Enables the user to change file attributes and add or append data to the file
Execute (X)	Enables the user to make changes to subfolders, display permissions, and display attributes	Enables the user to run a file if it is an executable and display attributes and permissions
Delete (D)	Enables the user to remove the folder	Enables the user to remove the file
Change Permission (P)	Enables the user to modify folder permissions	Enables the user to modify file permissions
Take Ownership (O)	Enables the user to take ownership of the folder	Enables the user to take ownership of a file

Table 11 lists the standard NTFS file permissions and the granular permissions that comprise them.

TABLE 11
STANDARD NTFS FILE PERMISSIONS

Standard File Permission	Individual NTFS Permissions
No Access	(None)
Read	(RX)
Change	(RWXD)
Full Control	(All Permissions)

Table 12 lists the standard NTFS folder permissions and the default file permissions for files within those folders.

You (or any user) can take ownership of an NTFS resource provided that you meet one or more of the following criteria:

◆ **You must be the owner of the file or folder.** You must be the user who created it.

◆ **You must have been granted Full Control.** This includes the ability to Change Permissions (P).

◆ **You must have been given special access to Change Permissions (P).** A user can be given just this one permission to a file or folder.

◆ **You must have been given special access to Take Ownership (O).** With the ability to Take Ownership, a user can give himself the right to Change Permissions (P).

◆ **You must be a member of the Administrators group.**

If a user is granted individual NTFS permissions to a resource and is also a member of one or more groups that have been granted access, the effective permission for the user is the cumulative permission from all the access levels. This is the case unless any level is No Access, in which case the No Access level prevails over all others.

When shared permissions are combined with NTFS permissions for accessing a resource over the network, the lowest permission (share or NTFS) prevails. If the user is accessing locally, however, only NTFS permission applies.

TABLE 12
STANDARD NTFS FOLDER PERMISSIONS

Standard Folder Permissions	Individual NTFS Folder Permissions	Individual NTFS File Permissions
No Access	(None)	(None)
Read	(RX)	(RX)
Change	(RWXD)	(RWXD)
Add	(WX)	(Not Applicable)
Add & Read	(RWX)	(RX)
List	(RX)	(Not Applicable)
Full Control	(All)	(All)

When you copy a file from one folder to another, the permissions of the destination folder are applied to the new copy of the file. When you move a file from one folder to another and the folders are on different partitions, the permissions on the destination folder apply to the moved file. When you move a file from one folder to another on the same partition, the file retains its original permissions.

It's important that you remember the definitions of the following printing terms:

◆ **Printer**. The software component for printing. Also referred to as a *logical printer*, it is the software interface between the application and the print device.

◆ **Print device.** The actual hardware the paper comes out of. This is what you would traditionally think of as a printer. In Windows NT terminology, however, it is called a print device.

◆ **Print job.** The information that is sent to the print device. It contains both the data and the commands for print processing.

◆ **Print spooler.** A collection of DLLs (Dynamic Link Libraries) that accept, process, schedule, and distribute print jobs.

◆ **Creating a printer.** The process of defining a printer from your Windows NT Workstation. When you create a printer, you specify that the machine on which you are creating it will be the print server for that print device. You must create a printer if no other Windows NT system has created it yet, or if the print device is on a non–Windows NT operating system such as Windows 95.

◆ **Connecting to a printer.** A process that is necessary when the print device has already been defined by another Windows NT system and a printer has been created on that Windows NT system. If that is the case, in order to use the printer, you just need to connect to the printer from your Windows NT Workstation.

◆ **Print server.** The computer that created the printer and on which the printer is defined. Typically this is a Windows NT Server. However, a Windows NT Workstation or even a Windows 95 system can act as a print server.

◆ **Print queue.** The list of print jobs on the print server that are waiting to print.

◆ **Printer driver.** The software that enables applications to communicate properly with the print device.

◆ **Spooling.** The process of storing documents on the hard disk and then sending them to the printer. After the document has been stored on the hard disk, the user regains control of the application.

You can configure a printer pool by assigning two or more printer ports to the same printer and enabling printer pooling.

To allow other users to access a printer over the network, you must share the printer. Printer permissions can be set to control access to a printer. Table 13 lists those permissions.

TABLE 13
CAPABILITIES GRANTED WITH PRINTER PERMISSIONS

Capability	Full Control	Manage Documents	Print	No Access
Print documents	X	X	X	
Pause, resume, restart, and cancel the user's own documents	X	X	X	
Connect to a printer	X	X	X	
Control job settings for all documents	X	X		
Pause, restart, and delete all documents	X	X		
Share a printer	X			
Change printer properties	X			
Delete a printer	X			
Change printer permissions		X		

In a printer's properties dialog box, you can set the availability of the printer to allow it to hold documents until a certain time of the day.

Spool settings include the following options:

❖ **Spool Print Documents So Program Finishes Printing Faster.** If you choose this option, the documents will spool. This option has two choices within it:

- *Start Printing After Last Page Is Spooled.* This prevents documents from printing until they are completely spooled. The application that is printing is not available during the spooling. To use this option, you must have enough space on the partition of the spool directory to hold the entire print job.

- *Start Printing Immediately.* This enables a document to start printing before it has spooled completely, which speeds up printing.

❖ **Print Directly to the Printer.** This prevents the document from spooling. Although it speeds up printing, this is not an option for a shared printer, which would must support multiple incoming documents simultaneously.

❖ **Hold Mismatched Documents.** This prevents incorrect documents from printing. Incorrect documents are those that do not match the configuration of the printer.

❖ **Print Spooled Documents First.** Spooled documents will print ahead of partially spooled documents, even if they have a lower priority. This speeds up printing.

❖ **Keep Documents After They Have Printed.** Documents remain in the spooler after they have been printed.

If the print queue becomes jammed, you can clear corrupted print items by stopping and restarting the Spooler service from the Services icon in the Control Panel. The spool directory is, by default, located in Systemroot\system32\spool\printers, but that location can be changed via the File menu in the printer properties dialog box.

CONNECTIVITY

Remember: Here are the elements that Microsoft says they test on in the "Connectivity" section of the exam.

◆ Add and configure the network components of Windows NT Workstation.

◆ Use various methods to access network resources.

◆ Implement Windows NT Workstation as a client in a NetWare environment.

◆ Use various configurations to install Windows NT Workstation as a TCP/IP client.

◆ Configure and install Dial-Up Networking in a given situation.

◆ Configure Microsoft Peer Web Services in a given situation.

NDIS 4.0 enables the following on an NT Workstation computer:

◆ An unlimited number of network adapter cards.

◆ An unlimited number of network protocols can be bound to a single network adapter card.

◆ Independence between protocols and adapter card drivers.

◆ Communication links between adapter cards and their drivers.

The major characteristics of TCP/IP include the following:

◆ Routing support

◆ Connectivity with the Internet

◆ Interoperability with most possible operating systems and computer types

◆ Support as a client for Dynamic Host Configuration Protocol (DHCP)

◆ Support as a client for Windows Internet Name Service (WINS)

◆ Support as a client for Domain Name System (DNS)

◆ Support for Simple Network Management Protocol (SNMP)

The following are the major characteristics of NWLink:

◆ Connectivity with NetWare resources

◆ Routing support

◆ Supported by a wide variety of other operating systems

◆ Large installation base

The main characteristics of NetBEUI include

◆ No routing support.

◆ Transmissions are broadcast-based and, therefore, generate a lot of traffic.

◆ Fast performance on small LANs.

◆ Small memory overhead.

◆ No tuning options.

DLC protocol is primarily used for connecting NT Workstations to printers directly attached to the network through network interface cards.

Two network programming interfaces are available to allow programmers to access the network:

◆ **NetBIOS (Network Basic Input/Output System).** The original network API supported by Microsoft. IBM originally developed NetBIOS.

◆ **Windows Sockets (also called WinSock).** A newer network API originally developed by the UNIX community. Now Microsoft also supports it.

Table 14 describes the IPC mechanisms available in NT Workstation.

The Network applet in the Control Panel allows you to change names, services, protocols, adapters, and bindings for network configuration.

In order to be part of an NT domain, an NT computer must have an account that was created by someone with the right to add computer accounts in the domain (by default, an administrator).

If NWLink is installed and NT is left to autoconfigure the frame type, NT will expect 802.2 frames unless others are detected, in which case it will configure to the frame type it sees first. To use multiple NWLink frame types, you must make a Registry setting change.

Client Services for NetWare gives an NT Workstation the capability to access files and printers from a NetWare server, provided that NWLink is also installed on the Workstation. When installed on an NT Workstation, NWLink allows the workstation to connect to an application running on a NetWare server.

TABLE 14
TYPES OF INTERPROCESS COMMUNICATIONS

IPC Mechanism	Typical Uses
Named pipes	Named pipes establish a guaranteed bidirectional communications channel between two computers. After the pipe is established, either computer can read data from or write data to the pipe.
Mailslots	Mailslots establish a unidirectional communications channel between two computers. Receipt of the message is not guaranteed, and no acknowledgment is sent if the data is received.
Windows Sockets (WinSock)	WinSock is an API that enables applications to access transport protocols such as TCP/IP and NWLink.
RPCs	RPCs enable the various components of distributed applications to communicate with one another via the network.
Network Dynamic Data Exchange (NetDDE)	NetDDE is an older version of an RPC that is based on NetBIOS.
Distributed ActiveX Component Object Model (DCOM)	DCOM is an RPC based on Microsoft technology; it enables the components of a distributed application to be located on multiple computers across a network simultaneously.

TCP/IP is the default protocol installed on NT Workstation and requires at least a TCP/IP address and subnet mask to function properly. You can configure an NT Workstation to automatically receive TCP/IP configuration information from a DHCP server by selecting the Obtain Address from DHCP Server option button in the TCP/IP Properties dialog box. Two tools, IPCONFIG and PING, can be used to test the configuration and function of TCP/IP on your NT Workstation.

NT Workstation can act as a RAS client or a RAS server with one concurrent incoming connection. As a client, it can connect to servers using the SLIP, PPP, and PPTP protocols; as a client, it supports incoming connections using PPP or PPTP. Whether acting as a RAS client or a RAS server, an NT Workstation must have the RAS service installed. Table 15 lists the features of the three line protocols mentioned here.

PPTP connections require a PPP or LAN connection to a server with a Virtual Private Network (VPN) configured on it and provide for secure and encrypted communication.

In order for a user to log on to an NT Workstation using RAS, the user account must be configured in User Manager to allow dialin.

Peer Web Services allows for FTP, WWW, and Gopher connections from Internet or intranet clients.

TABLE 15
RAS LINE PROTOCOLS AND FEATURES

Feature	SLIP	PPP	PPTP
Supports NT as server	No	Yes	Yes
Supports NT as client	Yes	Yes	Yes
Passes TCP/IP	Yes	Yes	Yes
Passes NetBEUI	No	Yes	Yes
Passes NWLink	No	Yes	Yes
Supports DHCP over RAS	No	Yes	No
Requires PPP or LAN connection	No	No	Yes
Supports VPNs	No	No	Yes
Supports password encryption	No	Yes	Yes
Supports transmission encryption	No	No	Yes

RUNNING APPLICATIONS

Remember: Here are the elements that Microsoft says they test on in the "Running Applications" section of the exam.

- Start applications on Intel and RISC platforms in various operating system environments.

- Start applications with various priorities.

NT Workstation supports (to a greater or lesser extent) applications written for the following operating systems:

- Windows NT and Windows 95

- MS-DOS

- Windows 3.x

- OS/2

- POSIX

MS-DOS applications invoke an NT Virtual DOS machine, which emulates a DOS environment. Windows 16-bit applications invoke an NT Virtual DOS machine (unless one is already running) and then run a Win16 emulator called WOW.EXE.

By default, Win16 applications all run in the same NTVDM. However, if desired, you can configure them to run in separate NTVDMs. The following list summarizes the advantages and disadvantages of running Win16 applications in separate NTVDMs.

Advantages:

- Win16 applications will now use preemptive multitasking. An ill-behaved Win16 application will no longer prevent other Win16 applications from executing normally because each Win16 application will have its own memory space and thread of execution.

- Win16 applications will now be more reliable because they will not be affected by the problems of other Win16 applications.

- Win16 applications can now take advantage of multiprocessor computers. When Win16 applications are run in a common NTVDM, they must share a single thread of execution. The generation of individual NTVDMs also creates individual threads of execution, and each thread can potentially be executed on a different processor. The operating system could now schedule each NTVDM's thread of execution to run on whichever processor is available. In a system with multiple processors, this can lead to multiprocessing. If the Win16 applications were running in a common NTVDM, their single thread of execution would be able to run only on a single processor, no matter how many processors existed on the computer.

- Windows NT will enable Win16 applications running in separate memory spaces to continue to participate in OLE and dynamic data exchange (DDE).

Disadvantages:

- There is additional overhead in running separate NTVDMs.

- Some older Win16 applications did not use the standards of OLE and DDE. These applications would not function properly if they were run in separate memory spaces. These applications must be run in a common memory space to function correctly. Lotus for Windows 1.0 is an example of this type of application.

NT offers four methods for running Win16 applications in separate NTVDMs:

◆ Anytime you start a Win16 application from the Start menu using the Run option, you can select the Run in Separate Memory Space option. This technique must be applied every time an application is run from the Run dialog box.

◆ At a command prompt, you can start a Win16 application using the command syntax start /separate *application*. For example, to start Word 6.0 you could type the following:

```
start /separate c:\office16\word\winword.exe
```

This technique must be applied every time the application is run from a command prompt.

◆ Shortcuts that point to Win16 applications can be configured to always run in a separate memory space. To do that, use the appropriate option on the Shortcut tab of the properties dialog box for the shortcut. Although this causes an application to run in a separate memory space every time the shortcut is used, it applies only to the particular shortcut that's modified, and not to any other shortcuts that have been created to that application.

◆ You can configure all files with a particular extension to always run in a separate memory space when the data document is double-clicked on in the Windows NT Explorer. To do this, you edit the File Types tab of the View, Options properties.

The OS/2 subsystem allows you to run OS/2 1.x character-based applications on Intel machines. On RISC machines, you must run OS/2 applications in NTVDMs by using the /FORCEDOS switch when running the applications from a command prompt or shortcut. You configure OS/2 applications by editing a CONFIG.SYS file using an OS/2 text editor. This creates a temporary file that is then converted to Registry settings (no CONFIG.SYS file is actually stored on the hard drive).

NT provides POSIX.1 support in its POSIX subsystem. This subsystem supports the following features for POSIX applications:

◆ **Case-sensitive file naming.** NTFS preserves case for both directory and filenames.

◆ **Hard links.** POSIX applications can store the same data in two differently named files.

◆ **An additional time stamp on files.** This tracks the last time the file was accessed. The default on FAT volumes is to track only the last time the file was modified.

Application support differs across different hardware platforms. Table 16 lists the kinds of support that applications have. *Binary* means that the same application will run across all hardware platforms; *source* means that a different compile is required for each hardware platform.

TABLE 16
APPLICATION COMPATIBILITY ACROSS WINDOWS NT PLATFORMS

Platform	MS-DOS	Win16	Win32	OS/2	POSIX
Intel	Binary	Binary	Source	Binary	Source
Alpha	Binary	Binary	Source*	Binary**	Source
Mips	Binary	Binary	Source	Binary**	Source
PowerPC	Binary	Binary	Source	Binary**	Source

* Third-party utilities such as Digital FX!32 enable Win32-based Intel programs to execute on Digital Alpha AXP microprocessors. Although these utilities are interpreting the code on-the-fly, they end up performing faster on the Alpha as a result of the increased processor speed.
** Only bound applications can be run on the three RISC hardware platforms. They will run in a Windows NTVDM because the OS/2 subsystem is not provided in RISC-based versions of Windows NT.

All applications run at a default priority set by the application itself (between 0 and 31). This priority determines its relative access to the CPU and, as a result, how quickly it responds to user interaction.

You can assign priority levels to applications through the use of command prompt switches. Table 17 lists the priority levels, their base priorities, and the commands you use to assign them.

NT boosts the priority of the application in the foreground by anywhere from 0 to 2 points (this ensures that foreground applications are more responsive than background applications). The "boost from" base is set on the Performance tab of the Control Panel's System application.

TABLE 17
BASE PRIORITY LEVELS UNDER WINDOWS NT

Priority Level	Base Priority	Command Line
Low	4	`start /low executable.exe`
Normal	8	`start /normal executable.exe`
High	13	`start /high executable.exe`
Realtime	24	`start /realtime executable.exe`

MONITORING AND OPTIMIZATION

Remember: Here are the elements that Microsoft says they test on in the "Monitoring and Optimization" section of the exam.

◆ Monitor system performance by using various tools.

◆ Identify and resolve a given performance problem.

◆ Optimize system performance in various areas.

Task Manager (accessible by right-clicking the taskbar and choosing Task Manager) allows you to see and end applications and processes on your system.

Performance Monitor allows you to monitor counters for specific computer and application objects and to tune the performance of your computer based on what you find.

In order to monitor disk counters, you must first enable them through the use of the command DISKPERF -y (or DISKPERF -YE for volume sets and RAID disks).

Table 18 describes the objects you will find in the Performance Monitor (others may be present depending on the services or applications you have installed).

Four views are available in the Performance Monitor:

◆ **Chart view.** Real-time line graphs of counters.

◆ **Log view.** Stored statistics useable by other views at a later time.

◆ **Alert view.** Monitored thresholds that generate events if the thresholds are crossed.

◆ **Report view.** Real-time text-displayed statistics on counters.

Performance Monitor can be used to monitor a local machine or an NT Server or Workstation to which the user has Administrative rights.

TABLE 18

COMMON OBJECTS ALWAYS AVAILABLE IN THE PERFORMANCE MONITOR

Object	Description
Cache	The file system cache is an area of physical memory that holds recently used data.
Logical Disk	Disk partitions and other logical views of disk space.
Memory	Random access memory used to store code and data.
Objects	Certain system software objects.
Paging File	File used to support virtual memory allocated by the system.
Physical Disk	Hardware disk unit.
Process	Software object that represents a running program.
Processor	Hardware unit that executes program instructions.
Redirector	File system that diverts file requests to network servers.
System	Counters that apply to all system hardware and software.
Thread	The part of a process that uses the processor.

The Server Manager allows you to see who is currently logged on to a computer and what resources they are using, to see available shares on your Workstation, to start or stop sharing resources, and to see what type of access is being made to all in-use resources.

WINMSD allows you to view configuration information about your computer.

You may want to monitor and tune the following components:

- ◆ Memory
- ◆ Processor
- ◆ Disks
- ◆ Network

The Event Viewer allows you to view information logged to any of three logs:

- ◆ **System log.** A log of events detected by NT that have to do with system functioning (the starting and stopping of services or their failure).
- ◆ **Security log.** A log of audited events that have to do with resource access (success or failure).
- ◆ **Application log.** A log of events recorded by applications running on NT that are configured to create such events.

You can archive any of these logs for viewing at a later time or for event archive.

An emergency repair disk enables you to recover Registry and system settings should they become corrupt. By performing the following two steps, you can be sure your ERD remains up-to-date:

1. Using the RDISK.EXE utility, update the Repair directory to save the repair information on your hard drive.

2. Using the RDISK.EXE utility, write the Repair information to a floppy disk.

You can perform a repair by booting to and using the three installation disks required to install NT from a CD-ROM and by specifying that you want to repair your system when asked.

The LastKnownGood configuration is a set of Registry settings that record the state of the NT configuration at the time of the last successful login. If you encounter problems with your system resulting from a change you've made in the current session, reboot and choose to restore LastKnownGood. Every time you log in, the LastKnownGood configuration is overwritten with the current configuration of your hardware (whether it functions properly or not).

TROUBLESHOOTING

Remember: Here are the elements that Microsoft says they test on in the "Troubleshooting" section of the exam.

- ◆ Choose the appropriate course of action to take when the boot process fails.
- ◆ Choose the appropriate course of action to take when a print job fails.
- ◆ Choose the appropriate course of action to take when the installation process fails.
- ◆ Choose the appropriate course of action to take when an application fails.
- ◆ Choose the appropriate course of action to take when a user cannot access a resource.
- ◆ Modify the Registry using the appropriate tool in a given situation.
- ◆ Implement advanced techniques to resolve various problems.

The acronym DETECT can be used to define the troubleshooting process:

D	Discover the problem
E	Explore the boundaries
T	Track the possible approaches
E	Execute an approach
C	Check for success
T	Tie up loose ends

Table 19 identifies the files involved in the boot process for both Intel and RISC machines.

TABLE 19
BOOT PROCESS FILES

Intel	*RISC*
NTLDR	OSLOADER.EXE
BOOT.INI	NTOSKRNL.EXE
NTDETECT.COM	
NTOSKRNL.EXE	
NTBOOTDD.SYS (for SCSI drives with BIOS disabled)	

In the NT boot process (in BOOT.INI), ARC paths define the physical position of the NT operating system files. ARC paths follow one of two formats:

scsi(0)disk(0)rdisk(0)partition(1)*folder*

multi(0)disk(0)rdisk(0)partition(1)*folder*

The first type, scsi ARC paths, define hard drives that are SCSI but have the BIOS disabled. The relevant parameters are

◆ **scsi.** The SCSI controller, starting from 0.

◆ **disk.** The physical disk, starting from 0.

◆ **partition.** The partition on the disk, starting from 1.

◆ *folder.* The folder in which the NT files are located.

The second type, multi ARC paths, define hard drives that are non-SCSI or are SCSI with the BIOS enabled. The relevant parameters are

◆ **multi.** The controller, starting from 0.

◆ **rdisk.** The physical disk, starting from 0.

◆ **partition.** The partition on the disk, starting from 1.

◆ *folder.* The folder in which the NT files are located.

Partitions are numbered according to the following pattern:

1. The first primary partition on each disk gets the number 1.

2. Each additional primary partition is then given a number, incrementing up from 1.

3. Each logical drive is then given a number in the order they appear in the Disk Administrator.

Switches on boot lines in the BOOT.INI file define additional boot parameters. Table 20 lists the switches you need to know and their functions.

TABLE 20
BOOT.INI SWITCHES

Switch	Function
/basevideo	Loads standard VGA video driver (640×480, 16-color)
/sos	Displays each driver as it is loaded
/noserialmice	Prevents autodetection of serial mice on COM ports, which can disable a UPS connected to the port

A recovery disk can be used to bypass problems with a system partition. This disk must be formatted in NT and will contain the files listed in Table 21 (broken down by hardware platform).

TABLE 21
FILES ON THE RECOVERY DISK

Intel	RISC
NTLDR	OSLOADER.EXE
NTDETECT.COM	HAL.DLL
BOOT.INI	*.PAL (for Alpha machines)
BOOTSECT.DOS (allows you to boot to DOS)	
NTBOOTDD.SYS (the SCSI driver for a hard drive with SCSI BIOS not enabled)	

An emergency repair disk can be used to repair an NT system if the Registry becomes corrupted. The repair disk must be used in conjunction with the three setup disks used to install NT.

The RDISK program allows you to update the \REPAIR folder, which in turn is used to update your repair disk.

The following list identifies possible sources of installation problems:

♦ Media errors

♦ Insufficient disk space

♦ Non-supported SCSI adapters

♦ Failure of dependency service to start

♦ Inability to connect to the domain controller

♦ Error in assigning domain names

Application failures generally result from incorrect application configuration, not from incorrect NT configuration.

If applications do not run, check the following:

♦ An MS-DOS application may be trying to access hardware directly.

♦ Two Win16 applications running in the same NTVDM may be conflicting.

♦ Win32 applications may be compiled for a different processor.

Services are interrelated: If one service fails, it may affect others as well. Therefore, you need to make sure that you get to the root of a service failure, and you're not just treating the symptoms.

Two programs are available for viewing and modifying the Registry:

♦ REGEDIT.EXE

♦ REGEDT32.EXE

The Network Monitor tool can be used to analyze network traffic in and out of the adapter on an NT Workstation computer.

Study and Exam Prep Tips

This chapter provides you with some general guidelines for preparing for the exam. It is organized into three sections. The first section addresses your pre-exam preparation activities, covering general study tips. This is followed by an extended look at the Microsoft Certification exams, including a number of specific tips that apply to the Microsoft exam formats. Finally, it addresses changes in Microsoft's testing policies and how they might affect you.

To better understand the nature of preparation for the test, it is important to understand learning as a process. You probably are aware of how you best learn new material. Maybe outlining works best for you, or maybe you are a visual learner who needs to "see" things. Whatever your learning style, test preparation takes time. While it is obvious that you can't start studying for these exams the night before you take them, it is very important to understand that learning is a developmental process. Understanding the process helps you focus on what you know and what you have yet to learn.

Thinking about how you learn should help you recognize that learning takes place when we are able to match new information to old. You have some previous experience with computers and networking, and now you are preparing for this certification exam. Using this book, software, and supplementary materials will not just add incrementally to what you know. As you study, you actually change the organization of your knowledge to integrate this new information into your existing knowledge base. This will lead you to a more comprehensive understanding of the tasks and concepts outlined in the objectives and related to computing in general. Again, this happens as an iterative process rather than a singular event. Keep this model of learning in mind as you prepare for the exam, and you will make better decisions on what to study and how much to study.

STUDY TIPS

There are many ways to approach studying, just as there are many different types of material to study. However, the tips that follow should work well for the type of material covered on the certification exams.

Study Strategies

Although individuals vary in the ways they learn information, some basic principles of learning apply to everyone. You should adopt some study strategies that take advantage of these principles. One of these principles is that learning can be broken into various depths. *Recognition* (of terms, for example) exemplifies a surface level of learning: You rely on a prompt of some sort to elicit recall. *Comprehension or understanding* (of the concepts behind the terms, for instance) represents a deeper level of learning. The ability to analyze a concept and apply your understanding of it in a new way or to address a unique setting represents further depth of learning.

Your learning strategy should enable you to know the material a level or two deeper than mere recognition. This will help you to do well on the exam(s). You will know the material so thoroughly that you can easily handle the recognition-level types of questions used in multiple-choice testing. You will also be able to apply your knowledge to solve novel problems.

Macro and Micro Study Strategies

One strategy that can lead to this deeper learning includes preparing an outline that covers all the objectives and subobjectives for the particular exam you are working on. You should then delve a bit further into the material and include a level or two of detail beyond the stated objectives and subobjectives for the exam. Finally, flesh out the outline by coming up with a statement of definition or a summary for each point in the outline.

This outline provides two approaches to studying. First, you can study the outline by focusing on the organization of the material. Work your way through the points and subpoints of your outline with the goal of learning how they relate to one another. For example, be sure you understand how each of the main objective areas is similar to and different from one another. Then do the same thing with the subobjectives. Also, be sure you know which subobjectives pertain to each objective area and how they relate to one another.

Next, you can work through the outline and focus on learning the details. Memorize and understand terms and their definitions, facts, rules and strategies, advantages and disadvantages, and so on. In this pass through the outline, attempt to learn detail as opposed to the big picture (the organizational information that you worked on in the first pass through the outline).

Research shows that attempting to assimilate both types of information at the same time seems to interfere with the overall learning process. Separate your studying into these two approaches, and you will perform better on the exam than if you attempt to study the material in a more conventional manner.

Active Study Strategies

In addition, the process of writing down and defining the objectives, subobjectives, terms, facts, and definitions promotes a more active learning strategy than merely reading the material does. In human information processing terms, writing forces you to engage in more active encoding of the information. Simply reading over it constitutes passive processing.

Next, determine whether you can apply the information you have learned by attempting to create examples and scenarios of your own. Think about how or where you could apply the concepts you are learning. Again, write down this information to process the facts and concepts in a more active fashion.

The hands-on nature of the Step by Step tutorials and the exercises at the end of the chapters provide further active learning opportunities that will reinforce concepts.

Common Sense Strategies

Finally, you should also follow common sense practices in studying: Study when you are alert, reduce or eliminate distractions, take breaks when you become fatigued, and so on.

Pre-Testing Yourself

Pre-testing allows you to assess how well you are learning. One of the most important aspects of learning is what has been called "meta-learning." Meta-learning has to do with realizing when you know something well or when you need to study some more. In other words, you recognize how well or how poorly you have learned the material you are studying. For most people, this can be difficult to assess objectively on their own. Therefore, practice tests are useful because they reveal more objectively what you have and have not learned. You should use this information to guide review and further studying. Developmental learning takes place as you cycle through studying, assessing how well you have learned, reviewing, and assessing again, until you feel you are ready to take the exam.

You may have noticed the practice exam included in this book. Use it as part of this process. In addition to the Practice Exam, the Top Score software on the CD-ROM also provides a variety of ways to test yourself before you take the actual exam. By using the Top Score Practice Exams, you can take an entire practice test. By using the Top Score Study Cards, you can take an entire practice exam or you can focus on a particular objective area, such as Planning, Troubleshooting, or Monitoring and Optimization. By using the Top Score Flash Cards, you can test your knowledge at a level beyond that of recognition; you must come up with the answers in your own words. The Flash Cards also enable you to test your knowledge of particular objective areas.

You should set a goal for your pre-testing. A reasonable goal would be to score consistently in the 90-percent range (or better). See Appendix D, "Using the Top Score Software," for more detailed explanation of the test engine.

EXAM PREP TIPS

Having mastered the subject matter, the final preparatory step is to understand how the exam will be presented. Make no mistake about it, a Microsoft Certified Professional (MCP) exam will challenge both your knowledge and your test-taking skills! This section starts with the basics of exam design, reviews a new type of exam format, and concludes with hints that are targeted to each of the exam formats.

The MCP Exam

Every MCP exam is released in one of two basic formats. What's being called *exam format* here is really little more than a combination of the overall exam structure and the presentation method for exam questions.

Each exam format utilizes the same types of questions. These types or styles of questions include multiple-rating (or scenario-based) questions, traditional multiple-choice questions, and simulation-based questions. It's important to understand the types of questions you will be asked and the actions required to properly answer them.

Understanding the exam formats is essential to good preparation because the format determines the number of questions presented, the difficulty of those questions, and the amount of time allowed to complete the exam.

Exam Format

There are two basic formats for the MCP exams: the traditional fixed-form exam and the adaptive form. As its name implies, the fixed-form exam presents a fixed set of questions during the exam session. The adaptive format, however, uses only a subset of questions drawn from a larger pool during any given exam session.

Fixed-Form

A fixed-form, computerized exam is based on a fixed set of exam questions. The individual questions are presented in random order during a test session. If you take the same exam more than once, you won't necessarily see the exact same questions. This is because two or three final forms are typically assembled for every fixed-form exam Microsoft releases. These are usually labeled Forms A, B, and C.

The final forms of a fixed-form exam are identical in terms of content coverage, number of questions, and allotted time, but the questions themselves are different. You may have noticed, however, that some of the same questions appear on, or rather are shared across, different final forms. When questions are shared across multiple final forms of an exam, the percentage of sharing is generally small. Many final forms share no questions, but some older exams may have ten to fifteen percent duplication of exam questions on the final exam forms.

Fixed-form exams also have a fixed time limit in which you must complete the exam. The Top Score software on the CD-ROM that accompanies this book provides fixed-form exams.

Finally, the score you achieve on a fixed-form exam (which is always reported for MCP exams on a scale of 0 to 1,000) is based on the number of questions you answer correctly. The exam passing score is the same for all final forms of a given fixed-form exam.

The typical format for the fixed-form exam is this:

◆ 50–60 questions

◆ 75–90 minute testing time

◆ Question review is allowed, including the opportunity to change your answers

Adaptive Form

An adaptive form exam has the same appearance as a fixed-form exam, but it differs in both how questions are selected for presentation and how many questions actually are presented. Although the statistics of adaptive testing are fairly complex, the process is concerned with determining your level of skill or ability with the exam subject matter. This ability assessment begins with the presentation of questions of varying levels of difficulty and ascertains at what difficulty level you can reliably answer them. Finally, the ability assessment determines if that ability level is above or below the level required to pass that exam.

Examinees at different levels of ability will then see quite different sets of questions. Examinees who demonstrate little expertise with the subject matter will

continue to be presented with relatively easy questions. Examinees who demonstrate a high level of expertise will be presented progressively more-difficult questions. Both individuals may answer the same number of questions correctly, but because the higher-expertise examinee can correctly answer more-difficult questions, he or she will receive a higher score and is more likely to pass the exam.

The typical design for the adaptive form exam is this:

◆ 20–25 questions

◆ 90 minute testing time (although this is likely to be reduced to 45–60 minutes in the near future)

◆ Question review is not allowed, providing no opportunity to change your answers

The Adaptive Exam Process

Your first adaptive exam will be unlike any other testing experience you have had. In fact, many examinees have difficulty accepting the adaptive testing process because they feel they were not provided the opportunity to adequately demonstrate their full expertise.

You can take consolation in the fact that adaptive exams are painstakingly put together after months of data gathering and analysis and are just as valid as a fixed-form exam. The rigor introduced through the adaptive testing methodology means that there is nothing arbitrary about what you'll see! It is also a more efficient means of testing that requires less time to conduct and complete.

As you can see from Figure 1, a number of statistical measures drive the adaptive examination process. The one that's most immediately relevant to you is the ability estimate. Accompanying this test statistic are the standard error of measurement, the item characteristic curve, and the test information curve.

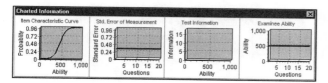

FIGURE 1
Microsoft's adaptive testing demonstration program.

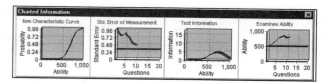

FIGURE 2
The changing statistics in an adaptive exam.

The standard error, which is the key factor in determining when an adaptive exam will terminate, reflects the degree of error in the exam ability estimate. The item characteristic curve reflects the probability of a correct response relative to examinee ability. Finally, the test information statistic provides a measure of the information contained in the set of questions the examinee has answered, again relative to the ability level of the individual examinee.

When you begin an adaptive exam, the standard error has already been assigned a target value below which it must drop for the exam to conclude. This target value reflects a particular level of statistical confidence in the process. The examinee ability is initially set to the mean possible exam score, which is 500 for MCP exams.

As the adaptive exam progresses, questions of varying difficulty are presented. Based on your pattern of responses to those questions, the ability estimate is recalculated. Simultaneously, the standard error estimate is refined from its first estimated value of one toward the target value. When the standard error reaches its target value, the exam terminates. Thus, the more consistently you answer questions of the same degree of difficulty, the more quickly the standard error estimate drops and the fewer questions you will end up seeing during the exam session. This situation is depicted in Figure 2.

As you might suspect, one good piece of advice for taking an adaptive exam is to treat every exam question as if it is the most important. The adaptive scoring algorithm is attempting to discover a pattern of responses that reflects some level of proficiency with the subject matter. Incorrect responses almost guarantee that additional questions must be answered (unless, of course, you get every question wrong). This is because the scoring algorithm must adjust to information that is not consistent with the emerging pattern.

New Question Types

A variety of question types can appear on MCP exams. Examples of multiple-choice questions and scenario-based questions appear throughout this book and the Top Score software. Simulation-based questions are new to the MCP exam series.

Simulation Questions

Simulation-based questions reproduce the look and feel of key Microsoft product features for the purpose of testing. The simulation software used in MCP exams has been designed to look and act, as much as possible, just like the actual product. Consequently, answering simulation questions in an MCP exam entails completing one or more tasks just as if you were using the product itself.

The format of a typical Microsoft simulation question is straightforward. It presents a brief scenario or problem statement along with one or more tasks that must be completed to solve the problem. The next section provides an example of a simulation question for MCP exams.

A Typical Simulation Question

It sounds obvious, but the first step when you encounter a simulation is to carefully read the question (see Figure 3). Do not go straight to the simulation application! Assess the problem being presented and identify the conditions that make up the problem scenario. Note the tasks that must be performed or outcomes that must be achieved to answer the question, and then review any instructions on how to proceed.

The next step is to launch the simulator by using the button provided. After clicking the Show Simulation button, you will see a feature of the product, like the dialog box shown in Figure 4. The simulation application will partially cover the question text on many test center machines. Feel free to reposition the simulation or to move between the question text screen and the simulation using hot-keys and point-and-click navigation or even by clicking the simulation launch button again.

It is important to understand that your answer to the simulation question is not recorded until you move on to the next exam question. This gives you the added capability to close and reopen the simulation application (using the launch button) on the same question without losing any partial answer you may have made.

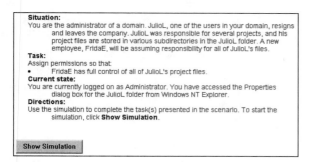

FIGURE 3
Typical MCP exam simulation question with directions.

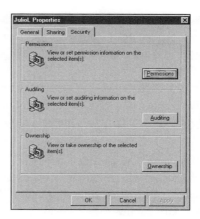

FIGURE 4
Launching the simulation application.

The third step is to use the simulator as you would the actual product to solve the problem or perform the defined tasks. Again, the simulation software is designed to function, within reason, just as the product does. But don't expect the simulation to reproduce product behavior perfectly. Most importantly, do not allow yourself to become flustered if the simulation does not look or act exactly like the product. Figure 5 shows the solution to the sample simulation problem.

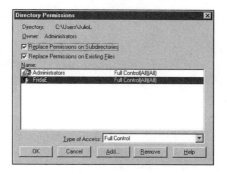

FIGURE 5
The solution to the simulation example.

There are two final points that will help you tackle simulation questions. First, respond only to what is being asked in the question. Do not solve problems that you are not asked to solve. Second, accept what is being asked of you. You may not entirely agree with conditions in the problem statement, the quality of the desired solution, or sufficiency of defined tasks to adequately solve the problem. Always remember that you are being tested on your ability to solve the problem as it has been presented.

The solution to the simulation problem shown in Figure 5 perfectly illustrates both of these points. As you'll recall from the question scenario (refer to Figure 3), you were asked to assign appropriate permissions to a new user called FridaE. You were not instructed to make any other changes in permissions. Thus, if you had modified or removed Administrator permissions, this item would have been scored wrong on an MCP exam.

Putting It All Together

Given all these different pieces of information, the task is now to assemble a set of tips that will help you successfully tackle the different types of MCP exams.

More Pre-Exam Preparation Tips

Generic exam preparation advice is always useful. Follow these general guidelines:

◆ Become familiar with the product. Hands-on experience is one of the keys to success on any MCP exam. Review the exercises and the Step by Step tutorials in the book.

◆ Review the current exam preparation guide on the Microsoft MCP Web site. The documentation Microsoft makes publicly available over the Web identifies the skills every exam is intended to test.

◆ Memorize foundational technical detail as appropriate. But remember, MCP exams are generally heavy on problem solving and application of knowledge more than they are on questions that require only rote memorization.

◆ Take any of the available practice tests. We recommend the one included in this book and those you can create using the Top Score software on the CD-ROM. While these are fixed-format exams, they provide preparation that is also valuable for taking an adaptive exam. Because of the nature of adaptive testing, it is not possible for these practice exams to be offered in the adaptive format. However, fixed-format exams provide the same types of questions as adaptive exams and are the most effective way to prepare for either type of exam. As a supplement to the material included with this book, try the free practice tests available on the Microsoft MCP Web site.

◆ Look on the Microsoft MCP Web site for samples and demonstration items. These tend to be particularly valuable for one significant reason: They allow you to become familiar with any new testing technologies before you encounter them on an MCP exam.

During the Exam Session

Similarly, the generic exam-taking advice you've heard for years applies when taking an MCP exam:

◆ Take a deep breath and try to relax when you first sit down for your exam. It is very important to control the pressure you may (naturally) feel when taking exams.

◆ You will be provided scratch paper. Take a moment to write down any factual information and technical detail that you committed to short-term memory.

◆ Carefully read all information and instruction screens. These displays have been put together to give you information relevant to the exam you are taking.

◆ Accept the Non-Disclosure Agreement and preliminary survey as part of the examination process. Complete them accurately and quickly move on.

◆ Read the exam questions carefully. Reread each question to identify all relevant detail.

◆ Tackle the questions in the order they are presented. Skipping around won't build your confidence; the clock is always counting down.

◆ Don't rush, but at the same time, don't linger on difficult questions. The questions vary in degree of difficulty. Don't let yourself be flustered by a particularly difficult or verbose question.

Fixed-Form Exams

Building from this basic preparation and test-taking advice, you also need to consider the challenges presented by the different exam designs. Because a fixed-form exam is composed of a fixed, finite set of questions, add these tips to your strategy for taking a fixed-form exam:

◆ Note the time allotted and the number of questions appearing on the exam you are taking. Make a rough calculation of how many minutes you can spend on each question, and use that number to pace yourself through the exam.

◆ Take advantage of the fact that you can return to and review skipped or previously answered questions. Mark the questions you can't answer confidently, noting the relative difficulty of each question on the scratch paper provided. When you reach the end of the exam, return to the more difficult questions.

◆ If there is session time remaining when you have completed all questions (and you aren't too fatigued!), review your answers. Pay particular attention to questions that seem to have a lot of detail or that required graphics.

◆ As for changing your answers, the rule of thumb here is *don't*! If you read the question carefully and completely and you felt like you knew the right answer, you probably did. Don't second-guess yourself. If, as you check your answers, one stands out as clearly incorrect, however, of course you should change it. But if you are at all unsure, go with your first impression.

Adaptive Exams

If you are planning to take an adaptive exam, keep these additional tips in mind:

◆ Read and answer every question with great care. When reading a question, identify every relevant detail, requirement, or task that must be performed and double-check your answer to be sure you have addressed every one of them.

◆ If you cannot answer a question, use the process of elimination to reduce the set of potential answers, and then take your best guess. Stupid mistakes invariably mean additional questions will be presented.

◆ Forget about reviewing questions and changing your answers. Once you leave a question, whether you've answered it or not, you cannot return to it. Do not skip any questions either. If you do, that question is counted as incorrect!

Simulation Questions

You may encounter simulation questions on either the fixed-form or adaptive form exam. If you do, keep these tips in mind:

◆ Avoid changing any simulation settings that don't pertain directly to the problem solution. Solve the problem you are being asked to solve and nothing more.

◆ Assume default settings when related information has not been provided. If something has not been mentioned or defined, it is a non-critical detail that does not factor in to the correct solution.

◆ Be sure your entries are syntactically correct, paying particular attention to your spelling. Enter relevant information just as the product would require it.

◆ Close all simulation application windows after you complete the simulation tasks. The testing system software is designed to trap errors that could result when using the simulation application, but trust yourself over the testing software.

◆ If simulations are part of a fixed-form exam, you can return to skipped or previously answered questions and change your answer. However, if you choose to change your answer to a simulation question, or if you even attempt to review the settings you've made in the simulation application, your previous response to that simulation question will be deleted. If simulations are part of an adaptive exam, you cannot return to previous questions.

FINAL CONSIDERATIONS

Finally, a number of changes in the MCP program will impact how frequently you can repeat an exam and what you will see when you do.

◆ Microsoft has instituted a new exam retake policy. This new rule is "two and two, then one and two." That is, you can attempt any exam twice with no restrictions on the time between attempts. But after the second attempt, you must wait two weeks before you can attempt that exam again. After that, you will be required to wait two weeks between subsequent attempts. Plan to pass the exam in two attempts; if that's not possible, increase your time horizon for receiving an MCP credential.

◆ New questions are being seeded into the MCP exams. After performance data has been gathered on new questions, they will replace older questions on all exam forms. This means that the questions appearing on exams will change regularly.

◆ Many of the current MCP exams will be republished in adaptive format in the coming months. Prepare yourself for this significant change in testing format, as it is entirely likely that this will become the new preferred MCP exam format.

These changes mean that the brute-force strategies for passing MCP exams may soon completely lose their viability. So if you don't pass an exam on the first or second attempt, it is entirely possible that the exam will change significantly in form. It could be updated from fixed-form to adaptive form, or it might have a different set of questions or question types.

The intention of Microsoft is clearly not to make the exams more difficult by introducing unwanted change. Their intent is to create and maintain valid measures of the technical skills and knowledge associated with the different MCP credentials. Preparing for an MCP exam has always involved not only studying the subject matter, but also planning for the testing experience itself. With these changes, this is now more true than ever.

Practice Exam

EXAM QUESTIONS

1. Which are media?

   A. Twisted-pair wire

   B. Television

   C. Radio waves

   D. Microwave signals

   E. Disk drive

   F. Backup tapes

   G. All

   H. None

2. 10BASE2 uses which type of cable?

   A. RG59

   B. RG62

   C. RG58

   D. UTP

3. Which is not a protocol?

   A. TCP/IP

   B. NetBEUI

   C. AppleTalk

   D. ARP

   E. NFS

   F. Ethernet

4. RAID 0 is also known as

   A. Striping

   B. Mirror set

   C. Striping with parity

   D. None of the above

5. Which type of cable will operate at 100 Mbs?

   A. Category 3 cable

   B. Category 5 cable

   C. Category 2 cable

   D. 10BASE2

6. Which network access method does LocalTalk use?

   A. CSMA/CD

   B. CSMA/CA

   C. Token passing

   D. AppleTalk

7. CSMA/CA networks are typically slower than CSMA/CD networks because

   A. There are more collisions on CSMA/CA networks.

   B. CSMA/CA networks must wait a random amount of time before transmitting on the media.

   C. CSMA/CA networks must wait for a token before transmitting on the cable.

   D. CSMA/CA networks use twisted-pair cable and CSMA/CD networks use coaxial cable.

8. Which is not an example of client/server computing?

    A. A workstation application accessing a SQL database on a server.

    B. A workstation application accessing the corporate mail server to find an address.

    C. A terminal accessing a mainframe database.

9. Which is not an advantage of storing applications on network servers instead of on the client's computer?

    A. Lower licensing cost

    B. Easier to upgrade

    C. Greater uptime because application is on the server

    D. Requires less disk space because the application is only installed on the server

10. In a peer-to-peer network, which network security model is used?

    A. User-level security

    B. Share-level security

    C. Password-protected shares

    D. Access permissions

11. Which type of access is not associated with directory shares?

    A. Read

    B. Change

    C. Add

    D. No Access

12. Windows NT domain model is a

    A. Peer-to-peer network

    B. Server-based network

    C. Application server

13. In which type of network does the computer act as a client and as a server?

    A. A Windows NT domain server network

    B. A peer-to-peer network

    C. A server-based network

14. Which Internet protocol is connection-oriented?

    A. NetBEUI

    B. TCP/IP

    C. UDP/IP

    D. None of the above

15. Which description is associated with connectionless-oriented mode protocols?

    A. Fast but unreliable

    B. Used for microwave communication links

    C. Guaranteed delivery of packets

    D. Used in wireless systems

16. Which protocol is typically found in older dial-up systems?

    A. SLIP

    B. PPP

    C. TCP

17. Which device resides at the OSI Network Layer?

    A. Bridge

    B. Router

    C. Gateway

    D. Repeater

18. Which device resides at the OSI Data Link Layer?

    A. Cable

    B. Bridge

    C. Repeater

    D. Router

19. Which device does not build routing tables?

    A. Bridge

    B. Router

    C. Brouter

    D. Repeater

20. In which layer would you find a redirector?

    A. The Application layer

    B. The Presentation layer

    C. The Data Link layer

    D. The Physical layer

    E. The Network layer

21. What is the maximum number of segments between any two nodes on an 802.3 network?

    A. 2

    B. 5

    C. 3

    D. 4

22. Token ring is a physical

    A. Bus network

    B. Ring network

    C. Star network

23. Propagation delay is

    A. Signal attenuation due to long cable lengths

    B. The amount of time it takes a signal to travel through a medium

    C. Reflections caused by poorly terminated systems

24. Which network access method does Ethernet use?

    A. CSMA/CD

    B. CSMA/CA

    C. Token passing

    D. AppleTalk

25. When installing a network, you must heed the distance limitations on the cable because the primary limiting factor for data transmission in a very long cable is

    A. Crosstalk

    B. Collisions

    C. Attenuation

    D. EMI

26. In a multiplexing environment in which efficient line utilization is most important, what is used?

    A. Repeaters

    B. A transmission control mux

    C. Capacity-sensitive allocation units

    D. Stat-TDM

27. You will use BNC-style connectors to connect

    A. Transceivers to AUI ports

    B. 10BASE-T cable segments

    C. Thick coax cable segments

    D. Thin coax segments

28. You are troubleshooting a thicknet LAN. Which of the following cable lengths that you found is/are legal?

    A. 150 meters

    B. 200 meters

    C. 500 meters

    D. All of the above

29. A standard, cabled LAN that includes some wireless components is known as

    A. A hybrid LAN

    B. A point-to-point LAN

    C. A wireless LAN

    D. A spread-spectrum LAN

30. Under heavy traffic loads, token passing networks

    A. Perform worse than contention based networks

    B. Perform better than contention based networks

    C. Have many collisions

    D. Stop exhibiting deterministic behavior

31. You are designing the Ethernet network for a new office building that will hold several hundred computer users on several floors. What type of Ethernet should you use to minimize your total cost of ownership?

    A. 10BASE5 (Thicknet)

    B. 10BASE2 (Thinnet)

    C. 10BASE-F (fiber-optic)

    D. 10BASE-T (UTP)

32. Your office is very dynamic, with existing users needing to move their computers frequently. Which type of Ethernet best accommodates this environment?

    A. 10BASE5 (Thicknet)

    B. 10BASE2 (Thinnet)

    C. 10BASE-F (fiber-optic)

    D. 10BASE-T (UTP)

33. What type of Ethernet is an easy upgrade from 10BASE-T if you have Category 5 wiring installed?

    A. 10BASE5

    B. 100BASE-TX

    C. 100BASE-T4

    D. 100BASE-FX

34. You are called in to troubleshoot a coax-based Ethernet network. You see that they have four repeaters in the network data path between some stations. This

    A. Will always create problems

    B. Always breaks the 5-4-3 rule

    C. May break the 5-4-3 rule if there are computers on more than three segments

    D. Is never a problem

35. Token ring uses an access arbitration method that can be considered

    A. Deterministic

    B. Stochastic

    C. Probabilistic

    D. Simple

36. What protocol should you configure if your network needs access to the Internet?

    A. DLC

    B. AppleTalk

    C. NWLink IPX

    D. TCP/IP

37. One of the advantages of TCP over UDP is

    A. TCP uses very small packets.

    B. TCP uses link-state route discovery.

    C. TCP provides error correction.

    D. TCP is faster than any other protocol for small networks.

38. You have a Hewlett-Packard JetDirect-family printer to install for shared network use on the same LAN segment as the Windows NT Server. What is the easiest protocol to install for it?

    A. DLC

    B. AppleTalk

    C. NWLink IPX

    D. TCP/IP

39. You need to use the Simple Network Management Protocol (SNMP) to monitor the health of some UNIX database servers at a remote site. What protocol does your network need to support?

    A. DLC

    B. AppleTalk

    C. NWLink IPX

    D. TCP/IP

40. You need to subnet your TCP/IP network. Which of the following protocols might your routers use to communicate routes to each other?

    A. RIP

    B. SNMP

    C. ICMP

    D. OSPF

41. Which Novell protocol is most like TCP?

    A. IPX

    B. SPX

    C. NCP

    D. ODI

42. What protocol should you configure if you need to connect to Novell NetWare servers?

    A. NWLink IPX

    B. TCP/IP

    C. DLC

    D. AppleTalk

43. Which Novell protocol is most like UDP?

    A. IPX

    B. SPX

    C. NCP

    D. ODI

44. Using a Web browser to connect with www.microsoft.com uses which protocols?

    A. NWLink, NetBIOS, and NetBEUI

    B. TCP, OSPF, and DLC

    C. NWLink, RIP, and SMB

    D. TCP, ARP, and DNS

45. You need to use 10Base-T to connect two computers that are 180 meters apart. What is the least expensive device you could use?

    A. Repeater

    B. Bridge

    C. Router

    D. Gateway

46. Scenario:
    You have a 200- PC network running a mixture of NWLink IPX and NetBEUI. Broadcast storms are already a frequent problem, and you need to add 100 more PCs.

Required:	You need to implement a strategy to minimize broadcasts while allowing for continued growth.
Desirable:	1. Minimal reconfiguration 2. Minimum expense
Proposed solution:	Replace the cabling with Category 5 and implement 100Base-TX switching to the desktop.

    A. Meets the requirement and both desirable goals

    B. Meets the requirement and one of the desirable goals

    C. Meets the requirement but neither of the desirable goals

    D. Does not meet the requirement

47. Scenario:
    You have a 200-PC network running a mixture of NWLink IPX and NetBEUI. Broadcast storms are already a frequent problem, and you need to add 100 more PCs.

Required:	You need to implement a strategy to minimize broadcasts while allowing for continued growth.
Desirable:	1. Minimal reconfiguration 2. Minimum expense
Proposed solution:	Configure the stations running NetBEUI to use NWLink IPX instead and install an IPX router.

    A. Meets the requirement and both desirable goals

    B. Meets the requirement and one of the desirable goals

    C. Meets the requirement but neither of the desirable goals

    D. Does not meet the requirement

48. You have decided to subnet your network to reduce the broadcast levels. Which device do you use?

    A. Repeater

    B. Bridge

    C. Router

    D. None of the above

49. You need to build a WAN that connects offices in China, France, and Australia. What WAN connection type is best suited for this type of requirement?

    A. Leased T1

    B. X.25

    C. ISDN BRI

    D. Frame relay

50. One of the advantages of ATM's using such small cells is that

    A. It means there is less overhead than larger cells would have.

    B. Each cell can contain complete, end-to-end addressing.

    C. Time-sensitive data can be safely multiplexed with non-time-sensitive data.

    D. Software-based cell switching is much faster.

51. Which of the following is used to simplify user management?

    A. Groups

    B. User Manager for Domains

    C. Syscon

    D. The ACL (Access Control List)

52. Access permissions applied to a shared resource

    A. Describes sharing an item with two passwords, one for read-only one for full access.

    B. Must be enabled to grant access to the network resource.

    C. Is the act of adding users to a shared resource.

    D. Requires a Windows NT or Novell NetWare server.

The following two questions use this situation as a scenario.

Network type: Windows NT servers, NetWare servers

Protocols: NetBEUI, IPX

Workstations: 30 Windows NT workstations

Servers: 7 servers, NetWare, and Windows NT

Your network contains some mission-critical data. If a disaster caused the data to be permanently lost, the company would have no choice but to go out of business. However, it is acceptable to roll back to the previous day's work. Traffic and network performance are operating within normal baseline parameters. The office has three locations, connected via a WAN.

You want to implement a backup plan.

Required objectives:

- The network must have no more than eight hours of downtime.

- If one site goes down, the others must be able to function.

Desired objectives:

- Network performance should not be adversely impacted by the strategy.

- Cost should be kept to reasonable levels.

53. You decide to implement a fully redundant backup network. You use an isolated network segment and a centralized tape backup server. You also keep a spare server in reserve. This plan will

    A. Perform both of the required objectives and both of the desired objectives.

    B. Perform both of the required objectives and one of the desired objectives.

    C. Perform both of the required objectives and none of the desired objectives.

    D. Not perform the required objectives.

54. You decide to use single tape units on each server. You maintain a spare server just in case. In addition, you do daily full backups and move the tapes to each of the other locations. This plan will

A. Perform both of the required objectives and both of the desired objectives.

B. Perform both of the required objectives and one of the desired objectives.

C. Perform both of the required objectives and none of the desired objectives.

D. Not perform the required objectives.

The following question uses this situation as a scenario.

Network type: Windows NT servers, multiple domains

Protocols: NetBEUI, IPX, TCP/IP

Workstations: 30 Windows NT workstations

You decide to implement a NetBIOS naming scheme for your network. You are currently part of a standalone network with one server, but you are scheduled to be connected to the multidomain corporate WAN in several months. Your users have email accounts on the corporate WAN mail hub.

Required objectives:

• The naming scheme must contain unique names.

• The naming scheme must continue to function after the WAN integration.

Desired objectives:

• The naming scheme should help streamline user administration.

• The naming scheme should be informative about the computer's role.

55. The Network Card *driver* is responsible for

A. Enabling the hardware and binding the software.

B. Managing the network path of the protocol software.

C. Pushing the data across the network.

D. Beaconing to the other adapter cards to limit network traffic.

56. Once the NIC is installed and is not conflicting with other devices, it is important to

A. Load the token and insert it into the frame.

B. Load the frame type into the protocol stack.

C. Create a unique token based on the MAC address.

D. Load the driver, protocols, and clients and attach the network cable.

57. You create a naming convention that uses a three-character building code, followed by a four-character floor code, followed by the user's email address. This plan will

A. Perform both of the required objectives and both of the desired objectives.

B. Perform both of the required objectives and one of the desired objectives.

C. Perform both of the required objectives and none of the desired objectives.

D. Not perform the required objectives.

58. You can use Performance Monitor to track such items as

A. Protocol use, drive use, and processor use.

B. A user's performance while using certain applications.

C. How long a computer takes to boot up.

D. Whether the user is suffering from a protocol mismanagement issue.

59. Protocol analysis tools measure performance by

   A. Decoding frames.

   B. Filtering packets through NetBEUI, IPX, and TCP/IP.

   C. Must use a gateway.

   D. Checking current network performance against a baseline.

60. Suppose Computer A can't seem to ping computer B on a TCP/IP network. You know that TCP/IP is installed on both PCs. The next thing you should check is

   A. The network utilization.

   B. The protocol binding.

   C. To see whether a competing protocol has control of the adapter.

   D. To see whether the Server service is running on Computer A.

61. Which of the following can you use to look for breaks in network cables by measuring cable voltage?

   A. Protocol analyzer

   B. DVM

   C. TDR

   D. MSDL

62. Which of the following sends sonar-like pulses down the cable to look for imperfections?

   A. DVM

   B. Oscilloscope

   C. TDR

   D. None of the above

63. A broadcast storm is

   A. A network broadcast that begins properly but doesn't terminate.

   B. An infinite loop caused by a faulty redirector.

   C. A sudden deluge of network traffic.

   D. A hard drive consecutively outputting all its bits to the network.

64. Which two of the following problems are the most common causes of network broadcast storms?

   A. A malfunctioning network adapter card.

   B. A short in a section of the transmission medium.

   C. Incorrect transport protocol assignments.

   D. A device on the network that is unable to contact another device because the other device either does not exist or, for some reason, does not respond.

65. Which three of the following could degrade network performance?

   A. A generator or mechanical device near the network

   B. A computer game

   C. A sudden disorderly shutdown of a workstation

   D. New hardware

66. Which one of the following devices is a solution for power fluctuation problems?

   A. Uninterruptible Power Supply (UPS)

   B. NT Clustering

   C. RAID

   D. Grounded circuit

67. Suppose there appears to be some interference on network cables installed over an acoustic tile ceiling. What is a possible (probable) cause for the interference?

    A. Fluorescent lights

    B. Adverse weather

    C. Electrical motors and devices

    D. Network cables tied together with monitor wires

68. Which of the following is the most fault tolerant of network types?

    A. Mesh

    B. Ring

    C. Star

    D. Ring

ANSWERS TO PRACTICE EXAM

1. **G.**   All of the above items are forms of media.

2. **C.**   10BASE2 uses 50-ohm RG58 coaxial cable.

3. **F.**   Ethernet is a physical network topology not a protocol.

4. **A.**   Raid level 0 refers to disk striping. Other popular implementations are Raid level 1, called disk mirroring, and Raid level 5, called disk striping with parity.

5. **B.**   Category 5. Remember that, as the number gets larger, the cable can support higher data rates and the expense also rises.

6. **B.**   LocalTalk employs collision-avoidance access.

7. **B.**   CSMA/CA networks are typically slower than CSMA/CD because CSMA/CA network must wait a random amount of time before transmitting on the media.

8. **C.**   In client/sever computing, both the client and the server share the task of processing. Terminals do not process data; they simply display data from the mainframe.

9. **C.**   This is not true. If the server goes down, then all users of the application stored on the server cannot run the application.

10. **B.**   Peer-to-peer networks implement share-level security. There is not a database of users in the peer-to-peer network architecture.

11. **C.**   Add access is not associated with directory shares. Add access is a security attribute for disk files and directories under NTFS.

12. **B.**   The Windows NT domain model is a server-based networking architecture that is centrally managed by the Primary Domain Controller (PDC).

13. **B.**   In a peer-to-peer network, each computer that shares resources is a server. It is also a client if it uses resources shared by other computers.

14. **B.**   TCP/IP is a connection-oriented protocol. NetBEUI is not a member of the Internet protocol suite, and UDP/IP is connectionless-oriented.

15. **A.**   Connectionless oriented communications are not responsible for error detection or delivering packets in correct sequence. Without this overhead, this mode is faster but not reliable.

16. **A.**   SLIP was developed before PPP; thus, it is found on older dial-up systems.

17. **B.**   The router resides at the Network layer. The router requires network configuration information to build internal network routing tables.

18. **B.** The bridge resides at the Data Link layer and requires address information to pass the frame to the correct next segment.

19. **D.** The repeater has no knowledge of segments or routes; thus, it does not build routing tables.

20. **B.** The redirector is found at the Presentation layer. This is an important component of many operating systems that make remote devices appear to be local.

21. **B.** Remember the 5-4-3 rule, in which 5 is the maximum number of repeated segments, 4 is the maximum number of repeaters and 3 is the maximum number of segments of the 5 that can be populated.

22. **C.** Token ring is a physical star because each workstation is connected to a central hub.

23. **B.** Propagation delay is the amount of time it takes a signal to travel through a medium.

24. **A.** Ethernet employs collision detection access.

25. **C.** Attenuation is the limiting factor for data transmission in very long cables. The longer the cable, the weaker the signal at the end.

26. **D.** Stat-TDM can use a line more efficiently than a fixed TDM configuration.

27. **D.** BNC connectors are only used with thin coax (10Base2) segments.

28. **D.** Thicknet cable can support cable segments of up to 500 meters, so all the choices listed are correct.

29. **A.** A LAN that has both wireless and standard cabled components is called a hybrid LAN.

30. **B.** Under heavy traffic loads, token-passing networks typically perform better than contention-based networks because they do not use any more bandwidth arbitrating access with a heavy load than they do with a light load.

31. **D.** The star wiring that 10BASE-T uses is inexpensive and much easier to troubleshoot and maintain than coaxial wiring like thicknet or thinnet.

32. **D.** 10BASE-T (UTP) is the best choice when computers move frequently because a single cable can be moved without affecting other users.

33. **B.** 100BASE-TX and 10BASE-T can both use Category 5 copper wiring, and 100BASE-TX is 10 times faster than 10BASE-T.

34. **C.** The 5-4-3 rule only allows four repeaters in the path if there are computers on no more than three of the cable segments.

35. **A.** Because each station gets a turn to transmit when the token arrives, token rings are considered deterministic.

36. **D.** TCP/IP is the protocol used on the Internet.

37. **C.** TCP is a reliable protocol and, as such, provides error correction that unreliable protocols, such as UDP, do not.

38. **A.** DLC is often considered the easiest protocol to configure because it has so few options.

39. **D.** Although SNMP *can* be carried inside of other protocols, it is almost always used with TCP/IP. The fact that the devices you are monitoring run UNIX makes this an easy question because UNIX devices almost exclusively support TCP/IP.

40. **A, D.** RIP and OSPF are both routing protocols that you might use.

41. **B.** SPX is the Novell protocol most like TCP.

42. **A.** NWLink IPX is used to connect to Novell NetWare servers.

43. **A.** IPX is the Novell protocol most like UDP.

44. **D.** TCP, ARP, & DNS are all used. DNS resolves the name into an address, ARP finds the hardware address of your default router, and TCP is used for the actual connection.

45. **A.** A repeater is the least expensive device listed, and it would allow each 10Base-T cable to be up to 100 meters.

46. **D.** Replacing the cabling with Category 5 and implementing 100Base-TX switching to the desktop does not meet the requirement because it does nothing to change the broadcast levels.

47. **A.** Configuring the stations running NetBEUI to use NWLink IPX instead and installing an IPX router reduces broadcasts while requiring minimal reconfiguration and expense. You might even be able to use an existing NT Server or NetWare server for the IPX router if you really have no budget.

48. **C.** Routers are the only type of device that can divide a network into subnets.

49. **B.** X.25 is best suited to international WANs.

50. **C.** Because ATM cells are so small, time-sensitive data can be safely multiplexed with non-time-sensitive data.

51. **A.** Groups are used to simplify user management.

52. **A.** This method of access, called Access Permissions, is applied to a shared resource. (This is not true if you are using NT Server or NT Workstation to share the resouce as it is then shared by granting permissions to individual users.)

53. **D.** If the centralized tape server fails, the entire network is without a backup.

54. **A.** Network performance will not suffer because the tape units are directly connected to each server.

55. **A.** Without a *driver*, or software, the NIC will fail to function. In addition to enabling the NIC, the driver also binds the protocols to the adapter.

56. **D.** Installation of the NIC is only a small step.

57. **A.** This plan will work perfectly, but the email address portion can contain only eight characters or less, because you will have used seven characters on the building and floor codes.

58. **A.** The Performance Monitor has a very high level of detail.

59. **A.** Protocol analysis tools decode frames in order to determine such items as packet source, packet destination, packet size, and data.

60. **B.** You must bind a protocol to a specific adapter in order to use it. The NDIS and ODI standards ensure that you don't have "competing protocols" fighting for control of the adapter. The Server service enables you to share resources, but it isn't required for a simple diagnostic check such as a ping.

61. **B.** A DVM (Digital Voltage Meter) measures cable voltage.

62. **C.** TDRs (Time-Domain Reflectometers) send sonar-like pulses.

63. **C.** A broadcast storm is a large, sudden increase in network traffic.

64. **A, D.** The most common causes of broadcast storms are a malfunctioning adapter and a device looking for a missing network node.

65. **A, B, D.** A shutdown of a workstation typically won't affect network performance. A mechanical device could cause electrical interference. A computer game or a faulty new device could disrupt or slow down the network.

66. **A.** A UPS protects the network from power fluctuations.

67. **A.** If you are experiencing interference in network cables installed over an acoustic tile ceiling, fluorescent lights are a logical first guess for the cause.

68. **A.** Mesh provides one link from each PC to every other PC. If one link goes down, the network still would function.

PART

VI

APPENDIXES

Glossary

100BASE-X 100BASE-X provides a data transmission speed of 100 Mbps using baseband. 100BASE-X supports many different cable standards.

100VG-AnyLAN Defined in the IEEE 802.12 standard for the transmitting of Ethernet and token-ring packets at 100 Mbps. Uses four twisted pair cables.

10BASE2 An Ethernet topology that supports 10 Mbps, uses baseband signals and can span 200 meters. Also called Thinnet.

10BASE5 An Ethernet topology that supports 10 Mbps, uses baseband signals and can span 500 meters. Also called Thicknet.

10BASE-FL An Ethernet topology that supports 10 Mbps, uses baseband signals and fiber-optic cable.

10BASE-T An Ethernet topology that supports 10 Mbps, uses baseband signals and twisted-pair wiring. Also known as UTP.

802.2 frame The default frame type used on Ethernet networks by all NetWare versions 3.12 and later.

802.3 frame This was the default frame type used in all Novell NetWare products versions 3.11 and earlier.

A

active hub A hub that has the ability to act as a repeater at the same time.

Address Resolution Protocol (ARP) ARP determines the physical address used by the device containing the IP address. ARP maintains tables of address resolution data and can broadcast packets to discover addresses on the network segment or use previously cached entries.

analog signal Analog signals constantly vary in one or more values, and these changes in values can be used to represent data. Analog waveforms frequently take the form of sine waves.

AppleTalk AppleTalk is the computing architecture developed by Apple Computer for the Macintosh family of personal computers. Although AppleTalk originally supported only Apple's proprietary LocalTalk cabling system, the suite has been expanded to incorporate both Ethernet and token-ring Physical layers. Within Microsoft operating systems, AppleTalk is only supported by Windows NT Server.

Application layer The seventh and top layer of the OSI model. This layer is concerned with the services provided on a network.

application server A server that provides some high end application used by many different computers.

ARCNet An older architecture that physically followed a physical bus or star topology and used a form of token passing to transmit data.

Asymmetric Digital Subscriber Line (ADSL) One new type of broadband WAN connectivity that is being tested by the telephone companies. Available only since 1997, ADSL is a Physical layer standard of sending data across existing telephone wires. By using a special ADSL modem, users can receive data at rates over 8 Mbps and send data at rates of up to 640 Kbps.

asynchronous modems Do not use a clocking mechanism to keep the sending and receiving devices synchronized. Instead, this type of transmission uses bit synchronization to synchronize the devices for each frame that is transmitted.

Asynchronous Transfer Mode (ATM) A high-bandwidth switching technology developed by the ITU Telecommunications Standards Sector (ITU-TSS). An organization called the ATM Forum is responsible for defining ATM implementation characteristics. ATM can be layered on other Physical layer technologies, such as Fiber Distributed Data Interface (FDDI) and SONET.

attenuation The degradation of a signal, caused by travelling too far of a distance.

auditing The process of creating a database that records particular events that occur on your network.

B

Backup Domain Controller (BDC) The Backup Domain Controller's user account database is a replicated copy of that from the PDC.

bandwidth The amount of data that a transmission medium can transfer.

base I/O port address Defines a memory address through which data will flow to and from the adapter.

base memory address A place in the computer's memory that marks the beginning of a buffer area reserved for the network adapter.

baseband The entire bandwidth is used by a signal. Found in digital communications.

baseline A sampling of how the network functions in its equilibrium state.

Basic Rate ISDN (BRI) Basic Rate ISDN uses three channels. Two channels (called *B channels*) carry the digital data at 64 Kbps. A third channel (called the *D channel*) provides link and signaling information at 16 Kbps. Basic Rate ISDN thus is referred to as *2B+D*. A single PC transmitting through ISDN can use both B channels simultaneously, providing a maximum data rate of 128 Kbps (or higher with compression).

bindery An administrative model that is used by Novell NetWare versions up to NetWare 3.2 (All Novell servers that are version 4 or higher use directory services.)

block interleaving A process that involves distributing the data block-by-block across the disk array in the same location across each disk. This is used by RAID 0.

Boot PROM Boot PROM allows the network card to boot up and connect over the network, as the Boot PROM has the necessary connection software to use.

bounded media A physical form of media, such as a cable.

boundless media A wireless form of media, such as radio waves.

bridges Bridges know the side of the bridge on which a node is located. A bridge passes only packets addressed to computers across the bridge, so a bridge can thus filter traffic, reducing the load on the transmission medium.

broadband The bandwidth contains many signals at once.

Broadband ISDN (B-ISDN) A refinement of ISDN that is defined to support higher-bandwidth applications, such as video, imaging, and multimedia. Physical layer support for B-ISDN is provided by Asynchronous Transfer Mode (ATM) and the Synchronous Optical Network (SONET).

broadcast storm A sudden flood of broadcast messages that clogs the transmission medium, approaching use of 100 percent of the bandwidth. Broadcast storms cause performance to decline and, in the worst case, computers cannot even access the network.

brouter A device that is a combination of a Bridge and router.

bus topology A topology in which all devices connect to a common shared cable.

C

cable modem   This device allows networks to interconnect through existing cable TV lines. Some areas that offer this service have a full duplex version that allows transmission rates of 4 to 10 Mbps. Other areas have cable standards in place that only allow the coaxial TV cable to receive data, relying upon an analog dial-up connection to be used to send data.

Campus Area Network (CAN)   A network that spans a campus.

centralized computing   A form of computing where all the processing is done by one central computer.

circuit switching   A mechanism for moving data requiring a constant physical circuit.

client/server   A networking model where a specific role of providing services or acting as a client (but not both) is performed by a computer.

clocking   The mechanism used to count and pace the number of signals being sent and received.

coaxial cable   A type of cabling using a solid metal core surrounded by a plastic sheath.

collaborative or cooperative computing   A form of computing where certain tasks are processed by one computer, and other specific tasks are performed by other computers.

concentrator   This is a term for a hub or MSAU. A connectivity device used to connect multiple twisted-pair cables together.

connection oriented   In connection-oriented mode, the chain of links between the source and destination nodes forms a kind of logical pathway connection. The nodes forwarding the data packet can track which packet is part of which connection. This enables the internal nodes to provide flow control as the data moves along the path.

connectionless   Connectionless mode does not provide elaborate internal control mechanisms; instead, connectionless mode relegates all error-correcting and retransmitting processes to the source and destination nodes. The end nodes acknowledge the receipt of packets and retransmit if necessary, but internal nodes do not participate in flow control and error correction (other than simply forwarding messages between the end nodes).

connector type   The connection between the network adapter card and the transmission media.

contention   Computers contend for use of the transmission medium. Any computer in the network can transmit at any time (first come, first serve).

Copy   This is the other Microsoft NT NTBACKUP utility-specific command. This command backs up all selected files, but does not modify the archive bit of those files being backed up. This is a useful option if you wish to do a backup outside the regular backup schedule and do not wish to alter the normal backup routine.

current state   A mechanism that uses the clock count to analyze the current state of the signal during that count. Thus the signal is either "on" or "off" during the clock count.

D

Daily Copy   This is a Microsoft NT NTBACKUP utility-specific command. This command backs up only those files that were changed the day that this option is selected, when doing a Daily Copy backup, and does not modify the archive bit of the files being backed up. This is a useful option if you wish to do a backup outside the regular back up schedule and do not wish to alter the normal backup routine.

data bus   A pathway inside your computer that carries data between the hardware components.

Data Link Control (DLC)   DLC is not a protocol that can be used to connect Windows NT or 95 computers together.

Data Link layer   The second from the bottom layer of the OSI model. This layer is concerned with relating the access methods to the transmission media.

data migration   The moving of data from one location to another.

data striping   The capability of arranging data in different sequences across drives. Microsoft calls this disk striping.

database services   A service that provides access to a database by many different computers.

datagram packet switching   Datagram services treat each packet as an independent message. Each packet is routed through the internetwork independently, and each switch node determines which network segment should be used for the next step in the packet's route. This capability enables switches to bypass busy segments and take other steps to speed packets through the internetwork.

differential backup   Backs up the specified files if the files have changed since the last backup. This type doesn't mark the files as having been backed up, however. (A differential backup is somewhat like a copy command. Because the file is not marked as having been backed up, a later differential or incremental backup will back up the file again.)

Digital Data Service (DDS)   A very basic form of digital service. DDS transmits point-to-point at 2.4, 4.8, 9.6, or 56 Kbps. In its most basic form, DDS provides a dedicated line.

digital signal   Signals that have two discrete states. These states are either "off" or "on."

digital volt meters   Hand-held electronic measuring tools that enable you to check the voltage of network cables. They also can be used to check the resistance of terminators.

directory services   A hierarchical distributed database model. This model allows for the management of all resources through one utility as well as providing a high level of fault tolerance within the system.

directory services   A service that provides location information of devices and services on the network. Also known as x.500.

disk duplexing   Disk mirroring when adding a separate drive controller for each drive. Duplexing is a form of mirroring that enables you to configure a more robust hardware environment. Known also as RAID 1.

disk mirroring   Two hard drives—one primary, one secondary—that use the same disk channel or controller cards and cable. Disk mirroring is most commonly configured by using disk drives contained in the server. Known also as RAID 1.

disk striping   *See* data striping.

disk striping with parity   Also known as RAID 5, this form of fault-tolerance requires three or more drives. It involves striping data and a parity across all drives being used. If any one drive fails, the data on that drive can be reconstructed by using the parity bits and data found on the other drives.

distance vector routing   A routing algorithm that utilizes constant broadcasts to send out routing tables to other routers.

distributed computing   A form of computing where all the processing is shared by many different computers.

DMA channel   The DMA or Direct Memory Access channel is an address used for quicker access to the CPU by the adapter card.

domain   A security model that uses a flat user account database similar to the bindery model. The main difference is that this database is stored on one or more computers known as Domain Controllers.

Domain Name System (DNS)   The Domain Name System (DNS) protocol provides host name and IP address resolution as a service to client applications. DNS servers enable humans to use logical node names, utilizing a fully qualified domain name structure, to access network resources. Host names can be up to 260 characters long.

Dynamic Host Configuration Protocol (DHCP) DHCP allows for the automatic assignment of IP addresses. This is usually performed by one or more computers (DHCP servers) that will assign IP addresses and subnet masks, along with other configuration information, to a computer as a computer initializes on the network.

dynamic router   A router that can utilize a routing protocol to exchange information with other routers to build a routing table.

E

ElectroMagnetic Interference (EMI)   Interference caused by electromagnetic waves.

electromagnetic spectrum   The range of electromagnetic waves.

email   Electronic mail.

encryption   Encryption codes the information sent on the network using a special algorithm and then decodes it on the other end. This technique offers varying degrees of safety, largely based on the length and complexity of the code used to encrypt the data.

Ethernet   A network architecture that follows the IEEE 802.3 set of standards.

Ethernet II frame type   Ethernet II frame types are similar to 802.3 frame types, except they contain a type field instead of a length field. This frame type can also be used with TCP/IP and AppleTalk.

Ethernet_SNAP frame   Ethernet_SNAP can be used for TCP/IP and AppleTalk Phase II transport protocols, as well as for IPX/SPX on Ethernet networks.

Event Viewer   A Windows NT utility that creates logs containing a record of previous errors, warnings, and other messages from the system. Studying the event log can help you find recurring errors and discover when a problem first appeared.

F

fax service   Services providing a shared fax to many computers.

FDDI   A token passing architecture that uses fiber-optic cable.

fiber-optic cable   A type of cable that uses light to transmit data.

file archiving   The movement of files to a near or off-line storage.

file service   Services allowing for the storage and access of files.

file transfer   The moving of a file from one location to another.

file transfer protocol (FTP)   FTP is a protocol for sharing files between networked hosts. FTP enables users to log on to remote hosts. Logged-on users can inspect directories, manipulate files, execute commands, and perform other commands on the host. FTP also has the capability of transferring files between dissimilar hosts by supporting a file request structure that is independent of specific operating systems.

file-level security   Security applied to files and directories on NTFS partitions.

file-update synchronization   The updating of many copies of a file at once.

Frame Relay Designed to support the Broadband Integrated Services Digital Network (B-ISDN), which was discussed in the previous section. The specifications for Frame Relay address some of the limitations of X.25. As with X.25, Frame Relay is a packet-switching network service, but Frame Relay was designed around newer, faster fiber-optic networks.

frequency-division multiplexing Multiplexing that sends different data using different signals.

full backup Backs up all specified files.

G

gateway A device that can translate the different protocols used by different networks. Gateways can be implemented starting at the Network layer or at higher layers in the OSI model, depending on where the protocol translation is required. A gateway replaces the necessary protocol layers of a packet so that the packet can circulate in the destination environment.

global groups Created only on the Primary Domain Controller of a Microsoft domain. Backup Domain Controllers receive a copy of this database, thus they also contain global groups. These groups function primarily as containers for user accounts. Global Groups are designed to contain general groupings of people, such as Sales, Accounting, or the IS department. Global groups cannot contain other groups; only users from the domain the global group is created in, are permitted to be part of a global group.

groups Administrative units that are comprised of one or more users with similar needs for network resources. Often users are placed into groups, and resource access is managed on a group basis, as opposed to an individual user basis.

groupware An application that allows access to many users at once for the distribution of information.

H

hop count This method describes the number of routers that a message might cross before it reaches its destination. If all hops are assumed to take the same amount of time, the optimum path is the path with the smallest hop count.

I, J, K

IBM cabling Another name for STP cabling.

IEEE The Institute of Electronic and Electrical Engineers. This is an international body that sets standards for electronic devices.

IEEE 802 family A set of networking standards developed by the IEEE.

incremental backup Backs up only those files that have changed since the last full or incremental backup.

infrared transmissions Infrared transmissions typically are limited to 100 feet. Within this range, however, infrared is relatively fast. Infrared's high bandwidth supports transmission speeds of up to 10 Mbps.

Integrated Services Digital Network (ISDN) A group of ITU (CCITT) standards designed to provide voice, video, and data transmission services on digital telephone networks. ISDN uses multiplexing to support multiple channels on high-bandwidth circuits.

intelligent hub A hub that can allow management and/or the ability to perform switching.

International Standards Organization (ISO) International body responsible for setting standards for many things, including certain network standards.

Internet The term used to describe the far-flung, worldwide set of services provided by the interconnection of LANs and WANs through the TCP/IP networking protocol.

Internet Control Message Protocol (ICMP)
ICMP enhances the error control provided by IP.
Connectionless protocols, such as IP, cannot detect
internetwork errors, such as congestion or path failures.
ICMP can detect such errors and notify IP and upper-
layer protocols.

Internet Protocol (IP)   A connectionless protocol
that provides datagram service, and IP packets are most
commonly referred to as IP datagrams. IP is a packet-
switching protocol that performs the addressing and
route selection. IP operates at the Network layer of the
OSI model.

internetwork   Multiple independent networks that
are connected and can share remote resources.

Internetwork Packet Exchange (IPX)   A Network
layer protocol that provides connectionless (datagram)
service. IPX is responsible for internetwork routing and
maintaining network logical addresses.

intranet   A term used to describe your network.

IPX/SPX   A protocol suite developed by Xerox and
used by Novell operating systems.

IRQ   The IRQ (Interrupt Request Line) setting
reserves an interrupt request line for the adapter to use
when contacting the CPU.

L

laser transmissions   High-powered laser transmitters
can transmit data for several thousand yards when line-
of-sight communication is possible. Lasers can be used
in many of the same situations as microwave links
without requiring an FCC license.

learning bridge   Also known as a transparent bridge.
This type of bridge is transparent to the device sending
the packet. At the same time, this bridge will learn over
time what devices exist on each side of it.

leased lines   Telephone lines that are leased for dedicated use by a company or individual.

link state routing   A routing algorithm that only
sends out route table changes.

local area network (LAN)   A network characterized
by high throughput, short distances to be traveled, and
all systems controlled by the company owning the network.

local groups   Local groups can be created on
Windows NT Server or Workstation and can include
both user accounts and global groups. Moreover, these
groups are assigned permissions.

logical topology   Describes the logical pathway a signal follows as it passes among the network nodes.

M

MAC address   These addresses are hexadecimal in
nature and are unique for each card. Each MAC
address is assigned by the manufacturer. It is sometimes
referred to as the network adapter card's hardware
address.

Management Information Base (MIB)   A MIB is a
database of information that can be read by management software designed to work with SNMP. Some
examples of this management software is IBM's
OpenView.

mesh topology   A topology in which every device is
connected to every other device on the network. When
a new device is added, a connection to all existing
devices must be made.

message switching   A store-and-forward mechanism
of moving data.

message/communication services   A service that
transfers messages and or communications to many
different computers.

modem   A device that converts a computer's digital signal to an analog signal for transmission of information over a telephone line.

multiplexing   The ability to send many different signals over a single transmission media.

Municipal Area Network (MAN)   A network that spans a municipality.

N

narrow-band radio   In narrow-band radio communications (also called single-frequency radio), transmissions occur at a single radio frequency.

NDIS (Network Data Link Interface Standard)   A Microsoft standard for network card drivers.

NetBEUI   A transport protocol that serves as an extension to Microsoft's Network Basic Input/Output System (NetBIOS). Because NetBEUI was developed for an earlier generation of DOS-based PCs, it is small, easy to implement, and fast. NetBEUI is non-routable, making it somewhat anachronistic in today's diverse and interconnected networking environment. NetBEUI is also a broadcast-based protocol, which can cause congestion in larger networks.

NetWare Core Protocol (NCP)   The NetWare Core Protocol provides numerous function calls that support network services, such as file service, printing, name management, file locking, and synchronization. NetWare client software interfaces with NCP to access NetWare services.

NetWare Link Services Protocol (NLSP)   A link state routing protocol used by routers (NetWare servers with two or more adapter cards can act as routers) to advertise networks when their address tables change.

network   A set of interconnected systems with something to share.

Network File System (NFS)   Developed by Sun Microsystems, NFS is a family of file-access protocols that are a considerable advancement over FTP and Telnet. Since Sun made the NFS specifications available for public use, NFS has achieved a high level of popularity.

Network layer   The third layer of the OSI model. This layer is is concerned with the addressing locations on the network.

Network Monitor   A Microsoft program that analyzes frames coming and going, in real time, from the computer on which they run. Network Monitor records a number of statistics, including the percent of network utilization and the broadcasts per second. In addition, Network Monitor tabulates frame statistics (such as frames sent and received) for each network address.

NWLink   Microsoft's implementation of the IPX/SPX protocol suite.

O

ODI   Open Data Link Interface. A Novell standard for network card drivers.

Open Shortest Path First (OSPF)   The OSPF protocol is a link-state route-discovery protocol that is designed to overcome the limitations of RIP. On large internetworks, OSPF can identify the internetwork topology and improve performance by implementing load balancing and class-of-service routing.

oscilloscope   An oscilloscope measures fluctuations in signal voltage and can help find faulty or damaged cabling. Oscilloscopes are often more expensive electronic devices that show the signal fluctuations on a monitor.

OSI   The Open Systems Interconnection model. A reference model developed by the ISO to provide a framework for explaining networking concepts.

P, Q

packet   A unit of data that is transmitted across the transmission media.

packet switching   A mechanism for moving data by breaking the data down into many small packets. These packets are transported over many different routes and are reassembled at their destination.

peer-to-peer   A networking model where both the services and the client are performed by the same computer.

Performance Monitor   A Windows NT program that lets you monitor important system parameters for the computers on your network in real time. Performance Monitor can keep an eye on a large number of system parameters, providing a graphical or tabular profile of system and network trends.

Permanent Virtual Circuit (PVC)   A permanent route through the network that is always available to the customer. With a PVC, charges are still billed on a per-use basis.

Physical layer   Bottom layer of the OSI model. This layer of the OSI model deals with the transmission media.

physical topology   Describes the actual layout of the network transmission media.

Point-to-Point Protocol (PPP)   A standard similar to SLIP, but more robust. This standard will support NetBEUI and NWLink as well as TCP/IP.

polling   One device is responsible for polling the other devices to see if they are ready for the transmission or reception of data.

Presentation layer   The sixth layer from the bottom of the OSI model. This layer is concerned with hiding the bottom layers from the Application layer of the OSI model.

Primary Domain Controller (PDC)   Primary and Backup Domain Controllers perform essentially the same function. It is their role to store the user account database. The difference is that a PDC stores the master copy of this database. It is on this master copy that changes can occur. When a new user is added, the PDC's database is affected.

Primary Rate   Primary Rate supports 23 64 Kbps B channels and one 64 Kbps D channel. The D channel is used for signaling and management, and the B channels provide the data throughput.

printing services   Services that allow the sharing of a printer.

protocol   A set of rules used for communications.

protocol analyzers   Hardware or software products that are used to monitor network traffic, track network performance, and analyze packets. Protocol analyzers can identify bottlenecks, protocol problems, and malfunctioning network components.

PSTN (Public Switched Telephone Network)   Your typical phone system.

R

redirector service   A service that provides connectivity to a server service.

relative expense   This method calculates any defined measure of the cost (including the monetary cost) to use a given link.

Remote Terminal Emulation (Telnet)   Telnet enables PCs and workstations to function as dumb terminals in sessions with hosts on internetworks. Telnet implementations are available for most end-user platforms, including UNIX (of course), DOS, Windows, and Macintosh OS.

Repeaters   Repeaters regenerate a signal and are used to expand LANs beyond cabling limits.

Resource   Any component that you would like to use on the network. This could be anything from a file on another machine, to a printer located at the end of the hall, to even a certain task available by a specific program.

ring speed   The data transfer speed of a token-ring network. Possible values are 8 Mbps and 16 Mbps.

ring topology   Ring topologies are wired in a circle. Each node is connected to its neighbors on either side, and data passes around the ring in one direction only.

routers   Routers forward packets based on a logical (as opposed to a physical) address. Some routers can determine the best path for a packet based on routing algorithms.

Routing Information Protocol (RIP)   A protocol used in both the TCP/IP and IPX/SPX protocol suites for the automatic building and distribution of routing tables.

S

satellite microwave   Satellite microwave systems relay transmissions through communication satellites that operate in geosynchronous orbits 22,300 miles above the earth.

security   The process of giving "rights" or "permissions" to groups or users, so that they can access resources on the network. Different network operating systems use different terms to describe these types of security issues.

security services   A service that provides security on the network.

Sequenced Packet Exchange (SPX)   A Transport layer protocol that extends IPX to provide connection-oriented service with reliable delivery. Reliable delivery is ensured by retransmitting packets in the event of an error.

Serial Line Internet Protocol (SLIP)   This is a standard for moving data across a telephone line using the TCP/IP transport protocol.

Server Messaging Blocks (SMB)   Microsoft's equivalent to NCP packets. Like NCP packets, SMBs operate at the Application layer of the OSI model. SMBs allow machines on a Microsoft network to communicate with one another. Through the use of SMBs, file and print services can be shared. SMBs can use TCP/IP, NWLink (IPX/SPX), or NetBEUI.

server mirroring   The capability to have one server completely mirrored in all forms to another server. This would mean that if Server A went down for any reason whatsoever, such as a failed hard drive, a failed network card, or even a blown motherboard, the mirrored Server B would take over the duties of Server A.

server service   A service on Microsoft NT computers that provides file and print services.

Service Advertising Protocol (SAP)   The Service Advertising Protocol (SAP) provides location information by a device indicating what services it is offering. Devices can see each other on the network by listing the SAPs each server issues.

Session layer   This is the fifth layer from the bottom of the OSI model. This layer addresses session establishment between computers.

share-level security   Security applied to resources such as directories and printers that have been shared on the network.

sharing   Only by specifying that you want to grant others access to a resource—be it a directory, a CD-ROM drive, or a printer—do you make the resource available for use from remote computers and devices. A shared resource is simply a resource whose owner has leveraged networking to make it available for use by others.

shielded twisted-pair cable (STP) A form of twisted-pair cabling that has EMI shielding.

Simple Mail Transport Protocol (SMTP) A protocol for routing mail through internetworks. SMTP uses the TCP and IP protocols.

Simple Network Management Protocol (SNMP) A general purpose method of managing remote devices on the network.

spanning tree algorithm Enables complex Ethernet networks to use bridges while redundant routes exist. The algorithm enables the bridges to communicate and construct a logical network without redundant paths. The logical network is reconfigured if one of the paths fails.

spread-spectrum radio Spread-spectrum radio transmission is a technique originally developed by the military to solve several communication problems. Spread-spectrum improves reliability, reduces sensitivity to interference and jamming, and is less vulnerable to eavesdropping than single-frequency radio.

star topology Star topologies require that all devices connect to a central hub. The hub receives signals from other network devices and routes the signals to the proper destinations.

state transmission State transmission relies on the change of the state of a network signal to represent a new transmission of data.

static router A router that must have a manually programmed routing table.

Super Server A hardware solution offered by several different hardware manufacturers. The idea behind a Super Server is that almost any piece of equipment can be changed on the Super Server without needing to shut down the server.

Switched 56 A dial-up version of the 56 Kbps DDS. With Switched 56, users can dial other Switched 56 sites and pay only for the connect time.

Switched Multimegabit Digital Service (SMDS) Developed by Bell Communications Research in 1991, SMDS technology is related to ATM in that it transports data in 53-byte cells. SMDS is a connectionless Data Link layer service that supports cell switching at data rates of 1.544 to 45 Mbps.

Switched Virtual Circuit (SVC) SVC is created for a specific communication session and then disappears after the session. The next time the computers communicate, a different virtual circuit might be used.

synchronous modems A simple, inexpensive technology ideally suited for transmitting small frames at irregular intervals by using start, stop, and parity bits added to each character being transmitted. Overhead for asynchronous transmission is high, often in the neighborhood of nearly 20 to 30 percent.

Synchronous Optical Network (SONET) Bell Communications Research developed SONET, which has been accepted as an ANSI standard. As the "optical" in the name implies, SONET is a standard for communication over fiber-optic networks. Data rates for SONET are organized in a hierarchy based on the Optical Carrier (OC) speed and the corresponding Synchronous Transport Signals (STS) employed. The basic OC and STS data rate is 51.84 Mbps, but higher data rates are provided in multiples of the basic rate.

System Monitor A program that collects information on a Windows 95 machine in real time. System Manager collects information on different categories of items on the system.

T

T1 This leased line provides point-to-point connections and transmits a total of 24 channels across two wire pairs—one pair for sending and one for receiving—for a transmission rate of 1.544 Mbps. A T1 is known as an E1 line in Europe.

T3   T3 (E3 in Europe) is similar to T1, but T3 has an even higher capacity. In fact, a T3 line can transmit at up to 45 Mbps. This is because a T3 line is made up of 672 64 Kbps channels.

T-connector   A T-shaped device used to connect network cards to Thinnet cable.

TCP/IP   Transmission Control Protocol / Internet Protocol. A set of protocols (protocol suite) and services used by many different operating systems and the Internet.

terrestrial microwave   Terrestrial microwave communication employs Earth-based transmitters and receivers. The frequencies used are in the low-gigahertz range, which limits all communications to line-of-sight.

Thicknet   A form of coaxial cable that's thicker than Thinnet.

Thinnet   A form of coaxial cable that's thinner than Thicknet.

tic count   This method provides an actual time estimate used in routers. A tic is a time unit as defined by the routing implementation.

time-division multiplexing   Multiplexing using different time intervals to send data.

Time-Domain Reflectometer (TDM)   TDMs send sound waves along a cable and look for imperfections that might be caused by a break or a short in the line. A good TDR will often be able to detect faults on a cable to within a few feet.

token passing   The computers take turns using the transmission medium. This is facilitated by the passing of a token. The machine in possession of the token is allowed to transmit.

token-ring   A network architecture that follows the IEEE 802.5 set of standards.

token-ring frame   There are two types of token-ring frames. One is used to carry management information, and the other is used to transfer data. Token-ring frames are used on token-ring networks, and not Ethernet networks.

Token-Ring_SNAP frame   The Token-Ring_SNAP provides a similar function as the Ethernet_SNAP frame type, but for token-ring networks.

Transmission Control Protocol (TCP)   An internetwork connection-oriented protocol that corresponds to the OSI Transport layer. TCP provides full-duplex end-to-end connections.

transmission medium   A pathway used to connect different resources on a network.

transparent bridge   *See* learning bridge.

Transport layer   The fourth layer of the OSI model. This layer covers the movement of data on the network.

twisted-pair cable   A type of cable that has two or more wires twisted around each other. Telephone wire is a twisted-pair cable.

U, V

Uninterruptible Power Supply (UPS)   A special battery (or sometimes a generator) that supplies power to an electronic device in the event of a power failure.

unshielded twisted-pair cable (UTP)   A form of twisted-pair that has no shielding from EMI.

user   Anyone who requests network resources. In most cases, you assign a unique username and password to every individual on your network.

User Datagram Protocol (UDP)   The User Datagram Protocol (UDP) is a connectionless Transport (host-to-host) layer protocol. UDP does not provide message acknowledgments; rather, it simply transports datagrams. UDP operates at the Transport layer of the OSI model.

vampire clamp   A device used to connect drop cables to Thicknet cables.

virtual circuit packet switching   Virtual circuits operate by establishing a formal connection between two devices in communication. When devices begin a session, they negotiate communication parameters, such as maximum message size, communication windows, and network paths. This negotiation establishes a *virtual circuit*, which is a well-defined path through the internetwork by which the devices communicate. This virtual circuit generally remains in effect until the devices stop communicating.

viruses   Viruses are created intentionally with the aim of injuring or altering your machines. Viruses can be spread through computer systems in many ways, but the most common is through an executable file.

voice mail   The storage and movement of voice messages.

W, X, Y, Z

wide area network (WAN)   A network characterized by low throughput, long distances to be traveled, and not all systems controlled by the company owning the network.

Windows Internet Naming Service (WINS)   WINS provides a function similar to that of DNS, with the exception that it provides NetBIOS names to IP address resolution.

wireless media   Transmission media that does not use a cable to transmit data.

workgroup   An administrative model used by peer-to-peer networking systems such as Windows 95 and Windows for Workgroups.

X.25   A packet-switching network standard developed by the International Telegraph and Telephone Consultative Committee (CCITT), which has been renamed the International Telecommunications Union (ITU). The standard, referred to as *Recommendation X.25*, was introduced in 1974 and is now implemented most commonly in WANs.

zone   An AppleTalk version of a workgroup. Multiple network segments can be joined to form a single zone, and a single segment can have multiple zones.

Overview of the Certification Process

You must pass rigorous certification exams to become a Microsoft Certified Professional. These certification exams provide a valid and reliable measure of your technical proficiency and expertise. The closed-book exams are developed in consultation with computer industry professionals who have on-the-job experience with Microsoft products in the workplace. These exams are conducted by an independent organization—Sylvan Prometric—at more than 1,200 Authorized Prometric Testing Centers around the world.

Currently Microsoft offers six types of certification, based on specific areas of expertise:

- **Microsoft Certified Professional (MCP).** Persons who attain this certification are qualified to provide installation, configuration, and support for users of at least one Microsoft desktop operating system, such as Windows NT Workstation. In addition, candidates can take elective exams to develop areas of specialization. MCP is the initial or first level of expertise.

- **Microsoft Certified Professional + Internet (MCP+Internet).** Persons who attain this certification are qualified to plan security, install and configure server products, manage server resources, extend service to run CGI scripts or ISAPI scripts, monitor and analyze performance, and troubleshoot problems. The expertise required is similar to that of an MCP with a focus on the Internet.

- **Microsoft Certified Systems Engineer (MCSE).** Persons who attain this certification are qualified to effectively plan, implement, maintain, and support information systems with Microsoft Windows NT and other Microsoft advanced systems and workgroup products, such as Microsoft Office and Microsoft BackOffice. MCSE is a second level of expertise.

- **Microsoft Certified Systems Engineer + Internet (MCSE+Internet).** Persons who attain this certification are qualified in the core MCSE areas and are qualified to enhance, deploy, and manage sophisticated intranet and Internet solutions that include a browser, proxy server, host servers, database, and messaging and commerce components. In addition, an MCSE+Internet–certified professional will be able to manage and analyze Web sites.

- **Microsoft Certified Solution Developer (MCSD).** Persons who attain this certification are qualified to design and develop custom business solutions by using Microsoft development tools, technologies, and platforms, including Microsoft Office and Microsoft BackOffice. MCSD is a second level of expertise with a focus on software development.

- **Microsoft Certified Trainer (MCT).** Persons who attain this certification are instructionally and technically qualified by Microsoft to deliver

Microsoft Education Courses at Microsoft-authorized sites. An MCT must be employed by a Microsoft Solution Provider Authorized Technical Education Center or a Microsoft Authorized Academic Training site.

NOTE

Stay in Touch For up-to-date information about each type of certification, visit the Microsoft Training and Certification World Wide Web site at http://www.microsoft.com/ train_cert. You must have an Internet account and a WWW browser to access this information. You also can call the following sources:

- Microsoft Certified Professional Program:
  800-636-7544

- Sylvan Prometric Testing Centers:
  800-755-EXAM

- Microsoft Online Institute (MOLI):
  800-449-9333

How to Become a Microsoft Certified Professional (MCP)

To become an MCP, you must pass one operating system exam. The following list contains the names and exam numbers of all the operating system exams that will qualify you for your MCP certification (a * denotes an exam that is scheduled to be retired):

- Implementing and Supporting Microsoft Windows 95, #70-064 (formerly #70-063)

- Implementing and Supporting Microsoft Windows NT Workstation 4.02, #70-073

- Implementing and Supporting Microsoft Windows NT Workstation 3.51, #70-042*

- Implementing and Supporting Microsoft Windows NT Server 4.0, #70-067

- Implementing and Supporting Microsoft Windows NT Server 3.51, #70-043*

- Microsoft Windows for Workgroups 3.11–Desktop, #70-048*

- Microsoft Windows 3.1, #70-030*

- Microsoft Windows Architecture I, #70-160

- Microsoft Windows Architecture II, #70-161

How to Become a Microsoft Certified Professional + Internet (MCP+Internet)

To become an MCP with a specialty in Internet technology, you must pass the following three exams:

- Internetworking Microsoft TCP/IP on Microsoft Windows NT 4.0, #70-059

- Implementing and Supporting Microsoft Windows NT Server 4.0, #70-067

- Implementing and Supporting Microsoft Internet Information Server 3.0 and Microsoft Index Server 1.1, #70-077

  OR Implementing and Supporting Microsoft Internet Information Server 4.0, #70-087

How to Become a Microsoft Certified Systems Engineer (MCSE)

MCSE candidates must pass four operating system exams and two elective exams. The MCSE certification path is divided into two tracks: the Windows NT 3.51 track and the Windows NT 4.0 track.

The following lists show the core requirements (four operating system exams) for the Windows NT 3.51 track, the core requirements for the Windows NT 4.0 track, and the elective courses (two exams) you can choose from for either track.

The four Windows NT 3.51 track core requirements for MCSE certification are:

- Implementing and Supporting Microsoft Windows NT Server 3.51, #70-043*

- Implementing and Supporting Microsoft Windows NT Workstation 3.51, #70-042*

- Microsoft Windows 3.1, #70-030*

  OR Microsoft Windows for Workgroups 3.11, #70-048*

  OR Implementing and Supporting Microsoft Windows 95, #70-064

  OR Implementing and Supporting Microsoft Windows 98, #70-098

- Networking Essentials, #70-058

The four Windows NT 4.0 track core requirements for MCSE certification are:

- Implementing and Supporting Microsoft Windows NT Server 4.0, #70-067

- Implementing and Supporting Microsoft Windows NT Server 4.0 in the Enterprise, #70-068

- Microsoft Windows 3.1, #70-030*

  OR Microsoft Windows for Workgroups 3.11, #70-048*

  OR Implementing and Supporting Microsoft Windows 95, #70-064

  OR Implementing and Supporting Microsoft Windows NT Workstation 4.0, #70-073

  OR Implementing and Supporting Microsoft Windows 98, #70-098

- Networking Essentials, #70-058

For both the Windows NT 3.51 and the Windows NT 4.0 track, you must pass two of the following elective exams for MCSE certification:

- Implementing and Supporting Microsoft SNA Server 3.0, #70-013

  OR Implementing and Supporting Microsoft SNA Server 4.0, #70-085

- Implementing and Supporting Microsoft Systems Management Server 1.0, #70-014*

  OR Implementing and Supporting Microsoft Systems Management Server 1.2, #70-018

  OR Implementing and Supporting Microsoft Systems Management Server 2.0, #70-086

- Microsoft SQL Server 4.2 Database Implementation, #70-021

  OR Implementing a Database Design on Microsoft SQL Server 6.5, #70-027

  OR Implementing a Database Design on Microsoft SQL Server 7.0, #70-029

- Microsoft SQL Server 4.2 Database Administration for Microsoft Windows NT, #70-022

OR System Administration for Microsoft SQL Server 6.5 (or 6.0), #70-026

OR System Administration for Microsoft SQL Server 7.0, #70-028

◆ Microsoft Mail for PC Networks 3.2-Enterprise, #70-037

◆ Internetworking with Microsoft TCP/IP on Microsoft Windows NT (3.5–3.51), #70-053

OR Internetworking with Microsoft TCP/IP on Microsoft Windows NT 4.0, #70-059

◆ Implementing and Supporting Microsoft Exchange Server 4.0, #70-075*

OR Implementing and Supporting Microsoft Exchange Server 5.0, #70-076

OR Implementing and Supporting Microsoft Exchange Server 5.5, #70-081

◆ Implementing and Supporting Microsoft Internet Information Server 3.0 and Microsoft Index Server 1.1, #70-077

OR Implementing and Supporting Microsoft Internet Information Server 4.0, #70-087

◆ Implementing and Supporting Microsoft Proxy Server 1.0, #70-078

OR Implementing and Supporting Microsoft Proxy Server 2.0, #70-088

◆ Implementing and Supporting Microsoft Internet Explorer 4.0 by Using the Internet Explorer Resource Kit, #70-079

How to Become a Microsoft Certified Systems Engineer + Internet (MCSE+Internet)

MCSE+Internet candidates must pass seven operating system exams and two elective exams. The following lists show the core requirements and the elective courses (of which you need to pass two exams).

The seven MCSE+Internet core exams required for certification are:

◆ Networking Essentials, #70-058

◆ Internetworking with Microsoft TCP/IP on Microsoft Windows NT 4.0, #70-059

◆ Implementing and Supporting Microsoft Windows 95, #70-064

OR Implementing and Supporting Microsoft Windows NT Workstation 4.0, #70-073

OR Implementing and Supporting Microsoft Windows 98, #70-098

◆ Implementing and Supporting Microsoft Windows NT Server 4.0, #70-067

◆ Implementing and Supporting Microsoft Windows NT Server 4.0 in the Enterprise, #70-068

◆ Implementing and Supporting Microsoft Internet Information Server 3.0 and Microsoft Index Server 1.1, #70-077

OR Implementing and Supporting Microsoft Internet Information Server 4.0, #70-087

◆ Implementing and Supporting Microsoft Internet Explorer 4.0 by Using the Internet Explorer Resource Kit, #70-079

You must also pass two of the following elective exams:

◆ System Administration for Microsoft SQL Server 6.5, #70-026

◆ Implementing a Database Design on Microsoft SQL Server 6.5, #70-027

◆ Implementing and Supporting Web Sites Using Microsoft Site Server 3.0, #70-056

◆ Implementing and Supporting Microsoft Exchange Server 5.0, #70-076

   OR Implementing and Supporting Microsoft Exchange Server 5.5, #70-081

◆ Implementing and Supporting Microsoft Proxy Server 1.0, #70-078

   OR Implementing and Supporting Microsoft Proxy Server 2.0, #70-088

◆ Implementing and Supporting Microsoft SNA Server 4.0, #70-085

How to Become a Microsoft Certified Solution Developer (MCSD)

MCSD candidates must pass two core technology exams and two elective exams. The following lists show the required technology exams, plus the elective exams that apply toward obtaining the MCSD.

You must pass the following two core technology exams to qualify for MCSD certification:

◆ Microsoft Windows Architecture I, #70-160

◆ Microsoft Windows Architecture II, #70-161

You must also pass two of the following elective exams to become an MSCD:

◆ Microsoft SQL Server 4.2 Database Implementation, #70-021

   OR Implementing a Database Design on Microsoft SQL Server 6.5, #70-027

   OR Implementing a Database Design on Microsoft SQL Server 7.0, #70-029

◆ Developing Applications with C++ Using the Microsoft Foundation Class Library, #70-024

◆ Implementing OLE in Microsoft Foundation Class Applications, #70-025

◆ Programming with Microsoft Visual Basic 4.0, #70-065

   OR Developing Applications with Microsoft Visual Basic 5.0, #70-165

◆ Microsoft Access 2.0 for Windows-Application Development, #70-051

   OR Microsoft Access for Windows 95 and the Microsoft Access Development Toolkit, #70-069

◆ Developing Applications with Microsoft Excel 5.0 Using Visual Basic for Applications, #70-052

◆ Programming in Microsoft Visual FoxPro 3.0 for Windows, #70-054

Becoming a Microsoft Certified Trainer (MCT)

To understand the requirements and process for becoming a Microsoft Certified Trainer (MCT), you need to obtain the Microsoft Certified Trainer Guide document from the following WWW site:

```
http://www.microsoft.com/train_cert/mct/
```

From this page, you can read the document as Web pages, or you can display or download it as a Word file.

The MCT Guide explains the four-step process of becoming an MCT. The general steps for the MCT certification are described here:

1. Complete and mail a Microsoft Certified Trainer application to Microsoft. You must include proof of your skills for presenting instructional material. The options for doing so are described in the MCT Guide.

2. Obtain and study the Microsoft Trainer Kit for the Microsoft Official Curricula (MOC) course(s) for which you want to be certified. You can order Microsoft Trainer Kits by calling 800-688-0496 in North America. Other regions should review the MCT Guide for information on how to order a Trainer Kit.

3. Pass the Microsoft certification exam for the product for which you want to be certified to teach.

4. Attend the Microsoft Official Curriculum (MOC) course for which you want to be certified. You do this so that you can understand how the course is structured, how labs are completed, and how the course flows.

> **WARNING**
>
> **Be Sure to Get the MCT Guide!**
> You should consider the preceding steps to be a general overview of the MCT certification process. The precise steps that you need to take are described in detail on the WWW site mentioned earlier. Do not mistakenly believe the preceding steps make up the actual process you need to take.

If you are interested in becoming an MCT, you can receive more information by visiting the Microsoft Certified Training (MCT) WWW site at `http://www.microsoft.com/train_cert/mct/` or call 800-688-0496.

What's on the CD-ROM

This appendix offers a brief rundown of what you'll find on the CD-ROM that comes with this book. For a more detailed description of the newly developed Top Score test engine, exclusive to Macmillan Computer Publishing, see Appendix D, "Using the Top Score Software."

TOP SCORE

Top Score is a test engine developed exclusively for Macmillan Computer Publishing. It is, we believe, the best test engine available because it closely emulates the format of the standard Microsoft exams. In addition to providing a means of evaluating your knowledge of the exam material, Top Score features several innovations that help you to improve your mastery of the subject matter. For example, the practice tests allow you to check your score by exam area or category, which helps you determine which topics you need to study further. Other modes allow you to obtain immediate feedback on your response to a question, explanation of the correct answer, and even hyperlinks to the chapter in an electronic version of the book where the topic of the question is covered. Again, for a complete description of the benefits of Top Score, see Appendix D.

Before you attempt to run the Top Score software, make sure that autorun is enabled. If you prefer not to use autorun, you can run the application from the CD by double-clicking the START.EXE file from within Explorer.

EXCLUSIVE ELECTRONIC VERSION OF TEXT

As alluded to above, the CD-ROM also contains the electronic version of this book in Portable Document Format (PDF). In addition to the links to the book that are built into the Top Score engine, you can use that version of the book to help you search for terms you need to study or other book elements. The electronic version comes complete with all figures as they appear in the book.

COPYRIGHT INFORMATION AND DISCLAIMER

Macmillan Computer Publishing's Top Score test engine: Copyright 1998 New Riders Publishing. All rights reserved. Made in U.S.A.

Using the Top Score Software

GETTING STARTED

The installation procedure is very simple and typical of Windows 95 or Window NT 4 installations.

1. Put the CD into the CD-ROM drive. The autorun function starts, and after a moment, you see a CD-ROM Setup dialog box asking you if you are ready to proceed.

2. Click OK, and you are prompted for the location of the directory in which the program can install a small log file. Choose the default (C:\Program Files\), or type the name of another drive and directory, or select the drive and directory where you want it placed. Then click OK.

3. The next prompt asks you to select a start menu name. If you like the default name, click OK. If not, enter the name you would like to use. The Setup process runs its course.

When setup is complete, icons are displayed in the MCSE Top Score Software Explorer window that is open. For an overview of the CD's contents, double-click the CD-ROM Contents icon.

If you reach this point, you have successfully installed the exam(s). If you have another CD, repeat this process to install additional exams.

INSTRUCTIONS ON USING THE TOP SCORE SOFTWARE

Top Score software consists of the following three applications:

◆ Practice Exams

◆ Study Cards

◆ Flash Cards

The Practice Exams application provides exams that simulate the Microsoft certification exams. The Study Cards serve as a study aid organized around specific exam objectives. Both are in multiple-choice format. Flash Cards are another study aid that require responses to open-ended questions, which test your knowledge of the material at a level deeper than that of recognition memory.

To start the Study Cards, Practice Exams, or Flash Cards applications, follow these steps:

1. Begin from the overview of the CD contents (double-click the CD-ROM Contents icon). The left window provides you with options for obtaining further information on any of the Top Score applications as well as a way to launch them.

2. Click a "book" icon, and a listing of related topics appears below it in Explorer fashion.

3. Click an application name. This displays more detailed information for that application in the right window.

4. To start an application, click its book icon. Then click on the Starting the Program option. Do this for Practice Exams, for example. Information appears in the right window. Click on the button for the exam, and the opening screens of the application appear.

Further details on using each of the applications follow.

Using Top Score Practice Exams

The Practice Exams interface is simple and straightforward. Its design simulates the look and feel of the Microsoft certification exams. To begin a practice exam, click the button for the exam name. After a moment, you see an opening screen similar to the one shown in Figure D.1.

Click on the Next button to see a disclaimer and copyright screen. Read the information, and then click Top Score's Start button. A notice appears, indicating that the program is randomly selecting questions for the practice exam from the exam database (see Figure D.2). Each practice exam contains the same number of items as the official Microsoft exam. The items are selected from a larger set of 150–900 questions. The random selection of questions from the database takes some time to retrieve. Don't reboot; your machine is not hung!

> **NOTE**
>
> **Some Exams Follow a New Format**
> The number of questions will be the same for traditional exams. However, this will not be the case for exams that incorporate the new "adaptive testing" format. In that format, there is no set number of questions. See the chapter entitled "Study and Exam Prep Tips" in the Final Review section of the book for more details on this new format.

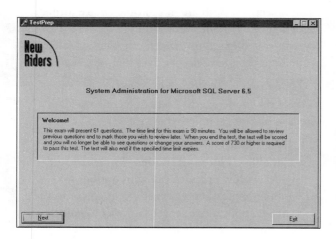

FIGURE D.1
Top Score Practice Exams opening screen.

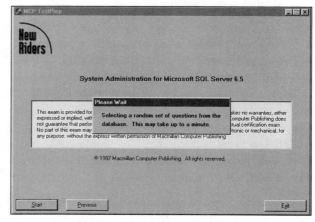

FIGURE D.2
Top Score's Please Wait notice.

After the questions have been selected, the first test item appears. See Figure D.3 for an example of a test item screen.

Notice several important features of this window. The question number and the total number of retrieved questions appears in the top-left corner of the window in the control bar. Immediately below that is a check box labeled Mark, which enables you to mark any exam item you would like to return to later. Across the screen from the Mark check box, you see the total time remaining for the exam.

The test question is located in a colored section (it's gray in the figure). Directly below the test question, in the white area, are response choices. Be sure to note that immediately below the responses are instructions about how to respond, including the number of responses required. You will notice that question items requiring a single response, such as that shown in Figure D.3, have radio buttons. Items requiring multiple responses have check boxes (see Figure D.4).

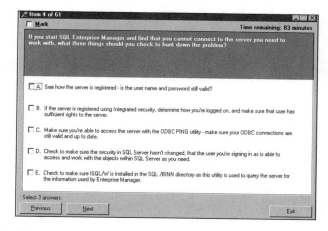

FIGURE D.4
A Top Score test item requiring multiple responses.

Some questions and some responses do not appear on the screen in their entirety. You will recognize such items because a scroll bar appears to the right of the question item or response. Use the scroll bar to reveal the rest of the question or response item.

The buttons at the bottom of the window enable you to move back to a previous test item, proceed to the next test item, or exit Top Score Practice Exams.

Some items require you to examine additional information referred to as *exhibits*. These screens typically include graphs, diagrams, or other types of visual information that you will need in order to respond to the test question. You can access Exhibits by clicking the Exhibit button, also located at the bottom of the window.

After you complete the practice test by moving through all of the test questions for your exam, you arrive at a summary screen titled Item Review (see Figure D.5).

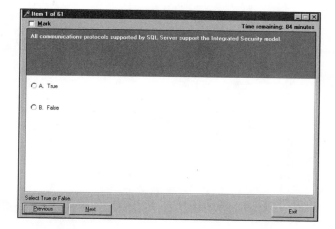

FIGURE D.3
A Top Score test item requiring a single response.

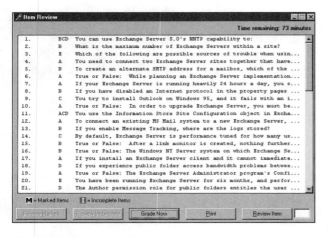

FIGURE D.5
The Top Score Item Review window.

This window enables you to see all the question numbers, your response(s) to each item, any questions you have marked, and any you've left incomplete. The buttons at the bottom of the screen enable you to review all the marked items and incomplete items in numeric order.

If you want to review a specific marked or incomplete item, simply type the desired item number in the box in the lower-right corner of the window and click the Review Item button. This takes you to that particular item. After you review the item, you can respond to the question. Notice that this window also offers the Next and Previous options. You can also select the Item Review button to return to the Item Review window.

> **NOTE**
>
> **Your Time Is Limited** If you exceed the time allotted for the test, you do not have the opportunity to review any marked or incomplete items. The program will move on to the next screen.

After you complete your review of the practice test questions, click the Grade Now button to find out how you did. An Examination Score Report is generated for your practice test (see Figure D.6). This report provides you with the required score for this particular certification exam, your score on the practice test, and a grade. The report also breaks down your performance on the practice test by the specific objectives for the exam. Click the Print button to print out the results of your performance.

You also have the option of reviewing those items that you answered incorrectly. Click the Show Me What I Missed button to view a summary of those items. You can print out that information if you need further practice or review; such printouts can be used to guide your use of Study Cards and Flash Cards.

Using Top Score Study Cards

To start the software, begin from the overview of the CD contents. Click the Study Cards icon to see a listing of topics. Clicking Study Cards brings up more detailed information for this application in the right window.

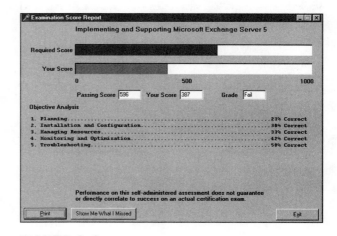

FIGURE D.6
The Top Score Examination Score Report window.

To launch Study Cards, click on Starting the Program. In the right window, click on the button for the exam in which you are interested. After a moment, an initial screen similar to that of the Practice Exams appears.

Click on the Next button to see the first Study Cards screen (see Figure D.7).

The interface for Study Cards is very similar to that of Practice Exams. However, several important options enable you to prepare for an exam. The Study Cards material is organized according to the specific objectives for each exam. You can opt to receive questions on all the objectives, or you can use the check boxes to request questions on a limited set of objectives. For example, if you have already completed a Practice Exam and your score report indicates that you need work on Planning, you can choose to cover only the Planning objectives for your Study Cards session.

You can also determine the number of questions presented by typing the number of questions you want into the option box at the right of the screen. You can control the amount of time you will be allowed for a review by typing the number of minutes into the Time Limit option box immediately below the one for the number of questions.

When you're ready, click the Start Test button, and Study Cards randomly selects the indicated number of questions from the question database. A dialog box appears, informing you that this process could take some time. After the questions are selected, the first item appears, in a format similar to that in Figure D.8.

Respond to the questions in the same manner you did for the Practice Exam questions. Radio buttons signify that a single answer is required, while check boxes indicate that multiple answers are expected.

Notice the menu options at the top of the window. You can pull down the File menu to exit from the program. The Edit menu contains commands for the copy function and even allows you to copy questions to the Windows clipboard.

Should you feel the urge to take some notes on a particular question, you can do so via the Options menu. When you pull it down, choose Open Notes, and Notepad opens. Type any notes you want to save for later reference. The Options menu also allows you to start over with another exam.

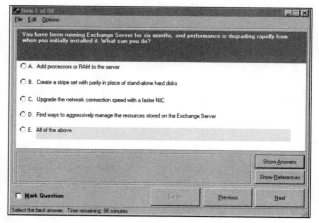

FIGURE D.8
A Study Cards item.

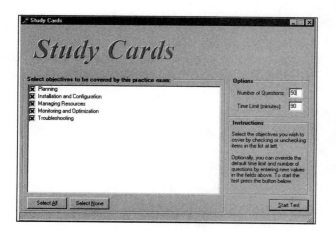

FIGURE D.7
The first Study Cards screen.

The Study Cards application provides you with immediate feedback of whether you answered the question correctly. Click the Show Answers button to see the correct answer, and it appears highlighted on the screen as shown in Figure D.9.

Study Cards also includes Item Review, Score Report, and Show Me What I Missed features that function the same as those in the Practice Exams application.

Using Top Score Flash Cards

Flash Cards offer a third way to use the exam question database. The Flash Cards items do not offer you multiple-choice answers to choose from; instead, they require you to respond in a short answer/essay format. Flash Cards are intended to help you learn the material well enough to respond with the correct answers in your own words, rather than just by recognizing the correct answer. If you have the depth of knowledge to answer questions without prompting, you will certainly be prepared to pass a multiple-choice exam.

You start the Flash Cards application in the same way you did Practice Exams and Study Cards. Click the Flash Cards icon, and then click Start the Program.

Click the button for the exam you are interested in, and the opening screen appears. It looks similar to the example shown in Figure D.10.

You can choose Flash Cards according to the various objectives, as you did Study Cards. Simply select the objectives you want to cover, enter the number of questions you want, and enter the amount of time you want to limit yourself to. Click the Start Test button to start the Flash Cards session, and you see a dialog box notifying you that questions are being selected.

The Flash Cards items appear in an interface similar to that of Practice Exams and Study Cards (see Figure D.11).

Notice, however, that although a question is presented, no possible answers appear. You type your answer in the white space below the question (see Figure D.12).

Compare your answer to the correct answer by clicking the Show Answers button (see Figure D.13).

You can also use the Show Reference button in the same manner as described earlier in the Study Cards sections.

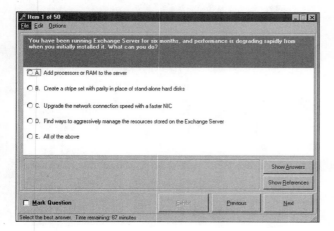

FIGURE D.9
The correct answer is highlighted.

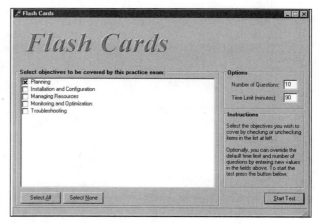

FIGURE D.10
The Flash Cards opening screen.

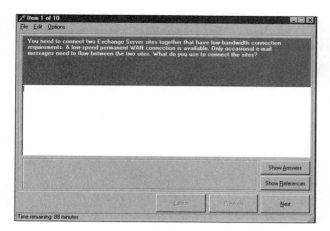

FIGURE D.11
A Flash Cards item.

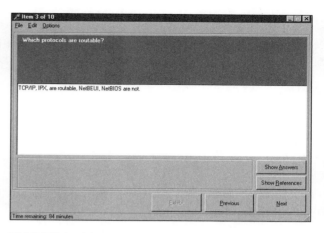

FIGURE D.12
A typed answer in Flash Cards.

The pull-down menus provide nearly the same functionality as those in Study Cards, with the exception of a Paste command on the Edit menu instead of the Copy Question command.

Flash Cards provide simple feedback; they do not include an Item Review or Score Report. They are intended to provide you with an alternative way of assessing your level of knowledge that will encourage you to learn the information more thoroughly than other methods do.

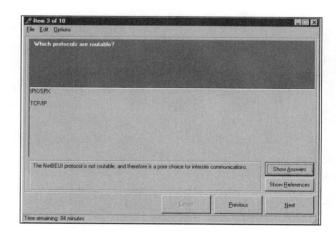

FIGURE D.13
The correct answer is shown.

Summary

The Top Score software's suite of applications provides you with several approaches to exam preparation. Use Practice Exams to do just that—practice taking exams, not only to assess your learning, but also to prepare yourself for the test-taking situation. Use Study Cards and Flash Cards as tools for more focused assessment and review and to reinforce the knowledge you are gaining. You will find that these three applications are the perfect way to finish off your exam preparation.

Index

Q - R

S

SAP (Service Advertising Protocol), 272
satellite microwave transmission, 140
security
  auditing options, 372
  data encryption, 372
  equipment security, 373
  network models
    bindery based, 348, 352
    directory services, 348, 356-357
    domains, 348, 354-355
    workgroups, 348-349
  permissions, 348
  user rights, 348
  virus protection software, 373
  Windows 95
    share-level, 367
    user-level, 367
security events (Event Viewer), 402
selecting
  RAID levels, 328-329
  transmission media, 108
    attentuation, 113
    band usage, 110
    bandwidth, 109-110
    cost factors, 109
    installation requirements, 109
    electromagnetic interference (EMI), 113-114
    multiplexing, 110-111
Server Messaging Blocks (SMB), 459
server mirroring as fault tolerance tool, 332
Server service, I/O request routing, 19
service addresses (Network layer), 63
Session layer (OSI model), 72-73
  dialog forms
    full-duplex, 73
    half-duplex, 73
    simplex, 72-73
  session administration phases, 74-75
share-level security
  full access, 368-369
  passwords, 367-368
  read-only access, 368-369
shared folders, permissions, 521-523
  assigning, 364-365
  creating, 364-365

sharing
  applications versus local applications, 514
  printers
    Windows 95, 371
    Windows NT, 366-367
  resources on Microsoft networks, 347
shielded twisted-pair cable
  characteristics
    attentuation, 124
    capacity, 124
    connector types, 125
    cost, 123
    EMI characteristics, 124-125
    installation, 123-124
  diagram, 121
  electromagnetic intereference reduction, 121-122
  grounding properties, 122
short-haul modems, 225
signal regeneration, 232
signals
  analog, measurement of, 204
  attentuation, 56
  clocking, 201-202
  digital, measurement of, 202-203
  network adapter cards
    analog, 199-200
    digital, 201
  regeneration, 232
Simple Network Management Protocol (SNMP), 465
simplex dialogs (Session layer), 72-73
SLIP (Serial Line Internet Protocol), 48, 452-453
  dial-up configuration requirements, 81
  OSI model relationship, 80
  TCP/IP dial-up connections, 80
SMB (Server Messaging Blocks), 277
SMDS (Switched Multimegabit Digital Service)
  data rates, 307
  development, 307
SMTP (Simple Mail Transfer Protocol), mail routing functions, 265
sneaker-net, 23
SNMP (Simple Network Monitoring Protocol), 397
  IBM OpenView software, 397
  management information base (MIB), 397
  traps, issuing, 398

TRAINING GUIDES
THE NEXT GENERATION

MCSE Training Guide: Networking Essentials, Second Edition

1-56205-919-X, $49.99, 9/98

MCSE Training Guide: TCP/IP, Second Edition

1-56205-920-3, $49.99, 10/98

MCSD Training Guide: Microsoft Visual Basic 6, Exam 70-176

0-7357-0031-1, $49.99, Q1/99

MCSE Training Guide: Windows NT Server 4, Second Edition

1-56205-916-5, $49.99, 9/98

MCSE Training Guide: SQL Server 7 Administration

0-7357-0003-6, $49.99, Q1/99

TRAINING GUIDES
FIRST EDITIONS
Your Quality Elective Solution

MCSE Training Guide: Systems Management Server 1.2, 1-56205-748-0

MCSE Training Guide: SQL Server 6.5 Administration, 1-56205-726-X

MCSE Training Guide: SQL Server 6.5 Design and Implementation, 1-56205-830-4

MCSE Training Guide: Windows 95, 70-064 Exam, 1-56205-880-0

MCSE Training Guide: Exchange Server 5, 1-56205-824-X

MCSE Training Guide: Internet Explorer 4, 1-56205-889-4

MCSE Training Guide: Microsoft Exchange Server 5.5, 1-56205-899-1

MCSE Training Guide: IIS 4, 1-56205-823-1

MCSD Training Guide: Visual Basic 5, 1-56205-850-9

MCSD Training Guide: Microsoft Access, 1-56205-771-5

MCSE Training Guide: Windows NT Server 4 Enterprise, Second Edition

1-56205-917-3, $49.99, 9/98

MCSE Training Guide: SQL Server 7 Design and Implementation

0-7357-0004-4, $49.99, Q1/99

MCSE Training Guide: Windows NT Workstation 4, Second Edition

1-56205-918-1, $49.99, 9/98

MCSD Training Guide: Solution Architectures

0-7357-0026-5, $49.99, Q1/99

MCSE Training Guide: Windows 98

1-56205-890-8, $49.99, Q4/98

MCSD Training Guide: Visual Basic 6, Exam 70-175

0-7357-0002-8, $49.99, Q1/99

FAST TRACK SERIES

The Accelerated Path to Certification Success

Fast Tracks provide an easy way to review the key elements of each certification technology without being bogged down with elementary-level information.

These guides are perfect for when you already have real-world, hands-on experience. They're the ideal enhancement to training courses, test simulators, and comprehensive training guides. *No fluff, simply what you really need to pass the exam!*

LEARN IT FAST

Part I contains only the essential information you need to pass the test. With over 200 pages of information, it is a concise review for the more experienced MCSE candidate.

REVIEW IT EVEN FASTER

Part II averages 50–75 pages, and takes you through the test and into the real-world use of the technology, with chapters on:

1) Fast Facts Review Section
2) Hotlists of Exam-Critical Concepts
3) Sample Test Questions
4) The Insider's Spin (on taking the exam)
5) Did You Know? (real-world applications for the technology covered in the exam)

 MCSE Fast Track: Networking Essentials
1-56205-939-4, $19.99, 9/98

 MCSE Fast Track: TCP/IP
1-56205-937-8, $19.99, 9/98

 MCSE Fast Track: Windows 98
0-7357-0016-8, $19.99, Q4/98

 MCSE Fast Track: Internet Information Server 4
1-56205-936-X, $19.99, 9/98

 MCSE Fast Track: Windows NT Server 4
1-56205-935-1, $19.99, 9/98

 MCSD Fast Track: Solution Architectures
0-7357-0029-X, $19.99, Q1/99

 MCSE Fast Track: Windows NT Server 4 Enterprise
1-56205-940-8, $19.99, 9/98

 MCSD Fast Track: Visual Basic 6, Exam 70-175
0-7357-0018-4, $19.99, Q4/98

 MCSE Fast Track: Windows NT Workstation 4
1-56205-938-6, $19.99, 9/98

 MCSD Fast Track: Visual Basic 6, Exam 70-176
0-7357-0019-2, $19.99, Q4/98

TESTPREP SERIES

Practice and cram with the new, revised Second Edition TestPreps

Questions. Questions. And more questions. That's what you'll find in our New Riders *TestPreps*. They're great practice books when you reach the final stage of studying for the exam. We recommend them as supplements to our *Training Guides*.

What makes these study tools unique is that the questions are the primary focus of each book. All the text in these books support and explain the answers to the questions.

- ✓ **Scenario-based questions** challenge your experience.

- ✓ **Multiple-choice questions** prep you for the exam.

- ✓ **Fact-based questions** test your product knowledge.

- ✓ **Exam strategies** assist you in test preparation.

- ✓ **Complete yet concise explanations of answers** make for better retention.

- ✓ **Two practice exams** prepare you for the real thing.

- ✓ **Fast Facts** offer you everything you need to review in the testing center parking lot.

Practice, practice, practice, pass with New Riders TestPreps*!*

MCSE TestPrep: Networking Essentials, Second Edition

0-7357-0010-9, $19.99, 11/98

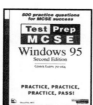

MCSE TestPrep: Windows 95, Second Edition

0-7357-0011-7, $19.99, 11/98

MCSE TestPrep: Windows NT Server 4, Second Edition

0-7357-0012-5, $19.99, 12/98

MCSE TestPrep: Windows NT Server 4 Enterprise, Second Edition

0-7357-0009-5, $19.99, 11/98

MCSE TestPrep: Windows NT Workstation 4, Second Edition

0-7357-0008-7, $19.99, 11/98

MCSE TestPrep: TCP/IP, Second Edition

0-7357-0025-7, $19.99, 12/98

MCSE TestPrep: Windows 98

1-56205-922-X, $19.99, Q4/98

FIRST EDITIONS

MCSE TestPrep: SQL Server 6.5 Administration, 0-7897-1597-X

MCSE TestPrep: SQL Server 6.5 Design and Implementation, 1-56205-915-7

MCSE TestPrep: Windows 95 70-64 Exam, 0-7897-1609-7

MCSE TestPrep: Internet Explorer 4, 0-7897-1654-2

MCSE TestPrep: Exchange Server 5.5, 0-7897-1611-9

MCSE TestPrep: IIS 4.0, 0-7897-1610-0

How to Contact Us

IF YOU NEED THE LATEST UPDATES ON A TITLE THAT YOU'VE PURCHASED:

1) Visit our Web site at www.newriders.com.

2) Click on the DOWNLOADS link, and enter your book's ISBN number, which is located on the back cover in the bottom right-hand corner.

3) In the DOWNLOADS section, you'll find available updates that are linked to the book page.

IF YOU ARE HAVING TECHNICAL PROBLEMS WITH THE BOOK OR THE CD THAT IS INCLUDED:

1) Check the book's information page on our Web site according to the instructions listed above, or

2) Email us at support@mcp.com, or

3) Fax us at (317) 817-7488 attn: Tech Support.

IF YOU HAVE COMMENTS ABOUT ANY OF OUR CERTIFICATION PRODUCTS THAT ARE NON-SUPPORT RELATED:

1) Email us at certification@mcp.com, or

2) Write to us at New Riders, 201 W. 103rd St., Indianapolis, IN 46290-1097, or

3) Fax us at (317) 581-4663.

IF YOU ARE OUTSIDE THE UNITED STATES AND NEED TO FIND A DISTRIBUTOR IN YOUR AREA:

Please contact our international department at international@mcp.com.

IF YOU WISH TO PREVIEW ANY OF OUR CERTIFICATION BOOKS FOR CLASSROOM USE:

Email us at pr@mcp.com. Your message should include your name, title, training company or school, department, address, phone number, office days/hours, text in use, and enrollment. Send these details along with your request for desk/examination copies and/or additional information.

WE WANT TO KNOW WHAT YOU THINK

To better serve you, we would like your opinion on the content and quality of this book. Please complete this card and mail it to us or fax it to 317-581-4663.

Name _____

Address _____

City _____ State _____ Zip _____

Phone _____ Email Address _____

Occupation _____

Which certification exams have you already passed? _____
_____
_____
_____

Which certification exams do you plan to take? _____
_____
_____
_____

What influenced your purchase of this book?
❏ Recommendation   ❏ Cover Design
❏ Table of Contents   ❏ Index
❏ Magazine Review   ❏ Advertisement
❏ Reputation of New Riders ❏ Author Name

How would you rate the contents of this book?
❏ Excellent   ❏ Very Good
❏ Good   ❏ Fair
❏ Below Average   ❏ Poor

What other types of certification products will you buy/have you bought to help you prepare for the exam?
❏ Quick reference books   ❏ Testing software
❏ Study guides   ❏ Other

What do you like most about this book? Check all that apply.
❏ Content   ❏ Writing Style
❏ Accuracy   ❏ Examples
❏ Listings   ❏ Design
❏ Index   ❏ Page Count
❏ Price   ❏ Illustrations

What do you like least about this book? Check all that apply.
❏ Content   ❏ Writing Style
❏ Accuracy   ❏ Examples
❏ Listings   ❏ Design
❏ Index   ❏ Page Count
❏ Price   ❏ Illustrations

What would be a useful follow-up book to this one for you?_____
Where did you purchase this book? _____
Can you name a similar book that you like better than this one, or one that is as good? Why?_____
_____
_____

How many New Riders books do you own? _____
What are your favorite certification or general computer book titles? _____
_____

What other titles would you like to see us develop?_____
_____

Any comments for us? _____
_____
_____
_____

Fold here and Scotch tape to mail

Place
Stamp
Here

New Riders
201 W. 103rd St.
Indianapolis, IN 46290

NEW RIDERS TOP SCORE TEST SIMULATION SOFTWARE SUITE

Practice Exams simulate the actual Microsoft exams. Option buttons and check boxes indicate whether there is one or more than one correct answer. All test questions are presented randomly to create a unique exam each time you practice—the ideal way to prepare.

The Item Review shows you the answers you've already selected and the questions you need to revisit before grading the exam.

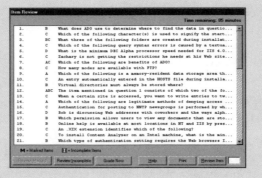

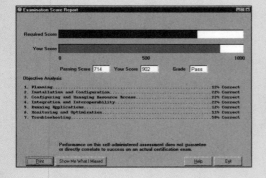

The Score Report displays your score for each objective category, helping you to define which objectives you need to study more. It also shows you what score you need to pass and your total score.

Study Cards allow you to test yourself and receive immediate feedback and an answer explanation. Link to the text for more in-depth explanations.